Mazda MPV Automotive Repair Manual

by Mark Ryan and John H Haynes
Member of the Guild of Motoring Writers

Models covered:
All Mazda MPV models
1989 through 1994

(2C6 - 61020)
(2047)

ABCDE
FGHIJ
K

Haynes Publishing Group
Sparkford Nr Yeovil
Somerset BA22 7JJ England

Haynes North America, Inc
861 Lawrence Drive
Newbury Park
California 91320 USA

Acknowledgements

We are grateful to the Mazda Motor Company for assistance with technical information, certain illustrations and vehicle photos. Technical writers who contributed to this project include Robert Maddox, Mike Stubblefield and Larry Warren.

A book in the Haynes Automotive Repair Manual Series

Printed in the U.S.A.

ISBN 1 56392 142 1

Library of Congress Catalog Card Number 95-075694

While every attempt is made to ensure that the information in this manual is correct, no liability can be accepted by the authors or publishers for loss, damage or injury caused by any errors in, or omissions from, the information given.

Contents

Haynes mechanic, author and photographer with 1990 Mazda MPV

About this manual

Its purpose

The purpose of this manual is to help you get the best value from your vehicle. It can do so in several ways. It can help you decide what work must be done, even if you choose to have it done by a dealer service department or a repair shop; it provides information and procedures for routine maintenance and servicing; and it offers diagnostic and repair procedures to follow when trouble occurs.

We hope you use the manual to tackle the work yourself. For many simpler jobs, doing it yourself may be quicker than arranging an appointment to get the vehicle into a shop and making the trips to leave it and pick it up. More importantly, a lot of money can be saved by avoiding the expense the shop must pass on to you to cover its labor and overhead costs. An added benefit is the sense of satisfaction and accomplishment that you feel after doing the job yourself.

Using the manual

The manual is divided into Chapters. Each Chapter is divided into numbered Sections, which are headed in bold type between horizontal lines. Each Section consists of consecutively numbered paragraphs.

At the beginning of each numbered Section you will be referred to any illustrations which apply to the procedures in that Section. The reference numbers used in illustration captions pinpoint the pertinent Section and the Step within that Section. That is, illustration 3.2 means the illustration refers to Section 3 and Step (or paragraph) 2 within that Section.

Procedures, once described in the text, are not normally repeated. When it's necessary to refer to another Chapter, the reference will be given as Chapter and Section number. Cross references given without use of the word "Chapter" apply to Sections and/or paragraphs in the same Chapter. For example, "see Section 8" means in the same Chapter.

References to the left or right side of the vehicle assume you are sitting in the driver's seat, facing forward.

Even though we have prepared this manual with extreme care, neither the publisher nor the author can accept responsibility for any errors in, or omissions from, the information given.

NOTE

A **Note** provides information necessary to properly complete a procedure or information which will make the procedure easier to understand.

CAUTION

A **Caution** provides a special procedure or special steps which must be taken while completing the procedure where the Caution is found. Not heeding a Caution can result in damage to the assembly being worked on.

WARNING

A **Warning** provides a special procedure or special steps which must be taken while completing the procedure where the Warning is found. Not heeding a Warning can result in personal injury.

Introduction to the Mazda MPV

These models are equipped with either a 2.6L four-cylinder or a 3.0L V6 engine. Transmissions used are a five-speed overdrive manual and four-speed overdrive automatic.

Chassis layout is conventional, with the engine mounted at the front and the power being transmitted through either a manual or automatic transmission to a driveshaft and solid rear axle on 2WD models. On 4WD models a transfer case transmits power through a driveshaft to the front axle, then to the wheels by way of driveaxles.

Front suspension on all models is independent using coil springs and struts. The rear suspension uses a solid rear axle suspended by coil springs and located by trailing arms.

All models are equipped with power assisted front disc and rear drum brakes. Rear wheel Anti-lock Brake System (ABS) is used on later models.

Vehicle identification numbers

Modifications are a continuing and unpublicized part of vehicle manufacturing. Since spare parts manuals and lists are compiled on a numerical basis, the individual vehicle numbers are essential to correctly identify the component required.

Chassis number

The vehicle chassis number is stamped on the right (passenger) side firewall in the engine compartment **(see illustration)**.

Certification label

The certification label on the left (driver's) door pillar. The label contains the name of the manufacturer, the month and year of manufacture, vehicle weight and the certification statement.

Vehicle Identification Number (VIN)

The VIN is very important because it's used for title and registration purposes. The VIN is stamped into a metal plate fastened to the dashboard close to the windshield on the driver's side of the vehicle, on the driver's door jamb and on the firewall in the engine compart-ment. It contains valuable information such as where and when the vehicle was manufactured, the model year and the body style.

Tire pressure label

The tire pressure label is found on the driver's door and contains the recommended tire pressures.

Vehicle emission Control Information label

The Vehicle emission Control Information (VECI) label is located on the underside of the hood. It contains information on the emission controls with which your vehicle is equipped. California models also have a vacuum hose routing diagram label.

Oil label

Located on the underside of the hood, the oil label contains information on the specified lubricants for these models.

Engine identification numbers

The engine identification number is stamped on a pad adjacent to the distributor **(see illustration)**.

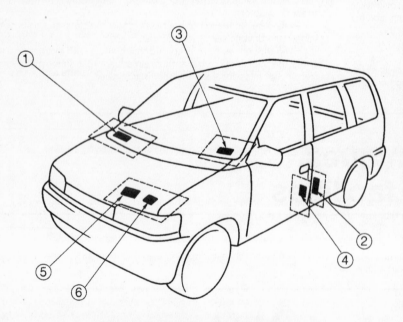

Vehicle identification number locations

1   Chassis number
2   Certification number
3   Vehicle Identification Number (VIN)
4   Tire pressure label
5   Vehicle Emission Control Identification (VECI) and (on California models) vacuum hose routing diagram)
6   Oil label

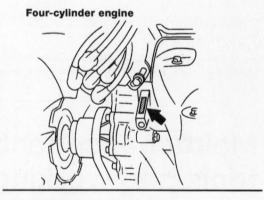

Four-cylinder engine

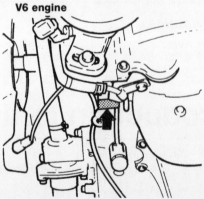

V6 engine

Engine identification number locations

Buying parts

Replacement parts are available from many sources, which generally fall into one of two categories - authorized dealer parts departments and independent retail auto parts stores. Our advice concerning these parts is as follows:

Retail auto parts stores: Good auto parts stores will stock frequently needed components which wear out relatively fast, such as clutch components, exhaust systems, brake parts, tune-up parts, etc. These stores often supply new or reconditioned parts on an exchange basis, which can save a considerable amount of money. Discount auto parts stores are often very good places to buy materials and parts needed for general vehicle maintenance such as oil, grease, filters, spark plugs, belts, touch-up paint, bulbs, etc. They also usually sell tools and general accessories, have convenient hours, charge lower prices and can often be found not far from home.

Authorized dealer parts department: This is the best source for parts which are unique to the vehicle and not generally available elsewhere (such as major engine parts, transmission parts, trim pieces, etc.).

Warranty information: If the vehicle is still covered under warranty, be sure that any replacement parts purchased - regardless of the source - do not invalidate the warranty!

To be sure of obtaining the correct parts, have engine and chassis numbers available and, if possible, take the old parts along for positive identification.

Maintenance techniques, tools and working facilities

Maintenance techniques

There are a number of techniques involved in maintenance and repair that will be referred to throughout this manual. Application of these techniques will enable the home mechanic to be more efficient, better organized and capable of performing the various tasks properly, which will ensure that the repair job is thorough and complete.

Fasteners

Fasteners are nuts, bolts, studs and screws used to hold two or more parts together. There are a few things to keep in mind when working with fasteners. Almost all of them use a locking device of some type, either a lockwasher, locknut, locking tab or thread adhesive. All threaded fasteners should be clean and straight, with undamaged threads and undamaged corners on the hex head where the wrench fits. Develop the habit of replacing all damaged nuts and bolts with new ones. Special locknuts with nylon or fiber inserts can only be used once. If they are removed, they lose their locking ability and must be replaced with new ones.

Rusted nuts and bolts should be treated with a penetrating fluid to ease removal and prevent breakage. Some mechanics use turpentine in a spout-type oil can, which works quite well. After applying the rust penetrant, let it work for a few minutes before trying to loosen the nut or bolt. Badly rusted fasteners may have to be chiseled or sawed off or removed with a special nut breaker, available at tool stores.

If a bolt or stud breaks off in an assembly, it can be drilled and removed with a special tool commonly available for this purpose. Most automotive machine shops can perform this task, as well as other repair procedures, such as the repair of threaded holes that have been stripped out.

Flat washers and lockwashers, when removed from an assembly, should always be replaced exactly as removed. Replace any damaged washers with new ones. Never use a lockwasher on any soft metal surface (such as aluminum), thin sheet metal or plastic.

Fastener sizes

For a number of reasons, automobile manufacturers are making wider and wider use of metric fasteners. Therefore, it is important to be able to tell the difference between standard (sometimes called U.S. or SAE) and metric hardware, since they cannot be interchanged.

All bolts, whether standard or metric, are sized according to diameter, thread pitch and length. For example, a standard 1/2 - 13 x 1 bolt is 1/2 inch in diameter, has 13 threads per inch and is 1 inch long. An M12 - 1.75 x 25 metric bolt is 12 mm in diameter, has a thread pitch of 1.75 mm (the distance between threads) and is 25 mm long. The two bolts are nearly identical, and easily confused, but they are not interchangeable.

In addition to the differences in diameter, thread pitch and length, metric and standard bolts can also be distinguished by examining the bolt heads. To begin with, the distance across the flats on a standard bolt head is measured in inches, while the same dimension on a metric bolt is sized in millimeters (the same is true for nuts). As a result, a standard wrench should not be used on a metric bolt and a metric wrench should not be used on a standard bolt. Also, most standard bolts have slashes radiating out from the center of the head to denote the grade or strength of the bolt, which is an indication of the amount of torque that can be applied to it. The greater the number of slashes, the greater the strength of the bolt. Grades 0 through 5 are commonly used on automobiles. Metric bolts have a property class (grade) number, rather than a slash, molded into their heads to indicate bolt strength. In this case, the higher the number, the stronger the bolt. Property class numbers 8.8, 9.8 and 10.9 are commonly used on automobiles.

Strength markings can also be used to distinguish standard hex nuts from metric hex nuts. Many standard nuts have dots stamped into one side, while metric nuts are marked with a number. The greater the number of dots, or the higher the number, the greater the strength of the nut.

Metric studs are also marked on their ends according to property class (grade). Larger studs are numbered (the same as metric bolts), while smaller studs carry a geometric code to denote grade.

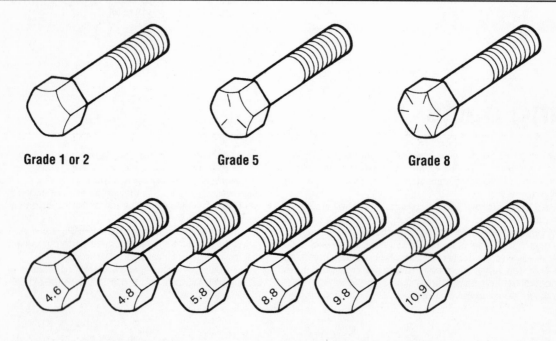

Bolt strength markings (top - standard/SAE/USS; bottom - metric)

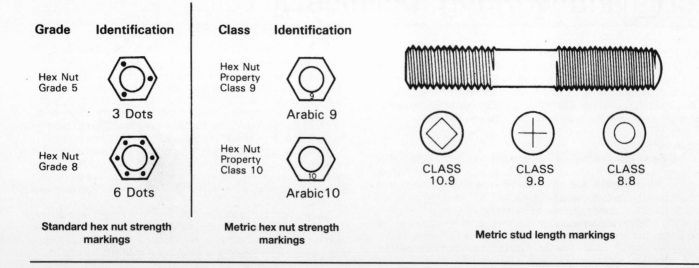

Grade	Identification
Hex Nut Grade 5	3 Dots
Hex Nut Grade 8	6 Dots

Standard hex nut strength markings

Class	Identification
Hex Nut Property Class 9	Arabic 9
Hex Nut Property Class 10	Arabic 10

Metric hex nut strength markings

CLASS 10.9   CLASS 9.8   CLASS 8.8

Metric stud length markings

It should be noted that many fasteners, especially Grades 0 through 2, have no distinguishing marks on them. When such is the case, the only way to determine whether it is standard or metric is to measure the thread pitch or compare it to a known fastener of the same size.

Standard fasteners are often referred to as SAE, as opposed to metric. However, it should be noted that SAE technically refers to a non-metric fine thread fastener only. Coarse thread non-metric fasteners are referred to as USS sizes.

Since fasteners of the same size (both standard and metric) may have different strength ratings, be sure to reinstall any bolts, studs or nuts removed from your vehicle in their original locations. Also, when replacing a fastener with a new one, make sure that the new one has a strength rating equal to or greater than the original.

Tightening sequences and procedures

Most threaded fasteners should be tightened to a specific torque value (torque is the twisting force applied to a threaded component such as a nut or bolt). Overtightening the fastener can weaken it and cause it to break, while undertightening can cause it to eventually come loose. Bolts, screws and studs, depending on the material they are made of and their thread diameters, have specific torque values, many of which are noted in the Specifications at the beginning of each Chapter. Be sure to follow the torque recommendations closely. For fasteners not assigned a specific torque, a general torque value chart is presented here as a guide. These torque values are for dry (unlubricated) fasteners threaded into steel or cast iron (not aluminum). As was previously mentioned, the size and grade of a fastener determine the amount of torque that can safely be applied to it. The figures listed

Metric thread sizes	Ft-lbs	Nm
M-6	6 to 9	9 to 12
M-8	14 to 21	19 to 28
M-10	28 to 40	38 to 54
M-12	50 to 71	68 to 96
M-14	80 to 140	109 to 154
Pipe thread sizes		
1/8	5 to 8	7 to 10
1/4	12 to 18	17 to 24
3/8	22 to 33	30 to 44
1/2	25 to 35	34 to 47
U.S. thread sizes		
1/4 - 20	6 to 9	9 to 12
5/16 - 18	12 to 18	17 to 24
5/16 - 24	14 to 20	19 to 27
3/8 - 16	22 to 32	30 to 43
3/8 - 24	27 to 38	37 to 51
7/16 - 14	40 to 55	55 to 74
7/16 - 20	40 to 60	55 to 81
1/2 - 13	55 to 80	75 to 108

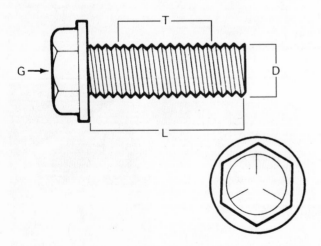

Standard (SAE and USS) bolt dimensions/grade marks

    G   *Grade marks (bolt length)*
    L   *Length (in inches)*
    T   *Thread pitch (number of threads per inch)*
    D   *Nominal diameter (in inches)*

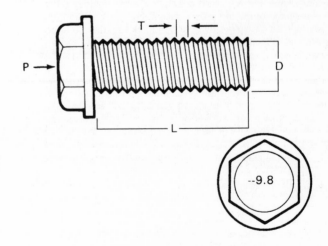

Metric bolt dimensions/grade marks

    P   *Property class (bolt strength)*
    L   *Length (in millimeters)*
    T   *Thread pitch (distance between threads in millimeters)*
    D   *Diameter*

here are approximate for Grade 2 and Grade 3 fasteners. Higher grades can tolerate higher torque values.

Fasteners laid out in a pattern, such as cylinder head bolts, oil pan bolts, differential cover bolts, etc., must be loosened or tightened in sequence to avoid warping the component. This sequence will normally be shown in the appropriate Chapter. If a specific pattern is not given, the following procedures can be used to prevent warping.

Initially, the bolts or nuts should be assembled finger-tight only. Next, they should be tightened one full turn each, in a criss-cross or diagonal pattern. After each one has been tightened one full turn, return to the first one and tighten them all one-half turn, following the same pattern. Finally, tighten each of them one-quarter turn at a time until each fastener has been tightened to the proper torque. To loosen and remove the fasteners, the procedure would be reversed.

Component disassembly

Component disassembly should be done with care and purpose to help ensure that the parts go back together properly. Always keep track of the sequence in which parts are removed. Make note of special characteristics or marks on parts that can be installed more than one way, such as a grooved thrust washer on a shaft. It is a good idea to lay the disassembled parts out on a clean surface in the order that they were removed. It may also be helpful to make sketches or take instant photos of components before removal.

When removing fasteners from a component, keep track of their locations. Sometimes threading a bolt back in a part, or putting the washers and nut back on a stud, can prevent mix-ups later. If nuts and bolts cannot be returned to their original locations, they should be kept in a compartmented box or a series of small boxes. A cupcake or muffin tin is ideal for this purpose, since each cavity can hold the bolts and nuts from a particular area (i.e. oil pan bolts, valve cover bolts, engine mount bolts, etc.). A pan of this type is especially helpful when working on assemblies with very small parts, such as the carburetor, alternator, valve train or interior dash and trim pieces. The cavities can be marked with paint or tape to identify the contents.

Whenever wiring looms, harnesses or connectors are separated, it is a good idea to identify the two halves with numbered pieces of masking tape so they can be easily reconnected.

Gasket sealing surfaces

Throughout any vehicle, gaskets are used to seal the mating surfaces between two parts and keep lubricants, fluids, vacuum or pressure contained in an assembly.

Many times these gaskets are coated with a liquid or paste-type gasket sealing compound before assembly. Age, heat and pressure can sometimes cause the two parts to stick together so tightly that they are very difficult to separate. Often, the assembly can be loosened by striking it with a soft-face hammer near the mating surfaces. A regular hammer can be used if a block of wood is placed between the hammer and the part. Do not hammer on cast parts or parts that could be easily damaged. With any particularly stubborn part, always recheck to make sure that every fastener has been removed.

Avoid using a screwdriver or bar to pry apart an assembly, as they can easily mar the gasket sealing surfaces of the parts, which must remain smooth. If prying is absolutely necessary, use an old broom handle, but keep in mind that extra clean up will be necessary if the wood splinters.

After the parts are separated, the old gasket must be carefully scraped off and the gasket surfaces cleaned. Stubborn gasket material can be soaked with rust penetrant or treated with a special chemical to soften it so it can be easily scraped off. A scraper can be fashioned from a piece of copper tubing by flattening and sharpening one end. Copper is recommended because it is usually softer than the surfaces to be scraped, which reduces the chance of gouging the part. Some gaskets can be removed with a wire brush, but regardless of the method used, the mating surfaces must be left clean and smooth. If for some reason the gasket surface is gouged, then a gasket sealer thick enough to fill scratches will have to be used during reassembly of the components. For most applications, a non-drying (or semi-drying) gasket sealer should be used.

Hose removal tips

Warning: *If the vehicle is equipped with air conditioning, do not disconnect any of the A/C hoses without first having the system depressurized by a dealer service department or a service station.*

Hose removal precautions closely parallel gasket removal precautions. Avoid scratching or gouging the surface that the hose mates against or the connection may leak. This is especially true for radiator hoses. Because of various chemical reactions, the rubber in hoses can bond itself to the metal spigot that the hose fits over. To remove a hose, first loosen the hose clamps that secure it to the spigot. Then, with slip-joint pliers, grab the hose at the clamp and rotate it around the spigot. Work it back and forth until it is completely free, then pull it off. Silicone or other lubricants will ease removal if they can be applied between the hose and the outside of the spigot. Apply the same lubricant to the inside of the hose and the outside of the spigot to simplify installation.

As a last resort (and if the hose is to be replaced with a new one anyway), the rubber can be slit with a knife and the hose peeled from the spigot. If this must be done, be careful that the metal connection is not damaged.

If a hose clamp is broken or damaged, do not reuse it. Wire-type clamps usually weaken with age, so it is a good idea to replace them with screw-type clamps whenever a hose is removed.

Tools

A selection of good tools is a basic requirement for anyone who plans to maintain and repair his or her own vehicle. For the owner who has few tools, the initial investment might seem high, but when compared to the spiraling costs of professional auto maintenance and repair, it is a wise one.

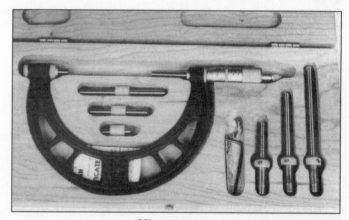

Micrometer set

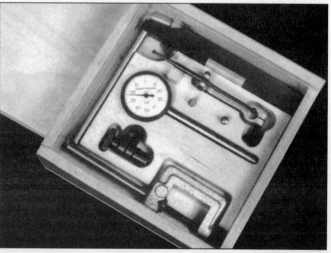

Dial indicator set

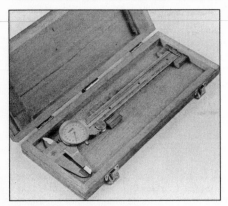

Dial caliper

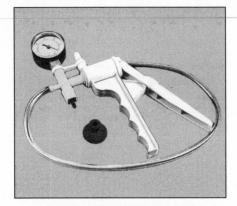

Hand-operated vacuum pump

Timing light

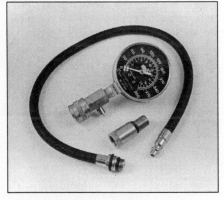

Compression gauge with spark plug hole adapter

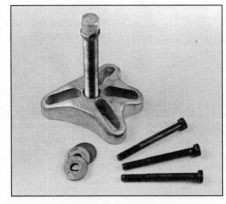

Damper/steering wheel puller

General purpose puller

Hydraulic lifter removal tool

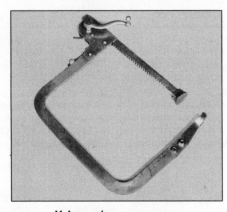

Valve spring compressor

Valve spring compressor

Ridge reamer

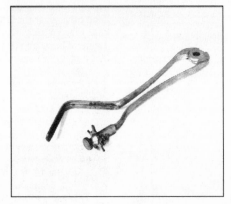

Piston ring groove cleaning tool

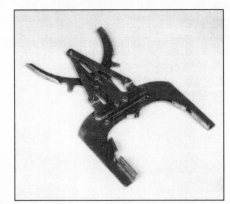

Ring removal/installation tool

Ring compressor

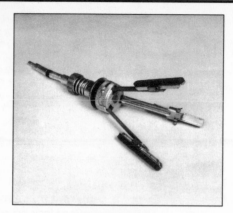

Cylinder hone

Brake hold-down spring tool

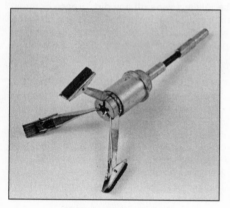

Brake cylinder hone

Clutch plate alignment tool

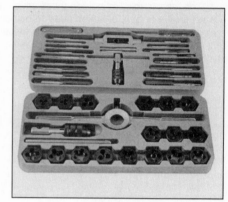

Tap and die set

To help the owner decide which tools are needed to perform the tasks detailed in this manual, the following tool lists are offered: *Maintenance and minor repair, Repair/overhaul* and *Special.*

The newcomer to practical mechanics should start off with the *maintenance and minor repair* tool kit, which is adequate for the simpler jobs performed on a vehicle. Then, as confidence and experience grow, the owner can tackle more difficult tasks, buying additional tools as they are needed. Eventually the basic kit will be expanded into the *repair and overhaul* tool set. Over a period of time, the experienced do-it-yourselfer will assemble a tool set complete enough for most repair and overhaul procedures and will add tools from the special category when it is felt that the expense is justified by the frequency of use.

Maintenance and minor repair tool kit

The tools in this list should be considered the minimum required for performance of routine maintenance, servicing and minor repair work. We recommend the purchase of combination wrenches (box-end and open-end combined in one wrench). While more expensive than open end wrenches, they offer the advantages of both types of wrench.

    Combination wrench set (1/4-inch to 1 inch or 6 mm to 19 mm)
    Adjustable wrench, 8 inch
    Spark plug wrench with rubber insert
    Spark plug gap adjusting tool
    Feeler gauge set
    Brake bleeder wrench
    Standard screwdriver (5/16-inch x 6 inch)
    Phillips screwdriver (No. 2 x 6 inch)
    Combination pliers - 6 inch
    Hacksaw and assortment of blades
    Tire pressure gauge
    Grease gun
    Oil can
    Fine emery cloth
    Wire brush

    Battery post and cable cleaning tool
    Oil filter wrench
    Funnel (medium size)
    Safety goggles
    Jackstands (2)
    Drain pan

Note: *If basic tune-ups are going to be part of routine maintenance, it will be necessary to purchase a good quality stroboscopic timing light and combination tachometer/dwell meter. Although they are included in the list of special tools, it is mentioned here because they are absolutely necessary for tuning most vehicles properly.*

Repair and overhaul tool set

These tools are essential for anyone who plans to perform major repairs and are in addition to those in the maintenance and minor repair tool kit. Included is a comprehensive set of sockets which, though expensive, are invaluable because of their versatility, especially when various extensions and drives are available. We recommend the 1/2-inch drive over the 3/8-inch drive. Although the larger drive is bulky and more expensive, it has the capacity of accepting a very wide range of large sockets. Ideally, however, the mechanic should have a 3/8-inch drive set and a 1/2-inch drive set.

    Socket set(s)
    Reversible ratchet
    Extension - 10 inch
    Universal joint
    Torque wrench (same size drive as sockets)
    Ball peen hammer - 8 ounce
    Soft-face hammer (plastic/rubber)
    Standard screwdriver (1/4-inch x 6 inch)
    Standard screwdriver (stubby - 5/16-inch)
    Phillips screwdriver (No. 3 x 8 inch)
    Phillips screwdriver (stubby - No. 2)
    Pliers - vise grip
    Pliers - lineman's

Pliers - needle nose
Pliers - snap-ring (internal and external)
Cold chisel - 1/2-inch
Scribe
Scraper (made from flattened copper tubing)
Centerpunch
Pin punches (1/16, 1/8, 3/16-inch)
Steel rule/straightedge - 12 inch
Allen wrench set (1/8 to 3/8-inch or 4 mm to 10 mm)
A selection of files
Wire brush (large)
Jackstands (second set)
Jack (scissor or hydraulic type)

Note: Another tool which is often useful is an electric drill with a chuck capacity of 3/8-inch and a set of good quality drill bits

Special tools

The tools in this list include those which are not used regularly, are expensive to buy, or which need to be used in accordance with their manufacturer's instructions. Unless these tools will be used frequently, it is not very economical to purchase many of them. A consideration would be to split the cost and use between yourself and a friend or friends. In addition, most of these tools can be obtained from a tool rental shop on a temporary basis.

This list primarily contains only those tools and instruments widely available to the public, and not those special tools produced by the vehicle manufacturer for distribution to dealer service departments. Occasionally, references to the manufacturer's special tools are included in the text of this manual. Generally, an alternative method of doing the job without the special tool is offered. However, sometimes there is no alternative to their use. Where this is the case, and the tool cannot be purchased or borrowed, the work should be turned over to the dealer service department or an automotive repair shop.

Valve spring compressor
Piston ring groove cleaning tool
Piston ring compressor
Piston ring installation tool
Cylinder compression gauge
Cylinder ridge reamer
Cylinder surfacing hone
Cylinder bore gauge
Micrometers and/or dial calipers
Hydraulic lifter removal tool
Balljoint separator
Universal-type puller
Impact screwdriver
Dial indicator set
Stroboscopic timing light (inductive pick-up)
Hand operated vacuum/pressure pump
Tachometer/dwell meter
Universal electrical multimeter
Cable hoist
Brake spring removal and installation tools
Floor jack

Buying tools

For the do-it-yourselfer who is just starting to get involved in vehicle maintenance and repair, there are a number of options available when purchasing tools. If maintenance and minor repair is the extent of the work to be done, the purchase of individual tools is satisfactory. If, on the other hand, extensive work is planned, it would be a good idea to purchase a modest tool set from one of the large retail chain stores. A set can usually be bought at a substantial savings over the individual tool prices, and they often come with a tool box. As additional tools are needed, add-on sets, individual tools and a larger tool box can be purchased to expand the tool selection. Building a tool set gradually allows the cost of the tools to be spread over a longer period of time and gives the mechanic the freedom to choose only those tools that will actually be used.

Tool stores will often be the only source of some of the special tools that are needed, but regardless of where tools are bought, try to avoid cheap ones, especially when buying screwdrivers and sockets, because they won't last very long. The expense involved in replacing cheap tools will eventually be greater than the initial cost of quality tools.

Care and maintenance of tools

Good tools are expensive, so it makes sense to treat them with respect. Keep them clean and in usable condition and store them properly when not in use. Always wipe off any dirt, grease or metal chips before putting them away. Never leave tools lying around in the work area. Upon completion of a job, always check closely under the hood for tools that may have been left there so they won't get lost during a test drive.

Some tools, such as screwdrivers, pliers, wrenches and sockets, can be hung on a panel mounted on the garage or workshop wall, while others should be kept in a tool box or tray. Measuring instruments, gauges, meters, etc. must be carefully stored where they cannot be damaged by weather or impact from other tools.

When tools are used with care and stored properly, they will last a very long time. Even with the best of care, though, tools will wear out if used frequently. When a tool is damaged or worn out, replace it. Subsequent jobs will be safer and more enjoyable if you do.

Working facilities

Not to be overlooked when discussing tools is the workshop. If anything more than routine maintenance is to be carried out, some sort of suitable work area is essential.

It is understood, and appreciated, that many home mechanics do not have a good workshop or garage available, and end up removing an engine or doing major repairs outside. It is recommended, however, that the overhaul or repair be completed under the cover of a roof.

A clean, flat workbench or table of comfortable working height is an absolute necessity. The workbench should be equipped with a vise that has a jaw opening of at least four inches.

As mentioned previously, some clean, dry storage space is also required for tools, as well as the lubricants, fluids, cleaning solvents, etc. which soon become necessary.

Sometimes waste oil and fluids, drained from the engine or cooling system during normal maintenance or repairs, present a disposal problem. To avoid pouring them on the ground or into a sewage system, pour the used fluids into large containers, seal them with caps and take them to an authorized disposal site or recycling center. Plastic jugs, such as old antifreeze containers, are ideal for this purpose.

Always keep a supply of old newspapers and clean rags available. Old towels are excellent for mopping up spills. Many mechanics use rolls of paper towels for most work because they are readily available and disposable. To help keep the area under the vehicle clean, a large cardboard box can be cut open and flattened to protect the garage or shop floor.

Whenever working over a painted surface, such as when leaning over a fender to service something under the hood, always cover it with an old blanket or bedspread to protect the finish. Vinyl covered pads, made especially for this purpose, are available at auto parts stores.

Jacking and towing

Jacking

When lifting the vehicle with either the supplied jack or a floor jack, block the wheel that is diagonally opposite the one being lifted to prevent the vehicle from moving. Warning: If equipped with an under-chassis mounted spare tire, remove the tire or tire carrier from the rack before the vehicle is raised in order to avoid sudden weight release from the chassis.

When using the vehicle jack, the manufacturer recommends positioning the jack under the axles, shock absorber or jacking bracket, as close to the wheel to be removed as possible (see illustrations).

When raising the vehicle for service, always place jackstands under the frame rails. NEVER work under the vehicle when it is supported only by a jack!

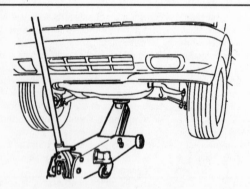

Front floor jack jacking point

Towing

Manual transmission

Vehicles with a manual transmission can be towed with all four wheels on the ground. The transmission should be in Neutral and the ignition key in the Accessory position.

Automatic transmission

The vehicle can be towed with all four wheels on the ground only forward at a speed of 35 mph for a distance no farther then 35 miles. Exceeding these speed and distance limitations will result in damage to the transmission.

4WD

A 4WD model can be towed with all four wheels on the ground after first setting the center differential in the unlocked position and the driving mode in 2WD.

All models

When the vehicle is towed with the rear wheels raised, the steering wheel must be clamped in the straight ahead position with a special device designed for use during towing. **Warning:** *Don't use the steering column lock to keep the front wheels pointed straight ahead. It's not strong enough for this purpose.*

Equipment specifically designed for towing should be used. It should be attached to the frame members of the vehicle, not the bumpers or brackets.

Safety is a major consideration when towing and all applicable state and local laws must be obeyed. A safety chain system must be used at all times. Remember that power steering and power brakes will not work with the engine off.

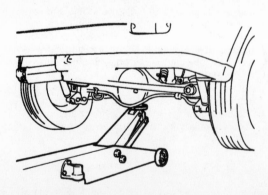

Rear floor jack jacking point

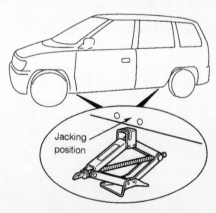

Jacking position

Vehicle supplied jacking points

Booster battery (jump) starting

Observe these precautions when using a booster battery to start a vehicle:

a) Before connecting the booster battery, make sure the ignition switch is in the Off position.

b) Turn off the lights, heater and other electrical loads.

c) Your eyes should be shielded. Safety goggles are a good idea.

d) Make sure the booster battery is the same voltage as the dead one in the vehicle.

e) The two vehicles MUST NOT TOUCH each other!

f) Make sure the transaxle is in Neutral (manual) or Park (automatic).

g) If the booster battery is not a maintenance-free type, remove the vent caps and lay a cloth over the vent holes.

Connect the red jumper cable to the positive (+) terminals of each battery (see illustration).

Connect one end of the black jumper cable to the negative (-) terminal of the booster battery. The other end of this cable should be connected to a good ground on the vehicle to be started, such as a bolt or bracket on the body.

Start the engine using the booster battery, then, with the engine running at idle speed, disconnect the jumper cables in the reverse order of connection.

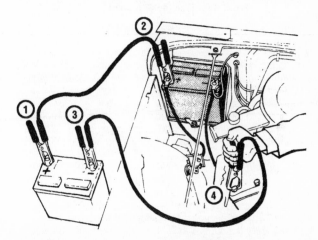

Make the booster battery cable connections in the numerical order shown (note that the negative cable of the booster battery is NOT attached to the negative terminal of the dead battery)

Automotive chemicals and lubricants

A number of automotive chemicals and lubricants are available for use during vehicle maintenance and repair. They include a wide variety of products ranging from cleaning solvents and degreasers to lubricants and protective sprays for rubber, plastic and vinyl.

Cleaners

Carburetor cleaner and choke cleaner is a strong solvent for gum, varnish and carbon. Most carburetor cleaners leave a dry-type lubricant film which will not harden or gum up. Because of this film it is not recommended for use on electrical components

Brake system cleaner is used to remove grease and brake fluid from the brake system, where clean surfaces are absolutely necessary. It leaves no residue and often eliminates brake squeal caused by contaminants.

Electrical cleaner removes oxidation, corrosion and carbon deposits from electrical contacts, restoring full current flow. It can also be used to clean spark plugs, carburetor jets, voltage regulators and other parts where an oil-free surface is desired.

Demoisturants remove water and moisture from electrical components such as alternators, voltage regulators, electrical connectors and fuse blocks. They are non-conductive, non-corrosive and non-flammable.

Degreasers are heavy-duty solvents used to remove grease from the outside of the engine and from chassis components. They can be sprayed or brushed on and, depending on the type, are rinsed off either with water or solvent.

Lubricants

Motor oil is the lubricant formulated for use in engines. It normally contains a wide variety of additives to prevent corrosion and reduce foaming and wear. Motor oil comes in various weights (viscosity ratings) from 5 to 80. The recommended weight of the oil depends on the season, temperature and the demands on the engine. Light oil is used in cold climates and under light load conditions. Heavy oil is used in hot climates and where high loads are encountered. Multi-viscosity oils are designed to have characteristics of both light and heavy oils and are available in a number of weights from 5W-20 to 20W-50.

Gear oil is designed to be used in differentials, manual transmissions and other areas where high-temperature lubrication is required.

Chassis and wheel bearing grease is a heavy grease used where increased loads and friction are encountered, such as for wheel bearings, balljoints, tie-rod ends and universal joints.

High-temperature wheel bearing grease is designed to withstand the extreme temperatures encountered by wheel bearings in disc brake equipped vehicles. It usually contains molybdenum disulfide (moly), which is a dry-type lubricant.

White grease is a heavy grease for metal-to-metal applications where water is a problem. White grease stays soft under both low and high temperatures (usually from -100 to +190-degrees F), and will not wash off or dilute in the presence of water.

Assembly lube is a special extreme pressure lubricant, usually containing moly, used to lubricate high-load parts (such as main and rod bearings and cam lobes) for initial start-up of a new engine. The assembly lube lubricates the parts without being squeezed out or washed away until the engine oiling system begins to function.

Silicone lubricants are used to protect rubber, plastic, vinyl and nylon parts.

Graphite lubricants are used where oils cannot be used due to contamination problems, such as in locks. The dry graphite will lubricate metal parts while remaining uncontaminated by dirt, water, oil or acids. It is electrically conductive and will not foul electrical contacts in locks such as the ignition switch.

Moly penetrants loosen and lubricate frozen, rusted and corroded fasteners and prevent future rusting or freezing.

Heat-sink grease is a special electrically non-conductive grease that is used for mounting electronic ignition modules where it is essential that heat is transferred away from the module.

Sealants

RTV sealant is one of the most widely used gasket compounds. Made from silicone, RTV is air curing, it seals, bonds, waterproofs, fills surface irregularities, remains flexible, doesn't shrink, is relatively easy to remove, and is used as a supplementary sealer with almost all low and medium temperature gaskets.

Anaerobic sealant is much like RTV in that it can be used either to seal gaskets or to form gaskets by itself. It remains flexible, is solvent resistant and fills surface imperfections. The difference between an anaerobic sealant and an RTV-type sealant is in the curing. RTV cures when exposed to air, while an anaerobic sealant cures only in the absence of air. This means that an anaerobic sealant cures only after the assembly of parts, sealing them together.

Thread and pipe sealant is used for sealing hydraulic and pneumatic fittings and vacuum lines. It is usually made from a Teflon compound, and comes in a spray, a paint-on liquid and as a wrap-around tape.

Chemicals

Anti-seize compound prevents seizing, galling, cold welding, rust and corrosion in fasteners. High-temperature ant-seize, usually made with copper and graphite lubricants, is used for exhaust system and exhaust manifold bolts.

Anaerobic locking compounds are used to keep fasteners from vibrating or working loose and cure only after installation, in the absence of air. Medium strength locking compound is used for small nuts, bolts and screws that may be removed later. High-strength locking compound is for large nuts, bolts and studs which aren't removed on a regular basis.

Oil additives range from viscosity index improvers to chemical treatments that claim to reduce internal engine friction. It should be noted that most oil manufacturers caution against using additives with their oils.

Gas additives perform several functions, depending on their chemical makeup. They usually contain solvents that help dissolve gum and varnish that build up on carburetor, fuel injection and intake parts. They also serve to break down carbon deposits that form on the inside surfaces of the combustion chambers. Some additives contain upper cylinder lubricants for valves and piston rings, and others contain chemicals to remove condensation from the gas tank.

Miscellaneous

Brake fluid is specially formulated hydraulic fluid that can withstand the heat and pressure encountered in brake systems. Care must be taken so this fluid does not come in contact with painted surfaces or plastics. An opened container should always be resealed to prevent contamination by water or dirt.

Weatherstrip adhesive is used to bond weatherstripping around doors, windows and trunk lids. It is sometimes used to attach trim pieces.

Undercoating is a petroleum-based, tar-like substance that is designed to protect metal surfaces on the underside of the vehicle from corrosion. It also acts as a sound-deadening agent by insulating the bottom of the vehicle.

Waxes and polishes are used to help protect painted and plated surfaces from the weather. Different types of paint may require the use of different types of wax and polish. Some polishes utilize a chemical or abrasive cleaner to help remove the top layer of oxidized (dull) paint on older vehicles. In recent years many non-wax polishes that contain a wide variety of chemicals such as polymers and silicones have been introduced. These non-wax polishes are usually easier to apply and last longer than conventional waxes and polishes.

Safety first

Regardless of how enthusiastic you may be about getting on with the job at hand, take the time to ensure that your safety is not jeopardized. A moment's lack of attention can result in an accident, as can failure to observe certain simple safety precautions. The possibility of an accident will always exist, and the following points should not be considered a comprehensive list of all dangers. Rather, they are intended to make you aware of the risks and to encourage a safety conscious approach to all work you carry out on your vehicle.

Essential DOs and DON'Ts

DON'T rely on a jack when working under the vehicle. Always use approved jackstands to support the weight of the vehicle and place them under the recommended lift or support points.

DON'T attempt to loosen extremely tight fasteners (i.e. wheel lug nuts) while the vehicle is on a jack - it may fall.

DON'T start the engine without first making sure that the transmission is in Neutral (or Park where applicable) and the parking brake is set.

DON'T remove the radiator cap from a hot cooling system - let it cool or cover it with a cloth and release the pressure gradually.

DON'T attempt to drain the engine oil until you are sure it has cooled to the point that it will not burn you.

DON'T touch any part of the engine or exhaust system until it has cooled sufficiently to avoid burns.

DON'T siphon toxic liquids such as gasoline, antifreeze and brake fluid by mouth, or allow them to remain on your skin.

DON'T inhale brake lining dust - it is potentially hazardous (see Asbestos below)

DON'T allow spilled oil or grease to remain on the floor - wipe it up before someone slips on it.

DON'T use loose fitting wrenches or other tools which may slip and cause injury.

DON'T push on wrenches when loosening or tightening nuts or bolts. Always try to pull the wrench toward you. If the situation calls for pushing the wrench away, push with an open hand to avoid scraped knuckles if the wrench should slip.

DON'T attempt to lift a heavy component alone - get someone to help you.

DON'T rush or take unsafe shortcuts to finish a job.

DON'T allow children or animals in or around the vehicle while you are working on it.

DO wear eye protection when using power tools such as a drill, sander, bench grinder, etc. and when working under a vehicle.

DO keep loose clothing and long hair well out of the way of moving parts.

DO make sure that any hoist used has a safe working load rating adequate for the job.

DO get someone to check on you periodically when working alone on a vehicle.

DO carry out work in a logical sequence and make sure that everything is correctly assembled and tightened.

DO keep chemicals and fluids tightly capped and out of the reach of children and pets.

DO remember that your vehicle's safety affects that of yourself and others. If in doubt on any point, get professional advice.

Asbestos

Certain friction, insulating, sealing, and other products - such as brake linings, brake bands, clutch linings, torque converters, gaskets, etc. - contain asbestos. Extreme care must be taken to avoid inhalation of dust from such products, since it is hazardous to health. If in doubt, assume that they do contain asbestos.

Fire

Remember at all times that gasoline is highly flammable. Never smoke or have any kind of open flame around when working on a vehicle. But the risk does not end there. A spark caused by an electrical short circuit, by two metal surfaces contacting each other, or even by static electricity built up in your body under certain conditions, can ignite gasoline vapors, which in a confined space are highly explosive. Do not, under any circumstances, use gasoline for cleaning parts. Use an approved safety solvent.

Always disconnect the battery ground (-) cable at the battery before working on any part of the fuel system or electrical system. Never risk spilling fuel on a hot engine or exhaust component.It is strongly recommended that a fire extinguisher suitable for use on fuel and electrical fires be kept handy in the garage or workshop at all times. Never try to extinguish a fuel or electrical fire with water.

Fumes

Certain fumes are highly toxic and can quickly cause unconsciousness and even death if inhaled to any extent. Gasoline vapor falls into this category, as do the vapors from some cleaning solvents. Any draining or pouring of such volatile fluids should be done in a well ventilated area.

When using cleaning fluids and solvents, read the instructions on the container carefully. Never use materials from unmarked containers.

Never run the engine in an enclosed space, such as a garage. Exhaust fumes contain carbon monoxide, which is extremely poisonous. If you need to run the engine, always do so in the open air, or at least have the rear of the vehicle outside the work area.

If you are fortunate enough to have the use of an inspection pit, never drain or pour gasoline and never run the engine while the vehicle is over the pit. The fumes, being heavier than air, will concentrate in the pit with possibly lethal results.

The battery

Never create a spark or allow a bare light bulb near a battery. They normally give off a certain amount of hydrogen gas, which is highly explosive.

Always disconnect the battery ground (-) cable at the battery before working on the fuel or electrical systems.

If possible, loosen the filler caps or cover when charging the battery from an external source (this does not apply to sealed or maintenance-free batteries). Do not charge at an excessive rate or the battery may burst.

Take care when adding water to a non maintenance-free battery and when carrying a battery. The electrolyte, even when diluted, is very corrosive and should not be allowed to contact clothing or skin.

Always wear eye protection when cleaning the battery to prevent the caustic deposits from entering your eyes.

Household current

When using an electric power tool, inspection light, etc., which operates on household current, always make sure that the tool is correctly connected to its plug and that, where necessary, it is properly grounded. Do not use such items in damp conditions and, again, do not create a spark or apply excessive heat in the vicinity of fuel or fuel vapor.

Secondary ignition system voltage

A severe electric shock can result from touching certain parts of the ignition system (such as the spark plug wires) when the engine is running or being cranked, particularly if components are damp or the insulation is defective. In the case of an electronic ignition system, the secondary system voltage is much higher and could prove fatal.

Conversion factors

Length (distance)

Inches (in)	X	25.4	= Millimetres (mm)	X	0.0394	= Inches (in)
Feet (ft)	X	0.305	= Metres (m)	X	3.281	= Feet (ft)
Miles	X	1.609	= Kilometres (km)	X	0.621	= Miles

Volume (capacity)

Cubic inches (cu in; in³)	X	16.387	= Cubic centimetres (cc; cm³)	X	0.061	= Cubic inches (cu in; in³)
Imperial pints (Imp pt)	X	0.568	= Litres (l)	X	1.76	= Imperial pints (Imp pt)
Imperial quarts (Imp qt)	X	1.137	= Litres (l)	X	0.88	= Imperial quarts (Imp qt)
Imperial quarts (Imp qt)	X	1.201	= US quarts (US qt)	X	0.833	= Imperial quarts (Imp qt)
US quarts (US qt)	X	0.946	= Litres (l)	X	1.057	= US quarts (US qt)
Imperial gallons (Imp gal)	X	4.546	= Litres (l)	X	0.22	= Imperial gallons (Imp gal)
Imperial gallons (Imp gal)	X	1.201	= US gallons (US gal)	X	0.833	= Imperial gallons (Imp gal)
US gallons (US gal)	X	3.785	= Litres (l)	X	0.264	= US gallons (US gal)

Mass (weight)

Ounces (oz)	X	28.35	= Grams (g)	X	0.035	Ounces (oz)
Pounds (lb)	X	0.454	= Kilograms (kg)	X	2.205	= Pounds (lb)

Force

Ounces-force (ozf; oz)	X	0.278	= Newtons (N)	X	3.6	= Ounces-force (ozf; oz)
Pounds-force (lbf; lb)	X	4.448	= Newtons (N)	X	0.225	= Pounds-force (lbf; lb)
Newtons (N)	X	0.1	= Kilograms-force (kgf; kg)	X	9.81	= Newtons (N)

Pressure

Pounds-force per square inch (psi; lbf/in²; lb/in²)	X	0.070	= Kilograms-force per square centimetre (kgf/cm²; kg/cm²)	X	14.223	= Pounds-force per square inch (psi; lbf/in²; lb/in²)
Pounds-force per square inch (psi; lbf/in²; lb/in²)	X	0.068	= Atmospheres (atm)	X	14.696	= Pounds-force per square inch (psi; lbf/in²; lb/in²)
Pounds-force per square inch (psi; lbf/in²; lb/in²)	X	0.069	= Bars	X	14.5	= Pounds-force per square inch (psi; lbf/in²; lb/in²)
Pounds-force per square inch (psi; lbf/in²; lb/in²)	X	6.895	= Kilopascals (kPa)	X	0.145	= Pounds-force per square inch (psi; lbf/in²; lb/in²)
Kilopascals (kPa)	X	0.01	= Kilograms-force per square centimetre (kgf/cm²; kg/cm²)	X	98.1	= Kilopascals (kPa)

Torque (moment of force)

Pounds-force inches (lbf in; lb in)	X	1.152	= Kilograms-force centimetre (kgf cm; kg cm)	X	0.868	= Pounds-force inches (lbf in; lb in)
Pounds-force inches (lbf in; lb in)	X	0.113	= Newton metres (Nm)	X	8.85	= Pounds-force inches (lbf in; lb in)
Pounds-force inches (lbf in; lb in)	X	0.083	= Pounds-force feet (lbf ft; lb ft)	X	12	= Pounds-force inches (lbf in; lb in)
Pounds-force feet (lbf ft; lb ft)	X	0.138	= Kilograms-force metres (kgf m; kg m)	X	7.233	= Pounds-force feet (lbf ft; lb ft)
Pounds-force feet (lbf ft; lb ft)	X	1.356	= Newton metres (Nm)	X	0.738	= Pounds-force feet (lbf ft; lb ft)
Newton metres (Nm)	X	0.102	= Kilograms-force metres (kgf m; kg m)	X	9.804	= Newton metres (Nm)

Power

Horsepower (hp)	X	745.7	= Watts (W)	X	0.0013	= Horsepower (hp)

Velocity (speed)

Miles per hour (miles/hr; mph)	X	1.609	= Kilometres per hour (km/hr; kph)	X	0.621	= Miles per hour (miles/hr; mph)

Fuel consumption*

Miles per gallon, Imperial (mpg)	X	0.354	= Kilometres per litre (km/l)	X	2.825	= Miles per gallon, Imperial (mpg)
Miles per gallon, US (mpg)	X	0.425	= Kilometres per litre (km/l)	X	2.352	= Miles per gallon, US (mpg)

Temperature

Degrees Fahrenheit = (°C x 1.8) + 32   Degrees Celsius (Degrees Centigrade; °C) = (°F − 32) x 0.56

*It is common practice to convert from miles per gallon (mpg) to litres/100 kilometres (l/100km),
where mpg (Imperial) x l/100 km = 282 and mpg (US) x l/100 km = 235

Troubleshooting

Contents

This section provides an easy reference guide to the more common problems which may occur during the operation of your vehicle. These problems and possible causes are grouped under various components or systems; i.e. Engine, Cooling System, etc., and also refer to the Chapter and/or Section which deals with the problem.

Remember that successful troubleshooting is not a mysterious black art practiced only by professional mechanics. It's simply the result of a bit of knowledge combined with an intelligent, systematic approach to the problem. Always work by a process of elimination, starting with the simplest solution and working through to the most complex - and never overlook the obvious. Anyone can forget to fill the gas tank or leave the lights on overnight, so don't assume that you are above such oversights.

Finally, always get clear in your mind why a problem has occurred and take steps to ensure that it doesn't happen again. If the electrical system fails because of a poor connection, check all other connections in the system to make sure that they don't fail as well. If a particular fuse continues to blow, find out why - don't just go on replacing fuses. Remember, failure of a small component can often be indicative of potential failure or incorrect functioning of a more important component or system.

Engine

1   Engine will not rotate when attempting to start

1   Battery terminal connections loose or corroded. Check the cable terminals at the battery. Tighten the cable or remove corrosion as necessary.
2   Battery discharged or faulty. If the cable connections are clean and tight on the battery posts, turn the key to the On position and switch on the headlights and/or windshield wipers. If they fail to function, the battery is discharged.
3   Automatic transmission not completely engaged in Park or Neutral or clutch pedal not completely depressed.
4   Broken, loose or disconnected wiring in the starting circuit. Inspect all wiring and connectors at the battery, starter solenoid and ignition switch.
5   Starter motor pinion jammed in flywheel ring gear. If manual transmission, place transmission in gear and rock the vehicle to manually turn the engine. Remove starter and inspect pinion and flywheel at earliest convenience (Chapter 5).
6   Starter solenoid faulty (Chapter 5).
7   Starter motor faulty (Chapter 5).
8   Ignition switch faulty (Chapter 12).

2   Engine rotates but will not start

1   Fuel tank empty.
2   Fault in the fuel injection system (Chapter 4).
3   Battery discharged (engine rotates slowly). Check the operation of electrical components as described in the previous Section.
4   Battery terminal connections loose or corroded (see previous Section).
5   Fuel pump faulty (Chapter 4).
6   Excessive moisture on, or damage to, ignition components (see Chapter 5).
7   Worn, faulty or incorrectly gapped spark plugs (Chapter 1).
8   Broken, loose or disconnected wiring in the starting circuit (see previous Section).
9   Broken, loose or disconnected wires at the ignition coil or distributor (Chapter 5).
10   Low fuel line pressure (Chapter 4).
11   Incorrect ignition timing with engine hot. Check the timing with the engine at normal operating temperature (Chapter 1).

3   Starter motor operates without rotating engine

1   Starter pinion sticking. Remove the starter (Chapter 5) and inspect.
2   Starter pinion or flywheel teeth worn or broken. Remove the flywheel/driveplate access cover and inspect.

4   Engine hard to start when cold

1   Battery discharged or low. Check as described in Section 1.
2   Fault in the fuel or electrical systems (Chapters 4 and 5).
3   Faulty water temperature sensor (Chapter 6).
4   Fault in the ISC system (Chapter 4).

5   Engine hard to start when hot

1   Air filter clogged (Chapter 1).
2   Fault in the fuel or electrical systems (Chapters 4 and 5).
3   Fuel not reaching the injectors (see Chapter 4).

6   Starter motor noisy or excessively rough in engagement

1   Pinion or flywheel gear teeth worn or broken. Remove the cover at the rear of the engine (if equipped) and inspect.
2   Starter motor mounting bolts loose or missing.

7   Engine starts but stops immediately

1   Loose or faulty electrical connections at distributor, coil or alternator.
2   Fault in the fuel or electrical systems (Chapters 4 and 5).
3   Vacuum leak at the gasket surfaces of the intake manifold or throttle body. Make sure all mounting bolts/nuts are tightened securely and all vacuum hoses connected to the manifold are positioned properly and in good condition.
4   Faulty airflow meter (Chapter 4).
5   Low fuel pressure. Check the fuel pressure regulator (Chapter 4).

8   Engine lopes while idling or idles erratically

1   Vacuum leakage. Check the mounting bolts/nuts at the throttle body and intake manifold for tightness. Make sure all vacuum hoses are connected and in good condition. Use a stethoscope or a length of fuel hose held against your ear to listen for vacuum leaks while the engine is running. A hissing sound will be heard. A soapy water solution will also detect leaks.
2   Fault in the fuel or electrical systems (Chapters 4 and 5).
3   Plugged PCV valve (see Chapters 1 and 6).
4   Air filter clogged (Chapter 1).
5   Fuel pump not delivering sufficient fuel to the fuel injectors (see Chapter 4).
6   Leaking head gasket. Perform a compression check (Chapter 2).
7   Camshaft lobes worn (Chapter 2).
8   Faulty oxygen sensor (Chapter 6).

9   Engine misses at idle speed

1   Spark plugs worn, fouled or not gapped properly (Chapter 1).
2   Fault in the fuel or electrical systems (Chapters 4 and 5).

3   Faulty spark plug wires (Chapter 1).
4   Vacuum leaks at intake or hose connections. Check as described in Section 8.
5   Uneven or low cylinder compression. Check compression as described in Chapter 1.

10   Engine misses throughout driving speed range

1   Fuel filter clogged and/or impurities in the fuel system (Chapter 1).
2   Faulty or incorrectly gapped spark plugs (Chapter 1).
3   Fault in the fuel or electrical systems (Chapters 4 and 5).
4   Defective spark plug wires (Chapter 1).
5   Faulty emissions system components (Chapter 6).
6   Low or uneven cylinder compression pressures. Remove the spark plugs and test the compression with a gauge (Chapter 2).
7   Weak or faulty ignition system (Chapter 5).
8   Vacuum leaks at the throttle body, intake manifold or vacuum hoses (see Section 8).
9   Faulty oxygen sensor (Chapter 6).

11   Engine stalls

1   Idle speed incorrect (Chapter 1)..
2   Fuel filter clogged and/or water and impurities in the fuel system (Chapter 1).
3   Fault in the fuel system or sensors (Chapters 4 and 6).
4   Faulty emissions system components (Chapter 6).
5   Faulty or incorrectly gapped spark plugs (Chapter 1). Also check the spark plug wires (Chapter 1).
6   Vacuum leak at the throttle body, intake manifold or vacuum hoses. Check as described in Section 8.

12   Engine lacks power

1   Fault in the fuel or electrical systems (Chapters 4 and 5).
2   Faulty or incorrectly gapped spark plugs (Chapter 1).
3   Faulty coil (Chapter 5).
4   Brakes binding (Chapter 1).
5   Automatic transmission fluid level incorrect (Chapter 1).
6   Clutch slipping (Chapter 8).
7   Fuel filter clogged and/or impurities in the fuel system (Chapter 1).
8   Emissions control system not functioning properly (Chapter 6).
9   Use of substandard fuel. Fill the tank with the proper octane fuel.
10   Low or uneven cylinder compression pressures. Test with a compression tester, which will detect leaking valves and/or a blown head gasket (Chapter 2).

13   Engine backfires

1   Emissions system not functioning properly (Chapter 6).
2   Fault in the fuel or electrical systems (Chapters 4 and 5).
3   Faulty secondary ignition system (cracked spark plug insulator or faulty plug wires) (Chapters 1 and 5).
4   Fuel injection system in need of adjustment or worn excessively (Chapter 4).
5   Vacuum leak at the throttle body, intake manifold or vacuum hoses. Check as described in Section 8.
6   Valves sticking (Chapter 2).
7   Crossed plug wires (Chapter 1).

14   Pinging or knocking engine sounds during acceleration or uphill

1   Incorrect grade of fuel. Fill the tank with fuel of the proper octane rating.
2   Fault in the fuel or electrical systems (Chapters 4 and 5).
3   Improper spark plugs. Check the plug type against the VECI label located in the engine compartment. Also check the plugs and wires for damage (Chapter 1).
4   Faulty emissions system (Chapter 6).
5   Vacuum leak. Check as described in Section 8.

15   Engine diesels (continues to run) after switching off

1   Idle speed too high. Refer to Chapter 1.
2   Fault in the fuel or electrical systems (Chapters 4 and 5).
3   Excessive engine operating temperature. Probable causes of this are a low coolant level (see Chapter 1), malfunctioning thermostat, clogged radiator or faulty water pump (see Chapter 3).

Engine electrical system

16   Battery will not hold a charge

1   Alternator drivebelt defective or not adjusted properly (Chapter 1).
2   Electrolyte level low or battery discharged (Chapter 1).
3   Battery terminals loose or corroded (Chapter 1).
4   Alternator not charging properly (Chapter 5).
5   Loose, broken or faulty wiring in the charging circuit (Chapter 5).
6   Short in the vehicle wiring causing a continuous drain on the battery (refer to Chapter 12 and the Wiring Diagrams).
7   Battery defective internally.

17   Ignition light fails to go out

1   Fault in the alternator or charging circuit (Chapter 5).
2   Alternator drivebelt defective or not properly adjusted (Chapter 1).

18   Ignition light fails to come on when key is turned on

1   Instrument cluster warning light bulb defective (Chapter 12).
2   Alternator faulty (Chapter 5).
3   Fault in the instrument cluster printed circuit, dashboard wiring or bulb holder (Chapter 12).

Fuel system

19   Excessive fuel consumption

1   Dirty or clogged air filter element (Chapter 1).
2   Emissions system not functioning properly (Chapter 6).
3   Fault in the fuel or electrical systems (Chapters 4 and 5).
4   Fuel injection system internal parts excessively worn or damaged (Chapter 4).
5   Low tire pressure or incorrect tire size (Chapter 1).

20　Fuel leakage and/or fuel odor

1　Leak in a fuel feed or vent line (Chapter 4).
2　Tank overfilled. Fill only to automatic shut-off.
3　Evaporative emissions system canister clogged (Chapter 6).
4　Vapor leaks from system lines (Chapter 4).
5　Fuel injection system internal parts excessively worn or out of adjustment (Chapter 4).

Cooling system

21　Overheating

1　Insufficient coolant in the system (Chapter 1).
2　Water pump drivebelt defective or not adjusted properly (Chapter 1).
3　Radiator core blocked or radiator grille dirty and restricted (see Chapter 3).
4　Thermostat faulty (Chapter 3).
5　Fan blades broken or cracked (Chapter 3).
6　Radiator cap not maintaining proper pressure. Have the cap pressure tested by gas station or repair shop.

22　Overcooling

1　Thermostat faulty (Chapter 3).
2　Inaccurate temperature gauge (Chapter 12).

23　External coolant leakage

1　Deteriorated or damaged hoses or loose clamps. Replace hoses and/or tighten the clamps at the hose connections (Chapter 1).
2　Water pump seals defective. If this is the case, water will drip from the weep hole in the water pump body (Chapter 3).
3　Leakage from the radiator core or side tank(s). This will require the radiator to be professionally repaired (see Chapter 3 for removal procedures).
4　Engine drain plug leaking (Chapter 1) or water jacket core plugs leaking (see Chapter 2).

24　Internal coolant leakage

Note: *Internal coolant leaks can usually be detected by examining the oil. Check the dipstick and inside of the valve cover for water deposits and an oil consistency like that of a milkshake.*
1　Leaking cylinder head gasket. Have the cooling system pressure tested.
2　Cracked cylinder bore or cylinder head. Dismantle the engine and inspect (Chapter 2).

25　Coolant loss

1　Too much coolant in the system (Chapter 1).
2　Coolant boiling away due to overheating (see Section 15).
3　External or internal leakage (see Sections 23 and 24).
4　Faulty radiator cap. Have the cap pressure tested.

26　Poor coolant circulation

1　Inoperative water pump. A quick test is to pinch the top radiator hose closed with your hand while the engine is idling, then let it loose. You should feel the surge of coolant if the pump is working properly (see Chapter 1).
2　Restriction in the cooling system. Drain, flush and refill the system (Chapter 1). If necessary, remove the radiator (Chapter 3) and have it reverse flushed.
3　Water pump drivebelt defective or not adjusted properly (Chapter 1).
4　Thermostat sticking (Chapter 3).

Clutch

27　Fails to release (pedal pressed to the floor - shift lever does not move freely in and out of Reverse)

1　Leak in the clutch hydraulic system. Check the master cylinder, slave cylinder and lines (Chapter 8).
2　Clutch plate warped or damaged (Chapter 8).

28　Clutch slips (engine speed increases with no increase in vehicle speed)

1　Clutch plate oil soaked or lining worn. Remove clutch (Chapter 8) and inspect.
2　Clutch plate not seated. It may take 30 or 40 normal starts for a new one to seat.
3　Pressure plate worn (Chapter 8).

29　Grabbing (chattering) as clutch is engaged

1　Oil on clutch plate lining. Remove (Chapter 8) and inspect. Correct any leakage source.
2　Worn or loose engine or transmission mounts. These units move slightly when the clutch is released. Inspect the mounts and bolts (Chapter 2).
3　Worn splines on clutch plate hub. Remove the clutch components (Chapter 8) and inspect.
4　Warped pressure plate or flywheel. Remove the clutch components and inspect.

30　Squeal or rumble with clutch fully engaged (pedal released)

Release bearing binding on transmission bearing retainer. Remove clutch components (Chapter 8) and check bearing. Remove any burrs or nicks; clean and relubricate bearing retainer before installing.

31　Squeal or rumble with clutch fully disengaged (pedal depressed)

1　Worn, defective or broken release bearing (Chapter 8).
2　Worn or broken pressure plate springs (or diaphragm fingers) (Chapter 8).

32 Clutch pedal stays on floor when disengaged

1   Linkage or release bearing binding. Inspect the linkage or remove the clutch components as necessary.
2   Make sure proper pedal stop (bumper) is installed.

Manual transmission

Note: *All the following references are in Chapter 7, unless noted.*

33 Noisy in Neutral with engine running

1   Input shaft bearing worn.
2   Damaged main drive gear bearing.
3   Worn countershaft bearings.
4   Worn or damaged countershaft endplay shims.

34 Noisy in all gears

1   Any of the above causes, and/or:
2   Insufficient lubricant (see the checking procedures in Chapter 1).

35 Noisy in one particular gear

1   Worn, damaged or chipped gear teeth for that particular gear.
2   Worn or damaged synchronizer for that particular gear.

36 Slips out of high gear

1   Transmission loose on clutch housing.
2   Dirt between the transmission case and engine or misalignment of the transmission (Chapter 7).

37 Difficulty in engaging gears

1   Clutch not releasing completely (see clutch adjustment in Chapter 1).
2   Loose, damaged or out-of-adjustment shift linkage. Make a thorough inspection, replacing parts as necessary (Chapter 7).

38 Oil leakage

1   Excessive amount of lubricant in the transmission (see Chapter 1 for correct checking procedures). Drain lubricant as required.
2   Driveaxle oil seal or speedometer oil seal in need of replacement (Chapter 7).

Automatic transmission

Note: *Due to the complexity of the automatic transmission, it's difficult for the home mechanic to properly diagnose and service this component. For problems other than the following, the vehicle should be taken to a dealer service department or a transmission shop.*

39 General shift mechanism problems

1   Chapter 7 deals with checking and adjusting the shift linkage on automatic transmissions. Common problems which may be attributed

to poorly adjusted linkage are:
   a) Engine starting in gears other than Park or Neutral.
   b) Indicator on shifter pointing to a gear other than the one actually being selected.
   c) Vehicle moves when in Park.
2   Refer to Chapter 7 to adjust the linkage.

40 Transmission slips, shifts rough, is noisy or has no drive in forward or reverse gears

1   There are many probable causes for the above problems, but the home mechanic should be concerned with only one possibility - fluid level.
2   Before taking the vehicle to a repair shop, check the level and condition of the fluid as described in Chapter 1. Correct fluid level as necessary or change the fluid and filter if needed. If the problem persists, have a professional diagnose the probable cause.
3   If the transmission shifts late and the shifts are harsh, suspect a faulty vacuum diaphragm.

41 Fluid leakage

1   Automatic transmission fluid is a deep red color. Fluid leaks should not be confused with engine oil, which can easily be blown by air flow to the transmission.
2   To pinpoint a leak, first remove all built-up dirt and grime from around the transmission. Degreasing agents and/or steam cleaning will achieve this. With the underside clean, drive the vehicle at low speeds so air flow will not blow the leak far from its source. Raise the vehicle and determine where the leak is coming from. Common areas of leakage are:
   a) **Pan:** Tighten the mounting bolts and/or replace the pan gasket as necessary (see Chapter 7).
   b) **Filler pipe:** Replace the rubber seal where the pipe enters the transmission case.
   c) **Transmission oil lines:** Tighten the connectors where the lines enter the transmission case and/or replace the lines.
   d) **Vent pipe:** Transmission overfilled and/or water in fluid (see checking procedures, Chapter 1).
   e) **Speedometer connector:** Replace the O-ring where the speedometer cable enters the transmission case (Chapter 7).

Transfer case

42 Transfer case is difficult to shift into the desired range

1   Speed may be too great to permit engagement. Stop the vehicle and shift into the desired range.
2   Insufficient battery voltage to fully engage the transfer case. Check the battery (Chapter 1) and make sure the electrical connections are secure (Chapter 7).
3   Insufficient or incorrect grade of lubricant. Drain and refill the transfer case with the specified lubricant (Chapter 1).
4   Worn or damaged internal components. Disassembly and overhaul of the transfer case may be necessary (Chapter 7).

43 Transfer case noisy in all gears

Insufficient or incorrect grade of lubricant. Drain and refill (Chapter 1).

44   Noisy or jumps out of four-wheel drive Low range

1   Transfer case not fully engaged. Stop the vehicle, shift into Neutral and then engage 4L.
2   Insufficient battery voltage to fully engage the transfer case. Check the battery (Chapter 1 and make sure the electrical connections are secure (Chapter 7).
3   Shift linkage loose, worn or binding. Tighten, repair or lubricate linkage as necessary.
4   Shift fork cracked, inserts worn or fork binding on the rail. Disassemble and repair as necessary (Chapter 7).

45   Lubricant leaks from the vent or output shaft seals

1   Transfer case is overfilled. Drain to the proper level (Chapter 1).
2   Vent is clogged or jammed closed. Clear or replace the vent.
3   Output shaft seal incorrectly installed or damaged. Replace the seal and check contact surfaces for nicks and scoring.

Driveshaft

46   Oil leak at seal end of driveshaft

Defective transmission or transfer case oil seal. See Chapter 7 for replacement procedures. While this is done, check the splined yoke for burrs or a rough condition which may be damaging the seal. Burrs can be removed with crocus cloth or a fine whetstone.

47   Knock or clunk when the transmission is under initial load (just after transmission is put into gear)

1   Loose or disconnected rear suspension components. Check all mounting bolts, nuts and bushings (see Chapter 10).
2   Loose driveshaft bolts. Inspect all bolts and nuts and tighten them to the specified torque.
3   Worn or damaged universal joint bearings. Check for wear (see Chapter 8).

48   Metallic grinding sound consistent with vehicle speed.

Pronounced wear in the universal joint bearings. Check as described in Chapter 8.

49   Vibration

Note: *Before assuming that the driveshaft is at fault, make sure the tires are perfectly balanced and perform the following test.*

1   Install a tachometer inside the vehicle to monitor engine speed as the vehicle is driven. Drive the vehicle and note the engine speed at which the vibration (roughness) is most pronounced. Now shift the transmission to a different gear and bring the engine speed to the same point.
2   If the vibration occurs at the same engine speed (rpm) regardless of which gear the transmission is in, the driveshaft is NOT at fault since the driveshaft speed varies.
3   If the vibration decreases or is eliminated when the transmission is in a different gear at the same engine speed, refer to the following probable causes.
4   Bent or dented driveshaft. Inspect and replace as necessary (see Chapter 8).

5   Undercoating or built-up dirt, etc. on the driveshaft. Clean the shaft thoroughly and recheck.
6   Worn universal joint bearings. Remove and inspect (see Chapter 8).
7   Driveshaft and/or companion flange out of balance. Check for missing weights on the shaft. Remove the driveshaft (see Chapter 8) and reinstall 180-degrees from original position, then retest. Have the driveshaft professionally balanced if the problem persists.

Axles

50   Noise

1   Road noise. No corrective procedures available.
2   Tire noise. Inspect tires and check tire pressures (Chapter 1).
3   Rear axle bearings worn or damaged (Chapter 8).

51   Vibration

See probable causes under *Driveshaft*. Proceed under the guidelines listed for the driveshaft. If the problem persists, check the rear axle bearings by raising the rear of the vehicle and spinning the rear wheels by hand. Listen for evidence of rough (noisy) bearings. Remove and inspect (see Chapter 8).

52   Oil leakage

1   Pinion seal damaged (see Chapter 8).
2   Axleshaft oil seals damaged (see Chapter 8).

Brakes

Note: *Before assuming that a brake problem exists, make sure that the tires are in good condition and inflated properly (see Chapter 1), that the front end alignment is correct and that the vehicle is not loaded with weight in an unequal manner.*

53   Vehicle pulls to one side during braking

1   Defective, damaged or oil contaminated disc brake pads or shoes on one side. Inspect as described in Chapter 9.
2   Excessive wear of brake shoe or pad material or drum/disc on one side. Inspect and correct as necessary.
3   Loose or disconnected front suspension components. Inspect and tighten all bolts to the specified torque (Chapter 10).
4   Defective drum brake or caliper assembly. Remove the drum or caliper and inspect for a stuck piston or other damage (Chapter 9).

54   Noise (high-pitched squeal with the brakes applied)

1   Disc brake pads worn out. The noise comes from the wear sensor rubbing against the disc (does not apply to all vehicles) or the actual pad backing plate itself if the material is completely worn away. Replace the pads with new ones immediately (Chapter 9). If the pad material has worn completely away, the brake discs should be inspected for damage as described in Chapter 9.
2   Missing or damaged brake pad insulators (disc brakes). Replace pad insulators (see Chapter 9).
3   Linings contaminated with dirt or grease. Replace pads or shoes.
4   Incorrect linings. Replace with correct linings.

55 Excessive brake pedal travel

1   Partial brake system failure. Inspect the entire system (Chapter 9) and correct as required.
2   Insufficient fluid in the master cylinder. Check (Chapter 1), add fluid and bleed the system if necessary (Chapter 9).
3   Rear brakes not adjusting properly. Make a series of starts and stops while the vehicle is in Reverse. If this does not correct the situation, remove the drums and inspect the self-adjusters (Chapter 9).

56 Brake pedal feels spongy when depressed

1   Air in the hydraulic lines. Bleed the brake system (Chapter 9).
2   Faulty flexible hoses. Inspect all system hoses and lines. Replace parts as necessary.
3   Master cylinder mounting bolts/nuts loose.
4   Master cylinder defective (Chapter 9).

57 Excessive effort required to stop vehicle

1   Power brake booster not operating properly (Chapter 9).
2   Excessively worn linings or pads. Inspect and replace if necessary (Chapter 9).
3   One or more caliper pistons or wheel cylinders seized or sticking. Inspect and rebuild as required (Chapter 9).
4   Brake linings or pads contaminated with oil or grease. Inspect and replace as required (Chapter 9).
5   New pads or shoes installed and not yet seated. It will take a while for the new material to seat against the drum (or disc).

58 Pedal travels to the floor with little resistance

1   Little or no fluid in the master cylinder reservoir caused by leaking wheel cylinder(s), lea
king caliper piston(s), loose, damaged or disconnected brake lines. Inspect the entire system and correct as necessary.
2   Worn master cylinder seals (Chapter 9).

59 Brake pedal pulsates during brake application

1   Caliper improperly installed. Remove and inspect (Chapter 9).
2   Disc or drum defective. Remove (Chapter 9) and check for excessive lateral runout and parallelism. Have the disc or drum resurfaced or replace it with a new one.

Suspension and steering systems

60 Vehicle pulls to one side

1   Tire pressures uneven (Chapter 1).
2   Defective tire (Chapter 1).
3   Excessive wear in suspension or steering components (Chapter 10).
4   Front end in need of alignment.
5   Front brakes dragging. Inspect the brakes as described in Chapter 9.

61 Shimmy, shake or vibration

1   Tire or wheel out-of-balance or out-of-round. Have professionally balanced.
2   Loose or worn front hub/wheel bearing assembly(ies) (Chapter 10).
3   Shock absorbers and/or suspension components worn or damaged (Chapter 10).

62 Excessive pitching and/or rolling around corners or during braking

1   Defective shock absorbers. Replace as a set (Chapter 10).
2   Broken or weak springs and/or suspension components. Inspect as described in Chapter 10.

63 Excessively stiff steering

1   Lack of fluid in power steering fluid reservoir (Chapter 1).
2   Incorrect tire pressures (Chapter 1).
3   Lack of lubrication at steering joints (see Chapter 1).
4   Front end out of alignment.
5   Lack of power assistance (see Section 62).

64 Excessive play in steering

1   Worn front hub/wheel bearing assembly(ies) (Chapters 10).
2   Excessive wear in suspension or steering components (Chapter 10).
3   Steering gearbox damaged or out of adjustment (Chapter 10).

65 Lack of power assistance

1   Steering pump drivebelt faulty or not adjusted properly (Chapter 1).
2   Fluid level low (Chapter 1).
3   Hoses or lines restricted. Inspect and replace parts as necessary.
4   Air in power steering system. Bleed the system (Chapter 10).

66 Excessive tire wear (not specific to one area)

1   Incorrect tire pressures (Chapter 1).
2   Tires out-of-balance. Have professionally balanced.
3   Wheels damaged. Inspect and replace as necessary.
4   Suspension or steering components excessively worn (Chapter 10).

67 Excessive tire wear on outside edge

1   Inflation pressures incorrect (Chapter 1).
2   Excessive speed in turns.
3   Front end alignment incorrect (excessive toe-in). Have professionally aligned.
4   Suspension arm bent or twisted (Chapter 10).

68 Excessive tire wear on inside edge

1   Inflation pressures incorrect (Chapter 1).

2　Front end alignment incorrect (toe-out). Have professionally aligned.
3　Loose or damaged steering components (Chapter 10).

69　Tire tread worn in one place

1　Tires out-of-balance.
2　Damaged or buckled wheel. Inspect and replace if necessary.
3　Defective tire (Chapter 1).

Chapter 1 Tune-up and routine maintenance

Contents

Specifications

Recommended lubricants and fluids

Note: *Listed here are manufacturer recommendations at the time this manual was written. Manufacturers occasionally upgrade their fluid and lubricant specifications, so check with your auto parts store for current recommendations.*

Engine oil
Type	API grade SG
Viscosity	See accompanying chart
Power steering fluid type	DEXRON II automatic transmission fluid
Brake fluid type	DOT 3 heavy duty brake fluid
Automatic transmission fluid type	DEXRON II or M-III automatic transmission fluid
Manual transmission lubricant type	API GL-5 SAE 75 gear lubricant
Transfer case lubricant type	API GL-5 SAE 75 gear lubricant
Differential lubricant	API GL-5 SAE 90-hypoid gear lubricant
Coolant type	50/50 mixture of ethylene glycol-based antifreeze and water

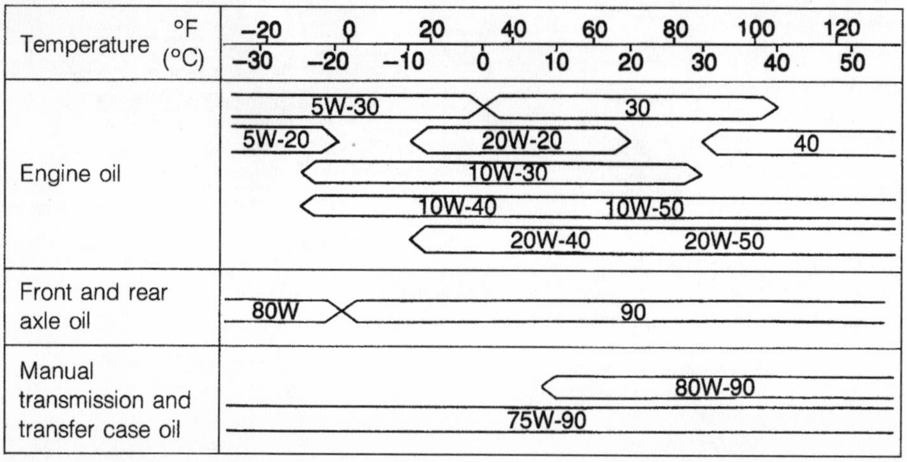

Temperature °F (°C)	−20 / −30	0 / −20	20 / −10	40 / 0	60 / 10	80 / 20	100 / 30	120 / 40	/ 50
Engine oil	5W-30	5W-20		20W-20	30		40		
			10W-30						
			10W-40		10W-50				
				20W-40		20W-50			
Front and rear axle oil	80W				90				
Manual transmission and transfer case oil				75W-90	80W-90				

Lubrication viscosity chart (engine, front and rear axle (differential) and manual transmission lubricant)

Capacities (approximate)

Engine oil with filter change..	5 qts
Cooling system	
Four cylinder engine..	7.2 qts
V6 engine	10.1 qts
Transmission	
Automatic	
Drain and refill..	4.2 qts
From dry	9.1 qts
Manual..	2.6 qts
Transfer case	1.6 qts
Differential	
Front...	1.8 qts
Rear..	1.6 qts

Brakes

Disc brake pad thickness (minimum)..	1/8-inch
Drum brake shoe lining thickness (minimum)...........................	1/16-inch

Ignition system

Spark plug	
Type	Champion RC12YC or equivalent
Gap	0.039 to 0.043 inch
Ignition timing	
V6 engine	5-degrees BTDC
Four-cylinder engine	11-degrees BTDC
Idle speed	
V6 engine	800 rpm
Four-cylinder engine	
Manual transmission...	750 rpm
Automatic transmission	770 rpm

Torque specifications

	Ft-lbs (unless otherwise indicated)
Automatic transmission pan bolt..	48 to 72 in-lbs
Spark plug	11 to 17
Oxygen sensor..	22 to 36
Wheel lug nuts..	65 to 87

Four-cylinder

The blackened terminal shown on the distributor cap indicates the Number One spark plug wire position

V6 engine

Cylinder location and distributor rotation

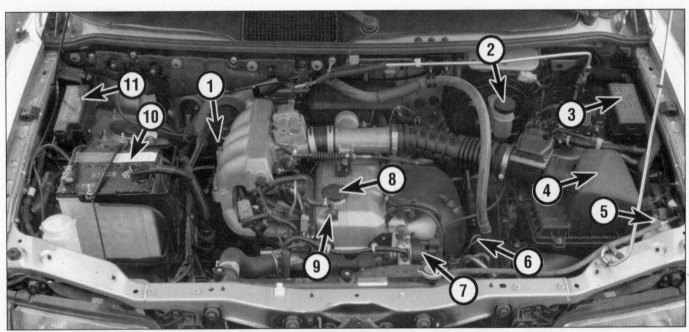

Typical engine compartment components (four-cylinder engine)

1	Automatic transmission dipstick location	4	Air cleaner housing	8	Engine oil filler cap
2	Brake fluid reservoir	5	Engine coolant reservoir	9	PCV valve
3	Main relay block	6	Oil dipstick	10	Battery
		7	Distributor	11	Fuse box

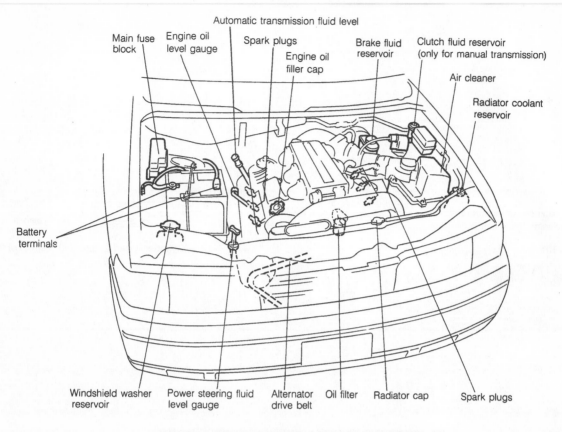

Typical engine compartment components (V6 engine)

Typical engine compartment underside components (2WD model)

1	Radiator drain	4	Lower radiator hose	7	Automatic transmission fluid pan
2	Engine drivebelt	5	Front disc brake	8	Engine oil drain plug
3	Radiator	6	Steering gear boot	9	Fuel filter

Typical engine compartment underside components (4WD model)

1	Radiator drain	5	Lower radiator hose	8	Exhaust system
2	Engine drivebelt	6	Front disc brake	9	Automatic transmission fluid pan
3	Engine oil drain plug	7	Front driveaxle boot	10	Front differential drain plug
4	Radiator				

Typical rear underside components

1	Muffler	4	Fuel filler hose
2	Rear axle differential fill plug	5	Rear differential drain plug
3	Rear shock absorber	6	Driveshaft

1 Mazda MPV
Maintenance schedule

The following maintenance intervals are based on the assumption that the vehicle owner will be doing the maintenance or service work, as opposed to having a dealer service department do the work. Although the time/mileage intervals are loosely based on factory recommendations, most have been shortened to ensure, for example, that such items as lubricants and fluids are checked/changed at intervals that promote maximum engine/driveline service life. Also, subject to the preference of the individual owner interested in keeping his or her vehicle in peak condition at all times, and with the vehicle's ultimate resale in mind, many of the maintenance procedures may be performed more often than recommended in the following schedule. We encourage such owner initiative.

When the vehicle is new it should be serviced initially by a factory authorized dealer service department to protect the factory warranty. In many cases the initial maintenance check is done at no cost to the owner (check with your dealer service department for more information).

Every 250 miles or weekly, whichever comes first

Check the engine oil level (Section 4)
Check the engine coolant level (Section 4)
Check the brake fluid level (Section 4)
Check the clutch fluid level (Section 4)
Check the washer fluid level (Section 4)
Check the tires and tire pressures (Section 5)

Every 3,000 miles or 3 months, whichever comes first

All items listed above, plus
Change the engine oil and oil filter (Section 6)
Check the power steering fluid level (Section 7)
Check the automatic transmission fluid level (Section 8)
Rotate the tires (Section 9)

Every 15,000 miles or 12 months, whichever comes first

All items listed above, plus . . .
Inspect/replace the underhood hoses (Section 10)
Check/adjust the drivebelts (Section 11)
Check/service the battery (Section 12)
Check/replace the spark plugs (Section 13)
Check/replace the spark plug wires, distributor cap and rotor (Section 14)
Check/replenish the manual transmission lubricant (Section 15)
Check the differential lubricant level (Section 16)
Check the transfer case lubricant level (Section 17)
Replace the air filter (Section 18)
Check/replace the PCV valve (Section 19)
Check the fuel system (Section 20)
Inspect the cooling system (Section 21)
Inspect the exhaust system (Section 22)
Inspect the steering and suspension components (Section 23)
Front driveaxle boot check (4WD models only) (Section 24)
Inspect the brakes (Section 25)
Inspect/replace the windshield wiper blades (Section 26)

Every 30,000 miles or 24 months, whichever comes first

All items listed above plus . . .
Change the automatic transmission fluid and filter (Section 27)
Service the cooling system (drain, flush and refill) (Section 28)
Check/replace the fuel filter (Section 29)
Change the manual transmission lubricant (Section 30)
Change the differential lubricant (Section 31)
Change the transfer case lubricant (Section 32)
Lubricate the driveshafts(4WD) (Section 33)
Check the evaporative emissions system (Section 34)
Check and adjust, if necessary, the engine idle speed (Section 35)
Check and adjust, if necessary, the ignition timing (Section 36)

Every 60,000 miles

Reset the Check Engine Sensor warning light (Section 37)
Replace the engine timing belt (V6 engine only) (Chapter 2B)

Every 80,000 miles

Replace the oxygen sensor (Section 38)

2   Introduction

This Chapter is designed to help the home mechanic maintain his or her vehicle with the goals of maximum performance, economy, safety and reliability in mind. Included is a master maintenance schedule (page 1-5), followed by procedures dealing specifically with each item on the schedule. Visual checks, adjustments, component replacement and other helpful items are included. Refer to the accompanying illustrations of the engine compartment and the underside of the vehicle for the locations of various components. Servicing the vehicle, in accordance with the mileage/time maintenance schedule and the step-by-step procedures will result in a planned maintenance program that should produce a long and reliable service life. Keep in mind that it is a comprehensive plan, so maintaining some items but not others at specified intervals will not produce the same results.

As you service the vehicle, you will discover that many of the procedures can - and should - be grouped together because of the nature of the particular procedure you're performing or because of the close proximity of two otherwise unrelated components to one another. For example, if the vehicle is raised for chassis lubrication, you should inspect the exhaust, suspension, steering and fuel systems while you're under the vehicle. When you're rotating the tires, it makes good sense to check the brakes since the wheels are already removed. Finally, let's suppose you have to borrow or rent a torque wrench. Even if you only need it to tighten the spark plugs, you might as well check the torque of as many critical fasteners as time allows.

The first step in this maintenance program is to prepare yourself before the actual work begins. Read through all the procedures you're planning to do, then gather up all the parts and tools needed. If it looks like you might run into problems during a particular job, seek advice from a mechanic or an experienced do-it-yourselfer.

3   Tune-up general information

The term tune-up is used in this manual to represent a combination of individual operations rather than one specific procedure.

If, from the time the vehicle is new, the routine maintenance schedule is followed closely and frequent checks are made of fluid levels and high wear items, as suggested throughout this manual, the engine will be kept in relatively good running condition and the need for additional work will be minimized.

More likely than not, however, there will be times when the engine is running poorly due to a lack of regular maintenance. This is even more likely if a used vehicle, which has not received regular and frequent maintenance checks, is purchased. In such cases, an engine tune-up will be needed outside of the regular maintenance intervals.

The first step in any tune-up or diagnostic procedure to help correct a poor running engine is a cylinder compression check. A compression check (see Chapter 2C) will help determine the condition of internal engine components and should be used as a guide for tune-up and repair procedures. If, for instance, a compression check indicates serious internal engine wear, a conventional tune-up will not improve the performance of the engine and would be a waste of time and money. Because of its importance, the compression check should be done by someone with the right equipment and the knowledge to use it properly.

The following procedures are those most often needed to bring as generally poor running engine back into a proper state of tune.

Minor tune-up

>   Clean, inspect and test the battery (see Section 12)
>   Check all engine related fluids (see Section 4)
>   Check and adjust the drivebelts (see Section 11)
>   Replace the spark plugs (see Section 13)
>   Inspect the spark plug wires, distributor cap and rotor (see Section 14)
>   Check the PCV valve (see Section 19)
>   Check the air filter (see Section 18)
>   Check the cooling system (see Section 21)
>   Check all underhood hoses (see Section 10)

4.4a The engine oil dipstick (arrow) is located on the right side on V6 engines

Major tune-up

All items listed under minor tune-up, plus . . .

>   Check the ignition system (see Chapter 5)
>   Check the charging system (see Chapter 5)
>   Check the fuel system (see Chapter 4)
>   Replace the spark plug wires distributor cap and rotor (Section 14)
>   Check the engine idle speed (Section 35)
>   Check the ignition timing (Section 36)

4   Fluid level checks (every 250 miles or weekly)

Refer to illustrations 4.4a, 4.4b, 4.4c, 4.6, 4.9, 4.14, 4.16, 4.22 and 4.23

Note: *The following are fluid level checks to be done on a 250 mile or weekly basis. Additional fluid level checks can be found in specific maintenance procedures which follow. Regardless of intervals, be alert to fluid leaks under the vehicle which would indicate a fault to be corrected immediately.*

1   Fluids are an essential part of the lubrication, cooling, brake and windshield washer systems. Because the fluids gradually become depleted and/or contaminated during normal operation of the vehicle, they must be periodically replenished. See *Recommended lubricants and fluids* at the beginning of this Chapter before adding fluid to any of the following components. **Note:** *The vehicle must be on level ground when fluid levels are checked.*

Engine oil

2   Engine oil is checked with a dipstick, which is located on the side of the engine (refer to the underhood illustrations at the front of this Chapter for dipstick location). The dipstick extends through a metal tube down into the oil pan.

3   The engine oil should be checked before the vehicle has been driven, or about 15 minutes after the engine has been shut off. If the oil is checked immediately after driving the vehicle, some of the oil will remain in the upper part of the engine, resulting in an inaccurate reading on the dipstick.

4   Pull the dipstick out of the tube **(see illustrations)** and wipe all of the oil away from the end with a clean rag or paper towel. Insert the clean dipstick all the way back into the tube and pull it out again. Note the oil at the end of the dipstick. At its highest point, the oil should be between the F and L marks **(see illustration)**.

5   It takes one quart of oil to raise the level from the L mark to the F mark on the dipstick. Do not allow the level to drop below the L mark or oil starvation may cause engine damage. Conversely, overfilling the engine (adding oil above the F mark) may cause oil fouled spark plugs, oil leaks or oil seal failures.

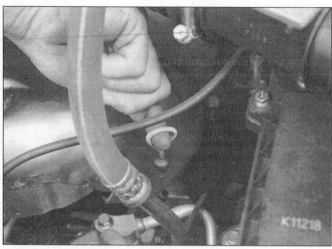

4.4b On four-cylinder engines the dipstick is on the left side

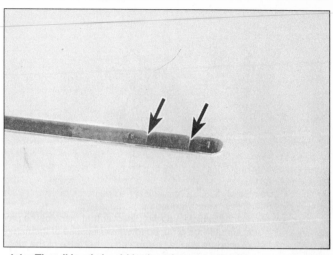

4.4c The oil level should be kept between the two notches, at or near the F - if it isn't, add enough oil to bring the level to near the F notch (it takes one full quart to raise the level from the L to the F mark)

4.6 The threaded oil filler cap is located in the valve cover - always make sure the area around the opening is clean before unscrewing the cap

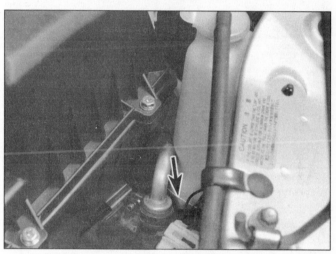

4.9 The coolant reservoir is located in the left front corner of the engine compartment - make sure the level is kept at or near the Full mark (arrow)

6   To add oil, remove the filler cap located on the valve cover **(see illustration)**. After adding oil, wait a few minutes to allow the level to stabilize, then pull the dipstick out and check the level again. Add more oil if required. Install the filler cap and tighten it by hand only.

7   Checking the oil level is an important preventive maintenance step. A consistently low oil level indicates oil leakage through damaged seals, defective gaskets or past worn rings or valve guides. The condition of the oil should also be noted. If the oil looks milky in color or has water droplets in it, the cylinder head gasket(s) may be blown or the head(s) or block may be cracked. The engine should be repaired immediately. Whenever you check the oil level, slide your thumb and index finger up the dipstick before wiping off the oil. If you see small dirt or metal particles clinging to the dipstick, the oil should be changed (see Section 6).

Engine coolant

Warning: *Do not allow antifreeze to come in contact with your skin or painted surfaces of the vehicle. Rinse off spills immediately with plenty of water. Antifreeze is highly toxic if ingested. Never leave antifreeze lying around in an open container or in puddles on the floor; children and pets are attracted by it's sweet smell and may drink it. Check with local authorities about disposing of used antifreeze. Many communities have collection centers which will see that antifreeze is disposed of safely.*

8   All vehicles covered by this manual are equipped with a pressurized coolant recovery system. A white plastic coolant reservoir located at the left front corner of the engine compartment is connected by a hose to the radiator filler neck. If the engine overheats, coolant escapes through a valve in the radiator cap and travels through the hose into the reservoir. As the engine cools, the coolant is automatically drawn back into the cooling system to maintain the correct level.

9   The coolant level in the reservoir **(see illustration)** should be checked regularly. **Warning:** *Do not remove the radiator cap to check the coolant level when the engine is warm!* The level in the reservoir varies with the temperature of the engine. When the engine is cold, the coolant level should be above the LOW mark on the reservoir. Once the engine has warmed up, the level should be at or near the FULL mark. If it isn't, allow the engine to cool, then remove the cap from the reservoir and add a 50/50 mixture of ethylene glycol based antifreeze and water. Don't use rust inhibitors or additives.

10   Drive the vehicle and recheck the coolant level. If only a small amount of coolant is required to bring the system up to the proper level, water can be used. However, repeated additions of water will dilute the antifreeze and water solution. In order to maintain the proper ratio of antifreeze and water, always top up the coolant level with the correct mixture. An empty plastic milk jug or bleach bottle makes an excellent container for mixing coolant.

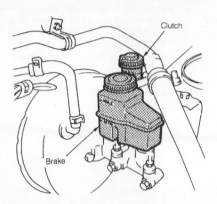

4.14 On manual transmission-equipped models the clutch fluid reservoir is located next to the brake reservoir

4.16 The brake fluid level should be kept above the MIN mark on the translucent reservoir - unscrew the cap to add fluid

4.22 The windshield washer fluid reservoir is located in the right front corner of the engine compartment - fluid can be added after flipping up the cap

4.23 The rear window washer fluid reservoir is located in the right side of the rear compartment under a cover - flip up the cap to add fluid

11   If the coolant level drops consistently, there may be a leak in the system. Inspect the radiator, hoses, filler cap, drain plugs and water pump (see Section 21). If no leaks are noted, have the radiator cap pressure tested by a service station.

12   If you have to remove the radiator cap, wait until the engine has cooled completely, then wrap a thick cloth around the cap and turn it to the first stop. If coolant or steam escapes, let the engine cool down longer, then remove the cap.

13   Check the condition of the coolant as well. It should be relatively clear. If it's brown or rust colored, the system should be drained, flushed and refilled. Even if the coolant appears to be normal, the corrosion inhibitors wear out, so it must be replaced at the specified intervals.

Brake and clutch fluid

Warning: *Brake fluid can harm your eyes and damage painted surfaces, so use extreme caution when handling or pouring it. Do not use brake fluid that has been standing open or is more than one year old. Brake fluid absorbs moisture from the air, which can cause a dangerous loss of brake effectiveness. Use only the specified type of brake fluid. Mixing different types (such as DOT 3 or 4 and DOT 5) can cause brake failure.*

14   The brake master cylinder is mounted at the left (driver's side) rear corner of the engine compartment. The clutch fluid reservoir (used on models with manual transmissions) is mounted adjacent to it **(see illustration)**.

15   To check the clutch fluid level, observe the level through the translucent reservoir. The level should be at or near the step molded into the reservoir. If the level is low, remove the reservoir cap to add the specified fluid.

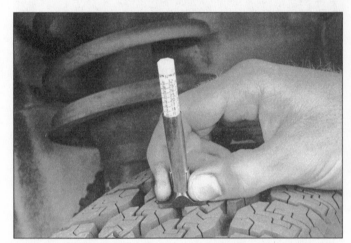

5.2 A tire tread depth indicator should be used to monitor tire wear - they are available at auto parts stores and service stations and cost very little

16   The brake fluid level is checked by looking through the plastic reservoir mounted on the master cylinder. The fluid level should be between the MAX and MIN lines on the reservoir **(see illustration)**. If the fluid level is low, wipe the top of the reservoir and the cap with a clean rag to prevent contamination of the system as the cap is unscrewed. Top up with the recommended brake fluid, but do not overfill.

17   While the reservoir cap is off, check the master cylinder reservoir for contamination. If rust deposits, dirt particles or water droplets are

Condition	Probable cause	Corrective action	Condition	Probable cause	Corrective action
Shoulder wear	• Underinflation (both sides wear) • Incorrect wheel camber (one side wear) • Hard cornering • Lack of rotation	• Measure and adjust pressure. • Repair or replace axle and suspension parts. • Reduce speed. • Rotate tires.	Feathered edge **Toe wear**	• Incorrect toe	• Adjust toe-in.
Center wear	• Overinflation • Lack of rotation	• Measure and adjust pressure. • Rotate tires.	**Uneven wear**	• Incorrect camber or caster • Malfunctioning suspension • Unbalanced wheel • Out-of-round brake drum • Lack of rotation	• Repair or replace axle and suspension parts. • Repair or replace suspension parts. • Balance or replace. • Turn or replace. • Rotate tires.

5.3 This chart will help you determine the condition of the tires, the probable cause(s) of abnormal wear and the corrective action necessary

5.4a If a tire loses air on a steady basis, check the valve core first to make sure it's snug (special inexpensive wrenches are commonly available at auto parts stores)

present, the system should be drained and refilled by a dealer service department or repair shop.

18   After filling the reservoir to the proper level, make sure the cap is seated to prevent fluid leakage and/or contamination.

19   The fluid level in the master cylinder will drop slightly as the disc brake pads wear. A very low level may indicate worn brake pads. Check for wear (see Section 25).

20   If the brake fluid level drops consistently, check the entire system for leaks immediately. Examine all brake lines, hoses and connections, along with the calipers, wheel cylinders and master cylinder (see Section 25).

21   When checking the fluid level, if you discover one or both reservoirs empty or nearly empty, the brake or clutch hydraulic system should be checked for leaks and bled (see Chapters 8 and 9).

Wiper washer fluid

22   Fluid for the front windshield washer system is stored in a plastic

reservoir in the engine compartment **(see illustration)**.

23   Fluid for the rear windshield washer system is stored in a reservoir in the right rear corner of the passenger compartment, under a cover **(see illustration)**.

24   In milder climates, plain water can be used in the reservoir, but it should be kept no more than two-thirds full to allow for expansion if the water freezes. In colder climates, use windshield washer system antifreeze, available at any auto parts store, to lower the freezing point of the fluid. This comes in concentrated or pre-mixed form. If you purchase concentrated antifreeze, mix the antifreeze with water in accordance with the manufacturer's directions on the container. **Caution:** *Do not use cooling system antifreeze - it will damage the vehicle's paint.*

---

5   Tire and tire pressure checks (every 250 miles or weekly)

Refer to illustrations 5.2, 5.3, 5.4a, 5.4b and 5.8

1   Periodic inspection of the tires may save you the inconvenience of being stranded with a flat tire. It can also provide you with vital information regarding possible problems in the steering and suspension systems before major damage occurs.

2   Tires are equipped with 1/2-inch wide bands that will appear when tread depth reaches 1/16-inch, at which time the tires can be considered worn out. Tread wear can be monitored with a simple, inexpensive device known as a tread depth indicator **(see illustration)**.

3   Note any abnormal tire wear **(see illustration)**. Tread pattern irregularities such as cupping, flat spots and more wear on one side that the other are indications of front end alignment and/or balance problems. If any of these conditions are noted, take the vehicle to a tire shop or service station to correct the problem.

4   Look closely for cuts, punctures and embedded nails or tacks. Sometimes a tire will hold air pressure for a short time or leak down very slowly after a nail has embedded itself in the tread. If a slow leak persists, check the valve stem core to make sure it is tight **(see illustration)**. Examine the tread for an object that may have embedded itself in the tire or for a "plug" that may have begun to leak (radial tire punctures are repaired with a plug that is installed in the puncture). If a puncture is suspected, it can be easily verified by spraying a solution

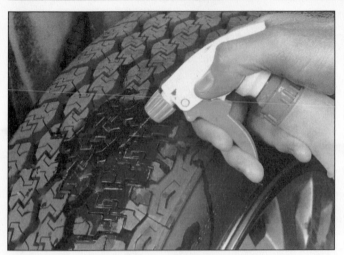

5.4b If the valve core is tight, raise the corner of the vehicle with the low tire and spray a soapy water solution onto the tread as the tire is turned slowly - leaks will cause small bubbles to appear

5.8 To extend the life of the tires, check the air pressure at least once a week with an accurate gauge (don't forget the spare!)

of soapy water onto the puncture **(see illustration)**. The soapy solution will bubble if there is a leak. Unless the puncture is unusually large, a tire shop or service station can usually repair the tire.

5   Carefully inspect the inner sidewall of each tire for evidence of brake fluid leakage. If you see any, inspect the brakes immediately.

6   Correct air pressure adds miles to the lifespan of the tires, improves mileage and enhances overall ride quality. Tire pressure cannot be accurately estimated by looking at a tire, especially if it's a radial. A tire pressure gauge is essential. Keep an accurate gauge in the glove compartment. The pressure gauges attached to the nozzles of air hoses at gas stations are often inaccurate.

7   Always check tire pressure when the tires are cold. Cold, in this case, means the vehicle has not been driven over a mile in the three hours preceding a tire pressure check. A pressure rise of four to eight pounds is not uncommon once the tires are warm.

8   Unscrew the valve cap protruding from the wheel or hubcap and push the gauge firmly onto the valve stem **(see illustration)**. Note the reading on the gauge and compare the figure to the recommended tire pressure shown in your owner's manual or on the tire placard on the passenger side door or door pillar. Be sure to reinstall the valve cap to keep dirt and moisture out of the valve stem mechanism. Check all four tires and, if necessary, add enough air to bring them to the recommended pressure.

9   Don't forget to keep the spare tire inflated to the specified pressure (refer to your owner's manual or the placard attached to the door pillar). Note that the pressure recommended for temporary (mini) spare tires is higher than for the tires on the vehicle.

6   Engine oil and filter change (every 3000 miles or 3 months)

Refer to illustrations 6.2, 6.7, 6.12 and 6.16

1   Frequent oil changes are the most important preventive maintenance procedures that can be done by the home mechanic. As engine oil ages, it becomes diluted and contaminated, which leads to premature engine wear.

2   Make sure that you have all the necessary tools before you begin this procedure **(see illustration)**. You should also have plenty of rags or newspapers handy for mopping up oil spills.

3   Start the engine and allow it to reach normal operating temperature - oil and sludge will flow more easily when warm. If new oil, a filter or tools are needed, use the vehicle to go get them and warm up the engine oil at the same time. Park on a level surface and shut off the engine when it's warmed up. Remove the oil filler cap from the valve cover.

4   Access to the oil drain plug and filter will be improved if the vehicle can be lifted on a hoist, driven onto ramps or supported by jack-

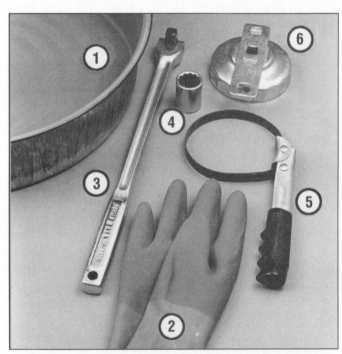

6.2 These tools are required when changing the engine oil and filter

1   *Drain pan - It should be fairly shallow in depth, but wide to prevent spills*
2   *Rubber gloves - When removing the drain plug and filter, you will get oil on your hands (the gloves will prevent burns)*
3   *Breaker bar - Sometimes the oil drain plug is tight, and a long breaker bar is needed to loosen it*
4   *Socket - To be used with the breaker bar or a ratchet (must be the correct size to fit the drain plug - six-point preferred)*
5   *Filter wrench - This is a metal band-type wrench, which requires clearance around the filter to be effective*
6   *Filter wrench - This type fits on the bottom of the filter and can be turned with a ratchet or breaker bar (different-size wrenches are available for different types of filters)*

6.7 Use a proper size box-end wrench or six-point socket to remove the oil drain plug to avoid rounding it off

6.12 The oil filter is usually on very tight and will normally require a special wrench for removal - DO NOT use the wrench to tighten the filter!

6.16 Lubricate the oil filter gasket with clean engine oil before installing the filter on the engine

stands. **Warning:** *DO NOT work under a vehicle supported only by a bumper, hydraulic or scissors-type jack - always use jackstands!*

5   Raise the vehicle and support it on jackstands. Make sure it is safely supported!

6   If you haven't changed the oil on this vehicle before, get under it and locate the drain plug and the oil filter. The exhaust components will be hot as you work, so note how they are routed to avoid touching them.

7   Being careful not to touch the hot exhaust components, position a drain pan under the plug in the bottom of the engine. Clean the area around the plug, then remove the plug **(see illustration)**. It's a good idea to wear an old glove while unscrewing the plug the final few turns to avoid being scalded by hot oil. It will also help to hold the drain plug against the threads as you unscrew it, then pull it away from the drain hole suddenly. This will place your arm out of the way of the hot oil, as well as reducing the chances of dropping the drain plug into the drain pan.

8   It may be necessary to move the drain pan slightly as oil flow slows to a trickle. Inspect the old oil for the presence of metal particles.

9   After all the oil has drained, wipe off the drain plug with a clean rag. Any small metal particles clinging to the plug would immediately contaminate the new oil.

10   Reinstall the plug and tighten it securely, but don't strip the threads.

11   Move the drain pan into position under the oil filter.

12   Loosen the oil filter by turning it counterclockwise with a filter

wrench. Any standard filter wrench will work **(see illustration)**.

13   Sometimes the oil filter is screwed on so tightly that it can't be loosened. If it is, punch a metal bar or long screwdriver directly through it, as close to the engine as possible, and use it as a T-bar to turn the filter. Be prepared for oil to spurt out of the canister as it's punctured.

14   Once the filter is loose, use your hands to unscrew it from the block. Just as the filter is detached from the block, immediately tilt the open end up to prevent oil inside the filter from spilling out.

15   Using a clean rag, wipe off the mounting surface on the block. Also, make sure that none of the old gasket remains stuck to the mounting surface. It can be removed with a scraper if necessary.

16   Compare the old filter with the new one to make sure they are the same type. Smear some engine oil on the rubber gasket of the new filter and screw it into place **(see illustration)**. Overtightening the filter will damage the gasket, so don't use a filter wrench. Most filter manufacturers recommend tightening the filter by hand only. Normally, they should be tightened 3/4-turn after the gasket contacts the block, but be sure to follow the directions on the filter or container.

17   Remove all tools and materials from under the vehicle, being careful not to spill the oil in the drain pan, then lower the vehicle.

18   Add new oil to the engine through the oil filler cap in the valve cover. Use a funnel to prevent oil from spilling onto the top of the engine. Pour four quarts of fresh oil into the engine. Wait a few minutes to allow the oil to drain into the pan, then check the level on the dipstick (see Section 4 if necessary). If the oil level is in the SAFE range, install the filler cap.

19   Start the engine and run it for about a minute. While the engine is running, look under the vehicle and check for leaks at the oil pan drain plug and around the oil filter. If either one is leaking, stop the engine and tighten the plug or filter slightly.

20   Wait a few minutes, then recheck the level on the dipstick. Add oil as necessary to bring the level into the SAFE range.

21   During the first few trips after an oil change, make it a point to check frequently for leaks and proper oil level.

22   The old oil drained from the engine cannot be reused in its present state and should be discarded. Oil reclamation centers will normally accept the oil, which can be recycled. After the oil has cooled, it can be drained into a container (plastic jugs, bottles, milk cartons, etc.) for transport to a disposal site.

---

7   Power steering fluid level check (every 3000 miles or 3 months)

Refer to illustrations 7.2, 7.4 and 7.5

1   Check the power steering fluid level periodically to avoid steering system problems, such as damage to the pump. **Caution:** *DO NOT hold the steering wheel against either stop (extreme left or right turn)*

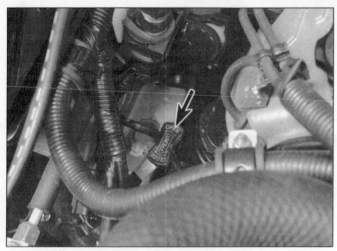

7.2 The power steering reservoir dipstick (arrow) is located on the right side of the engine compartment

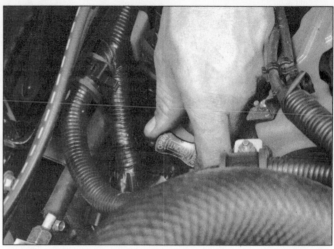

7.4 Rotate the dipstick cap counterclockwise and pull it up

7.5 The power steering fluid level should be kept near the top of the hatched area on the dipstick

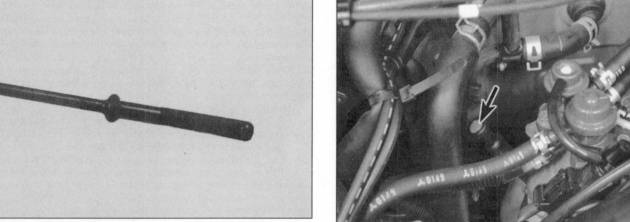

8.5 The automatic transmission dipstick (arrow) is located near the firewall on the right side of the engine compartment

for more than five seconds. If you do, the power steering pump could be damaged.

2   The power steering pump, located at the right front corner of the engine on all models, is equipped with a twist-off cap with an integral fluid level dipstick **(see illustration)**.

3   Park the vehicle on level ground and apply the parking brake.

4   Run the engine until it has reached normal operating temperature. With the engine at idle, turn the steering wheel back-and-forth several times to get any air out of the steering system. Shut the engine off, remove the cap by turning it counterclockwise, wipe the dipstick clean and reinstall the cap **(see illustration)**.

5   Remove the cap again and note the fluid level. It should be near the top of the hatched area on the dipstick **(see illustration)**.

6   Add small amounts of fluid until the level is correct. **Caution:** *Do not overfill the pump. If too much fluid is added, remove the excess with a clean syringe or suction pump.* Insert the dipstick and make sure the cap is seated with the arrow pointing forward.

7   Check the power steering hoses and connections for leaks and wear (see Section 10).

8   Check the condition and tension of the drivebelt (see Section 11).

---

8   Automatic transmission fluid level check (every 3000 miles or 3 months)

Refer to illustrations 8.5 and 8.6

Caution: *The use of transmission fluid other than the type listed in this*

Chapter's Specifications could result in transmission malfunctions or failure.

1   The automatic transmission fluid level should be carefully maintained. Low fluid level can lead to slipping or loss of drive, while overfilling can cause foaming and loss of fluid. Either condition can cause transmission damage.

2   Since transmission fluid expands as it heats up, the fluid level should only be checked when the transmission is warm (at normal operating temperature). If the vehicle has just been driven over 20 miles, the transmission can be considered warm. **Caution:** *If the vehicle has just been driven for a long time at high speed or in city traffic, in hot weather, or if it has been pulling a trailer, an accurate fluid level reading cannot be obtained. Allow the transmission to cool down for about 30 minutes. You can also check the transmission fluid level when the transmission is cold. If the vehicle has not been driven for over five hours and the fluid is about room temperature (70 to 95-degrees F), the transmission is cold. However, the fluid level is normally checked with the transmission warm to ensure accurate results.*

3   Immediately after driving the vehicle, park it on a level surface, set the parking brake and start the engine. While the engine is idling, depress the brake pedal and move the selector lever through all the gear ranges, beginning and ending in Park.

4   Locate the automatic transmission dipstick tube in the right rear corner of the engine compartment.

5   With the engine still idling, pull the dipstick out from the tube **(see illustration)**, wipe it off with a clean rag, push it all the way back into

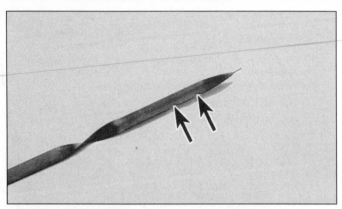

8.6 With the fluid hot, the level should be kept between the two dipstick notches, near the upper one

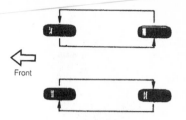

9.2 The tire rotation pattern for these models

the tube and withdraw it again, then note the fluid level.

6   The level should be between the two notches **(see illustration)**. If the level is low, add the specified automatic transmission fluid through the dipstick tube - use a clean funnel to prevent spills.

7   Add just enough of the recommended fluid to fill the transmission to the proper level. It takes about one pint to raise the level from the low mark to the high mark when the fluid is hot, so add the fluid a little at a time and keep checking the level until it's correct.

8   The condition of the fluid should also be checked along with the level. If the fluid is black or a dark reddish-brown color, or if it smells burned, it should be changed (see below). If you are in doubt about its condition, purchase some new fluid and compare the two for color and smell.

---

9   Tire rotation (every 3000 miles or 3 months)

Refer to illustration 9.2

1   The tires should be rotated at the specified intervals and whenever uneven wear is noticed. Since the vehicle will be raised and the tires checked anyway, check the brakes also (see Section 25). **Note:** *Even if you don't rotate the tires, at least check the lug nut tightness.*

2   It is recommended that the tires be rotated in a specific pattern **(see illustration)**.

3   Refer to the information in *Jacking and towing* at the front of this manual for the proper procedure to follow when raising the vehicle and changing a tire. If the brakes must be checked, don't apply the parking brake as stated.

4   The vehicle must be raised on a hoist or supported on jackstands to get all four tires off the ground. Make sure the vehicle is safely supported!

5   After the rotation procedure is finished, check and adjust the tire pressures as necessary and be sure to check the lug nut tightness.

---

10   Underhood hose check and replacement (every 15,000 miles or 12 months)

Warning: *Replacement of air conditioning hoses must be left to a dealer service department or air conditioning shop that has the equipment to depressurize the system safely. Never disconnect air conditioning hoses or components until the system has been depressurized.*

General

1   High temperatures under the hood can cause deterioration of the rubber and plastic hoses used for engine, accessory and emission systems operation. Periodic inspection should be made for cracks, loose clamps, material hardening and leaks.

2   Information specific to the cooling system can be found in Section 21.

3   Most (but not all) hoses are secured to the fitting with clamps.

Where clamps are used, check to be sure they haven't lost their tension, allowing the hose to leak. If clamps aren't used, make sure the hose has not expanded and/or hardened where it slips over the fitting, allowing it to leak.

Vacuum hoses

4   It's quite common for vacuum hoses, especially those in the emissions system, to be color coded or identified by colored stripes molded into them. Various systems require hoses with different wall thicknesses, collapse resistance and temperature resistance. When replacing hoses, be sure the new ones are made of the same material.

5   Often the only effective way to check a hose is to remove it completely from the vehicle. If more than one hose is removed, be sure to label the hoses and fittings to ensure correct installation.

6   When checking vacuum hoses, be sure to include any plastic T-fittings in the check. Inspect the fittings for cracks and the hose where it fits over each fitting for distortion, which could cause leakage.

7   A small piece of vacuum hose can be used as a stethoscope to detect vacuum leaks. Hold one end of the hose to your ear and probe around vacuum hoses and fittings, listening for the "hissing" sound characteristic of a vacuum leak. **Warning:** *When probing with the vacuum hose stethoscope, be careful not to come into contact with moving engine components such as the drivebelt, cooling fan, etc.*

Fuel hoses

Warning: *There are certain precautions which must be taken when servicing or inspecting fuel system components. Work in a well ventilated area and do not allow open flames (cigarettes, appliance pilot lights, etc.) or bare light bulbs near the work area. Mop up any spills immediately and do not store fuel-soaked rags where they could ignite.*

8   The fuel lines are usually under pressure, so if any fuel lines are to be disconnected be prepared to catch spilled fuel. **Warning:** *Your vehicle is equipped with fuel injection and you must relieve the fuel system pressure before servicing the fuel lines. Refer to Chapter 4 for the fuel system pressure relief procedure.*

9   Check all rubber fuel lines for deterioration and chafing. Check especially for cracks in areas where the hose bends and just before fittings, such as where a hose attaches to the fuel pump, fuel filter and fuel injection system.

10   High quality fuel line, usually identified by the word *Fluoroelastomer* printed on the hose, should be used for fuel line replacement. Never, under any circumstances, use unreinforced vacuum line, clear plastic tubing or water hose for fuel lines.

11   Spring-type clamps are commonly used on fuel lines. These clamps often lose their tension over a period of time, and can be "sprung" during removal. Replace all spring-type clamps with screw clamps whenever a hose is replaced.

Metal lines

12   Sections of metal line are often used for fuel line between the fuel pump and fuel injection system. Check carefully to make sure the line isn't bent, crimped or cracked.

13   If a section of metal fuel line must be replaced, use seamless steel tubing only, since copper and aluminum tubing do not have the strength necessary to withstand the vibration caused by the engine.

14   Check the metal brake lines where they enter the master cylinder

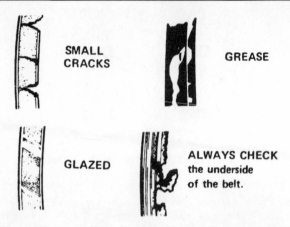

SMALL CRACKS

GREASE

GLAZED

ALWAYS CHECK the underside of the belt.

11.3 Here are some of the more common problems associated with drivebelts (check the belts very carefully to prevent an untimely breakdown)

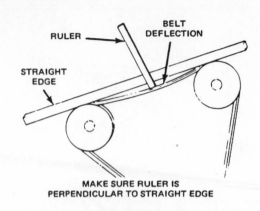

RULER

BELT DEFLECTION

STRAIGHT EDGE

MAKE SURE RULER IS PERPENDICULAR TO STRAIGHT EDGE

11.4 Measuring drivebelt deflection with a straightedge and ruler

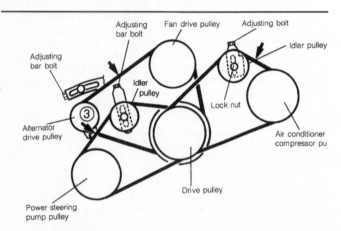

11.6a Drivebelt layout on the V6 engine

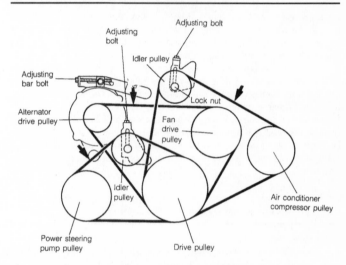

11.6b Drivebelt layout on the four-cylinder engine

and brake proportioning unit (if used) for cracks in the lines and loose fittings. Any sign of brake fluid leakage calls for an immediate thorough inspection of the brake system.

Nylon fuel lines

15   Nylon fuel lines are used at several points in fuel injection systems. These lines require special materials and methods for repair. Refer to Chapter 4 for details.

Power steering hoses

16   Check the power steering hoses for leaks, loose connections and worn clamps. Tighten loose connections. Worn clamps or leaky hoses should be replaced.

11   Drivebelt check, adjustment and replacement (every 15,000 miles or 12 months)

Refer to illustrations 11.3, 11.4, 11.6a and 11.6b

Check

1   The drivebelts, sometimes called V-belts or simply "fan" belts, are located at the front of the engine and play an important role in the overall operation of the vehicle and its components. Due to their function and material make up, the belts are prone to failure after a period of time and should be inspected and adjusted periodically to prevent major engine damage.
2   The number of belts used on a particular vehicle depends on the

accessories installed. Drivebelts are used to turn the alternator, power steering pump, water pump and air conditioning compressor. Depending on the pulley arrangement, a single belt may be used to drive more than one of these components.
3   With the engine off, open the hood and locate the various belts at the front of the engine. Using your fingers (and a flashlight, if necessary), move along the belts checking for cracks and separation of the belt plies. Also check for fraying and glazing, which gives the belt a shiny appearance **(see illustration)**. Both sides of the belts should be inspected, which means you will have to twist each belt to check the underside.
4   The tension of each belt is checked by pushing firmly with your thumb and see how much the belt moves (deflects). Measure the deflection with a ruler **(see illustration)**. A good rule of thumb is that the belt should deflect 1/4-inch if the distance from pulley center-to-pulley center is between 7 and 11 inches. The belt should deflect 1/2-inch if the distance from pulley center-to-pulley center is between 12 and 16 inches.

Adjustment

5   If it is necessary to adjust the belt tension, either to make the belt tighter or looser, it is done by moving the belt driven accessory on the bracket.
6   For each component there will be an adjusting bolt and a pivot bolt. Both bolts must be loosened slightly to enable you to move the component. On some components the drivebelt tension can be adjusted turning an adjusting bolt after loosening the lock-bolt **(see illustrations)**.

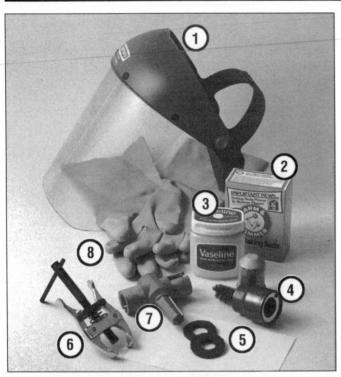

12.1 Tools and materials required for battery maintenance

1 **Face shield/safety goggles** - When removing corrosion with a brush, the acidic particles can easily fly up into your eyes
2 **Baking soda** - A solution of baking soda and water can be used to neutralize corrosion
3 **Petroleum jelly** - A layer of this on the battery posts will help prevent corrosion
4 **Battery post/cable cleaner** - This wire brush cleaning tool will remove all traces of corrosion from the battery posts and cable clamps
5 **Treated felt washers** - Placing one of these on each post, directly under the cable clamps, will help prevent corrosion
6 **Puller** - Sometimes the cable clamps are very difficult to pull off the posts, even after the nut/bolt has been completely loosened. This tool pulls the clamp straight up and off the post without damage
7 **Battery post/cable cleaner** - Here is another cleaning tool which is a slightly different version of Number 4 above, but it does the same thing
8 **Rubber gloves** - Another safety item to consider when servicing the battery; remember that's acid inside the battery!

7   After the two bolts have been loosened, move the component away from the engine to tighten the belt or toward the engine to loosen the belt. Hold the accessory in position and check the belt tension. If it is correct, tighten the two bolts until just snug, then recheck the tension. If the tension is correct, tighten the bolts.
8   It will often be necessary to use some sort of prybar to move the accessory while the belt is adjusted. If this must be done to gain the proper leverage, be very careful not to damage the component being moved or the part being pried against.

Replacement

9   To replace a belt, follow the instructions above for adjustment, however completely remove the belt from the pulleys.
10   In some cases you will have to remove more then one belt because of their arrangement on the front of the engine. Due to this and

12.4 Remove the cell caps to check the water level in the battery - if the level is low, add distilled water only

the fact that belts will tend to fail at the same time, it is wise to replace all belts together. Mark each belt and its appropriate pulley groove so all replacement belts can be installed in their proper positions.
11   It is a good idea to take the old belts with you when buying new ones in order to make a direct comparison for length, width and design.

12   Battery check, maintenance and charging (every 15,000 miles or 12 months)

Check and maintenance

Refer to illustrations 12.1, 12.4, 12.8a, 12.8b, 12.8c and 12.8d
Warning: Certain precautions must be followed when checking and servicing the battery. Hydrogen gas, which is highly flammable, is always present in the battery cells, so keep lighted tobacco and all other flames and sparks away from it. The electrolyte inside the battery is actually dilute sulfuric acid, which will cause injury if splashed on your skin or in your eyes. It will also ruin clothes and painted surfaces. When removing the battery cables, always detach the negative cable first and hook it up last!
1   Battery maintenance is an important procedure which will help ensure that you are not stranded because of a dead battery. Several tools are required for this procedure **(see illustration)**.
2   Before servicing the battery, always turn the engine and all accessories off and disconnect the cable from the negative terminal of the battery.
3   A sealed (sometimes called maintenance free) battery is standard equipment. The cell caps cannot be removed, no electrolyte checks are required and water cannot be added to the cells. However, if an aftermarket battery has been installed and it is a type that requires regular maintenance, the following procedures can be used.
4   Check the electrolyte level in each of the battery cells **(see illustration)**. It must be above the plates. There's usually a split-ring indicator in each cell to indicate the correct level. If the level is low, add distilled water only, then install the cell caps. **Caution:** Overfilling the cells may cause electrolyte to spill over during periods of heavy charging, causing corrosion and damage to nearby components.
5   If the positive terminal and cable clamp on your vehicle's battery is equipped with a rubber protector, make sure that it's not torn or damaged. It should completely cover the terminal.
6   The external condition of the battery should be checked periodically. Look for damage such as a cracked case.
7   Check the tightness of the battery cable clamps to ensure good electrical connections and inspect the entire length of each cable, looking for cracked or abraded insulation and frayed conductors.

12.8a Battery terminal corrosion usually appears as light, fluffy powder

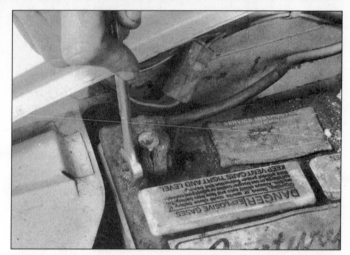

12.8b Removing the cable from a battery post with a wrench - sometimes special battery pliers are required for this procedure if corrosion has caused deterioration of the nut hex (always remove the ground cable first and hook it up last!)

12.8c Regardless of the type of tool used on the battery posts, a clean, shiny surface should be the result

12.8d When cleaning the cable clamps, all corrosion must be removed (the inside of the clamp is tapered to match the taper on the post, so don't remove too much material)

8   If corrosion (visible as white, fluffy deposits) is evident, remove the cables from the terminals, clean them with a battery brush and re-install them **(see illustrations)**. Corrosion can be kept to a minimum by installing specially treated washers available at auto parts stores or by applying a layer of petroleum jelly or grease to the terminals and cable clamps after they are assembled.

9   Make sure that the battery carrier is in good condition and that the hold-down clamp bolt is tight. If the battery is removed (see Chapter 5 for the removal and installation procedure), make sure that no parts remain in the bottom of the carrier when it's reinstalled. When re-installing the hold-down clamp, don't overtighten the bolt.

10   Corrosion on the carrier, battery case and surrounding areas can be removed with a solution of water and baking soda. Apply the mixture with a small brush, let it work, then rinse it off with plenty of clean water.

11   Any metal parts of the vehicle damaged by corrosion should be coated with a zinc-based primer, then painted.

12   Additional information on the battery and jump starting can be found in Chapter 5 and the front of this manual.

Charging

13   Remove all of the cell caps (if equipped) and cover the holes with a clean cloth to prevent spattering electrolyte. Disconnect the negative battery cable and hook the battery charger leads to the battery posts (positive to positive, negative to negative), then plug in the charger. Make sure it is set at 12-volts if it has a selector switch.

14   If you're using a charger with a rate higher than two amps, check the battery regularly during charging to make sure it doesn't overheat. If you're using a trickle charger, you can safely let the battery charge overnight after you've checked it regularly for the first couple of hours.

15   If the battery has removable cell caps, measure the specific gravity with a hydrometer every hour during the last few hours of the charging cycle. Hydrometers are available inexpensively from auto parts stores - follow the instructions that come with the hydrometer. Consider the battery charged when there's no change in the specific gravity reading for two hours and the electrolyte in the cells is gassing (bubbling) freely. The specific gravity reading from each cell should be very close to the others. If not, the battery probably has a bad cell(s).

16   Some batteries with sealed tops have built-in hydrometers on the top that indicate the state of charge by the color displayed in the hydrometer window. Normally, a bright-colored hydrometer indicates a full charge and a dark hydrometer indicates the battery still needs charging. Check the battery manufacturer's instructions to be sure you know what the colors mean.

17   If the battery has a sealed top and no built-in hydrometer, you can hook up a digital voltmeter across the battery terminals to check the charge. A fully charged battery should read 12.6-volts or higher.

18   Further information on the battery and jump starting can be found in Chapter 5 and at the front of this manual.

Common spark plug conditions

NORMAL

Symptoms: Brown to grayish-tan color and slight electrode wear. Correct heat range for engine and operating conditions.

Recommendation: When new spark plugs are installed, replace with plugs of the same heat range.

WORN

Symptoms: Rounded electrodes with a small amount of deposits on the firing end. Normal color. Causes hard starting in damp or cold weather and poor fuel economy.

Recommendation: Plugs have been left in the engine too long. Replace with new plugs of the same heat range. Follow the recommended maintenance schedule.

CARBON DEPOSITS

Symptoms: Dry sooty deposits indicate a rich mixture or weak ignition. Causes misfiring, hard starting and hesitation.

Recommendation: Make sure the plug has the correct heat range. Check for a clogged air filter or problem in the fuel system or engine management system. Also check for ignition system problems.

ASH DEPOSITS

Symptoms: Light brown deposits encrusted on the side or center electrodes or both. Derived from oil and/or fuel additives. Excessive amounts may mask the spark, causing misfiring and hesitation during acceleration.

Recommendation: If excessive deposits accumulate over a short time or low mileage, install new valve guide seals to prevent seepage of oil into the combustion chambers. Also try changing gasoline brands.

OIL DEPOSITS

Symptoms: Oily coating caused by poor oil control. Oil is leaking past worn valve guides or piston rings into the combustion chamber. Causes hard starting, misfiring and hesitation.

Recommendation: Correct the mechanical condition with necessary repairs and install new plugs.

GAP BRIDGING

Symptoms: Combustion deposits lodge between the electrodes. Heavy deposits accumulate and bridge the electrode gap. The plug ceases to fire, resulting in a dead cylinder.

Recommendation: Locate the faulty plug and remove the deposits from between the electrodes.

TOO HOT

Symptoms: Blistered, white insulator, eroded electrode and absence of deposits. Results in shortened plug life.

Recommendation: Check for the correct plug heat range, over-advanced ignition timing, lean fuel mixture, intake manifold vacuum leaks, sticking valves and insufficient engine cooling.

PREIGNITION

Symptoms: Melted electrodes. Insulators are white, but may be dirty due to misfiring or flying debris in the combustion chamber. Can lead to engine damage.

Recommendation: Check for the correct plug heat range, over-advanced ignition timing, lean fuel mixture, insufficient engine cooling and lack of lubrication.

HIGH SPEED GLAZING

Symptoms: Insulator has yellowish, glazed appearance. Indicates that combustion chamber temperatures have risen suddenly during hard acceleration. Normal deposits melt to form a conductive coating. Causes misfiring at high speeds.

Recommendation: Install new plugs. Consider using a colder plug if driving habits warrant.

DETONATION

Symptoms: Insulators may be cracked or chipped. Improper gap setting techniques can also result in a fractured insulator tip. Can lead to piston damage.

Recommendation: Make sure the fuel anti-knock values meet engine requirements. Use care when setting the gaps on new plugs. Avoid lugging the engine.

MECHANICAL DAMAGE

Symptoms: May be caused by a foreign object in the combustion chamber or the piston striking an incorrect reach (too long) plug. Causes a dead cylinder and could result in piston damage.

Recommendation: Repair the mechanical damage. Remove the foreign object from the engine and/or install the correct reach plug.

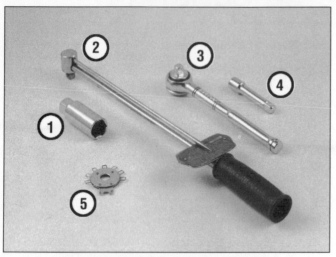

13.1 Tools required for changing spark plugs

1 **Spark plug socket** - *This will have special padding inside to protect the spark plug's porcelain insulator*
2 **Torque wrench** - *Although not mandatory, using this tool is the best way to ensure the plugs are tightened properly*
3 **Ratchet** - *Standard hand tool to fit the spark plug socket*
4 **Extension** - *Depending on model and accessories, you may need special extensions and universal joints to reach one or more of the plugs*
5 **Spark plug gap gauge** - *This gauge for checking the gap comes in a variety of styles. Make sure the gap for your engine is included*

---

13 Spark plug check and replacement (every 15,000 miles or 12 months)

Refer to illustrations 13.1, 13.4a, 13.4b, 13.5, 13.7, 13.9a, 13.9b and 13.9c

1 Before beginning, obtain the necessary tools, which will include a spark plug socket and a gap gauge **(see illustration)**.
2 The best procedure to follow when replacing the spark plugs is to purchase the new spark plugs beforehand, adjust them to the proper gap, and then replace each plug one at a time. When buying the new

13.4a Spark plug manufacturers recommend using a wire-type gauge when checking the gap - if the wire does not slide between the electrodes with a slight drag, adjustment is required

spark plugs it is important to obtain the correct plugs for your specific engine. This information can be found on the Vehicle Emissions Control Information label located under the hood, in the Specifications section in the front of this Chapter or in the owner's manual. If differences exist between these sources, purchase the spark plug type specified on the Emissions Control label, because the information was printed for your specific engine.
3 With the new spark plugs at hand, allow the engine to cool completely before attempting plug removal. During this time, each of the new spark plugs can be inspected for defects and the gaps can be checked.
4 The gap is checked by inserting the proper thickness gauge between the electrodes at the tip of the plug **(see illustration)**. The gap between the electrodes should be the same as that given in the Specifications or on the Emissions Control label. The wire should just touch each of the electrodes. If the gap is incorrect, use the notched adjuster to bend the curved side of the electrode slightly until the proper gap is achieved **(see illustration)**. **Note:** *When adjusting the gap of a new plug, bend only the base of the ground electrode, do not touch the tip. If the side electrode is not exactly over the center electrode, use the notched adjuster to align the two. Check for cracks in the porcelain insulator, indicating the spark plug should not be used.*
5 With the engine cool, remove the spark plug wire from one spark plug. Do this by grabbing the boot at the end of the wire, not the wire itself **(see illustration)**. Sometimes it is necessary to use a twisting motion while the boot and plug wire are pulled free.

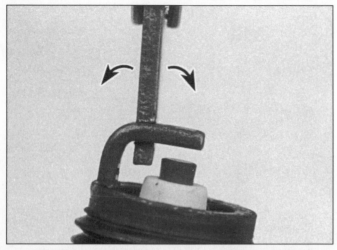

13.4b To change the gap, bend the side electrode only, as indicated by the arrows, and be very careful not to crack or chip the porcelain insulator surrounding the center electrode

13.5 When removing the spark plug wires, pull only on the boot and twist it back-and-forth

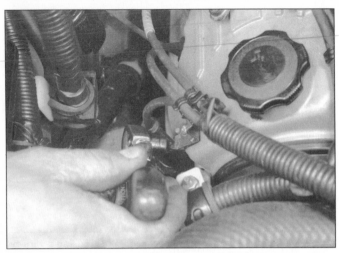

13.7 Use a ratchet and socket with an extension to unscrew the spark plugs

13.9a Apply a thin coat of anti-seize compound to the spark plug threads to prevent damage to the cylinder head

6   If compressed air is available, use it to blow any dirt or foreign material away from the spark plug area. A common bicycle pump will also work. The idea here is to eliminate the possibility of debris falling into the cylinder as the spark plug is removed.

7   Place the spark plug socket over the plug and remove it from the engine by turning in a counterclockwise direction **(see illustration)**.

8   Compare the spark plug with those shown in the accompanying color photos to get an indication of the overall running condition of the engine.

9   Apply a small amount of anti-seize compound to the spark plug threads **(see illustration)**. Install the plug into the head, turning it with your fingers until it no longer turns, then tighten it with the socket. Where there might be difficulty in inserting the spark plugs into the spark plug holes, or the possibility of cross threading them into the head, a short piece of 5/16-inch rubber tubing can be fitted over the end of the spark plug **(see illustration)**. The flexible tubing will act as a universal joint to help align the plug with the plug hole, and should the plug begin to cross thread, the hose will slip on the spark plug, preventing thread damage **(see illustration)**. If one is available, use a torque wrench to tighten the plug to ensure that it is seated correctly. The correct torque figure is included in the Specifications.

10   Before pushing the spark plug wire onto the end of the plug, inspect it following the procedures outlined in Section 14.

11   Attach the plug wire to the new spark plug, again using a twisting motion on the boot until it is firmly seated on the spark plug.

12   Follow the above procedure for the remaining spark plugs, replacing them one at a time to prevent mixing up the spark plug wires.

---

14   Spark plug wire, distributor cap and rotor check and replacement (every 15,000 miles or 12 months)

Refer to illustrations 14.11a, 11.14b, 11.14c and 14.11d

1   The spark plug wires should be checked at the recommended intervals and whenever new spark plugs are installed in the engine.

2   Begin this procedure by making a visual check of the spark plug wires while the engine is running. In a darkened garage (make sure there is ventilation) start the engine and observe each plug wire. Be careful not to come into contact with any moving engine parts. If there is a break in the wire, you will see arcing or a small spark at the damaged area. If arcing is noticed, make a note to obtain new wires, then allow the engine to cool.

3   Disconnect the negative cable from the battery.

4   The wires should be inspected one at a time to prevent mixing up the order, which is essential for proper engine operation.

5   Disconnect the plug wire from the spark plug. A removal tool can be used for this purpose or you can grab the plastic boot, twist slightly and pull the wire free. Do not pull on the wire itself, only on the boot.

6   Inspect inside the boot for corrosion, which will look like a white crusty powder. Push the wire and boot back onto the end of the spark

13.9b A length of 5/16-inch ID rubber hose will save time and prevent damaged threads when installing the spark plugs

13.9c Thread the spark plug into the cylinder head until the hose starts to slip, then remove the hose and finish tightening with your fingers

14.11a Loosen the screws and lift the distributor cap up so you can inspect the inside

14.11b Use a socket and ratchet to remove the screw, then lift the rotor off the shaft

plug. It should be a tight fit on the plug end. If it is not, remove the wire and use pliers to carefully crimp the metal connector inside the boot until it fits securely on the end of the spark plug.

7   Using a clean rag, wipe the entire length of the wire to remove any built-up dirt and grease. Once the wire is clean, check for burns,

cracks and other damage. Do not bend the wire excessively, since the conductor might break.

8   Disconnect the wire from the distributor. Again, pull only on the boot. Check for corrosion and a tight fit in the same manner as the spark plug end. Replace the wire in the distributor.

9   Check the remaining spark plug wires, making sure they are securely fastened at the distributor and spark plug when the check is complete.

10   If new spark plug wires are required, purchase a set for your specific engine model. Wire sets are available pre-cut, with the boots already installed. Remove and replace the wires one at a time to avoid mix-ups in the firing order.

11   Check the distributor cap and rotor for wear. Loosen the screws and remove the distributor cap **(see illustration)**. Remove the screw and pull the rotor off the shaft **(see illustration)**. Look for cracks, carbon tracks and worn, burned or loose contacts **(see illustrations)**. Replace the cap and rotor with new parts if defects are found. It is common practice to install a new cap and rotor whenever new spark plug wires are installed. When installing a new cap, remove the wires from the old cap one at a time and attach them to the new cap in the exact same location - do not simultaneously remove all the wires or firing order mix-ups may occur.

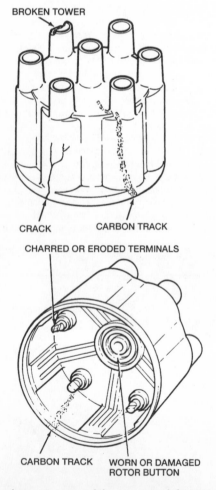

14.11c Shown here are some of the common defects to look for when inspecting the distributor cap (if in doubt about its condition, install a new one)

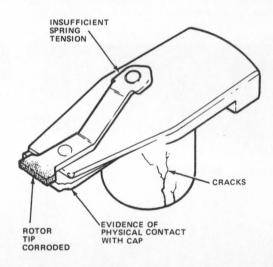

14.11d The ignition rotor should be checked for wear and corrosion as indicated here (if in doubt about its condition, buy a new one)

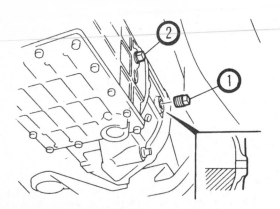

15.2 Check the lubricant level at the check plug opening (1) - if it's low, add lubricant at the fill plug opening (2)

15   Manual transmission lubricant level check (every 15,000 miles or 12 months)

Refer to illustration 15.2

1   The transmission has a check and fill plugs which must be removed to check the lubricant level If the vehicle is raised to gain access to the plug, be sure to support it safely on jackstands - DO NOT crawl under a vehicle which is supported only by a jack!

2   Remove the check plug from the transmission **(see illustration)** and use your little finger to reach inside and feel the lubricant level. It should be at or very near the bottom of the plug hole.

3   If it isn't, remove the fill plug and add the recommended lubricant through the plug hole with a syringe or squeeze bottle.

4   Install and tighten both plugs securely and check for leaks after the first few miles of driving.

16   Differential lubricant level check (every 15,000 miles or 12 months)

Refer to illustrations 16.2a and 16.2b

Note: *This procedure applies to both the front and rear differential.*

1   The differential has a check/fill plug which must be removed to check the lubricant level. If the vehicle is raised to gain access to the plug, be sure to support it safely on jackstands - DO NOT crawl under the vehicle when it's supported only by the jack!

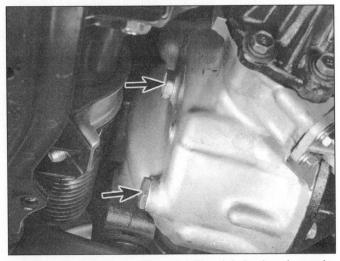

16.2b 4WD model front differential fill and drain plugs (arrows)

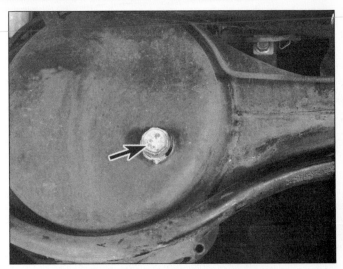

16.2a Rear axle check/fill plug location (arrow)

2   Remove the lubricant check/fill plug from the differential **(see illustrations)**.

3   Use your little finger as a dipstick to make sure the lubricant level is even with the bottom of the plug hole. If not, use a syringe or a squeeze bottle to add the recommended lubricant until it just starts to run out of the opening.

4   Install the plug and tighten it securely.

17   Transfer case lubricant level check (4WD models only) (every 15,000 miles or 12 months)

Refer to illustration 17.2

1   The transfer case has check and fill plugs on the sides of the case which must be removed to check the lubricant level. If the vehicle is raised to gain access to the plugs, be sure to support it safely on jackstands - DO NOT crawl under a vehicle which is supported only by a jack!

2   Remove the level (check) plug from the transfer case and use your little finger to reach inside the housing and feel the lubricant level **(see illustration)**. It should be at or very near the bottom of the plug hole.

3   If it isn't, remove the upper plug and add the recommended lubricant through the plug hole with a syringe or squeeze bottle.

4   Install and tighten the plugs securely and check for leaks after the first few miles of driving.

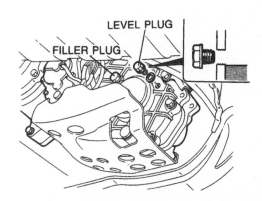

17.2 Check the lubricant level at the level plug - if it's low, add lubricant at the filler plug opening

18.2 Unplug the MAF sensor

18.3 Loosen the air hose clamp screw

18.4 Use a socket with an extension to remove the air cleaner cover bolts

18.5 Rotate the cover up and lift the air filter element out

18   Air filter replacement (every 15,000 miles or 12 months)

Refer to illustrations 18.2, 18.3, 18.4 and 18.5

1   Purchase a new filter element.
2   Unplug the electrical connector from the Mass Air Flow (MAF) sensor **(see illustration)**.
3   Loosen the throttle body air hose clamp **(see illustration)**.
4   Remove the cover screws **(see illustration)**.
5   Rotate the cover up, lift it off and remove the element, noting the direction it faces **(see illustration)**.
6   Wipe the inside of the air cleaner housing with a clean cloth. If the element is marked TOP be sure the marked side faces up.
7   Reinstall the cover and retaining screws. Don't overtighten the screws!
8   Tighten the air hose screw and plug in the electrical connector.

19   Positive Crankcase Ventilation (PCV) valve check and replacement (every 15,000 miles or 12 months)

Refer to illustrations 19.1a, 19.1b, 19.1c and 19.2

1   To check the valve, first pull it out of the grommet in the valve cover **(see illustrations)**. Shake the valve **(see illustration)**. It should rattle, indicating that it is not clogged with deposits. If the valve does not rattle, replace it with a new one. If it does rattle, reinstall it.

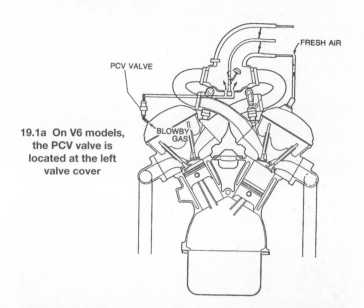

19.1a On V6 models, the PCV valve is located at the left valve cover

2   Start the engine and allow it to idle, then disconnect the PCV hose. If vacuum is felt, the PCV valve system is working properly **(see illustration)** (see Chapter 6 for additional PCV system information).
3   If no vacuum is felt, the oil filler cap, hoses or valve cover gasket

19.1b On four-cylinder engines the PCV valve is located in a grommet at the front of the valve cover

19.1c Shake the valve back and forth - if it rattles, it's OK

19.2 You should feel suction on your thumb with the engine running if the valve is working properly

20.5 Check the rubber filler hose carefully for cracks

may be leaking or the PCV valve may be bad. Check for vacuum leaks at the valve, filler cap and all hoses.

4   Pull straight up on the valve to remove it. Check the rubber grommet for cracks and distortion. If it's damaged, replace it.

5   If the valve is clogged, the hose is also probably plugged. Remove the hose and clean with solvent.

6   After cleaning the hose, inspect it for damage, wear and deterioration. Make sure it fits snugly on the fittings.

7   If necessary, install a new PCV valve. **Note:** *The elbow (if equipped) is not part of the PCV valve. A new valve will not include the elbow. The original must be transferred to the new valve. If a new elbow is purchased, it may be necessary to soak it in warm water for up to an hour to slip it onto the new valve. Do not attempt to force the elbow onto the valve or it will break.*

8   Install the clean PCV system hose. Make sure that the PCV valve and hose are secure.

---

20   Fuel system check (every 15,000 miles or 12 months)

Refer to illustration 20.5

Warning: *Certain precautions should be observed when inspecting or servicing the fuel system components. Work in a well ventilated area and don't allow open flames (cigarettes, appliance pilot lights, etc.) near the work area. Mop up spills immediately. Do not store fuel soaked rags where they could ignite. It is a good idea to keep a dry*
chemical (Class B) fire extinguisher near the work area any time the fuel system is being serviced.

1   If you smell gasoline while driving or after the vehicle has been sitting in the sun, inspect the fuel system immediately.

2   Remove the fuel filler cap and inspect it for damage and corrosion. The gasket should have an unbroken sealing imprint. If the gasket is damaged or corroded, install a new cap.

3   Inspect the fuel feed and return lines for cracks. Make sure that the connections between the fuel lines and the fuel injection system and between the fuel lines and the in-line fuel filter are tight. **Warning:** *The fuel system pressure must be relieved before servicing fuel system components. The fuel system pressure relief procedure is outlined in Chapter 4.*

4   Since some components of the fuel system - the fuel tank and some of the fuel feed and return lines, for example - are underneath the vehicle, they can be inspected more easily with the vehicle raised on a hoist. If that's not possible, raise the vehicle and support it on jackstands.

5   With the vehicle raised and safely supported, inspect the gas tank and filler neck for punctures, cracks or other damage. The connection between the filler neck and the tank is particularly critical. Sometimes a rubber filler neck will leak because of loose clamps or deteriorated rubber **(see illustration)**. Inspect all fuel tank mounting brackets and straps to be sure the tank is securely attached to the vehicle. **Warning:** *Do not, under any circumstances, try to repair a fuel tank (except rubber components). A welding torch or any open flame can easily cause fuel vapors inside the tank to explode.*

21.3 The radiator cap sealing surfaces in the radiator filler neck should be checked for built-up corrosion - the radiator cap should be replaced if the gasket is brittle or deteriorated

6   Carefully check all rubber hoses and metal or nylon lines leading away from the fuel tank. Check for loose connections, deteriorated hoses, crimped lines and other damage. Repair or replace damaged sections as necessary (see Chapter 4).

21   Cooling system check (every 15,000 miles or 12 months)

Refer to illustrations 21.3 and 21.4

1   Many major engine failures can be attributed to a faulty cooling system. If the vehicle is equipped with an automatic transmission, the cooling system also plays an important role in prolonging transmission life because it cools the fluid.
2   The engine should be cold for the cooling system check, so perform the following procedure before the vehicle is driven for the day or after it has been shut off for at least three hours.
3   Remove the radiator cap **(see illustration)** and clean it thoroughly, inside and out, with clean water. Also clean the filler neck on the radiator. The presence of rust or corrosion in the filler neck means the coolant should be changed (see Section 28). The coolant inside the radiator should be relatively clean and transparent. If it's rust colored, drain the system and refill with new coolant.
4   Carefully check the radiator hoses and smaller diameter heater hoses. Inspect each coolant hose along its entire length, replacing any hose which is cracked, swollen or deteriorated **(see illustration)**. Cracks will show up better if the hose is squeezed. Pay close attention to hose clamps that secure the hoses to cooling system components. Hose clamps can pinch and puncture hoses, resulting in coolant leaks.
5   Make sure all hose connections are tight. A leak in the cooling system will usually show up as white or rust colored deposits on the area adjoining the leak. If wire-type clamps are used on the hoses, it may be a good idea to replace them with screw-type clamps.
6   Clean the front of the radiator and air conditioning condenser with compressed air, if available, or a soft brush. Remove all bugs, leaves, etc. embedded in the radiator fins. Be extremely careful not to damage the cooling fins or cut your fingers on them.
7   If the coolant level has been dropping consistently and no leaks are detectable, have the radiator cap and cooling system pressure checked at a service station.

22   Exhaust system check (every 15,000 miles or 12 months)

Refer to illustrations 22.4a and 22.4b

1   With the engine cold (at least three hours after the vehicle has been driven), check the complete exhaust system from the engine to

ALWAYS CHECK hose for chafed or burned areas that may cause an untimely and costly failure.

SOFT hose indicates inside deterioration. This deterioration can contaminate the cooling system and cause particles to clog the radiator.

HARDENED hose can fail at any time. Tightening hose clamps will not seal the connection or stop leaks.

SWOLLEN hose or oil soaked ends indicate danger and possible failure from oil or grease contamination. Squeeze the hose to locate cracks and breaks that cause leaks.

21.4 Hoses, like drivebelts, have a habit of failing at the worst possible time - to prevent the inconvenience of a blown radiator or heater hose, inspect them carefully as shown here

end of the tailpipe. Ideally, the inspection should be done with the vehicle on a hoist to permit unrestricted access. If a hoist isn't available, raise the vehicle and support it securely on jackstands.
2   Check the exhaust pipes and connections for evidence of leaks, severe corrosion and damage. Make sure that all brackets and hangers are in good condition and are tight.
3   At the same time, inspect the underside of the body for holes, corrosion, open seams, etc. which may allow exhaust gases to enter the passenger compartment. Seal all body openings with silicone or body putty.
4   Rattles and other noises can often be traced to the exhaust system, especially the mounts, hangers and heat shields. Try to move the pipes, muffler and catalytic converter **(see illustrations)**. If the components can come in contact with the body or suspension parts, secure the exhaust system with new mounts.
5   Check the running condition of the engine by inspecting inside the end of the tailpipe. The exhaust deposits here are an indication of engine state-of-tune. If the pipe is black and sooty or coated with white deposits, the engine may need a tune-up, including a thorough fuel system inspection.

23   Steering and suspension check (every 15,000 miles or 12 months)

Note: *The steering linkage and suspension components should be checked periodically. Worn or damaged suspension and steering linkage components can result in excessive and abnormal tire wear, poor ride quality and vehicle handling and reduced fuel economy. For detailed illustrations of the steering and suspension components, refer to Chapter 10.*

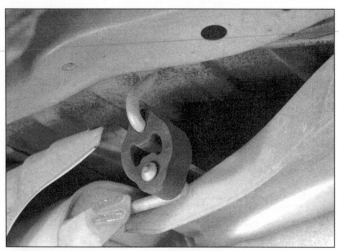

22.4a Check the rubber exhaust system hangers for cracks

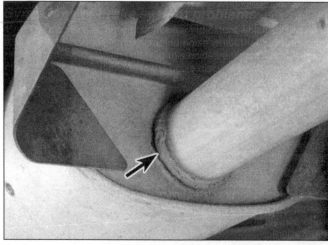

22.4b Inspect the exhaust system welds for cracks and corrosion

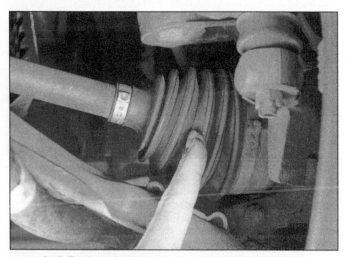

24.2 Push on the driveaxle boots to check for cracks

Shock absorber check

1   Park the vehicle on level ground, turn the engine off and set the parking brake. Check the tire pressures.

2   Push down at one corner of the vehicle, then release it while noting the movement of the body. It should stop moving and come to rest in a level position with one or two bounces.

3   If the vehicle continues to move up-and-down or if it fails to return to its original position, a worn or weak shock absorber is probably the reason.

4   Repeat the above check at each of the three remaining corners of the vehicle.

5   Raise the vehicle and support it on jackstands.

6   Check the shock absorbers for evidence of fluid leakage. A light film of fluid is no cause for concern. Make sure that any fluid noted is from the shocks and not from any other source. If leakage is noted, replace the shocks as a set.

7   Check the shock absorbers to be sure that they are securely mounted and undamaged. Check the upper mounts for damage and wear. If damage or wear is noted, replace the shock absorbers as a set.

8   If the shock absorbers must be replaced, refer to Chapter 10 for the procedure.

Steering and suspension check

9   Visually inspect the steering system components for damage and distortion. Look for leaks and damaged seals, boots and fittings.

10   Clean the lower end of the steering knuckle. Have an assistant

grasp the lower edge of the tire and move the wheel in-and-out while you look for movement at the steering knuckle-to-control arm balljoints. If there is any movement, the balljoint must be replaced.

11   Grasp each front tire at the front and rear edges, push in at the front, pull out at the rear and feel for play in the steering linkage. If any freeplay is noted, check the steering gear mounts and the tie-rod balljoints for looseness. If the steering gear mounts are loose, tighten them. If the tie-rods are loose, the balljoints may be worn (check to make sure the nuts are tight). Additional steering and suspension system illustrations can be found in Chapter 10.

24   Front driveaxle boot check (4WD models only) (every 15,000 miles or 12 months)

Refer to illustration 24.2

1   The front driveaxle boots are very important because they prevent dirt, water and foreign material from entering and damaging the constant velocity (CV) joints. Oil and grease can cause the boot material to deteriorate prematurely, so it's a good idea to wash the boots with soap and water.

2   Inspect the boots for tears and cracks as well as loose clamps **(see illustration)**. If there is any evidence of cracks or leaking lubricant, the boot must be replaced with a new one (see Chapter 8).

25   Brake system check (every 15,000 miles or 12 months)

Refer to illustrations 25.11 and 25.14

Warning: *Dust produced by lining wear and deposited on brake components may contain asbestos, which is hazardous to your health. DO NOT blow it out with compressed air and DO NOT inhale it! DO NOT use gasoline or solvents to remove the dust. Brake system cleaner should be used to flush the dust into a drain pan. After the brake components are wiped with a damp rag, dispose of the contaminated rag(s) and brake cleaner in a covered and labeled container. Try to use non-asbestos replacement parts whenever possible.*

Note: *In addition to the specified intervals, the brake system should be inspected each time the wheels are removed or a malfunction is indicated. Because of the obvious safety considerations, the following brake system checks are some of the most important maintenance procedures you can perform on your vehicle.*

Symptoms of brake system problems

1   The disc brakes have built-in wear indicators which should make a high-pitched squealing or scraping noise when they're worn to the replacement point. When you hear this noise, replace the pads immediately or expensive damage to the brake discs could result.

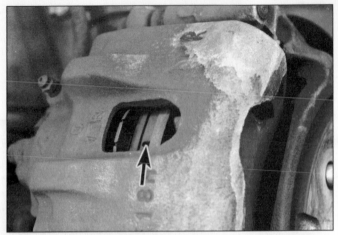

25.11 Look through the caliper inspection window to inspect the brake pads - the pad lining (arrow) which rubs against the disc can also be inspected by looking at each end of the caliper

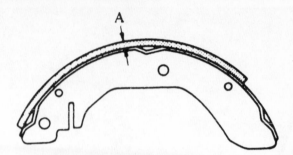

25.14 If the lining is bonded to the brake shoe, measure the lining thickness from the outer surface to the metal shoe, as shown here; if the lining is riveted to the shoe, measure from the lining outer surface to the rivet head

2   Any of the following symptoms could indicate a potential brake system defect. The vehicle pulls to one side when the brake pedal is depressed, the brakes make squealing or dragging noises when applied, brake travel is excessive, the pedal pulsates and brake fluid leaks are noted (usually on the inner side of the tire or wheel). If any of these conditions are noted, inspect the brake system immediately.

Brake lines and hoses

Note: *Steel tubing is used throughout the brake system, with the exception of flexible, reinforced hoses at the front wheels and as connectors at the rear axle. Periodic inspection of these lines is very important.*

3   Park the vehicle on level ground and turn the engine off.
4   Remove the wheel covers. Loosen, but do not remove, the lug nuts on all four wheels.
5   Raise the vehicle and support it securely on jackstands.
6   Remove the wheels (see *Jacking and towing* at the front of this book, or refer to your owner's manual, if necessary).
7   Check all brake lines and hoses for cracks, chafing of the outer cover, leaks, blisters and distortion. Check the brake hoses at front and rear of the vehicle for softening, cracks, bulging, or wear from rubbing on other components. Check all threaded fittings for leaks and make sure the brake hose mounting bolts and clips are secure.
8   If leaks or damage are discovered, they must be fixed immediately. Refer to Chapter 9 for detailed brake system repair procedures.

Disc brakes

9   If it hasn't already been done, raise the vehicle and support it securely on jackstands. Remove the front wheels.
10   The disc brake calipers, which contain the pads, are now visible. Each caliper has an outer and an inner pad - all pads should be checked.
11   Note the pad thickness by looking through the inspection hole in the caliper **(see illustration)**. If the lining material is 1/8-inch thick or less, or if it is tapered from end-to-end, the pads should be replaced (see Chapter 9). Keep in mind that the lining material is riveted or bonded to a metal plate or shoe - the metal portion is not included in this measurement.
12   Check the condition of the brake disc. Look for score marks, deep scratches and overheated areas (they will appear blue or discolored). If damage or wear is noted, the disc can be removed and resurfaced by an automotive machine shop or replaced with a new one. Refer to Chapter 9 for more detailed inspection and repair procedures.

Drum brakes

13   Refer to Chapter 9 and remove the rear brake drums.
14   Note the thickness of the lining material on the rear brake shoes and look for signs of contamination by brake fluid or grease (see illus-

tration). If the material is within 1/16-inch of the recessed rivets or metal shoes, replace the brake shoes with new ones. The shoes should also be replaced if they are cracked, glazed (shiny lining surfaces), or contaminated with brake fluid or grease. See Chapter 9 for the replacement procedure.
15   Check the shoe return and hold-down springs and the adjusting mechanism to make sure they are installed correctly and in good condition. Deteriorated or distorted springs, if not replaced, could allow the linings to drag and wear prematurely.
16   Check the wheel cylinders for leakage by carefully peeling back the rubber boots Slight moisture behind the boots is acceptable. If brake fluid is noted behind the boots or if it runs out of the wheel cylinder, the wheel cylinders must be overhauled or replaced (see Chapter 9).
17   Check the drums for cracks, score marks, deep scratches and hard spots, which will appear as small discolored areas. If imperfections cannot be removed with emery cloth, the drums must be resurfaced by an automotive machine shop (see Chapter 9 for more detailed information).
18   Refer to Chapter 9 and install the brake drums.
19   Install the wheels, but don't lower the vehicle yet.

Parking brake

20   The easiest, and perhaps most obvious, method of checking the parking brake is to park the vehicle on a steep hill with the parking brake set and the transmission in Neutral. If the parking brake doesn't prevent the vehicle from rolling, refer to Chapter 9 and adjust it.

---

26   Wiper blade check and replacement (every 15,000 miles or 12 months)

---

1   Road film can build up on the wiper blades and affect their efficiency, so they should be washed regularly with a mild detergent solution.

Check

2   The wiper and blade assembly should be inspected periodically. Even if you don't use your wipers, the sun and elements will dry out the rubber portions, causing them to crack and break apart. If inspection reveals hardened or cracked rubber, replace the wiper blades. If inspection reveals nothing unusual, wet the windshield, turn the wipers on, allow them to cycle several times, then shut them off. An uneven wiper pattern across the glass or streaks over clean glass indicate that the blades should be replaced.
3   The operation of the wiper mechanism can loosen the fasteners, so they should be checked and tightened, as necessary, at the same time the wiper blades are checked (see Chapter 12 for further information regarding the wiper mechanism).

Wiper blade replacement

Refer to illustrations 26.5, 26.6, 26.8a and 26.8b
4   Pull the wiper/blade assembly away from the glass.

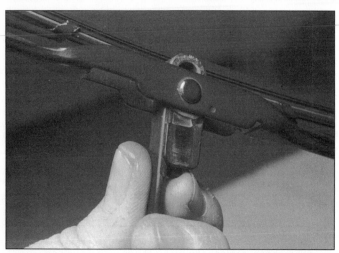

26.5 Press the retaining tab in, then slide the wiper blade assembly down and out of the hook in the end of the wiper arm

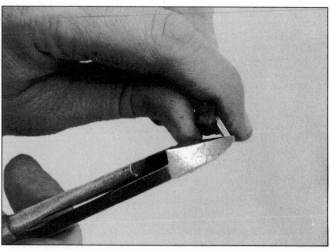

26.6 Wire cutters or needle-nose pliers can be used to pull the two support rods out of the blade element

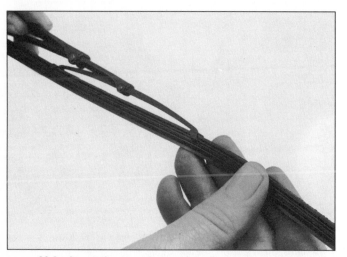

26.8a Insert the new element into the blade assembly

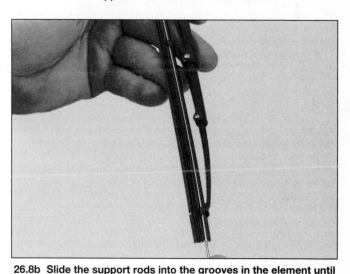

26.8b Slide the support rods into the grooves in the element until they lock the element in the blade assembly

7   Compare the new element with the old for length, design, etc.
8   Slide the new element into place **(see illustration)**. Insert the support rods into the element to lock it in place **(see illustration)**.
9   Reinstall the blade assembly on the arm, wet the glass and check for proper operation.

---

27   Automatic transmission fluid and filter change (every 30,000 miles or 24 months)

Refer to illustrations 27.7, 27.10a and 27.10b
1   At the specified intervals, the transmission fluid should be drained and replaced. Since the fluid will remain hot long after driving, perform this procedure only after the engine has cooled down completely.
2   Before beginning work, purchase the specified transmission fluid (see *Recommended lubricants and fluids* at the beginning of this Chapter) and a new filter.
3   Other tools necessary for this job include jackstands to support the vehicle in a raised position, a drain pan, newspapers and clean rags.
4   Raise the vehicle and support it securely on jackstands.
5   With a drain pan in place, remove the front and side pan mounting bolts.
6   Loosen the rear pan bolts approximately four turns.
7   Carefully pry the transmission pan loose with a screwdriver, allowing the fluid to drain **(see illustration)**

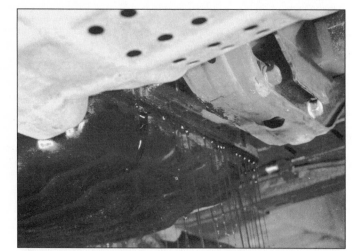

27.7 Pry the pan free and let it hang down so the fluid can drain

5   Squeeze the retaining lever and slide the off the wiper arm **(see illustration)**.
6   Bend the end of the element out of the way and pull out the two support rods, using needle-nose pliers or wire cutters **(see illustration)**.

27.10a Remove the bolts . . .

27.10b . . . and rotate the fluid filter out of the bracket

8   Remove the remaining bolts, pan and gasket. Carefully clean the gasket surface of the transmission to remove all traces of the old gasket and sealant.
9   Drain the fluid from the transmission pan, clean it with solvent and dry it with compressed air. Be sure to clean the metal filings from the magnet.
10   Remove the filter from the mount inside the transmission **(see illustrations)**.
11   Install a new filter, being sure to tighten the bolts securely.
12   Make sure the gasket surface on the transmission pan is clean, the install a new gasket. Put the pan in place against the transmission and install the bolts. Working around the pan, tighten each bolt a little at a time until the torque listed in this Chapter's Specifications Section is reached. Don't overtighten the bolts!
13   Lower the vehicle and add the specified amount of fluid through the filler tube (Section 8).
14   With the transmission in Park and the parking brake set, run the engine at fast idle, but don't race it.
15   Move the gear selector through each range and back to Park. Check the fluid level.
16   Check under the vehicle for leaks during the first few trips.

28.4 Before opening the drain valve located at the bottom of the radiator, push a short section of 3/8-inch diameter hose on the fitting to prevent the coolant from splashing as it drains

28   Cooling system servicing (draining, flushing and refilling) (every 30,000 miles or 24 months)

Refer to illustration 28.4
Warning: *Do not allow antifreeze to come in contact with your skin or painted surfaces of the vehicle. Rinse off spills immediately with plenty of water. Antifreeze is highly toxic if ingested. Never leave antifreeze lying around in an open container or in puddles on the floor; children and pets are attracted by it's sweet smell and may drink it. Check with local authorities about disposing of used antifreeze. Many communities have collection centers which will see that antifreeze is disposed of safely.*
1   Periodically, the cooling system should be drained, flushed and refilled to replenish the antifreeze mixture and prevent formation of rust and corrosion, which can impair the performance of the cooling system and cause engine damage. When the cooling system is serviced, all hoses and the radiator cap should be checked and replaced if necessary.

Draining

2   Apply the parking brake and block the wheels. If the vehicle has just been driven, wait several hours to allow the engine to cool down before beginning this procedure.
3   Once the engine is completely cool, remove the radiator cap.
4   Move a large container under the radiator drain to catch the coolant. Attach a 3/8-inch diameter hose to the drain fitting to direct the coolant into the container **(see illustration)**, then open the drain

fitting (a pair of pliers may be required to turn it).
5   While the coolant is draining, check the condition of the radiator hoses, heater hoses and clamps (see Section 21 if necessary).
6   Replace any damaged clamps or hoses (see Chapter 3 for detailed replacement procedures).

Flushing

7   Once the system is completely drained, flush the radiator with fresh water from a garden hose until the water runs clear at the drain. The flushing action of the water will remove sediments from the radiator but will not remove rust and scale from the engine and cooling tube surfaces.
8   These deposits can be removed by a chemical cleaner. Follow the procedure outlined in the manufacturer's instructions. If the radiator is severely corroded, damaged or leaking, it should be removed (see Chapter 3) and taken to a radiator repair shop.
9   The heater core should be back flushed whenever the cooling system is flushed. To do this, disconnect the heater return hose from the thermostat housing or engine. Slide a female garden hose fitting into the heater hose and secure it with a clamp. This will allow you to attach a garden hose securely.
10   Attach the end of a garden hose to the fitting you installed in the heater hose.
11   Disconnect the heater inlet hose and position it to act as a drain.
12   Turn the water on and off several times to create a surging action through the heater core. Then turn the water on full force and allow it to run for approximately five minutes.

29.2 The fuel filter (arrow) is located on the right side of the engine compartment

29.3 Use needle-nose pliers to slide the clip off, then detach the inlet hose

29.5a Remove the nut . . .

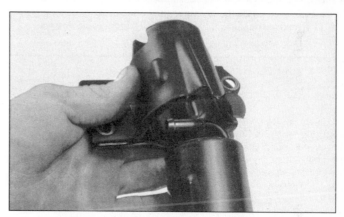

29.5b . . . and detach the filter from the bracket

29.6 Install the filter with the word OUT facing up

to the radiator until it is full. Add coolant to the reservoir up to the lower mark.
18   Leave the radiator cap off and run the engine in a well-ventilated area until the thermostat opens (coolant will begin flowing through the radiator and the upper radiator hose will become hot).
19   Turn the engine off and let it cool. Add more coolant mixture to bring the coolant level back up to the lip on the radiator filler neck.
20   Squeeze the upper radiator hose to expel air, then add more coolant mixture if necessary. Replace the radiator cap.
21   Start the engine, allow it to reach normal operating temperature and check for leaks.

29   Fuel filter replacement (every 30,000 miles or 24 months)

Refer to illustrations 29.2, 29.3, 29.5a, 29.5b and 29.6
Warning: *Gasoline is extremely flammable so extra safety precautions must be observed when working on any part of the fuel system. Do not smoke and do not allow bare light bulbs or open flames near the vehicle. Also, do not perform this maintenance procedure in a garage if a natural gas type appliance with a pilot light is present.*
1   Depressurize the system (see Chapter 4).
2   The fuel filter is located on the wheelhouse on the right (passenger) side of the engine compartment **(see illustration)**.
3   Place a pan or rags under the fuel filter to catch any spilled gasoline, then use needle-nose pliers to remove the clamp, then detach the inlet hose **(see illustration)**.
4   Detach the outlet hose and remove the bracket bolts, then lift the filter and bracket assembly out of the engine compartment.
5   Remove the bracket bolt and detach the filter from the bracket **(see illustrations)**.
6   Installation is the reverse of removal, making sure that the end of the filter marked OUT is facing up **(see illustration)**.

13   Turn off the water and disconnect the garden hose from the female fitting. Remove the fitting from the heater return hose, then reconnect the hoses to the engine.
14   Remove the overflow hose from the coolant recovery reservoir. Drain the reservoir and flush it with clean water, then reconnect the hose.

Refilling
15   Close and tighten the radiator drain. Install and tighten the block drain plug(s).
16   Place the heater temperature control in the maximum heat position.
17   Slowly add new coolant (a 50/50 mixture of water and antifreeze)

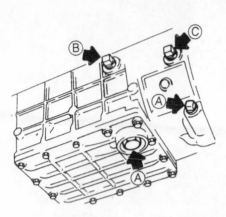

**30.6 Some models have more than one drain and fill plug -
remove the upper plugs (B and C) before removing the
drain plugs (A)**

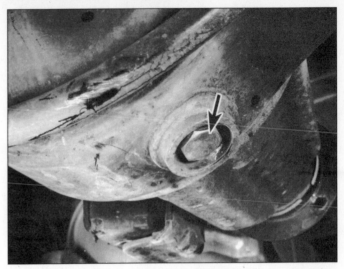

**31.5 A socket will be required to remove the drain plug from the
rear axle**

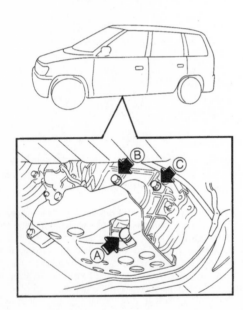

**32.3 Remove the check/fill plugs (B and C) from the transfer
case, followed by the drain plug (A)**

30   Manual transmission lubricant change (every 30,000 miles or 24 months)

Refer to illustration 30.6

1   At the specified time intervals the transmission lubricant should be changed to ensure trouble free operation. Before proceeding, purchase the specified type of lubricant.

2   Tools necessary for this job include jackstands to support the vehicle in a raised position, a wrench to remove the drain plugs, a drain pan capable of holding at least four quarts, newspapers and clean rags.

3   The lubricant should be drained immediately after the vehicle has been driven. This will remove any contaminants better than if the lubricant were cold. Because of this, it may be wise to wear rubber gloves while removing the drain plug.

4   After the vehicle has been driven to warm up the oil, raise it and place it on jackstands. Make sure it is safely supported and as level as

possible.

5   Move the necessary equipment under the vehicle, being careful not to touch any of the hot exhaust components.

6   Place the drain pan under the transmission and remove the check/fill plug(s) from the side of the transmission **(see illustration)**. Loosen the drain plug(s) **(see illustration)**.

7   Carefully unscrew the plug(s) with your fingers. Be careful not to burn yourself on the lubricant.

8   Allow the oil to drain completely. Clean the drain plug(s) then reinstall and tighten securely.

9   Refer to Section 15, fill the transmission to the correct level with new lubricant and install the check/fill plug(s).

31   Differential lubricant change (every 30,000 miles or 24 months)

Refer to illustration 31.5

1   Drive the vehicle for several miles to warm up the differential oil, then raise the vehicle and support it securely on jackstands.

2   Move a drain pan, rags and newspapers under the vehicle.

3   On the front differential (4WD models), remove the bolts and detach the undercover for access.

4   Remove the check/fill plug from the differential. It's the upper of the two plugs.

5   With the drain pan under the differential, loosen the drain plug. It's the lower of the two plugs **(see illustration)**.

6   Once loosened, carefully unscrew it with your fingers until you can remove it from the case.

7   Allow all of the oil to drain into the pan, then replace the drain plug and tighten it securely.

8   Refer to Section 16 and fill the differential with lubricant.

9   Reinstall the fill plug and tighten it securely.

10   Lower the vehicle. Check for leaks at the drain plug after the first few miles of driving.

32   Transfer case lubricant change (4WD models only) (every 30,000 miles or 24 months)

Refer to illustration 32.3

1   After driving the vehicle to warm up the lubricant, raise the vehicle and support it securely on jackstands.

2   Move a drain pan, rags and newspapers under the vehicle.

3   With the drain pan under the transfer case, remove the check/fill plugs, followed by the drain plug **(see illustration)**.

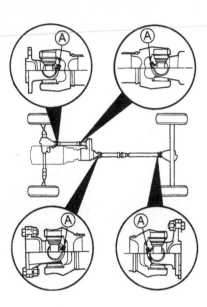

33.3 4WD model driveshaft grease fitting (A) locations

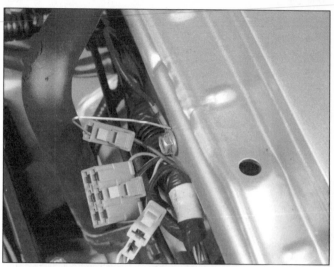

35.6 A paper clip can be used to ground the check connector to the body

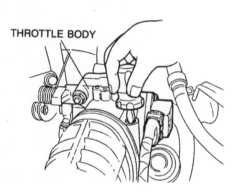

35.8 Turn the screw on top of the throttle body to adjust the idle speed

4   Wipe the plug clean, then install the drain plug securely, using a new washer.

5   Refer to Section 17, fill the transfer case with lubricant and install the check/fill plugs.

6   Lower the vehicle. Check for leaks at the drain plug after the first few miles of driving.

33   Driveshaft lubrication (4WD models only) (every 30,000 miles or 24 months)

Refer to illustration 33.3

1   A grease gun and cartridge filled with the recommended grease (along with some clean rags) and equipment needed to raise the vehicle safely are required to lubricate the driveshafts on these models.

2   Raise the vehicle and support it securely on jackstands.

3   Locate the grease fittings on the driveshafts **(see illustration)**. Wipe the fittings clean before attaching the grease gun.

4   Pump grease into each fitting until a slight amount of resistance is felt when operating the grease gun.

34   Evaporative Emissions Control (EVAP) system check (every 30,000 miles or 24 months)

1   The function of the Evaporative Emissions Control system is to draw fuel vapors from the tank and fuel system, store them in a charcoal canister and then burn them during normal engine operation.

2   The most common symptom of a fault in the evaporative emissions system is a strong fuel odor in the engine compartment. If a fuel odor is detected, inspect the charcoal canister and system hoses for cracks. The canister is located in the engine compartment on the lower right (passenger) side of the firewall.

3   The evaporative emissions control system is explained in more detail in Chapter 6.

35   Engine idle speed check and adjustment (every 30,000 miles or 24 months)

Refer to illustrations 35.6 and 35.8

1   Engine idle speed is the speed at which the engine operates when no accelerator pedal pressure is applied. This speed is critical to the performance of the engine itself, as well as many engine sub-systems.

2   A hand held tachometer must be used when adjusting idle speed to get an accurate reading. The exact hook-up for these meters varies with the manufacturer, so follow the particular directions included with the meter.

3   The fuel/air mixture on these vehicles is controlled by the computer, but the idle speed can be adjusted if a suitable tachometer is available.

4   Connect the tachometer to the engine by following the instructions supplied by the tachometer manufacturer. Keep in mind that some tachometers are not compatible with electronic ignition systems and remember that these vehicles are equipped with electronic ignition.

5   Before the idle speed is checked and adjusted, make sure that the air cleaner, the air intake system hoses, the vacuum lines and any EFI system wiring connectors are all properly installed. In addition, the engine must be at normal operating temperature, all accessories must be OFF and the transmission must be in NEUTRAL. Apply the parking brake and block the wheels to prevent accidental movement of the vehicle.

6   Use a jumper wire or paper clip to ground the test connector located in the left front corner of the engine compartment **(see illustration)**.

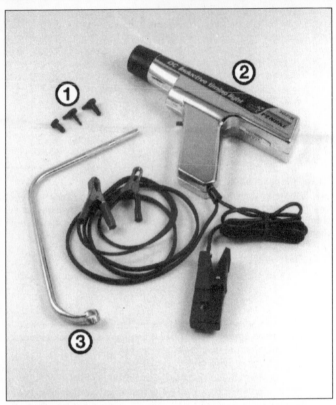

36.2 Tools needed to check and adjust the ignition timing

1   ***Vacuum plugs*** - *Vacuum hoses will, in most cases, have to be disconnected and plugged. Molded plugs in various shapes and sizes are available for this*
2   ***Inductive pick-up timing light*** - *Flashes a bright, concentrated beam of light when the number one spark plug fires. Connect the leads according to the instructions supplied with the light*
3   ***Distributor wrench*** - *On some models, the hold-down bolt for the distributor is difficult to reach and turn with conventional wrenches or sockets. A special wrench like this must be used*

36.11b Distributor hold-down bolt (arrow) on the four-cylinder engine

36.11a Distributor hold-down bolt (arrow) on the V6 engine

37.3 Use a Phillips-head screwdriver to remove the screw from the NO hole and move it to the NC hole on the back of the instrument cluster

7   Check the engine idle speed with the tachometer and compare it to those listed in the Specifications Section at the beginning of this Chapter.
8   If the idle speed is incorrect turn the idle speed adjusting screw to change it **(see illustration)**.
9   Once the procedure is complete, be sure to disconnect the tachometer and test connector jumper wire.

---

36   Ignition timing check and adjustment (every 30,000 miles or 24 months)

Refer to illustrations 36.2, 36.11a and 36.11b
1   These vehicles are equipped with an Emission Control Information label inside the engine compartment. This label gives important ignition timing settings and procedures to be followed specific to that vehicle. If information on the label is different than the information given in the Specifications Section at the beginning of this Chapter, the label should be followed.
2   At the specified intervals or whenever the distributor is removed, the ignition timing must be checked and adjusted if necessary. Some special tools are required for this procedure **(see illustration)**.

3   Before attempting to check the timing, make sure the engine is at normal operating temperature, the idle speed is as specified (see Section 35) and the distributor air gap is correct (see Chapter 5).

4   Ground the test connector by installing a jumper wire **(see illustration 35.6)**.

5   Connect a timing light in accordance with the manufacturer's instructions. Generally, the light will be connected to power and ground sources and the number one spark plug in some fashion. The number one spark plug is the very front one on four-cylinder models or the front one on the right (passenger side) bank on V6 engines.

6   Locate the numbered timing scale on the front cover of the engine. It is just behind the crankshaft pulley. Clean it off with solvent if necessary to read the printing and small grooves.

7   Locate the notched groove across the crankshaft pulley. It may be necessary to have an assistant temporarily turn the ignition off and on in short bursts without starting the engine to bring this groove into a position where it can easily be cleaned and marked. Stay clear of all moving engine components if the engine is turned over in this manner.

8   Use white soap-stone chalk or paint to mark the groove on the crankshaft pulley. Also put a mark on the timing tab in accordance with the number of degrees called for in the Specifications Section at the beginning of this Chapter or on the Emission Control Information label inside the engine compartment. Each notch on the timing tab represents five degrees. The 0 indicates Top Dead Center (TDC). If your vehicle specifications call for 12 degrees BTDC (Before Top Dead Center), you will make a mark on the timing tab between the second and third notches.

9   Check that the wiring for the timing light is clear of all moving engine components, then start the engine.

10   Point the flashing timing light at the timing marks, again being careful not to come in contact with moving parts. The marks you made should appear stationary. If the marks are in alignment, the timing is correct. If the marks are not aligned, turn off the engine.

11   Loosen the bolt at the base of the distributor **(see illustrations)**.

Loosen the bolt only slightly, just enough to turn the distributor.

12   Now restart the engine and turn the distributor until the timing marks coincide.

13   Shut off the engine and tighten the distributor bolt, being careful not to move the distributor.

14   Start the engine and recheck the timing to make sure the marks are still in alignment.

15   Disconnect the timing light.

---

37   Check engine light resetting (every 60,000 miles or 60 months)

Refer to illustration 37.3

1   At the specified interval, on some models the check engine light will go on and stay on as a reminder to replace the oxygen sensor system. . After the oxygen sensor has been replaced the check engine light must be turned off manually.

2   Remove the instrument cluster (see Chapter 12).

3   Remove the screw from the NO position on the back of the cluster and install it in the NC position **(see illustration)**.

4   Install the cluster.

---

38   Oxygen sensor replacement (every 80,000 miles)

---

1   The oxygen sensor is located in the exhaust manifold. Starting at the oxygen sensor, follow the wire back to the connector. Unplug the oxygen sensor wire at the connector.

2   Use a wrench to unscrew the oxygen sensor from the manifold.

3   Install the new oxygen sensor and tighten it to the torque listed in the Specifications Section at the beginning of this Chapter.

4   Plug in the electrical connector.

1

NOTES

Chapter 2 Part A   Four-cylinder engine

Contents

Specifications

General

Firing order	1-3-4-2
Cylinder numbers (front-to-rear)	1-2-3-4
Bore	3.62 inches
Stroke	3.86 inches
Displacement	158.97 cubic inches (2.6 liters)
Intake/exhaust manifold warpage limit	0.006 inch
Balance shaft chain slack	1/8-inch

The blackened terminal shown on the distributor cap indicates the Number One spark plug wire position

Cylinder location and distributor rotation

Camshaft

Endplay	
Standard	0.0008 to 0.0059 inch
Maximum	0.008 inch
Runout	0.0012 inch (maximum)

Camshaft (continued)

Camshaft journal diameter
  Standard
    Journal nos. 1 and 5 .... 1.1788 to 1.1797 inches
    Journal nos. 2, 3 and 4 .... 1.1776 to 1.1785 inches
Journal oil clearance
  Standard
    Journal nos. 1 and 5 .... 0.0014 to 0.0033 inch
    Journal nos. 2, 3 and 4 .... 0.0026 to 0.0045 inch
  Service limit .... 0.006 inch

Oil pump

Side clearance .... .0039 inch maximum
Tooth tip clearance .... .0071 inch maximum
Outer rotor-to-pump body clearance .... .0071 inch maximum
Pressure relief valve spring - free length .... 1.827 inches

Torque specifications   Ft-lbs (unless otherwise indicated)

Camshaft bearing cap bolts .... 14 to 19
Valve cover bolts .... 52 to 78 in-lbs
Balance shaft chain guide bolts .... 156 in-lbs
Timing chain guide bolts .... 70 to 95 in-lbs
Camshaft sprocket bolt .... 37 to 40
Crankshaft pulley bolt .... 131 to 144
Cylinder head bolts **(see illustration 13.8)**
  First step 21
  Second step 42
  Third step .... 59 to 64
Cylinder head-to-timing chain cover bolts (bolt A) .... 12 to 16
Flywheel/driveplate-to-crankshaft bolts .... 68 to 72
Intake manifold bolts .... 14 to 18
Exhaust manifold bolts .... 16 to 20
Balance shaft sprocket bolt .... 27 to 39
Oil pan-to-engine bolts .... 70 to 95 in-lbs
Oil pump pick-up tube bolts .... 70 to 95 in-lbs
Oil pump body bolts .... 14 to 18
Oil pump pressure relief valve .... 28 to 44
Rear main oil seal housing bolts .... 70 to 95 in-lbs
Timing chain/balance shaft chain access cover
  Bolts .... 70 to 95 in-lbs
  Nuts .... 61 to 86 in-lbs
Timing chain cover bolts .... 14 to 18
Water pump bolts .... See Chapter 3

1   General information

This Part of Chapter 2 is devoted to in-vehicle repair procedures for the four-cylinder engine. All information concerning engine removal and installation and engine block and cylinder head overhaul can be found in Part C of this Chapter.

The following repair procedures are based on the assumption that the engine is installed in the vehicle. If the engine has been removed from the vehicle and mounted on a stand, many of the steps outlined in this Part of Chapter 2 will not apply.

The Specifications included in this Part of Chapter 2 apply only to the procedures contained in this chapter. Chapter 2C contains the Specifications necessary for cylinder head and engine block rebuilding.

The 2.6L engine is an inline vertical four, with a chain-driven overhead camshaft and a balance shaft system which cancels the engine's power pulses and produces relatively vibration-free operation. The crankshaft rides in five renewable insert-type main bearings, with the center bearing (the thrust bearing) assigned the additional task of controlling crankshaft endplay.

The pistons have two compression rings and one oil control ring. The semi-floating piston pins are press fitted into the small end of the connecting rod. The connecting rod big ends are also equipped with renewable insert-type plain bearings.

The engine is liquid-cooled, utilizing a centrifugal impeller-type pump, driven by a belt, to circulate coolant around the cylinders and combustion chambers and through the intake manifold.

Lubrication is handled by a rotor-type oil pump mounted on the front of the engine under the timing chain cover. It is driven by the balance shaft chain. The oil is filtered continuously by a cartridge-type filter mounted on the radiator side of the engine.

2   Repair operations possible with the engine in the vehicle

Clean the engine compartment and the exterior of the engine with some type of degreaser before any work is done. It will make the job easier and help keep dirt out of the internal areas of the engine.

Depending on the components involved, it may be helpful to remove the hood to improve access to the engine as repairs are performed (refer to Chapter 11 if necessary). Cover the fenders to prevent damage to the paint. Special pads are available, but an old bedspread or blanket will also work.

If vacuum, exhaust, oil or coolant leaks develop, indicating a need for gasket or seal replacement, the repairs can generally be made with the engine in the vehicle. The intake and exhaust manifold gaskets, oil pan gasket, crankshaft oil seals and cylinder head gasket are all accessible with the engine in place.

Exterior engine components, such as the intake and exhaust

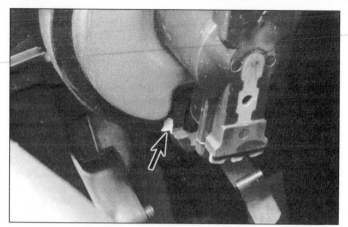

3.6 Mark the distributor housing directly beneath the number one spark plug wire terminal (double check the distributor cap to verify that the rotor points to the number 1 spark plug wire)

3.8 Align the notch in the pulley with the 0 on the timing scale then check to see if the distributor rotor is pointing to the number 1 cylinder (if not, the camshaft is 180-degrees out of time [number 4 is at TDC] - the crankshaft will have to be rotated 360-degrees)

manifolds, the oil pan, the water pump, the starter motor, the alternator, the distributor and the fuel system components can be removed for repair with the engine in place.

Since the cylinder head can be removed without pulling the engine, camshaft and valve component servicing can also be accomplished with the engine in the vehicle. Replacement of the timing chain and sprockets is also possible with the engine in the vehicle.

In extreme cases caused by a lack of necessary equipment, repair or replacement of piston rings, pistons, connecting rods and rod bearings is possible with the engine in the vehicle. However, this practice is not recommended because of the cleaning and preparation work that must be done to the components involved.

3   Top Dead Center (TDC) for number one piston - locating

Refer to illustrations 3.6 and 3.8

Note: *The following procedure is based on the assumption that the spark plug wires and distributor are correctly installed. If you are trying to locate TDC to install the distributor correctly, piston position must be determined by feeling for compression at the number one spark plug hole, then aligning the ignition timing marks as described in Step 8.*

1   Top Dead Center (TDC) is the highest point in the cylinder that each piston reaches as it travels up-and-down when the crankshaft turns. Each piston reaches TDC on the compression stroke and again on the exhaust stroke, but TDC generally refers to piston position on the compression stroke.

2   Positioning the piston(s) at TDC is an essential part of many procedures such as camshaft and timing chain/sprocket removal and distributor removal.

3   Before beginning this procedure, be sure to place the transmission in Neutral and apply the parking brake or block the rear wheels. Also, disable the ignition system by detaching the primary (low voltage) electrical connectors from the ignition coil. Remove the spark plugs (see Chapter 1).

4   In order to bring any piston to TDC, the crankshaft must be turned using one of the methods outlined below. When looking at the front of the engine, normal crankshaft rotation is clockwise.

  a) The preferred method is to turn the crankshaft with a socket and ratchet attached to the bolt threaded into the front of the crankshaft.

  b) A remote starter switch, which may save some time, can also be used. Follow the instructions included with the switch. Once the piston is close to TDC, use a socket and ratchet as described in the previous paragraph.

  c) If an assistant is available to turn the ignition switch to the Start position in short bursts, you can get the piston close to TDC with-

out a remote starter switch. Make sure your assistant is out of the vehicle, away from the ignition switch, then use a socket and ratchet as described in Paragraph a) to complete the procedure.

5   Note the position of the terminal for the number one spark plug wire on the distributor cap. If the terminal isn't marked, follow the plug wire from the number one cylinder spark plug to the cap.

6   Mark the distributor body directly under the terminal **(see illustration)**.

7   Detach the cap from the distributor and set it aside (see Chapter 1 if necessary).

8   Locate the timing marks on the timing chain cover. You'll see the timing increments directly above the front pulley. Turn the crankshaft (see Paragraph 3 above) until the TDC mark (zero) on the timing chain cover is aligned with the groove in the front pulley **(see illustration)**.

9   Look at the distributor rotor - it should be pointing directly at the mark you made on the distributor body. If the rotor is pointing at the mark, go to Step 12. If it isn't, go to Step 10.

10   If the rotor is 180-degrees off, the number one piston is at TDC on the exhaust stroke.

11   To get the piston to TDC on the compression stroke, turn the crankshaft one complete turn (360-degrees) clockwise. The rotor should now be pointing at the mark on the distributor. When the rotor is pointing at the number one spark plug wire terminal in the distributor cap and the ignition timing marks are aligned, the number one piston is at TDC on the compression stroke.

12   After the number one piston has been positioned at TDC on the compression stroke, TDC for any of the remaining pistons can be located by turning the crankshaft and following the firing order. Mark the remaining spark plug wire terminal locations on the distributor body just like you did for the number one terminal, then number the marks to correspond with the cylinder numbers. As you turn the crankshaft, the rotor will also turn. When it's pointing directly at one of the marks on the distributor, the piston for that particular cylinder is at TDC on the compression stroke.

4   Valve cover - removal and installation

Refer to illustration 4.7

Removal

1   Detach the cable from the negative battery terminal.

2   Remove the air cleaner inlet hose and housing assembly from the throttle body and the top of the valve cover (see Chapter 4).

3   Remove the distributor cap and wires from their cylinder head and valve cover connections (see Chapter 1). Be sure to mark each wire for correct installation.

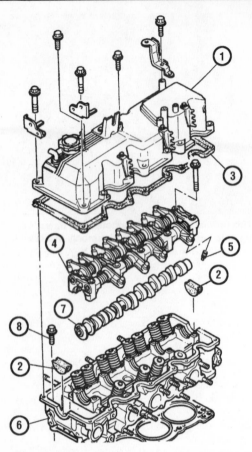

4.7 An exploded view of the valve cover and related components

1	Valve cover	6	Cylinder head
2	Semi-circular seal	7	Camshaft
3	Valve cover gasket	8	Cylinder head-to-
4	Rocker arm assembly		timing chain cover bolt
5	Hydraulic lash adjuster		

4   Mark and detach any hoses or wires from the throttle body or valve cover that will interfere with the removal of the valve cover.
5   Disconnect the accelerator cable from the throttle body and un-bolt it from the valve cover (see Chapter 4).
6   Wipe off the valve cover thoroughly to prevent debris from falling onto the exposed cylinder head or camshaft/valve train assembly.
7   Remove the valve cover bolts **(see illustration)**.
8   Carefully lift off the valve cover and gasket. If the gasket is stuck to the cylinder head, tap it with a rubber mallet to break the seal. Do not pry between the cover and cylinder head or you'll damage the gasket mating surfaces.

Installation

9   Use a gasket scraper to remove any traces of old gasket material from the gasket mating surfaces of the cylinder head and the valve cover. Clean the surfaces with a rag soaked in lacquer thinner or acetone.
10   Be sure to install the semi-circular cover seal (camshaft plug) on top of the cylinder head near both ends of the camshaft. Apply beads of RTV sealant to the points where the seal meets the valve cover mating surfaces.
11   Install a new gasket onto the valve cover. Install the molded rubber gasket onto the cover by pushing the new gasket into the slot that circles the valve cover perimeter. Apply beads of RTV sealant where the cylinder head and camshaft bearing cap meet. Wait five minutes or so and let the RTV "set-up" (slightly harden) and then install the cover

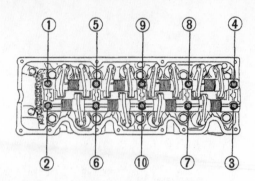

5.3 REMOVAL sequence for the rocker arm assembly bolts

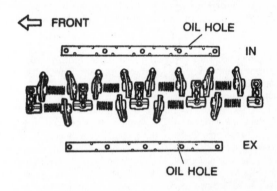

5.5 An exploded view of the rocker arms and shafts

and bolts and tighten them to the torque listed in this Chapter's Specifications.
12   The remainder of installation is the reverse of removal.

5   Rocker arm assembly - removal, inspection and installation

Note 1: *The camshaft bearing caps are removed together with the rocker arm assembly. To prevent the opposite end (transmission end) of the camshaft from popping up (from timing-chain tension) after the assembly is removed, have an assistant hold the opposite end of the camshaft down, then reinstall the bearing cap on that end to hold it in place until reassembly.*
Note 2: *While the camshaft bearing caps are off, inspect them, as well as the camshaft bearing journals, as described in Section 12.*

Removal
Refer to illustration 5.3
1   Remove the valve cover (see Section 4).
2   Position the number one piston at Top Dead Center (see Section 3).
3   Have an assistant hold down the transmission end of the camshaft, then loosen the camshaft bearing cap bolts 1/4-turn at a time, in the order shown, until the spring pressure is relieved **(see illustration)**. Do not remove the bolts from the bearing caps. Reinstall the bearing cap at the transmission end to hold the camshaft in place.
4   Lift the rocker arms and shaft assembly from the cylinder head.

Inspection
Refer to illustrations 5.5 and 5.6
5   If you wish to disassemble and inspect the rocker arm assemblies (a good idea as long as you have them off), remove the retaining bolts

5.6 Check the contact face and hydraulic lash adjuster tip for damage or wear (arrows)

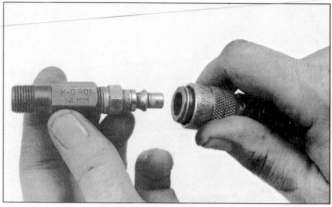

6.4 This is what the air hose adapter that threads into the spark plug hole looks like - they're commonly available from auto parts stores

6.9 Use a valve spring compressor to compress the springs, then remove the keepers from the valve stem with a magnet or small needle-nose pliers

and slip the rocker arms, springs and bearing caps off the shafts **(see illustration)**. Mark the relationship of the shafts to the bearing caps and keep the parts in order so you can reassemble them in the same positions.

6   Thoroughly clean the parts and inspect them for wear and damage. Check the rocker arm faces that contact the camshaft and the rocker arm tips **(see illustration)**. Check the surfaces of the shafts that the rocker arms ride on, as well as the bearing surfaces inside the rocker arms, for scoring and excessive wear. Replace any parts that are damaged or excessively worn. Also, make sure the oil holes in the shafts are not plugged.

Installation

7   Lubricate all components with assembly lube or engine oil and reassemble the shafts. When installing the rocker arms, shafts and springs, note the markings and the difference between the left and right side parts. Place the marks in the end of the shaft directly in line with the marks on the caps to keep them aligned until they are ready to be installed onto the cylinder head.

8   Coat the cam lobes and journals with camshaft installation lubricant. Apply anaerobic-type sealant to the cylinder head contact surfaces of bearing caps 1 and 5 and install the rocker arm assembly.

9   Tighten the camshaft bearing cap bolts a little at a time, to the torque listed in this Chapter's Specifications, following a sequence *opposite* the one shown in illustration 5.3.

10   The remainder of installation is the reverse of removal.

11   Run the engine and check for oil leaks and proper operation.

6   Valve springs, retainers and seals - replacement

Refer to illustrations 6.4, 6.9 and 6.17
Note: *Broken valve springs and defective valve stem seals can be replaced without removing the cylinder heads. Two special tools and a compressed air source are normally required to perform this operation, so read through this Section carefully and rent or buy the tools before beginning the job. If compressed air isn't available, a length of nylon rope can be used to keep the valves from falling into the cylinder during this procedure.*

1   Refer to Section 4 and remove the valve cover.

2   Remove the spark plug from the cylinder which has the defective component. If all of the valve stem seals are being replaced, all of the spark plugs should be removed.

3   Turn the crankshaft until the piston in the affected cylinder is at top dead center on the compression stroke (refer to Section 3 for instructions). If you're replacing all of the valve stem seals, begin with cylinder number one and work on the valves for one cylinder at a time. Move from cylinder-to-cylinder following the firing order sequence (see this Chapter's Specifications).

4   Thread an adapter into the spark plug hole and connect an air hose from a compressed air source to it **(see illustration)**. Most auto parts stores can supply the air hose adapter. **Note:** *Many cylinder compression gauges utilize a screw-in fitting that may work with your air hose quick-disconnect fitting.*

5   Remove the rocker arms and shafts (see Section 5).

6   Apply compressed air to the cylinder. **Warning:** *The piston may be forced down by compressed air, causing the crankshaft to turn suddenly. If the wrench used when positioning the number one piston at TDC is still attached to the bolt in the crankshaft nose, it could cause damage or injury when the crankshaft moves.*

7   The valves should be held in place by the air pressure. If the valve faces or seats are in poor condition, leaks may prevent air pressure from retaining the valves - refer to the alternative procedure below.

8   If you don't have access to compressed air, an alternative method can be used. Position the piston at a point about 45-degrees before TDC on the compression stroke, then feed a long piece of nylon rope through the spark plug hole until it fills the combustion chamber. Be sure to leave the end of the rope hanging out of the engine so it can be removed easily. Use a large ratchet and socket to rotate the crankshaft in the normal direction of rotation until slight resistance is felt.

9   Stuff shop rags into the cylinder head holes around the valves to prevent parts and tools from falling into the engine, then use a valve spring compressor to compress the spring **(see illustration)**. Remove the keepers with small needle-nose pliers or a magnet.

10   Remove the spring retainer, shield and valve spring, then remove the umbrella type guide seal. **Note:** *If air pressure fails to hold the valve*

6.17 Apply a small dab of grease to each keeper as shown here before installation - it'll hold them in place on the valve stem as the spring is released

in the closed position during this operation, the valve face or seat is probably damaged. If so, the cylinder head will have to be removed for additional repair operations.

11   Wrap a rubber band or tape around the top of the valve stem so the valve won't fall into the combustion chamber, then release the air pressure. **Note:** *If a rope was used instead of air pressure, turn the crankshaft slightly in the direction opposite normal rotation.*

12   Inspect the valve stem for damage. Rotate the valve in the guide and check the end for eccentric movement, which would indicate that the valve is bent.

13   Move the valve up-and-down in the guide and make sure it doesn't bind. If the valve stem binds, either the valve is bent or the guide is damaged. In either case, the head will have to be removed for repair.

14   Reapply air pressure to the cylinder to retain the valve in the closed position, then remove the tape or rubber band from the valve stem. If a rope was used instead of air pressure, rotate the crankshaft in the normal direction of rotation until slight resistance is felt.

15   Lubricate the valve stem with engine oil and install a new guide seal.

16   Install the spring(s) in position over the valve.

17   Install the valve spring retainer. Compress the valve spring and carefully position the keepers in the groove. Apply a small dab of grease to the inside of each keeper to hold it in place **(see illustration)**.

18   Remove the pressure from the spring tool and make sure the keepers are seated.

19   Disconnect the air hose and remove the adapter from the spark plug hole. If a rope was used in place of air pressure, pull it out of the cylinder.

20   Refer to Section 5 and install the rocker arm assembly.

21   Refer to Section 4 and install the valve cover.

22   Install the spark plug(s) and hook up the wire(s).

23   Start and run the engine, then check for oil leaks and unusual sounds coming from the valve cover area.

---

7   Intake manifold - removal and installation

Warning: *Gasoline is extremely flammable, so take extra precautions when you work on any part of the fuel system. Don't smoke or allow open flames or bare light bulbs near the work area, and don't work in a garage where a natural gas-type appliance (such as a water heater or clothes dryer) with a pilot light is present. If you spill any fuel on your skin, rinse it off immediately with soap and water. When you perform any kind of work on the fuel system, wear safety glasses and have a Class B type fire extinguisher on hand.*

Removal

1   Detach the cable from the negative battery terminal.

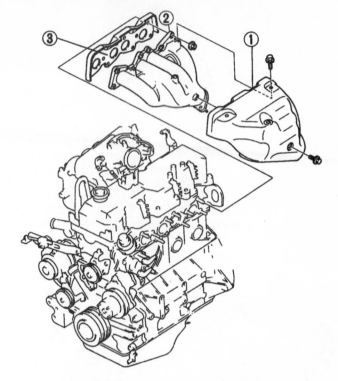

8.4 Exhaust manifold installation details

1   *Heat shield*   3   *Gasket*
2   *Exhaust manifold*

---

2   Drain the cooling system (see Chapter 1).

3   Remove the air cleaner (see Chapter 4).

4   Clearly label and detach any vacuum lines and electrical connectors which will interfere with removal of the manifold.

5   Detach the accelerator cable from the throttle lever (see Chapter 4).

6   Remove the throttle body unit from the intake manifold plenum (see Chapter 4).

7   Remove the coolant hoses from the intake manifold.

8   Disconnect the fuel feed and return lines at the fuel rail (see Chapter 4).

9   Remove the intake manifold bolts and remove the manifold from the engine.

Installation

10   Clean the manifold bolts with solvent and dry them with compressed air, if available. **Warning:** *Wear eye protection!*

11   Check the mating surfaces of the manifold for flatness with a precision straightedge and feeler gauges. Refer to this Chapter's Specifications for the warpage limit.

12   Inspect the manifold for cracks and distortion. If the manifold is cracked or warped, replace it or see if it can be resurfaced at an automotive machine shop.

13   Check carefully for any stripped or broken intake manifold bolts. Replace any defective bolts with new parts.

14   Using a scraper, remove all traces of old gasket material from the cylinder head and manifold mating surfaces. Clean the surfaces with lacquer thinner or acetone.

15   Install the intake manifold with a new gasket and tighten the bolts finger-tight. Starting at the center and working out in both directions, tighten the bolts in a criss-cross pattern until the torque listed in this Chapter's Specifications is reached.

16   The remainder of the installation procedure is the reverse of removal.

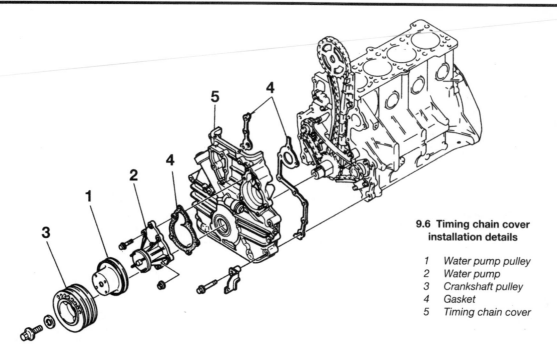

2A

9.6 Timing chain cover installation details

1   Water pump pulley
2   Water pump
3   Crankshaft pulley
4   Gasket
5   Timing chain cover

---

8   Exhaust manifold - removal and installation

Refer to illustration 8.4

Removal

1   Disconnect the negative battery cable from the battery.
2   Remove the air cleaner (see Chapter 4).
3   Raise the front of the vehicle and support it securely on jack-stands. Detach the exhaust pipe from the exhaust manifold (see Chapter 4). Apply penetrating oil to the fastener threads if they are difficult to remove.
4   Remove the heat shield from the exhaust manifold **(see illustration)**. Be sure to soak the bolts and nuts with penetrating oil before attempting to remove them from the manifold.
5   Remove the exhaust manifold bolts and detach the exhaust manifold from the cylinder head.

Installation

6   Discard the old gasket and use a scraper to clean the gasket mating surfaces on the manifold and head, then clean the surfaces with a rag soaked in lacquer thinner or acetone.
7   Place the exhaust manifold in position on the cylinder head and install the nuts. Starting at the center, tighten the nuts in a criss-cross pattern until the torque listed in this Chapter's Specifications is reached.
8   The remainder of installation is the reverse of removal.
9   Start the engine and check for exhaust leaks between the manifold and the cylinder head and between the manifold and the exhaust pipe.

---

9   Balance shafts chain/sprockets - removal, inspection and installation

Note: *When a loose balance shaft drive chain is suspected as the cause of excessive noise, the tension must be adjusted. It is possible to do this procedure without removing the timing chain cover (see Step 17).*

Removal

Refer to illustrations 9.6 and 9.8

1   Position the number one cylinder at top dead center (see Section 3). Disconnect the cable from the negative terminal of the battery.

2   Remove the valve cover and the oil pan (see Sections 4 and 14).
3   Remove the large bolt at the front of the crankshaft and slide the pulley off. **Note:** *To keep the crankshaft from turning while you're removing this bolt, remove the starter (see Chapter 5) and wedge a large screwdriver into the flywheel/driveplate ring gear. If the pulley won't slide off, pullers are available at auto parts stores that will make removal easy.*
4   Remove the cooling fan and the water pump (see Chapter 3).
5   Remove the alternator and brackets from the timing chain cover (see Chapter 5).
6   Remove the bolts attaching the timing chain cover to the engine block **(see illustration)**. Draw a simple diagram showing the location and length of each of the bolts so they can be returned to the same holes from which they were removed.
7   Tap the timing chain cover with a soft-faced hammer to break the gasket seal, then remove the cover from the engine block. **Caution:** *Prying between the cover and the engine block can damage the gasket sealing surfaces.*
8   Remove the chain guides labeled A, B and C **(see illustration)**. Each guide is held in place by two bolts. Again, draw a simple diagram showing the location of each bolt so they can be returned to the same holes from which they were removed.
9   Reinstall the large bolt in the end of the crankshaft. Hold it in place with a wrench to prevent the crankshaft from turning while loos-

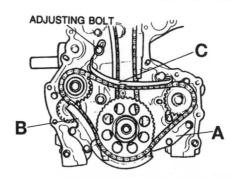

9.8 Locations of balance shaft chain guides A, B, and C

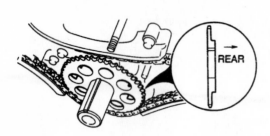

9.14a Assembly direction of the balance shaft gear on the crankshaft

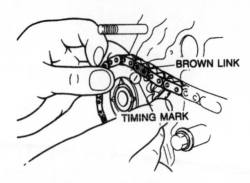

9.14b Line up the brown link of the balance shaft chain with the mark on the idler gear

ening the bolt on the end of the right (passenger side) balance shaft, the bolt attaching the right balance shaft drive sprocket to the oil pump shaft and the bolt in the end of the left balance shaft.

10   Slide the crankshaft sprocket, the balance shaft sprockets and the chain off the engine as an assembly. Leave the bolt in the end of the crankshaft in place. Do not lose the keys that index the sprockets to the shafts.

Inspection

11   Check the balance shafts chain, guides and sprockets for wear, damage or cracks. Replace parts as necessary. **Note :** *If the balance shaft or the idler sprocket is to be replaced, replace both as an assembly.*

Installation

Refer to illustrations 9.14a, 9.14b, 9.14c, 9.17a, 9.17b and 9.17c

12   Before installing the balance shaft chain and sprockets, make sure the timing chain is properly installed and the Number One piston is at TDC on the compression stroke. Both balance shafts and the oil pump must also be in place. Retract the timing chain tensioner and hold it in this position following the procedure described in Section 10, Step 9.

13   Slide the crankshaft sprocket part way onto the front of the crankshaft by lining up the keyway in the sprocket with the key on the shaft.

14   Install the balance shaft sprocket part way onto the crankshaft. The raised side of the gear faces to the rear, towards the engine block **(see illustration)**. Install the sprockets part way onto the idler shaft and the left side balance shaft. Install the balance shaft chain onto the sprocket. Line up the brown link on the chain with the mark on the idler sprocket (which drives the right side balance shaft). Install the

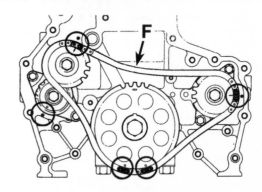

9.14c Make sure all five marks are in alignment when the balance shaft chain is installed (F indicates the point where excess chain slack is taken up during adjustment)

chain over the other balance shaft sprocket and make sure all of the marks are in alignment **(see illustrations)**.

15   Push the sprockets all the way onto their respective shafts. Recheck the position of the mating marks, then install the balance shaft sprocket bolts and tighten them to the torque listed in this Chapter's Specifications.

16   Apply a coat of moly-based grease to the chain and chain guides. Install the chain guides **(see illustration 9.8)** and tighten the mounting bolts for chain guides A and B securely (leave the mounting bolts for chain guide C finger-tight). Note the difference between the upper and lower chain guide C mounting bolts. Make sure they are installed in the proper location.

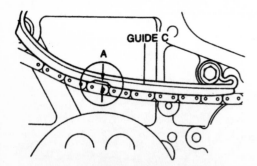

9.17a Adjust chain guide C until the clearance between the chain and the guide is correct

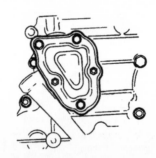

9.17b Remove this cover from the timing chain cover for access to the balance shaft chain tensioner and the timing chain tensioner

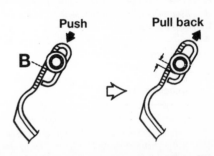

9.17c Loosen bolt B, push down on the chain guide, then pull it up 1/8-inch and tighten the bolt

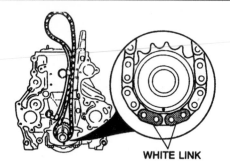

10.7 Install the timing chain on the crankshaft sprocket with the plated chain links flanking the mark on the crank gear

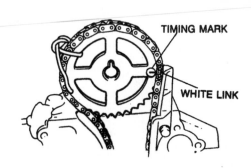

10.8 Mesh the camshaft sprocket and the timing chain with the mark on the sprocket directly opposite the plated link on the chain (wire the chain to the sprocket so this relationship isn't lost)

17   Adjust the chain slack as follows: rotate the right (passenger side) balance shaft clockwise and the left (driver's side) balance shaft counterclockwise so the chain slack is collected at point F **(see illustration 9.14c)**. Pull the chain with your finger tips in the direction of arrow F, then move the lower end of chain guide C up or down, as required, until the clearance between the chain and the guide (chain slack) **(see illustration)** is as listed in this Chapter's Specifications. Tighten the mounting bolts for chain guide C securely, then recheck the slack to make sure it hasn't changed. If the chain is not tensioned properly, engine noise will result. **Note:** *To adjust the chain without removing the timing chain cover, remove the access cover mounted on the front of the timing chain cover* **(see illustration)**. *Loosen bolt "B"* **(see illustration)** *and using your finger push chain guide "C" down until it bottoms out. Don't use a screwdriver or other implement. Now pull the chain guide up 1/8-inch (3 mm) and tighten bolt "B". Reinstall the access cover.*
18   Install a new crankshaft front oil seal in the timing chain cover (see Section 11).
19   Using a new gasket and RTV sealant, install the timing chain cover onto the engine **(see illustration 9.6)**. Tighten the bolts to the torque listed in this Chapter's Specifications. If the gasket protrudes beyond the top or bottom of the case and engine block, trim off the excess with a razor blade.
20   Apply a thin layer of multi-purpose grease to the seal contact surface of the crankshaft pulley, then slide it onto the crankshaft. Install the bolt and tighten it finger-tight only. **Note:** *The bolt should be tightened to the specified torque only after the cylinder head and camshaft have been installed.*
21   The remainder of installation is the reverse of removal. Once the camshaft sprocket has been bolted to the camshaft, remove the pin from the timing chain tensioner, push the chain guide in (towards the driver's side), then install the access cover. Be sure to use a new gasket.

---

10   Timing chain and sprockets - removal, inspection and installation

Refer to illustrations 10.7, 10.8 and 10.9

Removal

1   Remove the balance shaft chain, guides and the sprocket on the crankshaft for access to the timing chain (see Section 9).
2   Push the right (passenger side) timing chain guide to the right and remove the sprocket from the camshaft. Pull off the lower sprocket from the crankshaft and remove the timing chain from the engine. Don't lose the key that indexes the crankshaft sprocket in the proper place.

Inspection

3   Inspect the sprocket teeth for wear and damage. Check the chain for cracked plates and pitted or worn rollers. Check the chain guides

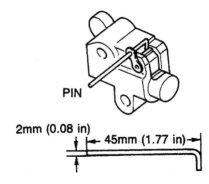

10.9 Insert a pin fabricated from a piece of coat hanger or welding rod through the tensioner lock lever to keep the tensioner plunger in the retracted position

for wear and damage. Check the timing chain tensioner. If there are more than 13 teeth exposed on the plunger, the chain has stretched too far to be reused. Also check the condition of the teeth on the tensioner plunger. Replace any worn parts with new ones.

Installation

4   Install the chain guides onto the engine block. Tighten the bolts securely. Coat the entire length of the chain contact surfaces of the guides with moly-based grease.
5   Check to make sure the number one piston is still at Top Dead Center (TDC) (see Section 3).
6   Position the timing chain sprocket on the end of the crankshaft. Line up the keyway in the sprocket with the key on the crankshaft.
7   Slip the chain over the crankshaft sprocket, lining up the plated links on the chain with the mark on the sprocket **(see illustration)**.
8   Install the chain over the camshaft sprocket, lining up the plated link on the chain with the mark on the sprocket **(see illustration)**. **Caution:** *Do not rotate the crankshaft until the cylinder head and camshaft have been properly installed.*
9   Push the timing chain tensioner plunger into the tensioner, lift the lever on the tensioner to lock it in place, then insert a fabricated pin through the hole in the lever to hold the lever in place **(see illustration)**. **Note:** *Leave the pin in this position until the cylinder head is installed and the camshaft sprocket is bolted to the camshaft.*
10   After installation of the timing chain cover and the cylinder head (and the camshaft sprocket has been bolted to the camshaft, remove the tensioner access cover from the timing chain cover and remove the retaining pin from the chain tensioner. Reinstall the service cover with a new gasket and tighten the bolts to the torque listed in this Chapter's Specifications.
11   The remainder of installation is the reverse of removal.

11.3 Crankshaft front oil seal location in the timing chain cover

11   Crankshaft front oil seal - replacement

Refer to illustration 11.3

1   Remove the drivebelts (see Chapter 1).
2   Remove the crankshaft pulley.
3   Carefully pry the seal out of the timing chain cover **(see illustration)** with a seal removal tool or a screwdriver. Don't scratch the seal bore or damage the crankshaft in the process (if the crankshaft is damaged, the new seal will end up leaking).
4   Clean the bore in the timing chain cover and coat the outer edge of the new seal with engine oil or multi-purpose grease. Using a socket with an outside diameter slightly smaller than the outside diameter of the seal, carefully drive the seal into place with a hammer. If a socket is not available, a short section of a large diameter pipe will work. Check the seal after installation to be sure the spring did not pop out.
5   Lubricate the sleeve of the crankshaft pulley with engine oil or multi-purpose grease, then install the crankshaft pulley. The remainder of installation is the reverse of removal.
6   Run the engine and check for leaks.

12   Camshaft - removal, inspection and installation

Removal

Refer to illustrations 12.4, 12.5a and 12.5b

1   Remove the valve cover (see Section 4).
2   Remove the distributor (see Chapter 5).

12.5a Position a screwdriver between the projection on the camshaft and the cylinder head to prevent it from turning when the bolt is loosened (place a rag under the screwdriver so the head doesn't get gouged)

12.4 Before removing the camshaft sprocket, wedge the tensioner locking tool between the chain runs in the timing chain cover - be sure the tool has a cord or wire attached to the end of it so it can be easily removed after the job - if the tool is not available, a wedge-shaped block of wood and a length of mechanic's wire will also work.

3   Set the engine at TDC for cylinder number one (see Section 3), then remove the rocker arm assembly (see Section 5). If the camshaft bearing caps do not have numbers on them, number them before removal. Be sure to put the marks on the same ends of all the caps to prevent incorrect orientation of the caps during installation.
4   To keep the tensioner from collapsing once the sprocket has been removed, install a special retaining tool between the timing chain, near the tensioner **(see illustration)**. The tool will extend down into the timing chain cover, so be sure the strap or wire hanger on the tool does not fall into the cover or it will be very difficult to remove the tool when the camshaft has been installed.
5   Remove the camshaft sprocket bolt and distributor drive gear **(see illustration)**. **Note:** *Prevent the camshaft from turning by inserting a screwdriver between the projection on the camshaft and the cylinder head* **(see illustration)**. Detach the timing chain and camshaft sprocket from the camshaft. Suspend the camshaft sprocket, with the chain still attached, out of the way.
6   Lift out the camshaft, wipe it off with a clean shop towel and set it aside.

Inspection

Refer to illustrations 12.7, 12.9 and 12.10

7   To check camshaft endplay:

12.5b Remove the camshaft sprocket bolt and detach the sprocket and distributor drive gear from the camshaft

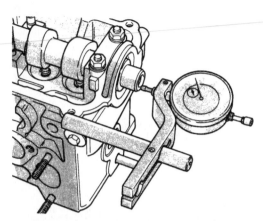

12.7 To check camshaft endplay, set a dial indicator like this, with the gauge plunger touching the nose of the camshaft

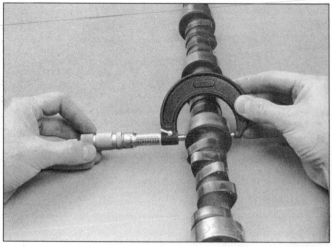

12.9 Check the diameter of each camshaft bearing journal to pinpoint excessive wear and out-of-round conditions

a) Install the camshaft and secure it with caps 1 and 5.
b) Mount a dial indicator on the head **(see illustration)**.
c) Using a large screwdriver as a lever at the opposite end, move the camshaft forward-and-backward and note the dial indicator reading.
d) Compare the reading with the endplay listed in this Chapter's Specifications.
e) If the indicated reading is higher, either the camshaft or the head is worn. Replace parts as necessary.

8   To check camshaft runout:
a) Support the camshaft with a pair of V-blocks and set up a dial indicator with the plunger resting against the center bearing journal on the camshaft.
b) Rotate the camshaft and note the indicated runout.
c) Compare the results to the camshaft runout listed in this Chapter's Specifications.
d) If the indicated runout exceeds the specified runout, replace the camshaft.

9   Check the camshaft bearing journals and caps for scoring and signs of wear. If they are worn, replace the cylinder head with a new or rebuilt unit. Measure the journals on the camshaft with a micrometer, comparing your readings with this Chapter's Specifications. If the diameter of any of the journals is out of specification, replace the camshaft.

10   Check the cam lobes for wear:
a) Check the toe and ramp areas of each cam lobe for score marks and uneven wear. Also check for flaking and pitting.

b) If there's wear on the toe or the ramp, replace the camshaft, but first try to find the cause of the wear. Look for abrasive substances in the oil and inspect the oil pump and oil passages for blockage. Lobe wear is usually caused by inadequate lubrication or dirty oil.
c) Using a micrometer, measure the cam lobe height **(see illustration)**. If the lobe wear is greater than listed in this Chapter's Specifications, replace the camshaft.

11   Inspect the rocker arms for wear, galling and pitting of the contact surfaces.

12   If any of the conditions described above are noted, the cylinder head is probably getting insufficient lubrication or dirty oil, so make sure you track down the cause of this problem (low oil level, low oil pump capacity, clogged oil passage, etc.) before installing a new head, camshaft or rocker arms.

Installation

Refer to illustration 12.14a and 12.14b

13   Thoroughly clean the camshaft, the bearing surfaces in the head and caps and the rocker arms. Remove all sludge and dirt. Wipe off all components with a clean, lint-free cloth.

14   Lubricate the camshaft bearing surfaces in the head and the bearing journals and lobes on the camshaft with camshaft assembly lube or moly-base grease. Carefully lower the camshaft into position with the dowel pin pointing up **(see illustrations)**. **Caution:** *Failure to*

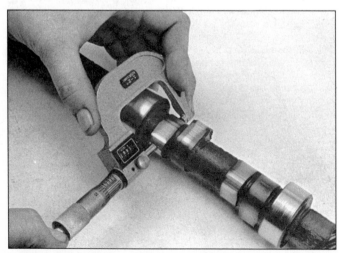

12.10 Measure the camshaft lobe heights with a micrometer

12.14a Be sure to apply camshaft lube to the cam lobes and bearing journals before installing the camshaft

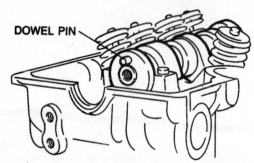

12.14b Install the camshaft with the dowel pin in the 12 o'clock position

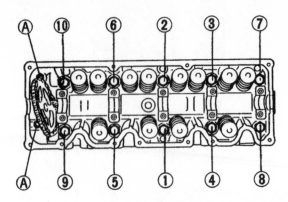

13.16 Cylinder head bolt TIGHTENING sequence (tighten the bolts marked A after the others have been tightened completely)

adequately lubricate the camshaft and related components can cause serious damage to bearing and friction surfaces during the first few seconds after engine start-up, when the oil pressure is low or nonexistent.

15   Install the rocker arm assembly (see Section 5).

16   Install the camshaft sprocket and timing chain and related components (see Section 10). If you suspended the camshaft sprocket out of the way and didn't disturb the timing chain or sprockets, the valve timing should still be correct. Rotate the camshaft as necessary to reattach the sprocket to the camshaft. If the valve timing was disturbed, align the sprockets and install the chain as described in Section 10.

17   Remove the spark plugs and rotate the crankshaft by hand to make sure the valve timing is correct. After two revolutions, the timing marks on the sprockets should still be aligned. If they're not, reindex the timing chain to the sprockets (see Section 10). **Note:** *If you feel resistance while rotating the crankshaft, stop immediately and check the valve timing by referring to Section 10.*

18   The remainder of installation is the reverse of removal.

---

13   Cylinder head - removal and installation

Refer to illustration 13.16

Caution: *Allow the engine to cool completely before beginning this procedure.*

Removal

1   Position the number one piston at Top Dead Center (see Section 3).

2   Disconnect the negative cable from the battery.

3   Drain the cooling system and remove the spark plugs (see Chapter 1).

4   Remove the intake and exhaust manifold (see Sections 7 and 8). **Note:** *If you're only replacing the cylinder head gasket, it isn't necessary to remove the manifolds. If you leave the manifolds attached, you may need an assistant to help lift the head off the engine, since it will be quite heavy.*

5   Remove the valve cover (see Section 4).

6   Remove the distributor (see Chapter 5), including the cap and wires.

7   Install a tensioner locking tool **(see illustration 12.4)** to hold the chain and tensioner in place while the cylinder head is off the engine. This will save time you by not having to remove the timing chain and balance shaft chain assemblies. Be sure to install the tool very tightly to prevent it from popping out when the engine is shaken or jarred. Unbolt the camshaft sprocket from the camshaft (see Section 12).

8   Loosen the head bolts in 1/4-turn increments until they can be removed by hand. Work in a pattern that's the reverse of the tightening sequence **(see illustration 13.16)** to avoid warping the head. Note where each bolt goes so it can be returned to the same location on installation.

9   Lift the head off the engine. If resistance is felt, don't pry between the head and block gasket mating surfaces - damage to the mating surfaces will result. Instead, pry against the casting protrusions on the sides of the cylinder head. Set the head on blocks of wood to prevent damage to the gasket sealing surfaces.

10   Cylinder head disassembly and inspection procedures are covered in detail in Chapter 2, Part C. It's a good idea to have the head checked for warpage, even if you're just replacing the gasket.

Installation

11   The mating surfaces of the cylinder head and block must be perfectly clean when the head is installed.

12   Use a gasket scraper to remove all traces of carbon and old gasket material, then clean the mating surfaces with lacquer thinner or acetone. If there's oil on the mating surfaces when the head is installed, the gasket may not seal correctly and leaks may develop. When working on the block, stuff the cylinders with clean shop rags to keep out debris. Use a vacuum cleaner to remove material that falls into the cylinders. Since the head is made of aluminum, aggressive scraping can cause damage. Be extra careful not to nick or gouge the mating surfaces with the scraper.

13   Check the block and head mating surfaces for nicks, deep scratches and other damage. If damage is slight, it can be removed with a file; if it's excessive, machining may be the only alternative.

14   Use a tap of the correct size to chase the threads in the head bolt holes. Mount each head bolt in a vise and run a die down the threads to remove corrosion and restore the threads. Dirt, corrosion, sealant and damaged threads will affect torque readings.

15   Place a new gasket on the block. Check to see if there are any markings (such as "TOP") on the gasket that say how it is to be installed. Those identification marks must face UP. Also, apply sealant to the edges of the timing chain cover where it mates with the engine block. Set the cylinder head in position.

16   Lubricate the threads and the seats of the cylinder head bolts, then install them. They must be tightened in a specific sequence **(see illustration)**, in three stages and to the torque listed in this Chapter's Specifications.

17   Attach the camshaft sprocket to the camshaft (see Section 12) and remove the tensioner locking tool.

18   Reinstall the remaining parts in the reverse order of removal.

19   Be sure to refill the cooling system and check all fluid levels.

20   Rotate the crankshaft clockwise slowly by hand through two complete revolutions. **Caution:** *If you feel any resistance while turning the engine over, stop and re-check the camshaft timing. The valves may be hitting the pistons.*

21   Start the engine and check the ignition timing (see Chapter 1).

22   Run the engine until normal operating temperature is reached. Check for leaks and proper operation.

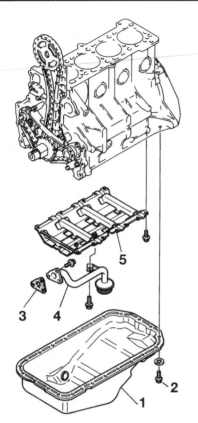

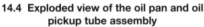

14.4 Exploded view of the oil pan and oil pickup tube assembly

1   Oil pan
2   Bolt
3   Pickup tube gasket
4   Pickup tube
5   Vibration reducing stiffener

15.5 Exploded view of the oil pump assembly

1	Pump cover	5	Oil seal
2	Outer rotor	6	Timing chain cover
3	Inner rotor	7	Water inlet pipe
4	Pressure relief valve		gasket

2A

14   Oil pan - removal and installation

Refer to illustration 14.4

1   Warm up the engine, then drain the oil and replace the oil filter (see Chapter 1).
2   Detach the cable from the negative battery terminal.
3   Raise the vehicle and support it securely on jackstands. **Note:** *On some models it may be necessary to unbolt the engine mounts and raise the engine several inches to make additional clearance for the oil pan. If this is the case, be sure to place wood blocks between the engine mounts and the frame while the engine is in the raised position.*
4   Remove the bolts securing the oil pan to the engine block **(see illustration)**.
5   Tap on the pan with a soft-face hammer to break the gasket seal, then detach the oil pan from the engine. Don't pry between the block and oil pan mating surfaces.
6   Using a gasket scraper, remove all traces of old gasket and/or sealant from the engine block and oil pan. Remove the seals from each end of the engine block or oil pan. Clean the mating surfaces with lacquer thinner or acetone. Make sure the threaded bolt holes in the block are clean.
7   Clean the oil pan with solvent and dry it thoroughly. Check the gasket flanges for distortion, particularly around the bolt holes. If necessary, place the pan on a block of wood and use a hammer to flatten and restore the gasket surfaces.
8   Apply a 1/8-inch wide bead of RTV sealant to the oil pan gasket surfaces. Make sure the sealant is applied to the inside edge of the

bolt holes.
9   Carefully place the oil pan in position.
10   Install the bolts and tighten them in small increments to the torque listed in this Chapter's Specifications. Start with the bolts closest to the center of the pan and work out in a spiral pattern. Don't overtighten them or leakage may occur.
11   Add oil (see Chapter 1), run the engine and check for oil leaks.

15   Oil pump - removal, inspection and installation

Removal

Refer to illustration 15.5

1   Remove valve cover (see Section 4) and unscrew the two bolts attaching the cylinder head to the timing chain cover (bolts "A" in illustration 13.8).
2   Remove the oil pan (see Section 14)
3   Remove oil pickup tube and screen from pump housing.
4   Remove timing chain cover (see Section 9).
5   Remove the screws and disassemble the oil pump **(see illustration)**. You may need to use an impact screwdriver to loosen the pump cover screws without stripping the heads out.

Inspection

Refer to illustrations 15.6a, 15.6b, 15.6c and 15.7

6   Check the oil pump clearances on both inner and outer rotors to each other and to the pump body **(see illustrations)**. Compare your

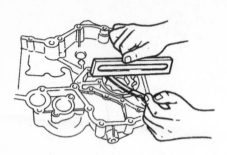
15.6a Using a feeler gauge and straightedge to check the side clearance

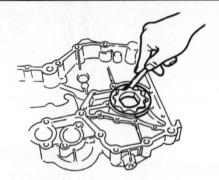
15.6b Using a feeler gauge to check the tooth-tip clearance between the inner and outer rotors

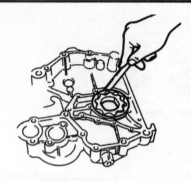
15.6c Using a feeler gauge to check the outer rotor-to-pump body clearance

measurements to the figures listed in this Chapter's Specifications. Replace the pump if any of the measurements are outside of the specified limits.

7   Extract the spring and oil pump relief valve from the pump housing **(see illustration 15.5)**. Measure the free length of the oil pressure relief valve spring **(see illustration)** and compare your measurement with the value listed in this Chapter's Specifications. Replace the spring if its length is not as specified.

8   Install the rotors with the dimples in alignment and facing the pump cover. Install the pump cover and tighten the screws to the torque listed in this Chapter's Specifications. Install the oil pressure relief valve and spring assembly.

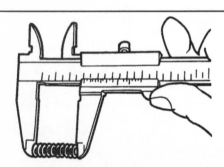
15.7 Measuring the free length of the oil pump pressure relief spring with a vernier caliper

Installation

9   Install the timing chain cover (see Section 9).
10   Install the oil pick-up tube and screen, using a new gasket. Tighten the bolts to the torque listed in this Chapter's Specifications.
11   Install the oil pan (see Section 14).
12   Remainder of installation is the reverse of removal. Add the specified type and quantity of oil and coolant (see Chapter 1), run the engine and check for leaks.

16   Flywheel/driveplate - removal and installation

Removal

Refer to illustrations 16.3 and 16.4

1   Raise the vehicle and support it securely on jackstands, then refer to Chapter 7 and remove the transmission.
2   Remove the pressure plate and clutch disc (see Chapter 8) (manual transmission equipped vehicles). Now is a good time to check/replace the clutch components and pilot bearing.
3   Make alignment marks on the flywheel/driveplate and crankshaft to ensure correct alignment during reinstallation **(see illustration)**.
4   Remove the bolts that secure the flywheel/driveplate to the crankshaft **(see illustration)**. If the crankshaft turns, remove the starter (see Chapter 5) and wedge a screwdriver in the ring gear teeth (manual transmission models), or insert a long punch through one of the holes

16.3 Mark the relationship of the flywheel /driveplate to the crankshaft prior to removal

16.4 If you're working on a model with an automatic transmission, insert a punch through one of the holes and let it rest against a projection on the engine block - this will prevent the driveplate from turning as the bolts are loosened

17.3a Carefully pry the oil seal out with a removal tool or a screwdriver - don't nick or scratch the crankshaft or the new seal will be damaged and leaks will develop

17.3b Because the seal lip is stiff, it won't slide over the end of the crankshaft easily - if you lubricate the journal and the seal lip with multi-purpose grease and carefully work the seal over the journal with a smooth, blunt object, it should go on without damage

2A

in the driveplate and allow it to rest against a projection on the engine block (automatic transmission models).

5   Remove the flywheel/driveplate from the crankshaft. Since the flywheel is fairly heavy, be sure to support it while removing the last bolt.

6   Clean the flywheel to remove grease and oil. Inspect the surface for cracks, rivet grooves, burned areas and score marks. Light scoring can be removed with emery cloth. Check for cracked and broken ring gear teeth. Lay the flywheel on a flat surface and use a straightedge to check for warpage.

7   Clean and inspect the mating surfaces of the flywheel/driveplate and the crankshaft. If the crankshaft rear seal is leaking, replace it before reinstalling the flywheel/driveplate (see Section 17).

Installation

8   Position the flywheel/driveplate against the crankshaft. Be sure to align the marks made during removal. Note that some engines have an alignment dowel or staggered bolt holes to ensure correct installation. Before installing the bolts, apply thread locking compound to the threads.

9   Prevent the flywheel/driveplate from turning by using one of the methods described in Step 4. Tighten the bolts to the torque listed in this Chapter's Specifications.

10   The remainder of installation is the reverse of the removal procedure.

17   Rear main oil seal - replacement

Refer to illustrations 17.3a and 17.3b

1   The transmission must be removed from the vehicle for this procedure (see Chapter 7).

2   Remove the flywheel/driveplate (see Section 16).

3   The seal can be replaced without removing the oil pan or seal retainer. Use a screwdriver and a rag to carefully pry the seal out of the housing **(see illustration)**. Use the rag to be sure no nicks are made in the crankshaft seal surface. Apply a film of clean oil to the crankshaft seal journal and the lip of the new seal and carefully tap the new seal into place **(see illustration)**. The lip is stiff so carefully work it onto the seal journal of the crankshaft with a smooth object like the end of a socket extension. Tap the seal into the retainer with a seal driver. If a seal driver isn't available, a large socket or piece of pipe, with an outside diameter slightly smaller than that of the seal, can be used. Don't rush it or you may damage the seal. **Note:** *Removal of the oil seal retainer and replacement of the seal are covered in Chapter 2, Part C.*

4   *The remaining steps are the reverse of removal.*

5   Run the engine and check for oil leaks.

18   Engine mounts - check and replacement

Refer to illustrations 18.4 and 18.9

1   Engine mounts seldom require attention, but broken or deteriorated mounts should be replaced immediately or the added strain placed on the driveline components may cause damage or wear.

Check

2   During the check, the engine must be raised slightly to remove the weight from the mounts.

3   Raise the vehicle and support it securely on jackstands, then position a jack under the engine oil pan. Place a large block of wood between the jack head and the oil pan, then carefully raise the engine just enough to take the weight off the mounts. **Warning:** *DO NOT place any part of your body under the engine when it's supported only by a jack!*

4   Check the mount insulators **(see illustration)** to see if the rubber is cracked, hardened or separated from the metal plates. Sometimes the rubber will split right down the center.

18.4 Check the rubber portion of the engine mount (arrow) for cracking or fluid leakage

5   Check for relative movement between the mount plates and the engine or frame (use a large screwdriver or pry bar to attempt to move the mounts). If movement is noted, lower the engine and tighten the mount fasteners.

6   Rubber preservative should be applied to the insulators to slow deterioration.

Replacement

7   Disconnect the negative battery cable from the battery, then raise the vehicle and support it securely on jackstands (if not already done). Support the engine as described in Step 3.

8   Remove the fasteners, raise the engine with the jack and detach the mount from the frame bracket and engine. **Warning:** *Don't apply heat to the engine mount or dispose of it in a fire. The mount is fluid filled and could explode.*

9   Install the new mount, making sure it is correctly positioned in its bracket **(see illustration)**. Install the fasteners and tighten them securely.

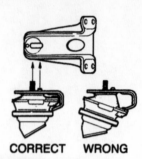

18.9 Make sure the edge of the engine mount doesn't get caught on the bracket

Chapter 2 Part B V6 engine

Contents

Specifications

General

Displacement..	180.2 cubic inches (3.0 liters)
Bore	3.54 inches
Stroke	3.05 inches
Compression ratio	8.5:1
Firing order	1-2-3-4-5-6
Cylinder numbers (front to rear)	
Right (passenger's side)..	1-3-5
Left (driver's side)..	2-4-6

Camshaft

Camshaft endplay	
Standard..	0.002 to 0.007
inch	
Maximum..	0.008 inch
Camshaft runout limit	0.0012 inch
Camshaft lobe height	
Standard	
Intake	1.6163 inches
Exhaust	1.6257 inches
Minimum	
Intake	1.6084 inches

Cylinder location and distributor rotation

Camshaft (continued)

Camshaft journal diameter
    Journals 1 and 4.. 1.9268 to 1.9274 inches
    Journals 2 and 3.. 1.9258 to 1.9266 inches
Journal out-of-round .... 0.0012 inch
Journal bore diameter .... 1.9297 to 1.9303 inches
Journal oil clearance
    Journals 1 and 4.. 0.0024 to 0.0035 inch
    Journals 2 and 3.. 0.0031 to 0.0045 inch

Cylinder head bolt length

Standard
    Intake side.. 4.25 inches
    Exhaust side... 5.43 inches
Maximum
    Intake side.. 4.29 inches
    Exhaust side... 5.47 inches

Oil pump

Outer rotor-to-pump body.. 0.0091 inch (maximum)
Inner rotor tooth tip-to-outer rotor clearance .... 0.0094 inch (maximum)
Rotor side clearance.. 0.0051 inch (maximum)

Torque specifications   **Ft-lbs** (unless otherwise indicated)

Rocker arm shaft bolts .... 14 to 19
Intake manifold nuts .... 14 to 19
Exhaust manifold nuts .... 16 to 21
Crankshaft pulley bolt.. 116 to 122
Camshaft sprocket bolt .... 53 to 59
Cylinder head bolts
    Step 1 14
    Step 2 .... Rotate an additional 90-degrees (1/4-turn)
    Step 3 .... Rotate an additional 90-degrees (1/4-turn)
Flywheel/driveplate bolts... 76 to 81
Oil pan bolts .... 69 to 95 in-lbs
Oil pump (front cover) bolts... 14 to 19
Oil pump pressure relief valve .... 57 to 65 in-lbs
Oil pick-up tube-to-pump bolts.. 70 to 95 in-lbs
Timing belt idler pulley bolt.. 27 to 38
Timing belt tensioner bolts .... 14 to 19
Timing belt tensioner pulley bolt.. 17 to 22
Valve cover bolts .... 21 to 39 in-lbs

1   General information

This Part of Chapter 2 is devoted to in-vehicle repair procedures for the V6 engine. All information concerning engine removal and installation and engine block and cylinder head overhaul can be found in Chapter 2C.

The following repair procedures are based on the assumption that the engine is installed in the vehicle. If the engine has been removed from the vehicle and mounted on a stand, many of the steps outlined in this Part of Chapter 2 will not apply.

The Specifications included in this Part of Chapter 2 apply only to the procedures contained in this Part. Chapter 2C contains the Specifications necessary for cylinder head and engine block rebuilding.

The 60-degree V6 has a cast iron block and aluminum heads with a camshaft in each head. The block has thin walled sections for light weight.

Both camshafts are driven off the crankshaft by a cog belt. A spring loaded tensioner, adjusted by an eccentric type locknut, maintains belt tension. Each camshaft actuates three valves per cylinder through hydraulic lash adjusters and shaft-mounted rocker arms.

Each cast aluminum three-ring piston has two compression rings and a three-piece oil control ring. The piston pins are pressed into forged steel connecting rods.

The rotor type oil pump is mounted in the front cover. It is driven by the crankshaft. From the oil pump, oil travels through the filter to the main oil gallery, from which it is routed either directly to the main bearings, crankshaft, connecting rod bearings and pistons and cylinder walls or to the cylinder heads.

2   Repair operations possible with the engine in the vehicle

Many major repair operations can be accomplished without removing the engine from the vehicle.

Clean the engine compartment and the exterior of the engine with some type of degreaser before any work is done. It will make the job easier and help keep dirt out of the internal areas of the engine.

Depending on the components involved, it may be helpful to remove the hood to improve access to the engine as repairs are performed (refer to Chapter 11 if necessary). Cover the fenders to prevent damage to the paint. Special pads are available, but an old bedspread or blanket will also work.

If vacuum, exhaust, oil or coolant leaks develop, indicating a need for gasket or seal replacement, the repairs can generally be made with the engine in the vehicle. The intake and exhaust manifold gaskets, oil pan gasket, camshaft and crankshaft oil seals and cylinder head gaskets are all accessible with the engine in place.

4.3 Unbolt the fuel pressure regulator from the valve cover and move it aside

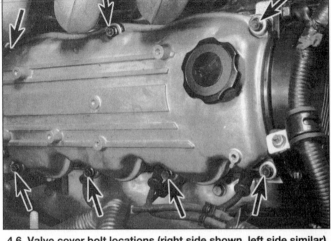

4.6 Valve cover bolt locations (right side shown, left side similar)

Exterior engine components, such as the intake and exhaust manifolds, the oil pan (and the oil pump), the water pump, the starter motor, the alternator, the distributor and the fuel system components can be removed for repair with the engine in place.

Since the cylinder heads can be removed without pulling the engine, camshaft and valve component servicing can also be accomplished with the engine in the vehicle. Replacement of the timing belt and sprockets is also possible with the engine in the vehicle.

In extreme cases caused by a lack of necessary equipment, repair or replacement of piston rings, pistons, connecting rods and rod bearings is possible with the engine in the vehicle. However, this practice is not recommended because of the cleaning and preparation work that must be done to the components involved.

---

3 Top Dead Center (TDC) for number one piston - locating

This procedure is essentially the same for all engines. Refer to Chapter 2A and follow the procedure outlined there.

---

4 Valve cover(s) - removal and installation

Refer to illustrations 4.3 and 4.6

Removal

1   Relieve the fuel system pressure (see Chapter 4).
2   Disconnect the negative cable from the battery.

Right (passenger side) cover

3   Remove the fuel pressure regulator from the valve cover **(see illustration)**.
4   Remove the spark plug wires from the spark plugs. Mark them clearly with pieces of numbered tape to prevent confusion during installation.
5   Disconnect the electrical connectors and vacuum hoses necessary for removal. Label and move the wiring and hoses aside.
6   Remove the valve cover bolts and washers and lift off the valve cover **(see illustration)**. **Caution**: *If the cover is stuck to the head, bump one end with a block of wood and a hammer to jar it loose. If that doesn't work, try to slip a flexible putty knife between the head and cover to break the gasket seal. Don't pry at the cover-to-head joint or damage to the sealing surfaces may occur (leading to oil leaks in the future).*

Left (driver's side) cover

7   Detach the breather hose from the valve cover.
8   Remove the spark plug wires from the spark plugs. Mark them clearly with pieces of masking tape to prevent confusion during installation.
10   Remove the throttle body, then detach the intake air pipe from the dynamic chamber (see Chapter 4). Plug the coolant lines to prevent spillage.
11   Disconnect the coolant lines attached to the top of the valve cover and move them aside to get clearance for cover removal.
12   Remove the valve cover bolts and washers **(see illustration 4.6)**.
13   Detach the valve cover. Read the Caution in Step 6 if the cover sticks to the head.

Installation

14   The mating surfaces of each cylinder head and valve cover must be perfectly clean when the covers are installed. Use a gasket scraper to remove all traces of sealant and old gasket material, then clean the mating surfaces with lacquer thinner or acetone. If there's sealant or oil on the mating surfaces when the cover is installed, oil leaks may develop.
16   If necessary, clean the mounting bolt threads with a die to remove any corrosion and restore damaged threads. Make sure the threaded holes in the head are clean - run a tap into them to remove corrosion and restore damaged threads.
17   The gaskets should be mated to the covers before the covers are installed. Apply a bead of RTV sealant to the cover, then position the gasket inside the cover and allow the sealant to set up so the gasket adheres to the cover. If the sealant isn't allowed to set, the gasket may fall out of the cover as it's installed on the engine.
18   Carefully position the cover on the head and install the bolts.
19   Tighten the bolts in three or four steps to the torque listed in this Chapter's Specifications.
20   The remaining installation steps are the reverse of removal. If the left valve cover was removed, be sure to check the coolant level and add some, if necessary.
21   Start the engine and check carefully for oil leaks as the engine warms up.

---

5 Rocker arm components - removal and installation

Refer to illustrations 5.2 and 5.5

1   Position the engine at TDC compression for the number 1 cylinder (see Section 3). Remove the valve cover (see Section 4).

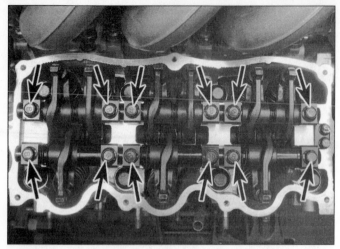

5.2 Loosen the rocker arm shaft bolts, a little at a time, working from the ends of the shafts to the center (keep all pieces in order and on the same shaft it was removed from)

2   Loosen the rocker arm shaft bolts **(see illustration)** in two or three stages, working your way from the ends toward the middle of the shafts. **Caution:** *Some of the valves will be open when you loosen the rocker arm shaft bolts and the rocker arm shafts will be under a certain amount of valve spring pressure. Therefore, the bolts must be loosened gradually. Loosening a bolt all at once near a rocker arm under spring pressure could bend or break the rocker arm shaft.*

3   Prior to removal, scribe or paint identifying marks on the rocker arms to ensure they will be installed in their original locations.

4   Remove the bolts and lift off the rocker arm shaft assemblies one at a time. Lay them down on a workbench in the same relationship to each other that they're in when installed. They must be reinstalled on the same cylinder head, in the same positions.

5   Installation is the reverse of the removal procedure. **Note:** *Tighten the rocker arm shaft bolts in the sequence shown* **(see illustration)**, *in three steps, to the torque listed in this Chapter's Specifications.*

---

6   Hydraulic lash adjusters - check, removal and installation

Check

Refer to illustration 6.2

1   Remove the rocker arm and shaft components (see Section 5). **Note:** *Be sure to label each rocker arm and adjuster and place them in a partitioned box or something suitable to keep them from getting mixed with each other.*

2   Check the rocker arm pad and the hydraulic lash adjuster tip for

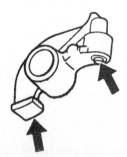

6.2 Typical rocker arm with the hydraulic lash adjuster in place (arrows indicate the points where each should be checked for wear)

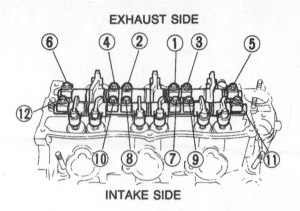

5.5 Bolt tightening sequence for the rocker arm shafts

---

wear **(see illustration)**. Replace if necessary. **Note:** *Do not remove the hydraulic lash adjuster from the rocker arm unless absolutely necessary. Oil leakage will occur if the O-ring is damaged.*

Removal and installation

3   Remove the rocker arm shaft components, if not already done (see Section 5).

4   Pull the hydraulic lash adjuster out of the rocker arm, using pliers if necessary.

5   Installation is the reverse of removal, but be sure to apply a film of clean engine oil to the O-ring.

---

7   Intake manifold - removal and installation

Removal

Refer to illustration 7.8

1   Relieve the fuel system pressure (see Chapter 4).

2   Disconnect the cable from the negative terminal of the battery.

3   Drain the cooling system (don't forget to drain the cylinder block) (see Chapter 1).

4   Label and disconnect any vacuum lines and electrical connectors that would interfere with removal of the manifold.

5   Remove the intake air pipe, intake manifold, extension manifolds and air plenum (see Chapter 4).

6   Detach the fuel lines from the fuel rail (see Chapter 4).

7.8 Location of the intake manifold nuts (arrows)

7.12 Installing the intake manifold gaskets - no sealant is needed on these metal gaskets, but make sure they are installed in the proper positions (they're marked LEFT and RIGHT) and the UP marks are facing up

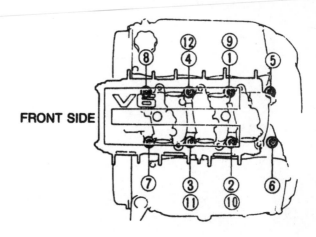

7.14 Intake manifold nut tightening sequence

sure to refill the cooling system (see Chapter 1). Start the engine and check carefully for oil and coolant leaks at the intake manifold joints.

7 Label and remove any remaining hoses, wires or cables attached to the intake manifold or its components.

8 Loosen the manifold mounting nuts in 1/4-turn increments until they can be removed by hand. Loosen the outer bolts first, then the inner bolts **(see illustration)**.

9 Remove the intake manifold. The manifold will probably be stuck to the cylinder heads and force may be required to break the gasket seal. If this is the case, tapping the manifold with a rubber mallet or plastic hammer may break it loose. If it still sticks, insert a wooden dowel (such as a broom handle) into one of the ports and pry it upward. **Caution:** *Don't pry between the manifold and the heads or damage to the gasket sealing surfaces may occur, leading to vacuum leaks.*

Installation

Refer to illustrations 7.12 and 7.14

Note: *The mating surfaces of the cylinder heads and manifold must be perfectly clean when the manifold is installed. Gasket removal solvents in aerosol cans are available at most auto parts stores and may be helpful when removing old gasket material that's stuck to the heads and manifold (since they're made of aluminum, aggressive scraping can cause damage). Be sure to follow the directions printed on the container.*

10 Use a gasket scraper to carefully remove all traces of sealant and old gasket material, then clean the mating surfaces with lacquer thinner or acetone. If there's old sealant or oil on the mating surfaces when the manifold is installed, oil or vacuum leaks may develop. Use a vacuum cleaner to remove any material that falls into the intake ports in the heads.

11 If necessary, use a die of the correct size to clean up the threads on the mounting studs, then use compressed air (if available) to remove the debris from the area. **Warning:** *Wear safety glasses or a face shield to protect your eyes when using compressed air!*

12 Position the gaskets on the cylinder heads. Make sure they are installed in the correct positions - they are marked LEFT and RIGHT and each gasket also has an UP mark. No sealant is required; however, follow the instructions included with the new gaskets **(see illustration)**.

13 Carefully set the manifold in place. Be careful not to disturb the gaskets.

14 Install the nuts and tighten them to the torque listed in this Chapter's Specifications, following the recommended sequence **(see illustration)**. Work up to the final torque in two steps.

15 The remaining installation steps are the reverse of removal. Be

8 Exhaust manifold(s) - removal and installation

Refer to illustrations 8.3, 8.5 and 8.6

Note: *The engine must be completely cool when this procedure is done.*

Removal

1 Disconnect the negative cable from the battery. Raise the vehicle and support it securely on jackstands.

2 Spray penetrating oil on the exhaust manifold fasteners and allow it to soak in. Disconnect the oxygen sensor electrical connector.

3 If you're removing the left manifold, remove the nuts that retain the exhaust pipe to the manifold, and also the bolt that retains the exhaust pipe bracket to the engine block **(see illustration)**.

4 If you're removing the left manifold, remove the oxygen sensor (see Chapter 6).

5 Lower the vehicle and remove the bolts retaining the heat shield(s)

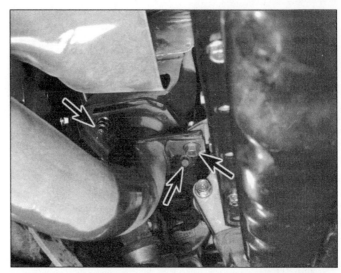

8.3 If you're removing the left exhaust manifold unbolt the exhaust pipe from the manifold and block

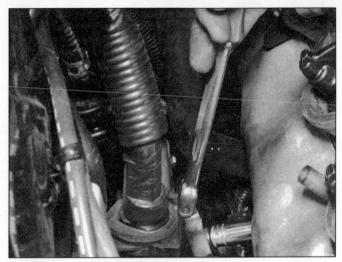

8.5 Removal of the exhaust manifold heat shield (one per side) - a ratchet with a pivoting head makes access to the bolt much easier

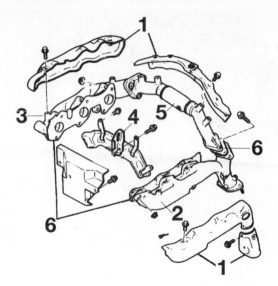

8.6 Details of the exhaust manifolds and crossover pipe

1	Heat shield	4	Engine lifting bracket
2	Left exhaust manifold	5	Crossover pipe
3	Right exhaust manifold	6	Gasket

to the manifold(s) and remove **(see illustration)**. If you're removing the left side manifold, it may be helpful to remove the air intake duct (see Chapter 4).

6   Unbolt the crossover pipe from the manifold **(see illustration)**.

7   Remove the nuts that retain the manifold to the cylinder head and lift the exhaust manifold off.

8   Clean both the head and manifold surfaces to remove any carbon deposits. Carefully inspect the manifolds and fasteners for cracks and damage.

Installation

9   Position new gaskets over the cylinder head studs. Also be sure to install a new gasket between the manifold and crossover pipe

10   Install the manifold and thread the mounting nuts and bolts into place.

11   Working from the center out, tighten the nuts to the torque listed in this Chapter's Specifications in three or four equal steps. Tighten the crossover pipe-to-manifold bolts *after* the manifold-to-cylinder head nuts have been tightened.

12   Reinstall the remaining parts in the reverse order of removal. Use new gaskets when connecting the exhaust pipes.

13   Run the engine and check for exhaust leaks.

---

9   Crankshaft pulley - removal and installation

Refer to illustration 9.4

Removal

1   Disconnect the negative cable from the battery.

2   Raise the front of the vehicle and support it securely on jackstands.

3   Remove the drivebelts (see Chapter 1).

4   Thread a bolt into one of the holes in the pulley **(see illustration)**.

5   Using a socket and ratchet on the center bolt, place a large prybar or screwdriver between the bolt installed in the previous Step and the socket to prevent the pulley from turning.

6   Remove the bolt from the crankshaft.

7   Slide the pulley off the crankshaft nose. If the pulley sticks, use a puller to remove it. **Caution:** *Don't use a puller with jaws that grip the outer edge of the pulley. The puller must be the type that uses bolts to apply pressure to the pulley hub only.*

Installation

8   Align the keyway in the pulley with the key in the crankshaft and push the pulley into place.

9.4 Thread a bolt into one of the holes in the crankshaft pulley, then wedge a large screwdriver or prybar between the socket and bolt to prevent the pulley from turning as the pulley bolt is loosened (shown from above, but actual access to the pulley is easier from below)

9   Prevent the crankshaft from turning as described in Step 5, then install the pulley bolt and tighten it to the torque listed in this Chapter's Specifications.

10   Reinstall the remaining parts in the reverse order of removal.

---

10   Timing belt - removal, installation and adjustment

Removal

Refer to illustrations 10.12, 10.13, 10.14a and 10.14b

1   Disconnect the cable from the negative terminal of the battery.

2   Drain the cooling system (see Chapter 1).

3   Remove the upper radiator hose.

4   Remove the coolant bypass hose.

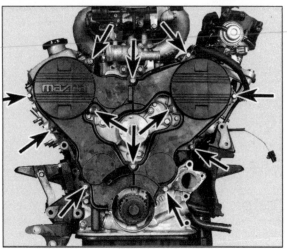

10.12 Timing belt cover bolt locations (arrows)

10.13 Camshaft and crankshaft sprocket alignment details - when cylinder no. 1 is at TDC on the compression stroke, these marks must be in alignment

5   Remove fresh air duct, the radiator shroud, cooling fan assembly and pulley (see Chapter 3).

6   Label and remove the spark plug wires from the distributor to the right side of the engine, to gain better access to the timing belt cover.

7   Remove the air conditioning belt idler pulley.

8   Position the number one piston at TDC on the compression stroke (see Section 3).

9   Remove the drivebelts (see Chapter 1).

10   Raise the front of the vehicle and support it securely on jackstands.

11   Remove the crankshaft pulley (see Section 9). Don't let the crankshaft turn - if the crankshaft moves, the number one piston will no longer be at TDC.

12   Remove the bolts securing the timing belt right and left covers **(see illustration)**. Note the various type and sizes of bolts by drawing a diagram or making specific notes while the timing belt cover is being removed. The bolts must be reinstalled in their original locations.

13   Confirm that the number one piston is still at TDC on the compression stroke by verifying that the timing marks on all three timing belt sprockets are aligned with their respective stationary timing marks **(see illustration)**.

14   Relieve tension on the timing belt by removing the timing belt automatic tensioner **(see illustration)**. Also remove the tensioner pulley and inspect it for smooth operation **(see illustration)**. If it feels loose or rough, replace it. **Note:** *The pulley is a sealed unit and is lubricated for life - don't immerse it in solvent.*

10.14a Installation details of the timing belt and related components

1   Crankshaft pulley
2   Left side timing belt cover
3   Right side timing belt cover
4   Upper idler pulley
5   Timing belt
6   Timing belt automatic tensioner
7   Lower idler pulley
8   Tensioner pulley
9   Timing belt cover seals

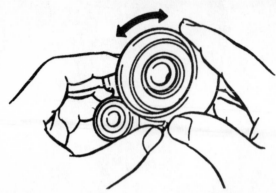

10.14b If the tensioner pulley feels loose or rough when turning, it's worn out and must be replaced

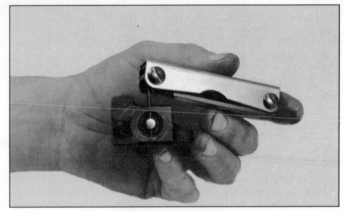

10.18 Once the tensioner is compressed in vise or press, insert a small Allen wrench or drill bit through the holes to keep the tensioner retracted

15   Remove the upper idler pulley.

16   Check to see that the timing belt is marked with an arrow as to which side faces out. If there isn't a mark, paint one on (only if the same belt will be reinstalled). Slide the timing belt off the sprockets.

Installation

Refer to illustrations 10.18 and 10.19

17   Check the automatic tensioner for oil leakage. Replace it if necessary.

18   Compress the tensioner in a vise or press to align the hole in the rod with the hole in the housing, then insert a small Allen wrench or drill bit to keep the rod retracted until reassembly **(see illustration)**. **Note**: *Place a flat washer under the body of the tensioner when compressing to avoid damage to the body plug.*

19   Install the timing belt, starting with the crankshaft sprocket, then around the lower idler pulley and left (driver's side) camshaft sprocket, tensioner sprocket and then the right camshaft sprocket **(see illustration)**. Be careful not to disturb any of the alignment marks. If you're installing the old belt, make sure the directional arrow made in Step 16 is pointing out.

20   Reinstall the upper idler pulley, tightening the bolt to the torque listed in this Chapter's Specifications.

21   Reinstall the automatic tensioner pulley and tensioner, tightening the bolts to the torque values listed in this Chapter's Specifications.

22   Checking to see that the belt is properly installed around all sprockets and pulleys, remove the Allen wrench or drill bit from the tensioner.

23   Install the crankshaft pulley bolt and slowly turn the crankshaft clockwise two full revolutions, returning the number one piston to TDC

on the compression stroke. **Caution**: *If excessive resistance is felt while turning the crankshaft, it's an indication that the pistons are coming into contact with the valves. Go back over the procedure to correct the situation before proceeding.*

24   Check to be sure all three timing marks are still aligned **(see illustration 10.13)**. If the belt seems loose, replace the automatic tensioner assembly.

25   Install the various components removed during disassembly, referring to the appropriate Sections as necessary.

11   Camshaft oil seal - replacement

Refer to illustrations 11.3 and 11.6

1   Disconnect the negative battery cable from the battery. Position the engine at TDC on the compression stroke for cylinder number 1 (see Section 3).

2   Remove the drivebelts (see Chapter 1), crankshaft pulley (see Section 9) and timing belt (see Section 10).

3   Hold the camshaft sprocket stationary by holding it with Mazda tool no. 49 H012 010, or equivalent **(see illustration)**, then unscrew the sprocket bolt. **Note:** *Because of the special composite material of the cam sprocket extreme care must be taken not to fracture or damage the sprocket in any way.* Slide the sprocket off the camshaft.

4   Carefully remove the old oil seal with a screwdriver or other pick type tool. Don't nick or scratch the camshaft or seal bore in the process.

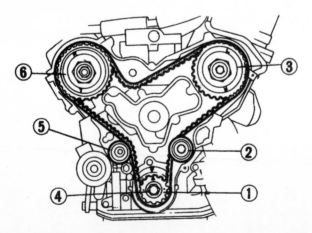

10.19 Install the timing belt over the sprockets and pulleys in the order shown

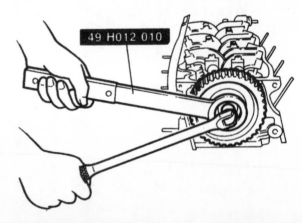

11.3 Use this Mazda tool (or an equivalent substitute) to hold the sprocket stationary while the bolt is loosened

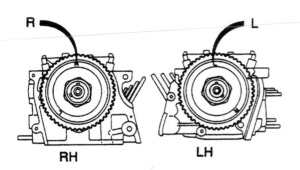

11.6 Make sure the proper letter is in the 12 o'clock position when installing the camshaft sprockets (remember - left is the driver's side, right is the passenger's side)

13.5 Remove the seal plates, which bolt to each end of the cylinder heads

Installation

5   Clean all surfaces before installation of the new seal. Apply a light coating of oil to the seal surfaces and lightly drive the seal into place with a seal driver. If a seal driver isn't available, a large socket or section of pipe, with an outside diameter slightly smaller than that of the seal, can be used.

6   Install the sprocket, making sure the notch in the sprocket is aligned with the key on the camshaft, and the R or L mark (depending on which sprocket is being installed) is in the 12 o'clock position **(see illustration)**. Also make sure the timing mark on the sprocket is aligned with its corresponding mark on the cylinder head **(see illustration 10.13)**.

7   Installation of the remaining components is the reverse of removal.

12   Valve springs, retainers and seals - replacement

This procedure is essentially the same as for the four-cylinder engine. Refer to Chapter 2A and follow the procedure outlined there.

13   Cylinder head(s) - removal and installation

Note: *Allow the engine to cool completely before beginning this procedure.*

Removal

Refer to illustrations 13.5 and 13.8

1   Position the engine at TDC on the compression stroke for the number 1 cylinder (see Section 3). Drain the engine coolant (see Chapter 1). Disconnect the cable from the negative terminal of the battery.

2   Remove the timing belt cover and timing belt (see Section 10).

3   Remove the intake manifold (see Section 7).

4   Remove the exhaust manifold(s) as described in Section 8. **Note:** *If desired, each manifold may remain attached to the cylinder head until after the head is removed from the engine. However, the manifold must still be disconnected from the exhaust system.*

5   Remove the seal plates from the front and rear of the cylinder heads **(see illustration)**.

6   Remove the valve cover (see Section 4).

7   If you're removing the left (driver's side) cylinder head, remove the distributor (see Chapter 5).

8   If you're removing the right (passenger side) cylinder head, unbolt the transmission fluid dipstick tube, if equipped with an automatic transmission **(see illustration)**.

9   Mark and detach any hoses, wires and brackets that may interfere with removal of the head.

10   Loosen the cylinder head bolts in 1/4-turn increments, in an order opposite that of the tightening sequence **(see illustration 13.20a)** until they can be removed by hand.

13.8 If you're removing the right cylinder head, unbolt the automatic transmission dip stick tube

11   Lift the head off the block. If resistance is felt, dislodge the head by striking it with a wood block and hammer. If prying is required, pry only on a casting protrusion - not between the gasket mating surfaces. Be very careful not to damage the head or block!

12   Set the head on two wood blocks to avoid damaging the gasket mating surface or the valves.

Installation

Refer to illustration 13.18, 13.20a and 13.20b

13   Remove all traces of old gasket material from the cylinder head and the engine block gasket mating surfaces. Clean the mating surfaces with lacquer thinner or acetone. If there's oil on the mating surfaces when the heads are installed, the gaskets may not seal correctly and leaks may develop. Use a vacuum cleaner to remove any debris that falls into the cylinders.

14   Check the block and head mating surfaces for nicks, deep scratches and other damage. If damage is slight, it can be removed with a file - if it's excessive, machining may be the only alternative. It's also a good idea to check the head for warpage, even if you're just replacing the gasket (see Chapter 2C).

15   Use a tap of the correct size to chase the threads in the head bolt holes. Also, mount each bolt in a vise and run a die down the threads to remove corrosion and restore the threads. Dirt, corrosion, sealant

2B

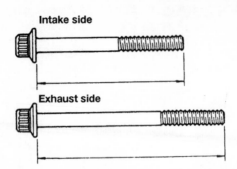

13.18 Measure the length of the head bolts to determine if they have stretched beyond the allowable limit (compare your measurements to the values listed in this Chapter's Specifications)

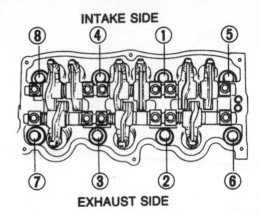

13.20a Cylinder head bolt TIGHTENING sequence

and damaged threads will affect torque readings. Ensure that the threaded holes in the block are clean and dry.

16   Position the new gaskets over the dowel pins on the block. Be sure the Right and/or Left mark on the head gasket(s) face up.

17   Carefully position the heads on the block without disturbing the gaskets. **Note**: *Be careful not to damage the O-ring on the oil control plug projection when installing the cylinder head.*

18   Measure the cylinder head bolt length (stretch) and replace them if they have stretched beyond the maximum length **(see illustration)**.

19   Lightly oil the threads and install the bolts in their original locations. Tighten them finger tight.

20   Follow the recommended sequence and tighten the bolts in three steps to the torque listed in this Chapter's Specifications **(see illustrations)**.

21   The remaining installation steps are the reverse of removal.

22   Add coolant and change the engine oil and filter (see Chapter 1), then start the engine and check carefully for oil and coolant leaks.

14   Camshaft(s) - removal and installation

Refer to illustrations 14.4 and 14.5

Removal

1   Position the engine at TDC on the compression stroke for the number 1 cylinder (see Section 3). Remove the timing belt and camshaft sprocket(s) (see Sections 10 and 11).

2   If you're removing the left (driver's side) camshaft, gently pry off the distributor drive gear.

3   Remove the rocker arm assembly (see Section 5).

13.20b Cylinder head bolts each marked with a white mark to be used as a reference point when angle torque is used for the final two rounds of tightening

4   Before removing the camshaft, measure the endplay with a dial indicator **(see illustration)**. If the endplay exceeds the limit listed in this Chapter's Specifications, replace the thrust plate with a new one

14.4 Position the dial indicator in line with the camshaft and use a screwdriver to pry the camshaft all the way back, then forward (the total indicated reading is the amount of camshaft endplay)

14.5 Location of the camshaft thrust plate (arrow)

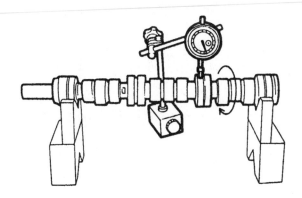

15.2 Checking camshaft runout with a dial indicator and V-blocks

and measure the endplay again. If the endplay is still excessive, replace the camshaft.

5　Unscrew the two bolts and remove the thrust plate **(see illustration)**.

6　Carefully pry the camshaft oil seal out of the cylinder head with a seal removal tool or a thin screwdriver. Be careful to not scratch the camshaft or any cylinder head bearing surface when removing either the oil seal or the camshaft.

7　Carefully pull the camshaft from the cylinder head. Inspect the camshaft as described in Section 15.

Installation

8　Lubricate the camshaft bearing journals and lobes with moly-base grease or engine assembly lube, then install it carefully in the head. Don't scratch the bearing surfaces with the cam lobes!

9　Check to make sure the mark on the crankshaft sprocket is still aligned with its mark on the front cover. Slide the camshaft sprocket(s) onto the camshaft(s) and align the mark(s) on the sprocket(s) with the corresponding mark(s) on the cylinder head(s) (see Sections 10 and 11).

10　The remaining steps are the reverse of the removal procedure.

15　Camshaft and bearing surfaces - inspection

Refer to illustrations 15.2, 15.3 and 15.4

1　Visually check the camshaft and cylinder head bearing surfaces for pitting, score marks, galling and abnormal wear. If the bearing surfaces are damaged, the head will have to be replaced. Get the advise of an automotive machine shop.

2　Check camshaft runout by placing the camshaft between two V-blocks and set up a dial indicator on one of the center journals **(see illustration)**. Zero the dial indicator. Turn the camshaft slowly and note the total indicator reading. Record your readings and compare them with the specified runout in this Chapter. If the measured runout exceeds the runout specified in this Chapter, replace the camshaft.

3　Check the camshaft lobe height by measuring each lobe with a micrometer **(see illustration)**. Compare the measurement to the cam lobe height specified in this Chapter. If it's less than specified, replace the camshaft.

4　Using a micrometer, measure each journal diameter and compare it to the journal diameter listed in this Chapter's Specifications **(see illustration)**. If the journals measure less than the standard journal diameter, replace the camshaft.

5　Inspect the contact and sliding surfaces of each hydraulic lash adjuster for scoring or damage (see Section 6). Replace any defective parts.

6　Check the rocker arms and shafts for abnormal wear, pits, galling, score marks and rough spots. Don't attempt to restore rocker arms by grinding the pad surfaces. Replace any defective parts.

16　Oil pan - removal and installation

Refer to illustrations 16.5a, 16.5b, 16.6a and 16.6b

Removal

1　Disconnect the negative cable from the battery.

2　Raise the vehicle and support it securely on jackstands.

3　Remove the under-vehicle splash pan.

4　Drain the engine oil and install a new oil filter (see Chapter 1).

5　Remove the oil pan bolts **(see illustrations)**.

6　Detach the oil pan from the engine. If the pan is stuck, dislodge it with a hammer and a block of wood. If that doesn't work, pry carefully

2B

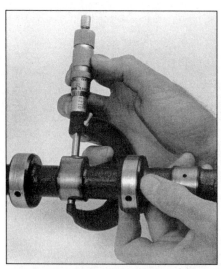

15.3 Measure the lobe heights on each camshaft with a micrometer - if any lobe height is less than the allowable minimum, replace the camshaft

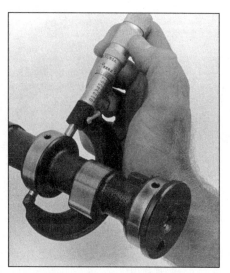

15.4 Check the diameter of each camshaft bearing journal to pinpoint excessive wear and out-of-round conditions

16.5a When removing the oil pan bolts a ratchet with a long extension and a swivel socket make this procedure much easier

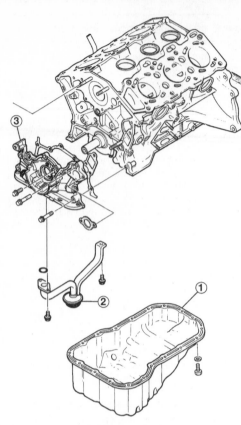

16.5b Exploded view of the oil pan, pick-up tube and screen, and oil pump assembly

1	*Oil pan*	*3*	*Front cover/oil pump*
2	*Pick-up tube and screen*		

between the pan and block, but don't distort the flange on the pan or mar the mating surface on the engine block **(see illustrations)**.

7   Use a gasket scraper to remove all traces of old gasket material and sealant from the block and pan. Clean the mating surfaces with lacquer, thinner or acetone.

Installation

8   Ensure that the threaded holes in the block are clean (use a tap to remove any sealant or corrosion from the threads).

16.6b View of removing the oil pan - there is sufficient clearance to remove it without lifting the engine

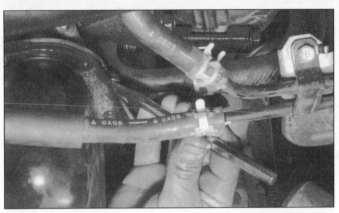

16.6a When removing the oil pan it may be necessary to pry the pan from the block to break the gasket material bond

9   Apply a continuous bead of RTV sealant to the oil pan, if no oil pan gasket is used. If your engine uses a gasket, apply sealant to the seams where the front cover and rear main oil seal retainer contact the block.

10   Apply a thread locking compound to the oil pan bolts. Install the oil pan and tighten the bolts to the torque listed in this Chapter's Specifications.

11   The remaining installation steps are the reverse of removal.

12   Allow at least 30 minutes for the sealant to dry, then fill the crankcase with oil (see Chapter 1), start the engine and check for oil pressure and leaks.

17   Oil pump - removal, inspection and installation

Removal

Refer to illustration 17.3 and 17.5

1   Remove the timing belt and the crankshaft sprocket (see Sections 10 and 14).

2   Remove the oil pan (see Section 16).

3   Remove the oil pump pick-up tube **(see illustration)**.

4   Remove the front cover/oil pump-to-engine block bolts from the front of the engine.

5   Use a block of wood and a hammer to break the oil pump loose (If necessary) and remove the pump assembly **(see illustration)**.

6   Use a scraper to remove old gasket material and sealant from the oil pump and engine block mating surfaces. Clean the mating surfaces with lacquer thinner or acetone.

17.3 Unbolt the oil pump pick-up tube from the bottom of the pump housing, remove the brace bolt and detach the pick-up tube

17.5 After removing the pump housing bolts, remove the front cover/oil pump assembly

17.7 With the oil pump assembly supported properly underneath, loosen all the screws with an impact screwdriver

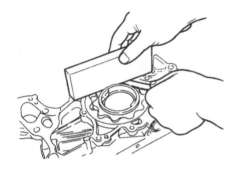

17.10a Using a feeler gauge and straightedge to measure rotor side clearance

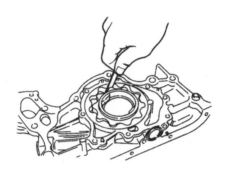

17.10b Using a feeler gauge to measure the tooth-tip clearance between the inner and outer rotors

Inspection

Refer to illustrations 17.7, 17.10a, 17.10b 17.10c and 17.11

7   Remove the screws holding the rear cover to the oil pump. An impact screwdriver will probably be needed, as the screws are very tight **(see illustration)**.

8   Clean all components with solvent, then inspect them for wear and damage.

9   Remove the oil pressure relief valve plug, washer, spring and valve (plunger). Check the oil pressure relief valve sliding surface and valve spring. If either the spring or the valve is damaged, they must be replaced as a set.

10   Check the oil pump clearances: a) side clearance, (b) tooth tip clearance and (c) outer rotor to pump body clearance **(see illustra-**

tions). Compare your measurements with the values listed in this Chapter's Specifications.

Reassembly and installation

11   Assemble the oil pump with the dimples in the rotors in alignment and facing the cover **(see illustration)**. Pack the cavities in the pump with petroleum jelly to prime it, then install the cover. **Note:** *Don't apply any sealant to the cover - install it dry.* Apply a thread locking compound to the screws and tighten them securely. Install the oil pressure

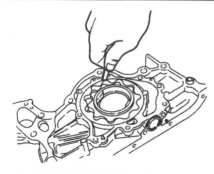

17.10c Using a feeler gauge to measure the outer rotor-to-pump body clearance

17.11 Align the dimples on the rotors and install them in the pump housing with the dimples facing the pump cover

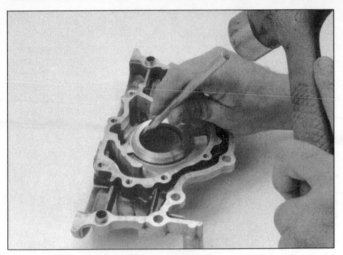

18.9 With the pump housing supported properly, drive the seal out from behind with a small punch and hammer

18.11 Install the new oil seal using a socket with an outside diameter slightly less than that of the oil seal

relief valve, spring and washer, then tighten the oil pressure relief valve plug to the torque listed in this Chapter's Specifications.

12   Installation is the reverse of the removal procedure. Align the flats on the crankshaft with the flats in the inner rotor of the oil pump. Tighten all fasteners to the torque values listed in this Chapter's Specifications.

18   Crankshaft front oil seal - replacement

Refer to illustrations 18.9 and 18.11

Removal

1   Disconnect the negative cable from the battery.
2   Remove the timing belt (see Section 10).
3   Drain the engine oil.
4   Remove the oil pan (see Section 16).
5   Unbolt the oil pump pick-up tube from the oil pump body (see Section 17).
6   Remove the crankshaft gear and key, sliding it by hand, from the crankshaft nose.
7   Remove the oil pump assembly from the engine (see Section 17).
Caution: *DO NOT try to remove the front oil seal with the oil pump on the engine. Damage to the crankshaft and possibly the aluminum pump housing can occur when trying to pry out the seal.*
8   Remove the oil pump (see Section 17).
9   Supporting the pump body squarely on a bench, drive the oil seal out from behind by using a small punch and hammer **(see illustration)**.

Installation

10   Clean both the seal outer surface and the housing surface and

apply a thin coating of sealant to outer edge of the seal.
11   Place the seal in position in the opening of the housing and drive it into place with a socket or pipe with an outside diameter slightly less than that of the seal diameter **(see illustration)**.
12   Clean both the engine block and the pump body surfaces of all gasket material and reassemble the oil pump to the engine block with a new gasket.
13   Installation of the remaining components is the reverse of removal. Be sure to refer to Section 10 for the timing belt installation and adjustment procedure. Tighten all bolts to the torque values listed in this Chapter's Specifications.

19   Flywheel/driveplate - removal and installation

This procedure is essentially the same for all engines. Refer to Chapter 2A and follow the procedure outlined there, but use the bolt torque listed in this Chapter's Specifications.

20   Rear main oil seal - replacement

This procedure is essentially the same for all engines. Refer to Chapter 2A and follow the procedure outlined there.

21   Engine mounts - check and replacement

This procedure is essentially the same for all engines. See Chapter 2A and follow the procedure outlined there.

Chapter 2 Part C
General engine overhaul procedures

Contents

Specifications

Four-cylinder engine

General

Displacement	158.97 cubic inches (2.6 liters)
Bore	3.62 inches
Stroke	3.86 inches
Cylinder compression pressure	
Standard	185 psi
Minimum	142 psi
Oil pressure	
At 1000 rpm	16 to 29 psi
At 3000 rpm	45 to 58 psi

Four-cylinder engine (continued)

Engine block

Cylinder taper limit..	0.0007 inch
Cylinder out-of-round limit	0.0007 inch

Pistons and rings

Piston diameter
  Standard
    1989 .... 3.6194 to 3.6202 inches
    1990 and 1991 .... 3.6195 to 3.6203 inches
    1992 .... 3.6194 to 3.6202 inches
    1993 on .... 3.6195 to 3.6202 inches
Piston ring side clearance
  1989 through 1992
    Top compression ring
      Standard .... 0.0012 to 0.0028 inch
      Service limit .... 0.006 inch
    Second compression ring
      Standard .... 0.0012 to 0.0028 inch
      Service limit .... 0.006 inch
  1993 on
    Top compression ring
      Standard .... 0.0012 to 0.0027 inch
      Service limit .... 0.006 inch
    Second compression ring
      Standard .... 0.0012 to 0.0027 inch
      Service limit .... 0.006 inch
Piston ring end gap
  Top compression ring
    Standard .... 0.008 to 0.014 inch
    Service limit .... Not available
  Second compression ring
    Standard .... 0.010 to 0.016 inch
    Service limit .... Not available
  Oil ring
    Standard .... 0.008 to 0.028 inch
    Service limit .... 0.039 inch
Piston-to-cylinder wall clearance
  Standard.. 0.0023 to 0.0029 inch
  Service limit... 0.006 inch

Crankshaft and connecting rods

Endplay
  Standard
    1989 through 1992... 0.0031 to 0.0071 inch
    1993 on .... 0.0032 to 0.0070 inch
    Service limit (all)... 0.0118 inch
Crankshaft runout.. 0.0012 inch
Main bearing journals
  Diameter
    Standard
      1989 through 1992 .... 2.3597 to 2.3604 inches
      1993 on.. 2.3598 to 2.3604 inches
    Minimum (all).. 2.358 inches
  Out-of-round... 0.0020 inch
Main bearing oil clearance
  Standard.. 0.0010 to 0.0017 inch
  Service limit... 0.0031 inch
Connecting rod journal
  Diameter
    Standard
      1989 through 1992 .... 2.0055 to 2.0061 inches
      1993 on.. 2.0056 to 2.0061 inches
    Minimum .... 2.004 inches
  Out-of-round... 0.0020 inch
Connecting rod bearing oil clearance
  Standard.. 0.0011 to 0.0026 inch
  Service limit... 0.0039 inch

Connecting rod endplay (side clearance)
    Standard.. 0.0044 to 0.0103 inch
    Service limit.. 0.012 inch

Balance shafts

Journal diameters
    Front journal .... 1.6514 to 1.6520 inches
    Center journal .... 1.5727 to 1.5732 inches
    Rear journal .... 0.8247 to 0.8251 inch
Oil clearances
    Front journal .... 0.0020 to 0.0045 inch
    Center journal .... 0.0031 to 0.0057 inch
    Rear journal .... 0.0031 to 0.0057 inch

Cylinder head and valves

Head warpage limit.. 0.006 inch
Head warpage at manifold surfaces... 0.006 inch
Valve seat angle.. 45-degrees
Valve face angle.. 45-degrees
Valve margin width
    Intake .... 0.039 inch
    Exhaust .... 0.059 inch
Valve stem-to-guide clearance
    Standard
        1989 through 1992
            Intake.. 0.0010 to 0.0024 inch
            Exhaust... 0.0012 to 0.0026 inch
        1993 on
            Intake.. 0.0010 to 0.0023 inch
            Exhaust... 0.0012 to 0.0025 inch
    Service limit (all) .... 0.008 inch
Valve length
    1989
        Intake.. 4.3660 inches
        Exhaust... 4.811 inches
    1990 through 1991
        Intake.. 4.4367 inches
        Exhaust... 4.4812 inches
    1992
        Intake.. 4.3660 inches
        Exhaust... 4.4811 inches
    1993 on
        Intake.. 4.4367 inches
        Exhaust... 4.4811 inches
Valve stem diameter
    1989 through 1992
        Intake.. 0.2744 to 0.2750 inch
        Exhaust... 0.2743 to 0.2748 inch
    1993 on
        Intake.. 0.2745 to 0.2750 inch
        Exhaust... 0.2743 to 0.2748 inch
Valve spring
    Free length
        1989 through 1993
            Standard... 1.970 inches
            Minimum... 1.963 inches
        1994
            Standard... 1.955 inches
            Minimum... 1.963 inches
    Out-of-square limit .... 0.069 inch
Valve stem installed height **(dimension L in illustration 11.8)**
    Standard
        Intake.. 1.929 to 1.948 inches
        Exhaust... 1.929 to 1.948 inches
    Service limit
        Intake.. 1.949 to 1.988 inches
        Exhaust... 1.949 to 1.988 inches

2C

Four-cylinder engine (continued)

Cylinder head and valves (continued)

Valve guides (continued)
    Inside diameter
        1989 through 1992
            Intake.. 0.2760 to 0.2768 inch
            Exhaust.. 0.2760 to 0.2768 inch
    Inside diameter
        1993 on
            Intake.. 0.2760 to 0.2767 inch
            Exhaust.. 0.2743 to 0.2767 inch
Rocker shafts
    Diameter
        1989 through 1992.. 0.8252 to 0.8260 inch
        1993 on.. 0.8252 to 0.8259 inch
    Oil clearance
        Standard... 0.0008 to 0.0029 inch
        Service limit.. 0.004 inch
Rocker arms
    Inside diameter
        1989 through 1992.. 0.8268 to 0.8281 inch
        1993 on.. 0.8268 to 0.8280 inch

Torque specifications*

Ft-lbs (unless otherwise indicated)

Main bearing cap bolts... 61 to 65
Connecting rod bearing cap nuts....................................... 48 to 50
Oil jet valves.. 104 to 156 in-lbs
Balance shaft thrust plate bolts... 69 to 95 in-lbs

* Refer to Part A for additional torque specifications.

V6 engine

General

Displacement.. 181 cubic inches (3.0 liters)
Bore .... 3.54 inches
Stroke .... 3.05 inches
Cylinder compression pressure
    Standard.. 164 psi
    Minimum.. 121 psi
Oil pressure
    At 1000 rpm
        1989 through 1992.. 17 to 31 psi
        1993 on.. 13 to 35 psi
    At 3000 rpm.. 53 to 75 psi

Engine block

Cylinder taper limit.. 0.0007 inch
Cylinder out-of-round limit .... 0.0007 inch
Main bearing cap bolt length
    Standard.. 3.35 inches
    Maximum.. 3.37 inches

Pistons and rings

Piston diameter
    Standard
        1989 through 1991.. 3.5411 to 3.5419 inches
        1992 on.. 3.5417 to 3.5429 inches
Piston ring side clearance (top and second compression rings)
    Standard
        1989 through 1992.. 0.0012 to 0.0028 inch
        1993 on.. 0.0012 to 0.0027 inch
    Service limit.. 0.006 inch
Piston ring end gap
    Top compression ring
        1989 through 1992.. 0.008 to 0.014 inch
        1993 on.. 0.008 to 0.013 inch
    Second compression ring
        1989 through 1992.. 0.006 to 0.012 inch
        1993 on.. 0.006 to 0.013 inch

Oil ring
   Standard
      1989 though 1992 .... 0.008 to 0.028 inch
      1993 on... 0.008 to 0.027 inch
   Service limit .... 0.039 inch
Piston-to-cylinder wall clearance
   Standard
      1989 through 1991 .... 0.0019 to 0.0026 inch
      1992 .... 0.0009 to 0.0022 inch
      1993 on... 0.0010 to 0.0020 inch
   Service limit .... 0.006 inch

Crankshaft and connecting rods

Endplay
   Standard... 0.0031 to 0.0111 inch
   Service limit .... 0.0118 inch
Runout
   1989 through 1991 .... 0.0016 inch
   1992 on .... 0.0012 inch
Main bearing journals
   Diameter
      1989 through 1992 .... 2.4385 to 2.4392 inches
      1993 on... 2.4385 to 2.4391 inches
   Out-of-round .... 0.0020 inch
   Oil clearance
      Standard
         1989 through 1992 .... 0.0010 to 0.0015 inch
         1993 on... 0.0010 to 0.0014 inch
      Service limit .... 0.0031 inch
Connecting rod journals
   Diameter
      1989 through 1992 .... 2.0842 to 2.0848 inches
      1993 on... 2.0843 to 2.0848 inches
   Out-of-round .... 0.0020 inch
   Oil clearance
      Standard
         1989 through 1992 .... 0.0009 to 0.0025 inch
         1993 on... 0.0010 to 0.0025 inch
      Service limit .... 0.004 inch
Connecting rod side clearance (endplay)
   Standard
      1989 through 1992 .... 0.0070 to 0.0130 inch
      1993 on... 0.0071 to 0.0129 inch
   Service limit .... 0.016 inch

Cylinder head and valves

Head warpage limit... 0.004 inch
Head warpage at manifold surfaces... 0.004 inch
Valve seat angle.. 45-degrees
Valve face angle.. 45-degrees
Valve margin width
   Intake .... 0.030 to 0.049 inch
   Exhaust
      1989 through 1992 .... 0.047 to 0.071 inch
      1993 on... 0.048 to 0.070 inch
Valve seat width
   1989 through 1992 .... 0.047 to 0.063 inch
   1993 on .... 0.048 to 0.062 inch
Valve stem-to-guide clearance
   Standard
      1989 through 1992
         Intake .... 0.0010 to 0.0024 inch
         Exhaust... 0.0012 to 0.0026 inch
      1993 on
         Intake .... 0.0010 to 0.0023 inch
         Exhaust... 0.0012 to 0.0025 inch
   Service limit .... 0.008 inch

2C

V6 engine (continued)

Cylinder head and valves

Valve length
  Standard
    Intake .... 4.7760 inches
    Exhaust .... 4.8279 inches
  Service limit
    Intake .... 4.7602 inches
    Exhaust .... 4.8122 inches
Valve stem diameter
  Intake .... 0.2744 to 0.2750 inch
  Exhaust .... 0.3159 to 0.3165 inch
Valve spring
  Out-of-square
    1989
      Intake springs
        Inner .... 0.064 inch
        Outer .... 0.070 inch
      Exhaust springs
        Inner .... 0.074 inch
        Outer .... 0.083 inch
    1990 on
      Intake springs
        Inner .... 0.064 inch
        Outer .... 0.070 inch
      Exhaust springs
        Inner .... 0.073 inch
        Outer .... 0.080 inch
Valve stem height **(dimension L in illustration 11.8)**
  Standard
    Intake .... 1.988 to 2.008 inches
    Exhaust .... 1.949 to 1.969 inches
  Service limit
    Intake .... 2.008 to 2.047 inches
    Exhaust .... 1.969 to 2.008 inches
Valve guide inner diameter
  Intake .... 0.2760 to 0.2767 inch
  Exhaust .... 0.3178 to 0.3185 inch

Torque specifications*   **Ft-lbs** (unless otherwise indicated)

Main bearing cap bolts
  Step 1 14
  Step 2 .... Rotate an additional 90-degrees
  Step 3 .... Rotate an additional 45-degrees
Connecting rod bearing cap nuts
  Step 1 22
  Step 2 .... Rotate an additional 90-degrees
Oil baffle plate bolts .... 70 to 95 in-lbs

* Refer to Part B for additional torque specifications.

---

1   General information

Included in this portion of Chapter 2 are the general overhaul procedures for the cylinder head(s) and internal engine components.

The information ranges from advice concerning preparation for an overhaul and the purchase of replacement parts to detailed, step-by-step procedures covering removal and installation of internal engine components and the inspection of parts.

The following Sections have been written based on the assumption the engine has been removed from the vehicle. For information concerning in-vehicle engine repair, as well as removal and installation of the external components necessary for the overhaul, see Part A (four-cylinder engine), or Part B (V6 engine) of this Chapter.

The Specifications included in this Part are only those necessary for the inspection and overhaul procedures which follow. Refer to Parts A and B for additional Specifications.

2   Engine overhaul - general information

It's not always easy to determine when, or if, an engine should be completely overhauled, as a number of factors must be considered.

High mileage isn't necessarily an indication an overhaul is needed, while low mileage doesn't preclude the need for an overhaul. Frequency of servicing is probably the most important consideration. An engine that's had regular and frequent oil and filter changes, as well as other required maintenance, will most likely give many thousands of miles of reliable service. Conversely, a neglected engine may require an overhaul very early in its life.

Excessive oil consumption is an indication that piston rings, valve seals and/or valve guides are in need of attention. Make sure oil leaks aren't responsible before deciding the rings and/or guides are bad. Perform a cylinder compression check to determine the extent of the work required (see Section 3).

Remove the oil pressure sending unit and check the oil pressure with a gauge installed in its place. Compare the results to this Chapter's Specifications. As a general rule, engines should have ten psi of oil pressure for every 1,000 rpm. If the pressure is extremely low, the bearings and/or oil pump are probably worn out.

Loss of power, rough running, knocking or metallic engine noises, excessive valve train noise and high fuel consumption rates may also point to the need for an overhaul, especially if they're all present at the same time. If a complete tune-up doesn't remedy the situation, major mechanical work is the only solution.

An engine overhaul involves restoring the internal parts to the specifications of a new engine. During an overhaul, the piston rings are replaced and the cylinder walls are reconditioned (rebored and/or honed). If a rebore is done by an automotive machine shop, new over-size pistons will also be installed. The main bearings, connecting rod bearings and camshaft bearings are generally replaced with new ones and, if necessary, the crankshaft may be reground to restore the journals. Generally, the valves are serviced as well, since they're usually in less-than-perfect condition at this point. While the engine is being overhauled, other components, such as the starter and alternator, can be rebuilt as well. The end result should be a like-new engine that will give many trouble free miles. **Note:** *Critical cooling system components such as the hoses, drivebelts, thermostat and water pump MUST be replaced with new parts when an engine is overhauled. The radiator should be checked carefully to ensure it isn't clogged or leaking (see Chapter 3). Also, we don't recommend overhauling the oil pump - always install a new one when an engine is rebuilt.*

Before beginning the engine overhaul, read through the entire chapter to familiarize yourself with the scope and requirements of the job. Overhauling an engine isn't particularly difficult, if you follow all of the instructions carefully, have the necessary tools and equipment and pay close attention to all specifications; however, it can be time consuming. Plan on the vehicle being tied up for a minimum of two weeks, especially if parts must be taken to an automotive machine shop for repair or reconditioning. Check on availability of parts and make sure any necessary special tools and equipment are obtained in advance. Most work can be done with typical hand tools, although a number of precision measuring tools are required for inspecting parts to determine if they must be replaced. Often an automotive machine shop will handle the inspection of parts and offer advice concerning reconditioning and replacement. **Note:** *Always wait until the engine has been completely disassembled and all components, especially the engine block, have been inspected before deciding what service and repair operations must be performed by an automotive machine shop. Since the block's condition will be the major factor to consider when determining whether to overhaul the original engine or buy a rebuilt one, never purchase parts or have machine work done on other components until the block has been thoroughly inspected. As a general rule, time is the primary cost of an overhaul, so it doesn't pay to install worn or substandard parts.*

As a final note, to ensure maximum life and minimum trouble from a rebuilt engine, everything must be assembled with care in a spotlessly clean environment.

3   Cylinder compression check

Refer to illustration 3.6

1   A compression check will tell you what mechanical condition the upper end (pistons, rings, valves, head gaskets) of the engine is in. Specifically, it can tell you if the compression is down due to leakage caused by worn piston rings, defective valves and seats or a blown head gasket. **Note:** *The engine must be at normal operating temperature and the battery must be fully charged for this check.*

2   Begin by cleaning the area around the spark plugs before you remove them. Compressed air should be used, if available, otherwise a small brush or even a bicycle tire pump will work. The idea is to prevent dirt from getting into the cylinders as the compression check is being done.

3   Remove all of the spark plugs from the engine (see Chapter 1).

4   Block the throttle wide open.

3.6 A compression gauge with a threaded fitting for the spark plug hole is preferred over the type that require hand pressure to maintain the seal

5   Disable the fuel system by removing the fuel pump fuse (see Chapter 4). Disable the ignition system by detaching the primary (low voltage) wires from the ignition coil (see Chapter 5).

6   Install the compression gauge in the number one spark plug hole **(see illustration)**.

7   Crank the engine over at least seven compression strokes and watch the gauge. The compression should build up quickly in a healthy engine. Low compression on the first stroke, followed by gradually increasing pressure on successive strokes, indicates worn piston rings. A low compression reading on the first stroke, which doesn't build up during successive strokes, indicates leaking valves or a blown head gasket (a cracked head could also be the cause). Deposits on the undersides of the valve heads can also cause low compression. Record the highest gauge reading obtained.

8   Repeat the procedure for the remaining cylinders and compare the results to this Chapter's Specifications.

9   If the readings are below normal, add some engine oil (about three squirts from a plunger-type oil can) to each cylinder, through the spark plug hole, and repeat the test.

10   If the compression increases significantly after the oil is added, the piston rings are definitely worn. If the compression doesn't increase significantly, the leakage is occurring at the valves or head gasket. Leakage past the valves may be caused by burned valve seats and/or faces or warped, cracked or bent valves.

11   If two adjacent cylinders have equally low compression, there's a strong possibility the head gasket between them is blown. The appearance of coolant in the combustion chambers or the crankcase would verify this condition.

12   If one cylinder is about 20-percent lower than the others, and the engine has a slightly rough idle, a worn exhaust lobe on the camshaft could be the cause.

13   If the compression is unusually high, the combustion chambers are probably coated with carbon deposits. If that's the case, the cylinder head(s) should be removed and decarbonized.

14   If compression is way down or varies greatly between cylinders, it would be a good idea to have a leak-down test performed by an automotive repair shop. This test will pinpoint exactly where the leakage is occurring and how severe it is.

4   Engine removal - methods and precautions

If you've decided the engine must be removed for overhaul or major repair work, several preliminary steps should be taken.

Locating a suitable place to work is extremely important. Adequate work space, along with storage space for the vehicle, will be needed. If a shop or garage isn't available, at the very least a flat, level, clean work surface made of concrete or asphalt is required.

Cleaning the engine compartment and engine before beginning

2C

5.6 Label each wire before unplugging the connector

5.18 Location of the gusset plate (arrow), one on each side of the engine, which bolts to the side of the engine block and to the transmission bellhousing

the removal procedure will help keep tools clean and organized.

An engine hoist or A-frame will also be necessary. Make sure the equipment is rated in excess of the combined weight of the engine and its accessories. Safety is of primary importance, considering the potential hazards involved in lifting the engine out of the vehicle.

If the engine is being removed by a novice, a helper should be available. Advice and aid from someone more experienced would also be helpful. There are many instances when one person cannot simultaneously perform all of the operations required when lifting the engine out of the vehicle.

Plan the operation ahead of time. Arrange for or obtain all of the tools and equipment you'll need prior to beginning the job. Some of the equipment necessary to perform engine removal and installation safely and with relative ease are (in addition to an engine hoist) a heavy duty floor jack, complete sets of wrenches and sockets as described in the front of this manual, wooden blocks and plenty of rags and cleaning solvent for mopping up spilled oil, coolant and gasoline. If the hoist must be rented, be sure to arrange for it in advance and perform all of the operations possible without it beforehand. This will save you money and time.

Plan for the vehicle to be out of use for quite a while. A machine shop will be required to perform some of the work which the do-it-yourselfer can't accomplish without special equipment. These shops often have a busy schedule, so it would be a good idea to consult them before removing the engine in order to accurately estimate the amount of time required to rebuild or repair components that may need work.

Always be extremely careful when removing and installing the engine. Serious injury can result from careless actions. Plan ahead, take your time and a job of this nature, although major, can be accomplished successfully.

5   Engine - removal and installation

Refer to illustrations 5.6, 5.18, 5.19a, 5.19b, 5.20, 5.21, 5.22, 5.30a, 5.30b, 5.30c and 5.32

Warning: *Gasoline is extremely flammable, so take extra precautions when you work on any part of the fuel system. Don't smoke or allow open flames or bare light bulbs near the work area, and don't work in a garage where a natural gas-type appliance (such as a water heater or clothes dryer) with a pilot light is present. If you spill any fuel on your skin, rinse it off immediately with soap and water. When you perform any kind of work on the fuel system, wear safety glasses and have a Class B type fire extinguisher on hand. Also, the air conditioning system is under high pressure - have a dealer service department or service station discharge the system before disconnecting any of the hoses or fittings.*

Note: *Read through the following steps carefully and familiarize yourself with the procedure before beginning work. Also at this point it may be helpful to use a penetrating fluid or spray on nuts and bolts that may be difficult to remove, such as exhaust manifolds, bellhousing, engine mounts, etc.*

Removal

1   Refer to Chapter 4 and relieve the fuel system pressure.
2   Disconnect the negative cable from the battery.

5.19a Remove the transmission shift linkage support braces . . .

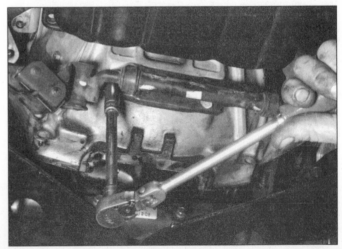

5.19b . . . then unbolt the transmission shift linkage from the bottom of the bellhousing

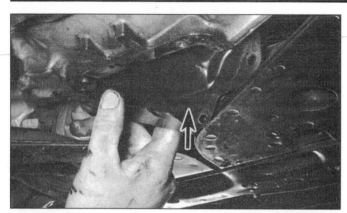

5.20 Remove the inspection/service cover to gain access to the torque converter bolts

5.21 Unbolt the transmission cooler line bracket from the power steering pump bracket

3   Cover the fenders and cowl and remove the hood (see Chapter 11). Special pads are available to protect the fenders, but an old bedspread or blanket will also work.

4   Remove the air cleaner assembly (see Chapter 4), and any fresh air duct work that is used.

5   If you're removing a V6 engine, remove the throttle body and intake air pipe (see Chapter 4).

6   Label the vacuum lines, emissions system hoses, electrical connectors, ground straps and fuel lines to ensure correct reinstallation, then detach them. Pieces of masking tape with numbers or letters written on them work well **(see illustration)**. If there's any possibility of confusion, make a sketch of the engine compartment and clearly label the lines, hoses and wires.

7   Label and detach all coolant hoses from the engine.

8   Remove the coolant reservoir, cooling fan, shroud and radiator (see Chapter 3).

9   Remove the drivebelt(s) and idler, if equipped (see Chapter 1).

10   Disconnect the fuel lines running from the engine to the chassis (see Chapter 4). Plug or cap all open fittings and lines.

11   Disconnect the accelerator linkage (and TV linkage/cruise control cable, if equipped) from the engine (see Chapters 4 and 7).

12   Unbolt the power steering pump and set it aside (see Chapter 10). Leave the lines/hoses attached and make sure the pump is kept in an upright position in the engine compartment.

13   Unbolt the air conditioning compressor (see Chapter 3) and set it aside. Do not disconnect the hoses.

14   If you're removing a V6 engine, unbolt the alternator and mounting strap and set it aside (see Chapter 5).

15   Raise the vehicle and support it securely on jackstands. Drain the cooling system (see Chapter 1).

16   Drain the engine oil and remove the filter (see Chapter 1).

17   Remove the starter (see Chapter 5).

18   Remove the gusset plates from the sides of the engine **(see illustration)**.

19   Remove the shift linkage assembly from under the transmission **(see illustrations)**.

20   Remove the inspection cover from the transmission bellhousing, which will give access to the torque converter **(see illustration)**.

21   Remove the bracket for the transmission cooler lines from the right side of the engine block **(see illustration)**.

22   Remove the crankshaft pulley and reinstall the bolt. Use a socket and a long breaker bar or ratchet to rotate the engine to position the torque converter bolts for removal **(see illustration)**. Remove the torque converter-to-driveplate bolts.

23   Remove the starter (see Chapter 5).

24   Disconnect the exhaust system from the engine (see Chapter 4).

25   Support the transmission with a jack (preferably a transmission jack). If you're not using a transmission jack, position a block of wood on the jack head to prevent damage to the transmission.

26   Attach an engine sling or a length of chain to the lifting brackets on the engine.

27   Roll the hoist into position and connect the sling to it. Take up the slack in the sling or chain, but don't lift the engine. **Warning:** *DO NOT place any part of your body under the engine when it's supported only by a hoist or other lifting device.*

28   Remove the driveshaft(s) (see Chapter 8).

29   Remove the engine mount-to-chassis bolts. Refer to the appropriate Chapter (2A or 2B) for complete illustrations of the engine mounts.

30   Remove the transmission-to-engine bolts **(see illustrations)**.
Note: *Lowering the rear of the transmission, by removal of the rear transmission crossmember, will give easier access to these bolts.*

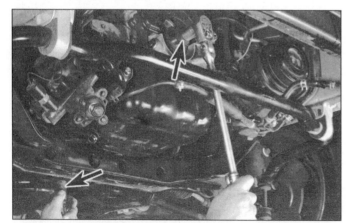

5.22 Use a large ratchet or breaker bar and socket to rotate the torque converter so each bolt can be removed through the inspection cover opening

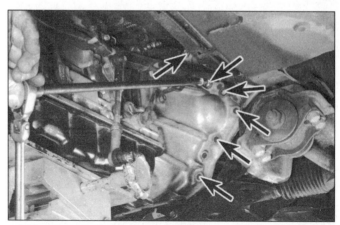

5.30a Use a swivel socket and a long extension to remove the transmission-to-engine bolts (passenger side shown)

5.30b On the drivers side, first remove the heat shield next to the transmission . . .

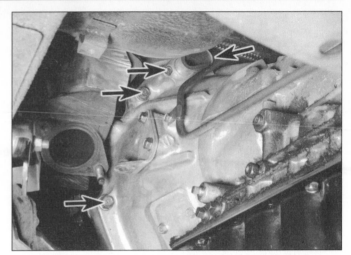

5.30c . . . then remove the bellhousing-to-engine bolts

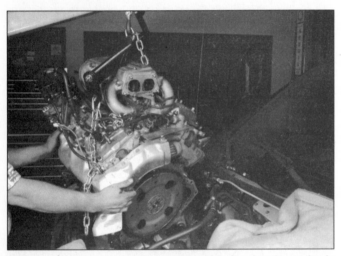

5.32 Engine being removed from the vehicle (turning the engine is necessary for clearance)

Raise and reconnect the crossmember when bolts have been removed to support the transmission in the vehicle.

31   Recheck to be sure nothing is still connecting the engine to the vehicle. Disconnect anything still remaining.

32   Raise the engine slightly to disengage the mounts. Also, slightly raise the jack supporting the transmission. Move the engine forward, disengaging it from the transmission. If the vehicle is equipped with a manual transmission, be sure the clutch pressure plate is clear of the transmission input shaft. If the vehicle is equipped with an automatic transmission, make sure the torque converter stays with the transmission and doesn't stick to the driveplate. Slowly raise the engine out of the engine compartment, turning it sideways, as necessary, for clearance. Check carefully to make sure nothing is hanging up as the hoist is raised **(see illustration)**. **Note:** *The front of the transmission can rest on the vehicle subframe/crossmember, but be sure it is supported in some way.*

33   Once the engine is out of the vehicle, be sure the torque converter (automatic transmission) stays in place (clamp a pair of locking pliers to the bellhousing to keep the converter from sliding out).

34   Lower the engine to the ground and support it with blocks of wood. Remove the clutch and flywheel or driveplate and mount the engine on an engine stand.

Installation

35   Check the engine and transmission mounts. If they're worn or damaged, replace them.

36   If you're working on a manual transmission equipped vehicle, install the clutch and pressure plate (see Chapter 8). Now is a good time to install a new clutch. Apply a dab of high-temperature grease to the input shaft.

37   Carefully lower the engine into the engine compartment and mate it to the transmission. **Caution:** *DO NOT use the bolts to force the transmission and engine together. If you're working on an automatic transmission equipped vehicle, take great care when installing the torque converter, following the procedure outlined in Chapter 7B.* Line up the holes in the engine mounts with the frame and install the bolts, tightening them securely.

38   Add coolant, oil, power steering and transmission fluid as needed (see Chapter 1).

39   Run the engine and check for leaks and proper operation of all accessories, then install the hood and test drive the vehicle.

40   If the air conditioning system was discharged, have it evacuated, recharged and leak tested by the shop that discharged it.

---

6   Engine rebuilding alternatives

The home mechanic is faced with a number of options when performing an engine overhaul. The decision to replace the engine block, piston/connecting rod assemblies and crankshaft depends on a number of factors, with the number one consideration being the condition of the block. Other considerations are cost, access to machine shop facilities, parts availability, time required to complete the project and the extent of prior mechanical experience.

Some of the rebuilding alternatives include:

Individual parts - If the inspection procedures reveal the engine block and most engine components are in reusable condition, purchasing individual parts may be the most economical alternative. The block, crankshaft and piston/connecting rod assemblies should all be inspected carefully. Even if the block shows little wear, the cylinder bores should be surface honed.

Short block - A short block consists of an engine block with a crankshaft and piston/connecting rod assemblies already installed. All new bearings are incorporated and all clearances will be correct. The existing camshaft, valve train components, cylinder head(s) and external parts can be bolted to the short block with little or no machine shop work necessary.

Long block - A long block consists of a short block plus an oil pump, oil pan, cylinder head(s), valve cover(s), camshaft and valve train components, timing sprockets and chain and timing chain cover. All components are installed with new bearings, seals and gaskets incorporated throughout. The installation of manifolds and external parts is all that's necessary.

Give careful thought to which alternative is best for you and dis-

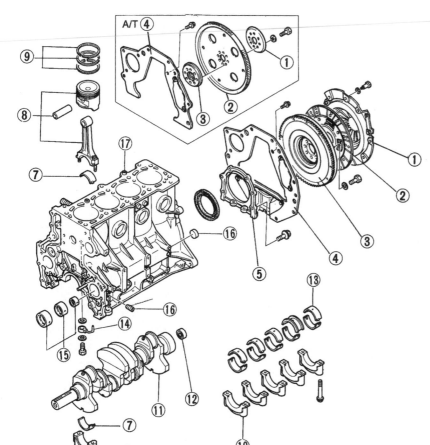

7.5a Exploded view of the four-cylinder engine block and internal components

1   Clutch pressure plate (manual transmission)
1   Bolt plate (automatic transmission)
2   Clutch disc (manual transmission)
2   Driveplate (automatic transmission)
3   Flywheel (manual transmission)
3   Adapter (automatic transmission)
4   End plate
5   Rear main oil seal retainer
6   Connecting rod cap
7   Connecting rod bearing
8   Connecting rod, piston and piston pin
9   Piston rings
10 Main bearing cap
11 Crankshaft
12 Pilot bearing (manual transmission)
13 Main bearing
14 Oil jet
15 Balance shaft bearings
16 Blind plug and screw
17 Cylinder block

2C

cuss the situation with local automotive machine shops, auto parts dealers and experienced rebuilders before ordering or purchasing replacement parts.

7   Engine overhaul - disassembly sequence

Refer to illustrations 7.5a, 7.5b and 7.5c

1   It's much easier to disassemble and work on the engine if it's mounted on a portable engine stand. A stand can often be rented quite cheaply from an equipment rental yard. Before it's mounted on a stand, the flywheel/driveplate should be removed from the engine.

2   If a stand isn't available, it's possible to disassemble the engine with it blocked up on the floor. Be extra careful not to tip or drop the engine when working without a stand.

3   If you're going to obtain a rebuilt engine, all external components must come off first, to be transferred to the replacement engine, just as they will if you're doing a complete engine overhaul yourself. These include:

Alternator and brackets
Power steering pump and brackets
Emissions control components
Distributor, spark plug wires and spark plugs
Thermostat and housing cover
Water pump and bypass pipe
Fuel injection components
Intake/exhaust manifolds
Oil filter
Engine mounts
Clutch and flywheel or driveplate

Note: *When removing the external components from the engine, pay close attention to details that may be helpful or important during instal-*

lation. Note the installed position of gaskets, seals, spacers, pins, brackets, washers, bolts, wiring and other small items.

4   If you're obtaining a short block, which consists of the engine block, crankshaft, pistons and connecting rods all assembled, then the cylinder head(s), oil pan and oil pump will have to be removed as well. See *Engine rebuilding alternatives* for additional information regarding the different possibilities to be considered.

5   If you're planning a complete overhaul, the engine must be disassembled and the internal components removed in the following general order **(see illustrations):**

Four-cylinder engine

Intake and exhaust manifolds
Oil cooler
Valve cover
Cylinder head with camshaft
Oil pan
Oil pick-up tube
Timing chain cover
Balance shafts
Vibration reducing stiffener
Piston/connecting rod assemblies
Rear main oil seal retainer
Crankshaft and main bearings

V6 engine

Intake manifold assembly
Exhaust manifolds and crossover pipe
Oil dipstick and tube
Left and right timing belt covers
Timing belt
Timing belt automatic tensioner and idler pulleys

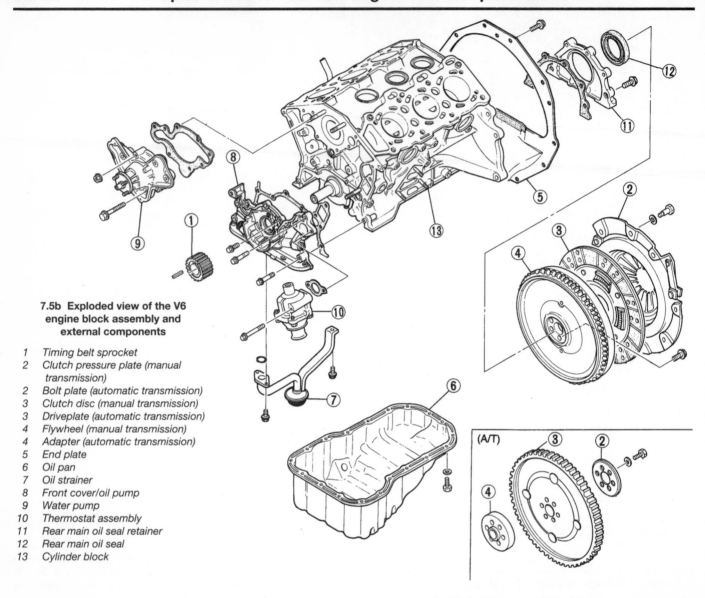

7.5b Exploded view of the V6 engine block assembly and external components

1   Timing belt sprocket
2   Clutch pressure plate (manual transmission)
2   Bolt plate (automatic transmission)
3   Clutch disc (manual transmission)
3   Driveplate (automatic transmission)
4   Flywheel (manual transmission)
4   Adapter (automatic transmission)
5   End plate
6   Oil pan
7   Oil strainer
8   Front cover/oil pump
9   Water pump
10 Thermostat assembly
11 Rear main oil seal retainer
12 Rear main oil seal
13 Cylinder block

Water pump
Oil pan
Oil pump pick-up assembly
Front cover (which includes the oil pump)
End plate
Valve covers
Cylinder heads with camshafts
Piston/connecting rod assemblies
Rear main oil seal retainer
Crankshaft and main bearings

6   Before beginning the disassembly and overhaul procedures, make sure the following items are available. Also, refer to *Engine overhaul - reassembly sequence* for a list of tools and materials needed for engine reassembly.

Common hand tools
Small cardboard boxes or plastic bags for storing parts
Gasket scraper
Ridge reamer
Vibration damper puller
Micrometers
Telescoping gauges
Dial indicator set
Valve spring compressor
Cylinder surfacing hone

Piston ring groove cleaning tool
Electric drill motor
Tap and die set
Wire brushes
Oil gallery brushes
Cleaning solvent

8   Cylinder head - disassembly

Refer to illustrations 8.2, 8.3a, 8.3b and 8.4

Note: *New and rebuilt cylinder heads are commonly available for most engines at dealer parts departments and auto parts stores. Due to the fact that some specialized tools are necessary for the disassembly and inspection procedures, and replacement parts aren't always readily available, it may be more practical and economical for the home mechanic to purchase replacement head(s) rather than taking the time to disassemble, inspect and recondition the original(s).*

1   Cylinder head disassembly involves removal of the intake and exhaust valves and related components. The rocker arm assemblies and camshaft(s) must be removed before beginning the cylinder head disassembly procedure (see Part A or B of this Chapter). Label the parts or store them separately so they can be reinstalled in their original locations.

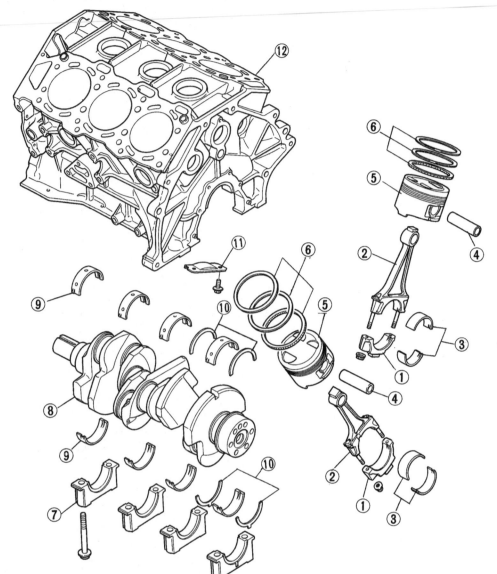

7.5c Exploded view of the V6 engine block and internal components

1 Connecting rod cap
2 Connecting rod
3 Connecting rod bearing
4 Piston pin
5 Piston
6 Piston rings
7 Main bearing cap
8 Crankshaft
9 Main bearing
10 Thrust bearing
11 Oil baffle plate
12 Cylinder block

8.2 A small plastic bag, with an appropriate label, can be used to store the valve train components so they can be kept together and reinstalled in the original position

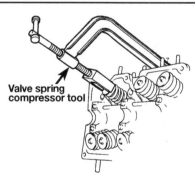

Valve spring compressor tool

8.3a Use a valve spring compressor to compress the springs . . .

2   Before the valves are removed, arrange to label and store them, along with their related components, so they can be kept separate and reinstalled in their original locations **(see illustration)**.

3   Compress the springs on the first valve with a spring compressor and remove the keepers **(see illustrations)**. Carefully release the valve spring compressor and remove the retainer, the spring and the spring seat (if used).

8.3b . . . then remove the keepers from the valve stem with a magnet or small needle-nose pliers

8.4 If the valve won't pull through the guide, deburr the edge of the stem end and the area around the top of the keeper groove with a file or whetstone

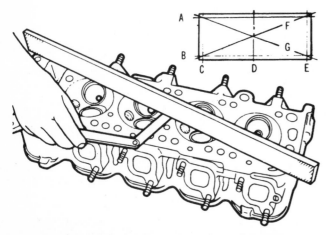

9.12 Check the cylinder head gasket surface for warpage by trying to slip a feeler gauge under the straightedge (see this Chapter's Specifications for the maximum warpage allowed and use a feeler gauge of that thickness)

4   Pull the valve out of the head, then remove the oil seal from the guide. If the valve binds in the guide (won't pull through), push it back into the head and deburr the area around the stem and the keeper groove with a fine file or whetstone **(see illustration)**.

5   Repeat the procedure for the remaining valves. Remember to keep all the parts for each valve together so they can be reinstalled in the same locations.

6   Once the valves and related components have been removed and stored in an organized manner, the head should be thoroughly cleaned and inspected. If a complete engine overhaul is being done, finish the engine disassembly procedures before beginning the cylinder head cleaning and inspection process.

---

9   Cylinder head - cleaning and inspection

---

1   Thorough cleaning of the cylinder head(s) and related valve train components, followed by a detailed inspection, will enable you to decide how much valve service work must be done during the engine overhaul. **Note:** *If the engine was severely overheated, the cylinder head is probably warped.*

Cleaning

2   Scrape all traces of old gasket material and sealant off the head gasket, intake manifold and exhaust manifold mating surfaces. Be very careful not to gouge the cylinder head. Special gasket removal solvents that soften gaskets and make removal much easier are available at auto parts stores.

3   Remove all built-up scale from the coolant passages.

4   Run a stiff wire brush through the various holes to remove deposits that may have formed in them.

5   Run an appropriate size tap into each of the threaded holes to remove corrosion and thread sealant that may be present. If compressed air is available, use it to clear the holes of debris produced by this operation. **Warning:** *Wear eye protection when using compressed air!*

6   Clean the camshaft bearing cap bolt threads with a wire brush.

7   Clean the cylinder head with solvent and dry it thoroughly. Compressed air will speed the drying process and ensure that all holes and recessed areas are clean. **Note:** *Decarbonizing chemicals are available and may prove very useful when cleaning cylinder heads and valve train components. They're very caustic and should be used with caution. Be sure to follow the instructions on the container.*

8   Clean the rocker arms and bearing caps with solvent and dry them thoroughly (don't mix them up during the cleaning process). Compressed air will speed the drying process and can be used to clean out the oil passages.

9   Clean all the valve springs, spring seats, keepers and retainers with solvent and dry them thoroughly. Do the components from one valve at a time to avoid mixing up the parts.

10   Scrape off any heavy deposits that may have formed on the valves, then use a motorized wire brush to remove deposits from the valve heads and stems. Again, make sure the valves don't get mixed up.

Inspection

Refer to illustrations 9.12, 9.14, 9.15, 9.16, 9.17, and 9.18

Note: *Be sure to perform all of the following inspection procedures before concluding machine shop work is required. Make a list of the items that need attention.*

Cylinder head

11   Inspect the head very carefully for cracks, evidence of coolant leakage and other damage. If cracks are found, check with an automotive machine shop concerning repair. If repair isn't possible, a new cylinder head should be obtained.

12   Using a straightedge and feeler gauge, check the head gasket mating surface for warpage **(see illustration)**. If the warpage exceeds the limit in this Chapter's Specifications, it can be resurfaced at an automotive machine shop. **Note:** *If the V6 engine heads are resurfaced, the intake manifold flanges will also require machining.*

13   Examine the valve seats in each of the combustion chambers. If they're pitted, cracked or burned, the head will require valve service that's beyond the scope of the home mechanic.

14   Check the valve stem-to-guide clearance by measuring the lateral movement of the valve stem with a dial indicator attached securely to the head **(see illustration)**. The valve must be in the guide and approximately 1/16-inch off the seat. The total valve stem movement indicated by the gauge needle must be divided by two to obtain the ac-

9.14 A dial indicator can be used to determine the valve stem-to-guide clearance (move the valve stem as indicated by the arrows)

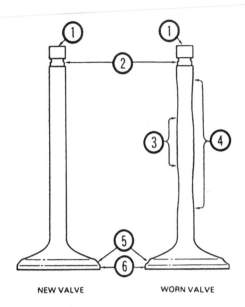

9.15 Check for valve wear at the points shown here

1	Valve tip	4	Stem (most worn area)
2	Keeper groove	5	Valve face
3	Stem (least worn area)	6	Margin

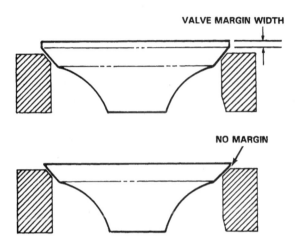

9.16 The margin width on each valve must be as specified (if no margin exists, the valve cannot be reused)

tual clearance. After this is done, if there's still some doubt regarding the condition of the valve guides, they should be checked by an automotive machine shop (the cost should be minimal).

Valves

15   Carefully inspect each valve face for uneven wear, deformation, cracks, pits and burned areas. Check the valve stem for scuffing and galling and the neck for cracks. Rotate the valve and check for any obvious indication that it's bent. Look for pits and excessive wear on the end of the stem **(see illustration)**. The presence of any of these conditions indicates the need for valve service by an automotive machine shop.

16   Measure the margin width on each valve **(see illustration)**. Any valve with a margin narrower than specified in this Chapter will have to be replaced with a new one.

Valve components

17   Check each valve spring for wear (on the ends) and pits. Measure the free length and compare it to this Chapter's Specifications **(see illustration)**. Any springs that are shorter than specified have sagged and shouldn't be reused. The tension of all springs should be checked with a special fixture before deciding they're suitable for use in a rebuilt engine (take the springs to an automotive machine shop for this check).

18   Stand each spring on a flat surface and check it for squareness **(see illustration)**. If any of the springs are distorted or sagged, replace all of them with new parts.

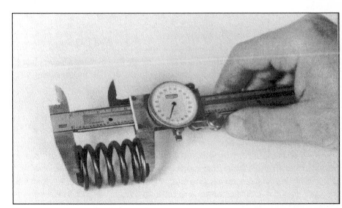

9.17 Measure the free length of each valve spring with a dial or vernier caliper

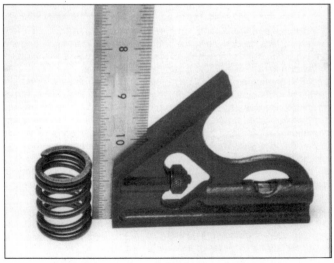

9.18 Check each valve spring for squareness

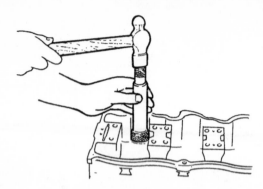

11.4 Installation of valve guide seals. Select a driver, socket or pipe of the proper diameter so the seal and guide are not damaged during installation

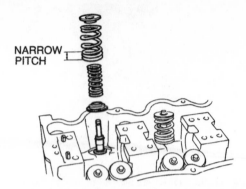

11.6a Exploded view of a typical valve shim, spring(s) and keeper assembly - be sure to install the springs with the narrow pitch coils at the bottom

11.6b Apply a small dab of grease to each keeper as shown here before installation - it'll hold them in place on the valve stem as the spring is released

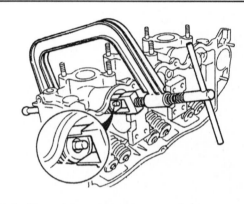

11.6c View of the valve spring reassembly set-up using a C-clamp type valve spring tool

19   Check the spring retainers and keepers for obvious wear and cracks. Any questionable parts should be replaced with new ones, as extensive damage will occur if they fail during engine operation.

20   If the inspection process indicates the valve components are in generally poor condition and worn beyond the limits specified, which is usually the case in an engine that's being overhauled, reassemble the valves in the cylinder head and refer to Section 10 for valve servicing recommendations.

10   Valves - servicing

1   Because of the complex nature of the job and the special tools and equipment needed, servicing of the valves, the valve seats and the valve guides, commonly known as a valve job, should be done by a professional.

2   The home mechanic can remove and disassemble the head, do the initial cleaning and inspection, then reassemble and deliver it to a dealer service department or an automotive machine shop for the actual service work. Doing the inspection will enable you to see what condition the head and valvetrain components are in and will ensure that you know what work and new parts are required when dealing with an automotive machine shop.

3   The dealer service department, or automotive machine shop, will remove the valves and springs, recondition or replace the valves and valve seats, recondition the valve guides, check and replace the valve springs, rotators, spring retainers and keepers (as necessary), replace the valve seals with new ones, reassemble the valve components and make sure the installed spring height is correct. The cylinder head gasket surface will also be resurfaced if it's warped.

4   After the valve job has been performed by a professional, the head will be in like new condition. When the head is returned, be sure

to clean it again before installation on the engine to remove any metal particles and abrasive grit that may still be present from the valve service or head resurfacing operations. Use compressed air, if available, to blow out all the oil holes and passages.

11   Cylinder head - reassembly

Refer to illustrations 11.4, 11.6a, 11.6b, 11.6c and 11.8

1   Regardless of whether or not the head was sent to an automotive repair shop for valve servicing, make sure it's clean before beginning reassembly.

2   If the head was sent out for valve servicing, the valves and related components will already be in place. Begin the reassembly procedure with Step 8.

3   Install the spring seats before the valve seals.

4   Install new seals on each of the valve guides. Using a hammer and a deep socket or seal installation tool, gently tap each seal into place until it's completely seated on the guide **(see illustration)**. Don't twist or cock the seals during installation or they won't seal properly on the valve stems.

5   Beginning at one end of the head, lubricate and install the first valve. Apply moly-base grease or clean engine oil to the valve stem.

6   Position the valve springs (and shims, if used) over the valves. Compress the springs with a valve spring compressor and carefully install the keepers in the groove, then slowly release the compressor and make sure the keepers seat properly. Apply a small dab of grease to each keeper to hold it in place if necessary **(see illustrations)**.

7   Repeat the procedure for the remaining valves. Be sure to return the components to their original locations - don't mix them up!

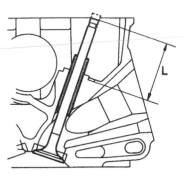

11.8 Be sure to check the valve stem installed height (the distance from the spring seat to the top of the valve stem)

12.1 A ridge reamer is required to remove the ridge from the top of each cylinder - do this before removing the pistons!

12.3 Check the connecting rod side clearance (endplay) with a feeler gauge

12.6 To prevent damage to the crankshaft journals and cylinder walls, slip sections of rubber or plastic hose over the rod bolts before removing the pistons

8   Check the installed valve stem height (dimension L) with a vernier or dial caliper **(see illustration)**. If the head was sent out for service work, the installed height should be correct (but don't automatically assume it is). The measurement is taken from the spring seat to the top of the valve stem. If the height is greater than listed in this Chapter's Specifications, shims can be added under the springs to correct it. **Caution:** *Do not, under any circumstances, shim the springs to the point where the installed height is less than specified.*

9   If you're working on a four-cylinder engine, apply moly-base grease to the rocker arm faces, the camshaft and the rocker shafts, then install the camshaft, rocker arms and shafts (refer to Chapter 2A).

10   If you're working on a V6 engine, install the camshafts, hydraulic lash adjusters and rocker arm assemblies onto the head. **Note:** *Check the head bolt stretch limitations as described in Chapter 2B.*

12   Pistons and connecting rods - removal

Refer to illustrations 12.1, 12.3 and 12.6

Note: *Prior to removing the piston/connecting rod assemblies, remove the cylinder head(s), the oil pan and the oil pump by referring to the appropriate Sections in Parts A or B of Chapter 2.*

1   Use your fingernail to feel if a ridge has formed at the upper limit of ring travel (about 1/4-inch down from the top of each cylinder). If carbon deposits or cylinder wear have produced ridges, they must be completely removed with a special tool **(see illustration)**. Follow the manufacturer's instructions provided with the tool. Failure to remove the ridges before attempting to remove the piston/connecting rod assemblies may result in piston breakage.

2   After the cylinder ridges have been removed, turn the engine upside-down so the crankshaft is facing up.

3   Before the connecting rods are removed, check the connecting rod side clearance (endplay) with feeler gauges. Slide them between the first connecting rod and the crankshaft throw until the play is removed **(see illustration)**. The endplay is equal to the thickness of the feeler gauge(s). If the endplay exceeds the service limit, new connecting rods will be required. If new rods (or a new crankshaft) are installed, the endplay may fall under the minimum listed in this Chapter's Specifications (if it does, the rods will have to be machined to restore it - consult an automotive machine shop for advice if necessary). Repeat the procedure for the remaining connecting rods.

4   Check the connecting rods and caps for identification marks. If they aren't plainly marked, use a small center-punch to make the appropriate number of indentations on each rod and cap (1, 2, 3, etc., depending on the engine type and cylinder they're associated with).

5   Loosen each of the connecting rod cap nuts 1/2-turn at a time until they can be removed by hand. Remove the number one connecting rod cap and bearing insert. Don't drop the bearing insert out of the cap.

6   Slip a short length of plastic or rubber hose over each connecting rod cap bolt to protect the crankshaft journal and cylinder wall as the piston is removed **(see illustration)**.

7   Remove the bearing insert and push the connecting rod/piston assembly out through the top of the engine. Use a wooden or plastic hammer handle to push on the upper bearing surface in the connecting rod. If resistance is felt, double-check to make sure all of the ridge was removed from the cylinder.

2C

13.1 Checking crankshaft endplay with a dial indicator

8   Repeat the procedure for the remaining cylinders.

9   After removal, reassemble the connecting rod caps and bearing inserts in their respective connecting rods and install the cap nuts finger tight. Leaving the old bearing inserts in place until reassembly will help prevent the connecting rod bearing surfaces from being accidentally nicked or gouged.

10   Don't separate the pistons from the connecting rods (see Section 17 for additional information).

13   Crankshaft and balance shafts - removal

Note: *It's assumed the flywheel or driveplate, crankshaft balancer/vibration damper, balance shafts chain, timing chain or belt, oil pan, oil pump and piston/connecting rod assemblies have already been removed. The rear main oil seal housing must be unbolted and separated from the block before proceeding with crankshaft removal.*

Crankshaft
Refer to illustrations 13.1 and 13.4

1   Before the crankshaft is removed, check the endplay. Mount a dial indicator with the stem in line with the crankshaft and touching one of the crank throws **(see illustration)**.

2   Push the crankshaft all the way to the rear and zero the dial indicator. Next, pry the crankshaft to the front as far as possible and check the reading on the dial indicator. The distance it moves is the

endplay. If it's greater than specified in this Chapter, check the crankshaft thrust surfaces for wear. If no wear is evident, new main bearings should correct the endplay.

3   If a dial indicator isn't available, feeler gauges can be used. Gently pry or push the crankshaft all the way to the front of the engine. Slip feeler gauges between the crankshaft and the front face of the thrust main bearing to determine the clearance.

4   Check the main bearing caps to see if they're marked to indicate their locations. They should be numbered consecutively from the front of the engine to the rear. If they aren't, mark them with number stamping dies or a center-punch **(see illustration)**. Main bearing caps generally have a cast-in arrow, which points to the front of the engine. Loosen the main bearing cap bolts 1/4-turn at a time each, until they can be removed by hand. Note if any stud bolts are used and make sure they're returned to their original locations when the crankshaft is reinstalled.

5   Gently tap the caps with a soft-face hammer, then separate them from the engine block. If necessary, use the bolts as levers to remove the caps. Try not to drop the bearing inserts if they come out with the caps.

6   Carefully lift the crankshaft out of the engine. It may be a good idea to have an assistant available, since the crankshaft is quite heavy. With the bearing inserts in place in the engine block and main bearing caps, return the caps to their respective locations on the engine block and tighten the bolts finger tight. **Caution:** *Before reinstalling the main bearing cap bolts, measure the length of the bolts and compare your findings with the value listed in this Chapter's Specifications (V6 engine only). Replace any bolt that has stretched beyond the maximum allowable length.*

Balance shafts (four-cylinder engine only)
Refer to illustrations 13.7 and 13.8

7   Remove the bolts from the balance shaft thrust plates **(see illustration)**.

8   Carefully pull the balance shafts out of the engine block **(see illustration)**. **Caution:** *Pull the shafts straight out, taking care not to damage the bushings. Mark the balance shafts (left for the driver's side, right for the passenger side) so they can be returned to their original locations.*

14   Engine block - cleaning

Refer to illustrations 14.4a, 14.4b, 14.8 and 14.10

1   Remove the main bearing caps and separate the bearing inserts

13.4 Use a center-punch or number stamping dies to mark the main bearing caps to ensure installation in their original locations on the block (make the punch marks near one of the bolt heads)

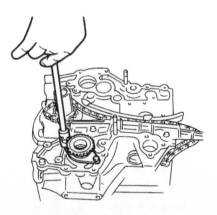

13.7 Remove the two bolts from the balance shaft thrust plate . . .

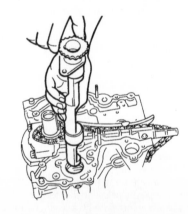

13.8 . . . then carefully withdraw the balance shaft

14.4a A hammer and a large punch can be used to knock the core plugs sideways in their bores

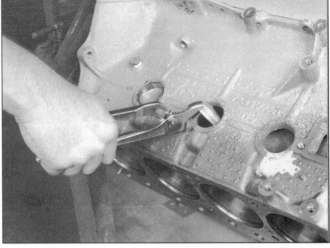

14.4b Pull the core plugs from the block with pliers

from the caps and the engine block. Tag the bearings, indicating which cylinder they were removed from and whether they were in the cap or the block, then set them aside.

2   Using a gasket scraper, remove all traces of gasket material from the engine block. Be very careful not to nick or gouge the gasket sealing surfaces.

3   Remove all of the covers and threaded oil gallery plugs from the block. The plugs are usually very tight - they may have to be drilled out and the holes retapped. Use new plugs when the engine is reassembled.

4   Remove the core plugs from the engine block. To do this, knock one side of the plug into the block with a hammer and a punch, then grasp them with large pliers and pull them out. **(see illustrations)**

5   If the engine is extremely dirty, it should be taken to an automotive machine shop to be steam cleaned or hot tanked.

6   After the block is returned, clean all oil holes and oil galleries one more time. Brushes specifically designed for this purpose are available at most auto parts stores. Flush the passages with warm water until the water runs clear, dry the block thoroughly and wipe all machined surfaces with a light, rust preventive oil. If you have access to compressed air, use it to speed the drying process and blow out all the oil holes and galleries. **Warning:** *Wear eye protection when using compressed air!*

7   If the block isn't extremely dirty or sludged up, you can do an adequate cleaning job with hot soapy water and a stiff brush. Take plenty of time and do a thorough job. Regardless of the cleaning method used, be sure to clean all oil holes and galleries very thoroughly, dry the block completely and coat all machined surfaces with light oil.

8   The threaded holes in the block must be clean to ensure accurate torque readings during reassembly. Run the proper size tap into each of the holes to remove rust, corrosion, thread sealant or sludge and restore damaged threads **(see illustration)**. If possible, use compressed air to clear the holes of debris produced by this operation. Now is a good time to clean the threads on the head bolts and the main bearing cap bolts as well.

9   Reinstall the main bearing caps and tighten the bolts finger tight.

10   After coating the sealing surfaces of the new core plugs with Permatex no. 2 sealant (or equivalent), install them in the engine block **(see illustration)**. Make sure they're driven in straight and seated properly or leakage could result. Special tools are available for this purpose, but a large socket, with an outside diameter that will just slip into the core plug, a 1/2-inch drive extension and a hammer will work just as well.

11   Apply non-hardening sealant (such as Permatex no. 2 or Teflon pipe sealant) to the new oil gallery plugs and thread them into the holes in the block. Make sure they're tightened securely.

2C

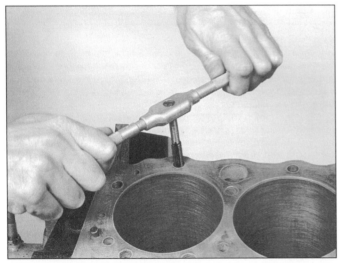

14.8 All bolt holes in the block - particularly the main bearing cap and head bolt holes - should be cleaned and restored with a tap (be sure to remove debris from the holes after this is done)

14.10 A large socket on an extension can be used to drive the new core plugs into the bores

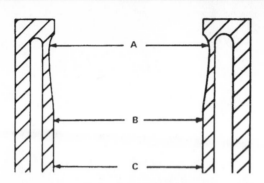

15.4a Measure the diameter of each cylinder just under the wear ridge (A), at the center (B) and at the bottom (C)

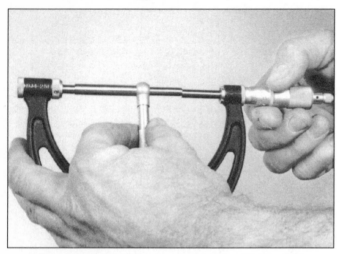

15.4c The gauge is then measured with a micrometer to determine the bore size

12   If the engine isn't going to be reassembled right away, cover it with a large plastic trash bag to keep it clean.

15   Engine block - inspection

Refer to illustrations 15.4a, 15.4b and 15.4c

1   Before the block is inspected, it should be cleaned as described in Section 14.

2   Visually check the block for cracks, rust and corrosion. Look for stripped threads in the threaded holes. It's also a good idea to have the block checked for hidden cracks by an automotive machine shop that has the special equipment to do this type of work. If defects are found, have the block repaired, if possible, or replaced.

3   Check the cylinder bores for scuffing and scoring.

4   Measure the diameter of each cylinder at the top (just under the ridge area), center and bottom of the cylinder bore, parallel to the crankshaft axis **(see illustrations)**. **Note:** *These measurements should not be made with the block mounted on an engine stand - the cylinders will be distorted and the measurements will be inaccurate.*

5   Next, measure each cylinder's diameter at the same three locations across the crankshaft axis. Compare the results to this Chapter's Specifications.

6   If the required precision measuring tools aren't available, the piston-to-cylinder clearances can be obtained, though not quite as accurately, using feeler gauge stock. Feeler gauge stock comes in 12-inch lengths and various thicknesses and is generally available at auto parts stores.

7   To check the clearance, select a feeler gauge and slip it into the cylinder along with the matching piston. The piston must be posi-

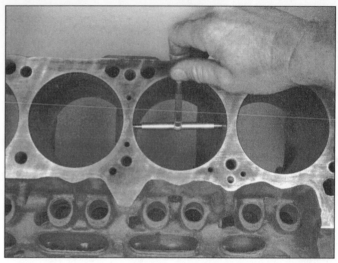

15.4b The ability to "feel" when the telescoping gauge is at the correct point will be developed over time, so work slowly and repeat the check until you're satisfied the bore measurement is accurate

tioned exactly as it normally would be. The feeler gauge must be between the piston and cylinder on one of the thrust faces (90-degrees to the piston pin bore).

8   The piston should slip through the cylinder (with the feeler gauge in place) with moderate pressure.

9   If it falls through or slides through easily, the clearance is excessive and a new piston will be required. If the piston binds at the lower end of the cylinder and is loose toward the top, the cylinder is tapered. If tight spots are encountered as the piston/feeler gauge is rotated in the cylinder, the cylinder is out-of-round.

10   Repeat the procedure for the remaining pistons and cylinders.

11   If the cylinder walls are badly scuffed or scored, or if they're out-of-round or tapered beyond the limits given in this Chapter's Specifications, have the engine block rebored and honed at an automotive machine shop. If a rebore is done, oversize pistons and rings will be required.

12   If the cylinders are in reasonably good condition and not worn to the outside of the limits, and if the piston-to-cylinder clearances can be maintained properly, they don't have to be rebored. Honing is all that's necessary (see Section 16).

16   Cylinder honing

Refer to illustrations 16.3a and 16.3b

1   Prior to engine reassembly, the cylinder bores must be honed so the new piston rings will seat correctly and provide the best possible combustion chamber seal. **Note:** *If you don't have the tools or don't want to tackle the honing operation, most automotive machine shops will do it for a reasonable fee.*

2   Before honing the cylinders, install the main bearing caps and tighten the bolts to the specified torque.

3   Two types of cylinder hones are commonly available - the flex hone or "bottle-brush" type and the more traditional surfacing hone with spring-loaded stones. Both will do the job, but for the less experienced mechanic the "bottle brush" hone will probably be easier to use. You'll also need some honing oil (kerosene will work if honing oil isn't available), rags and an electric drill motor. Proceed as follows:

a)   Mount the hone in the drill motor, compress the stones and slip it into the first cylinder **(see illustration)**. Be sure to wear safety goggles or a face shield!

b)   Lubricate the cylinder with plenty of honing oil, turn on the drill and move the hone up-and-down in the cylinder at a pace that will produce a fine crosshatch pattern on the cylinder walls. Ideally, the crosshatch lines should intersect at approximately a 60-

16.3a A "bottle brush" hone will produce better results if you've never honed cylinders before

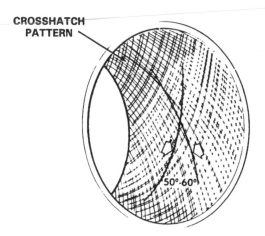

16.3b The cylinder hone should leave a smooth, crosshatch pattern with the lines intersecting at approximately a 60-degree angle

2C

17.4a The piston ring grooves can be cleaned with a special tool, as shown here, . . .

17.4b . . . or a section of a broken ring

degree angle **(see illustration)**. Be sure to use plenty of lubricant and don't take off any more material than is absolutely necessary to produce the desired finish. **Note:** *Piston ring manufacturers may specify a smaller crosshatch angle than the traditional 60-degrees - read and follow any instructions included with the new rings.*

  c) Don't withdraw the hone from the cylinder while it's running. Instead, shut off the drill and continue moving the hone up-and-down in the cylinder until it comes to a complete stop, then compress the stones and withdraw the hone. If you're using a -bottle brush" type hone, stop the drill motor, then turn the chuck in the normal direction of rotation while withdrawing the hone from the cylinder.

  d) Wipe the oil out of the cylinder and repeat the procedure for the remaining cylinders.

4   After the honing job is complete, chamfer the top edges of the cylinder bores with a small file so the rings won't catch when the pistons are installed. Be very careful not to nick the cylinder walls with the end of the file.

5   The entire engine block must be washed again very thoroughly with warm, soapy water to remove all traces of the abrasive grit produced during the honing operation. **Note:** *The bores can be considered clean when a lint-free white cloth - dampened with clean engine oil- used to wipe them out doesn't pick up any more honing residue, which will show up as gray areas on the cloth. Be sure to run a brush through all oil holes and galleries and flush them with running water.*

6   After rinsing, dry the block and apply a coat of light rust preven-

tive oil to all machined surfaces. Wrap the block in a plastic trash bag to keep it clean and set it aside until reassembly.

17 Pistons and connecting rods - inspection

Refer to illustrations 17.4a, 17,4b, 17.10 and 17.11

1   Before the inspection process can be carried out, the piston/connecting rod assemblies must be cleaned and the original piston rings removed from the pistons. **Note:** *Always use new piston rings when the engine is reassembled.*

2   Using a piston ring expander tool, carefully remove the rings from the pistons. Be careful not to nick or gouge the pistons in the process.

3   Scrape all traces of carbon from the top of the piston. A hand held wire brush or a piece of fine emery cloth can be used once the majority of the deposits have been scraped away. Do not, under any circumstances, use a wire brush mounted in a drill motor to remove deposits from the pistons. The piston material is soft and may be eroded away by the wire brush.

4   Use a piston ring groove cleaning tool to remove carbon deposits from the ring grooves. If a tool isn't available, a piece broken off the old ring will do the job. Be very careful to remove only the carbon deposits - don't remove any metal and do not nick or scratch the sides of the ring grooves **(see illustrations)**.

5   Once the deposits have been removed, clean the piston/rod assemblies with solvent and dry them with compressed air (if available).

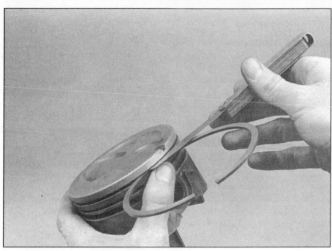

17.10 Check the ring side clearance with a feeler gauge at several points around the groove

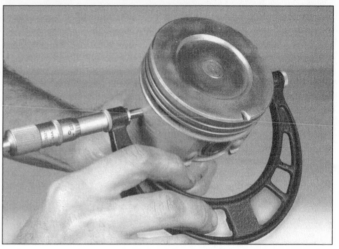

17.11 Measure the piston diameter at a 90-degree angle to the piston pin and in line with it

18.1 The oil holes should be chamfered so sharp edges don't gouge or scratch the new bearings

Warning: *Wear eye protection.* Make sure the oil return holes in the back sides of the ring grooves are clear.

6   If the pistons and cylinder walls aren't damaged or worn excessively, and if the engine block isn't rebored, new pistons won't be necessary. Normal piston wear appears as even vertical wear on the piston thrust surfaces and slight looseness of the top ring in its groove. New piston rings, however, should always be used when an engine is rebuilt.

7   Carefully inspect each piston for cracks around the skirt, at the pin bosses and at the ring lands.

8   Look for scoring and scuffing on the thrust faces of the skirt, holes in the piston crown and burned areas at the edge of the crown. If the skirt is scored or scuffed, the engine may have been suffering from overheating and/or abnormal combustion, which caused excessively high operating temperatures. The cooling and lubrication systems should be checked thoroughly. A hole in the piston crown is an indication that abnormal combustion (pre-ignition) was occurring. Burned areas at the edge of the piston crown are usually evidence of spark knock (detonation). If any of the above problems exist, the causes must be corrected or the damage will occur again. The causes may include intake air leaks, incorrect fuel/air mixture, low octane fuel, ignition timing and EGR system malfunctions.

9   Corrosion of the piston, in the form of small pits, indicates coolant is leaking into the combustion chamber and/or the crankcase. Again, the cause must be corrected or the problem may persist in the rebuilt engine.

10   Measure the piston ring side clearance by laying a new piston ring in each ring groove and slipping a feeler gauge in beside it **(see illustration)**. Check the clearance at three or four locations around each groove. Be sure to use the correct ring for each groove - they are different. If the side clearance is greater than specified in this Chapter, new pistons will have to be used.

11   Check the piston-to-bore clearance by measuring the bore (see Section 15) and the piston diameter. Make sure the pistons and bores are correctly matched. Measure the piston across the skirt, at a 90-degree angle to the piston pin **(see illustration)** below the axis of the piston pin.

12   Subtract the piston diameter from the bore diameter to obtain the clearance. If it's greater than listed in this Chapter's Specifications, the block will have to be rebored and new pistons and rings installed.

13   Check the piston-to-rod clearance by twisting the piston and rod in opposite directions. Any noticeable play indicates excessive wear, which must be corrected. The piston/connecting rod assemblies should be taken to an automotive machine shop to have the pistons and rods re-sized and new pins installed.

14   If the pistons must be removed from the connecting rods for any reason, they should be taken to an automotive machine shop. While they are there have the connecting rods checked for bend and twist, since automotive machine shops have special equipment for this purpose. **Note:** *Unless new pistons and/or connecting rods must be installed, do not disassemble the pistons and connecting rods.*

15   Check the connecting rods for cracks and other damage. Temporarily remove the rod caps, lift out the old bearing inserts, wipe the rod and cap bearing surfaces clean and inspect them for nicks, gouges and scratches. After checking the rods, replace the old bearings, slip the caps into place and tighten the nuts finger tight. **Note:** *If the engine is being rebuilt because of a connecting rod knock, be sure to install new rods.*

18   Crankshaft and balance shafts - inspection

Crankshaft

Refer to illustrations 18.1, 18.2, 18.4, 18.6 and 18.8

1   Remove all burrs from the crankshaft oil holes with a stone, file or scraper **(see illustration)**.

2   Clean the crankshaft with solvent and dry it with compressed air (if available). **Warning:** *Wear eye protection when using compressed air.* Be sure to clean the oil holes with a stiff brush **(see illustration)** and flush them with solvent.

3   Check the main and connecting rod bearing journals for uneven wear, scoring, pits and cracks.

4   Rub a penny across each journal several times **(see illustration)**.

18.2 Use a wire or stiff plastic bristle brush to clean the oil passages in the crankshaft

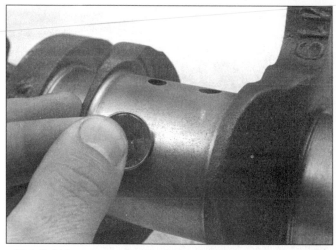

18.4 Rubbing a penny lengthwise on each journal will reveal its condition - if copper rubs off and is embedded in the crankshaft, the journals should be reground

18.6 Measure the diameter of each crankshaft journal at several points to detect taper and out-of-round conditions

18.8 If the seals have worn grooves in the crankshaft journals, or if the seal contact surfaces are nicked or scratched, the new seals will leak

If a journal picks up copper from the penny, it's too rough and must be reground.

5   Check the rest of the crankshaft for cracks and other damage. It should be magnafluxed to reveal hidden cracks - an automotive machine shop will handle the procedure.

6   Using a micrometer, measure the diameter of the main and connecting rod journals and compare the results to this Chapter's Specifications **(see illustration)**. By measuring the diameter at a number of points around each journal's circumference, you'll be able to determine whether or not the journal is out-of-round. Take the measurement at each end of the journal, near the crank throws, to determine if the journal is tapered.

7   If the crankshaft journals are damaged, tapered, out-of-round or worn beyond the limits given in the Specifications, have the crankshaft reground by an automotive machine shop. Be sure to use the correct size bearing inserts if the crankshaft is reconditioned.

8   Check the oil seal journals at each end of the crankshaft for wear and damage. If the seal has worn a groove in the journal, or if it's nicked or scratched **(see illustration)**, the new seal may leak when the engine is reassembled. In some cases, an automotive machine shop may be able to repair the journal by pressing on a thin sleeve. If repair isn't feasible, a new or different crankshaft should be installed.

9   Refer to Section 19 and examine the main and rod bearing inserts.

Balance shafts (four-cylinder engine only)

10   Check the journals of the balance shafts for signs of wear, scuffing and overheating (blue spots). Check the bushings in the cylinder block for the same conditions. If any undesirable conditions exist, the balance shafts and bushings must be replaced. Due to the special tools required to remove the balance shaft bushings and install the new ones, this job must be left to an automotive machine shop.

11   Using a micrometer, measure the diameter of the balance shaft journals and record these figures. Then measure the inside diameter of the corresponding bushings using a telescoping gauge and micrometer (similar to the technique shown in illustrations 15.4b and 15.4c). Subtract the diameter of each balance shaft journal from the inside diameter of its corresponding bushing to calculate the oil clearance. Compare your findings with the values listed in this Chapter's Specifications. If any of the oil clearances are excessive, compare the measurements of the balance shaft journals with the values listed in this Chapter's Specifications. If the journal diameters are within the specified range, have new balance shaft bushings installed.

---

19   Main and connecting rod bearings - inspection

Refer to illustration 19.1

1   Even though the main and connecting rod bearings should be replaced with new ones during the engine overhaul, the old bearings

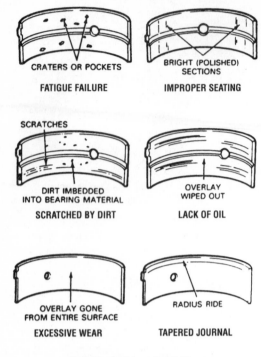

CRATERS OR POCKETS

FATIGUE FAILURE

BRIGHT (POLISHED) SECTIONS

IMPROPER SEATING

SCRATCHES

DIRT IMBEDDED INTO BEARING MATERIAL

SCRATCHED BY DIRT

OVERLAY WIPED OUT

LACK OF OIL

OVERLAY GONE FROM ENTIRE SURFACE

EXCESSIVE WEAR

RADIUS RIDE

TAPERED JOURNAL

19.1 Typical bearing failures

should be retained for close examination, as they may reveal valuable information about the condition of the engine **(see illustration)**.

2   Bearing failure occurs because of lack of lubrication, the presence of dirt or other foreign particles, overloading the engine and corrosion. Regardless of the cause of bearing failure, it must be corrected before the engine is reassembled to prevent it from happening again.

3   When examining the bearings, remove them from the engine block, the main bearing caps, the connecting rods and the rod caps and lay them out on a clean surface in the same general position as their location in the engine. This will enable you to match any bearing problems with the corresponding crankshaft journal.

4   Dirt and other foreign particles get into the engine in a variety of ways. It may be left in the engine during assembly, or it may pass through filters or the PCV system. It may get into the oil, and from there into the bearings. Metal chips from machining operations and normal engine wear are often present. Abrasives are sometimes left in engine components after reconditioning, especially when parts aren't thoroughly cleaned using the proper cleaning methods. Whatever the source, these foreign objects often end up embedded in the soft bearing material and are easily recognized. Large particles won't embed in the bearing and will score or gouge the bearing and journal. The best prevention for this cause of bearing failure is to clean all parts thoroughly and keep everything spotlessly clean during engine assembly. Frequent and regular engine oil and filter changes are also recommended.

5   Lack of lubrication (or lubrication breakdown) has a number of interrelated causes. Excessive heat (which thins the oil), overloading (which squeezes the oil from the bearing face) and oil leakage or throw off (from excessive bearing clearances, worn oil pump or high engine speeds) all contribute to lubrication breakdown. Blocked oil passages, which usually are the result of misaligned oil holes in a bearing shell, will also oil starve a bearing and destroy it. When lack of lubrication is the cause of bearing failure, the bearing material is wiped or extruded from the steel backing of the bearing. Temperatures may increase to the point where the steel backing turns blue from overheating.

6   Driving habits can have a definite effect on bearing life. Full throttle, low speed operation (lugging the engine) puts very high loads on bearings, which tends to squeeze out the oil film. These loads cause

the bearings to flex, which produces fine cracks in the bearing face (fatigue failure). Eventually the bearing material will loosen in pieces and tear away from the steel backing. Short trip driving leads to corrosion of bearings because insufficient engine heat is produced to drive off the condensed water and corrosive gases. These products collect in the engine oil, forming acid and sludge. As the oil is carried to the engine bearings, the acid attacks and corrodes the bearing material.

7   Incorrect bearing installation during engine assembly will lead to bearing failure as well. Tight fitting bearings leave insufficient oil clearance and will result in oil starvation. Dirt or foreign particles trapped behind a bearing insert result in high spots on the bearing which lead to failure.

20   Engine overhaul - reassembly sequence

1   Before beginning engine reassembly, make sure you have all the necessary new parts, gaskets and seals as well as the following items on hand:

Common hand tools
Torque wrench (1/2-inch drive)
Piston ring installation tool
Piston ring compressor
Short lengths of rubber or plastic hose to fit over connecting rod bolts
Plastigage
Feeler gauges
Fine-tooth file
New engine oil
Engine assembly lube or moly-base grease
Gasket sealant
Thread locking compound

2   To save time and avoid problems, engine reassembly must be done in the following general order:

Four-cylinder engine

Oil jets
Crankshaft and main bearings
Rear main oil seal retainer
Piston/connecting rod assemblies
Vibration reducing stiffener
Balance shafts
Timing chain and sprockets
Balance shaft chain and sprockets
Timing chain cover
Oil pump pick-up
Cylinder head, camshaft and rocker arms
Water pump
Oil pump pick-up
Oil pan
Intake and exhaust manifolds
Valve cover
End plate
Flywheel/driveplate

V6 engine

Oil baffle plate
Crankshaft and main bearings
Rear main oil seal housing
Piston/connecting rod assemblies
Cylinder heads, camshafts and rocker arms
Timing belt and sprockets
Water pump
Timing belt covers
Oil pump pick-up
Oil pan
Intake and exhaust manifolds
Valve covers
End plate
Flywheel/driveplate

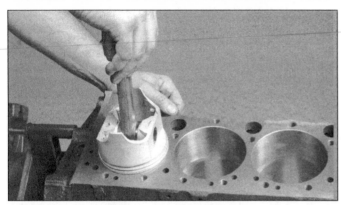

21.3 When checking piston ring end gap, the ring must be square in the cylinder bore (this is done by pushing the ring down with the top of a piston as shown)

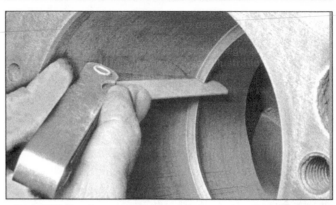

21.4 With the ring square in the cylinder, measure the end gap with a feeler gauge

21.5 If the end gap is too small, clamp a file in a vise and file the ring ends (from the outside in only) to enlarge the gap slightly

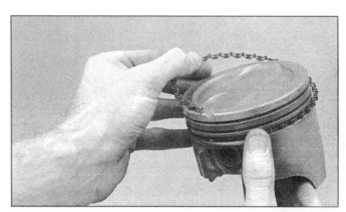

21.9a Installing the spacer/expander in the oil control ring groove

21 Piston rings - installation

Refer to illustrations 21.3, 21.4, 21.5, 21.9a, 21.9b and 21.12

1   Before installing the new piston rings, the ring end gaps must be checked. It's assumed the piston ring side clearance has been checked and verified correct (see Section 17).

2   Lay out the piston/connecting rod assemblies and the new ring sets so the ring sets will be matched with the same piston and cylinder during the end gap measurement and engine assembly.

3   Insert the top (number one) ring into the first cylinder and square it up with the cylinder walls by pushing it in with the top of the piston **(see illustration)**. The ring should be near the bottom of the cylinder, at the lower limit of ring travel.

4   To measure the end gap, slip feeler gauges between the ends of the ring until a gauge equal to the gap width is found **(see illustration)**. The feeler gauge should slide between the ring ends with a slight amount of drag. Compare the measurement to this Chapter's Specifications. If the gap is larger or smaller than specified, double-check to make sure you have the correct rings before proceeding.

5   If the gap is too small, it must be enlarged or the ring ends may come in contact with each other during engine operation, which can cause serious engine damage. The end gap can be increased by filing the ring ends very carefully with a fine file. Mount the file in a vise equipped with soft jaws, slip the ring over the file with the ends contacting the file teeth and slowly move the ring to remove material from the ends. When performing this operation, file only from the outside in **(see illustration)**.

6   Excess end gap isn't critical unless it's greater than 0.040-inch. Again, double-check to make sure you have the correct rings for the engine.

7   Repeat the procedure for each ring that will be installed in the

21.9b DO NOT use a piston ring installation tool when installing the oil ring side rails

first cylinder and for each ring in the remaining cylinders. Remember to keep rings, pistons and cylinders matched up.

8   Once the ring end gaps have been checked/corrected, the rings can be installed on the pistons.

9   The oil control ring (lowest one on the piston) is usually installed first. It's composed of three separate components. Slip the spacer/expander into the groove **(see illustration)**. If an anti-rotation tang is used, make sure it's inserted into the drilled hole in the ring groove. Next, install the lower side rail. Don't use a piston ring installation tool on the oil ring side rails, as they may be damaged. Instead, place one end of the side rail into the groove between the spacer/expander and the ring land, hold it firmly in place and slide a finger around the piston while pushing the rail into the groove **(see illustration)**. Next, install the upper side rail in the same manner.

21.12 Installing the compression rings with a ring expander - the mark (arrow) must face up

10   After the three oil ring components have been installed, check to make sure both the upper and lower side rails can be turned smoothly in the ring groove.

11   The number two (middle) ring is installed next. It's usually stamped with a mark, which must face up, toward the top of the piston. **Note:** *Always follow the instructions printed on the ring package or box - different manufacturers may require different approaches. Don't mix up the top and middle rings, as they have different cross sections.*

12   Use a piston ring installation tool and make sure the identification mark is facing the top of the piston, then slip the ring into the middle groove on the piston **(see illustration)**. Don't expand the ring any more than necessary to slide it over the piston.

13   Install the number one (top) ring in the same manner. Make sure the mark is facing up. Be careful not to confuse the number one and number two rings.

14   Repeat the procedure for the remaining pistons and rings.

22   Crankshaft and balance shafts - installation and main bearing oil clearance check

Refer to illustrations 22.6a, 22.6b, 22.11, and 22.15

1   It's assumed at this point that the engine block and crankshaft have been cleaned, inspected and repaired or reconditioned.

2   Position the engine with the bottom facing up. On the four-cylinder engine install the oil jets for each cylinder. For the V6 engine install the oil baffle plate. Apply thread locking compound to the bolts, then tighten them to the torque values listed in this Chapter's Specifications.

3   Remove the main bearing cap bolts and lift out the caps. Lay them out in the proper order to ensure correct installation. Also, read the Caution in Section 13, Step 6 (V6 engine only).

4   If they're still in place, remove the original bearing inserts from the block and the main bearing caps. Wipe the bearing surfaces of the block and caps with a clean, lint-free cloth. They must be kept spotlessly clean.

Main bearing oil clearance check

Note: *Don't touch the faces of the new bearing inserts with your fingers. Oil and acids from your skin can etch the bearings.*

5   Clean the back sides of the new main bearing inserts and lay one in each main bearing saddle in the block. If one of the bearing inserts from each set has a large groove in it, make sure the grooved insert is installed in the block. Lay the other bearing from each set in the corresponding main bearing cap. Make sure the tab on the bearing insert fits into the recess in the block or cap. **Caution:** *The oil holes in the block must line up with the oil holes in the bearing inserts. Do not hammer the bearing into place and don't nick or gouge the bearing faces. No lubrication should be used at this time.*

6   The flanged thrust bearing must be installed in the number four

22.6a Location of the number 4 (thrust bearing) main cap (arrow) on the V6 engine

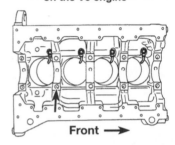

Front ➜

22.6b Location of the number 4 (thrust bearing) main cap (arrow) on the four-cylinder engine

cap and saddle (counting from the front of the engine) on either engine **(see illustrations)**.

7   Clean the faces of the bearings in the block and the crankshaft main bearing journals with a clean, lint-free cloth.

8   Check or clean the oil holes in the crankshaft, as any dirt here can go only one way - straight through the new bearings.

9   Once you're certain the crankshaft is clean, carefully lay it in position in the main bearings.

10   Before the crankshaft can be permanently installed, the main bearing oil clearance must be checked.

11   Cut several pieces of the appropriate size Plastigage (they should be slightly shorter than the width of the main bearings) and place one piece on each crankshaft main bearing journal, parallel with the journal axis **(see illustration)**.

12   Clean the faces of the bearings in the caps and install the caps in their original locations (don't mix them up) with the arrows pointing toward the front of the engine. Don't disturb the Plastigage.

13   Starting with the center main and working out toward the ends, tighten the main bearing cap bolts, in three steps, to the torque figure listed in this Chapter's Specifications. Don't rotate the crankshaft at any time during this operation.

14   Remove the bolts and carefully lift off the main bearing caps. Keep them in order. Don't disturb the Plastigage or rotate the crankshaft. If any of the main bearing caps are difficult to remove, tap them gently from side-to-side with a soft-face hammer to loosen them.

15   Compare the width of the crushed Plastigage on each journal to the scale printed on the Plastigage envelope to obtain the main bearing oil clearance **(see illustration)**. Check the Specifications at the beginning of this Chapter to make sure it's correct.

16   If the clearance is not as specified, the bearing inserts may be the wrong size (which means different ones will be required). Before deciding different inserts are needed, make sure no dirt or oil was between the bearing inserts and the caps or block when the clearance was measured. If the Plastigage was wider at one end than the other, the journal may be tapered (see Section 18).

17   Carefully scrape all traces of the Plastigage material off the main bearing journals and/or the bearing faces. Use your fingernail or the edge of a credit card - don't nick or scratch the bearing faces.

22.11 Lay the Plastigage strips (arrow) on the main bearing journals, parallel to the crankshaft centerline

22.15 Compare the width of the crushed Plastigage to the scale on the envelope to determine the main bearing oil clearance (always take the measurement at the widest point of the Plastigage); be sure to use the correct scale - standard and metric ones are included

Balance shafts installation (four-cylinder engine only)

30   Make sure the balance shafts and the bushings in the block are clean, then lubricate the bushings and journals with engine assembly lube.

31   Carefully guide the balance shafts into their bores. Make sure the shaft with the "L" on the thrust plate goes in the left (driver's side) bore and the shaft with the "R" goes in the right (passenger side) bore.

32   Install the thrust plate bolts and tighten them to the torque listed in this Chapter's Specifications. Rotate each balance shaft by hand to confirm smooth operation.

33   Install the timing chain and balance shaft chain following the procedure outlined in Chapter 2A.

23   Rear main oil seal - installation

Refer to illustrations 23.1 and 23.2

Note: The crankshaft must be installed and the main bearing caps bolted in place before the new seal and retainer assembly can be bolted to the block.

1   Remove the old seal from the retainer with a hammer and punch by driving it out from the back side **(see illustration)**. Be sure to note how far it's recessed into the retainer bore before removing it; the new seal will have to be recessed an equal amount. Be very careful not to scratch or otherwise damage the bore in the retainer or oil leaks could develop.

2   Make sure the retainer is clean, then apply a thin coat of engine oil to the outer edge of the new seal. The seal must be pressed squarely into the retainer bore, so hammering it into place isn't recommended. If you don't have access to a press, sandwich the retainer and seal between two smooth pieces of wood and press the seal into place with the jaws of a large vise. If you don't have a vise big enough, lay the retainer on a workbench and drive the seal into place with a block of wood and hammer **(see illustration)**. The piece of wood must be thick enough to distribute the force evenly around the entire circumference of the seal. Work slowly and make sure the seal enters the bore squarely.

3   If you're working on a four-cylinder engine, apply a continuous bead of RTV sealant to the seal retainer groove. If you're working on a V6 engine, be sure to install a new gasket.

4   Lubricate the seal lips with multi-purpose grease or engine oil before you slip the seal/retainer over the crankshaft and bolt it to the block.

5   Tighten the retainer bolts, a little at a time, to the torque listed in the Chapter 2A or 2B Specifications. If you're working on a V6 engine, trim the gasket flush with the oil pan gasket surface, being careful not to scratch it.

23.1 Support the retainer on wood blocks and drive out the old seal with a punch and hammer

Final crankshaft installation

18   Carefully lift the crankshaft out of the engine.

19   Clean the bearing faces in the block, then apply a thin, uniform layer of moly-base grease or engine assembly lube to each of the bearing surfaces. Be sure to coat the thrust faces as well as the journal face of the thrust bearing.

20   Make sure the crankshaft journals are clean, then lay the crankshaft back in place in the block.

21   Clean the faces of the bearings in the caps, then apply lubricant to them.

22   Install the caps in their original locations with the arrows pointing toward the front of the engine.

23   Install the bolts.

24   Tighten all except the thrust bearing cap bolts to the torque listed in this Chapter's Specifications (work from the center out and approach the final torque in three steps). Tighten the thrust bearing cap bolts to approximately 10 ft-lbs.

25   Tap the ends of the crankshaft forward and backward with a lead or brass hammer to line up the main bearing and crankshaft thrust surfaces.

26   Tighten all main bearing cap bolts to the torque listed in this Chapter's Specifications, starting with the center main and working out toward the ends.

27   Rotate the crankshaft a number of times by hand to check for any obvious binding.

28   The final step is to check the crankshaft endplay with feeler gauges or a dial indicator as described in Section 13. The endplay should be correct if the crankshaft thrust faces aren't worn or damaged and new bearings have been installed.

29   Refer to Section 23 and install the new rear main oil seal.

2C

23.2 Drive the new seal into the retainer with a wood block or a section of pipe, if you have one large enough - make sure you don't cock the seal in the retainer bore

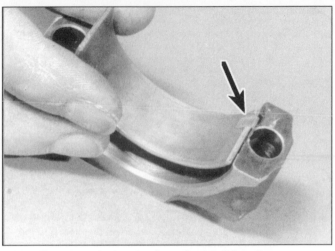

24.4 The tab on the bearing (arrow) must fit into the recess so that the bearing will seat properly

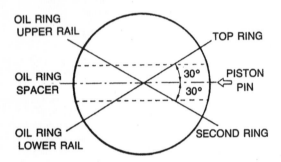

24.5 Position the ring gaps as shown before installing the piston/connecting rod assemblies into the engine

24.9a When installing the pistons in the four-cylinder engine be sure that the "F" casting mark on the piston faces forward in the block

24   Pistons and connecting rods - installation and rod bearing oil clearance check

Refer to illustrations 24.4, 24.5, 24.9a, 24.9b, 24.11 and 24.13

1   Before installing the piston/connecting rod assemblies, the cylinder walls must be perfectly clean, the top edge of each cylinder must be chamfered, and the crankshaft must be in place.

2   Remove the cap from the end of the number one connecting rod (check the marks made during removal). Remove the original bearing inserts and wipe the bearing surfaces of the connecting rod and cap with a clean, lint-free cloth. They must be kept spotlessly clean.

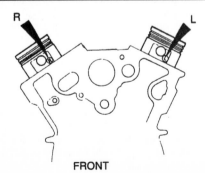

24.9b When installing the pistons in the V6 engine be sure the pistons with the "L" casting marks are in the left (driver's side) cylinder bank and the pistons with the "R" casting marks are in the right cylinder bank - all "L" and "R" marks should be facing forward in the block

Connecting rod bearing oil clearance check

Note: *Don't touch the faces of the new bearing inserts with your fingers. Oil and acids from your skin can etch the bearings.*

3   Clean the back side of the new upper bearing insert, then lay it in place in the connecting rod. Make sure the tab on the bearing fits into the recess in the rod. Don't hammer the bearing insert into place and be very careful not to nick or gouge the bearing face. Don't lubricate the bearing at this time.

4   Clean the back side of the other bearing insert and install it in the rod cap. Again, make sure the tab on the bearing fits into the recess in the cap **(see illustration)**, and don't apply any lubricant. It's critically important that the mating surfaces of the bearing and connecting rod are perfectly clean and oil free when they're assembled.

5   Position the piston ring gaps at intervals around the piston **(see illustration)**.

6   Slip a section of plastic or rubber hose over each connecting rod cap bolt.

7   Lubricate the piston and rings with clean engine oil and attach a piston ring compressor to the piston. Leave the skirt protruding about 1/4-inch to guide the piston into the cylinder. The rings must be compressed until they're flush with the piston.

8   Rotate the crankshaft until the number one connecting rod journal is at BDC (bottom dead center) and apply a coat of engine oil to the cylinder walls.

9   With the mark or notch on top of the piston facing the front of the engine **(see illustrations)**, gently insert the piston/connecting rod assembly into the number one cylinder bore and rest the bottom edge of the ring compressor on the engine block.

10   Tap the top edge of the ring compressor to make sure it's contacting the block around its entire circumference.

11   Gently tap on the top of the piston with the end of a wooden or plastic hammer handle **(see illustration)** while guiding the end of the

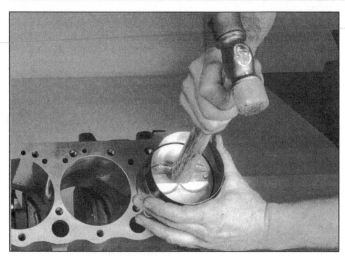

24.11 Drive the piston gently into the cylinder bore with the end of a wooden or plastic hammer handle

24.13 Lay the Plastigage strips on each rod bearing journal, parallel to the crankshaft centerline

connecting rod into place on the crankshaft journal. The piston rings may try to pop out of the ring compressor just before entering the cylinder bore, so keep some pressure on the ring compressor. Work slowly, and if any resistance is felt as the piston enters the cylinder, stop immediately. Find out what's hanging up and fix it before proceeding. Do not, for any reason, force the piston into the cylinder - you might break a ring and/or the piston.

12   Once the piston/connecting rod assembly is installed, the connecting rod bearing oil clearance must be checked before the rod cap is permanently bolted in place.

13   Cut a piece of the appropriate size Plastigage slightly shorter than the width of the connecting rod bearing and lay it in place on the number one connecting rod journal, parallel with the journal axis **(see illustration)**.

14   Clean the connecting rod cap bearing face, remove the protective hoses from the connecting rod bolts and install the rod cap. Make sure the mating mark on the cap is on the same side as the mark on the connecting rod.

15   Install the nuts and tighten them to the torque listed in this Chapter's Specifications. Work up to it in three steps. **Note:** *Use a thin-wall socket to avoid erroneous torque readings that can result if the socket is wedged between the rod cap and nut. If the socket tends to wedge itself between the nut and the cap, lift up on it slightly until it no longer contacts the cap. Do not rotate the crankshaft at any time during this operation.*

16   Remove the nuts and detach the rod cap, being very careful not to disturb the Plastigage.

17   Compare the width of the crushed Plastigage to the scale printed on the Plastigage envelope to obtain the oil clearance **(see illustration 22.15)**. Compare it to this Chapter's Specifications to make sure the clearance is correct.

18   If the clearance is not as specified, the bearing inserts may be the wrong size (which means different ones will be required). Before deciding different inserts are needed, make sure no dirt or oil was between the bearing inserts and the connecting rod or cap when the clearance was measured. Also, recheck the journal diameter. If the Plastigage was wider at one end than the other, the journal may be tapered.

Final connecting rod installation

19   Carefully scrape all traces of the Plastigage material off the rod journal and/or bearing face. Be very careful not to scratch the bearing - use your fingernail or the edge of a credit card.

20   Make sure the bearing faces are perfectly clean, then apply a uniform layer of clean moly-base grease or engine assembly lube to both of them. You'll have to push the piston into the cylinder to expose the face of the bearing insert in the connecting rod - be sure to slip the protective hoses over the rod bolts first.

21   Slide the connecting rod back into place on the journal, remove the protective hoses from the rod cap bolts, install the rod cap and tighten the nuts to the torque listed in this Chapter's Specifications. Again, work up to the torque in three steps. **Note:** *Again, make sure the mating mark on the cap is on the same side as the mark on the connecting rod.*

22   Repeat the entire procedure for the remaining pistons/connecting rods.

23   The important points to remember are:
   a)   Keep the back sides of the bearing inserts and the insides of the connecting rods and caps perfectly clean when assembling them.
   b)   Make sure you have the correct piston/rod assembly for each cylinder.
   c)   The arrow or mark on the piston must face the front of the engine.
   d)   Lubricate the cylinder walls with clean oil.
   e)   Lubricate the bearing faces when installing the rod caps after the oil clearance has been checked.

24   After all the piston/connecting rod assemblies have been properly installed, rotate the crankshaft a number of times by hand to check for any obvious binding.

25   As a final step, the connecting rod endplay must be checked. Refer to Section 12 for this procedure.

26   Compare the measured endplay to this Chapter's Specifications to make sure it's correct. If it was correct before disassembly and the original crankshaft and rods were reinstalled, it should still be right. If new rods or a new crankshaft were installed, the endplay may be inadequate. If so, the rods will have to be removed and taken to an automotive machine shop for re-sizing.

---

25   Initial start-up and break-in after overhaul

Warning: *Have a fire extinguisher handy when starting the engine for the first time.*

1   Once the engine has been installed in the vehicle, double-check the engine oil and coolant levels.

2   With the spark plugs out of the engine and the ignition system disabled (see Section 3), crank the engine until oil pressure registers on the gauge or the light goes out.

3   Install the spark plugs, hook up the plug wires and restore the ignition system functions.

4   Start the engine. It may take a few moments for the fuel system to build up pressure, but the engine should start without a great deal of effort. **Note:** *If backfiring occurs through the throttle body, recheck the valve timing and ignition timing.*

5   After the engine starts, it should be allowed to warm up to normal operating temperature. While the engine is warming up, make a thorough check for fuel, oil and coolant leaks.

2C

6   Shut the engine off and recheck the engine oil and coolant levels.

7   Drive the vehicle to an area with minimum traffic, accelerate at full throttle from 30 to 50 mph, then allow the vehicle to slow to 30 mph with the throttle closed. Repeat the procedure 10 or 12 times. This will load the piston rings and cause them to seat properly against the cylinder walls. Check again for oil and coolant leaks.

8   Drive the vehicle gently for the first 500 miles (no sustained high speeds) and keep a constant check on the oil level. It isn't unusual for an engine to use oil during the break-in period.

9   At approximately 500 to 600 miles, change the oil and filter.

10   For the next few hundred miles, drive the vehicle normally. Don't pamper it or abuse it.

11   After 2000 miles, change the oil and filter again and consider the engine broken in.

Chapter 3 Cooling, heating and air conditioning systems

Contents

Specifications

General

Coolant capacity..	See Chapter 1
Radiator cap pressure rating	See Chapter 1
Refrigerant capacity	
Without rear air conditioning unit	42-1/2 ounces
With rear air conditioning unit	58-1/4 ounces

Torque specifications

	Ft-lbs (unless otherwise indicated)
Thermostat cover bolts/nuts	14 to 19
Water pump mounting bolts/nuts...	14 to 19
Fan-to-water pump nuts..	70 to 95 in-lbs

3.7a Squeeze the hose clamp and slide it back so the radiator hose can be removed (four-cylinder engine)

3.7b On V6 models the thermostat is located down by the bottom of the engine

1   General information

Engine cooling system

All vehicles covered by this manual employ a pressurized engine cooling system with thermostatically controlled coolant circulation. An impeller type water pump mounted on the front of the engine pumps coolant through the engine and radiator. The coolant flows around each cylinder and back to the radiator. Cast-in coolant passages direct coolant around the intake and exhaust ports, near the spark plug areas and the exhaust valve guides.

A wax pellet type thermostat is located in a housing connected to the upper radiator hose. During warm up the closed thermostat prevents coolant from circulating through the radiator. As the engine nears normal operating temperature, the thermostat opens and allows hot coolant to travel through the radiator, where it's cooled before returning to the engine.

The cooling system is sealed by a pressure-type radiator cap, which raises the boiling point of the coolant and increases the cooling efficiency of the radiator. If the system pressure exceeds the cap pressure relief value, the excess pressure in the system forces the spring-loaded valve inside the cap off its seat and allows the coolant to escape through a hose into a coolant reservoir. When the system cools, the excess coolant is automatically drawn from the reservoir back into the radiator.

The coolant reservoir serves as both the point at which fresh coolant is added to the cooling system to maintain the proper level and as a holding tank for expelled coolant.

This type of cooling system is known as a closed design because coolant that escapes past the pressure cap is saved and reused.

Heating system

The heating system consists of a blower fan and heater core located in the heater box, the hoses connecting the heater core to the engine cooling system and the heater/air conditioning control head on the dashboard. Hot engine coolant is circulated through the heater core. When the heater mode is activated, a trap door opens to expose the heater box to the passenger compartment. A fan switch on the control head activates the blower motor, which forces air through the core, heating the air. Some models are equipped with an auxiliary heating unit which is designed to heat the rear of the passenger compartment. It is located underneath the driver's seat.

Air conditioning system

The air conditioning system consists of a condenser mounted in front of the radiator, an evaporator mounted adjacent to the heater core, a compressor mounted on the engine, a filter-drier (receiver-drier), which contains a high-pressure relief valve, and the hoses and lines connecting all of the above components. Some models are equipped with a rear air conditioning system with its own control panel

and blower fan.

A blower fan forces the warmer air of the passenger compartment through the evaporator core (sort of a radiator-in-reverse), transferring the heat from the air to the refrigerant. The liquid refrigerant boils off into low pressure vapor, taking the heat with it when it leaves the evaporator.

2   Antifreeze - general information

Warning: *Don't allow antifreeze to come in contact with your skin or painted surfaces of the vehicle. Rinse off spills immediately with plenty of water. Antifreeze is highly toxic if ingested. Never leave antifreeze lying around in an open container or in puddles on the floor; children and pets are attracted by its sweet smell and may drink it. Check with local authorities about disposing of used antifreeze. Many communities have collection centers which will see that antifreeze is disposed of safely. Antifreeze is also combustible, so don't store or use it near open flames.*

The cooling system should be filled with a water/ethylene glycol based antifreeze solution, which will prevent freezing down to at least -20-degrees F, or lower if local climate requires it. It also provides protection against corrosion and increases the coolant boiling point.

The cooling system should be drained, flushed and refilled at the specified intervals (see Chapter 1). Old or contaminated antifreeze solutions are likely to cause damage and encourage the formation of rust and scale in the system. Use distilled water with the antifreeze.

Before adding antifreeze, check all hose connections, because antifreeze tends to leak through very minute openings. Engines don't normally consume coolant, so if the level goes down, find the cause and correct it.

The exact mixture of antifreeze-to-water which you should use depends on the relative weather conditions. The mixture should contain at least 50-percent antifreeze, but should never contain more than 70-percent antifreeze. Consult the mixture ratio chart on the antifreeze container before adding coolant. Hydrometers are available at most auto parts stores to test the coolant. Use antifreeze which meets the vehicle manufacturer's specifications.

3   Thermostat - check and replacement

Refer to illustrations 3.7a, 3.7b, 3.9a, 3.9b, 3.11, 3.12a and 3.12b
Warning: *DO NOT remove the radiator cap, drain the coolant or replace the thermostat until the engine has cooled completely.*

Check

1   Before assuming the thermostat is to blame for a cooling system

3.9a Remove the bolts holding the thermostat housing together (V6 engine)

3.9b Separate the two halves to remove the thermostat - be sure to note which way the thermostat is installed (V6 engine)

3.11 When replacing the thermostat on a V6 model, be sure to replace the gasket

problem, check the coolant level (see Chapter 1), drivebelt tension (see Chapter 1) and temperature gauge (or light) operation.

2   If the engine seems to be taking a long time to warm up (based on heater output or temperature gauge operation), the thermostat is probably stuck open. Replace the thermostat with a new one.

3   If the engine runs hot, use your hand to check the temperature of the upper radiator hose. If the hose isn't hot, but the engine is, the thermostat is probably stuck closed, preventing the coolant inside the engine from escaping to the radiator. Replace the thermostat. **Caution**: *Don't drive the vehicle without a thermostat. The computer may stay in open loop and emissions and fuel economy will suffer.*

4   If the upper radiator hose is hot, it means the coolant is flowing and the thermostat is open. Consult the *Troubleshooting* section at the front of this manual for cooling system diagnosis.

Replacement

5   Disconnect the negative battery cable from the battery and drain the cooling system (see Chapter 1). If the coolant is relatively new or in good condition, save it and reuse it.

6   Follow the lower radiator hose (V6 engine) or upper radiator hose (four-cylinder engine) to the engine to locate the thermostat cover.

7   Loosen the hose clamp, then detach the hose from the fitting

(see illustrations). If the hose sticks, grasp it near the end with a pair of adjustable pliers and twist it to break the seal, then pull it off. If the hose is old or deteriorated, cut it off and install a new one.

8   If the outer surface of the large fitting that mates with the hose is severely deteriorated (corroded, pitted, etc.) it may be damaged further by hose removal. If it is, the thermostat cover will have to be replaced.

9   Remove the bolts/nuts and detach the thermostat cover **(see illustrations)**. If the cover is stuck, tap it with a soft-face hammer to jar it loose. Be prepared for some coolant to spill as the gasket seal is broken.

10   Note how it's installed (direction of the housing), then remove the thermostat. Clean all gasket material from both surfaces of the thermostat housing. Clean both mating surfaces with lacquer thinner or acetone.

11   If you're working on a V6 engine, replace the rubber gasket on the thermostat **(see illustration)**.

12   Install the new thermostat in the housing **(see illustrations)**. If you're working on a four-cylinder engine, be sure to use a new gasket, and make sure the jiggle pin is in the 12 o'clock position. Also make sure the thermostat is installed the correct way - the spring end is normally directed into the engine.

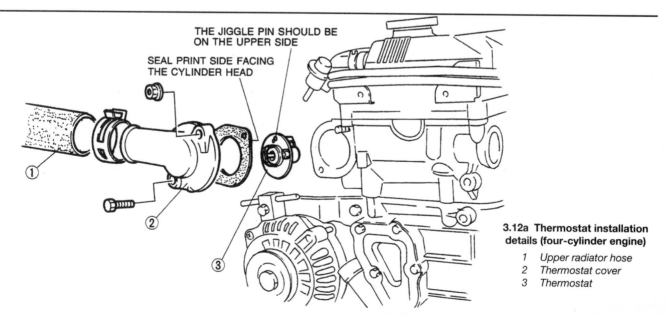

THE JIGGLE PIN SHOULD BE ON THE UPPER SIDE

SEAL PRINT SIDE FACING THE CYLINDER HEAD

3.12a Thermostat installation details (four-cylinder engine)

1   *Upper radiator hose*
2   *Thermostat cover*
3   *Thermostat*

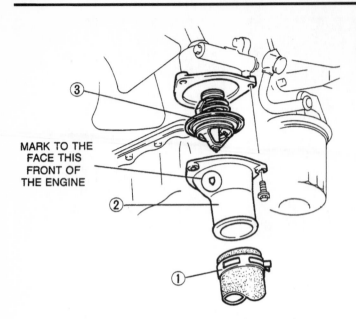

4.7 Remove the 4 nuts that hold the fan to the water pump (a screwdriver placed across two of the other studs or nuts will prevent the water pump from turning while you break the nuts loose)

3.12b Thermostat installation details (V6 engine)

1	Lower radiator hose	3	Thermostat
2	Thermostat cover		

13   Install the cover and bolts/nuts. If you're working on a V6 model, make sure the mark on the thermostat cover is facing the front of the vehicle. Tighten the bolts to the torque figure listed in this Chapter's Specifications.
14   The remaining steps are the reverse of removal.
15   Refill the cooling system (see Chapter 1).
16   Start the engine and allow it to reach normal operating temperature, then check for leaks and proper thermostat operation (as described in Step 3).

4   Engine cooling fan and clutch - check, removal and installation

Refer to illustrations 4.7, 4.8 and 4.9
Warning. *Keep hands, tools and clothing away from the fan. To avoid injury or damage DO NOT operate the engine with a damaged fan. Do not attempt to repair fan blades - replace a damaged fan with a new one.*

Check

1   Disconnect the negative battery cable and rock the fan back and forth by hand to check for excessive bearing play.
2   With the engine cold, turn the blades by hand. The fan should turn freely.
3   Visually inspect for substantial fluid leakage from the clutch assembly, a deformed bi-metal spring or grease leakage from the cooling fan bearing. If any of these conditions exist, replace the fan clutch.
4   When the engine is warmed up, turn off the ignition switch and disconnect the negative battery cable from the battery. Turn the fan by hand. Some resistance should be felt. If the fan turns easily, replace the fan clutch.

Removal and installation

5   Disconnect the negative battery cable.
6   Unbolt and remove the fresh air duct on top of the radiator.
7   Remove the nuts holding the fan assembly to the water pump flange **(see illustration)**.
8   Remove the fan shroud upper mounting bolts **(see illustration)** and carefully compress the lower two plastic fasteners with a long needle-nose pliers.
9   The cooling fan assembly can now be removed, while moving the shroud in order to gain clearance during removal **(see illustration)**.
10   Installation is the reverse of removal.

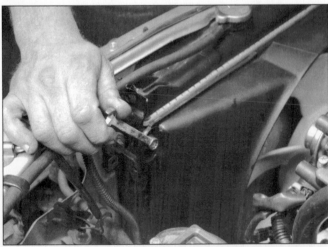

4.8 Remove the two upper bolts that hold the shroud to the radiator

4.9 With the nuts removed and the fan shroud loose, remove the fan assembly by sliding the shroud and fan up together

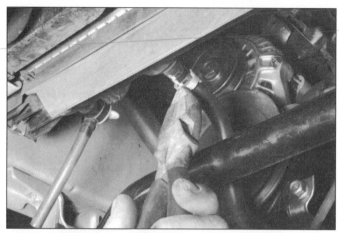

5.3a Disconnect the two transmission cooler lines from the lower radiator tank, then plug them - be ready with a drain pan for fluid coming from the lines when they are removed

5.3b Remove the bolts that hold the radiator to the radiator support

5 Radiator - removal and installation

Refer to illustrations 5.3a, 5.3b and 5.3c
Warning: *Wait until the engine is completely cool before beginning this procedure.*

Removal

1   Disconnect the negative battery cable from the battery.
2   Drain the cooling system (see Chapter 1). If the coolant is relatively new or in good condition, save it and reuse it.
3   Remove the fan and shroud (see Section 4).To remove the radiator follow the photo sequence **(see illustrations)**.
4   With the radiator removed, it can be inspected for leaks and damage. If it needs repair, have a radiator shop or dealer service department perform the work, as special techniques are required.
5   Bugs and dirt can be removed from the radiator with compressed air and a soft brush. Don't bend the cooling fins as this is done.
6   Check the radiator mounts for deterioration and make sure there's nothing in them when the radiator is installed.

Installation

7   Installation is the reverse of the removal procedure.
8   After installation, fill the cooling system with the proper mixture of antifreeze and water (see Chapter 1).

9   Start the engine and check for leaks. Allow the engine to reach normal operating temperature, indicated by the upper radiator hose becoming hot. Re-check the coolant level and add more if required.
10   Check and add automatic transmission fluid as needed (see Chapter 1).

6 Coolant reservoir - removal and installation

Refer to illustration 6.2
1   Disconnect the reservoir hose from the radiator neck.
2   The coolant reservoir is located in the left front corner of the engine compartment, mounted on two studs. Remove the mounting nuts **(see illustration)** and lift the coolant reservoir from the vehicle, being careful not to spill any coolant on the vehicle's paint.
3   Installation is the reverse of removal.

7 Water pump - check

Refer to illustrations 7.4 and 7.5
1   A failure in the water pump can cause serious engine damage due to overheating.
2   There are three ways to check the operation of the water pump while it's installed on the engine. If the pump is defective, it should be

5.3c Carefully lift the radiator out of the vehicle, looking for any pieces still attached

6.2 The coolant reservoir is located in the left front corner of the engine compartment

3

7.4 If coolant is leaking from the weep hole (arrow), the water pump must be replaced

7.5 To check for play in the water pump bearing, grab the flange and try to move it up and down (very little, if any, movement should be felt)

8.8 Locations of the water pump mounting bolts (arrows) - V6 engine

replaced with a new or rebuilt unit.

3   With the engine running at normal operating temperature, squeeze the upper radiator hose. If the water pump is working properly, a slight pressure surge should be felt as the hose is released. **Warning**: *Keep your hands away from the fan blades!*

4   Water pumps are equipped with weep or vent holes. If a failure occurs in the pump seal, coolant will leak from the hole **(see illustration)**. In most cases you'll need a flashlight and mirror to find the hole on the underside of the water pump to check for leaks.

5   If the water pump shaft bearings fail there may be a howling sound coming from the drivebelt area while the engine is running. With the engine off, shaft wear can be felt if the water pump pulley is rocked up-and-down **(see illustration)**. Don't mistake drivebelt slippage, which causes a squealing sound, for water pump bearing failure.

8   Water pump - removal and installation

Refer to illustration 8.8

Warning: *Wait until the engine is completely cool before beginning this procedure.*

Removal

1   Disconnect the negative battery cable from the battery.

2   If you're working on a V6 engine, position the No. 1 cylinder at TDC on the compression stroke (see Chapter 2C).

3   Remove the drivebelt(s) (see Chapter 1).

4   Drain the cooling system (see Chapter 1). If the coolant is rela-

tively new or in good condition, save it and reuse it.

5   Remove the cooling fan and shroud (see Section 4).

6   Remove the water pump pulley.

7   If you're working on a V6 engine, remove the timing belt (see Chapter 2B).

8   Unbolt and remove the water pump **(see illustration)**. If the water pump sticks, tap on it with a block of wood and a hammer to dislodge it. Don't pry between the sealing surfaces.

9   Clean the fastener threads and any threaded holes in the engine to remove corrosion and sealant.

10   Compare the new pump to the old one to make sure they're identical.

11   Remove all traces of old gasket material with a gasket scraper.

12   Clean the engine and water pump mating surfaces with lacquer thinner or acetone.

Installation

13   Apply a thin coat of RTV sealant to the engine side of the new gasket.

14   Apply a thin layer of RTV sealant to the gasket mating surface of the new pump, then carefully mate the gasket and the pump. Slip a couple of bolts through the pump mounting holes to hold the gasket in place.

15   Carefully attach the pump and gasket to the engine and start the bolts/nuts finger tight.

16   Tighten the bolts in 1/4-turn increments to the torque figure listed in this Chapter's Specifications. Don't over tighten them or the pump may be distorted.

17   Reinstall all parts removed for access to the pump.

18   Refill the cooling system (see Chapter 1). Run the engine and check for leaks.

9   Coolant temperature sending unit - check and replacement

Refer to illustration 9.1

Warning: *Wait until the engine is completely cool before beginning this procedure.*

Check

1   The coolant temperature indicator system is composed of a light or temperature gauge mounted in the instrument panel and a coolant temperature sending unit mounted on the thermostat housing (four-cylinder engine) **(see illustration)** or on the left (driver's) side of the water outlet on the front of the intake manifold (V6 engine).

2   If the light or gauge indicates the engine is overheating, check the coolant level in the system and then make sure the wiring between the light or gauge and the sending unit is secure and all fuses are intact.

9.1 Location of the coolant temperature sending unit for the temperature gauge or light (four-cylinder engine)

3   When the ignition switch is turned on and the starter motor is turning, the indicator light (if equipped) should be on (overheated engine indication). Once the engine has started the light should go out.

4   If the light isn't on, the bulb may be burned out, the ignition switch may be faulty or the circuit may be open. Test the circuit by grounding the wire to the sending unit while the ignition is on (engine not running for safety). If the gauge deflects full scale or the light comes on, replace the sending unit.

5   As soon as the engine starts, the light should go out and remain out unless the engine overheats. Failure of the light to go out may be due to a grounded wire between the light and the sending unit, a defective sending unit or a faulty ignition switch. Check the coolant to make sure it's the proper type (see Section 2). Plain water may have too low a boiling point to activate the sending unit.

Replacement

6   If the sending unit must be replaced, simply unscrew it from the engine and install the replacement. Use Teflon tape or a light coat of sealant on the threads. Make sure the engine is cool before removing the defective sending unit. There will be some coolant loss as the unit is removed, so be prepared to catch it. Check the level after the replacement sending unit has been installed, and add coolant if necessary (see Chapter 1).

---

10   Heater and air conditioning blower motor(s) and circuit - check and switch replacement

---

Refer to illustrations 10.8a and 10.8b

Note: *These vehicles are equipped with up to three blower motors. The front blower motor (all models) circulates air for the front heating and air conditioning. The rear heater and rear air conditioning systems (if equipped) have separate blower motors. The rear heater blower motor is powered through the front heater blower switch and resistor circuit. The rear air conditioning blower motor has a separate switch and resistor.*

Check

1   If the blower motor speed does not correspond to the setting selected on the blower switch, or the blower motor does not operate at all, the problem could be a bad fuse, relay, switch, blower motor resistor, blower motor or blower motor circuit wiring.

2   Before checking the blower motor or circuit, always check the fuse and relay (if equipped) first (see Chapter 12).

3   With the ignition key in the ON position, turn the blower switch to the faulty position(s) and, using a test light or voltmeter, check the voltage at the motor. If the motor is receiving voltage but not operating, either the motor ground is bad (on these models, the blower switch and resistor are part of the ground circuit) or the motor itself is faulty or the fan is binding.

4   To check for a bad ground, disconnect the electrical connector

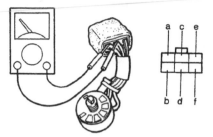

Position	Terminal					
	a	b	c	d	e	f
OFF						
First	○———————————————○					
Second			○———————○			
Third		○———————————○———————○				
Fourth		○———————————○———————————————○				

○———○: Indicates continuity

10.8a Terminal guide and continuity table for the front blower switch

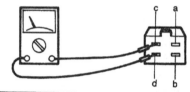

Switch	Terminal			
	a	b	c	d
OFF				
Lo (First)			○———————○	
Mid (Second)	○———————————————————○			
Hi (Third)		○———————○		

○———○ : Indicates continuity

10.8b Terminal guide and continuity table for the rear heater or air conditioner blower switch

from the blower motor, connect a jumper wire between the ground wire terminal on the blower motor and a good ground, then connect a fused jumper wire between the battery positive terminal and the positive terminal on the blower motor. If the motor now operates properly, the ground circuit is bad. Proceed to Step 6. If the motor does not operate, the fan is either binding or faulty.

5   If you suspect the blower motor fan is binding, remove the blower motor (see Section 11) to check for free operation of the fan.

6   Pull the blower switch out far enough to verify - with a test light or voltmeter - that voltage is reaching the blower switch. If the switch is not getting voltage, troubleshoot the circuit between the resistor and the switch.

7   Locate the electrical connector and wire for the heater blower motor resistor, usually attached to a heating/air conditioning duct or blower motor case. Verify that the resistor is getting current from the blower motor.

   a)   If the resistor is not getting current, check the wires and the connectors between the resistor and the motor. Check for loose or corroded connections and damaged wires.

   b)   If the wires and connectors are good and the blower switch is getting current, verify current is flowing out of the blower switch to ground. If it is not, replace the switch.

8   Unplug the electrical connector from the blower switch and check the continuity across the switch terminals **(see illustrations)** with an ohmmeter. If the switch fails any of the continuity checks, replace it.

3

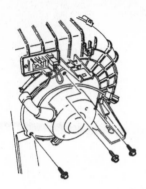

11.3 Front blower motor installation details

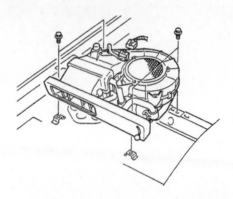

11.9 Rear heater unit mounting details

Switch replacement

Front blower switch

9 Remove the control knobs.
10 Remove the passenger side dash panel surrounding the control knobs (see Chapter 11).
11 Pull off the knob, remove the nut and disconnect the blower switch electrical connector.
12 Remove the blower switch from the dash.
13 Installation is the reverse of removal.

Rear heater blower switch

14 Remove the switch knob and cover.
15 Remove the screws and the rear heater blower motor switch, then disconnect the electrical connector from switch.
16 Installation is the reverse of removal.

Rear air conditioner blower switch

17 Pull out the rear cooler blower switch assembly (there are no screws). If necessary, carefully pry the panel out with a screwdriver.
18 Disconnect the blower switch electrical connector and remove the switch assembly.
19 Installation is the reverse of removal

---

11 Heater and air conditioning blower motor(s) - removal and installation

Front blower motor

Refer to illustration 11.3
1 Remove the passenger side lower trim panel to gain access to the motor.
2 Disconnect the blower motor electrical connector.
3 Remove the screws holding the motor to the blower unit case **(see illustration)**. Remove the blower motor.
4 Installation is the reverse of removal.

Rear heater blower motor

Refer to illustration 11.9
5 Set the temperature control knob to warm in order to open the water valve and drain the engine coolant.
6 Remove the drivers seat (see Chapter 11).
7 Disconnect the heater hoses from the heater unit. Plug the ends of the hoses to prevent excessive leakage.
8 Disconnect the blower motor electrical connector.
9 Remove the bolts that hold the heater unit to the floor **(see illustration)**.
10 Remove the screws that hold the blower motor to the case and remove the motor.
11 Installation is the reverse of removal. Check the coolant level and add, if necessary (see Chapter 1).

12.4 Disconnect the heater hoses from the heater core tubes

Rear air conditioning blower motor

Warning: *The air conditioning system is under high pressure. DO NOT loosen any hose or line fittings or remove any components until after the system has been discharged by a dealer service department or service station. Always wear eye protection when disconnecting air conditioning system fittings.*
12 Have the air conditioning system discharged at a service station or other repair shop (see Warning above).
13 Disconnect the negative cable from the battery.
14 Remove the left rear side trim panel (see Chapter 11).
15 Disconnect the high and low pressure refrigerant lines from the cooling unit.
16 Disconnect all electrical connections from the cooling unit assembly including the connector at the blower motor.
17 Disconnect the rear cooling unit nuts and bolts and remove the cooling unit.
18 Remove the screws holding the blower motor in place, and remove the motor.
19 Installation is the reverse of removal. Have the air conditioning system evacuated, charged and leak tested by the shop that discharged it.

---

12 Heater core(s) - removal and installation

Front heater core

Refer to illustrations 12.4, 12.5a, 12.5b, 12.6, 12.7a and 12.7b
1 Disconnect the cable from the negative terminal of the battery.
2 Drain the cooling system (see Chapter 1).
3 Working in the passenger compartment, remove the instrument panel (see Chapter 11).
4 Disconnect the heater hoses from the heater core **(see illustration)** from inside the engine compartment. Plug the ends of the hoses

12.5a Remove the instrument panel stays - one is located on the transmission tunnel . . .

12.5b . . .and the other is located at the top of the case, attached to the dash frame

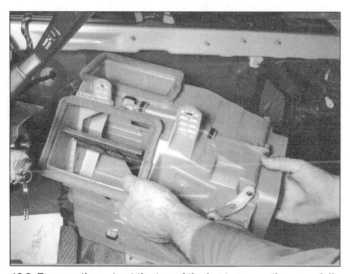

12.6 Remove the nuts at the top of the heater case, then carefully guide the case from the vehicle

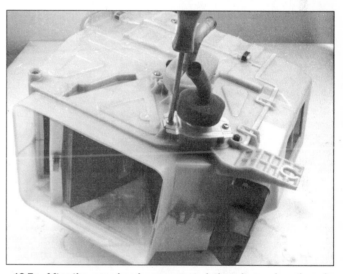

12.7a After the case has been removed place it on a bench and remove the screws that hold the heater core in the case . . .

and the ends of the heater core tubes.

5   Remove the nuts and the instrument panel stay **(see illustrations)**.

6   Remove the nuts attaching the heater case and remove the case **(see illustration)**.

7   The heater core can now be removed from the heater case. Follow the accompanying photographs **(see illustrations)**.

8   Installation is the reverse of removal. Be sure to refill the cooling system (see Chapter 1).

Rear heater core

9   Disconnect the cable from the negative terminal of the battery.

10   Drain the cooling system (see Chapter 1). If the coolant is relatively new or in good condition, save it and reuse it.

11   Remove the driver seat (see Chapter 11).

12   Disconnect the hoses from the heater core.

13   Disconnect the electrical connector from the heater case.

14   Remove the bolts holding the heater case to the floor **(see illustration 11.9)** and remove the assembly from the vehicle.

15   The heater unit case can now be split into an upper and lower halves by unbolting the two. This will allow access to the heater core

16   Remove heater core.

17   Installation is the reverse of the removal procedure. Be sure to refill the cooling system (see Chapter 1).

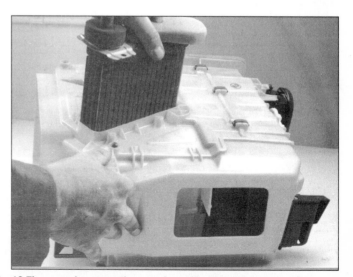

12.7b . . .and remove the core by pulling it straight out of the case

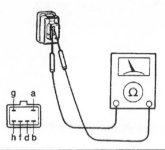

Switch	Terminal					
	a	b	d	f	g	h
OFF		○—○		○—○		
		○—○				
ON	○			○—○		○
				○▸—○		

○—○: Indicates continuity
○▸—○: Indicates diode

13.3a Terminal guide and continuity table for the front air conditioner main switch

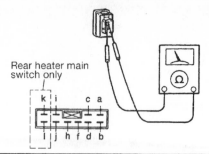

Rear heater main switch only

Switch	Terminal					
	c	d	f	h	i	j
OFF		○—○				
		○—○				
ON	○			○—○		○
				○▸—○		

○—○: Indicates continuity
○▸—○: Indicates diode

13.3b Terminal guide and continuity table for the rear heater or rear air conditioner main switch

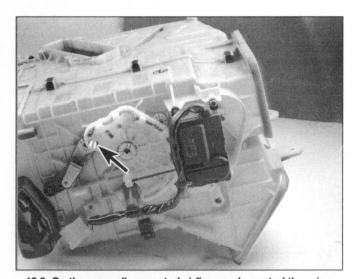

13.9 On the manually operated airflow mode control there is a wire from the control head to the mechanism on the heater case - reach in and disconnect the wire at the heater case (heater case removed for clarity)

13   Heater and air conditioning control assemblies - check, removal and installation

Main Switches

Refer to illustrations 13.3a and 13.3b

Removal and installation

1   Remove the main switches from the dash panel. There are no screws. The switches must be carefully pried out with a very thin tipped screwdriver. **Note:** *Be very careful not to damage the dash trim panel when removing the switches.*
2   Install switches by pushing them back into position until they snap back into place.

Check

3   Unplug the electrical connector(s) from the switch(es) and check for continuity between the indicated terminals of the switch **(see illustrations)**. If a switch fails any of the continuity checks, replace it.

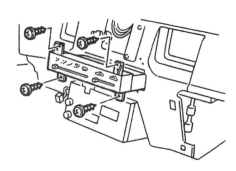

13.10 Mounting details of the airflow mode control assembly

Airflow mode control assembly

Note: *There are two types of airflow mode control assemblies. One which is manually operated, called the wire type, and another which is electrically controlled, called the logic type.*

Removal and installation

Refer to illustrations 13.9 and 13.10

4   Remove the interior trim lower panels and undercover (see Chapter 11).
5   Remove the steering column under cover (see Chapter 11).
6   Remove the instrument cluster (see Chapter 11).
7   Remove the nuts and washers and the switch cover panel (see Chapter 11).
8   Remove the center lower panel (see Chapter 11).
9   On the wire type control, disconnect the REC-FRESH wire at the heater unit **(see illustration)**.
10   Remove the screws holding the control assembly in place **(see illustration)**.
11   Remove the control assembly. While removing the logic type assembly, disconnect the electrical connector at this time.
12   Installation is the reverse of the removal procedure.

Check

13   The check procedure for the wire type is to manually move the levers and look for movement of the attached air door mechanisms. **Note:** *The check involving the logic type requires very involved testing*

procedures and should be left to a dealer service department or other qualified repair shop.

14 Air conditioning system - check and maintenance

Warning: *The air conditioning system is under high pressure. DO NOT loosen any hose or line fittings or remove any components until after the system has been discharged. Air conditioning refrigerant should be properly discharged into an EPA-approved container at a dealer service department or an automotive air conditioning repair facility. Always wear eye protection when disconnecting air conditioning system fittings.*

Caution: *The air conditioning system on 1994 models uses the non-ozone-depleting refrigerant, referred to as R-134a. The R-134a refrigerant and its lubricating oil are not compatible with the R-12 system used on 1993 and earlier models. Under no circumstances should R-12 refrigerant or refrigerant oil be added to an R-134a system, or vice versa. If the different types of refrigerant and/or oil are mixed, it will result in damage to the air conditioning system.*

Check

1   The following maintenance checks should be performed on a regular basis to ensure the air conditioner continues to operate at peak efficiency.
   a) Check the drivebelt. If it's worn or deteriorated, replace it (see Chapter 1).
   b) Check the system hoses. Look for cracks, bubbles, hard spots and deterioration. Inspect the hoses and all fittings for oil bubbles and seepage. If there's any evidence of wear, damage or leaks replace the hose(s).
   c) Inspect the condenser fins for leaves, bugs and other debris. Use a "fin comb" or compressed air to clean the condenser.
   d) Make sure the system has the correct refrigerant charge.
2   It's a good idea to operate the system for about 10 minutes at least once a month, particularly during the winter. Long term non-use can cause hardening, and subsequent failure, of the seals.
3   Because of the complexity of the air conditioning system and the special equipment necessary to service it, in-depth troubleshooting and repairs are not included in this manual (refer to the *Haynes Automotive Heating & Air Conditioning Manual*). However, simple checks and component replacement procedures are provided in this Chapter.
4   The most common cause of poor cooling is simply a low system refrigerant charge. If a noticeable loss of cool air output occurs, one of the following quick checks may help you determine if the refrigerant level is low.
5   Warm the engine up to normal operating temperature.
6   Place the air conditioning temperature selector at the coldest setting and put the blower at the highest setting. Open the doors (to make sure the air conditioning system doesn't cycle off as soon as it cools the passenger compartment).
7   With the compressor engaged - the compressor clutch will make an audible click and the center of the clutch will rotate - feel the orifice tube located adjacent to the right front frame rail near the radiator.
8   If a significant temperature drop is noticed, the refrigerant level is probably okay. Refer to Chapter 6 for information on the air conditioning clutch control system. Further inspection of the system is beyond the scope of the home mechanic and should be left to a professional.
9   If the inlet line has frost accumulation or feels cooler than the receiver-drier surface, the refrigerant charge is low. Add refrigerant.

Adding refrigerant (R-134a systems only)

Note: *Because of recent Environmental Protection Agency regulations, R-12 refrigerant is no longer available to the do-it-yourselfer.*
10   Buy a small can of R-134a refrigerant and a can tapper designed for use with the unique R-134a fitting. The tapper has a short section of hose that can be attached between the tapper valve and the system low side service valve. Because one can of refrigerant may not be suffi-

cient to bring the system charge up to the proper level, it's a good idea to buy a couple of additional cans. **Warning:** *Never add more than two cans of refrigerant to the system.*
11   Connect the tapper valve to the can and the end of the hose to the system low-side fitting, following the tapper valve manufacturer's instructions. Don't open the can at this time. Warning: Do not connect the hose to the system high side!
12   Warm up the engine and turn on the air conditioner. Keep the hose away from the fan and other moving parts.
13   Following the can tapper manufacturer's instructions, add refrigerant to the low side of the system until both the receiver-drier surface and the evaporator inlet line feel about the same temperature. Allow stabilization time between each addition.
14   Once the receiver-drier surface and the evaporator inlet line feel about the same temperature, add the contents remaining in the can.

15 Air conditioning receiver-drier - removal and installation

Warning: *The air conditioning system is under high pressure. DO NOT loosen any hose or line fittings or remove any components until after the system has been discharged by a dealer service department or service station. Always wear eye protection when disconnecting air conditioning system fittings.*
1   Have the system discharged (see Warning above).
2   Disconnect the negative battery cable from the battery.
3   Disconnect the right headlight and front combination light electrical connectors.
4   Remove the lower grille and radiator grille to gain access to the receiver-drier.
5   Remove the right side headlight and combination light assembly.
6   Disconnect the refrigerant lines from the receiver-drier.
7   Plug the open fittings to prevent the entry of dirt and moisture.
8   Loosen the mounting bracket bolt and remove the receiver-drier.
9   If a new receiver-drier is being installed, pour the oil out into a measuring cup, noting the amount. Add fresh refrigerant oil to the new receiver-drier equal to the amount removed from the old unit, plus one ounce.
10   Remove the old refrigerant line O-rings and replace with new ones. This should be done regardless of whether a new receiver-drier is being installed or not.
11   Installation is the reverse of removal, but be sure to lubricate the O-rings on the fittings with refrigerant oil before connecting the fittings.
12   Have the system evacuated, recharged and leak tested by the shop that discharged it.

16 Air conditioning compressor - removal and installation

Refer to illustrations 16.7 and 16.8

Warning: *The air conditioning system is under high pressure. DO NOT loosen any hose or line fittings or remove any components until after the system has been discharged by a dealer service department or service station. Always wear eye protection when disconnecting air conditioning system fittings.* **Note**: *The receiver-drier (see Section 14) should be replaced whenever the compressor is replaced.*
Note: *The receiver-drier (see Section 14) should be replaced whenever the compressor is replaced.*

Removal

1   Have the system discharged (see Warning above).
2   Disconnect the negative battery cable from the battery.
3   Disconnect and remove the fresh air duct from the top of the radiator.
4   Loosen the idler pulley adjusting bolt and locknut to loosen the compressor drivebelt.
5   Remove the drivebelt.
6   Disconnect the electrical connector from the compressor clutch.

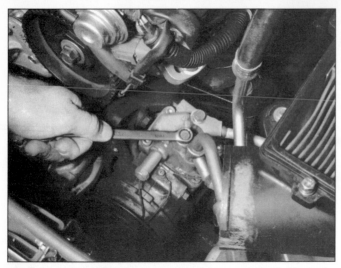

16.7 After the refrigerant system has been properly discharged, disconnect the lines at the compressor

16.8 Remove the bolts that hold the compressor to the mounting bracket (there are four of them)

7   Disconnect the refrigerant lines and plug the open fittings to prevent entry of dirt and moisture **(see illustration)**.
8   Unbolt the compressor from the mounting brackets **(see illustration)**.

Installation

9   If a new compressor is being installed, follow the directions with the compressor regarding the draining of excess oil prior to installation.
10   The clutch may have to be transferred from the original to the new compressor.
11   Installation is the reverse of removal. Replace all O-rings with new ones specifically made for air conditioning system use and lubricate them with refrigerant oil.
12   Have the system evacuated, recharged and leak tested by the shop that discharged it.

---

17   Air conditioning condenser cooling fan(s) - check, removal and installation

---

Refer to illustration 17.6
Note: *Models with a four-cylinder engine and an automatic transmission have dual electric cooling fans in front of the air conditioning condenser.*

Check

1   Disconnect the electrical connector from the fan(s).
2   Using jumper wires, connect battery voltage to terminal A and ground terminal B. The motor should operate.
3   If the fan(s) don't operate, disconnect the jumper wires and spin the fan(s) by hand to be sure that they aren't stuck.

Removal

4   Remove the lower grille and radiator grille.
5   Remove the hood latch assembly.
6   Unbolt the fan assembly by removing the bolts that hold the fan to the radiator support **(see illustration)**.
7   Disconnect the electrical connector at the fan motor(s).
8   Remove the fan(s).

Installation

9   On four-cylinder models install the right fan first.
10   Install the hood latch assembly.
11   Install the left side fan.
12   Reconnect the electrical connector(s).

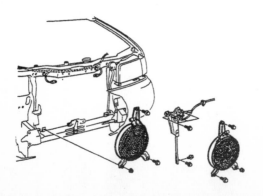

17.6 Mounting details of the condenser cooling fans

18.4 After the system has been properly discharged, disconnect the refrigerant lines from the front of the condenser (the arrow indicates one of the two condenser mounting bolts)

19.7 The air conditioning evaporator case is located on the passenger side, against the firewall

18 Air conditioning condenser - removal and installation

Refer to illustration 18.4
Warning: *The air conditioning system is under high pressure. DO NOT loosen any hose or line fittings or remove any components until after the system has been discharged by a dealer service department or service station. Always wear eye protection when disconnecting air conditioning system fittings.*

Removal

1   Have the air conditioning system discharged (see Warning above).
2   Disconnect the negative cable from the battery and on models so equipped, remove the condenser fan(s) (see Section 17).
3   Remove the electric cooling fan(s) from the front of the condenser (see Section 17).
4   Disconnect the refrigerant lines from the condenser **(see illustration)**.
5   Remove condenser mounting bolts and remove the condenser.

Installation

6   If a new condenser is being installed, pour one ounce of new refrigerant oil into it prior to installation.
7   Reinstall the components in the reverse order of removal. Be sure the rubber pads are in place under the condenser and that the refrigerant lines have new O-rings. **Note**: *Coat new O-rings with compressor oil before assembly.*
8   Have the system evacuated, recharged and leak tested by the shop that discharged it.

19 Evaporator core(s) - removal and installation

Refer to illustration 19.7
Warning: *The air conditioning system is under high pressure. DO NOT loosen any hose or line fittings or remove any components until after the system has been discharged by a dealer service department or service station. Always wear eye protection when disconnecting air conditioning system fittings.*

Front evaporator
Removal

1   Have the air conditioning system discharged (see Warning above).
2   Disconnect the negative cable from the battery and drain the cooling system (see Chapter 1).
3   Remove the passenger side lower trim and glovebox to expose the cooling unit case (see Chapter 11).
4   Locate the refrigerant lines to the evaporator under the hood, located at the firewall area, and disconnect them. Use a back-up wrench when removing the refrigerant lines to prevent twisting the tubing. **Note:** *Plug all refrigerant lines to keep moisture out of the system.*
5   Remove the grommets.
6   Disconnect the thermoswitch electrical connector.
7   Remove the attaching nuts and remove the evaporator case **(see illustration)**.
8   Disassemble the evaporator case by removing the screws separating the upper and lower halves, then remove the evaporator.

Installation

9   Installation is the reverse of the removal procedure. Be sure to refill the cooling system (see Chapter 1). Have the air conditioning system evacuated, recharged and leak tested by the shop that discharged it.

Rear evaporator
Removal

10   Have the air conditioning system discharged (see Warning above).
11   Disconnect the negative cable from the battery.
12   Remove the left rear side trim panel (see Chapter 11).
13   Disconnect the refrigerant lines from the evaporator.
14   Disconnect all electrical connections and hoses from the cooling unit assembly.
15   Disconnect the rear cooling unit nuts and bolts and remove the cooling unit.
16   Separate the upper and lower halves of the case to expose the evaporator.
17   Remove the evaporator from the case.

Installation

18   Installation is the reverse of the removal procedure. Have the air conditioning system evacuated, recharged and leak tested by the shop that discharged it.

3

NOTES

Chapter 4 Fuel and exhaust systems

Contents

4

Specifications

General

Throttle cable freeplay..	0.04 to 0.12 inches
Fuel injector resistance...	12 to 16 ohms

Fuel pressure

Fuel pump pressure (maximum)..	64 to 85 psi
Fuel pump hold pressure..	50 psi
Pressure regulator check (at idle)	
Vacuum hose detached	38 to 46 psi
Vacuum hose attached	31 to 38 psi
Fuel system hold pressure	21 psi

Torque specifications

	Ft-lbs
Throttle body nuts/bolts	14 to 19
Air intake plenum nuts/bolts (four-cylinder engine).........................	14
Extension manifold-to-dynamic chamber	
mounting nuts (V6 engine)...	14 to 19
Dynamic chamber mounting nuts (V6 engine)	
chamber (V6 engine)..	14 to 19
Front catalytic converter nuts/bolts..	44 to 54

---

1   General information

All engines are equipped with Electronic Fuel Injection (EFI). The EFI system consists of three basic sub-systems - the air intake system, the fuel system and the electronic control system.

Air intake system

The air intake system consists of the air filter housing, the airflow meter, the throttle body, the intake manifold and either an air intake plenum (four-cylinder engine) or a Variable Resonance Induction System (VRIS) (V6 engine). All components except the intake manifold are

2.6 Use a jumper wire or a paper clip and bridge the two terminals of the yellow 2-pin connector (four-cylinder engine shown - location and color is similar for the V6 engine)

3.6 Disconnect the fuel line from the pulsation damper (V6 engine shown) and install a fuel pressure gauge on the end of a 3-way fitting between the fuel filter and the fuel pulsation damper

covered in this Chapter; for information on removing and installing the intake manifold, refer to Chapter 2A or 2B.

The throttle valves inside the throttle body are actuated by the accelerator cable. When you depress the accelerator pedal, the throttle plates open and airflow through the intake system increases. A flap inside the airflow meter (V6 engine only) opens wider as the airflow increases. A potentiometer attached to the pivot shaft of the flap measures the angle of the flap (how much it's open) and converts this to a voltage signal which it sends to the computer. An intake air temperature sensor also sends an electrical signal to the computer. The air intake temperature is compared to a "map" - stored in computer memory - of the ideal injector opening duration for the prevailing operating conditions, and the computer alters injector duration accordingly.

Fuel system

An electric fuel pump, located inside the fuel tank, supplies fuel under constant pressure to the fuel rail(s), each of which distributes fuel to the injectors. A pulsation damper smoothes out the pulses of the electric fuel pump. A regulator controls the pressure in the fuel rails. The amount of fuel actually injected into the intake ports is precisely controlled by an electronic control unit (computer).

Electronic control system

Besides altering the injector opening duration as described above, the electronic control unit performs a number of other tasks related to fuel and emissions control. It accomplishes these tasks by comparing data relayed to it by a wide array of information sensors located throughout the engine compartment, comparing this information to its stored map and altering engine operation by controlling a number of different actuators. Since special equipment is required, most troubleshooting and repairing of the electronic control system is beyond the scope of the home mechanic. Additional information and testing procedures on the emissions system components (oxygen sensor, water thermosensor, EVAP system, PRC system etc.) is contained in Chapter 6.

Warranty information

These vehicles are covered by a Federally-mandated extended warranty (5 years or 50,000 miles at the time this manual was written) which covers nearly every fuel system component in this Chapter. Before working on the fuel system, check with a dealer service department for warranty terms on your particular vehicle.

***

2   Fuel pressure relief and fuel system priming

Refer to illustration 2.6
Warning: *Gasoline is extremely flammable, so take extra precautions*

when you work on any part of the fuel system. Don't smoke or allow open flames or bare light bulbs near the work area, and don't work in a garage where a natural gas-type appliance (such as a water heater or clothes dryer) with a pilot light is present. If you spill any fuel on your skin, rinse it off immediately with soap and water. When you perform any kind of work on the fuel system, wear safety glasses and have a Class B type fire extinguisher on hand.*

Relieving fuel pressure

1   Start the engine.
2   If you're working on a model with a V6 engine, detach the airflow meter electrical connector (see Section 12). If you're working on a model with a four-cylinder engine, disconnect the fuel pump electrical connector near the fuel tank.
3   Wait for the engine to stall, then turn off the ignition key.
4   Remove the fuel filler cap to relieve the fuel tank pressure.

Priming the fuel system

5   To avoid excessive cranking when you first start the engine after the fuel pressure has been relieved, prime the system.
6   Using a jumper wire, bridge the terminals of the yellow, two-pin check connector **(see illustration)**.
7   Turn the ignition switch to On for about 10 seconds, then check for leaks.
8   Turn the ignition switch to Off and remove the jumper wire.

***

3   Fuel pump/fuel pressure - check

***

Warning: *Gasoline is extremely flammable, so take extra precautions when you work on any part of the fuel system. Don't smoke or allow open flames or bare light bulbs near the work area, and don't work in a garage where a natural gas-type appliance (such as a water heater or clothes dryer) with a pilot light is present. If you spill any fuel on your skin, rinse it off immediately with soap and water. When you perform any kind of work on the fuel system, wear safety glasses and have a Class B type fire extinguisher on hand.*
Note: *The following checks assume the fuel filter is in good condition. If you doubt the condition of the fuel filter, replace it (see Chapter 1).*

Fuel pump operational check

1   Bridge the terminals of the yellow, two-pin check connector **(see illustration 2.6)**
2   Have an assistant turn the ignition key to On while you listen at the fuel tank (the fuel pump is inside the fuel tank). You should hear a whirring sound for a few seconds.
   a) If there is no whirring sound, there is a problem in the fuel pump circuit. Check the EGI main fuse first (see Chapter 12).

3.16 To check the maximum fuel pump pressure, attach the gauge directly after the fuel filter without allowing the fuel to enter the system

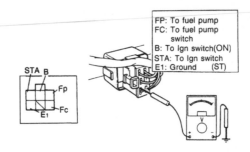

FP: To fuel pump
FC: To fuel pump switch
B: To Ign switch(ON)
STA: To Ign switch
E1: Ground   (ST)

VB: Battery voltage

Condition	Terminal	Fp	Fc	B	STA	E1
IG SW: ON		0V	VB	VB	0V	0V
At idling		VB	0V	VB	0V	0V
IG SW: ST		VB	0V	VB	VB	0

3.25 Terminal guide and voltage checks for the fuel pump relay

b) If the whirring sound continues for a long period of time, the fuel system is probably not pressurizing properly. Check the fuel system pressure (see below).

Fuel system pressure check

Refer to illustration 3.6

3   Relieve the system fuel pressure (see Section 2).
4   Detach the cable from the negative battery terminal.
5   Detach the fuel line from the pulsation damper on V6 engines or from the fuel filter to the main fuel line on four-cylinder engines.
6   Using a tee (three-way) fitting, a short section of high-pressure fuel hose and clamps, attach a fuel pressure gauge **(see illustration)**.
7   Attach the cable to the negative battery terminal.
8   Bridge the terminals of the yellow, two-pin check connector with a jumper wire **(see illustration 2.6)**.
9   Turn the ignition switch to ON.
10   Note the fuel pressure and compare it with this Chapter's specifications.
11   If the system fuel pressure is less than specified:
  a) Inspect the system for a fuel leak. Repair any leaks and recheck the fuel pressure.
  b) If there are no leaks, install a new fuel filter and recheck the fuel pressure.
  c) If the pressure is still low, check the fuel pump pressure (see below) and *the fuel pressure regulator* (see Section 17).
12   If the pressure is higher than specified, replace the fuel pressure regulator.
13   Turn the ignition switch to Off, wait five minutes and check the pressure reading on the gauge. Compare the reading with the hold pressure listed in this Chapter's specifications. If the hold pressure is less than specified:
  a) Inspect the fuel system for a fuel leak. Repair any leaks and recheck the fuel pressure.
  b) Check the fuel pump pressure (see below).
  c) Check the fuel pressure regulator (see Section 17).
  d) The fuel injectors may be leaking.

Fuel pump pressure check

Refer to illustration 3.16

14   Relieve the system fuel pressure (see Section 2).
15   Detach the cable from the negative battery terminal.
16   Detach the fuel feed hose from the fuel rail and attach a fuel pressure gauge **(see illustration)**. Note: *If the 3-way T fitting is still installed in the line, be sure to plug the other end of the 3-way fitting to avoid spilling fuel.*
17   Attach the cable to the negative battery terminal.
18   Using a jumper wire, bridge the terminals of the yellow, two-pin check connector **(see illustration 2.6)**.
19   Turn the ignition switch to On to operate the fuel pump.

20   Note the pressure reading on the gauge and compare the reading to the value listed in this Chapter's Specifications.
21   If the indicated pressure is less than specified, inspect the fuel line for leaks between the pump and gauge. If no leaks are found, replace the fuel pump.
22   Turn the ignition key to Off and wait five minutes. Note the reading on the gauge and compare it to the hold pressure listed in this Chapter's specifications. If the hold pressure is less than specified, check the fuel lines between the pump and gauge for leaks. If no leaks are found, replace the fuel pump.
23   Remove the jumper wire and gauge and reconnect the fuel line.

Fuel pump relay check

Refer to illustrations 3.25 and 3.26

24   The fuel pump relay is located behind the passenger side kick panel, next to the ECU (see Chapter 6).
25   With the relay intact, probe the terminals of the relay electrical connector and check for the proper voltage readings at all the terminals **(see illustration)**. Note: *Some tests will be performed either with the ignition On or with the ignition key turned to the Start position or with the engine at idle*
26   Disconnect the relay electrical connector and probe the terminals

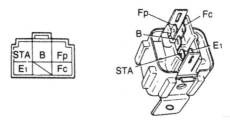

Between terminals	Resistance (Ω)
STA-E1	21—43
B-Fc	109—226
B-Fp	∞

Resistance checks

VB: Battery voltage

VB	Grounded	Correct result
STA	E1	B-Fp: Continuity
B	Fc	Fp: Battery voltage

Apply battery voltage and a ground, then check resistance and voltage

3.26 Terminal guide, resistance checks and continuity chart for the fuel pump relay

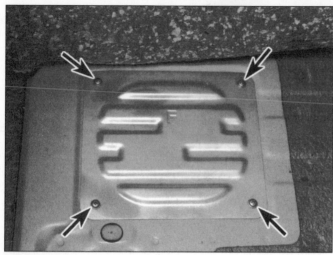

4.4 Remove the four screws (arrows) and pry the cover off the floor of the body

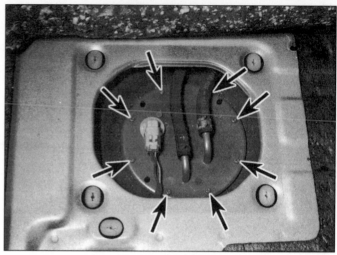

4.6 After disconnecting the electrical connectors and the fuel lines, remove the fuel pump assembly screws (arrows)

with an ohmmeter and check the resistance readings **(see illustration)**.

27   If any of the test results are incorrect, replace the relay with a new part.

---

4   Fuel pump - removal and installation

Refer to illustrations 4.4, 4.6, 4.7 and 4.8

Warning: *Gasoline is extremely flammable, so take extra precautions when you work on any part of the fuel system. Don't smoke or allow open flames or bare light bulbs near the work area, and don't work in a garage where a natural gas-type appliance (such as a water heater or clothes dryer) with a pilot light is present. If you spill any fuel on your skin, rinse it off immediately with soap and water. When you perform any kind of work on the fuel system, wear safety glasses and have a Class B type fire extinguisher on hand.*

1   Relieve the system fuel pressure (see Section 2).
2   Remove the fuel tank filler cap to relieve pressure in the tank.
3   Remove the middle seat (see Chapter 11).
4   Remove the floor mat and locate the fuel pump cover **(see illustration)**.
5   Remove the screws from the cover and lift it off the floor.
6   Unplug the fuel pump electrical connector from the pump **(see il-

lustration)**. Also, disconnect the fuel inlet and return lines.
7   Remove the fuel pump screws **(see illustration 4.6)**, and carefully lift the assembly from the fuel tank **(see illustration)**. It may be necessary to slightly twist the assembly to get the float to clear the opening.
8   Remove the clamp screw and separate the fuel pump from the assembly **(see illustration)**.
9   Installation is the reverse of removal. If the gasket between the fuel pump and fuel tank is dried, cracked or damaged, replace it.

---

5   Fuel lines and fittings - inspection and replacement

Warning: *Gasoline is extremely flammable, so take extra precautions when you work on any part of the fuel system. Don't smoke or allow open flames or bare light bulbs near the work area, and don't work in a garage where a natural gas-type appliance (such as a water heater or clothes dryer) with a pilot light is present. If you spill any fuel on your skin, rinse it off immediately with soap and water. When you perform any kind of work on the fuel system, wear safety glasses and have a Class B type fire extinguisher on hand.*

Inspection

1   Once in a while, you will have to raise the vehicle to service or replace some component (an exhaust pipe hanger, for example). When-

4.7 Carefully lift and twist the bottom section of the fuel pump assembly to clear the opening

4.8 Remove the clamp screw and disconnect the electrical connector to separate the fuel pump from the assembly

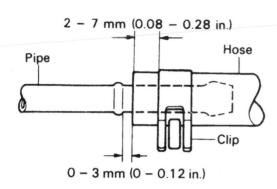

2 – 7 mm (0.08 – 0.28 in.)

Pipe

Hose

Clip

0 – 3 mm (0 – 0.12 in.)

5.6 When attaching a section of rubber fuel hose to a metal fuel line, be sure to overlap the hose as shown and secure it to the line with a new hose clamp of the proper type

6.4 Loosen the drain plug (arrow) and drain the fuel into a suitable container

ever you work under the vehicle, always inspect fuel lines and all fittings and connections for damage or deterioration.

2   Check all hoses and pipes for cracks, kinks, deformation or obstructions.

3   Make sure all hoses and pipe clips attach their associated hoses or pipes securely to the underside of the vehicle.

4   Verify all hose clamps attaching rubber hoses to metal fuel lines or pipes are snug enough to assure a tight fit between the hoses and pipes.

Replacement

Refer to illustration 5.6

5   If you must replace any damaged sections, use original equipment replacement hoses or pipes constructed from exactly the same material as the section you are replacing. Do not install substitutes constructed from inferior or inappropriate material or you could cause a fuel leak or a fire.

6   Always, before detaching or disassembling any part of the fuel line system, note the routing of all hoses and pipes and the orientation of all clamps and clips to assure that replacement sections are installed in exactly the same manner. When attaching hoses to metal lines, overlap them as shown **(see illustration)**.

7   Before detaching any part of the fuel system, be sure to relieve the fuel line and tank pressure by removing the fuel tank cap and disconnecting the battery. Cover the fitting being disconnected with a rag to absorb any fuel that may spray out.

6   Fuel tank - removal and installation

Refer to illustrations 6.4, 6.7a, 6.7b, 6.8a, 6.8b, 6.9 and 6.11

Warning: *Gasoline is extremely flammable, so take extra precautions when you work on any part of the fuel system. Don't smoke or allow open flames or bare light bulbs near the work area, and don't work in a garage where a natural gas-type appliance (such as a water heater or clothes dryer) with a pilot light is present. If you spill any fuel on your skin, rinse it off immediately with soap and water. When you perform any kind of work on the fuel system, wear safety glasses and have a Class B type fire extinguisher on hand.*

Note: *To avoid draining large amounts of fuel, make sure the fuel tank is nearly empty before beginning this procedure.*

1   Remove the fuel tank filler cap to relieve fuel tank pressure.

2   Relieve the fuel system pressure (see Section 2).

3   Detach the cable from the negative battery terminal.

4   Remove the drain plug **(see illustration)** and drain the fuel into an approved container.

5   Unplug the fuel pump electrical connector and detach the fuel feed and return hoses (see Section 4).

6   Raise the vehicle and place it securely on jackstands.

7   Remove the fuel tank shield **(see illustrations)**.

6.7a First remove the bolts from the side of the fuel tank cover . . .

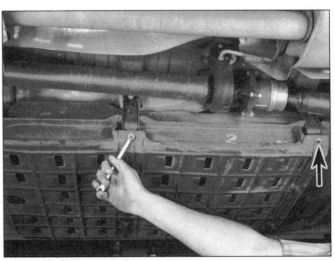

6.7b . . . then remove the bolts from the side

4

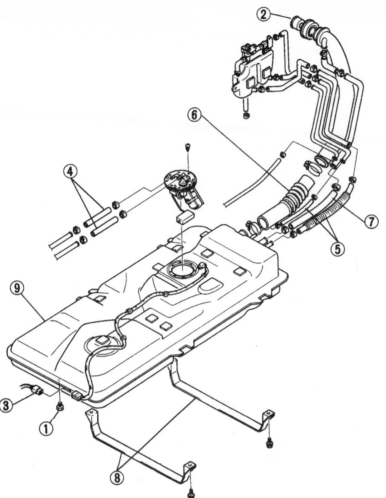

6.8a Details of the fuel tank assembly

1 Drain plug
2 Fuel filler cap
3 Fuel pump connector
4 Fuel hoses
5 Evaporative hoses
6 Fuel filler hose
7 Breather hose
8 Fuel tank straps
9 Fuel tank

8   Detach the fuel filler neck and breather hoses **(see illustrations)**.
9   Detach the electrical connector from the side of the fuel tank **(see illustration)**.
10   Support the tank with a floor jack or jackstands. Position a block of wood between the jack head and the fuel tank to protect the tank.

11   Unbolt both fuel tank retaining straps **(see illustration)** and pivot them down until they're hanging out of the way.
12   Lower the tank just enough so you can see the top and make sure you have detached everything. Finish lowering the tank and remove it from the vehicle.
13   Installation is the reverse of removal.

6.8b Disconnect the fuel filler neck and the evaporative emissions lines from the side of the fuel tank (arrows)

6.9 Disconnect the electrical connector from the side of the fuel tank

6.11 Remove the bolts (arrows) from the straps and lower the fuel tank

7 Fuel tank cleaning and repair - general information

1 All repairs to the fuel tank or filler neck should be carried out by a professional who has experience in this critical and potentially dangerous work. Even after cleaning and flushing of the fuel system, explosive fumes can remain and ignite during repair of the tank.

2 If the fuel tank is removed from the vehicle, it should not be placed in an area where sparks or open flames could ignite the fumes coming out of the tank. Be especially careful inside garages where a natural gas-type appliance is located, because the pilot light could cause an explosion.

8 Air cleaner assembly - removal and installation

Refer to illustrations 8.2a, 8.2b and 8.6

1 Detach the cable from the negative battery terminal.

2 Detach the air intake duct from the front side of the air cleaner **(see illustrations)**.

4

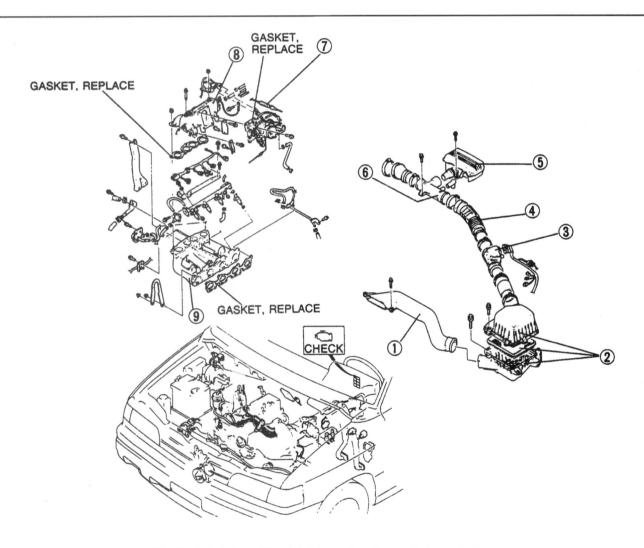

8.2a Exploded view of the air intake system (four-cylinder engine)

1 Air duct	4 Air hose	7 Accelerator cable
2 Air cleaner	5 Resonance chamber	8 Dynamic chamber
3 Airflow sensor	6 Air pipe	9 Intake manifold

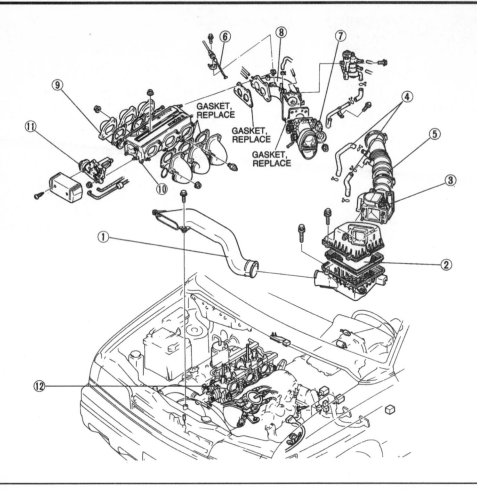

**8.2b Exploded view of
the air intake system
(V6 engine)**

1   Air duct
2   Air filter and housing
3   Airflow sensor
4   Air hose
5   Air funnel
6   Throttle cable
7   Throttle body
8   Intake air pipe
9   Extension manifold
10 Dynamic chamber
11 Shutter valve actuator
    and shutter valve
12 Intake manifold

3   Detach the duct between the air cleaner and the throttle body.
4   Remove the air filter (see Chapter 1).
5   Unplug the airflow meter electrical connector (see Section 12).
6   Remove the air cleaner mounting bolts **(see illustration)** and lift
the air cleaner assembly from the engine compartment.

9   Accelerator cable - check, adjustment and replacement

Check

1   Separate the air intake duct from the throttle body **(see illustrations 8.2a and 8.2b)**.
2   Have an assistant depress the accelerator pedal to the floor while
you watch the throttle valves. They should move to their fully open
(horizontal) positions.
3   Release the accelerator pedal and make sure the throttle valves
return smoothly to their fully closed position.

Adjustment

Refer to illustration 9.5

4   Warm the engine to normal operating temperature and turn it off.
Depress the accelerator pedal to the floor twice, then check the cable
freeplay at the throttle body. Compare it to the value listed in this
Chapter's Specifications.
5   If the freeplay isn't within specifications, adjust it by loosening the
nuts at the cable bracket and moving them in the required direction
(see illustration).
6   Have an assistant help you verify the throttle valves are fully open
when the accelerator pedal is depressed to the floor. If they're not, adjust the opening with the stop bolt near the top of the accelerator pedal.

**8.6 After removing the air filter, remove the bolts (arrows) that
retain the assembly to the fenderwell (V6 engine)**

Replacement

Refer to illustration 9.9

Note: *You'll need a flashlight for the under-dash portion of the following procedure.*

7   Detach the cable from the negative battery terminal.
8   Loosen the cable adjuster locknuts and detach the cable from its
support bracket behind the throttle body.
9   Rotate the throttle linkage to put some slack in the cable and de-

9.5 Loosen the nuts and move them in the required direction to achieve the desired freeplay

9.9 Rotate the throttle valve and remove the cable end from the slotted portion of the valve

tach the cable from the lever **(see illustration)**.
10   Working from underneath the driver's side of the dash, reach up and detach the cable from the top of the accelerator pedal. The cable end is sheathed in a small plastic bushing that pops out of the grooved upper end of the pedal.
11   With a flashlight, trace the path of the cable up to the firewall. You will see the cable disappear through a small plastic grommet with locking tabs on the top and bottom. Depress these tabs and push the grommet through the firewall.
12   Pull the cable through the firewall, from the engine compartment side.
13   Installation is the reverse of removal.

10   Fuel injection system - general information

Refer to illustrations 10.1a through 10.1d
Note: *On models since 1994, the designation for the ECU (Engine Control Unit) was changed to PCM (Powertrain Control Module). The unit operates the same as on prior models, only the name has been changed.*

All models covered by this manual are equipped with an Electronic Fuel Injection (EFI) system. The EFI system is composed of three basic sub systems: fuel delivery system, air intake system and electronic control system **(see illustrations)**.

4

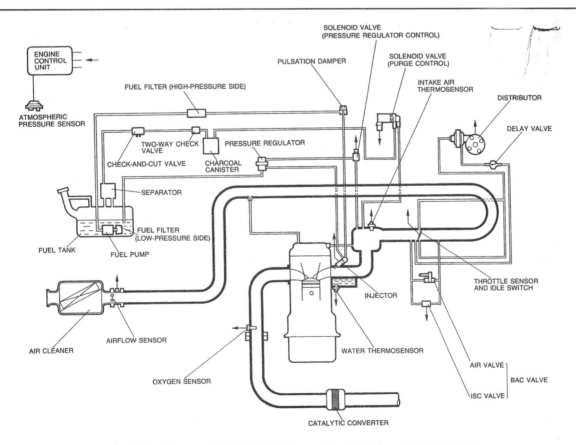

10.1a Diagram of the fuel injection system on the four-cylinder engine

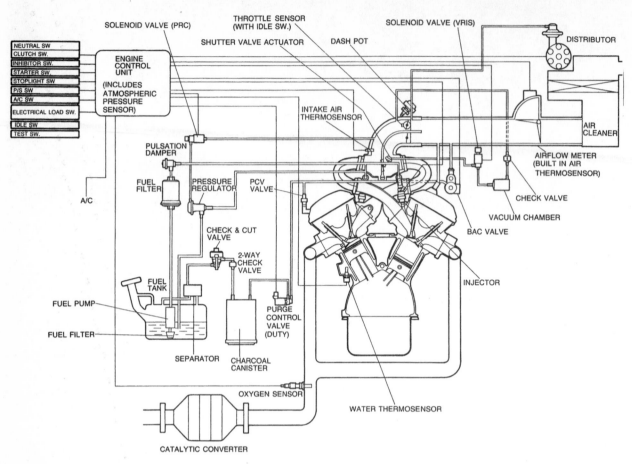

10.1b Diagram of the fuel injection system on the V6 engine

Fuel delivery system

An electric fuel pump located inside the fuel tank supplies fuel under constant pressure to the fuel rail, which distributes fuel evenly to all injectors. From the fuel rail, fuel is injected into the intake ports, just above each intake valve, by solenoid-operated fuel injectors. The amount of fuel supplied by the injectors is precisely controlled by an Electronic Control Unit (ECU). A pressure regulator controls system pressure in relation to intake manifold vacuum. A fuel filter between the fuel pump and the fuel rail filters fuel to protect the components of the system.

Air intake system

The air intake system consists of an air filter housing, an airflow meter and ducting between the components to the throttle body. The airflow meter is an information gathering device for the ECU. V6 engines are equipped with a vane-type airflow meter. A potentiometer measures intake airflow and a temperature sensor measures intake air temperature. Four-cylinder engines are equipped with a hot wire-type airflow sensor. A heated platinum wire (hot wire) is used as a sensing element. This sensor uses an electric current to measure airflow. This information helps the ECU determine the amount (duration) of fuel to be injected by the injectors.

Electronic control system

The Computer Control System controls the EFI and other systems by means of an Electronic Control Unit (ECU), which employs a microcomputer. The ECU receives signals from a number of information sensors which monitor such variables as intake air volume, intake air temperature, coolant temperature, engine rpm, acceleration/deceleration and exhaust oxygen content. These signals help the ECU determine the injection duration necessary for the optimum air/fuel ratio.

Some of these sensors and their corresponding ECU-controlled relays are not contained within EFI components, but are located throughout the engine compartment. For further information regarding the ECU and its relationship to the engine electrical and ignition system, refer to Chapter 6.

---

11   Fuel injection system - check

Refer to illustration 11.7

Warning: *Gasoline is extremely flammable, so take extra precautions when you work on any part of the fuel system. Don't smoke or allow open flames or bare light bulbs near the work area, and don't work in a garage where a natural gas-type appliance (such as a water heater or clothes dryer) with a pilot light is present. If you spill any fuel on your skin, rinse it off immediately with soap and water. When you perform any kind of work on the fuel system, wear safety glasses and have a Class B type fire extinguisher on hand.*

1   Check the ground wire connections. Check all wiring harness electrical connectors that are related to the system. Loose connectors and poor grounds can cause many problems that resemble more serious malfunctions.

2   Make sure the battery is fully charged, as the control unit and sensors depend on an accurate supply voltage in order to properly meter the fuel.

3   Check the air filter element - a dirty or partially blocked filter will severely impede performance and economy (see Chapter 1).

4   If a blown fuse is found, replace it and see if it blows again. If it does, search for a grounded wire in the harness related to the system.

5   Check the air intake duct from the airflow meter to the intake manifold for leaks, which will result in an excessively lean mixture. Also

10.1c Fuel and emissions control components - four-cylinder engine

1	Air intake duct	4	Relay control box	7	BAC valve	9	Air intake plenum
2	Airflow sensor	5	Distributor	8	Fuel pressure	10	Fuel filter
3	Air cleaner assembly	6	PCV valve		regulator	11	Solenoid valve

4

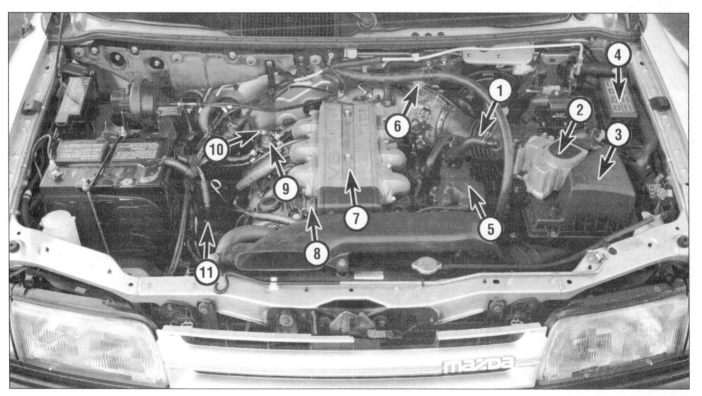

10.1d Fuel and emissions control components - V6 engine

1	Air intake duct	4	Relay control box	7	Dynamic chamber	10	Fuel pressure regulator
2	Airflow meter	5	Distributor	8	Shutter valve actuator	11	Fuel filter
3	Air cleaner assembly	6	BAC valve	9	Fuel pulsation damper		

11.7 Use a stethoscope or screwdriver to determine if the injectors are working properly - they should make a steady clicking sound that rises and falls with engine speed changes

12.1 Pull back the rubber boot from the electrical connector for access to the terminals (four-cylinder engine shown)

check the condition of the vacuum hoses connected to the intake manifold.

6   Remove the air intake duct from the throttle body and check for dirt, carbon and other residue build-up. If it's dirty, clean it with carburetor cleaner and a toothbrush.

7   With the engine running, place a screwdriver or a stethoscope against each injector, one at a time, and listen for a clicking sound, indicating operation **(see illustration)**.

8   The remainder of the system checks should be left to a dealer service department or other repair shop, since there's a chance the ECU may be damaged if the system isn't checked properly.

12   Airflow meter - check, removal and installation

Check

Four-cylinder engine

Refer to illustrations 12.1, 12.2a and 12.2b

Voltage check

1   Remove the rubber boot from the airflow meter electrical connec-

12.2a First check the power supply on the Black/white stripe wire (the wire colors are in the same order as listed in the chart in illustration 12.2b)

tor and slide it down the harness **(see illustration)**.

2   Probe the designated terminals **(see illustrations)** with the voltmeter and check for the proper voltage. **Note:** *Some tests will require the ignition key to be in the ON position.*

3   If the voltage readings are incorrect, check the wiring harness (see Chapter 12).

4   If necessary, check the burn-off control system as described in the next Step.

Burn-off control system check

5   The burn-off control system heats the hot wire (inside the airflow meter) to burn off contaminants that may have collected on the wire. Burn-off occurs after the engine has been stopped (ignition OFF) and:
   a) the engine has run at more than 1,500 rpm for 20 seconds after warm-up
   b) the prescribed amount of air has passed through the air intake system since the last burn-off.

6   Disconnect the negative battery terminal for 20 seconds. **Note:** *Do this only if the airflow meter output voltage is incorrect (see Step 2).* Reconnect the cable to the battery.

7   Warm up the engine to normal operating temperature.

8   Remove the rubber boot from the airflow meter electrical connector and slide it down the harness.

9   Run the engine for more than 5 seconds at approximately 2,000 rpm in Neutral. Turn the ignition key OFF and check for the voltage at

Terminal wire Condition	Ignition switch ON	Engine running
Black/white stripe (large wire) (Power supply)	Approximately 12V	
Green/orange stripe (Burn-off)	0V	
Green/black stripe (Airflow mass)	1.0 - 2.0V	1.9 - 5.0V
Black/white stripe (small wire) (Ground)	Approximately 12V	
Black/orange stripe (Ground)	Approximately 12V	

12.2b Check for the proper voltage readings across the airflow meter terminal connector on the four-cylinder engine

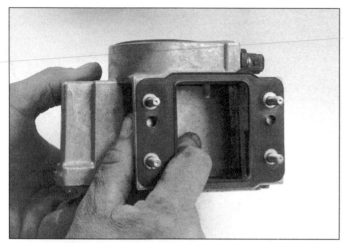

12.14 Make sure the measuring plate moves smoothly and opens fully

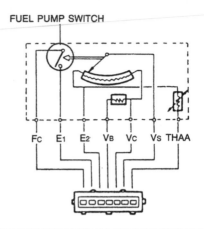

the terminal G/O **(see illustration 12.2b)**. The voltage should be 0 when the switch is turned OFF and then approximately 1 to 5 seconds later it should read 8 to 12 volts.

10   If the voltage readings are incorrect, have the ECU diagnosed by a dealer service department or other repair shop.

11   If the voltage readings are correct, replace the airflow meter.

V6 engines

Refer to illustrations 12.14, 12.15a and 12.15b

12   Remove the airflow meter (see Steps 17 through 21).

13   Check the airflow meter for cracks or any obvious damage.

14   Check that the measuring plate **(see illustration)** moves freely.

15   Carefully move the measuring plate from fully closed to fully open and check the terminals for the proper resistance **(see illustrations)**.

16   If the resistance readings are incorrect, replace the airflow meter.

Removal and installation (all engines)

Refer to illustrations 12.19a, 12.19b and 12.20

17   Remove the air cleaner assembly (see Section 8). **Note:** *On V6 engines, the airflow meter is attached to the air cleaner assembly.*

18   Disconnect the electrical connector.

19   Loosen the hose clamps **(see illustrations)**.

20   Remove the bolts **(see illustration)** and lift the airflow meter from the engine compartment (four-cylinder engine) or from the air cleaner assembly (V6 engine).

21   Installation is the reverse of removal.

Terminal	Resistance (Ω)	
	Fully closed	Fully open
E2↔Vs	20—400	20—1,000
E2↔Vc	100—300	
E2↔VB	200—400	
E2↔THAA (Intake air temp. sensor)	−20°C (−4°F) 13,600—18,400 20°C (68°F) 2,210— 2,690 60°C (140°F) 493— 667	
E1↔Fc	∞	0

12.15a Terminal guide and resistance table for the airflow meter (V6 engines)

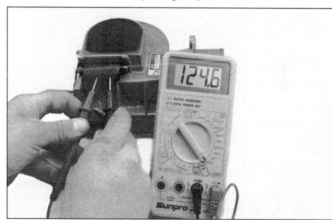

12.15b With the measuring plate fully closed, check the resistance between terminals E2 and Vs

12.19a Loosen the airflow meter clamps (four-cylinder engine)

12.19b Unscrew the bolts that hold the meter to the bracket

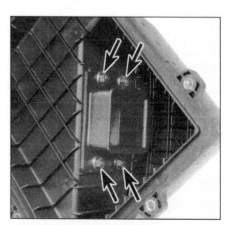

12.20 Remove the nuts (arrows) from the upper half of the air cleaner housing and detach the airflow meter

4

13.11a Remove the nuts and bolts (arrows) from the throttle body . . .

13.11b . . . and use a pair of needle-nose pliers to remove the clamp on the coolant hose before removing the throttle body unit

---

13   Throttle body - check, removal and installation

Check

1   Detach the air intake duct from the throttle body (see Section 8) and move the duct out of the way.
2   Have an assistant depress the throttle pedal while you watch the throttle valves. Check that the number one and number two throttle valves move smoothly when the throttle is moved from closed (idle position) to fully open (wide open throttle). **Note:** *The number two throttle valve is preset at the factory to begin opening simultaneously with the number one throttle valve.*
3   If the throttle valves are not working properly, replace the throttle body unit.

Removal and installation

Refer to illustrations 13.11a and 13.11b

Warning: *Wait until the engine has completely cooled before beginning this procedure.*
4   Detach the cable from the negative battery terminal.
5   Detach the air intake duct from the throttle body and set it aside (see Section 8).
6   Detach the accelerator cable from the throttle body **(see illustration 9.9)**.
7   Detach the cruise control cable, if equipped.

14.7 Remove the bolts and the two corner nuts (arrows) from the air intake plenum

8   Clearly label all electrical connectors (TPS, ISC valve and idle switch), then unplug them.
9   Clearly label all vacuum hoses, then detach them.
10   Clearly label the coolant hoses, then detach them. Plug the hoses to prevent excessive coolant loss. **Note:** *The rear coolant hose on V6 models may not be accessible until the throttle body is detached from the dynamic chamber.*
11   Remove the throttle body mounting nuts (upper) and bolts (lower) and detach the throttle body from the air intake plenum (four-cylinder engine) or intake air pipe (V6 engine) **(see illustrations)**.
12   Cover the air intake plenum (four-cylinder engine) or dynamic chamber (V6 engine) opening with a clean cloth to prevent foreign material from entering while the throttle body is removed.
13   Installation is the reverse of removal. Be sure to tighten the throttle body mounting nuts to the torque listed in this Chapter's Specifications and adjust the accelerator cable (see Section 9) when you're done. Check the coolant level and add, if necessary (see Chapter 1).

---

14   Air intake plenum (four-cylinder engine) - removal and installation

Refer to illustration 14.7

1   Remove the throttle body (see Section 13).
2   Remove the air intake plenum brackets.
3   Clearly label all vacuum hoses, then disconnect them.
4   Disconnect the PCV hose (see Chapter 1).
5   Clearly label all electrical connectors, then disconnect them.
6   Remove the ground wire bolt.
7   Remove the nuts and bolts that retain the air intake plenum **(see illustration)** and lift the plenum from the engine.
8   Installation is the reverse of removal. Tighten the nuts/bolts to the torque listed in this Chapter's Specifications.

---

15   Variable Resonance Induction System (VRIS) (V6 engine) - check and component replacement

Refer to illustration 15.1

1   The Variable Resonance Induction System (VRIS) is used to improve low speed torque. This system consists of the dynamic chamber, shutter valve actuator, extension manifolds, intake manifold, shutter valve and control system **(see illustration)**. The shutter valve is mounted on the dynamic chamber and it is controlled by the ECU. By the closing and opening of the intake valves (valve train), pressure waves are created within the dynamic chamber thereby building up a

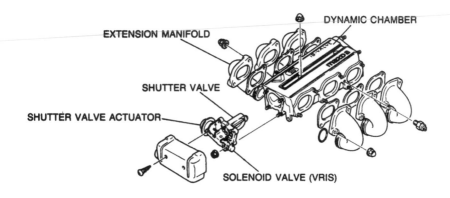

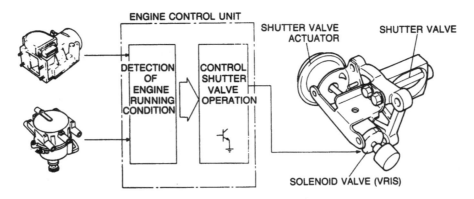

15.1 Diagram of the Variable Resonance Induction System (VRIS)

resonance charge. The resonance charge is forced into other cylinders (companion cylinders) as the engine cycles. The dynamic chamber controls the engine speed and length of the intake passage by the various switching valves (shutter valve, solenoid valve and shutter valve actuator). This in turn delivers a compressed air/fuel mixture at different speeds, resulting in more horsepower and torque. Follow the component checks and replace the proper parts if the system fails any of the tests.

Shutter valve actuator
Check

Refer to illustrations 15.2 and 15.3

2   Remove the actuator cover from the front of the dynamic chamber **(see illustration)**.

3   Connect a hand-held vacuum pump to the actuator **(see illustration)** and apply vacuum.

15.2 Exploded view of the shutter valve

1	Shutter valve actuator	5	C-clip
2	Solenoid valve bracket	6	Cover
3	Nut	7	Solenoid valve
4	Shutter valve and gasket		

15.3 Use a vacuum pump and apply vacuum to the shutter valve actuator

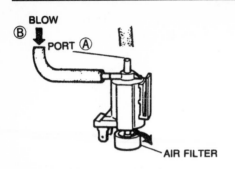

15.15 Blow into port B and check that air flows from the air filter side of the solenoid valve

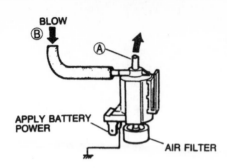

15.18 With the solenoid energized, blow into port B and check that air flows from port A of the solenoid valve

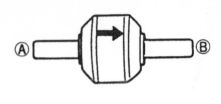

15.21 The check valve allows vacuum to travel through only in one direction

4   Make sure the rod is pulled into the actuator and the vacuum holds steady (no leaks).
5   Replace the shutter valve actuator if it is defective.

Replacement

6   Remove the C-clip **(see illustration 15.2)** and vacuum hose from the actuator.
7   Remove the nuts and lift the actuator from the chamber.
8   Installation is the reverse of removal.

Shutter valve

Check

9   Remove the actuator (see Steps 6 through 8) and make sure the shutter valve rod moves freely **(see illustration 15.2)**.
10   If it binds or does not move smoothly, replace it.

Replacement

11   Remove the shutter valve actuator (see Steps 6 through 8).
12   Remove the solenoid bracket **(see illustration 15.2)**.
13   Remove the nuts and lift the shutter valve from the chamber.
14   Installation is the reverse of removal.

Solenoid valve

Check

Refer to illustrations 15.15 and 15.18

15   Disconnect the vacuum hose from the solenoid valve (black hose) and blow through hose B **(see illustration)**.
16   Check that air flows out of the air filter.
17   Disconnect the solenoid valve electrical connector. Apply battery

voltage to one terminal and ground the other.
18   Disconnect the vacuum hose from the solenoid valve (black hose) and blow through hose B **(see illustration)**.
19   Air should flow out of port A.
20   If the solenoid valve doesn't pass these tests, replace it.

Check valve

Refer to illustration 15.21

21   Remove the check valve and blow through port A **(see illustration)** and check that airflows out of port B.
22   Now, blow through port B and make sure it does not blow back through port A. If it does, replace the check valve.

Vacuum chamber

Refer to illustration 15.23

23   Visually check the vacuum chamber for cracks, clogging or any obvious damage **(see illustration)**.
24   Replace it if necessary.

Dynamic chamber

Refer to illustrations 15.26, 15.27, 15.29a, 15.29b, 15.30a and 15.30b

25   Here are three important facts to remember concerning the order of removal of the VRIS system components. This will save time and extra work.
  a) If you're removing the dynamic chamber, remove the throttle body first (see Section 13), the intake air pipe, the extension manifolds and then the dynamic chamber. This removal order is recommended because it's easier to break the throttle body mounting nuts loose while the chamber is still bolted to the intake manifold.

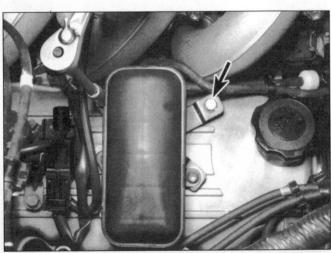

15.23 Be sure to remove only the mounting bolts (arrows) from the vacuum chamber when removing it from the valve cover

15.26 Remove the nuts (arrows) that hold the extension manifolds onto the dynamic chamber

15.27 Carefully lift the extension manifold from the intake manifold and dynamic chamber without breaking the O-rings

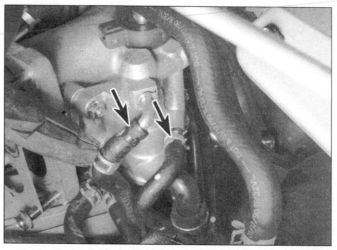

15.29a Use a pair of pliers to expand the clamps (arrows) and slide them down the coolant lines

b) If you're replacing the extension manifolds, the procedure can be performed without having to remove the dynamic chamber or the throttle body unit (proceed to Step 29 in this Section).

c) If you're stripping the engine block for disassembly, remove the throttle body and intake air pipe as one unit and the dynamic chamber and the extension manifolds as separate assemblies.

26   Remove the extension manifold retaining nuts **(see illustration)**.

Note: *Be sure to number the individual manifolds according to the cylinder position.*

27   Carefully lift the extension manifolds off the dynamic chamber without damaging the O-ring surfaces **(see illustration)**.

28   Remove the throttle body (see Section 13).

29   Detach the coolant hoses and plug them, remove the nuts and separate the intake air pipe from the dynamic chamber **(see illustrations)**.

30   Remove the nuts from the dynamic chamber and lift the assembly off the intake manifold **(see illustration)**. Be sure to remove the two rear bolts **(see illustration)**.

31   Carefully remove all traces of old gasket material from the gasket mating surfaces.

32   Installation is the reverse of removal. Be sure to use new gaskets and tighten the fasteners to the torque values listed in this Chapter's Specifications. Check the coolant level and add, if necessary (see Chapter 1).

15.29b Lift the intake air pipe from the dynamic chamber

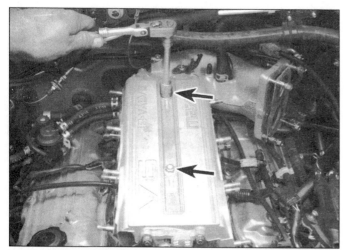

15.30a Remove the nuts from the top of the dynamic chamber . . .

15.30b . . . then unscrew the two bolts at the rear of the dynamic chamber (arrows) and lift it off

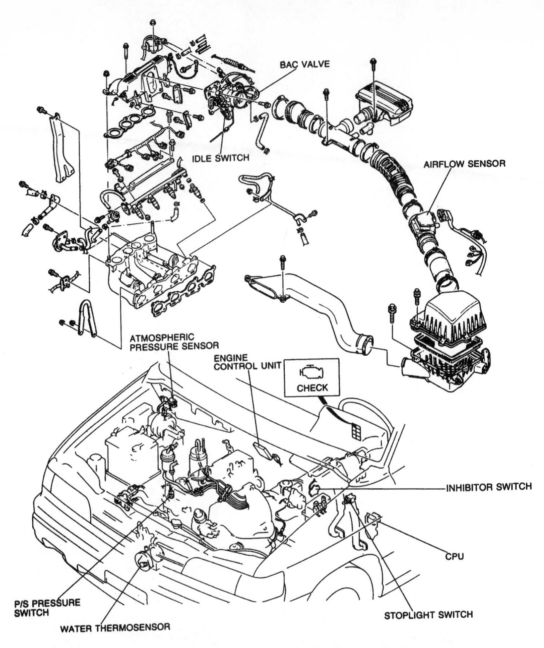

16.1a Diagram of the ISC system (and related components) on the four-cylinder engine

16 Idle Speed Control (ISC) system - check and component replacement

Refer to illustrations 16.1a and 16.1b

1 This system controls the amount of intake air at idle by regulating the volume of bypass air that passes through the throttle body. This is accomplished with the Bypass Air Control (BAC) valve. This system detects air volume, water temperature, engine speed etc. by the various sensors and the ECU incorporated in the fuel injection system **(see illustrations)**.

Check

Four-cylinder engine

Refer to illustrations 16.2, 16.4a and 16.4b

2 Disconnect the ISC electrical connector and measure the resis-

tance between the terminals at approximately 72-degrees F (if possible) **(see illustration)**.
3 The ohmmeter should read 7.7 to 9.3 ohms.
4 Remove the BAC valve **(see illustration)** and perform the following tests:
   a) Blow air through port A and make sure air comes out of port B when the unit is cold **(see illustration)**.
   b) Place the BAC valve into a pan of hot water (176-degrees F) for one minute and observe that after blowing air into port A, nothing comes out of port B.
   c) If the test results are incorrect, replace the BAC valve.

V6 engine

BAC valve

Refer to illustration 16.6

5 Disconnect the air hoses from the air funnel on the BAC valve.

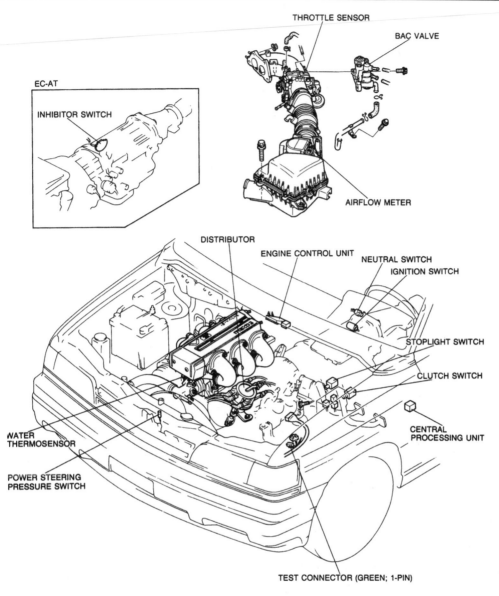

16.1b Diagram of the ISC system on the V6 engine

16.2 Check the resistance of the ISC solenoid by disconnecting the electrical connector (backside of air intake plenum) and probing the two terminals

16.4a Remove the four screws (arrows) and lift the BAC valve from the plenum

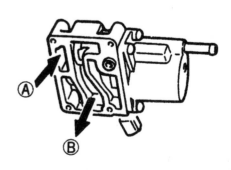

16.4b Blow air into passage A and verify airflow from passage B

16.6 Remove the hose and blow into port A

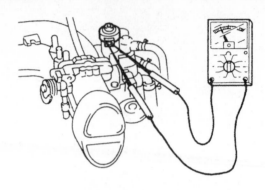

16.11 Check the resistance of the ISC valve

6   Perform this test when the engine is cold. Blow through the BAC valve from port A and check that air flows through the valve **(see illustration)**.

7   Warm up the engine.

8   Blow through the BAC valve from port A and check that air does not flow through the valve.

9   Here is another quick check to test the BAC valve:

a) Warm up the engine and run it·at idle speed.

b) Unplug the BAC valve electrical connector.

c) Verify the engine speed decreases when the electrical connector is unplugged.

d) If the engine speed does not decrease, check the ISC valve, as described in the following Steps.

ISC valve

Refer to illustration 16.11

10   Unplug the ISC valve electrical connector.

11   Check the valve resistance with an ohmmeter **(see illustration)**. It should be about 10.7 to 12.3 ohms. If it isn't, replace the ISC valve.

Replacement

Refer to illustration 16.12

12   Disconnect the coolant hoses from the BAC valve **(see illustration)**. Plug the hoses to prevent leakage.

13   Disconnect the air hose from the BAC valve.

14   Disconnect the BAC valve electrical connector.

15   Remove the nuts and lift the BAC valve from the dynamic chamber (V6 engine) or throttle body (four-cylinder engine).

16   Installation is the reverse of removal.

17   Fuel pressure regulator - check and replacement

Refer to illustrations 17.5, 17.11, and 17.16

Warning: *Gasoline is extremely flammable, so take extra precautions when you work on any part of the fuel system. Don't smoke or allow open flames or bare light bulbs near the work area, and don't work in a garage where a natural gas-type appliance (such as a water heater or clothes dryer) with a pilot light is present. If you spill any fuel on your skin, rinse it off immediately with soap and water. When you perform any kind of work on the fuel system, wear safety glasses and have a Class B type fire extinguisher on hand.*

Check

1   Relieve the fuel system pressure (see Section 2).

2   Detach the cable from the negative battery terminal.

3   Disconnect the fuel line from the fuel rail and install a fuel pressure gauge (see Section 3).

4   Start the engine and check for leakage around the gauge connections.

5   Detach the vacuum hose from the fuel pressure regulator and connect a hand-held vacuum pump to the fuel pressure regulator **(see illustration)**.

6   Read the fuel pressure gauge with vacuum applied to the pressure regulator and also with no vacuum applied. The fuel pressure should decrease as vacuum increases. Compare your readings with the values listed in this Chapter's Specifications.

7   Reconnect the vacuum hose to the regulator and check the fuel pressure at idle, comparing your reading with the value listed in this Chapter's Specifications. Disconnect the vacuum hose and watch the gauge - the pressure should jump up to the maximum specified pres-

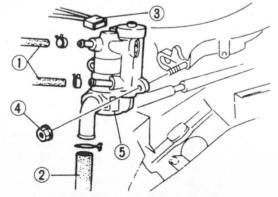

16.12 BAC valve installation details

1   *Coolant hoses*
2   *Air hose*
3   *BAC electrical connector*
4   *Nut*
5   *BAC valve*

17.5 Carefully watch the fuel pressure gauge as vacuum is applied - fuel pressure should increase as vacuum decreases

17.11 With the engine idling, the vacuum solenoid should allow vacuum to pass through

17.16 Disconnect the vacuum line and the fuel return hose (arrows), then remove the fuel pressure regulator mounting bolts (arrows) (four-cylinder engine shown)

sure as soon as the hose is disconnected.

8   If the fuel pressure is low, pinch the fuel return line shut and watch the gauge. If the pressure doesn't rise, the fuel pump is defective or there is a restriction or leak in the fuel feed line. If the pressure rises sharply, replace the pressure regulator.

9   If the indicated fuel pressure is too high, stop the engine. Disconnect the fuel return line from the regulator and blow through it to check for a blockage. If there is no blockage, replace the fuel pressure regulator.

10   If the pressure doesn't fluctuate as described in Step 7, check for vacuum at the pressure regulator vacuum hose. If there is vacuum, replace the fuel pressure regulator.

11   Connect a vacuum gauge to the vacuum solenoid and check for vacuum **(see illustration)**.

12   If there isn't any reading on the gauge, shut off the engine. Ground one terminal of the vacuum solenoid with a jumper wire and apply battery voltage to the other terminal. The solenoid should make a distinct "click" sound. This means the solenoid is working properly and it should allow vacuum to the fuel pressure regulator.

13   If the vacuum solenoid works properly but there still is no vacuum to the fuel pressure regulator, have the ECU and the fuel pressure regulator vacuum system diagnosed by a dealer service department or other repair shop.

Replacement

14   Relieve the system fuel pressure (see Section 2).

15   Detach the cable from the negative battery terminal.

16   Detach the vacuum hose and fuel hose from the pressure regulator, then unscrew the mounting bolts **(see illustration)**.

17   Remove the pressure regulator.

18   Installation is the reverse of removal. Be sure to use a new gasket.

19   Check for fuel leaks after installing the pressure regulator.

18   Pulsation damper - check and replacement

Refer to illustrations 18.5a and 18.5b

Warning: *Gasoline is extremely flammable, so take extra precautions when you work on any part of the fuel system. Don't smoke or allow open flames or bare light bulbs near the work area, and don't work in a garage where a natural gas-type appliance (such as a water heater or clothes dryer) with a pilot light is present. If you spill any fuel on your skin, rinse it off immediately with soap and water. When you perform any kind of work on the fuel system, wear safety glasses and have a Class B type fire extinguisher on hand.*

Check

1   Relieve the fuel system pressure (see Section 2). Connect a fuel pressure gauge between the pulsation damper and the fuel rail, using a "tee" fitting.

2   Start the engine and watch the needle on the gauge. If the needle fluctuates or oscillates, the pulsation damper is defective.

Replacement

3   Relieve the fuel system pressure (see Section 2).

4   Remove the fuel lines from the damper.

5   Unscrew the bolts and remove the pulsation damper **(see illustrations)**.

6   Installation is the reverse of removal.

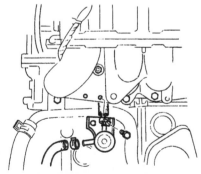

18.5a Location of the pulsation damper on the four-cylinder engine

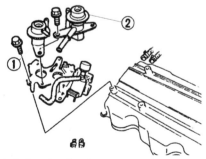

18.5b Installation details of the fuel pressure regulator and the pulsation damper (V6 engine)

1   *Fuel pressure regulator*   2   *Pulsation damper*

19.6 Remove the nuts (arrows) that hold the fuel rail to the intake manifold (V6 engine shown)

19.7 Lift the fuel rail assembly off the engine (V6 engine shown)

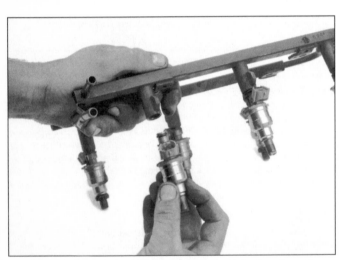

19.8 Using a twisting motion, pull the fuel injectors from the fuel rail

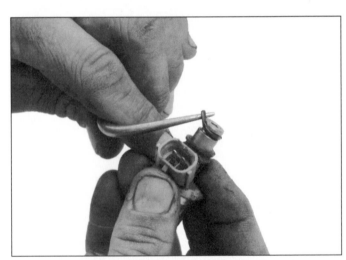

19.9 Be sure to replace the O-rings with new ones

---

19   Fuel injectors - check and replacement

Warning: *Gasoline is extremely flammable, so take extra precautions when you work on any part of the fuel system. Don't smoke or allow open flames or bare light bulbs near the work area, and don't work in a garage where a natural gas-type appliance (such as a water heater or clothes dryer) with a pilot light is present. If you spill any fuel on your skin, rinse it off immediately with soap and water. When you perform any kind of work on the fuel system, wear safety glasses and have a Class B type fire extinguisher on hand.*

Check

1   If you suspect any of the injectors are malfunctioning, start the engine and touch each injector with a stethoscope or screwdriver (which will work like a stethoscope if you put your ear to it) **(see illustration 11.7)**. Listen for a clicking sound proportional to engine speed; this indicates normal injector operation. If you hear no sound or an unusual sound from any injector, verify that the wiring connections are in good condition.

2   If you don't have a stethoscope, and you can't determine the condition of the injectors with a screwdriver, touch each injector with your finger and feel the injection pulses. You should feel a rhythmic clicking.

3   To measure the resistance of an injector, unplug the electrical connector, touch the probes of an ohmmeter to the injector terminals and compare your measurement to the resistance value listed in this Chapter's Specifications. If the indicated resistance of an injector is outside the specified range of resistance, replace the injector.

Replacement

Refer to illustrations 19.6, 19.7, 19.8 and 19.9

4   Remove the VRIS system on V6 engines (see Section 15) or the air intake plenum on four-cylinder engines (see Section 14) to expose the fuel injectors and the fuel rail.

5   Unplug the injector connectors.

6   Detach the fuel hoses from the fuel rail and remove the fuel rail mounting bolts or nuts **(see illustration)**.

7   Lift the fuel rail/injector assembly from the engine **(see illustration)**.

8   Detach the injectors from the fuel rail **(see illustration)**.

9   Installation is the reverse of removal. Be sure to replace all O-rings with new ones **(see illustration)**. Coat them with a little clean engine oil to prevent damage during installation. Be sure to prime the fuel system and check for leaks.

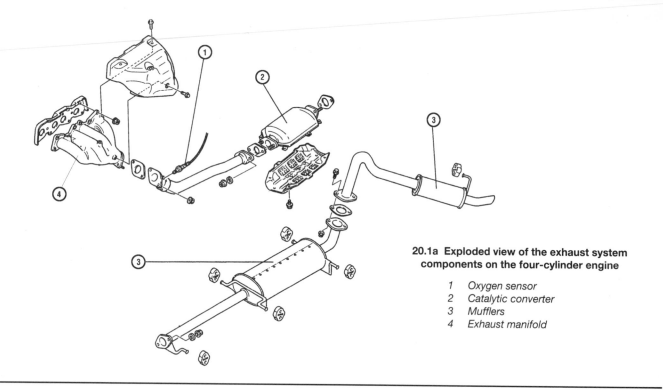

20.1a Exploded view of the exhaust system components on the four-cylinder engine

1   Oxygen sensor
2   Catalytic converter
3   Mufflers
4   Exhaust manifold

20   Exhaust system servicing - general information

Warning: *Inspect or repair exhaust system components only after enough time has elapsed after driving the vehicle to allow the system components to cool completely. Also, when working under the vehicle make sure it is securely supported by jackstands.*

Muffler and pipes

Refer to illustrations 20.1a and 20.1b

1   The exhaust system **(see illustrations)** consists of the exhaust manifold, catalytic converter, mufflers and all connecting pipes, brackets, hangers and clamps. The exhaust system is attached to the body with mounting brackets and rubber hangers. If any of the parts are im-

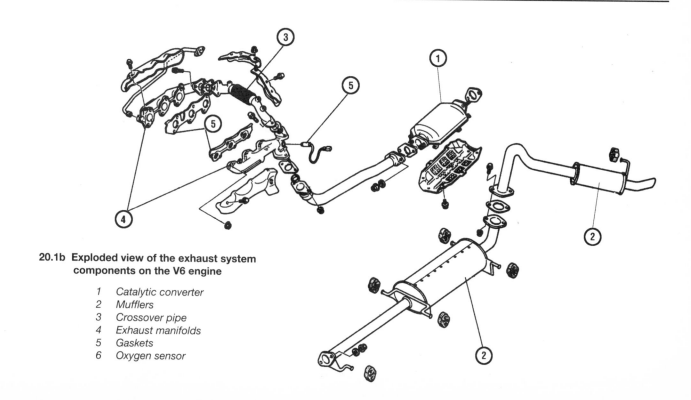

20.1b Exploded view of the exhaust system components on the V6 engine

1   Catalytic converter
2   Mufflers
3   Crossover pipe
4   Exhaust manifolds
5   Gaskets
6   Oxygen sensor

properly installed, excessive noise and vibration may be transmitted to the body.

2   Inspect the exhaust system regularly to keep it safe and quiet. Look for any damaged or bent parts, open seams, holes, loose connections, excessive corrosion or other defects which could allow exhaust fumes to enter the vehicle. Deteriorated exhaust system components should not be repaired; they should be replaced with new parts.

3   If the exhaust system components are ex
tremely corroded or rusted together, welding equipment will probably be required to remove them. The convenient way to accomplish this is to have a muffler repair shop remove the corroded sections with a cutting torch. If, however, you want to save money by doing it yourself (and you don't have a welding outfit with a cutting torch), cut off the old components with a hacksaw. If you have compressed air, a special pneumatic cutting chisel can also be used. If you decide to tackle the job at home, be sure to wear safety goggles to protect your eyes from metal chips and use work gloves to protect your hands.

4   Here are some simple guidelines to follow when repairing the exhaust system:

  a) Work from the back to the front of the vehicle when removing exhaust system components.

  b) Apply penetrating oil to the exhaust system fasteners to make them easier to remove.

  c) Use new gaskets, hangers and clamps when installing exhaust system components.

  d) Apply anti-seize compound to the threads of all exhaust system fasteners during reassembly.

  e) Be sure to allow sufficient clearance between newly installed parts and all points on the underbody to avoid overheating the floor pan and possibly damaging the interior carpet and insulation. Pay particularly close attention to the catalytic converters and heat shields.

Catalytic converters

5   Although the catalytic converters are emissions-related components, they are discussed here because, physically, they're integral parts of the exhaust system. Always check the converters whenever you raise the vehicle to inspect or service the exhaust system.

6   Raise the vehicle and place it securely on jackstands.

7   Visually inspect all catalytic converters on the vehicle for cracks or damage.

8   Check all converters for tightness.

9   Check the insulation covers welded onto the catalytic converters for damage or a loose fit.

10   Start the engine and run it at idle speed. Check all converter connections for exhaust gas leakage.

Chapter 5   Engine electrical systems

Contents

Specifications

Coil

Primary resistance
  Four-cylinder engine
    First stage .... 0.77 to 0.95 ohms
    Second stage .... 0.90 to 1.10 ohms
  V6 engine .... 0.81 to 0.99 ohms
Secondary resistance
  Four-cylinder engine .... 6 to 30K ohms
  V6 engine .... 6 to 30K ohms
Insulation resistance .... 10M ohms

Distributor

Pick-up coil/igniter resistance .... 900 to 1,200 ohms
Crank angle sensor resistance
  1992 models
    Between terminals Ne and Com .... 140 to 180 ohms
    Between terminals G1 and Com .... 140 to 180 ohms
    Between terminals G2 and Com .... 140 to 180 ohms
  1993 and later models
    Between terminals Ne and Com .... 205 to 255 ohms
    Between terminals G1 and Com .... 205 to 255 ohms
    Between terminals G2 and Com .... 205 to 255 ohms

Torque specifications

Crank angle sensor locknuts .... 70 inch-lbs

5

3.2 Always detach the cable from the negative battery terminal first, then detach the positive cable - to remove the hold-down assembly, simply remove both nuts (arrows)

7.4a Using an ohmmeter, measure the resistance between the primary terminals of the first stage (white terminal cover) (four-cylinder engine) . . .

1   General information

The engine electrical systems include all ignition, charging and starting components. Because of their engine-related functions, these components are discussed separately from chassis electrical devices such as the lights, the instruments, etc. (which are included in Chapter 12).

Always observe the following precautions when working on the electrical systems:

a) Be extremely careful when servicing engine electrical components. They are easily damaged if checked, connected or handled improperly.

b) Never leave the ignition switch on for long periods of time with the engine off.

c) Don't disconnect the battery cables while the engine is running.

d) Maintain correct polarity when connecting a battery cable from another vehicle during jump starting.

e) Always disconnect the negative cable first and hook it up last or the battery may be shorted by the tool being used to loosen the cable clamps.

It's also a good idea to review the safety-related information regarding the engine electrical systems located in the *Safety first* section near the front of this manual before beginning any operation included in this Chapter.

2   Battery - emergency jump starting

Refer to the *Booster battery (jump) starting* procedure at the front of this manual.

3   Battery - removal and installation

Refer to illustration 3.2

1   Disconnect the negative cable from the battery terminal.

2   Remove the battery hold-down bracket **(see illustration)**.

3   Remove the positive battery terminal and lift out the battery. Be careful - it's heavy.

4   While the battery is out, inspect the carrier (tray) for corrosion (see Chapter 1).

5   If you are replacing the battery, make sure that you get one that's identical, with the same dimensions, amperage rating, cold cranking rating, etc.

6   Installation is the reverse of removal. Be sure to connect the positive cable first, followed by the negative cable.

4   Battery cables - check and replacement

1   Periodically inspect the entire length of each battery cable for damage, cracked or burned insulation and corrosion. Poor battery cable connections can cause starting problems and decreased engine performance.

2   Check the cable-to-terminal connections at the ends of the cables for cracks, loose wire strands and corrosion. The presence of white, fluffy deposits under the insulation at the cable terminal connection is a sign that the cable is corroded and should be replaced. Check the terminals for distortion, missing mounting bolts and corrosion.

3   When removing the cables, always disconnect the negative cable first and hook it up last or the battery may be shorted by the tool used to loosen the cable clamps. Even if only the positive cable is being replaced, be sure to disconnect the negative cable from the battery first (see Chapter 1 for further information regarding battery cable removal).

4   Disconnect the old cables from the battery, then trace each of them to their opposite ends and detach them from the starter solenoid and ground terminals. Note the routing of each cable to ensure correct installation.

5   If you are replacing either or both of the old cables, take them with you when buying new cables. It is vitally important that you replace the cables with identical parts. Cables have characteristics that make them easy to identify: positive cables are usually red, larger in cross-section and have a larger diameter battery post clamp; ground cables are usually black, smaller in cross-section and have a slightly smaller diameter clamp for the negative post.

6   Clean the threads of the solenoid or ground connection with a wire brush to remove rust and corrosion. Apply a light coat of battery terminal corrosion inhibitor, or petroleum jelly, to the threads to prevent future corrosion.

7   Attach the cable to the solenoid or ground connection and tighten the mounting nut/bolt securely.

8   Before connecting a new cable to the battery, make sure that it reaches the battery post without having to be stretched.

9   Connect the positive cable first, followed by the negative cable.

5   Ignition system - general information and precautions

The ignition system includes the ignition switch, the battery, the crank angle sensor (1992 and later models), the pick-up coil/igniters (1989 through 1991 models), the primary (low voltage) and secondary (high voltage) wiring circuits and the spark plugs.

When working on the ignition system, take the following precautions:

7.4b . . . and then measure the resistance between the primary terminals of the second stage (black terminal cover) (four-cylinder engine)

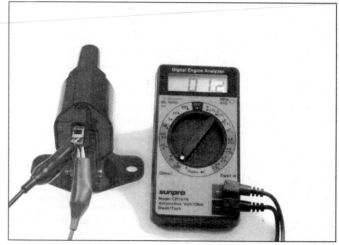

7.4c Using an ohmmeter, measure the resistance between the primary terminals of the coil (V6 engine) (coil removed for clarity)

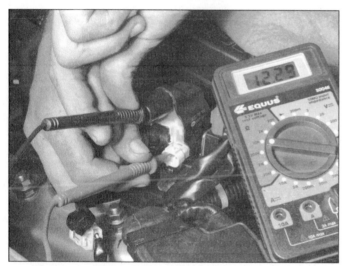

7.5a Using an ohmmeter, measure the secondary resistance of the coil (four-cylinder engine)

a) If the engine won't start, don't keep the ignition switch on for more than 10 seconds.
b) Never allow an ignition coil terminal to contact ground. Grounding the ignition coil can damage the igniter and/or the coil itself.
c) Don't disconnect the battery when the engine is running.
d) Make sure the igniter is properly grounded.

---

6   Ignition system - check

Warning: *Because of the high voltage generated by the ignition system, extreme care should be taken whenever an operation is performed involving ignition components. This not only includes the igniter, coil, distributor and spark plug wires, but related components such as spark plug connectors, tachometer and other test equipment.*
1   If the engine turns over but will not start, disconnect the spark plug wire from any spark plug and attach it to a calibrated spark tester (available at most auto parts stores). **Note:** *There are two different types of spark testers. Be sure to specify electronic (breakerless) ignition.* Connect the clip on the tester to a ground such as a metal bracket.
2   If you are unable to obtain a calibrated spark tester, remove the spark plug wire from one of the spark plugs. Using an insulated tool, hold the wire about 1/4-inch from a good ground.

3   Crank the engine and observe the tip of the tester or spark plug wire to see if a spark occurs. If bright blue, well-defined sparks occur, sufficient voltage is reaching the plugs to fire the engine. However, the plugs themselves may be fouled, so remove and check them as described in Chapter 1.
4   If there's no spark, check another wire in the same manner. A few sparks followed by no spark is the same condition as no spark at all.
5   If no spark occurs, remove the distributor cap and check the cap and rotor as described in Chapter 1. If moisture is present, use WD-40 (or something similar) to dry out the cap and rotor, then reinstall the cap and repeat the spark test.
6   If there's still no spark, disconnect the coil wire from the distributor, hold it about 1/4-inch from a good ground and crank the engine again.
7   If no spark occurs, check the primary wire connections at the coil to make sure they're clean and tight. Make any necessary repairs, then repeat the check again.
8   If sparks now occur, the distributor cap, rotor, plug wire(s) or spark plug(s) may be defective. If there's still no spark, the coil-to-cap wire may be bad. If a substitute wire doesn't make any difference, check the ignition coil (see Section 7).

---

7   Ignition coil - check and replacement

Refer to illustrations 7.4a, 7.4b, 7.4c, 7.5a and 7.5b
Caution: *If the coil terminals touch a ground source, the coil and/or pick-up coil/igniter could be damaged.*
1   Mark the wires and terminals with pieces of numbered tape, then remove the primary wires and the high-tension lead from the coil.
2   Remove the coil assembly from its mount, clean the outer case and check it for cracks and other damage.
3   Inspect the coil primary terminals and the coil tower terminal for corrosion. Clean them with a wire brush if any corrosion is found.
4   Check the coil primary resistance by attaching the leads of an ohmmeter to the positive and negative primary terminals **(see illustrations)**. Compare the measured resistance to the Specifications listed in this Chapter. **Note:** *Most digital ohmmeters will carry 0.2 to 0.3 ohms of resistance within the leads.*
5   Check the coil secondary resistance by hooking one of the ohmmeter leads to one of the primary terminals and the other ohmmeter lead to the coil high-tension terminal **(see illustrations)**. Compare the measured resistance to the Specifications listed in this Chapter.
6   Measure the insulation resistance by attaching the leads of an ohmmeter to the positive terminal and ground (the igniter body). Compare the measured resistance to the Specifications.
7   If the measured resistances are not as specified, the coil is probably defective and should be replaced with a new one.

5

7.5b   Measuring the secondary resistance of the coil (V6 engine)

8.2a   It is possible to check the resistance of the pick-up coil/igniter unit on either the electrical connector terminals (V6 engine shown) . . .

8.2b   . . . or directly on the terminals of the pick-up coil/igniter unit (V6 engine shown)

8.6a   Carefully pry the signal rotor off the distributor shaft

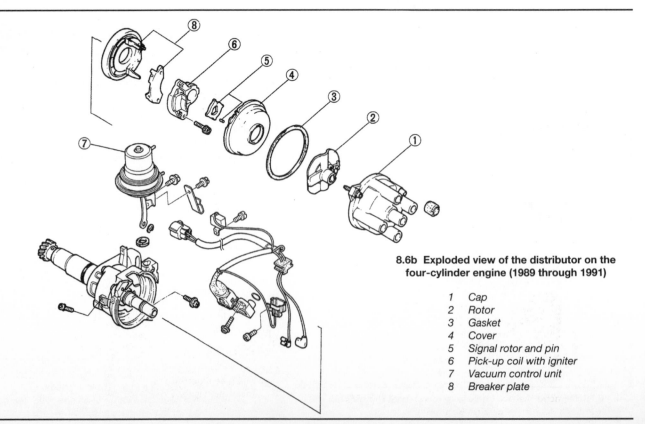

8.6b   Exploded view of the distributor on the four-cylinder engine (1989 through 1991)

1	Cap
2	Rotor
3	Gasket
4	Cover
5	Signal rotor and pin
6	Pick-up coil with igniter
7	Vacuum control unit
8	Breaker plate

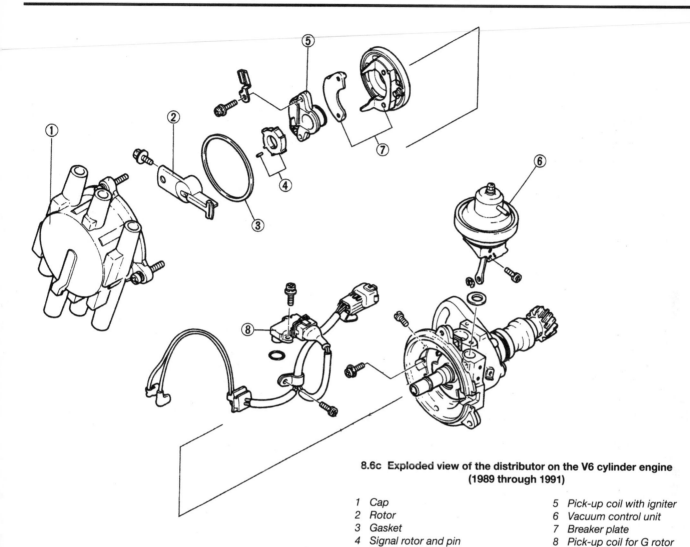

8.6c Exploded view of the distributor on the V6 cylinder engine (1989 through 1991)

1	Cap	5	Pick-up coil with igniter
2	Rotor	6	Vacuum control unit
3	Gasket	7	Breaker plate
4	Signal rotor and pin	8	Pick-up coil for G rotor

5

8   It is essential for proper ignition system operation that all coil terminals and wire leads to be kept clean and dry.

9   Install the coil in its mount and hook up the wires. Installation is the reverse of removal.

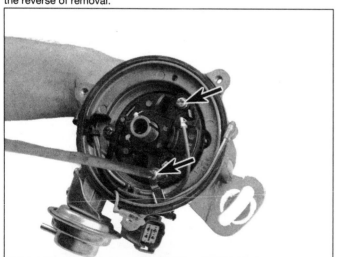

8.7a   Remove the two screws (arrows) from the pick-up coil igniter unit

8   Pick-up coil/igniter (1989 through 1991 models) - check and replacement

Check

Refer to illustrations 8.2a and 8.2b

1   Disconnect the electrical connector to the pick-up coil/igniter unit.

2   Connect an ohmmeter to the pick-up coil/igniter leads and measure the resistance **(see illustrations)**. Refer to the specifications listed in this Chapter.

3   If the readings are incorrect, replace the unit.

Replacement

Refer to illustrations 8.6a, 8.6b, 8.6c, 8.7a and 8.7b

4   Detach the cable from the negative terminal of the battery.

5   Remove the distributor from the engine (see Section 10).

6   Using two flat bladed screwdrivers, carefully pry the signal rotor up and off the distributor shaft **(see illustration)**. Be sure not to lose the alignment pin once the rotor is lifted from the assembly **(see illustrations)**.

7   Remove the pick-up coil/igniter mounting screws and nuts, disconnect the wires from the terminals and remove the pick-up coil/igniter unit **(see illustrations)**.

8   Installation is the reverse of removal.

8.7b Lift the assembly off the distributor

9   Crank angle sensor (1992 and later models) - check, removal and installation

Check

Refer to illustration 9.2

1   Unplug the electrical connector from the crank angle sensor.
2   Using an ohmmeter, check the resistance between the indicated terminals **(see illustration)**.
3   If the resistance is not as specified, replace the crank angle sensor.

Removal

Refer to illustrations 9.6a and 9.6b

4   Remove the distributor (see Section 10).
5   Unplug the electrical connector from the sensor if you haven't already done so.
6   Mark the base of the sensor housing and the front cover to assure proper alignment during reassembly **(see illustrations)**.
7   Remove the crank angle sensor locknut.
8   Lift the crank angle sensor straight up to remove it.

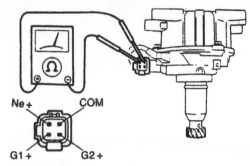

Terminals	Resistance
Ne — COM	140—180Ω
G1 — COM	at 20°C (68°F)
G2 — COM	

1992 models

Terminals	Resistance
Ne — COM	205—255Ω
G1 — COM	at 20°C (68°F)
G2 — COM	

1993 and later models

9.2 Measure the resistance of the crank angle sensor using the pin designations and the resistance values listed in the charts

Installation

9   Align the matching marks on the sensor housing and driven gear.
10   Verify the mark on the sensor housing is still set to the pointer.
11   Lower the crank angle sensor into the distributor, making sure the marks on the housing base and the front cover are in alignment. Loosely install the locknut and plug in the electrical connector.
12   Check the ignition timing (see Chapter 1).
13   Tighten the locknut securely.

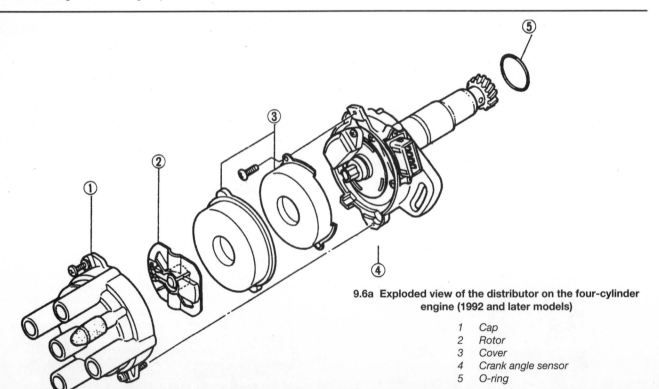

9.6a Exploded view of the distributor on the four-cylinder engine (1992 and later models)

1   *Cap*
2   *Rotor*
3   *Cover*
4   *Crank angle sensor*
5   *O-ring*

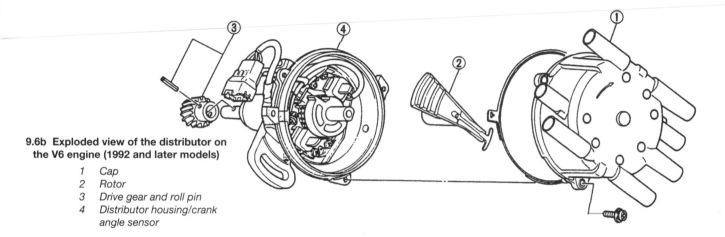

9.6b Exploded view of the distributor on the V6 engine (1992 and later models)

1 Cap
2 Rotor
3 Drive gear and roll pin
4 Distributor housing/crank angle sensor

10.7a Scribe or mark around the bolt/washer (four-cylinder engine shown)

10.7b Also make a mark to indicate the position of the rotor (arrows)

10 Distributor - removal and installation

Removal

Refer to illustrations 10.7a, 10.7b and 10.7c

1   After carefully marking them, remove the coil wire and spark plug wires from the distributor cap (see Chapter 1).

2   Remove the number one spark plug (the one nearest you when you are standing in front of the engine).

3   Manually rotate the engine to Top Dead Center on the compression stroke for number one piston (see Chapter 2A or 2B).

4   Carefully mark the vacuum hoses if more than one is connected on your distributor.

5   Disconnect the vacuum hose(s).

6   Disconnect the primary wires from the distributor.

7   Mark the relationship of the rotor position to the body of the distributor. Also mark the relationship of the distributor body to the engine **(see illustrations)**.

8   Remove the hold-down bolt and clamp.

9   Remove the distributor. **Note:** *Do not rotate the engine with the distributor out.*

Installation

10   Before installing the distributor, make certain the number one piston is still at TDC on the compression stroke.

10.7c Rotor alignment and distributor hold-down bolt marks on the V6 engine

11   Insert the distributor into the engine with the adjusting clamp centered over the hold-down hole. Make sure that the gear does not turn as the distributor is inserted.
12   Install the hold-down bolt. The marks previously made on the distributor housing and on the rotor and engine should line up before the bolt is tightened.
13   Install the distributor cap.
14   Connect the wiring for the distributor.
15   Install the spark plug wires.
16   Install the vacuum hoses as previously marked.
17   Adjust the ignition timing (see Chapter 1).

11   Charging system - description

Refer to illustration 11.1

The charging systems used on the vehicles covered in this manual are equipped with internal regulation systems. This system incorporates a rectifier(voltage regulator)/brush holder assembly that is mounted inside the alternator housing to the rear of the unit **(see illustration)**.

This alternator has an output amperage rating between 12 and 70 amps depending on the load and the engine rpm. Perform the charging system checks (see Section 14) to diagnose any problems with the alternator.

The purpose of the voltage regulator is to limit the alternator's voltage to a preset value. This prevents power surges, circuit overloads, etc., during peak voltage output.

The rectifier (voltage regulator) and the alternator brushes are mounted as a single assembly. This unit can be disassembled (see Section 15) and the components serviced individually.

The dashboard warning light should come on when the ignition key is turned to Start, then go off immediately. If it remains on, there is a malfunction in the charging system (see Section 11). Some vehicles are also equipped with a voltmeter. If the voltmeter indicates abnormally high or low voltage, check the charging system (see Section 13).

All charging systems mount the alternator on the right front of the engine and utilize a V-belt and pulley drive system. Drivebelt tension and battery service are the two primary maintenance requirements for these systems. See Chapter 1 for the procedures regarding engine drivebelt checking and battery servicing.

12   Charging system - general information and precautions

The charging system doesn't ordinarily require periodic maintenance. However, the drivebelt, battery and wires and connections should be inspected at the intervals outlined in Chapter 1.

Be very careful when making electrical circuit connections to a vehicle equipped with an alternator and note the following:
a)   When reconnecting wires to the alternator from the battery, be sure to note the polarity.
b)   Before using arc welding equipment to repair any part of the vehicle, disconnect the wires from the alternator and the battery terminals.
c)   Never start the engine with a battery charger connected.
d)   Always disconnect both battery leads before using a battery charger.
e)   The alternator is turned by an engine drivebelt which could cause serious injury if your hands, hair or clothes become entangled in it with the engine running.
f)   Because the alternator is connected directly to the battery, it could arc or cause a fire if overloaded or shorted out.
g)   Wrap a plastic bag over the alternator and secure it with rubber bands before steam cleaning the engine.

13   Charging system - check

1   If a malfunction occurs in the charging circuit, don't automatically assume that the alternator is causing the problem. First check the following items:
a)   Check the drivebelt tension and condition (see Chapter 1). Replace it if it's worn or deteriorated.

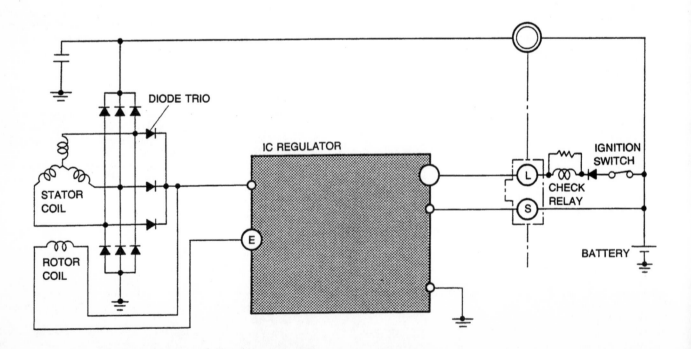

11.1 Schematic of the charging system

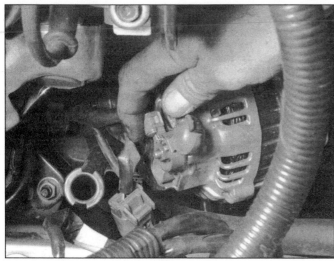

14.2 Press the tab out and pop off the plastic cover to gain access to the electrical connector on the backside of the alternator

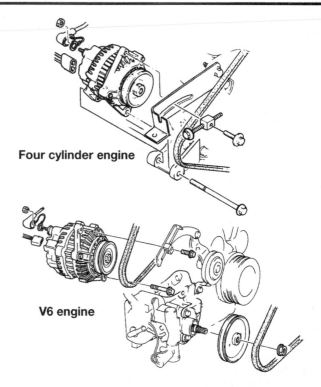

Four cylinder engine

V6 engine

14.3 Exploded views of the alternator mounting assemblies on the four-cylinder and V6 engines

b) Make sure the alternator mounting and adjustment bolts are tight.
c) Inspect the alternator wiring harness and the electrical connectors at the alternator and voltage regulator. They must be in good condition and tight.
d) Check the main fuse located in the main fuse block in the engine compartment. If it's blown, determine the cause, and replace the fuse (the vehicle won't start and/or the accessories won't work if the main fuse blows).
e) Start the engine and check the alternator for abnormal noises (a shrieking or squealing sound indicates a bad bearing).
f) Check the specific gravity of the battery electrolyte. If it's low, charge the battery (this doesn't apply to maintenance free batteries).
g) Make sure the battery is fully charged (one bad cell in a battery can cause overcharging by the alternator).
h) Disconnect the battery cables (negative first, then positive). Inspect the battery posts and the cable clamps for corrosion. Clean them thoroughly if necessary (see Chapter 1). Reconnect the cable to the negative terminal.
i) With the key off, connect a test light between the negative battery post and the disconnected negative cable clamp.
  1) If the test light does not come on, reattach the clamp and proceed to Step 3.
  2) If the test light comes on, there is a short (drain) in the electrical system of the vehicle. The short must be repaired before the charging system can be checked.
  3) Disconnect the alternator wiring harness.
    (a) If the light goes out, the alternator is bad.
    (b) If the light stays on, pull each fuse until the light goes out (this will tell you which component is shorted).
2   Using a voltmeter, check the battery voltage with the engine off. If should be approximately 12-volts.
3   Start the engine and check the battery voltage again. It should now be approximately 14-to-15 volts.
4   Turn on the headlights. The voltage should drop, and then come back up, if the charging system is working properly.
5   If the voltage reading is more than the specified charging voltage, replace the voltage regulator (refer to Section 13). If the voltage is less, the alternator diode(s), stator or rectifier may be bad or the voltage regulator may be malfunctioning.
6   If the battery is constantly discharging, the alternator drivebelt is loose (see Chapter 1), the alternator brushes are worn, dirty or disconnected (see Section 14), the voltage regulator is malfunctioning (see Section 13) or the rectifier, stator coil or rotor coil is defective. Repairing or replacing the rectifier, stator coil or rotor coil is beyond the scope of the home mechanic. Replace the alternator.

14   Alternator - removal and installation

Refer to illustrations 14.2 and 14.3
1   Detach the cable from the negative terminal of the battery.
2   Detach the electrical connectors from the alternator **(see illustration)**.
3   Loosen the alternator adjustment and pivot bolts **(see illustration)** and detach the drivebelt (see Chapter 1). **Note:** *On V6 engines, remove the power steering pump pulley (see Chapter 10).*
4   Remove the adjustment and pivot bolts and separate the alternator from the engine.
5   If you are replacing the alternator, take the old one with you when purchasing a replacement unit. Make sure the new/rebuilt unit looks identical to the old alternator. Look at the terminals - they should be the same in number, size and location as the terminals on the old alternator. Finally, look at the identification numbers - they will be stamped into the housing or printed on a tag attached to the housing. Make sure the numbers are the same on both alternators.
6   Many new/rebuilt alternators DO NOT have a pulley installed, so you may have to switch the pulley from the old unit to the new/rebuilt one. When buying an alternator, find out the shop's policy regarding pulleys - some shops will perform this service free of charge.
7   Installation is the reverse of removal.
8   After the alternator is installed, adjust the drivebelt tension (see Chapter 1).
9   Check the charging voltage to verify proper operation of the alternator (see Section 13).

15   Voltage regulator/rectifier and alternator brushes - check and replacement

Alternator brushes

Refer to illustrations 15.4 through 15.9, 15.11, 15.12, 15.13a, 15.13b and 15.14
1   Remove the alternator (see Section 14).

5

15.4 Remove the four bolts (arrows) that retain the front cover to the main assembly

15.5 Carefully lift the front cover off the alternator main assembly. It may be necessary to use a hammer (plastic head) to force the unit apart

2   Mark the alternator halves with paint or a scribe to ensure proper reassembly.

3   Remove the front pulley. If you do not have any air power tools, have the pulley removed at an auto service center.

4   Remove the through bolts **(see illustration)**.

5   Pull the alternator halves apart **(see illustration)**. Be sure to remove the front cover alone while leaving the stator attached to the rear cover. Tap on the alternator body with a soft-faced hammer if necessary, but don't use excessive force. If the two halves don't come apart fairly easily, clamp the alternator rear section into a vise along with a rag to prevent any cover damage.

6   Remove the rotor **(see illustration)**.

7   Remove the rectifier and brush holder mounting screws **(see illustration)**.

8   Separate the rear section of the alternator from the rotor and rectifier/brush assembly **(see illustration)**.

9   Using a soldering iron, remove the solder from the brush holder assembly **(see illustration)**. **Caution:** *Don't use the soldering iron for more than five seconds at a time - the rectifier may become damaged if it is overheated.*

10   Test the rectifier (voltage regulator) (see Steps 16 to 21).

11   Check the brushes before the alternator is disassembled. Check the length of the old brushes. The wear limit should not exceed 0.315

15.6 Remove the rotor from the assembly

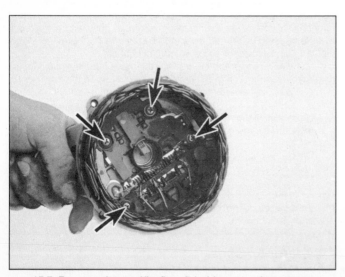

15.7 Remove the rectifier/brush holder mounting screws

15.8 Separate the stator and brush assembly from the rear section of the alternator

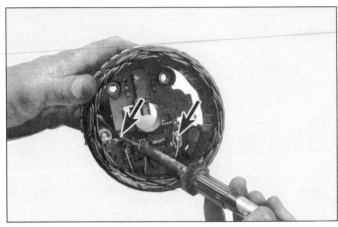

15.9 Be sure to insert a heat sink (pair of needle nose pliers) on the solder points (arrows) if the time to melt the solder exceeds 5 seconds

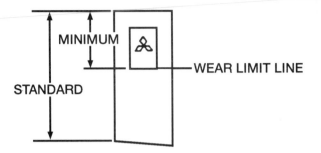

15.11 Wear and standard limits for the alternator brushes

Standard = 0.846 inches   *Minimum = 30.315 inches*

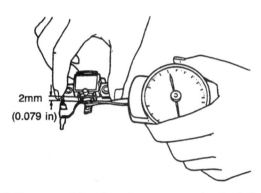

15.12 Use a special spring pressure gauge to check the force of the alternator brush spring. It should read 8.5 ounces at 0.079 inches

15.13a Use a screwdriver to push the rubber cap out of the hole in the rear section

5

15.13b Insert a paper clip into the slot to keep the brushes retracted. Make sure the wire clip is perfectly straight so it can be passed through the hole in the rear of the alternator cover when the unit is reassembled

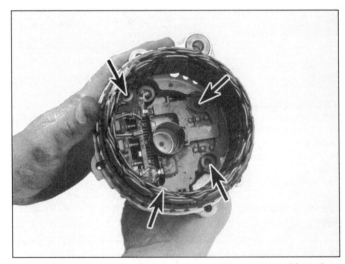

15.14 Once the stator and brush assembly are lowered into the rear section of the alternator, make sure the bolt holes (arrows) line up with the case. Another important procedure to remember is to install the long bolt first in order to clear the alternator body before the other bolts get tightened

inches from the end of the brush **(see illustration)**.
12   Also, check the force of the brush spring **(see illustration)**.
13   Before assembling the alternator, push the brushes into the brush holder and insert a rigid wire (a straightened-out paper clip will work) through the hole in the end frame to secure the brushes in position **(see illustrations)**.
14   Installation is otherwise the reverse of removal **(see illustration)**.

15   Remove the wire securing the brushes when you have completed reassembly.

Rectifier

Refer to illustrations 15.17 and 15.18
16   Disassemble the alternator (see Steps 1 through 9).

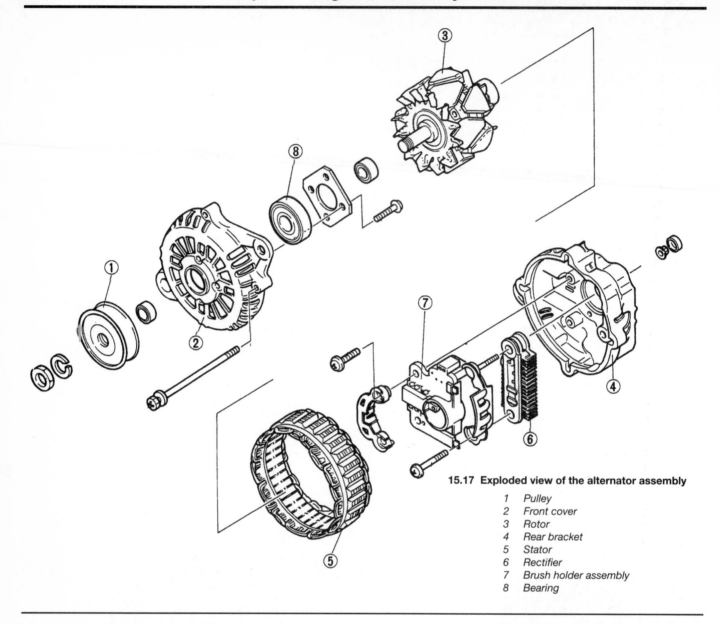

15.17 Exploded view of the alternator assembly

1   Pulley
2   Front cover
3   Rotor
4   Rear bracket
5   Stator
6   Rectifier
7   Brush holder assembly
8   Bearing

17   Separate the brush holder assembly from the rectifier **(see illustration)**.
18   Check the continuity of the diodes with an ohmmeter **(see illustration)**.
19   Installation is otherwise the reverse of removal (refer to Steps 13 through 15).
20   Be sure to pull the wire out after you have reassembled the alternator.

16   Starting system - general information and precautions

Refer to illustration 16.2

The sole function of the starting system is to turn over the engine quickly enough to allow it to start.

The starting system consists of the battery, the starter motor, the starter solenoid and the wires connecting them. The solenoid is mounted directly on the starter motor. V6 engines are equipped with a direct drive type starter/solenoid assembly while four-cylinder engines are equipped with the gear reduction type starter/solenoid assembly **(see illustration)**.

The starter/solenoid motor assembly is installed on the lower part of the engine, next to the transmission bellhousing.

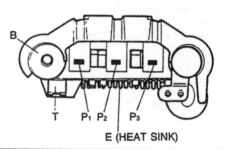

Negative (Black)	Positive (Red)	Continuity
E		Yes
B	P_1, P_2, P_3	No
T		No
P_1, P_2, P_3	E	No
	B	Yes

15.18 Use an ohmmeter and check the terminals of the rectifier for the correct continuity. This will tell you if any of the diodes are shorted

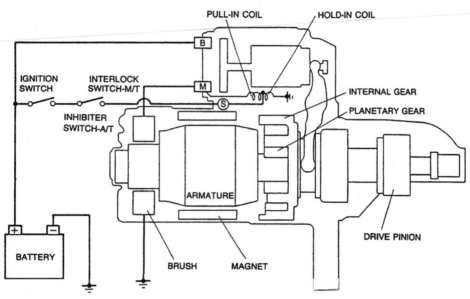

Six cylinder engine (direct drive type)

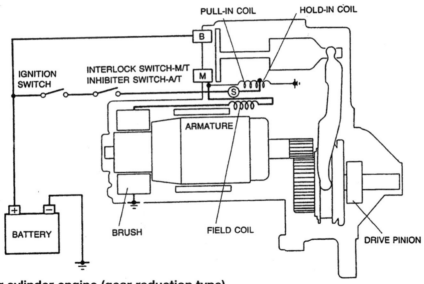

Four cylinder engine (gear reduction type)

16.2   Cross-sectional schematic of the starter/ solenoid assembly on the four-cylinder and V6 engines

When the ignition key is turned to the Start position, the starter solenoid is actuated through the starter control circuit. The starter solenoid then connects the battery to the starter. The battery supplies the electrical energy to the starter motor, which does the actual work of cranking the engine.

The starter motor on a vehicle equipped with a manual transmission can only be operated when the clutch pedal is depressed; the starter on a vehicle equipped with an automatic transmission can only be operated when the transmission selector lever is in Park or Neutral.

Always observe the following precautions when working on the starting system:

a)   Excessive cranking of the starter motor can overheat it and cause serious damage. Never operate the starter motor for more than 15 seconds at a time without pausing to allow it to cool for at least two minutes.

b)   The starter is connected directly to the battery and could arc or cause a fire if mishandled, overloaded or shorted out.

c)   Always detach the cable from the negative terminal of the battery before working on the starting system.

17   Starter motor - in-vehicle check

Note: *Before diagnosing starter problems, make sure the battery is fully charged.*

1   If the starter motor does not turn at all when the switch is operated, make sure that the shift lever is in Neutral or Park (automatic transmission) or that the clutch pedal is depressed (manual transmission).

2   Make sure that the battery is charged and that all cables, both at the battery and starter solenoid terminals, are clean and secure.

3   If the starter motor spins but the engine is not cranking, the overrunning clutch in the starter motor is slipping and the starter motor must be replaced.

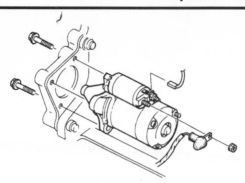

18. 3 Starter motor installation details

4   If, when the switch is actuated, the starter motor does not operate at all but the solenoid clicks, then the problem lies with either the battery, the main solenoid contacts or the starter motor itself (or the engine is seized).

5   If the solenoid plunger cannot be heard when the switch is actuated, the battery is bad, the fusible link is burned (the circuit is open) or

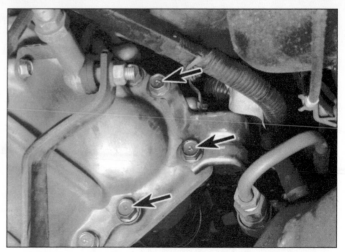

18.4 To remove the starter/solenoid assembly, detach the electrical connectors from the solenoid terminals, remove the starter bolts (arrows) and detach the assembly

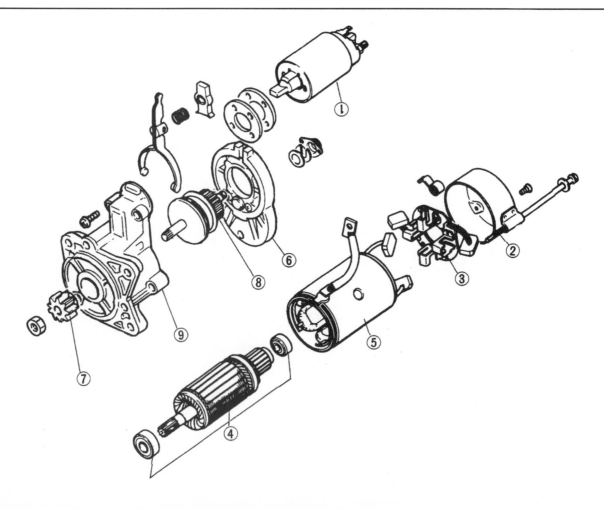

19.4a Starter/solenoid assembly on the four cylinder engine

1	Solenoid		6	Center bracket
2	Rear housing		7	Drive pinion
3	Brush holder assembly		8	Reduction gear
4	Armature		9	Front cover
5	Field coil			

the solenoid itself is defective.

6   To check the solenoid, connect a jumper lead between the battery (+) and the ignition switch wire terminal (the small terminal) on the solenoid. If the starter motor now operates, the solenoid is OK and the problem is in the ignition switch, neutral start switch or the wiring.

7   If the starter motor still does not operate, remove the starter/solenoid assembly for disassembly, testing and repair.

8   If the starter motor cranks the engine at an abnormally slow speed, first make sure that the battery is charged and that all terminal connections are tight. If the engine is partially seized, or has the wrong viscosity oil in it, it will crank slowly.

9   Run the engine until normal operating temperature is reached, then disconnect the coil wire from the distributor cap and ground it on the engine.

10   Connect a voltmeter positive lead to the positive battery post and connect the negative lead to the negative post.

11   Crank the engine and take the voltmeter readings as soon as a steady figure is indicated. Do not allow the starter motor to turn for more than 15 seconds at a time. A reading of 9 volts or more, with the starter motor turning at normal cranking speed, is normal. If the reading is 9 volts or more but the cranking speed is slow, the motor is faulty. If the reading is less than 9 volts and the cranking speed is slow, the solenoid contacts are probably burned, the starter motor is bad, the battery is discharged or there is a bad connection.

18   Starter motor - removal and installation

Refer to illustrations 18.3 and 18.4

1   Detach the cable from the negative terminal of the battery.

2   Raise the vehicle and support it securely on jackstands.

3   Clearly label, then disconnect the wires from the terminals on the starter motor and solenoid **(see illustration)**.

4   Remove the mounting bolts **(see illustration)** and detach the starter.

5   Installation is the reverse of removal.

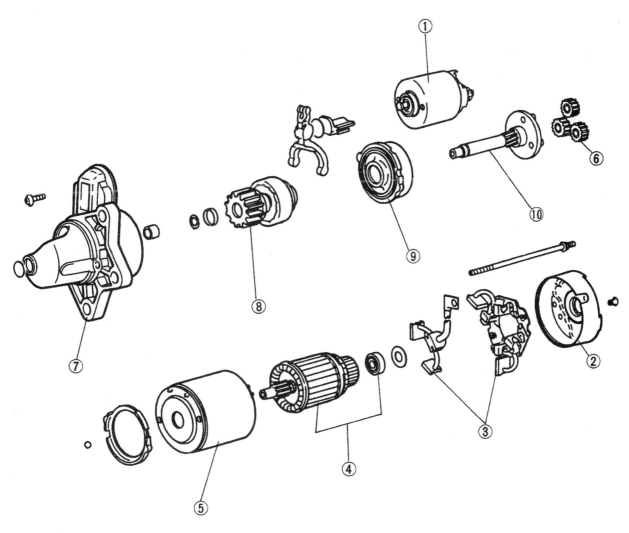

19.4b Starter/solenoid assembly on the V6 engine

1	Solenoid	6	Planetary gear
2	Rear housing	7	Front cover
3	Brush holder assembly	8	Drive pinion
4	Armature	9	Internal gear
5	Field coil	10	Gear shaft

5

19   Starter solenoid - removal and installation

Refer to illustrations 19.4a and 19.4b

1   Disconnect the cable from the negative terminal of the battery.
2   Remove the starter motor (see Section 18).
3   Disconnect the strap from the solenoid to the starter motor terminal.
4   Remove the screws which secure the solenoid to the starter motor **(see illustrations)**.
5   Detach the solenoid from the starter body.
6   Remove the plunger and plunger spring.
7   Installation is the reverse of removal.

Chapter 6 Emissions control systems

Contents

---

1 General information

Refer to illustrations 1.6a, 1.6b and 1.6c

To prevent pollution of the atmosphere from incompletely burned or evaporating gases, and to maintain good driveability and fuel economy, a number of emission control systems are used on these vehicles. They include the:

Air conditioning cut-off system
Catalytic converter system
Deceleration control system (V6 engines)
Evaporative emission control (EVAP) system
Positive crankcase ventilation (PCV) system
Pressure regulator control (PRC) system

The Sections in this Chapter include general descriptions, checking procedures within the scope of the home mechanic and component replacement procedures (when possible) for each of the systems listed above.

Before assuming that an emissions control system is malfunctioning, check the fuel and ignition systems carefully. The diagnosis of some emission control devices requires specialized tools, equipment and training. If checking and servicing become too difficult or if a procedure is beyond your ability, consult a dealer service department. Remember - the most frequent cause of emissions problems is simply a loose or broken vacuum hose or wire, so always check the hose and wiring connections first.

This doesn't mean, however, that emission control systems are particularly difficult to maintain and repair. You can quickly and easily

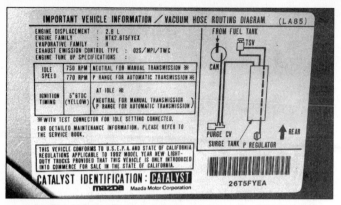

1.6a The Vehicle Emission Control Information (VECI) label contains such essential information as the types of emission control systems installed on the engine and the idle speed and ignition timing specifications

perform many checks and do most of the regular maintenance at home with common tune-up and hand tools. **Note**: *Because of a Federally mandated extended warranty which covers the emission control system components, check with your dealer about warranty coverage before working on any emissions-related systems. Once the warranty has expired, you may wish to perform some of the component checks and/or replacement procedures in this Chapter to save money.*

Pay close attention to any special precautions outlined in this Chapter. It should be noted that the illustrations of the various systems may not exactly match the system installed on your vehicle because of changes made by the manufacturer during production or from year to year.

A Vehicle Emissions Control Information label is located in the engine compartment **(see illustration)**. This label contains important emissions specifications and adjustment information. When servicing the engine or emissions systems, the VECI label in your particular vehicle should always be checked for up-to-date information. You will also find the accompanying vacuum hose diagrams helpful when you troubleshoot emissions problems **(see illustrations)**.

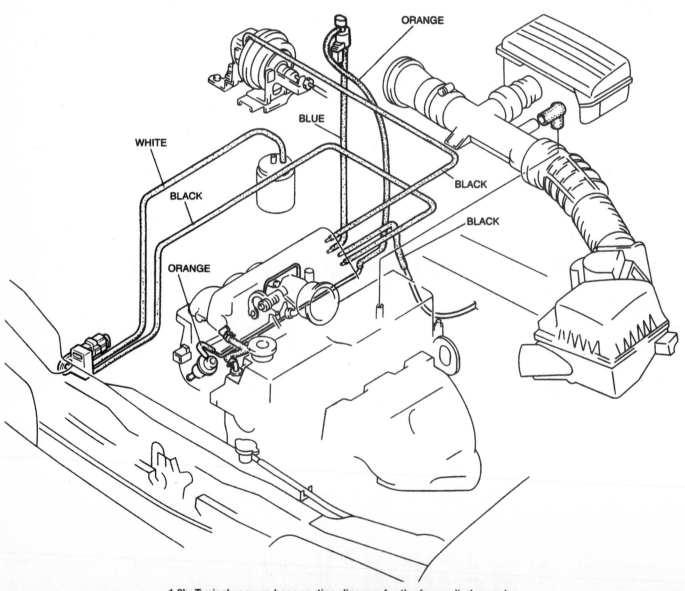

1.6b Typical vacuum hose routing diagram for the four-cylinder engine

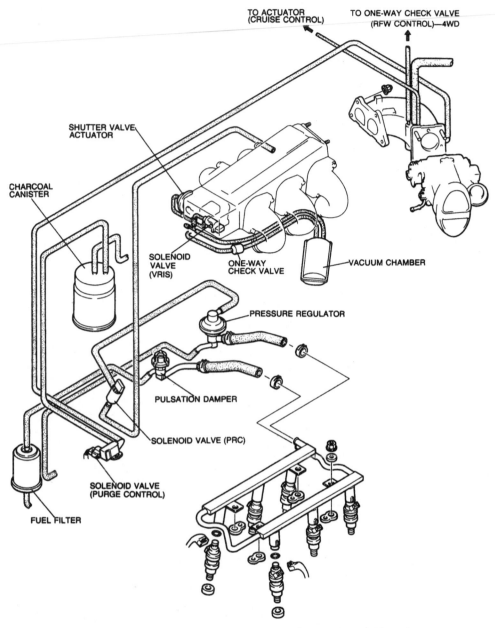

TO ACTUATOR
(CRUISE CONTROL)

TO ONE-WAY CHECK VALVE
(RFW CONTROL)—4WD

SHUTTER VALVE
ACTUATOR

CHARCOAL
CANISTER

SOLENOID
VALVE
(VRIS)

ONE-WAY
CHECK VALVE

VACUUM CHAMBER

PRESSURE REGULATOR

PULSATION DAMPER

SOLENOID VALVE (PRC)

SOLENOID VALVE
(PURGE CONTROL)

FUEL FILTER

1.6c Typical vacuum hose routing diagram for the V6 engine

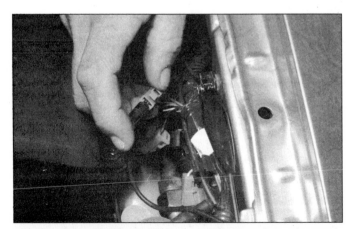

2.3 To retrieve the trouble codes, use a jumper wire and ground the green 1-pin electrical connector to a bolt on the body

2   EFI system self-diagnosis capability - general information

Refer to illustrations 2.3, 2.5a and 2.5b

The EFI system control unit (computer) has a built-in self-diagnosis system which detects malfunctions in the system sensors and alerts the driver by illuminating a CHECK ENGINE warning light in the instrument panel. The computer stores the failure code until the diagnostic system is cleared by disconnecting the negative battery cable then depressing the brake pedal for a period of five seconds or longer. The warning light goes out automatically when the malfunction is repaired.

The CHECK ENGINE warning light should come on when the ignition switch is placed in the On position. When the engine is started the warning light should go out. If the light remains on, the diagnostic system has detected a malfunction or abnormality in the system.

To determine which sensor or system component is malfunctioning, connect a jumper wire from the single green (1-pin) test connector **(see illustration)** and ground it to a suitable bolt in the engine com-

Malfunction display		Sensor or subsystem	Self-diagnosis	Fail-safe
Code No.	Pattern of output signal			
01	ON / OFF	Ignition pulse	No ignition signal	—
03	ON / OFF	G signal	No G signal	Cancels 2-group injection
08	ON / OFF	Airflow sensor	Open or short circuit	Basic fuel injection amount fixed as for two driving modes (1) Idle switch: ON (2) Idle switch: OFF
09	ON / OFF	Water thermosensor	Open or short circuit	Maintains constant 20°(68°F) command
11	ON / OFF	Intake air thermosensor (dynamic chamber)	Open or short circuit	Maintains constant 20°C (68°F) command
12	ON / OFF	Throttle sensor	Open or short circuit	Maintains constant command of throttle valve fully open
14	ON / OFF	Atmospheric pressure sensor	Open or short circuit	Maintains constant command of sea level pressure
15	ON / OFF	Oxygen sensor	Sensor output continues less than 0.45V 180 sec. after engine exceeds 1,500 rpm	Cancels engine feedback operation
17	ON / OFF	Feedback system	Sensor output not changed 20 sec. after engine exceeds 1,500 rpm	Cancels engine feedback operation
25	ON / OFF	Solenoid valve (pressure regulator control)	Open or short circuit	—
26	ON / OFF	Solenoid valve (purge control)		—
34	ON / OFF	Solenoid valve (idle speed control)		—

2.5a Trouble code chart for the four-cylinder engine

partment. Make sure the battery voltage is greater than 11 volts, the transmission is in Neutral, the accessories are off, the throttle valve is closed and the engine is at normal operating temperature, then turn the ignition switch to the On position but do not start the engine.

The diagnostic code is the number of flashes indicated on the CHECK ENGINE light. If no codes are stored, the CHECK ENGINE light will come on for a few moments, then go out. If any malfunction has been detected, the light will blink the first digit(s) of the code at a long interval(s) and then blink the second digit of the code at short interval(s). For example, a code 34 (BAC valve on V6 engines) will first

blink three long flashes and then pause and blink four quick flashes. **Note**: *If the code is simply a single digit number, the CHECK ENGINE light will flash in the quick mode.*

The accompanying tables explain the code that will be flashed for each of the malfunctions **(see illustrations)**. The accompanying tables indicate the diagnostic code - in blinks - along with the system, diagnosis and specific areas.

After the diagnosis check, remove the jumper wire and install the rubber cap in the CHECK ENGINE wire harness electrical connector. Check the indicated system or component or take the vehicle to a

Code No.	Input devices	Malfunction	Fail-safe function	Output signal pattern
01	Ignition pulse (Igniter, ignition coil)	Broken wire, short circuit	—	
03	Distributor (G-signal)	Broken wire, short circuit	—	
08	Airflow meter	Broken wire, short circuit	Basic fuel injection amount fixed as for 2 driving modes: 1) Idle switch: ON 2) Idle switch: OFF	
09	Water thermosensor	Broken wire, short circuit	Coolant temp. input fixed at 80°C (176°F)	
10	Intake air thermosensor (Airflow meter)	Broken wire, short circuit	Intake air temp. input fixed at 20°C (68°F)	
11	Intake air thermo-sensor (Dynamic chamber)	Broken wire, short circuit	Intake air temp. input fixed at 20°C (68°F)	
12	Throttle sensor	Broken wire, short circuit	Throttle valve opening angle input signal fixed at full open	
14	Atmospheric pressure sensor (within ECU)	Malfunction ECU	Atmospheric pressure input signal fixed at 760 mmHg (29.9 inHg)	
15	Oxygen sensor	Oxygen sensor output remains below 0.55V 120 sec after engine at 1,500 rpm	Feedback system canceled (for EGI)	
17	Feedback system	Oxygen sensor output remains 0.55V 60 sec. after engine above 1,500 rpm	Feedback system canceled (for EGI)	

Code No.	Output devices	Output signal pattern
25	Solenoid valve (Pressure regulator control)	
26	Solenoid valve (Purge control)	
34	Idle speed control valve (BAC valve)	
41	Solenoid valve (Variable resonance induction system)	

2.5b Trouble code chart for the V6 engine

3.4 Remove the nuts from the kick plate and lift it from the engine compartment

3.5 Be very careful when handling the ECU - take extra precautions and use an anti-static pad and gloves to avoid static discharge which could damage the ECU

dealer service department to have the malfunction repaired.

After repairs have been made, the diagnostic code must be canceled by detaching the cable from the negative terminal of the battery, then depressing the brake pedal for more than 5 seconds.

After cancellation, perform a road test and make sure the warning light does not come on. If the original trouble code is repeated, additional repairs are required.

---

3   Electronic Control Unit (ECU) - general information and replacement

Refer to illustrations 3.4 and 3.5

Note: *On models since 1994, the designation for the ECU (Engine Control Unit) was changed to PCM (Powertrain Control Module). The unit operates the same as on prior models, only the name has been changed.*

1   The Electronic Control Unit (ECU) is located inside the passenger compartment under the dashboard behind the kick panel (right side).
2   Disconnect the negative battery cable from the battery.
3   Remove the screws from the lower instrument panel and the under cover panel (see Chapter 11) under the right end of the dash. Remove these panels from the compartment.
4   Remove the kick plate to expose the relay panel and the ECU **(see illustration).**
5   Unplug both electrical connectors **(see illustration)** from the ECU. **Caution:** *The ignition switch must be turned OFF when pulling out or plugging in the electrical connectors to prevent damage to the ECU.*
6   Remove the retaining nut from the ECU bracket.
7   Carefully remove the ECU. **Note:** *Avoid any static electricity damage to the computer by using gloves and a special anti-static pad to store the ECU once it is removed.*
8   Installation is the reverse of removal.

---

4   Information sensors - check and replacement

Note: *Refer to Chapters 4 and 5 for additional information on the location and the diagnostics of the information sensors that are not covered in this section.*

Water thermosensor
General description

1   The water thermosensor is a thermistor (a resistor which varies the value of its voltage output in accordance with temperature

4.2a Check the resistance values of the water thermosensor at different operating temperatures (four-cylinder engine shown)

changes). The change in the resistance values will directly affect the voltage signal from the water thermosensor. As the sensor temperature DECREASES, the resistance values will INCREASE. As the sensor temperature INCREASES, the resistance values will DECREASE. A failure in this sensor circuit should set a Code 9. This code indicates a failure in the water thermosensor circuit, so in most cases the appropriate solution to the problem will be either repair of a wire or replacement of the sensor.

Check
Refer to illustrations 4.2a. 4.2b and 4.2c

2   To check the sensor, check the resistance value **(see illustrations)** of the sensor while it is completely cold (50 to 80 degrees F = 2,200 to 2,700 ohms). Next, start the engine and warm it up until it reaches operating temperature. The resistance should be lower (180 to 200 degrees F = 280 to 350 ohms). **Note:** *Access to the water thermosensor makes it difficult to position the tester probes on the terminals. If necessary, remove the sensor and perform the tests in a pan of heated water to simulate the conditions.*

Replacement
3   To remove the sensor, depress the locking tabs, unplug the electrical connector, then carefully unscrew the sensor. **Caution:** *Handle the sensor with care. Damage to this sensor will affect the operation of the entire fuel injection system.*
4   Before installing the new sensor, wrap the threads with Teflon

4.2b Checking the water thermosensor on the V6 engine

4.12a The oxygen sensor electrical connector is located toward the front of the engine near the thermostat housing on four-cylinder engines

Coolant temp.	Resistance (kΩ)
–20°C (–4°F)	14.5—17.8
20°C (68°F)	2.2—2.7
40°C (104°F)	1.0—1.3
60°C (140°F)	0.5—0.7
80°C (176°F)	0.28—0.35

4.2c Make sure the resistance of the water thermosensor decreases when the engine temperature increases

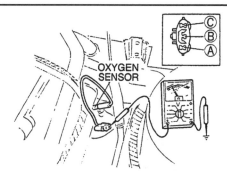

4.12b Oxygen sensor terminal designations on the V6 engine (1989 through 1991 models)

sealing tape to prevent leakage and thread corrosion.

5 Installation is the reverse of removal. Check the coolant level (see Chapter 1) and add, if necessary.

Oxygen sensor

General description

6 The oxygen sensor, which is located in the exhaust manifold, monitors the oxygen content of the exhaust gas stream. The oxygen content in the exhaust reacts with the oxygen sensor to produce a voltage output which varies from 0.1-volt (high oxygen, lean mixture) to 0.9-volts (low oxygen, rich mixture). The ECU constantly monitors this variable voltage output to determine the ratio of oxygen to fuel in the mixture. The ECU alters the air/fuel mixture ratio by controlling the pulse width (open time) of the fuel injectors. A mixture ratio of 14.7 parts air to 1 part fuel is the ideal mixture ratio for minimizing exhaust emissions, thus allowing the catalytic converter to operate at maximum efficiency. It is this ratio of 14.7 to 1 which the ECU and the oxygen sensor attempt to maintain at all times.

7 The oxygen sensor produces no voltage when it is below its normal operating temperature of about 600-degrees F. During this initial period before warm-up, the ECU operates in open loop mode.

8 If the engine reaches normal operating temperature and/or has been running for two or more minutes, and if the oxygen sensor is producing a steady signal voltage below 0.45-volts at 1,500 rpm or greater, the ECU will set a Code 15.

9 When there is a problem with the oxygen sensor or its circuit, the ECU operates in the open loop mode - that is, it controls fuel delivery in accordance with a programmed default value instead of feedback information from the oxygen sensor.

10 The proper operation of the oxygen sensor depends on four conditions:

a) **Electrical** - The low voltages generated by the sensor depend upon good, clean connections which should be checked whenever a malfunction of the sensor is suspected or indicated.

b) **Outside air supply** - The sensor is designed to allow air circulation to the internal portion of the sensor. Whenever the sensor is removed and installed or replaced, make sure the air passages are not restricted.

c) **Proper operating temperature** - The ECU will not react to the sensor signal until the sensor reaches approximately 600-degrees F. This factor must be taken into consideration when evaluating the performance of the sensor.

d) **Unleaded fuel** - The use of unleaded fuel is essential for proper operation of the sensor. Make sure the fuel you are using is of this type.

11 In addition to observing the above conditions, special care must be taken whenever the sensor is serviced.

a) The oxygen sensor has a permanently attached pigtail and electrical connector which should not be removed from the sensor. Damage or removal of the pigtail or electrical connector can adversely affect operation of the sensor.

b) Grease, dirt and other contaminants should be kept away from the electrical connector and the louvered end of the sensor.

c) Do not use cleaning solvents of any kind on the oxygen sensor.

d) Do not drop or roughly handle the sensor.

e) The silicone boot must be installed in the correct position to prevent the boot from being melted and to allow the sensor to operate properly.

Check

Refer to illustrations 4.12a, 4.12b, 4.12c, 4.15a and 4.15b

12 Warm up the engine and let it run at idle. Disconnect the oxygen sensor electrical connector and connect the positive probe of a voltmeter to the oxygen sensor connector terminal A **(see illustrations)** and the negative probe to ground.

13 Increase and then decrease the engine speed and monitor the voltage.

14 When the speed is increased, the voltage should increase to 0.5 to 1.0 volts. When the speed is decreased, the voltage should decrease to about 0 to 0.4 volts.

6

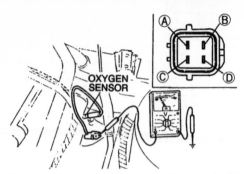

4.12c Oxygen sensor terminal designations on the V6 engine (1992 and later models)

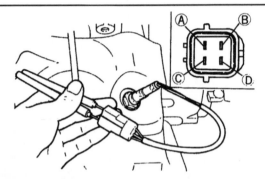

4.15b To check the oxygen sensor heater on the V6 engine (1992 and 1993 models), check for continuity between terminals D and C

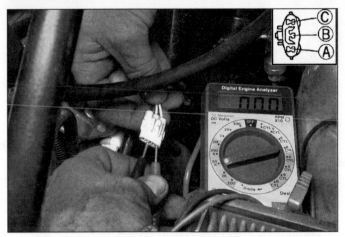

4.15a To check the oxygen sensor heater on the V6 engine (1989 through 1991 modes), check for continuity between terminals B and C

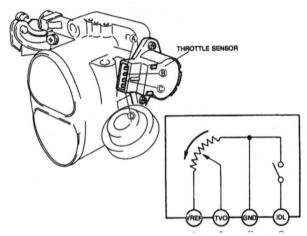

4.25 Diagram of a typical TPS (V6 engine)

15   On V6 engines, also inspect the oxygen sensor heater. Disconnect the oxygen sensor electrical connector and connect an ohmmeter between the B and C terminals on 1989 through 1991 models **(see Illustration)** or D and C terminals on 1992 and later models **(see Illustration).** There should be continuity.

16   If the oxygen sensor fails any of these tests, replace it with a new part.

Replacement

Note: *Because it is installed In the exhaust manifold or pipe, which contracts when cool, the oxygen sensor may be very difficult to loosen when the engine is cold. Rather than risk damage to the sensor (assuming you are planning to reuse it in another manifold or pipe), start and run the engine for a minute or two, then shut it off. Be careful not to burn yourself during the following procedure.*

17   Disconnect the cable from the negative terminal of the battery.

18   Raise the vehicle and place it securely on jackstands.

19   Carefully disconnect the electrical connector from the sensor.

20   Carefully unscrew the sensor from the exhaust manifold. **Caution:** *Excessive force may damage the threads.*

21   Anti-seize compound must be used on the threads of the sensor to facilitate future removal. The threads of new sensors will already be coated with this compound, but if an old sensor is removed and reinstalled, recoat the threads.

22   Install the sensor and tighten it securely.

23   Reconnect the electrical connector of the pigtail lead to the main engine wiring harness.

24   Lower the vehicle and reconnect the cable to the negative terminal of the battery.

Throttle Position Sensor (TPS)

General description

Refer to illustration 4.25

25   The Throttle Position Sensor (TPS) is located on the end of the throttle shaft on the throttle body **(see illustration).** By monitoring the output voltage from the TPS, the ECU can determine fuel delivery based on throttle valve angle (driver demand). A broken or loose TPS can cause intermittent bursts of fuel from the injector and an unstable idle because the ECU thinks the throttle is moving.

Check

Four-cylinder engine

Refer to illustrations 4.27 and 4.28

26   Follow the wire harness from the TPS to the back of the air intake plenum and remove it from the bracket. This will give you more room to probe the terminals.

27   Peel back the rubber to expose the wires and probe the terminals with sharp-ended tips **(see illustration)** directly behind the connector.

28   Follow the charts **(see illustration)** to verify that the voltage readings with the TPS fully closed and fully open coincide with each other. For example, with the throttle fully closed, if the power line (Red wire) is 5.0 volts then the signal voltage (Blue wire) should read about 0.5 volts. If the voltage does not coincide, loosen the screws and adjust the TPS.

V6 engine

Refer to illustration 4.29

29   To check the TPS with the throttle fully closed, connect the probes of an ohmmeter to terminals A and C (1989 through 1991 models) or A and D (1992 and later models) **(see illustration).** The sensor should read 3,000 to 6,500 ohms at idle.

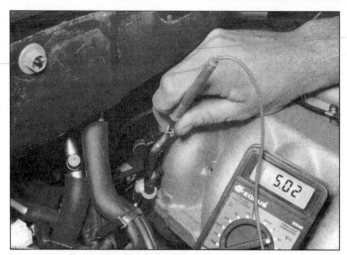

4.27 Pull the wire cover back far enough to get a probe into the back of the electrical connector

4.29 Checking the resistance of the TPS on a V6 model

RED wire voltage (V)	BLUE wire voltage (V)	RED wire voltage (V)	BLUE wire voltage (V)
4.50—4.59	0.37—0.54	5.10—5.19	0.42—0.61
4.60—4.69	0.38—0.55	5.20—5.29	0.43—0.62
4.70—4.79	0.39—0.56	5.30—5.39	0.44—0.63
4.80—4.89	0.40—0.57	5.40—5.49	0.44—0.64
4.90—4.99	0.40—0.58	5.50	0.44—0.66
5.00—5.09	0.41—0.60	**Throttle fully closed**	

RED wire voltage (V)	BLUE wire voltage (V)	RED wire voltage (V)	BLUE wire voltage (V)
4.50—4.59	3.58—4.23	5.10—5.19	4.05—4.79
4.60—4.69	3.66—4.32	5.20—5.29	4.13—4.88
4.70—4.79	3.74—4.41	5.30—5.39	4.21—4.98
4.80—4.89	3.82—4.51	5.40—5.49	4.29—5.07
4.90—4.99	3.90—4.60	5.50	4.29—5.17
5.00—5.09	3.97—4.70	**Throttle fully open**	

4.28 Supply and output voltages for the TPS (four-cylinder engine) fully closed and fully open

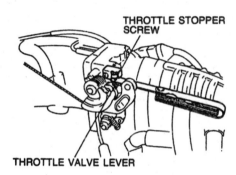

4.34 Insert a feeler gauge between the stopper screw and the valve lever and check for continuity

Feeler gauge thickness	continuity between C and D
0.020 inches.........................	continuity exists
0.028 inches.........................	no continuity

30   Also, check the resistance between terminals B and C (1989 through 1991 models) or B and D (1992 and later models). Gradually open the throttle valve and observe the TPS sensor resistance. With the throttle valve fully closed, the resistance should be below 1,000 ohms. Slowly move the throttle valve and observe a distinct change in the resistance values as the sensor travels from idle to full throttle. The resistance should increase to 3,000 to 6,500 ohms. If the readings are incorrect, adjust the TPS sensor.

31   A problem in any of the TPS circuits will set a Code 12. Once a trouble code is set, the ECU will use an artificial default value for TPS and some vehicle performance will return.

Adjustment

Note: *Adjust the TPS when installing a new one or when the original TPS was removed or diagnosed to be out of adjustment.*

Four-cylinder engine

32   Loosen the TPS screws and adjust the position by following the procedure described in Step 28.

V6 engine

Refer to illustration 4.34

33   Disconnect the TPS connector from the TPS and connect an ohmmeter between terminals C and D **(see illustration 4.29)**.

34   Insert a feeler gauge between the throttle stop screw and the throttle valve **(see illustration)** and check for continuity.

35   If the adjustment is not within specifications, loosen the screws on the TPS and rotate the TPS sensor into the correct adjustment.

36   Recheck the TPS sensor adjustment with the feeler gauge and the ohmmeter and if the readings are correct, reconnect the TPS harness connector.

Airflow Meter

General description

37   The airflow meter is located on the air intake duct. The airflow meter measures the amount of air entering the engine. The ECU uses this information to control fuel delivery. A large volume of air indicates acceleration, while a small volume of air indicates deceleration or idle. Refer to Chapter 4 for diagnostic checks and replacement procedures for the airflow meter.

Intake Air Temperature (IAT) sensor

General description

38   The Intake Air Temperature (IAT) sensor is located in the air intake plenum. This sensor acts as a resistor which changes values according to the temperature of the air entering the engine. Low temperatures produce a high resistance value (for example, at 77 degrees F the resistance is about 33,000 ohms) while high temperatures produce low resistance values (at 185 degrees F the resistance is 3,500 ohms).

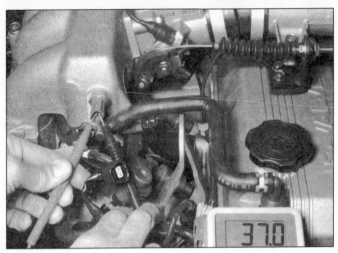

4.39a Checking the IAT sensor on the four-cylinder engine

4.39b Checking the IAT sensor on the V6 engine

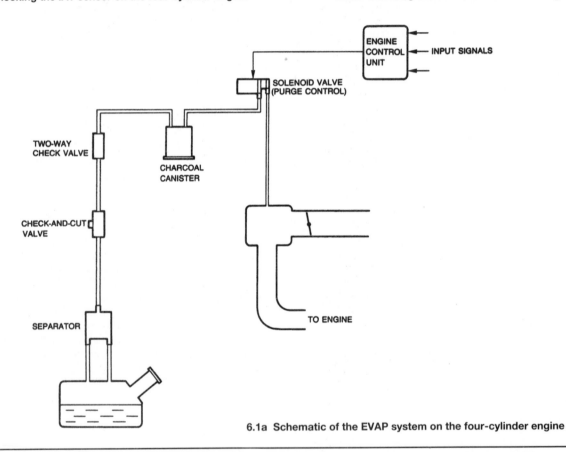

6.1a Schematic of the EVAP system on the four-cylinder engine

Check

Refer to illustrations 4.39a and 4.39b

39   To check the IAT sensor, disconnect the electrical connector and connect an ohmmeter to the sensor terminals **(see illustrations)**.

40   Measure the resistance of the sensor with the engine completely cold and with the engine warmed up to operating temperature.

41   With the temperature at 77 degrees F, the sensor resistance should be 29,000 to 36,000 ohms. With the temperature at 185 degrees F, the sensor resistance should be 3,300 to 3,700 ohms.

42   If the test readings are incorrect, replace the IAT sensor.

Replacement

43   Disconnect the IAT sensor electrical connector and remove the sensor.

44   Installation is the reverse of removal. Wrap the threads of the sensor with Teflon tape or other sealing compound to prevent air leaks.

5   Positive Crankcase Ventilation (PCV) system

1   The Positive Crankcase Ventilation (PCV) system reduces hydrocarbon emissions by scavenging crankcase vapors. It does this by circulating fresh air from the air cleaner through the crankcase, where it mixes with blow-by gases and is then rerouted through a PCV valve to the intake manifold.

2   The main components of the PCV system are the PCV valve, a fresh air inlet that incorporates a flame arrester and the vacuum hoses connecting these components with the engine.

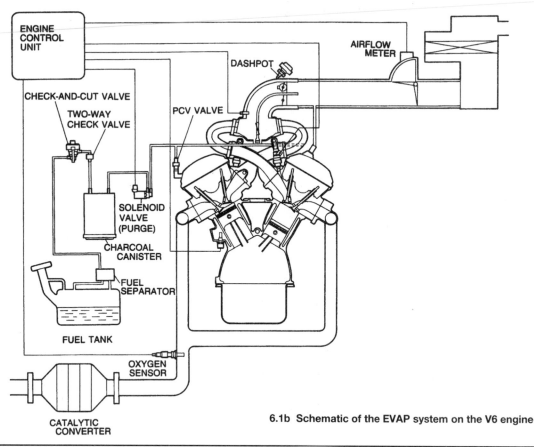

6.1b Schematic of the EVAP system on the V6 engine

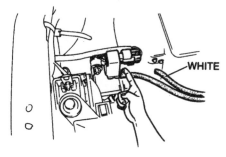

6.2 With the engine warmed up and idling, there should be no vacuum at the solenoid valve

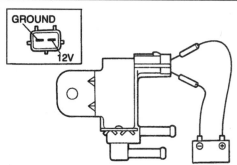

6.4 Apply 12 volts (battery voltage) to the solenoid valve and . . .

3   To maintain idle quality, the PCV valve restricts the flow when the intake manifold vacuum is high. If abnormal operating conditions (such as piston ring problems) arise, the system is designed to allow excessive amounts of blow-by gases to flow back through the crankcase vent tube into the air cleaner to be consumed by normal combustion.

4   Servicing of the PCV system is covered in Chapter 1.

6   Evaporative emission control (EVAP) system

General description

Refer to illustrations 6.1a and 6.1b

1   The evaporative emission control system **(see illustrations)** stores fuel vapors generated in the fuel tank in a charcoal canister when the engine isn't running. When the engine is started, the fuel vapors are drawn into the dynamic chamber and burned. The crankcase emission control system works like this: When the engine is cruising,

the purge control valve is opened slightly and a small amount of blow-by gas is drawn into the dynamic chamber and burned. At deceleration or heavy load conditions, the purge control valve is opened further and a larger amount of blow-by gas is drawn into the dynamic chamber.

Component check and replacement
Solenoid valve

Refer to illustrations 6.2, 6.4 and 6.5

2   Warm up the engine to normal operating temperature and let it idle. Detach the vacuum hose from the solenoid valve and check that no vacuum is felt at the solenoid valve **(see illustration)**.

3   Disconnect the vacuum hoses from the charcoal canister and the dynamic chamber and verify that no vacuum is reaching either component.

4   Disconnect the solenoid valve electrical connector and apply battery voltage to one side and ground the other side **(see illustration)**.

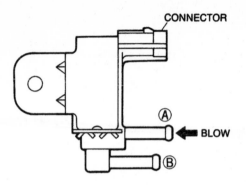

6.5 ... make sure air flows through port A and out port B

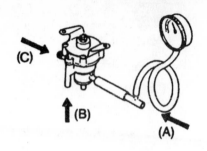

6.8 Blow into port A and make sure air comes out of port B

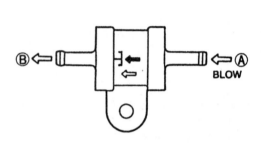

6.11 The check valve should allow air to flow only in one direction

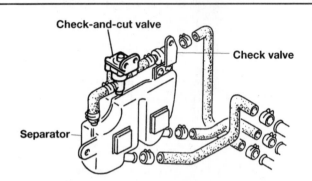

6.14 The check valve, the check and cut valve and separator should be removed as a single unit

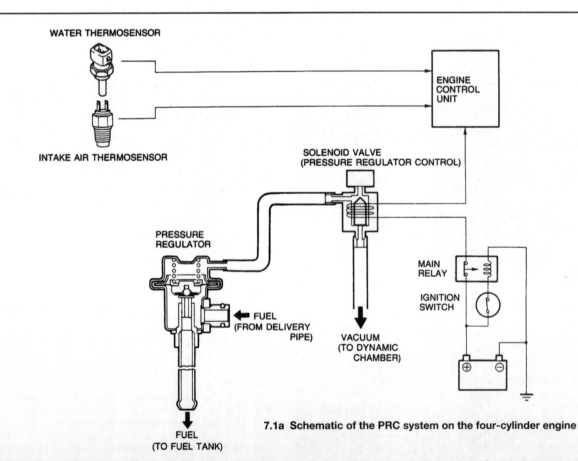

7.1a Schematic of the PRC system on the four-cylinder engine

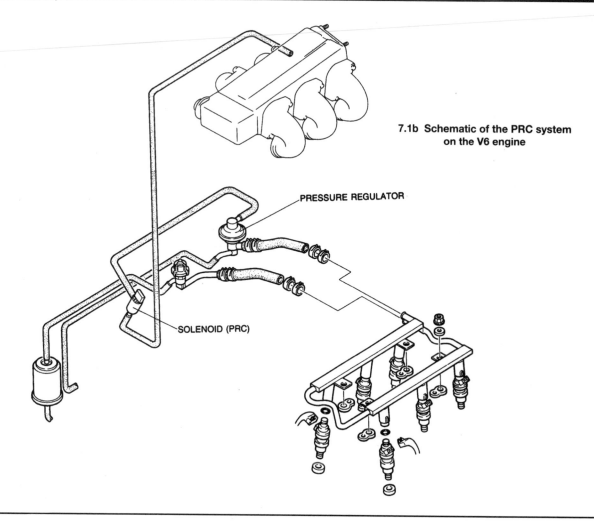

7.1b Schematic of the PRC system on the V6 engine

PRESSURE REGULATOR

SOLENOID (PRC)

6

5   Blow into pipe A. Air should flow through the valve **(see illustration)**.

6   If the test results are incorrect, replace the solenoid valve with a new part.

Check and cut valve

Refer to illustration 6.8

Note: *The check and cut valve is located behind the right trim panel in the rear of the vehicle above the tire.*

7   Remove the valve (see Step 14).

8   Blow through the valve from port A and verify air comes out port B **(see illustration)**. Block port B and verify air does not come out port C. If the test results are incorrect, replace the valve.

9   Block port B, attach a hand-held vacuum pump to port A, operate the pump and feel for vacuum at port C (the valve shouldn't hold vacuum unless ports B and C are plugged). If there is no vacuum at port C, replace the valve.

Check valve

Refer to illustration 6.11

10   Remove the check valve (see Step 14).

11   Blow through the valve at port A and verify that air flows through it **(see illustration)**.

12   Blow through the valve at port B - air should not flow through the valve.

13   If the valve doesn't operate as described, replace it.

Separator

Refer to illustration 6.14

14   Pull back the right rear side trim panel in the engine compartment

and remove the cover **(see illustration)**.

15   Visually check the separator for cracks or any obvious damage.

16   Replace the separator if necessary.

Canister

17   Label, then detach all hoses to the canister.

18   Slide the canister out of its mounting clip.

19   Visually examine the canister for leakage or damage.

20   Replace the canister if you find evidence of damage or leakage.

---

7   Pressure Regulator Control (PRC) system

Refer to illustrations 7.1a, 7.1b, 7.4a, 7.4b, 7.6a and 7.6b

General description

1   The Pressure Regulator Control (PRC) system prevents percolation of the fuel during idle after the engine has been restarted when warm **(see illustrations)**. Vacuum to the fuel pressure regulator is cut off and the fuel injection pressure increases to more than 41 psi.

Check

2   Start the engine and allow it to idle.

3   Disconnect the vacuum hose from the fuel pressure regulator (see Chapter 4) and verify that vacuum is available.

4   Locate the electrical connector on the solenoid valve **(see illustrations)** and ground terminal L/B with a jumper wire. **Note**: *Another quick method of checking the solenoid valve is to turn the ignition ON (engine not running) and ground the terminal L/B and listen for a "click-*

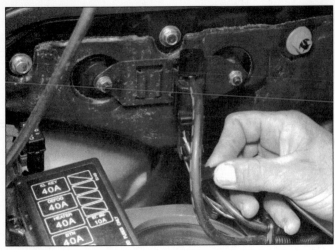

7.4a With the ignition key ON, ground terminal L/B and listen for a "click" as the solenoid activates (four-cylinder model shown)

7.4b Location of the vacuum solenoid on the V6 engine

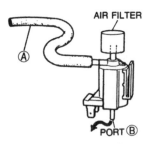

7.6a With no power applied to the solenoid, air blown into port A should flow through the solenoid valve and out port B

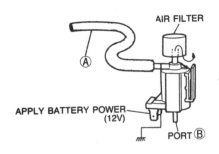

7.6b Apply battery voltage to the vacuum solenoid and blow into port A - air should flow through the solenoid and out the air filter

ing" sound. If the solenoid valve is silent, and the power is reaching the connector, replace the solenoid valve.

5   Now check for vacuum. There should not be any vacuum available at the fuel pressure regulator.

6   If vacuum exists, check the solenoid valve for correct operation. **Note**: *Before starting the test, make sure the solenoid valve electrical connector is reconnected.*

  a) First, disconnect the vacuum hose from the solenoid valve and vacuum pipe.
  b) Next, blow through the solenoid valve from port A and check that air comes out of port B **(see illustration)**.

  c) Disconnect the solenoid valve electrical connector and connect battery voltage to one terminal and ground the other.
  d) Now blow through the solenoid valve from port A and check that air flows out of the valve's air filter **(see illustration)**.
  e) If the test results are not correct, replace the solenoid valve with a new part.

Replacement

7   Remove the vacuum hoses, depress the tab and slide the solenoid valve out of the slotted bracket.

8   Installation is the reverse of removal.

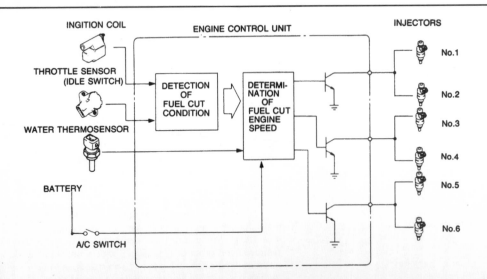

8.1 Schematic of the Deceleration Control System on the V6 engine

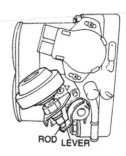

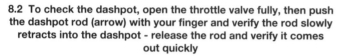

8.2 To check the dashpot, open the throttle valve fully, then push the dashpot rod (arrow) with your finger and verify the rod slowly retracts into the dashpot - release the rod and verify it comes out quickly

8.8 If the deceleration speed is incorrect, loosen the locknut and turn the dashpot until the rod contacts the throttle lever at approximately 3,200 to 3,800 rpm

8 Deceleration control system (V6 engine)

General description

Refer to illustration 8.1

1   The deceleration control system **(see illustration)** consists of a dashpot and a fuel cut control system. The dashpot prevents the throttle valves from closing too abruptly. The fuel cut control system improves fuel economy and prevents engine bucking during deceleration. These two components work in conjunction with the ignition coil, water thermosensor, throttle sensor and the ECU to control deceleration. If there is a problem with the system, which may be characterized by a failed emissions control test, high idle speed, stalling, backfiring or overheating of the exhaust system, and the following procedures do not remedy the problem, take the vehicle to a dealer service department or other repair shop for further diagnosis.

Check

Refer to illustration 8.2

Note: *Further testing of the deceleration control system can be performed by checking the water thermosensor and the TPS (see Section 4).*

2   Open the throttle valve fully, then push the dashpot rod **(see illustration)** with your finger and verify the rod slowly retracts into the

dashpot.

3   Release the rod and verify it comes out quickly.

4   Replace the dashpot if it doesn't perform as described.

Adjustment

Refer to illustration 8.8

5   Warm up the engine to its normal operating temperature and run it at idle speed.

6   Have an assistant watch the vehicle's tachometer.

7   Increase the engine speed to 4,000 rpm.

8   Slowly decrease the engine speed and verify the dashpot rod contacts the lever at 3,200 to 3,800 rpm **(see illustration)**.

9   If necessary, loosen the lock nut and adjust the dashpot by turning it, as necessary.

9 Air conditioning cut-off system

Refer to illustrations 9.1a and 9.1b

1   The air conditioning cut-off system improves idle smoothness directly after engine start-up and acceleration performance **(see illustrations)**. During acceleration, the air conditioning is cut-off for approximately five seconds when the following conditions have been met:

6

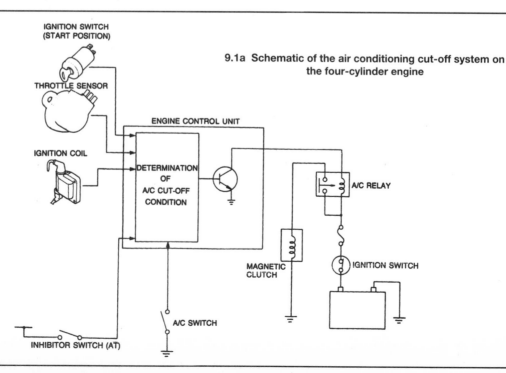

9.1a Schematic of the air conditioning cut-off system on the four-cylinder engine

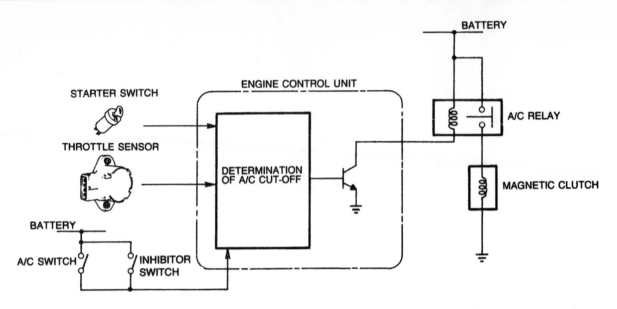

9.1b Schematic of the air conditioning cut-off system on the V6 engine

a) Air conditioning switch is ON
b) The manual transmission is in gear and the clutch pedal has been released
c) The automatic transmission is operating in gear (not P or N)
d) The throttle valve is opened more than 50 degrees (approximately half-throttle)

Check

2   Shift the transmission into gear (M/T) or into D range (A/T).
3   Turn the ignition switch, air conditioning switch and the blower fan switch to ON (engine not running).
4   Fully open the throttle valve and check that the condenser fan does not operate.
5   Shift the transmission into neutral (M/T) or P (A/T) and start the engine.
6   Check that the condenser fan does not operate for three seconds (V6 engine) or five seconds (four-cylinder engine).
7   If the test results are incorrect, check the TPS (see Section 4).

---

10   Catalytic converter system

Note: *Because of a Federally mandated extended warranty which cov-*ers emissions-related components such as the catalytic converter, check with a dealer service department before replacing the converter at your own expense.

General description

1   To reduce hydrocarbons (HC), carbon monoxide (CO) and oxides of nitrogen (NOx), the vehicles covered by this manual are equipped with a catalytic converter. The catalytic converter oxidizes these components and converts them to water, carbon dioxide and nitrogen.

Check

2   Visually examine the converters for cracks or damage. Make sure all fasteners are tight.
3   Inspect the insulation covers (if equipped) welded onto the converters - they should be tight. **Caution:** *If an insulation cover is touching a converter housing, excessive heat at the floor may result.*
4   Start the engine and run it at idle speed.
5   Check for exhaust gas leakage from the converter flanges. Check the body of each converter for holes.

Component replacement

6   See Chapter 4 for removal and installation procedures.

Chapter 7 Part A   Manual transmission

Contents

Specifications

Torque specifications

Transmission-to-engine bolts **(see illustration 3.15)**   **Ft-lbs** (unless otherwise indicated)

a	51 to 65
b	27 to 38
Drain and filler plugs...	20 to 30
Shift lever-to-transmission bolts	60 to 96 in-lbs
Transmission crossmember bolts	32 to 45
Transmission mount bolts	32 to 45

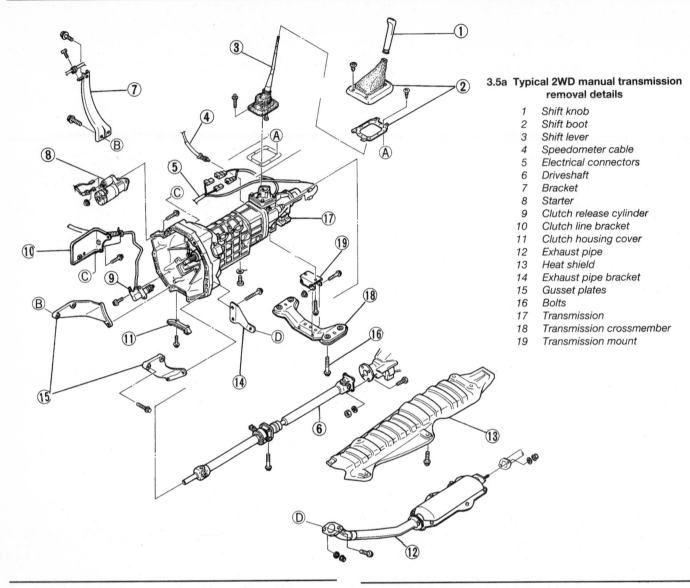

3.5a Typical 2WD manual transmission removal details

1   Shift knob
2   Shift boot
3   Shift lever
4   Speedometer cable
5   Electrical connectors
6   Driveshaft
7   Bracket
8   Starter
9   Clutch release cylinder
10 Clutch line bracket
11 Clutch housing cover
12 Exhaust pipe
13 Heat shield
14 Exhaust pipe bracket
15 Gusset plates
16 Bolts
17 Transmission
18 Transmission crossmember
19 Transmission mount

1   General information

All vehicles covered in this manual come equipped with either a five-speed manual transmission or an automatic transmission. All information on the manual transmission is included in this Part of Chapter 7. Information on the automatic transmission can be found in Part B of this Chapter.

The manual transmission used in these models is a five-speed unit with the fifth gear being an overdrive.

Due to the complexity, unavailability of replacement parts and the special tools necessary, internal repair by the home mechanic is not recommended. The information in this Chapter is limited to general information and removal and installation of the transmission.

Depending on the expense involved in having a faulty transmission overhauled, it may be a good idea to replace the unit with either a new or rebuilt one. Your local dealer or transmission shop should be able to supply you with information concerning cost, availability and exchange policy. Regardless of how you decide to remedy a transmission problem, you can still save a lot of money by removing and installing the unit yourself.

2   Manual transmission shift lever - removal and installation

1   Disconnect the negative cable at the battery.

2   Place the shift lever in Neutral.
3   Remove the shift boot (see Chapter 11).
4   Remove the three retaining bolts and lift the shift lever **straight up** and out of the transmission.
5   Coat both sides of a new gasket with sealant, place it **in** position, lubricate the shift lever base and lower it into the transmission.
6   Install the retaining bolts. Tighten the bolts to the torque listed in this Chapter's Specifications.
7   Install the shift boot and knob.

3   Manual transmission - removal and installation

Refer to illustrations 3.5a and 3.5b

Removal

1   Disconnect the negative cable from the battery.
2   Working inside the vehicle, remove the shift lever (see Section 2).
3   Raise the vehicle and support it securely on jackstands.
4   Remove the exhaust system components as necessary for clearance (see Chapter 4).
5   Disconnect the speedometer cable and wire harness connectors from the transmission **(see illustrations)**. Remove the starter (see Chapter 5) and the clutch release cylinder (see Chapter 8).
6   Remove the driveshaft(s) (see Chapter 8). Use a plastic bag to

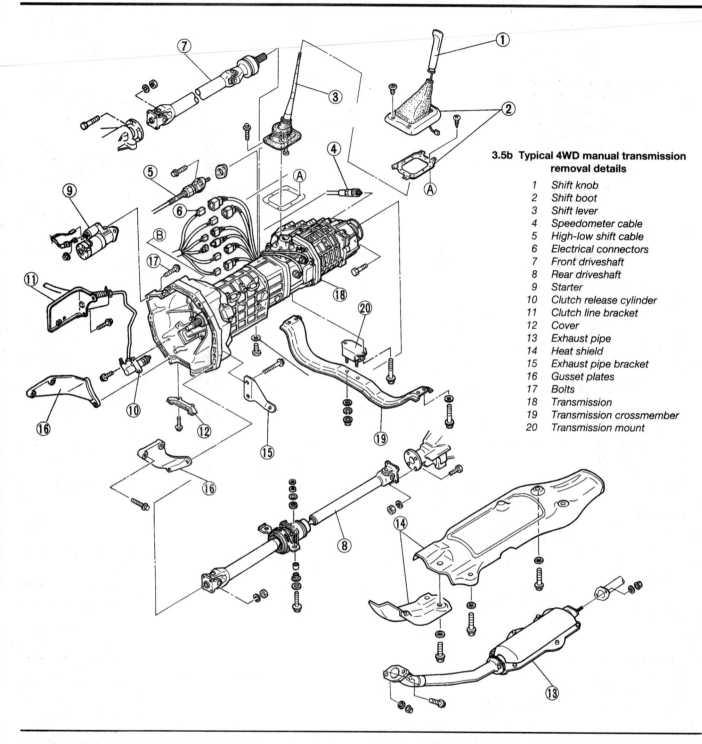

3.5b Typical 4WD manual transmission removal details

1 Shift knob
2 Shift boot
3 Shift lever
4 Speedometer cable
5 High-low shift cable
6 Electrical connectors
7 Front driveshaft
8 Rear driveshaft
9 Starter
10 Clutch release cylinder
11 Clutch line bracket
12 Cover
13 Exhaust pipe
14 Heat shield
15 Exhaust pipe bracket
16 Gusset plates
17 Bolts
18 Transmission
19 Transmission crossmember
20 Transmission mount

7A

cover the end of the transmission to prevent fluid loss and contamination.

7   Support the transmission with a jack - preferably a special jack made for this purpose. Safety chains will help steady the transmission on the jack.

8   Remove the transmission rear crossmember bolts.

9   Remove the bolts securing the transmission to the engine.

10   Make a final check that all wires and hoses have been disconnected from the transmission and then move the transmission and jack toward the rear of the vehicle until the transmission input shaft is clear of the clutch hub. Keep the transmission level as this is done.

11   Once the input shaft is clear, lower the transmission and remove it from under the vehicle. **Caution:** *Do not depress the clutch pedal while the transmission is out of the vehicle.*

12   The clutch components can be inspected at this time (see Chapter 8). In most cases, new clutch components should be routinely installed if the transmission is removed.

Installation

13   If removed, install the clutch components (see Chapter 8).

14   With the transmission secured to the jack as on removal, raise the transmission into position behind the engine and then carefully slide it forward, engaging the input shaft with the clutch plate hub. Do not use excessive force to install the transmission - if the input shaft does not slide into place, readjust the angle of the transmission so it is level and/or turn the input shaft so the splines engage properly with the clutch.

15   Install the transmission-to-engine bolts. Tighten the bolts to the

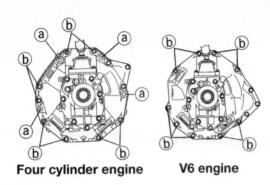

Four cylinder engine   **V6 engine**

3.15 Manual transmission-to-engine bolt torque details - refer to the Specifications Section for the specifications for your engine

torque listed in this Chapter's Specifications **(see illustration)**.
16   Install the crossmember bolts. Tighten the bolts securely.
17   Remove the jack supporting the transmission.
18   Install the various items removed previously, referring to Chapter 8 for the installation of the driveshaft(s) and Chapter 4 for information regarding the exhaust system components.

19   Make a final check that all wires, hoses and the speedometer cable have been connected and the transmission has been filled with lubricant to the proper level (see Chapter 1). Lower the vehicle.
20   Working inside the vehicle, install the shift lever (see Section 2).
21   Connect the negative battery cable. Road test the vehicle for proper operation and check for leakage.

---

4   Manual transmission overhaul - general information

Refer to illustrations 4.4a, 4.4b and 4.4c

Overhauling a manual transmission is a difficult job for the do-it-yourselfer. It involves the disassembly and reassembly of many small parts. Numerous clearances must be precisely measured and, if necessary, changed with select fit spacers and snap-rings. As a result, if transmission problems arise, it can be removed and installed by a competent do-it-yourselfer, but overhaul should be left to a transmission repair shop. Rebuilt transmissions may be available - check with your dealer parts department and auto parts stores. At any rate, the time and money involved in an overhaul is almost sure to exceed the cost of a rebuilt unit.

Nevertheless, it's not impossible for an inexperienced mechanic to rebuild a transmission if the special tools are available and the job is done in a deliberate step-by-step manner so nothing is overlooked.

The tools necessary for an overhaul include internal and external

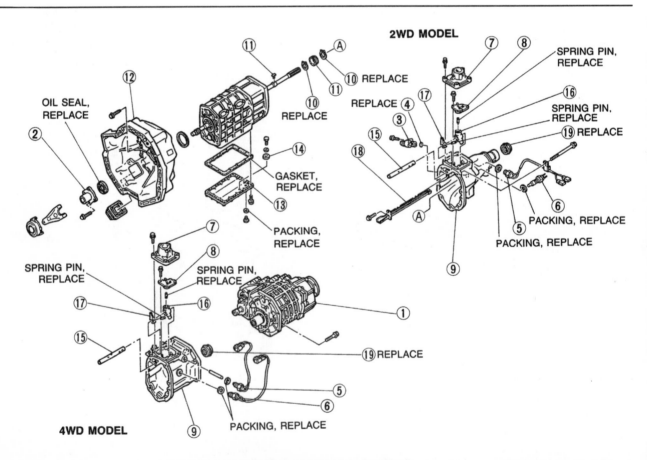

4.4a Typical manual transmission housing details

1	Transfer case (4WD models)	8	Shift lever guide	15	Control rod
2	Front cover	9	Extension housing	16	Control lever end
3	Speedometer drive gear	10	Snap-rings	17	Selector
4	Neutral safety switch	11	Speedometer driven gear and pin	18	Oil passage assembly
5	O-ring	12	Clutch housing	19	Rear oil seal
6	Backup light switch	13	Lower cover		
7	Shift lever housing	14	Magnet		

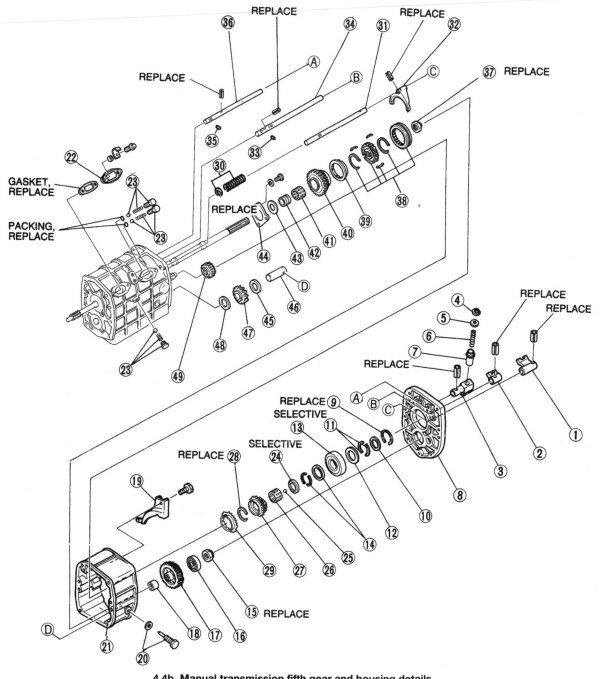

4.4b Manual transmission fifth gear and housing details

1	Fifth/reverse shift rod end	15	Locknut	29	Fifth gear synchronizer gear	40	Reverse gear
2	Third/fourth shift rod end	16	Countershaft rear bearing	30	Snap-ring and spring (4WD models)	41	Bearing
3	First/second shift rod end	17	Counter fifth gear	31	Fifth/reverse shift rod	42	Inner race
4	Retaining ring	18	Spacer	32	Fifth/reverse shift fork	43	Thrust washer
5	Spring retainer	19	Oil guide	33	Interlock pin	44	Bearing cover
6	Spring	20	Set bolt and washer	34	Third/fourth shift rod	45	Thrust washer
7	Pin and retaining ring	21	Center housing	35	Interlock pin	46	Reverse idler gear shaft
8	Bearing housing	22	Cover	36	First/second shift rod	47	Reverse idler gear
9	Snap-ring	23	Cap plug, spring and detent ball	37	Locknut	48	Thrust washer
10	Thrust washer	24	Thrust lock washer	38	Fifth/reverse clutch hub assembly	49	Reverse counter gear
11	C-washer	25	Steel ball	39	Reverse synchronizer ring		
12	Retaining ring	26	Bearing				
13	Mainshaft rear bearing	27	Fifth gear				
14	C-washer and retaining ring	28	Retaining ring				

snap-ring pliers, a bearing puller, a slide hammer, a set of pin punches, a dial indicator and possibly a hydraulic press. In addition, a large, sturdy workbench and a vise or transmission stand will be required.

During disassembly of the transmission, make careful notes of how each piece comes off, where it fits in relation to other pieces and what holds it in place. Exploded views are included **(see illustrations)** to show where the parts go - but actually noting how they are installed

when you remove the parts will make it much easier to get the transmission back together.

Before taking the transmission apart for repair, it will help if you have some idea what area of the transmission is malfunctioning. Certain problems can be closely tied to specific areas in the transmission, which can make component examination and replacement easier. Refer to the *Troubleshooting* section at the front of this manual for information regarding possible sources of trouble.

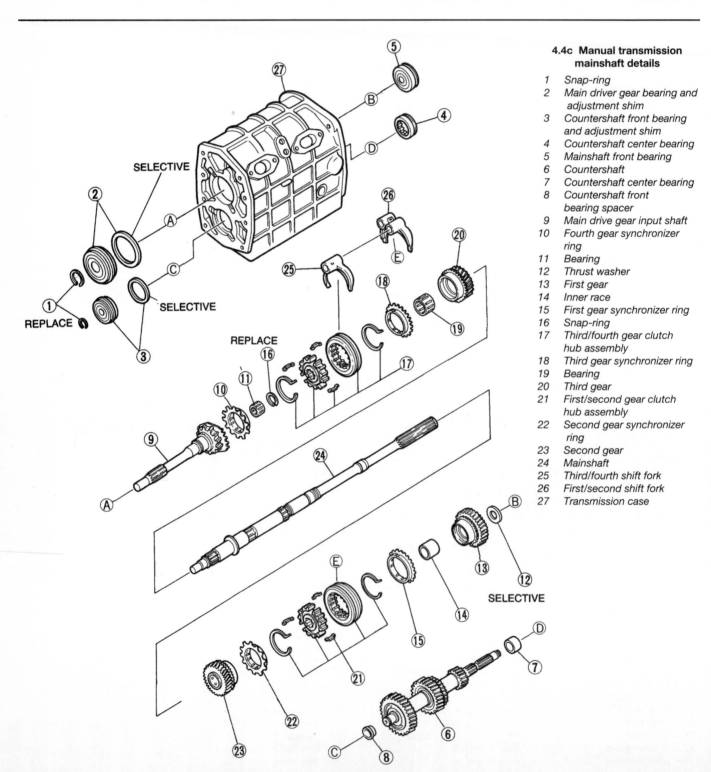

4.4c Manual transmission mainshaft details

1   Snap-ring
2   Main driver gear bearing and adjustment shim
3   Countershaft front bearing and adjustment shim
4   Countershaft center bearing
5   Mainshaft front bearing
6   Countershaft
7   Countershaft center bearing
8   Countershaft front bearing spacer
9   Main drive gear input shaft
10 Fourth gear synchronizer ring
11 Bearing
12 Thrust washer
13 First gear
14 Inner race
15 First gear synchronizer ring
16 Snap-ring
17 Third/fourth gear clutch hub assembly
18 Third gear synchronizer ring
19 Bearing
20 Third gear
21 First/second gear clutch hub assembly
22 Second gear synchronizer ring
23 Second gear
24 Mainshaft
25 Third/fourth shift fork
26 First/second shift fork
27 Transmission case

Chapter 7 Part B   Automatic transmission

Contents

7B

Specifications

General

Automatic transmission fluid type and capacity............................ See Chapter 1
Torque converter installation depth
    Electronically-controlled models.. 1.61 inches
    Hydraulically-controlled models.. 2.13 inches

Torque specifications   **Ft-lbs**

Torque converter-to-driveplate bolts .... 27 to 40
Transmission-to-engine bolts
    Electronically-controlled models .... 37 to 52
    Hydraulically-controlled models **(see illustration 7.25)**
        a .... 27 to 38
        b .... 51 to 65
        c .... 27 to 38
Fluid pan bolts... See Chapter 1

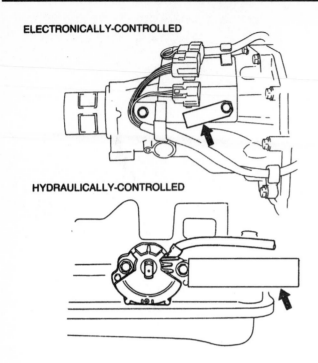

ELECTRONICALLY-CONTROLLED

HYDRAULICALLY-CONTROLLED

1.2 The electronically-controlled and hydraulically-controlled neutral safety switches can be differentiated by location of the serial number tag

1   General information

Refer to illustration 1.2

All vehicles covered in this manual come equipped with either a five-speed manual transmission or an automatic transmission. All information on the automatic transmission is included in this Part of Chapter 7. Information on the manual transmission can be found in Part A of this Chapter.

Two types of automatic transmissions are used in these models: hydraulically-controlled and electronically-controlled. The two transmissions can be differentiated by the location of the number tags; on electronically-controlled models the serial number tag is located by itself on the side of the case while on hydraulically-controlled models it is adjacent to the neutral start switch **(see illustration)**.

Due to the complexity of the automatic transmissions covered in this manual and the need for specialized equipment to perform most service operations, this Chapter contains only general diagnosis, routine maintenance, adjustment and removal and installation procedures.

If the transmission requires major repair work, it should be left to a dealer service department or an automotive or transmission repair shop. You can, however, remove and install the transmission yourself and save the expense, even if the repair work is done by a transmission shop.

2   Diagnosis - general

Note: *Automatic transmission malfunctions may be caused by five general conditions: poor engine performance, improper adjustments, hydraulic malfunctions, mechanical malfunctions or malfunctions in the computer or its signal network. Diagnosis of these problems should always begin with a check of the easily repaired items: fluid level and condition (see Chapter 1), shift linkage adjustment and throttle linkage adjustment. Next, perform a road test to determine if the problem has been corrected or if more diagnosis is necessary. If the problem persists after the preliminary tests and corrections are completed, addi-* *tional diagnosis should be done by a dealer service department or transmission repair shop. Refer to the* Troubleshooting *section at the front of this manual for information on symptoms of transmission problems.*

Preliminary checks

1   Drive the vehicle to warm the transmission to normal operating temperature.

2   Check the fluid level as described in Chapter 1:
   a) If the fluid level is unusually low, add enough fluid to bring the level within the designated area of the dipstick, then check for external leaks (see below).
   b) If the fluid level is abnormally high, drain off the excess, then check the drained fluid for contamination by coolant. The presence of engine coolant in the automatic transmission fluid indicates that a failure has occurred in the internal radiator walls that separate the coolant from the transmission fluid (see Chapter 3).
   c) If the fluid is foaming, drain it and refill the transmission, then check for coolant in the fluid or a high fluid level.

3   Check the engine idle speed. **Note:** *If the engine is malfunctioning, do not proceed with the preliminary checks until it has been repaired and runs normally.*

4   Inspect the shift linkage (see Section 4). Make sure that it's properly adjusted and that the linkage operates smoothly.

Fluid leak diagnosis

5   Most fluid leaks are easy to locate visually. Repair usually consists of replacing a seal or gasket. If a leak is difficult to find, the following procedure may help.

6   Identify the fluid. Make sure it's transmission fluid and not engine oil or brake fluid (automatic transmission fluid is a deep red color).

7   Try to pinpoint the source of the leak. Drive the vehicle several miles, then park it over a large sheet of cardboard. After a minute or two, you should be able to locate the leak by determining the source of the fluid dripping onto the cardboard.

8   Make a careful visual inspection of the suspected component and the area immediately around it. Pay particular attention to gasket mating surfaces. A mirror is often helpful for finding leaks in areas that are hard to see.

9   If the leak still cannot be found, clean the suspected area thoroughly with a degreaser or solvent, then dry it.

10   Drive the vehicle for several miles at normal operating temperature and varying speeds. After driving the vehicle, visually inspect the suspected component again.

11   Once the leak has been located, the cause must be determined before it can be properly repaired. If a gasket is replaced but the sealing flange is bent, the new gasket will not stop the leak. The bent flange must be straightened.

12   Before attempting to repair a leak, check to make sure that the following conditions are corrected or they may cause another leak. **Note:** *Some of the following conditions cannot be fixed without highly specialized tools and expertise. Such problems must be referred to a transmission repair shop or a dealer service department.*

Gasket leaks

13   Check the pan periodically. Make sure the bolts are tight, no bolts are missing, the gasket is in good condition and the pan is flat (dents in the pan may indicate damage to the valve body inside).

14   If the pan gasket is leaking, the fluid level or the fluid pressure may be too high, the vent may be plugged, the pan bolts may be too tight, the pan sealing flange may be warped, the sealing surface of the transmission housing may be damaged, the gasket may be damaged or the transmission casting may be cracked or porous. If sealant instead of gasket material has been used to form a seal between the pan and the transmission housing, it may be the wrong sealant.

Seal leaks

15   If a transmission seal is leaking, the fluid level or pressure may be too high, the vent may be plugged, the seal bore may be damaged, the seal itself may be damaged or improperly installed, the surface of

3.4 Insert the tip of large a screwdriver between the collar and the extension housing and pry the seal out of the transmission

3.6 Apply a thin layer of grease to the outer edge of the new seal and carefully tap it into the bore with a large socket and hammer

3.10 Remove the bolt and withdraw the speedometer driven gear from the transmission

3.11 Use a small screwdriver to remove the O-ring from the groove in the driven gear housing

the shaft protruding through the seal may be damaged or a loose bearing may be causing excessive shaft movement.

16   Make sure the dipstick tube seal is in good condition and the tube is properly seated. Periodically check the area around the speedometer gear for leakage. If transmission fluid is evident, check the O-ring for damage (see Chapter 7A).

Case leaks

17   If the case itself appears to be leaking, the casting is porous and will have to be repaired or replaced.

18   Make sure the oil cooler hose fittings are tight and in good condition.

Fluid comes out the vent pipe or fill tube

19   If this condition occurs, the transmission is overfilled, there is coolant in the fluid, the case is porous, the dipstick is incorrect, the vent is plugged or the drain back holes are plugged.

---

3   Oil seal replacement

Refer to illustrations 3.4, 3.6, 3.10 and 3.11

1   Oil leaks frequently occur due to wear of the extension housing oil seal and/or the speedometer drive gear O-ring. Replacement of these seals is relatively easy, since the repairs can usually be performed without removing the transmission from the vehicle.

2   The extension housing oil seal is located at the extreme rear of the transmission, where the driveshaft is attached. If leakage at the seal is suspected, raise the vehicle and support it securely on jackstands. If the seal is leaking, transmission lubricant will be built up on the front of the driveshaft and may be dripping from the rear of the transmission.

3   Refer to Chapter 8 and remove the driveshaft.

4   Using a screwdriver or pry bar, carefully pry the oil seal out of the rear of the transmission **(see illustration)**. Do not damage the splines on the transmission output shaft.

5   If the oil seal cannot be removed with a screwdriver or prybar, a special oil seal removal tool (available at auto parts stores) will be required.

6   Using a large section of pipe or a very large deep socket as a drift, install the new oil seal **(see illustration)**. Drive it into the bore squarely and make sure it's completely seated.

7   Lubricate the splines of the transmission output shaft and the outside of the driveshaft sleeve yoke with lightweight grease, then install the driveshaft. Be careful not to damage the lip of the new seal.

8   The speedometer cable and driven gear housing is located on the side of the extension housing. Look for transmission oil around the cable housing to determine if the O-ring is leaking.

9   Unscrew the collar and detach the speedometer cable.

10   Remove the driven gear housing **(see illustration)**.

11   Install a new O-ring in the driven gear housing and reinstall the driven gear housing and cable assembly on the extension housing **(see illustration)**.

7B

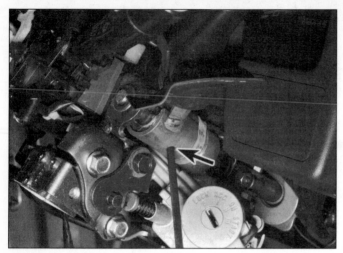

4.4 Insert a pin or small screwdriver into the shift linkage adjustment hole

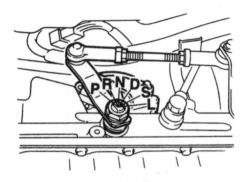

4.7 Make sure the shift lever on the transmission is in the Park position

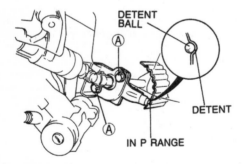

4.9 The detent ball must be in the center of the Drive range - loosen the bolts (A) to adjust the position

---

4   Shift linkage - check and adjustment

Check

1   Check the operation of the transmission in each shift lever position (try to start the engine in each gear - the starter should operate in Park and Neutral only). If the engine does not start or starts in any gear other than Park or Neutral, the shift linkage is in need of adjustment or the Neutral safety switch (see Section 4) is defective or in need of adjustment.

Adjustment

Refer to illustrations 4.4, 4.5, 4.7, 4.8, 4.9 and 4.10
2   Move the shift lever to the Park position.

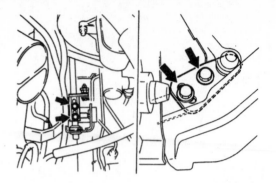

4.5 Loosen the shift lever and top lever bolts (arrows)

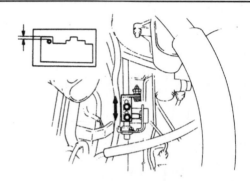

4.8 Remove any clearance between the lower bracket and the shift lever by sliding the lever

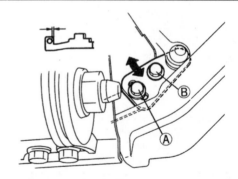

4.10 Turn the top lever to remove any clearance between the lower bracket and the shift lever bushing

---

3   Remove the steering column cover (see Chapter 11).
4   Pull the shift lever back and insert a 5 mm pin into the hole in the shift rod assembly **(see illustration)**.
5   In the engine compartment, remove the air cleaner hose for access and loosen the shift lever and top lever bolts **(see illustration)**.
6   Raise the vehicle and support it securely on jackstands.
7   Working under the vehicle, move the transmission shift lever to Park **(see illustration)**.
8   In the engine compartment, slide the shift lever to adjust out any clearance between the bracket and shift lever bushing, then tighten the shift lever bolts **(see illustration)**.
9   Inside the vehicle, make sure the detent ball is positioned in the center of the Park detent **(see illustration)**. Loosen the bolts and turn the bracket to adjust the position.
10   Check for clearance between the lower bracket and shift lever and turn the top lever to adjust it out if necessary **(see illustration)**.
11   Remove the pin from the shift rod and install the column covers.

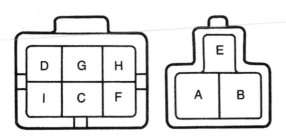

5.4a Electrical connector terminals for the neutral safety switch on electronically-controlled models

Position	Connector terminal								
	A	B	C	D	E	F	G	H	I
P	O——O		O——O						
R			O		O				
N	O——O		O			O			
D			O				O		
S			O					O	
L			O						O

O——O: Indicates continuity

5.4b Check for continuity between the neutral safety switch terminals indicated (electronically-controlled models)

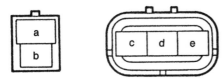

5.4c Hydraulically-controlled neutral safety switch terminals

Position	Connector terminal				
	a	b	c	d	e
P	O——O		O——O		
R			O——O		
N	O——O				
D, 1, 2					

O——O: Indicates continuity

5.4d Check for continuity between the neutral safety switch terminals indicated (hydraulically-controlled models)

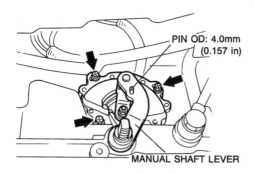

5.9a Insert an alignment pin (the shank of a 5/32-inch drill bit will work) into the hole in the Neutral safety switch - if the pin doesn't slide in fully, rotate the switch until it does (electronically-controlled models)

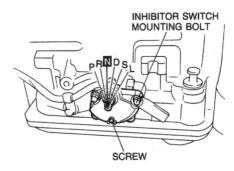

5.9b Remove the screw at the bottom of the switch, and with the bolts loose, insert a 5/64-inch drill bit into the hole, adjusting the switch position until it slides all the way in

7B

5 Neutral safety switch - check, adjustment and replacement

1   The neutral safety switch, located on the side of the transmission, prevents the engine from starting with the transmission in gear.

Check

Refer to illustrations 5.4a, 5.4b, 5.4c and 5.4d

2   Make sure the engine will start only with the selector lever in Park and Neutral. With the key in the On position, make sure the backup lights function when the lever is in Reverse only.

3   If a malfunction is noted, raise the vehicle and support it on jackstands.

4   Disconnect the switch wire harness, attach the leads of an ohmmeter to the terminals and check for continuity **(see illustrations)**.

5   Adjust the switch (see below) and then check that continuity is indicated between the switch terminals. If the switch does not operate properly after adjustment, replace it with a new one.

6   Disconnect the ohmmeter and reconnect the wire harness.

Adjustment

Refer to illustrations 5.9a and 5.9b

7   Shift the transmission into Neutral.

8   Loosen the retaining bolts.

9   On electronically-controlled models, rotate the switch and insert a 5/32-inch (4.0 mm) diameter pin into the alignment hole and through the internal rotor **(see illustration)**. On hydraulically-controlled transmissions, remove the screw at the bottom of the switch and insert a 5/64-inch (2.0 mm) pin **(see illustration)**.

10   On electronically-controlled models, tighten the mounting bolts and remove the pin. On hydraulically-controlled models, tighten the bolts, remove the pin, and install the screw in the hole.

11   Recheck the switch operation as described in Step 17.

Replacement

12   Disconnect the cable from the negative terminal of the battery.

13   Remove the retaining nut that secures the shift lever to the lever shaft and separate the lever from the shaft.

14   Unplug the electrical connector, remove the screw and the retaining bolts and lift the switch off.

15   Installation is the reverse of removal. Do not tighten the retaining bolts fully until the switch has been adjusted.

16   Connect the battery negative cable.

17   Start the engine in both Park and Neutral to verify that the switch is properly adjusted.

6 Transmission mount - check and replacement

Refer to illustrations 6.2, 6.3, 6.4a, 6.4b, 6.5a and 6.5b

1   Insert a large screwdriver or prybar into the space between the

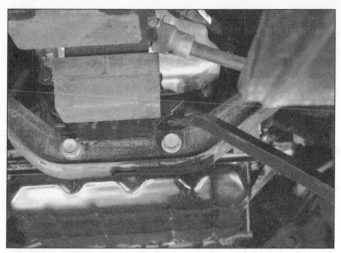

6.2 Pry between the transmission mount and the crossmember - there should be very little movement

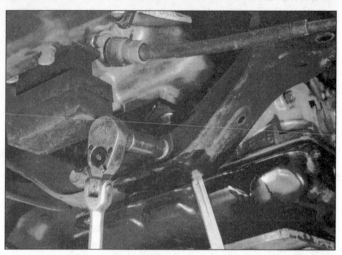

6.3 Use a socket and extension to remove the mount-to-crossmember bolts

6.4a With the transmission supported by a jack, remove the crossmember bolts and . . .

6.4b . . . lower the crossmember

transmission extension housing and the crossmember and try to pry the transmission up slightly.

2   The transmission should not move away from the crossmember much at all **(see illustration)**.

3   If it is necessary to replace the mount, support the transmission with a jack and remove the mount-to-crossmember bolts **(see illustration)**.

4   Remove the crossmember-to-chassis bolts and lower the crossmember from the vehicle **(see illustrations)**.

5   Unbolt the mount and separate it from the transmission **(see illustrations)**.

6   Install the new mount by reversing the removal procedure.

---

7   Automatic transmission - removal and installation

Refer to illustrations 7.11a, 7.11b, 7.11c, 7.21a, 7.21b and 7.25

Removal

1   Disconnect the negative cable from the battery.

2   Raise the vehicle and support it securely on jackstands.

3   Drain the transmission fluid (see Chapter 1), then reinstall the pan.

4   Remove any exhaust components which will interfere with transmission removal (see Chapter 4).

5   Remove the torque converter cover.

6   Mark the relationship of the torque converter to the driveplate so they can be installed in the same position.

6.5a Remove the nuts and . . .

7   Remove the torque converter-to-driveplate bolts. Turn the crankshaft for access to each bolt. Turn the crankshaft in a clockwise direction only (as viewed from the front).

8   Remove the starter motor (see Chapter 5).

9   Remove the driveshaft (see Chapter 8).

6.5b ... lower the mount from the transmission

10 Disconnect the speedometer cable.
11 Detach the electrical connectors from the transmission (**see illustrations**).
12 On models so equipped, disconnect the vacuum lines.
13 Disconnect the shift linkage.
14 Support the engine with a jack. Use a block of wood under the oil pan to spread the load.
15 Support the transmission with a jack - preferably a jack made for this purpose. Safety chains will help steady the transmission on the jack.
16 Remove the rear crossmember bolts.
17 Remove the bolts securing the transmission to the engine.
18 Lower the transmission slightly and disconnect and plug the transmission fluid cooler lines.
19 Remove the transmission dipstick tube.
20 Move the transmission to the rear to disengage it from the engine block dowel pins and make sure the torque converter is detached from the driveplate. Secure the torque converter to the transmission so it

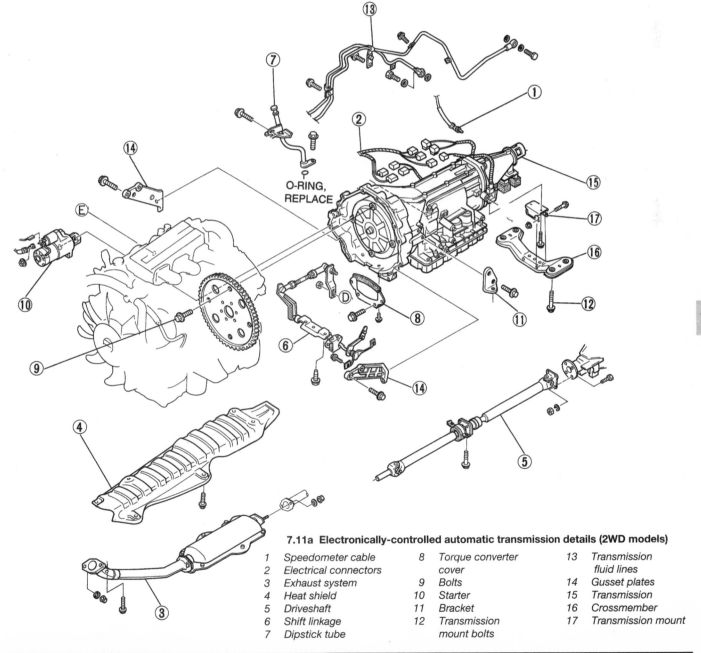

7.11a Electronically-controlled automatic transmission details (2WD models)

1	Speedometer cable	8	Torque converter cover	13	Transmission fluid lines
2	Electrical connectors	9	Bolts	14	Gusset plates
3	Exhaust system	10	Starter	15	Transmission
4	Heat shield	11	Bracket	16	Crossmember
5	Driveshaft	12	Transmission mount bolts	17	Transmission mount
6	Shift linkage				
7	Dipstick tube				

7B

won't fall out during removal. Lower the transmission slowly from the vehicle.

Installation

21   Prior to installation, make sure the torque converter hub is securely engaged in the pump **(see illustrations)**

22   With the transmission secured to the jack, raise it into position. Be sure to keep it level so the torque converter does not slide forward. Connect the transmission fluid cooler lines.

23   Turn the torque converter to line up the bolt holes with the holes

in the driveplate. The marks on the torque converter and the driveplate made in Step 6 must line up.

24   Move the transmission forward carefully until the dowel pins and the torque converter are engaged.

25   Install the transmission housing-to-engine bolts. Tighten them securely **(see illustration)**.

26   Install the torque converter-to-driveplate bolts. Tighten the bolts to the torque listed in this Chapter's Specifications.

27   Install the transmission mount crossmember and through-bolts. Tighten the bolts and nuts securely.

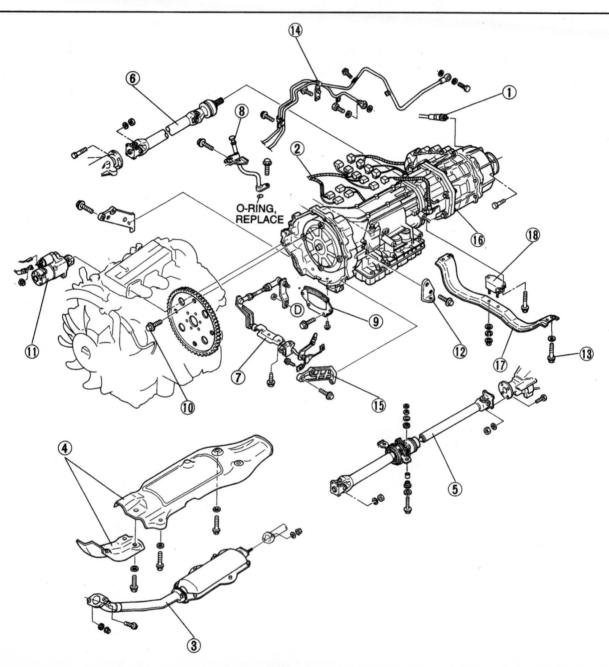

7.11b Electronically-controlled automatic transmission details (4WD models)

1	Speedometer cable	7	Shift linkgage	13	Transmission mount bolts
2	Electrical connectors	8	Dipstick tube	14	Transmission fluid lines
3	Exhaust system	9	Torque converter cover	15	Gusset plates
4	Heat shield	10	Bolts	16	Transmission/transfer case
5	Rear driveshaft	11	Starter	17	Crossmember
6	Front driveshaft	12	Bracket	18	Transmission mount

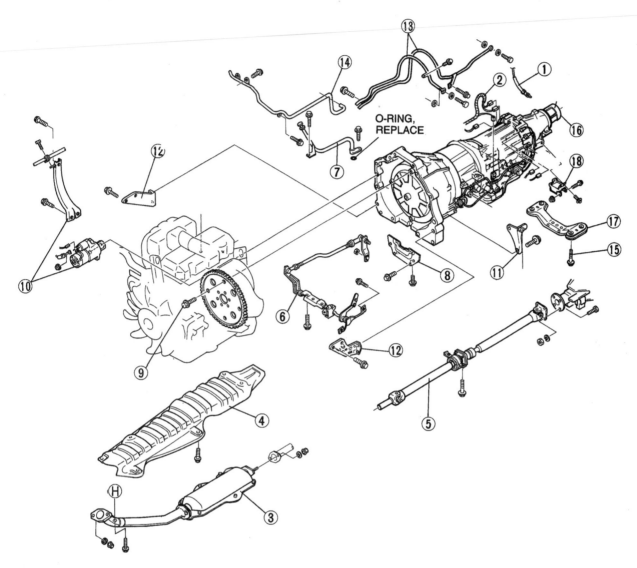

7.11c Hydraulically-controlled automatic transmission details

1	Speedometer cable	7	Dipstick tube	13	Transmission fluid lines
2	Electrical connectors	8	Torque converter cover	14	Vacuum lines
3	Exhaust system	9	Bolts	15	Transmission mount bolts
4	Heat shield	10	Starter	16	Transmission
5	Driveshaft	11	Bracket	17	Crossmember
6	Shift linkage	12	Gusset plates	18	Transmission mount

7B

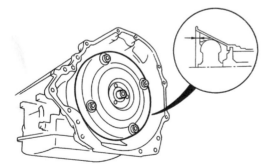

7.21a On electrically-controlled transmissions, the distance from the torque converter outer face to the transmission outer face must be as specified for the torque converter to be properly installed - refer to the Specifications Section

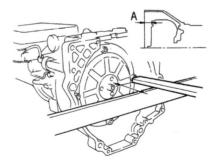

7.21b For the torque converter to be properly installed on hydraulically-controlled transmissions, the distance from the end of the torque converter to the end of the transmission housing (dimension A) must be as listed in the Specifications Section at the beginning of this Chapter

28   Remove the jacks supporting the transmission and the engine.
29   Install the dipstick tube, using a new O-ring.
30   Install the starter motor (see Chapter 5).
31   Connect the vacuum hose(s) (if equipped).
32   Connect the shift linkage.
33   Plug in the transmission wire harness connectors.
34   Install the torque converter cover.
35   Install the driveshaft.
36   Connect the speedometer cable.
37   Adjust the shift linkage (see Section 4).
38   Install any exhaust system components that were removed or disconnected.
39   Lower the vehicle.
40   Fill the transmission with the specified fluid (see Chapter 1), run the engine and check for fluid leaks.

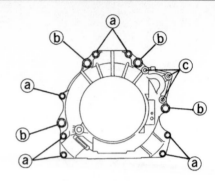

7.25 On hydraulically-controlled models, the transmission -to-engine bolts have different torques - refer to the Specifications Section

Chapter 7 Part C Transfer case

Contents

Specifications

Torque specifications

	Ft-lbs
Transfer case-to-transmission bolt	27 to 40
Transfer case mount bolt/nut	23 to 34
Crossmember bolt..	32 to 45

1 General information

Four-wheel drive (4WD) models are equipped with a transfer case mounted on the rear of the transmission. Drive is passed from the engine through the transmission and transfer case to the front and rear wheels by driveshafts.

Because of the special tools and techniques required, disassembly and overhaul of the transfer case should be left to a dealer or properly equipped shop. You can, however, remove and install the transfer case by yourself and save the expense, even if the repair work is done by a specialist.

2 Transfer case - removal and installation

Refer to illustrations 2.7 and 2.12

Removal

1 Disconnect the negative cable from the battery.
2 Raise the vehicle and support it securely on jackstands.

3 Drain the transfer case lubricant (see Chapter 1).
4 Remove any exhaust components which will interfere with the transfer case removal.
5 Remove the driveshafts.
6 Disconnect the speedometer cable.
7 Detach the electrical connectors **(see illustration)**.
8 Support the transmission with a jack.
9 Support the transfer case with a jack - preferably a jack made for this purpose. Safety chains will help steady the transfer case on the jack.
10 Remove the rear crossmember bolts.
11 Remove the bolts securing the transfer case to the transmission.
12 Move the transfer case to the rear to disengage it from the transmission. Sometimes the sealant between the transfer case and transmission makes removal difficult so it will be necessary to tap on the transfer case housing with a plastic hammer to break the seal **(see illustration)**. Lower the transfer case slowly from the vehicle.

Installation

13 Prior to installation, apply a bead of silicone sealant to the transfer case contact surface **(see illustration 2.7)**.
14 With the transfer case secured to the jack, raise it into position.

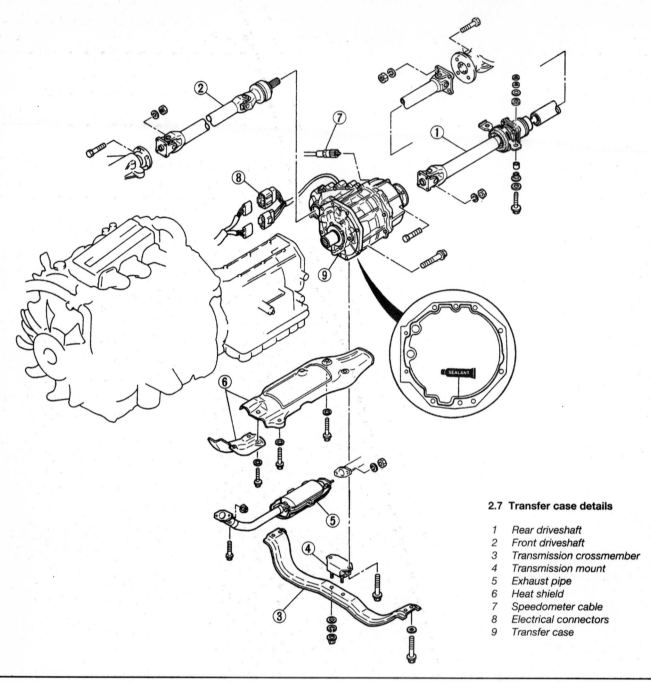

2.7 Transfer case details

1   Rear driveshaft
2   Front driveshaft
3   Transmission crossmember
4   Transmission mount
5   Exhaust pipe
6   Heat shield
7   Speedometer cable
8   Electrical connectors
9   Transfer case

15   Move the transfer case forward carefully until it is engaged in the transmission.

16   Install the transfer case-to-transmission bolts. Tighten the bolts to the torque listed in this Chapter's Specifications.

17   Install the transmission crossmember.

18   Remove the jacks supporting the transmission and transfer case.

19   Plug in the electrical connectors.

20   Install the driveshafts.

21   Connect the speedometer cable.

22   Install any exhaust system components that were removed or disconnected.

23   Fill the transfer case with the specified lubricant (see Chapter 1).

24   Lower the vehicle.

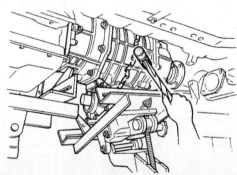

2.12 Use a plastic hammer to tap on the transfer case housing

Chapter 8 Clutch and driveline

Contents

Specifications

Clutch disc
Minimum lining thickness	1/32-inch above rivet heads
Maximum runout	0.039 inch

Clutch pedal
Pedal height	8-3/16 to 8-9/16 inches
Pedal freeplay	3/16 to 11/16 inch
Disengagement height	1-3/8 inch

Driveaxle standard length
Right side	22-5/16 inches
Left side	19-5/8 inches

Torque specifications
	Ft-lbs
Flywheel bolts	See Chapter 2
Pressure plate-to-flywheel bolts	13 to 20
Driveshafts	
Flange bolts/nuts	36 to 43
Center bearing support bolts	27 to 39
Front differential mounting bolts	49 to 72
Rear differential mounting bolts and nuts	17 to 20
Driveaxle hub nut (4WD models)	174 to 231
Pinion shaft companion flange nut	
Initial	94
Maximum	210
Brake backing plate-to-axle housing nuts	72 to 87
Front axle tube-to-differential bolts	27 to 40

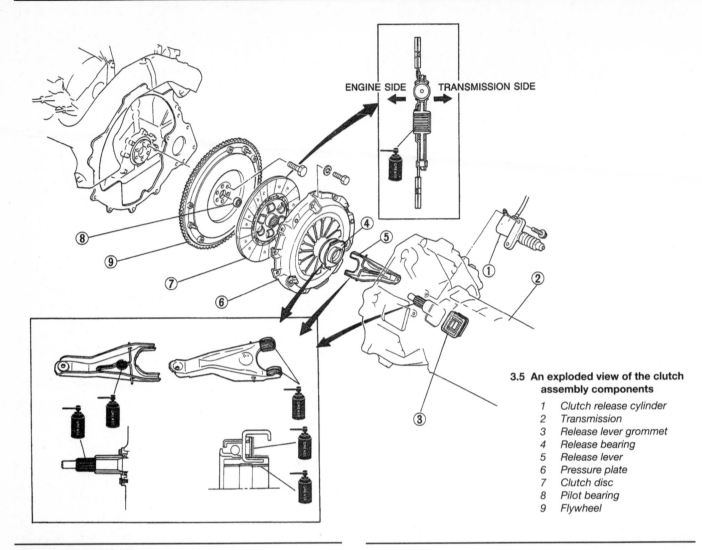

ENGINE SIDE   TRANSMISSION SIDE

**3.5 An exploded view of the clutch
assembly components**

1   *Clutch release cylinder*
2   *Transmission*
3   *Release lever grommet*
4   *Release bearing*
5   *Release lever*
6   *Pressure plate*
7   *Clutch disc*
8   *Pilot bearing*
9   *Flywheel*

1   General information

The information in this Chapter deals with the components that transmit power to the wheels, except for the transmission and transfer case, which are dealt with in Chapter 7. For the purposes of this Chapter, these components are grouped into three categories; clutch, driveshaft and axles. Separate Sections within this Chapter offer general descriptions and checking procedures for components in each of the three groups.

Since nearly all the procedures covered in this Chapter involve working under the vehicle, make sure it's securely supported on sturdy jackstands or on a hoist where the vehicle can be easily raised and lowered.

2   Clutch - description and check

1   All models with a manual transmission use a single dry plate, diaphragm spring type clutch. The clutch disc has a splined hub which allows it to slide along the splines of the transmission input shaft. The clutch and pressure plate are held in contact by spring pressure exerted by the diaphragm in the pressure plate.

2   The clutch release system is operated by hydraulic pressure. The hydraulic release system consists of the clutch pedal, a master cylinder and fluid reservoir, the hydraulic line, a release cylinder and the clutch release (or throwout) bearing.

3   Terminology can be a problem when discussing the clutch components because common names are in some cases different from

those used by the manufacturer. For example, the driven plate is also called the clutch plate or disc, the clutch release bearing is sometimes called a throw-out bearing, the release cylinder is sometimes called the operating or slave cylinder.

4   Other than to replace components with obvious damage, some preliminary checks should be performed to diagnose clutch problems.

  a) The first check should be of the fluid level in the clutch master cylinder. If the fluid level is low, add fluid as necessary and inspect the hydraulic system for leaks. If the master cylinder reservoir has run dry, bleed the system as described in Section 9 and retest the clutch operation.

  b) To check "clutch spin down time," run the engine at normal idle speed with the transmission in Neutral (clutch pedal up - engaged). Disengage the clutch (pedal down), wait several seconds and shift the transmission into Reverse. No grinding noise should be heard. A grinding noise would most likely indicate a problem in the pressure plate or the clutch disc.

  c) To check for complete clutch release, run the engine (with the parking brake applied to prevent movement) and hold the clutch pedal approximately 1/2-inch from the floor. Shift the transmission between first gear and Reverse several times. If the shift is hard or the transmission grinds, component failure is indicated. Watch the travel of the clutch release cylinder. With the clutch pedal depressed completely, the pushrod should extend substantially. If it doesn't, check the fluid level in the clutch master cylinder (see Chapter 1). Bleed the system (see Section 9).

  d) Visually inspect the pivot bushing at the top of the clutch pedal to make sure there is no binding or excessive play.

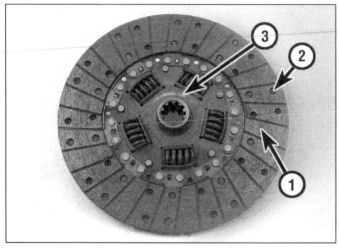

3.9 The clutch plate

1 **Lining** - This will wear down in use
2 **Rivets** - These secure the lining and will damage the flywheel or pressure plate if allowed to contact the surfaces
3 **Markings** - "Flywheel side" or something similar

---

3   Clutch components - removal, inspection and installation

Warning: *Dust produced by clutch wear and deposited on clutch components may contain asbestos, which is hazardous to your health. DO NOT blow it out with compressed air and DO NOT inhale it. DO NOT use gasoline or petroleum-based solvents to remove the dust. Brake system cleaner should be used to flush the dust into a drain pan. After the clutch components are wiped clean with a rag, dispose of the contaminated rags and cleaner in a covered, marked container.*

Removal

Refer to illustration 3.5

1   Access to the clutch components is normally accomplished by removing the transmission (and transfer case on 4WD models), leaving the engine in the vehicle. If, of course, the engine is being removed for major overhaul, then check the clutch for wear and replace worn components as necessary. However, the relatively low cost of the clutch components compared to the time and trouble spent gaining access to them warrants their replacement anytime the engine or transmission is removed, unless they are new or in near perfect condition. The following procedures are based on the assumption the engine will stay in place.

2   Referring to Chapter 7 Part A, remove the transmission from the vehicle. Support the engine while the transmission is out. Preferably, an engine hoist should be used to support it from above. However, if a jack is used underneath the engine, make sure a piece of wood is positioned between the jack and oil pan to spread the load. **Caution:** *The pick-up for the oil pump is very close to the bottom of the oil pan. If the pan is bent or distorted in any way, engine oil starvation could occur.*

3   To support the clutch disc during removal, install a clutch alignment tool through the clutch disc hub.

4   Carefully inspect the flywheel and pressure plate for indexing marks. The marks are usually an X, an O or a white letter. If they cannot be found, scribe marks yourself so the pressure plate and the flywheel will be in the same alignment during installation.

5   Turning each bolt a little at a time, loosen the pressure plate-to-flywheel bolts. Work in a criss-cross pattern until all spring pressure is relieved evenly. Then hold the pressure plate securely and completely remove the bolts, followed by the pressure plate and clutch disc **(see illustration).**

Inspection

Refer to illustrations 3.9 and 3.11

6   Ordinarily, when a problem occurs in the clutch, it can be at-

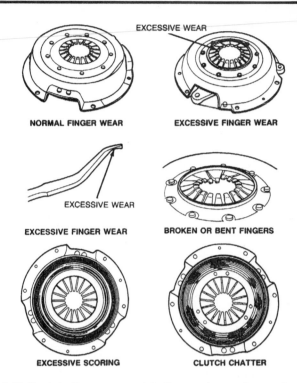

3.11 Replace the pressure plate if excessive or abnormal wear is noted

---

tributed to wear of the clutch driven plate assembly (clutch disc). However, all components should be inspected at this time.

7   Inspect the flywheel for cracks, heat checking, grooves and other obvious defects. If the imperfections are slight, a machine shop can machine the surface flat and smooth, which is highly recommended regardless of the surface appearance. Refer to Chapter 2 for the flywheel removal and installation procedure.

8   Inspect the pilot bearing (see Section 6).

9   Inspect the lining on the clutch disc. There should be at least 1/32-inch of lining above the rivet heads. Check for loose rivets, distortion, cracks, broken springs and other obvious damage **(see illustration).** As mentioned above, ordinarily the clutch disc is routinely replaced, so if in doubt about the condition, replace it with a new one.

10   The release bearing should also be replaced along with the clutch disc (see Section 5).

11   Check the machined surfaces and the diaphragm spring fingers of the pressure plate **(see illustration).** If the surface is grooved or otherwise damaged, replace the pressure plate. Also check for obvious damage, distortion, cracking, etc. Light glazing can be removed with medium grit emery cloth. If a new pressure plate is required, new and factory-rebuilt units are available.

Installation

Refer to illustration 3.13

12   Before installation, clean the flywheel and pressure plate machined surfaces with lacquer thinner or acetone. It's important that no oil or grease is on these surfaces or the lining of the clutch disc. Handle the parts only with clean hands.

13   Position the clutch disc and pressure plate against the flywheel with the clutch held in place with an alignment tool **(see illustration).** Make sure it's installed properly (most replacement clutch plates will be marked *"flywheel side"* or something similar - if not marked, install the clutch disc with the flat side of the hub toward the flywheel).

14   Tighten the pressure plate-to-flywheel bolts only finger tight, working around the pressure plate.

15   Center the clutch disc by ensuring the alignment tool extends through the splined hub and into the pilot bearing in the crankshaft. Wiggle the tool up, down or side-to-side as needed to bottom the tool

8

3.13 Hold the clutch disc in place with an alignment tool while you're tightening the pressure plate mounting bolts

5.4 To check the release bearing, hold the center of the bearing and rotate the outer portion while applying pressure - if it doesn't turn smoothly or if it's noisy, replace it

in the pilot bearing. Tighten the pressure plate-to-flywheel bolts a little at a time, working in a criss-cross pattern to prevent distorting the cover. After all of the bolts are snug, tighten them to the torque listed in this Chapter's Specifications. Remove the alignment tool.

16   If removed, install the clutch release bearing as described in Section 5.

17   Install the transmission and all components removed previously. Tighten all fasteners to the torque values listed in this Chapter's Specifications.

---

4   Flywheel - removal and installation

Refer to Chapter 2 for the flywheel removal and installation procedure.

---

5   Clutch release bearing - removal, inspection and installation

---

Warning: *Dust produced by clutch wear and deposited on clutch components may contain asbestos, which is hazardous to your health. DO NOT blow it out with compressed air and DO NOT inhale it. DO NOT use gasoline or petroleum-based solvents to remove the dust. Brake system cleaner should be used to flush the dust into a drain pan. After the clutch components are wiped clean with a rag, dispose of the contaminated rags and cleaner in a covered, marked container.*

Removal

Refer to illustration 5.3

1   Raise the front of the vehicle and place it securely on jackstands.

5.3 To remove the release bearing, slide it forward until the release lever is at its maximum travel, then disengage the release lever ends from the tangs on the bearing

2   Remove the transmission (see Chapter 7A).

3   The release bearing slides on a sleeve located around the transmission input shaft **(see illustration)**. Slide the bearing forward, to its maximum travel on the sleeve, disengage the tangs on the bearing from the release lever ends and slide the bearing off the input shaft. Give the release lever a sharp tug to pull it off its ballstud.

Inspection

Refer to illustration 5.4

4   Hold the center of the bearing and rotate the outer portion while applying pressure **(see illustration)**. If the bearing doesn't turn smoothly or if it's noisy, replace it with a new one. Wipe the bearing with a clean rag and inspect it for damage, wear and cracks. Don't immerse the bearing in solvent - it's sealed for life and to do so would ruin it.

Installation

5   Lightly lubricate the clutch lever ends and spring retention crown with high temperature grease where they contact the bearing **(see illustration 3.5).** Fill the inner groove of the bearing with the same grease.

6   Snap the release lever back into place on its ballstud. Guide the release bearing onto the input shaft sleeve, pull the release lever out to its maximum travel and engage the lever ends with the tangs on the bearing.

7   Apply a light coat of high-temperature grease to the face of the release bearing, where it contacts the pressure plate diaphragm fingers.

8   Prior to installing the transmission, apply a light coat of grease to the input shaft sleeve.

9   The remainder of installation is the reverse of the removal procedure.

---

6   Pilot bearing - inspection and replacement

Refer to illustrations 6.4, 6.5 and 6.10

1   The clutch pilot bearing is pressed into the rear of the crankshaft. It is greased at the factory and does not require additional lubrication. Its primary purpose is to support the front of the transmission input shaft. The pilot bearing should be inspected whenever the clutch components are removed from the engine. Due to its inaccessibility, if you are in doubt as to its condition, replace it with a new one. **Note:** *If the engine has been removed from the vehicle, disregard the following steps which do not apply.*

2   Remove the transmission (see Chapter 7A).

3   Remove the clutch components (see Section 3).

6.4 To check the pilot bearing, stick your finger in it and push out (toward the circumference), while rotating the bearing at the same time; if it sticks, feels rough or has excessive resistance, replace it

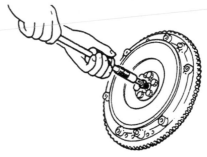

6.5 Use a special puller and slide hammer to remove the pilot bearing from the crankshaft (or use hydraulic pressure, as described in the text)

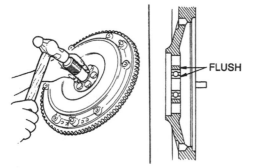

6.10 To install the new bearing, lightly lubricate the outside surface, then drive it into the recess until it's flush

4   Inspect for any excessive wear, scoring, lack of grease, dryness or obvious damage. If any of these conditions are noted, the bearing should be replaced. A flashlight will be helpful to direct light into the recess. Turn the bearing while applying force in the axial direction, i.e. push out, toward the circumference, while rotating the bearing with your finger **(see illustration)**. If it sticks or has excessive resistance, replace it.

5   Removal can be accomplished with a special puller and slide hammer **(see illustration)**, but an alternative method also works.

6   Find a solid steel bar which is slightly smaller in diameter than the bearing. Alternatives to a solid bar would be a wood dowel or a socket

with a bolt fixed in place to make it solid.

7   Check the bar for fit - it should just slip into the bearing with very little clearance.

8   Pack the bearing and the area behind it (in the crankshaft recess) with heavy grease. Pack it tightly to eliminate as much air as possible.

9   Insert the bar into the bearing bore and strike the bar sharply with a hammer which will force the grease to the back side of the bearing and push it out. Remove the bearing and clean all grease from the crankshaft recess.

10   To install the new bearing, lightly lubricate the outside surface with grease, then drive it into the recess until it's flush **(see illustration)**.

11   Install the clutch components, transmission and all other components removed previously, tightening all fasteners properly.

---

7   Clutch release cylinder - removal, overhaul and installation

Note: *Before beginning this procedure, contact local parts stores and dealer service departments concerning the purchase of a rebuild kit or a new release cylinder. Availability and cost of the necessary parts may dictate whether the cylinder is rebuilt or replaced with a new one. If you decide to rebuild the cylinder, inspect the bore as described in Step 7 before purchasing parts.*

Removal
Refer to illustration 7.2

1   Raise the front of the vehicle and place it securely on jackstands.

2   Disconnect the metal hydraulic line from the flexible hose at the

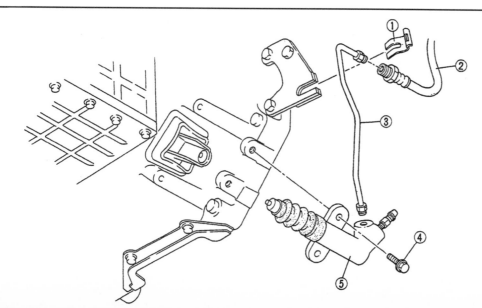

7.2 Clutch release cylinder mounting details

1   *Clip*
2   *Flexible hose*
3   *Metal line*
4   *Bolt*
5   *Clutch release cylinder*

8

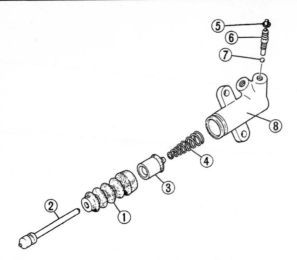

7.5 An exploded view of the clutch release cylinder components

1	Boot	5	Bleeder cap
2	Pushrod	6	Bleeder screw
3	Piston and seal assembly	7	Steel ball
4	Spring	8	Release cylinder body

threaded fitting **(see illustration)**. If available, use a flare nut wrench on the fitting to prevent the fitting from being rounded off. Plug the flexible hose to prevent fluid leakage. Disconnect the other end of the metal line from the release cylinder. Have some rags handy, as some fluid will be spilled as the line is removed.

3   Remove the two release cylinder mounting bolts.
4   Remove the release cylinder.

Overhaul

Refer to illustration 7.5

5   Remove the pushrod and the boot **(see illustration)**.
6   Tap the cylinder on a block of wood to eject the piston, seal and spring.
7   Carefully inspect the bore of the cylinder. Check for deep scratches, score marks and ridges. The bore must be smooth to the touch. If any imperfections are found, the release cylinder must be re-

placed with a new one.
8   Using the new parts in the rebuild kit, assemble the components using brake fluid for lubrication. Note that the lip on the piston cup faces away from the piston.

Installation

9   Install the release cylinder on the clutch housing. Make sure the pushrod is seated in the release fork pocket.
10   Reconnect the hydraulic line. Tighten the fittings securely.
11   Fill the clutch master cylinder with brake fluid conforming to DOT 3 specifications.
12   Bleed the system as described in Section 9.

8   Clutch master cylinder and reservoir - removal, overhaul and installation

Removal

Refer to illustration 8.2

Note: *The master cylinder and reservoir are separate units. You can remove either component separately.*
1   Disconnect the negative cable from the battery.
2   Detach the rubber hose between the reservoir and the master cylinder **(see illustration)**. **Caution:** *Brake fluid will damage painted surfaces. Be sure to use a container or rags to catch spilled fluid. If any spilled fluid does get on painted surfaces, wipe it off immediately.*
3   Remove the reservoir mounting bolts (skip this step if you're only removing the clutch master cylinder).
4   Disconnect the clutch hydraulic line from the master cylinder.
5   From inside the vehicle, remove the master cylinder mounting nuts; from the engine compartment side, remove the master cylinder.

Overhaul

Refer to illustration 8.6

6   Depress the piston and remove the snap-ring **(see illustration)**.
7   Tap the master cylinder on a block of wood to remove the piston, secondary cup, spacer, primary cup and return spring from the bore.
8   Remove the bolt and washer for the one-way valve, then use the same procedure outlined in Step 7 to remove the one-way valve and return spring.
9   Reassembly is the reverse of disassembly. Be sure lubricate all parts with brake fluid and use a new snap-ring.

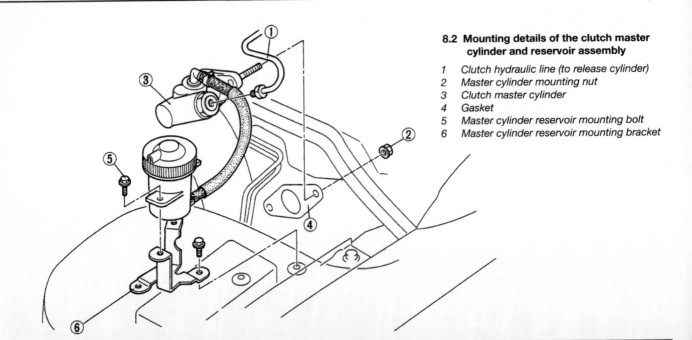

8.2 Mounting details of the clutch master cylinder and reservoir assembly

1	Clutch hydraulic line (to release cylinder)
2	Master cylinder mounting nut
3	Clutch master cylinder
4	Gasket
5	Master cylinder reservoir mounting bolt
6	Master cylinder reservoir mounting bracket

8.6 An exploded view of the clutch master cylinder and reservoir components

1	Snap-ring		11	Protector
2	Piston and secondary cup assembly		12	Hose
3	Spacer		13	Reservoir cap and baffle
4	Primary cup		14	Washer
5	Return spring		15	Reservoir
6	One-way valve bolt		16	Hose clamp
7	Washer		17	Bushing
8	One-way valve piston		18	Elbow fitting
9	Return spring		19	Master cylinder body
10	Hose clamp			

Installation

10   Installation is the reverse of removal.

11   Fill the clutch master cylinder reservoir with brake fluid conforming to DOT 3 specifications and bleed the clutch system (see Section 9).

9   Clutch hydraulic system - bleeding

Refer to illustration 9.5

1   The hydraulic system should be bled to remove all air whenever air enters the system. This occurs if the fluid level has been allowed to fall so low that air has been drawn into the master cylinder, or when-ever a hydraulic line has been detached from the master or release cylinder.

2   Fill the clutch master cylinder to the top with new brake fluid conforming to DOT 3 specifications. **Caution:** *Do not re-use any of the fluid coming from the system during the bleeding operation and don't use fluid which has been inside an open container for an extended period of time.*

3   Raise the vehicle and place it securely on jackstands to gain access to the bleeder valve, which is located on the clutch release cylinder.

4   Remove the dust cap from bleeder valve and push a length of clear plastic hose over the valve. Place the other end of the hose into a clear container.

5   Have an assistant slowly depress the clutch pedal. Open the

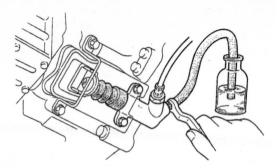

9.5 When bleeding the clutch hydraulic system, a hose is connected to the bleeder valve on the release cylinder and then submerged in brake fluid - when the pedal is depressed and the valve opened, air will be seen as bubbles in the hose and container

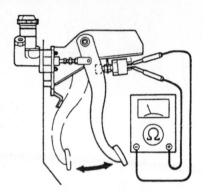

10.3 When the clutch pedal is depressed, there should be continuity through the switch; when the pedal is released, there should be no continuity

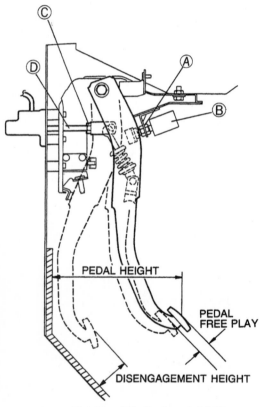

11.1 Clutch pedal adjustment details

bleeder valve **(see illustration)**. Fluid will run from the master cylinder, down the hydraulic line, into the release cylinder and out through the clear plastic tube. When your assistant signals you that the clutch pedal is near the bottom of its travel, close the bleeder valve (if you keep the bleeder valve open beyond this point, the lack of pressure in the line could allow air to enter the system at the bleeder valve. Repeat this procedure until the fluid is free of bubbles. **Note:** *Don't let the fluid level drop too low in the master cylinder, or air will be drawn into the hydraulic line and the whole process will have to be started over.*

6   Close the bleeder valve.

7   Slowly press and release the pedal five times, waiting for two seconds each time the pedal is released.

8   Fill the fluid reservoir.

9   The clutch should now be completely bled. If it isn't (indicated by failure to disengage completely), repeat Steps 5 through 8.

10   Install the dust cap and lower the vehicle. Check carefully for

proper operation before placing the vehicle in normal service. Check the fluid level.

10   Clutch start switch - check and replacement

Refer to illustration 10.3

1   Disconnect the negative cable from the battery.

2   Disconnect the electrical connector from the switch.

3   Check the switch for continuity with an ohmmeter **(see illustration)**. When you depress the pedal, there should be continuity; when you release the pedal, there should be no continuity.

4   If the continuity of the switch isn't as specified, adjust the switch by loosening the locknut and turning the switch in or out, as necessary. If the switch still doesn't work properly, replace it.

5   To replace the switch, simply unscrew the locknut and pull the switch out of its mounting bracket.

6   After you've installed the new switch, be sure to adjust the clutch pedal as described in Section 11.

11   Clutch pedal - adjustment

Refer to illustration 11.1

1   To check the pedal height, measure the distance from the upper surface of the pedal pad to the carpet **(see illustration)**. Compare your measurement with the pedal height listed in this Chapter's Specifications.

2   If necessary, adjust the pedal height as follows: Loosen locknut A and turn the clutch switch (B) until the height is correct. Tighten locknut A. Now check the pedal freeplay.

3   To check the pedal freeplay, depress the clutch pedal by hand until resistance is felt. Measure this distance **(see illustration 11.1)** and compare your measurement with the pedal freeplay listed in this Chapter's Specifications.

4   If necessary, adjust the pedal freeplay as follows: Loosen locknut C and turn pushrod D until pedal freeplay is correct. Verify that the disengagement height to the carpet is correct when the pedal is fully depressed. Tighten locknut C. Now check the pedal height again to make sure it's still in adjustment.

12   Driveshaft and universal joints - description and check

1   The driveshaft is a tube running between the transfer case or transmission and the rear axle or front axle. Universal joints (U-joints) are located at either end of the driveshaft, permitting power to be transmitted at varying angles.

2   The rear driveshaft on all models is a two-piece design with a

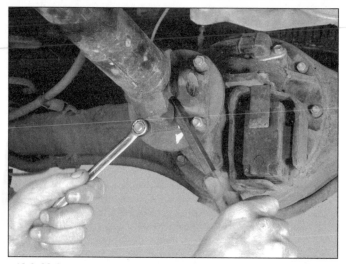

13.2 Make sure you mark the U-joint and companion flanges to ensure the driveshaft retains its balance when you reinstall it - jam a large screwdriver between the yoke spiders to immobilize the driveshaft when you break the flange nuts loose

center bearing support. On 4WD models, the front driveshaft is a one piece unit. The rear sections of all rear driveshafts are equipped with double-offset (constant velocity) type joints located right behind the center bearing support. As the rear axle travels up and down, the distance between the differential and the center bearing support changes. The double-offset joint slides in and out, allowing the rear section of the driveshaft to change its length.

3   The slip yokes on both 2WD and 4WD models have an oil seal to prevent leakage of fluid and keep dirt and contaminants from entering the transmission (or center bearing support). If leakage is evident at a seal, replace it (see Chapter 7B).

4   The driveshaft(s) require very little service. The U-joints on 2WD models are not serviceable, nor are the double-offset joints on any driveshafts. If these components develop problems, the driveshaft assembly must be replaced. However, you can overhaul the U-joints on 4WD models. The driveshafts must be removed from the vehicle for this procedure.

5   Since the driveshaft is a balanced unit, it's important that no undercoating, mud, etc. be allowed to stay on it. When the vehicle is raised for service it's a good idea to clean the driveshaft(s) and inspect it for any obvious damage. Make sure the small weights used to originally balance the driveshaft(s) are in place and securely attached. Whenever a driveshaft is removed it's important that it be reinstalled in the same relative position to preserve the balance, so always mark all flanges before removing a driveshaft.

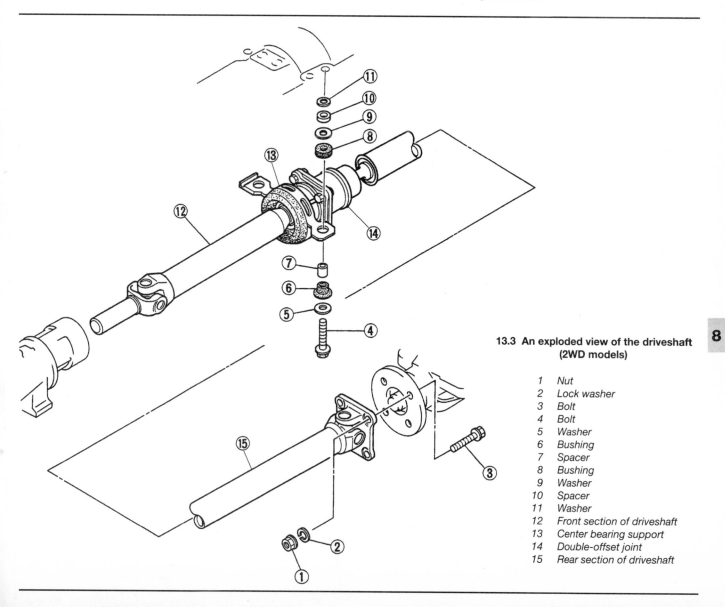

13.3 An exploded view of the driveshaft (2WD models)

1	Nut
2	Lock washer
3	Bolt
4	Bolt
5	Washer
6	Bushing
7	Spacer
8	Bushing
9	Washer
10	Spacer
11	Washer
12	Front section of driveshaft
13	Center bearing support
14	Double-offset joint
15	Rear section of driveshaft

8

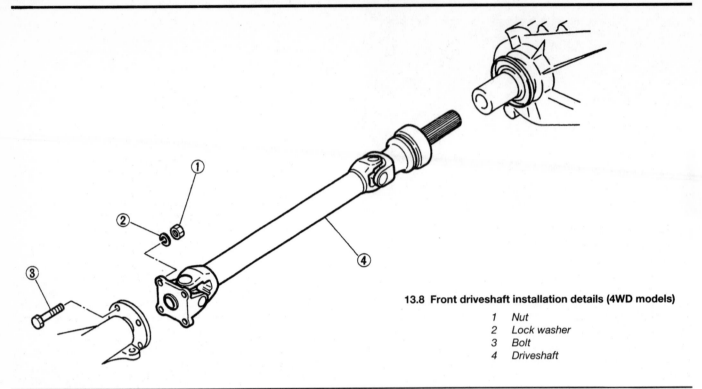

13.8 Front driveshaft installation details (4WD models)

1   Nut
2   Lock washer
3   Bolt
4   Driveshaft

6   Problems with the driveshaft(s) are usually indicated by a noise or vibration while driving the vehicle. A road test should verify if the problem is the driveshaft(s) or another vehicle component:
a) On an open road, free of traffic, drive the vehicle and note the engine speed (rpm) at which the problem is most evident.
b) With this noted, drive the vehicle again, this time manually keeping the transmission in first, then second, then third gear ranges and running the engine up to the engine speed noted.
c) If the noise or vibration decreased or was eliminated, visually inspect the driveshaft(s) for damage, material on the shaft which would effect balance, missing weights and damaged U-joints. Another possibility for this condition would be tires which are out-of-balance or a bent or damaged wheel(s).
d) If the noise or vibration occurs at the same engine speed regardless of which gear the transmission is in, the driveshaft is not at fault.
7   To check for worn U-joints:
a) On an open road, free of traffic, drive the vehicle slowly until the transmission is in High gear. Let off on the accelerator, allowing the vehicle to coast, then accelerate. A clunking or knocking noise will indicate worn U-joints.
b) Drive the vehicle at a speed of about 10 to 15 mph and then place the transmission in Neutral, allowing the vehicle to coast. Listen for abnormal driveline noises.
c) Raise the vehicle and support it securely on jackstands. With the transmission in Neutral, manually turn the driveshaft(s), watching the U-joints for excessive play.

13   Driveshafts - removal and installation

Rear driveshaft (all models)

Refer to illustrations 13.2 and 13.3

1   Raise the vehicle and support it securely on jackstands. Place the transmission in Neutral with the parking brake off.
2   Use a scribe, white paint or a hammer and punch to place alignment marks on all driveshaft flanges **(see illustration)** to ensure that the driveshaft is reinstalled in the same position so its dynamic balance is maintained.
3   On 2WD models, remove the bolts from the rear (differential)

flange, remove the bolts, washers, bushings and spacers from the center bearing support **(see illustration)**, lower the rear section of the driveshaft and slide the front end out of the transmission.
4   The procedure for removing the driveshaft from 4WD models is essentially the same as above, except that the forward end of the front section of the driveshaft must be unbolted from the companion flange on the transfer case.
5   While the driveshaft is removed, check the U-joints: While pushing and pulling on them, try to move them back and forth and side to side simultaneously. If there's any play in the U-joints, replace the driveshaft assembly; if there's any play in the U-joints on 4WD models, replace the U-joints (see Section 15).
6   Installation is the reverse of removal.
a) Make sure you match up the marks you made on all flanges.
b) Tighten all fasteners to the torque listed in this Chapter's Specifications.

Front driveshaft (4WD models)

Refer to illustration 13.8

7   Using a scribe, white paint or a hammer and punch, place marks on the driveshaft and differential flanges in line with each other to ensure that the driveshaft is reinstalled in the same position to preserve its balance.
8   Remove the bolts and nuts that attach the driveshaft flange to the front differential companion flange **(see illustration)**, slide the slip yoke out of the transfer case and remove the driveshaft.
9   Installation is the reverse of removal.
a) Make sure you align the marks you made on the flanges.
b) Be sure to tighten the flange bolts/nuts to the torque listed in this Chapter's Specifications.

14   Driveshaft center bearing - replacement

Refer to illustration 14.2

1   To perform this procedure, you need a special Mazda puller (SST 49 0839 425C and 49 0636 145) or equivalent, three adapters (SST 49 F026 102, 49 B025 001 and 49 H025 001) or equivalent, and a hydraulic press. If you don't have these tools, remove the driveshaft (see Section 13) and take it to a dealer service department or an automo-

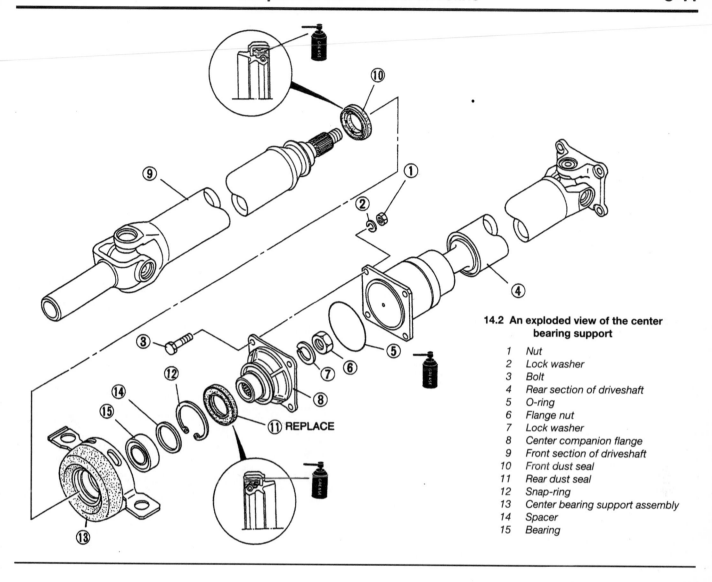

14.2 An exploded view of the center bearing support

1   Nut
2   Lock washer
3   Bolt
4   Rear section of driveshaft
5   O-ring
6   Flange nut
7   Lock washer
8   Center companion flange
9   Front section of driveshaft
10 Front dust seal
11 Rear dust seal
12 Snap-ring
13 Center bearing support assembly
14 Spacer
15 Bearing

8

tive machine shop to have the center bearing replaced. They will pull off the center companion flange and the center bearing support assembly and press off the bearing from the support assembly.

2   If you want to tackle this job yourself, remove the driveshaft (see Section 13), mark the center bearing and double-offset flanges, separate the front and rear sections of the driveshaft, then refer to the accompanying exploded view **(see illustration)**.

15   Universal joint (4WD models) - replacement

Refer to illustrations 15.2, 15.4a and 15.4b

Note: *A press or large vise will be required for this procedure. It may be a good idea to take the driveshaft to a repair or machine shop where the U-joints can be replaced for you, normally at a reasonable charge.*

1   Remove the driveshaft (see Section 13).

2   Place the driveshaft in a sturdy vise, mark the shaft and yoke for proper reassembly and remove the snap-rings from the spider **(see illustration)**.

3   Supporting the driveshaft, place it on a workbench equipped with a vise.

4   Place a piece of pipe or a large socket with the same inside diameter over one of the bearing cups. Position a socket which is of slightly smaller diameter than the cup on the opposite bearing cup **(see illustration)** and use the vise to force the cup out (inside the pipe or large

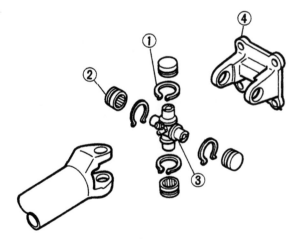

15.2 An exploded view of a U-joint assembly on a 4WD front driveshaft

1   Snap-ring
2   Bearing cup
3   Spider
4   U-joint yoke

15.4a Press out the U-joint bearing cups with a vise and sockets

15.4b Extract the bearing cup with locking pliers

socket), stopping just before it comes completely out of the yoke. Use the vise or large pliers to work the cup the rest of the way out **(see illustration)**.

5   Transfer the sockets to the other side and press the opposite bearing cup out in the same manner.

6   After the bearings have been removed, lift the spider from the yoke and thoroughly clean all dirt and debris from the yokes on both ends of the driveshaft.

7   Pack the new U-joint bearings with grease. Ordinarily, specific instructions for lubrication will be included with the U-joint servicing kit and should be followed carefully.

8   Position the spider in the yoke and partially install one bearing cup in the yoke. If the spider is equipped with a grease fitting, be sure it points in the proper direction **(see illustration 15.2).**

9   Start the spider into the bearing cup and then partially install the other cup. Align the spider and press the bearing cups into position, being careful not to damage the dust seals.

10   Install the snap-rings. If difficulty is encountered in seating the snap-rings, strike the driveshaft yoke sharply with a hammer. This will spring the yoke ears slightly and allow the snap-rings to seat in the groove. This should also be done if the joint feels tight after assembly.

11   Install the driveshaft (see Section 13). If the U-joint is equipped with a grease fitting, lubricate it as described in Chapter 1.

---

16   Rear axle - description and check

Description

1   The rear axle assembly is a "hypoid" (the centerline of the pinion gear is below the centerline of the ring gear) semi-floating type. The differential carrier is a casting bolted to the axle, which is a welded-up assembly consisting of the axle tubes and the differential housing.

2   Before you purchase any axle replacement parts, particularly the axleshafts, jot down the axle identification number, which is located on a small tag on the back of the differential housing, near the filler plug.

3   Often, an apparent "problem" in the rear axle is, in fact, somewhere else. Always perform a thorough check before assuming a rear axle problem.

4   The following noises are commonly associated with rear axle diagnosis procedures:

a)   Road noise is often mistaken for mechanical faults. Driving the vehicle on different surfaces will show whether the road surface is the cause of the noise. Road noise will remain the same if the vehicle is under power or coasting.

b)   Tire noise is sometimes mistaken for mechanical problems. Tires which are worn or low on air pressure are particularly susceptible to emitting vibrations and noises. Tire noise will remain about the same during varying driving situations, where rear axle noise will change during coasting, acceleration, etc.

17.6a A large screwdriver, positioned as shown, can be used to hold the companion flange stationary while the nut is loosened

c)   Engine and transmission noise can be deceiving because it will travel along the driveline. To isolate engine and transmission noises, make a note of the engine speed at which the noise is most pronounced. Stop the vehicle and place the transmission in Neutral and run the engine to the same speed. If the noise is the same, the rear axle is not at fault.

5   Because of the many special tools and critical measurements required, overhaul and general repair of the rear axle is beyond the scope of the home mechanic The following procedures are restricted to pinion oil seal replacement, axleshaft, bearing and oil seal replacement, differential removal and installation and removal and installation of the entire axle assembly for servicing.

---

17   Pinion oil seal - replacement

Refer to illustrations 17.6a, 17.6b, 17.7, 17.8 and 17.9
Note: *The following procedure applies to both front and rear differentials.*

1   A pinion shaft oil seal failure results in the leakage of differential gear lubricant past the seal and onto the driveshaft yoke or flange. The seal is replaceable without removing or disassembling the differential.

2   Raise the vehicle and support it securely on jackstands.

3   Drain the differential lubricant (see Chapter 1). After draining is complete, install the drain plug and tighten it securely.

4   Disconnect the driveshaft from the pinion shaft yoke (see Section 13). Support the driveshaft out of the way with a piece of wire.

17.6b Mark the relationship of the flange to the pinion shaft

17.7 Remove the companion flange from the pinion shaft with a two-jaw puller

17.8 It'll probably be necessary to drive the seal out with a hammer and punch - be careful not to damage the splines or threads on the pinion shaft

17.9 A hammer and a socket of the proper diameter can be used to drive the seal into place

5   Using an inch-pound torque wrench, measure the torque required to move the pinion shaft within its backlash (break-loose torque). Record this figure, as it will be used to set the pinion shaft preload during installation.

6   Using a large screwdriver or prybar, hold the companion flange stationary, then remove the companion flange nut (**see illustration**). Mark the relationship of the pinion shaft to the companion flange (**see illustration**).

7   Remove the companion flange from the pinion shaft with a two-jaw puller (**see illustration**).

8   Carefully pry the seal out of the differential with a screwdriver or prybar. It may be necessary to knock the seal out using a hammer and a punch (**see illustration**). Be careful not to damage the splines on the pinion shaft.

9   Lubricate the new seal lip with multi-purpose grease or differential lubricant and carefully install it in position in the differential. Using a hammer and a seal driver, large socket or a short section of pipe of the proper diameter, carefully drive the seal into place (**see illustration**).

10   Clean the sealing lip contact surface of the companion flange. Apply a thin coat of multi-purpose grease to the seal contact surface and the shaft spines. Slide the companion flange onto the shaft, making sure the match marks line up.

11   Coat the threads of the pinion shaft with multi-purpose grease. Install a new nut and, holding the flange stationary, tighten the nut to

the initial torque listed in this Chapter's Specifications.

12   Turn the companion flange several times to seat the bearing.

13   Using an inch-pound torque wrench, see how much torque is required to turn the pinion shaft within its backlash (break-loose torque). The desired preload is the previously recorded torque value plus five inch-pounds. If the preload is less than desired, retighten the nut in small increments until the desired preload is reached. If the maximum torque on the pinion shaft nut (see this Chapter's Specifications) is reached before the desired preload is obtained, the bearing spacer must be replaced by a repair shop. **Note:** *Do not back-off the pinion nut to reduce the preload.* After the preload is properly adjusted, proceed to the next Step.

14   Connect the driveshaft to the companion flange (see Section 13).

15   Fill the differential with the recommended lubricant (see Chapter 1).

16   Lower the vehicle to the ground and test drive the vehicle. Check around the companion flange for evidence of leakage.

---

18   Axleshafts, bearings and oil seals - replacement

Refer to illustrations 18.1, 18.6, 18.7, 18.8 and 18.9

1   The axleshafts can be removed without disturbing the differential assembly. They must be removed in order to replace the oil seals and when removing the differential carrier from the rear axle housing (**see**

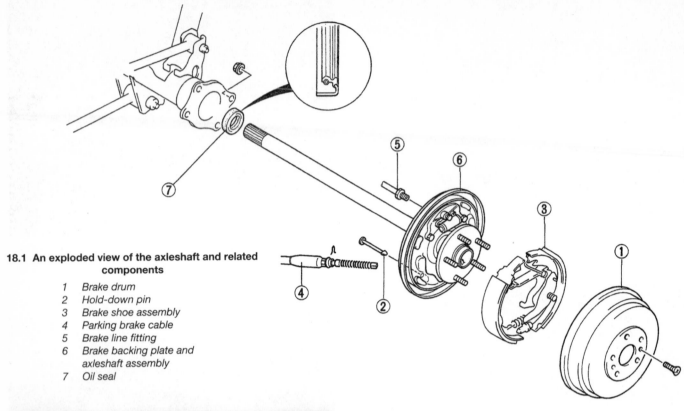

18.1 An exploded view of the axleshaft and related components

    1   *Brake drum*
    2   *Hold-down pin*
    3   *Brake shoe assembly*
    4   *Parking brake cable*
    5   *Brake line fitting*
    6   *Brake backing plate and*
         axleshaft assembly
    7   *Oil seal*

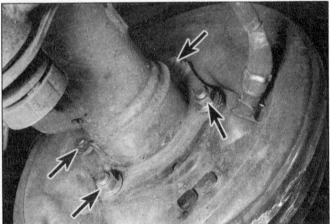

18.6 Remove the four nuts that attach the brake backing plate to the axle housing

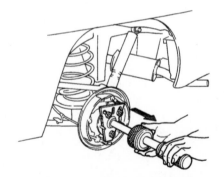

18.7 If the axleshaft is stuck, use a slide hammer and an axle flange adapter to remove it

illustration). Note: *Read this entire procedure before starting work.*
2   Raise the rear of the vehicle and support it securely on jackstands. Block the front wheels to keep the vehicle from rolling.
3   Remove the rear wheels and release the parking brake.
4   Remove the drain plug and drain the differential lubricant into a suitable container. When the draining is complete, tighten the drain plug securely.
5   Remove the brake drum, disconnect the parking brake cable and disconnect the brake line from the wheel cylinder (see Chapter 9).
6   Remove the four nuts that attach the brake backing plate to the axle housing **(see illustration).**
7   Remove the axleshaft, brake backing plate and brake assembly from the rear axle. If the shaft is stuck, use a slide hammer and axle flange adapter to remove it **(see illustration).**
8   Use a large screwdriver or seal removal tool (available at auto parts stores) to pry the seal out of the axle housing **(see illustration).**
9   Install the new seal with a seal driver or use a section of pipe or

18.8 Use a large screwdriver or a seal removal tool to remove the old seal from the axle housing

18.9 A large socket with an outside diameter slightly smaller than the outside diameter of the seal can be used to drive the seal into place

20.2 A screwdriver inserted through the caliper and into a disc cooling vane will hold the hub stationary while loosening the hub nut

large socket with an outside diameter slightly smaller than the outside diameter of the seal **(see illustration)**. Lubricate the lips of the seal with multi-purpose grease.

10   If the axleshaft bearing needs to be replaced, take the axleshaft to a dealer service department, an automotive machine shop or other repair shop. The bearing is pressed on and retained by a pressed on collar.

11   Installation is the reverse of removal. Be sure to tighten the brake backing plate-to-axle housing nuts to the torque listed in this Chapter's Specifications.

12   Following installation, fill the differential with the proper lubricant as listed in the Chapter 1 Specifications.

13   Bleed the brakes (see Chapter 9).

---

19   Driveaxles (4WD models) - general information and check

Power is transmitted from the front differential to the wheels through a pair of driveaxles. The inner end of each driveaxle is connected to the differential by an output shaft (flanged stub axle) splined to the differential side gear. The output shafts are lightly press-fitted and can be easily pried out if it becomes necessary to replace the output shaft oil seals (see Chapter 7B). The outer end of each driveaxle is splined to the wheel hub and locked in place by an axle nut.

The inner ends of the driveaxles are equipped with sliding constant velocity (CV) joints , which are capable of both angular and axial motion. Each inner joint assembly consists of an inner race, bearings, cage and a housing in which the joint is free to slide in and out as the driveaxle moves up and down with the wheel. The inner joints are rebuildable (see Section 21).

Each outer joint, which consists of ball bearings running between an inner race and an outer race (housing), is capable of angular but not axial movement. The outer joints are neither rebuildable nor removable. Should one of them fail, a new driveaxle/outer joint assembly must be installed.

The boots should be periodically inspected for damage, leaking lubricant and cuts. Damaged CV joint boots should be replaced immediately or the joints can be damaged. Boot replacement involves removal of the driveaxle (see Section 20). **Note:** *Some auto parts stores carry - "split" type replacement boots, which can be installed without removing the driveaxle from the vehicle. This is a convenient alternative; however, we recommended that the driveaxle be removed and the CV joint disassembled and cleaned to ensure that the joint is free from contaminants such as moisture and dirt, which will accelerate CV joint wear. The most common symptom of worn or damaged CV joints, besides lubricant leaks, is a clicking noise in turns, a clunk when accelerating from a coasting condition or vibration at highway speeds.*

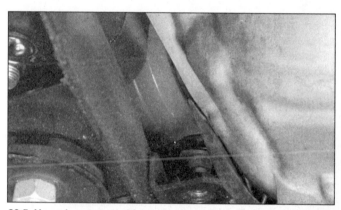

20.5 Use a large screwdriver or prybar to pry the inner joint out of the transaxle

To check for wear in the CV joints and driveaxle shafts, grasp each axle (one at a time) and rotate it in both directions while holding the CV joint housings, inspecting for movement, indicating worn splines or sloppy CV joints. Also check the driveaxle shafts for cracks, dents, twisting and bending.

---

20   Driveaxles (4WD models)- removal and installation

Removal

Refer to illustrations 20.2 and 20.5

1   Loosen the wheel lug nuts, raise the front of the vehicle and support it securely on jackstands. Apply the parking brake and block the rear wheels to keep the vehicle from rolling off the jackstands. Remove the front wheel.

2   Unstake and remove the driveaxle hub nut. To prevent the hub from turning, insert a screwdriver through the caliper and into a disc cooling vane, then unscrew the nut **(see illustration)**.

3   Unbolt the balljoint from the control arm (see Chapter 10).

4   Push the driveaxle out of the hub, then support the outer end of the driveaxle with a piece of wire to prevent damage to the inner CV joint. If the driveaxle sticks in the hub, thread the nut onto the driveaxle until it is flush with the end, then tap on the nut with a soft-faced hammer.

5   Use a large screwdriver or prybar to pry the inner joint out of the transaxle **(see illustration)**.

6   Support the CV joints and carefully remove the driveaxle from the vehicle.

20.7 Use a large brass drift to seat the CV joint in the differential side gear

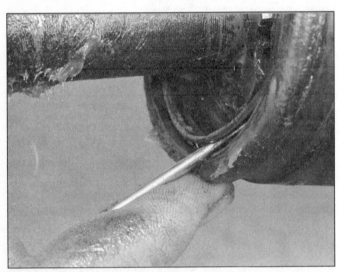

21.4 Pry the wire ring ball retainer out of the outer race, then slide the outer race (housing) off the bearing assembly

21.5a Use paint or a felt-tip marker to mark the outer race, cage, inner race and axleshaft - DO NOT use a punch or scribe

21.3 Pry the clamp retaining tabs up with a small screwdriver and slide the clamps off the boot

Installation

Refer to illustration 20.7

7   Lubricate the differential seal with multi-purpose grease. Raise the driveaxle into position while supporting the CV joints and insert the splined end of the inner CV joint into the differential side gear. Seat the CV joint in the side gear by tapping it into position with a hammer and brass drift **(see illustration)**.

8   Grasp the inner CV joint housing (not the driveaxle) and pull out to make sure the axle has seated securely.

9   Apply a light coat of multi-purpose grease to the outer CV joint splines, pull out on the strut/steering knuckle assembly and install the stub axle in the hub.

10   Connect the balljoint to the control arm (see Chapter 10).

11   Install a **new** hub nut. Lock the disc so it can't turn, using the method described in Step 2, then tighten the hub nut to the torque listed in this Chapter's Specifications. Be sure to stake the new nut.

12   Install the wheel and lower the vehicle. Tighten the lug nuts to the torque listed in the Chapter 1 Specifications.

---

21   Driveaxle boot replacement and constant velocity (CV) joint overhaul (4WD models)

Inner CV joint and boot

Disassembly

Refer to illustrations 21.3, 21.4, 21.5a, 21.5b 21.7, 21.9, 21.10a and 21.10b

1   Remove the driveaxle from the vehicle (see Section 20).

2   Mount the driveaxle in a vise. The jaws of the vise should be lined with wood or rags to prevent damage to the axleshaft.

3   Pry the boot clamp retaining tabs up with a small screwdriver and slide the clamps off the boot **(see illustration)**.

4   Slide the boot back on the axleshaft and pry the wire ring ball retainer from the outer race **(see illustration)**.

5   Mark the relationship of the outer race to the axleshaft and pull the outer race off the inner bearing assembly **(see illustrations)**.

6   Mark the inner race, cage and axleshaft end to ensure that they are reassembled in the same position.

7   Remove the snap-ring from the groove in the axleshaft with a pair of snap-ring pliers **(see illustration)**.

8   Slide the inner bearing assembly off the axleshaft.

9   Using a small screwdriver or a piece of wood, pry the balls from the cage **(see illustration)**. Be careful not to scratch the inner race, the balls or the cage.

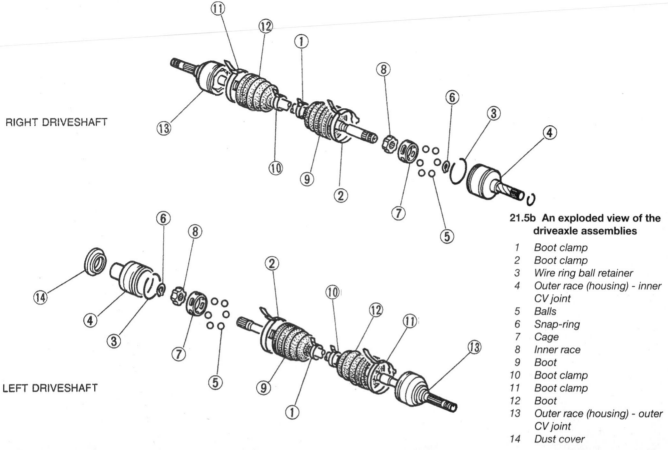

RIGHT DRIVESHAFT

LEFT DRIVESHAFT

21.5b An exploded view of the driveaxle assemblies

1   Boot clamp
2   Boot clamp
3   Wire ring ball retainer
4   Outer race (housing) - inner CV joint
5   Balls
6   Snap-ring
7   Cage
8   Inner race
9   Boot
10 Boot clamp
11 Boot clamp
12 Boot
13 Outer race (housing) - outer CV joint
14 Dust cover

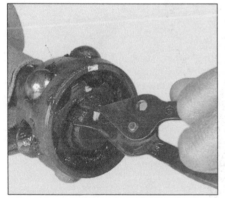

21.7 Remove the snap-ring from the end of the axleshaft

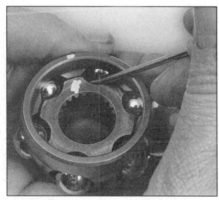

21.9 Pry the balls out of the cage, but be careful not to nick or scratch them

21.10a Align the lands of the inner race with the window of the cage . . .

8

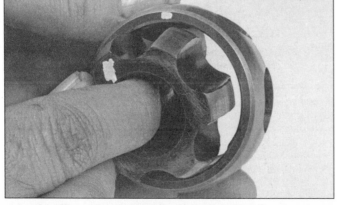

21.10b . . . then remove the inner race from the cage

10   Align the inner race lands with the cage windows and pull the race out of the cage **(see illustrations)**.

Inspection

Refer to illustrations 21.11a and 21.11b

11   Clean the components with solvent to remove all traces of grease. Inspect the cage and races for pitting, score marks, cracks and other signs of wear and damage. Shiny, polished spots are normal and will not adversely affect CV joint performance **(see illustrations)**.

Reassembly

Refer to illustrations 21.13, 21.14, 21.17, 21.19, 21.20, 21.21a and 21.21b

12   Insert the inner race into the cage and align the match marks.

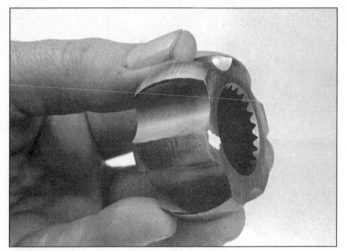

21.11a   Check the inner race lands and grooves for pitting and score marks

21.11b   Check the cage for cracks, pitting and score marks (shiny spots are normal and don't affect operation)

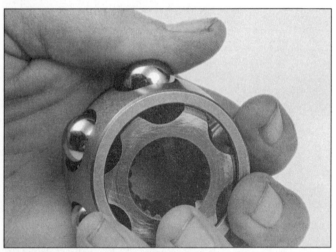

21.13   Press the balls into the cage through the windows using thumb pressure only

21.14   Wrap the splined area of the axle with tape to prevent damage to the boot when installing it

21.17   Pack the inner race and cage assembly full of CV joint grease (also note that the larger diameter side, or bulge, is facing the axleshaft end

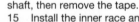

21.19   Before tightening the boot clamps, adjust the driveaxle to the proper length (see this Chapter's Specifications)

13   Press the balls into the cage windows with your thumbs **(see illustration)**.

14   Wrap the axleshaft splines with tape to avoid damaging the boot **(see illustration)**. Slide the small boot clamp and boot onto the axleshaft, then remove the tape.

15   Install the inner race and cage assembly on the axleshaft with the larger diameter side or bulge of the cage (and the previously applied marks) facing the axleshaft end.

16   Install the snap-ring in the groove. Make sure it's completely seated by pushing on the inner race and cage assembly.

17   Fill the outer race and boot with the specified type and quantity of CV joint grease (normally included with the new boot kit). Pack the inner race and cage assembly with grease, by hand, until grease is worked completely into the assembly **(see illustration)**.

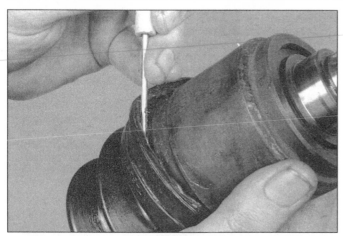

21.20 Also before tightening the clamps, equalize the pressure inside the boot by inserting a small, dull screwdriver between the boot and the outer race

21.21a To tighten a new clamp, bend the tang down and . . .

21.21b . . . fold the tabs over to hold it in place

21.26 After the old grease has been rinsed away and the solvent blown out with compressed air, rotate the outer joint housing through its full range of motion and inspect the bearing surfaces for wear and damage - if any of the balls, the race or the cage look damaged, replace the driveaxle and outer joint assembly

18   Slide the outer race (housing) down onto the inner race, aligning the matchmarks and install the wire ring retainer.

19   Wipe any excess grease from the axle boot groove on the outer race. Seat the small diameter of the boot in the recessed area on the axleshaft. Push the other end of the boot onto the outer race and move the race in or out to adjust the driveaxle to the length listed in this Chapter's Specifications **(see illustration)**.

20   With the axle set to the proper length, equalize the pressure in the boot by inserting a dull screwdriver between the boot and the outer race **(see illustration)**. Don't damage the boot with the tool.

21   Install the boot clamps **(see illustrations)**

22   Install the driveaxle as described in Section 20.

Outer CV joint and boot

Disassembly

23   Following Steps 1 through 10, remove the inner CV joint from the axleshaft and disassemble it.

24   Remove the outer CV joint boot clamps, using the technique described in Step 3. Slide the boot off the axleshaft.

Inspection

Refer to illustration 21.26

25   Thoroughly wash the inner and outer CV joints in clean solvent and blow them dry with compressed air, if available. **Note:** *Because the outer joint cannot be disassembled, it is difficult to wash away all the old grease and to rid the bearing of solvent once it's clean. But it's imperative the job be done thoroughly, so take your time and do it right.*

26   Bend the outer CV joint housing at an angle to the driveaxle to expose the bearings, inner race and cage **(see illustration)**. Inspect the bearing surfaces for signs of wear. If the bearings are damaged or worn, replace the driveaxle.

Reassembly

27   Slide the new outer boot onto the driveaxle. It's a good idea to wrap vinyl tape around the spline of the shaft to prevent damage to the boot **(see illustration 21.14)**. When the boot is in position, add the specified amount of grease (included in the boot replacement kit) to the outer joint and the boot (pack the joint with as much grease as it will hold and put the rest into the boot). Slide the boot on the rest of the way and install the new clamps **(see illustrations 21.21a and 21.21b)**.

28   Clean and reassemble the inner CV joint by following Steps 11 through 21, then install the driveaxle as described in Section 20.

---

22   Front axle shift motor (4WD models) - check, removal and installation

---

Check

Note: *Before beginning any of the checks below, inspect all vacuum hoses for kinks, cracks and other signs of damage and check the vacuum harness connectors for a good, tight fit on the vacuum ports.*

8

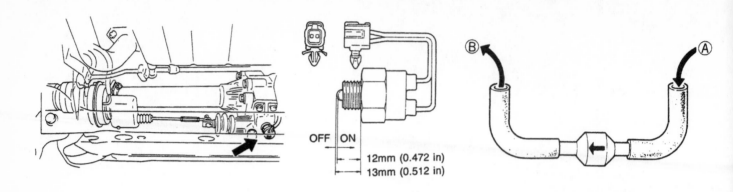

22.3 Unplug the AFW switch connector and remove the switch

22.4 Check the continuity of the switch with an ohmmeter - if it's not as specified, replace the switch

OFF | ON
12mm (0.472 in)
13mm (0.512 in)

22.5 Remove the one-way check valve, blow through hose A and verify that air flows from hose B, then blow through B and verify that air does not flow out A

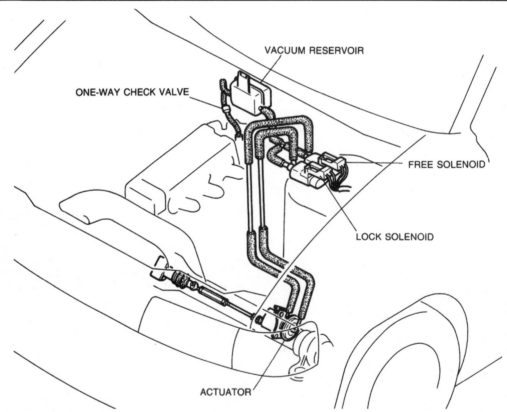

VACUUM RESERVOIR
ONE-WAY CHECK VALVE
FREE SOLENOID
LOCK SOLENOID
ACTUATOR

22.6 Disconnect the vacuum hoses and the electrical connector from each solenoid valve

Automatic Free Wheel (AFW) switch

Refer to illustrations 22.3 and 22.4

1   Detach the cable from the negative battery terminal.
2   Raise the front of the vehicle and support it securely on jackstands.
3   Unplug the AFW switch electrical connector and remove the switch **(see illustration)**.
4   Check the continuity of the switch with an ohmmeter **(see illustration)**. If it's not as specified, replace the switch.

One-way check valve

Refer to illustration 22.5

5   Remove the one-way check valve, blow through hose A and verify that air flows from hose B **(see illustration)**. Then blow through B

and verify that air does not flow out A. If the check valve doesn't work as described, replace it.

Solenoid valve

Refer to illustrations 22.6, 22.7 and 22.8

6   Disconnect the vacuum hoses and the electrical connector from each solenoid valve **(see illustration)**.
7   Blow through each valve from port B **(see illustration)** and verify that air flows from the air filter.
8   Hook up jumper wires to the terminals of the solenoid from the battery and ground **(see illustration)**.
9   Blow through each valve from port B and verify that air flows out port A.
10   If either solenoid valve fails to operate as described, replace it.

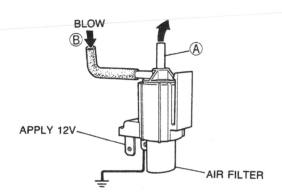

22.7 Blow through each valve from port B and verify that air flows from the air filter

22.8 With the solenoid valve energized, blow through each valve from port B and verify that air flows from port A

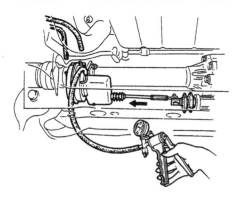

22.11 Attach a hand-held vacuum pump to the free side of the actuator, apply vacuum and verify that the rod moves in as shown

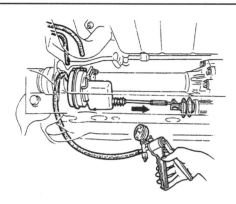

22.12 Apply vacuum to the lock side of the actuator and verify that the rod moves out as shown

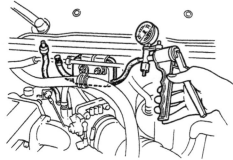

22.14 Detach the vacuum hoses from the reservoir, plug one of them, connect a hand-held vacuum pump to the other one and apply vacuum - if the reservoir doesn't hold vacuum, replace it

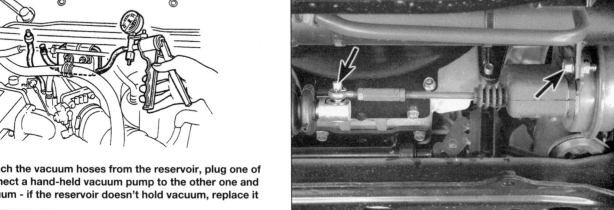

22.15 Remove the clip that secures the actuator rod, then unbolt the actuator

Actuator

Refer to illustrations 22.11 and 22.12

11   Attach a hand-held vacuum pump to the free side of the actuator **(see illustration)**. Apply vacuum and verify that the rod moves in as shown.

12   Detach the vacuum pump from the free side of the actuator and attach it to the lock side **(see illustration)**. Apply vacuum and verify that the rod moves out as shown.

13   If the actuator doesn't perform as described, replace it.

Vacuum reservoir

Refer to illustration 22.14

14   Detach the vacuum hoses from the reservoir **(see illustration)**, plug one of them, connect a hand-held vacuum pump to the other

one, apply vacuum and verify that the vacuum is held. If it isn't, re-place the vacuum reservoir.

Removal and installation

Refer to illustrations 22.15 and 22.17

15   If you're replacing the actuator, detach the vacuum hoses from the actuator vacuum ports, remove the clip that secures the actuator rod to the change rod **(see illustration)** and remove the nuts that attach the actuator to its mounting brackets on the front axleshaft tube. Installation is the reverse of removal.

16   If you're removing the control box assembly in order to remove

8

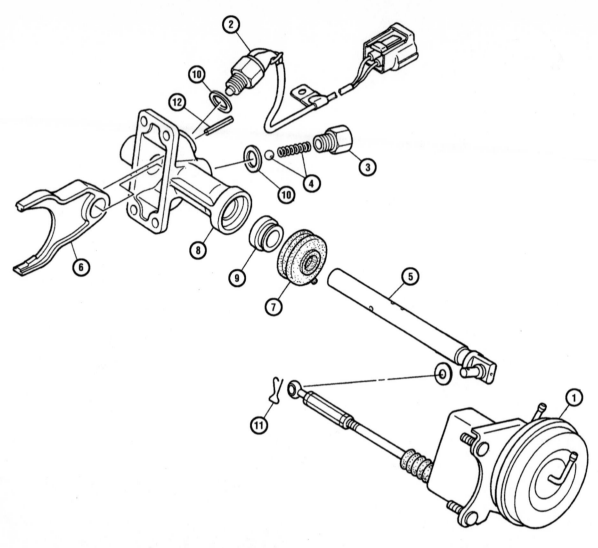

22.17 An exploded view of the front axle shift motor assembly

1	Actuator		7	Boot
2	Switch		8	Control box
3	Spring cap		9	Oil seal
4	Spring and ball		10	Washer
5	Change rod		11	Clip
6	Shift fork		12	Roll pin

the axleshaft from the tube, unplug the electrical lead from the AFW switch connector, disconnect the change rod from the actuator rod **(see illustration 22.15)**, unbolt the box and pull it off the tube. Installation is the reverse of removal. Be sure to liberally coat the shift fork and the hub sleeve with wheel bearing grease and make sure the fork is properly engaged with the hub sleeve before tightening the control box mounting bolts.

17   We don't recommend trying to rebuild the control box. However, if you wish to tackle this job, we have included the accompanying exploded view **(see illustration)**.

23   Front axleshaft and axle tube assembly (4WD models) - removal and installation

Refer to illustrations 23.4 and 23.8
Note: *You can replace the outer seal yourself, but special tools are re-*

quired to replace the bearings and the inner seal inside the axle tube. If the inner seal is leaking or either bearing is faulty, take the assembly to a dealer service department or other properly equipped shop to have the seal and/or bearings replaced.

1   Loosen the left front wheel lug nuts, raise the front of the vehicle and place it securely on jackstands. Remove the wheel.
2   Disconnect the left tie-rod end from the steering knuckle (see Chapter 10).
3   Disconnect the left control arm from the steering knuckle (see Chapter 10).
4   Remove the skid plate **(see illustration)**.
5   Remove the left driveaxle assembly (see Section 20).
6   Detach the front axle shift motor from the axle tube (see Section 22).
7   Unbolt the axle tube from the frame and differential, then remove it.
8   If the outer seal **(see illustration)** is leaking, remove it with a large screwdriver or seal removal tool. Install the new seal with a seal driver,

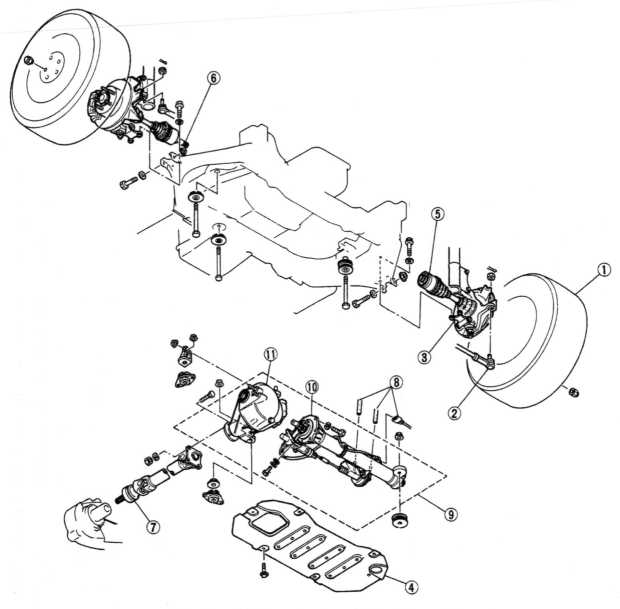

23.4 An exploded view of the front axle tube and differential assemblies

1	Wheel	8	Electrical connector and vacuum hoses for
2	Tie-rod end		control box assembly
3	Control arm balljoint	9	Front differential and front axleshaft and
4	Skid plate		tube assembly
5	Left driveaxle assembly	10	Axleshaft and tube assembly
6	Right driveaxle assembly	11	Front differential assembly
7	Front driveshaft assembly		

8

a large section of pipe or a large socket with an outside diameter slightly smaller than the outside diameter of the new seal.

9   Installation is the reverse of removal.

---

24   Differential assembly - removal and installation

Front differential

Refer to illustration 24.9

1   Loosen the wheel lug nuts, raise the front of the vehicle and place

it securely on jackstands. Remove the front wheels.

2   Disconnect the tie-rod ends (see Chapter 10).

3   Disconnect the lower arms from the steering knuckles (see Chapter 10).

4   Remove the skid plate **(see illustration 23.4)**.

5   Remove both driveaxles (see Section 20).

6   Remove the front driveshaft (see Section 13).

7   Clearly label and detach both vacuum hoses from the actuator and unplug the electrical connector from the control box assembly (see Section 22).

8   Support the front differential with a transmission jack.

23.8 An exploded view of the front axleshaft and axle tube assembly

1   Front axle shift motor assembly
    (control box and actuator)
2   Hub sleeve
3   Clip
4   Hub
5   Spacer
6   Retainer ring
7   Ball bearing
8   Adjustment shims
9   Dust seal
10 Bearing
11 Oil seal
12 Axleshaft
13 Needle bearing
14 Clip
15 Axle tube

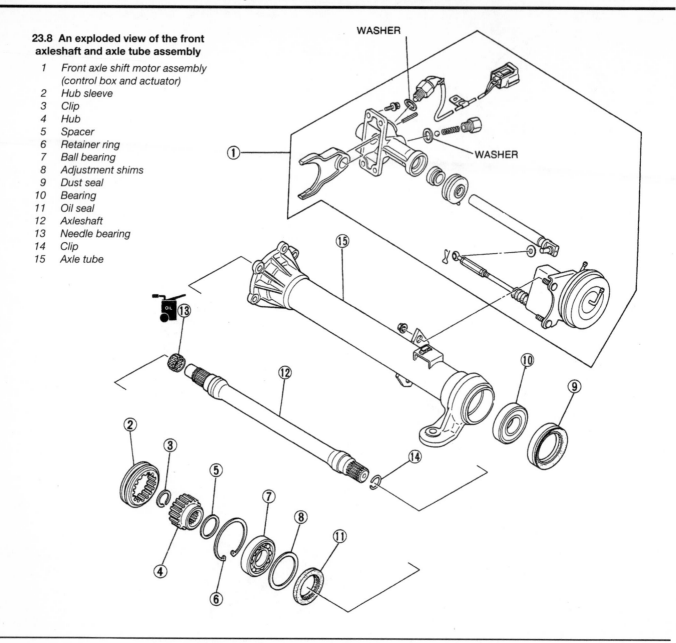

9   Remove the bolts and nuts as indicated **(see illustration)**.
10   Carefully lower the differential and axleshaft tube as a single as-sembly.
11   Separate the front axleshaft and tube assembly from the differen-tial (see Section 23).
12   Installation is the reverse of removal. Be sure to tighten the differ-ential mounting bolts to the torque listed in this Chapter's Specifica-tions.

Rear differential

Refer to illustrations 24.16
13   Loosen the wheel lug nuts, raise the rear of the vehicle and place it securely on jackstands. Remove the rear wheels.
14   Remove the axleshafts (see Section 18).
15   Remove the rear driveshaft (see Section 13).
16   Unplug the rear-wheel ABS sensor **(see illustration)**.
17   Remove the differential carrier bolts and nuts and remove the carrier assembly.
18   If you're replacing the differential assembly, remove the dynamic damper and bolt it onto the new carrier.

19   Installation is the reverse of removal. Clean all traces of old gas-ket material from the mating surfaces of the differential and housing, then apply a continuous bead of RTV sealant to the mating surface on the differential (install the differential within ten minutes of sealant ap-plication). Be sure to tighten the differential carrier mounting bolts and nuts to the torque listed in this Chapter's Specifications.

25   Rear axle assembly - removal and installation

Removal

Refer to illustrations 25.5 and 25.6
1   Disconnect the cable from the negative battery terminal.
2   Loosen, but do not remove the rear wheel lug nuts. Block the front wheels, raise the rear of the vehicle and support it securely on jackstands. Remove the rear wheels.
3   Disconnect the driveshaft from the differential flange (see Sec-tion 13).
4   Disconnect the parking brake cables from the spring clips on the

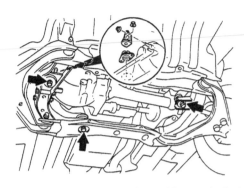

24.9 To remove the differential and front axleshaft and tube assemblies, remove these fasteners (arrows)

rear axle assembly and detach the cable brackets from the lower suspension arms (see Chapter 9).

5   Unplug the electrical connector for the rear wheel ABS from the differential carrier **(see illustration)**.

6   Disconnect the height sensor link for the Automatic Load Leveling (ALL) system, if equipped, from the rear axle assembly **(see illustration)**.

7   Detach the flexible brake hose from its bracket on top of the rear axle housing where it attaches to the metal brake line (see Chapter 9).

8   Place a floor jack under the differential and raise the rear axle assembly slightly.

9   Disconnect the lower end of the Panhard rod from the axle housing (see Chapter 10).

10   Disconnect the stabilizer bar from the rear axle assembly (see Chapter 10).

11   Disconnect the lower ends of the shock absorbers from the rear axle assembly (see Chapter 10).

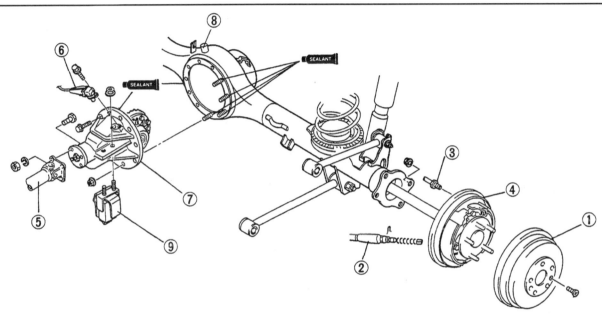

24.16 An exploded view of the rear differential assembly

1	Brake drum	
2	Parking brake cable	
3	Brake line fitting	
4	Backing plate and rear axleshaft assembly	
5	Rear driveshaft assembly	

6	Rear-wheel ABS sensor
7	Differential assembly
8	Air breather
9	Dynamic damper

8

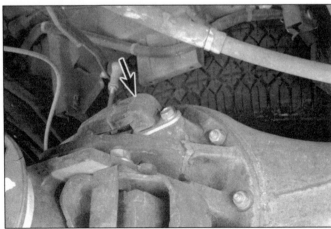

25.5 Unplug the electrical connector (arrow) for the ABS sensor from the top of the differential

25.6 Remove the nut and detach the height sensor link for the Automatic Load Leveling (ALL) system (1), detach the bracket for the electrical lead to the ABS sensor (2) and disconnect the flexible brake hose at its bracket (3)

12   Carefully lower the rear axle assembly until the coil springs are fully extended, then remove the springs (see Chapter 10).

13   Disconnect the upper and lower suspension arms from the rear axle assembly (see Chapter 10). **Caution:** *Once the suspension arms are disconnected from the axle assembly, it's no longer stable. Have an assistant help balance the axle on the floor jack pad.*

14   Roll the axle assembly out from underneath the vehicle on the floor jack.

15   If you're replacing the rear axle housing, refer to the appropriate Sections and remove the brakes, the metal brake lines, the axleshafts and the differential assembly from the housing, and install them on the new housing.

Installation

16   Raise the rear axle assembly into place and attach the upper and lower suspension arms (see Chapter 10). Don't fully tighten the nuts and bolts yet - just snug them.

17   Install the coil springs (see Chapter 10), raise the axle assembly to simulate normal ride height, then tighten the upper and lower suspension arm nuts and bolts to the torque listed in the Chapter 10 Specifications.

18   Attach the lower ends of the shock absorbers to the rear axle assembly and tighten the bolts securely (see Chapter 10).

19   Attach the stabilizer bar to the axle assembly (see Chapter 10).

20   Connect the driveshaft to the differential flange (see Section 13). Tighten the bolts to the torque listed in this Chapter's Specifications.

21   Connect the flexible brake hose to the metal brake line at the bracket on the top of the axle housing.

22   Plug in the electrical connector for the rear wheel ABS.

23   Attach the link rod for the ALL system.

24   Attach the parking brake cable spring clips to the axle assembly and attach the cable brackets to the lower suspension arms.

25   Bleed the brakes (see Chapter 9).

26   Install the wheels and hand tighten the lug nuts, then lower the vehicle. Tighten the wheel lug nuts to the torque listed in the Chapter 1 Specifications.

Chapter 9 Brakes

Contents

Specifications

General

Brake fluid type..	See Chapter 1
Power brake booster pushrod-to-master cylinder	
piston clearance	0.004 to 0.012 inch

Drum brakes

Drum maximum diameter*...	10.3 inches
Minimum lining thickness	See Chapter 1

Refer to the wear limit cast into the drum itself; it supersedes information printed here

Disc brakes

Minimum pad lining thickness...	See Chapter 1
Disc thickness	
Standard...	0.94 inch
Minimum*	0.87 inch
Maximum runout..	0.004 inch

Refer to the marks stamped on the disc (they supersede information printed here

Brake pedal

Pedal height..	7-1/2 to 7-29/32 inches
Pedal freeplay..	5/32 to 9/32 inch
Pedal-to-floor clearance	5-13/64 (minimum)

Torque specifications

	Ft-lbs (unless otherwise indicated)
Brake line-to-caliper banjo bolts	16 to 22
Brake caliper lock bolts	61 to 69
Brake caliper mount-to-steering knuckle	65 to 80
Master cylinder-to-brake booster nut.................................	86 to 144 in-lbs
Brake booster-to-firewall nuts	14 to 19

9

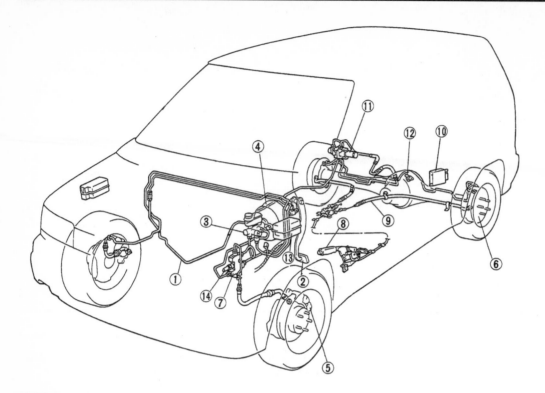

1.2 A schematic of the brake system

1   Brake hydraulic line
2   Brake pedal
3   Master cylinder
4   Power brake booster
5   Front brake caliper
6   Rear brake drum
7   Proportioning Bypass
    Valve (PBV)
8   Parking brake lever
9   Parking brake cable
10 Control unit for rear
    wheel ABS
11 Hydraulic unit for rear
    wheel ABS
12 Speed sensor for rear
    wheel ABS
13 Rear wheel ABS relay
14 Pressure differential
    switch for rear wheel ABS

1   General information

Refer to illustration 1.2

The vehicles covered by this manual are equipped with hydraulically operated front and rear brake systems. The front brakes are disc type and the rear brakes are drum type. Both the front and rear brakes are self adjusting. The front disc brakes automatically compensate for pad wear, while the rear drum brakes incorporate an adjustment mechanism which is activated as the brakes are applied when the vehicle is driven in reverse. A Load Sensing Proportioning Valve (LSPV) is standard on 1989 models (see Section 15); a Rear-Wheel Anti-Lock Brake System (Rear Wheel ABS) is standard on all 1990 and later models (see Section 16).

Hydraulic system

The hydraulic system **(see illustration)** consists of two separate circuits. The master cylinder has separate reservoirs for the two circuits and in the event of a leak or failure in one hydraulic circuit, the other circuit will remain operative. If one circuit fails, the other will remain functional and a warning indicator will light up on the instrument panel, showing that a failure has occurred.

Power brake booster

The power brake booster, utilizing engine manifold vacuum and atmospheric pressure to provide assistance to the hydraulically operated brakes, is mounted on the firewall in the engine compartment.

Parking brake system

The parking brake system is cable-actuated. It's activated by a lever mounted between the front seats.

Precautions

There are some general precautions involving the brake system on this vehicle:
a) Use only brake fluid conforming to DOT 3 specifications.
b) The brake pads and linings may contain asbestos fibers which are hazardous to your health if inhaled. Whenever you work on the brake system components, clean all parts with brake system

cleaner or denatured alcohol. Do not allow the fine dust to become airborne.
c) Safety should be paramount whenever any servicing of the brake components is performed. Do not use parts or fasteners which are not in perfect condition, and be sure that all clearances and torque specifications are adhered to. If you are at all unsure about a certain procedure, seek professional advice. Upon completion of brake system work, test the brakes carefully in a controlled area before putting the vehicle into normal service. If a problem is suspected in the brake system, don't drive the vehicle until it's fixed.

2   Front brake pads - replacement

Refer to illustrations 2.1 and 2.6a through 2.6j
Warning: *Disc brake pads must be replaced on both front wheels at the same time - never replace the pads on only one wheel. Also, the dust created by the brake system may contain asbestos, which is harmful to your health. Never blow it out with compressed air and don't inhale any of it. An approved filtering mask should be worn when working on the brakes. Do not, under any circumstances, use petroleum-based solvents to clean brake parts. Use brake cleaner or denatured alcohol only!*
Note: *When servicing the disc brakes, use only high quality, nationally recognized name brand pads.*
1   The caliper design for all models is basically the same **(see illustration)**.
2   Remove the cover from the brake fluid reservoir.
3   Apply the parking brake and block the rear wheels. Loosen the wheel lug nuts, raise the front of the vehicle and support it securely on jackstands.
4   Remove the front wheels. Work on one brake assembly at a time, using the assembled brake for reference if necessary.
5   Inspect the brake disc carefully as outlined in Section 4. If machining is necessary, follow the information in that Section to remove the disc, at which time the pads can be removed from the calipers as well.

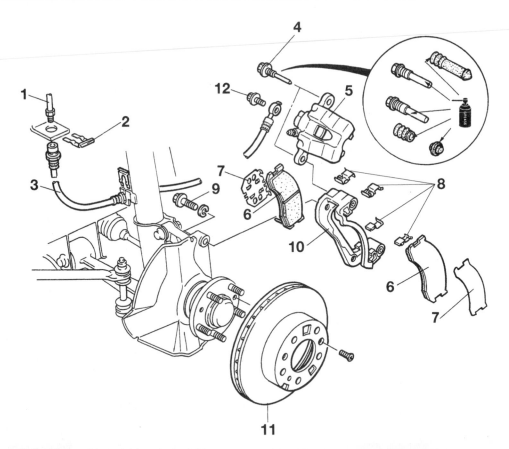

2.1 An exploded view of the front brake assembly

1. Metal brake line
2. Clip
3. Flexible brake hose
4. Caliper lock bolt
5. Brake caliper assembly
6. Disc brake pad
7. Shim
8. Guide plate (anti-rattle spring)
9. Caliper mount-to-steering knuckle bolt
10. Caliper mount
11. Disc
12. Brake hose-to-caliper banjo bolt

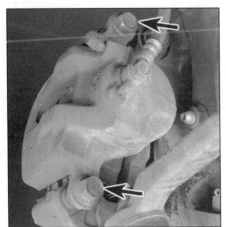

2.6a Remove the caliper bolts (arrows) . . .

2.6b . . . lift off the caliper. . .

2.6c . . . note how the inner brake pad shim is installed on the caliper piston and remove it from the piston

9

6   Follow the accompanying illustrations, beginning with 2.6a, for the pad removal procedure. Be sure to stay in order and read the caption under each illustration. As soon as you remove the caliper, be sure to push the piston(s) back into the bore - to provide room for the new brake pads - with a C-clamp. As the piston is depressed to the bottom of the caliper bore, the fluid in the master cylinder will rise. Make sure it doesn't overflow. If necessary, siphon off some of the fluid. **Caution:** *Don't use a screwdriver or similar tool to pry the piston away from the disc.* To install the new pads, reverse the removal procedure.

7   After the job has been completed, firmly depress the brake pedal a few times to bring the pads into contact with the disc.

8   Check for fluid leakage and make sure the brakes operate normally before driving in traffic.

3   Front brake caliper - removal, overhaul and installation

Warning: *Dust created by the brake system may contain asbestos, which is harmful to your health. Never blow it out with compressed air and don't inhale any of it. An approved filtering mask should be worn when working on the brakes. Do not, under any circumstances, use petroleum-based solvents to clean brake parts. Use brake cleaner or denatured alcohol only!*

Note: *If an overhaul is indicated (usually because of fluid leakage) explore all options before beginning the job. New and factory rebuilt calipers are available on an exchange basis, which makes this job quite easy. If it's decided to rebuild the calipers, make sure a rebuild kit is*

2.6d Use a C-clamp to push the piston(s) back into the bore to make room for the new brake pads (note how an old pad is used to protect the piston from damage)

2.6e Hang the caliper from the coil spring with a piece of wire as shown - don't allow the caliper to hang by the brake hose

2.6f Remove the shim from the outer brake pad

2.6g Remove the outer brake pad

2.6h Remove the inner brake pad

2.6i Inspect the upper guide plates (anti-rattle springs) (arrows); make sure they're neither bent nor damaged; if they are, replace them

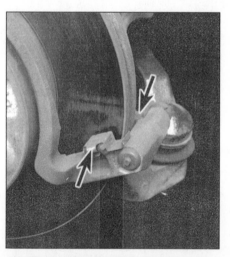

2.6j The lower guide plates (arrows) must also be in good shape and installed correctly before installing the pads

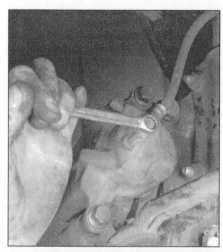

3.3 Remove the banjo bolt and separate the hose from the caliper

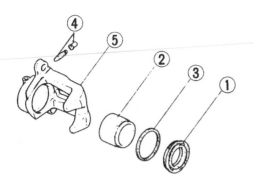

3.6 An exploded view of the single-piston caliper assembly

1	Dust boot	4	Cap and bleeder
2	Piston		screw
3	Piston seal	5	Caliper body

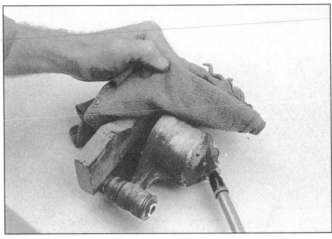

3.7 With the caliper padded to catch the piston, use compressed air to force the piston out of its bore - make sure your hands or fingers are not between the piston and the caliper

available before proceeding. Always rebuild the calipers in pairs - never rebuild just one of them.

Removal

Refer to illustration 3.3

1   Apply the parking brake and block the rear wheels. Loosen the wheel lug nuts, raise the front of the vehicle and support it securely on jackstands.

2   Remove the front wheels.

3   Remove the brake hose banjo bolt and detach the hose from the caliper **(see illustration)**. Have a rag handy to catch spilled fluid and wrap a plastic bag tightly around the end of the hose to prevent fluid loss and contamination. **Note:** *If the caliper will not be completely removed from the vehicle - as for pad inspection or disc removal - leave the hose connected and suspend the caliper with a length of wire. This will save the trouble of bleeding the system.*

4   Refer to the first few Steps in Section 2 to separate the caliper from the caliper mount - it's part of the brake pad replacement procedure.

Overhaul

Refer to illustrations 3.6, 3.7 and 3.8

Note: *The brakes on 1992 and 1993 models use two-piston calipers, but the procedure for rebuilding them is basically the same as the following procedure for single-piston calipers.*

5   Clean the exterior of the caliper with brake cleaner or denatured alcohol. Never use gasoline, kerosene or petroleum-based cleaning solvents. Place the caliper on a clean workbench.

6   Carefully pry the dust boot out of the caliper bore **(see illustration)**.

7   Position a wood block or several shop rags in the caliper as a cushion, then use compressed air to remove the piston from the caliper **(see illustration)**. Use only enough air pressure to ease the piston out of the bore. If the piston is blown out, even with the cushion in place, it may be damaged. On vehicles with two-piston calipers, both pistons will probably not come out at the same time, so to keep the air pressure from escaping through a bore where a piston has already come out, place the piston back into the bore far enough to seal off the bore, then hold it in place with a piece of wood. **Warning:** *Placing your fingers in front of the piston to catch or protect it when applying compressed air could result in serious injury.*

8   Using a wood or plastic tool, remove the piston seal from the groove in the caliper bore **(see illustration)**. Metal tools may cause bore damage.

9   Remove the caliper bleeder screw and discard all rubber parts.

10   Clean the remaining parts with brake system cleaner or denatured alcohol, then blow them dry with compressed air.

11   Carefully examine the piston for nicks and burrs and loss of plating. If surface defects are present, the parts must be replaced. Check the caliper bore in a similar way.

3.8 To avoid damage to the bore and seal groove, stay away from metal tools - instead, use a wood or plastic tool to remove the piston seal from the groove in the caliper bore (a pencil will do the job)

12   Discard the lock bolts if they're corroded or damaged.

13   Lubricate the piston bore and seal with clean brake fluid. Install the seal in the groove of the caliper bore. Make sure the seal does not become twisted and that it is firmly seated in the groove.

14   Lubricate the piston with clean brake fluid, insert it into the bore, then push it squarely to the bottom of its travel.

15   Place the lip of the dust boot in the groove on the piston. Seat the outer diameter of the dust boot in the caliper bore.

16   Install the bleeder screw.

Installation

17   Refer to Section 2 for the caliper installation procedure, as it is part of the brake pad replacement procedure.

18   Install a new sealing washer on each side of the brake hose fitting, then install the banjo bolt and tighten it to the torque listed in this Chapter's Specifications.

19   Bleed the brakes as outlined in Section 12. This is not necessary if the banjo bolt was not loosened or removed from the caliper.

20   Install the wheels and lower the vehicle. Tighten the lug nuts to the torque listed in the Chapter 1 Specifications.

21   Test the operation of the brakes before placing the vehicle in normal service.

9

4.4a Use a dial indicator to check disc runout - if the reading exceeds the maximum allowable runout limit, the disc will have to be machined or replaced

4.4b Using a swirling motion, remove the glaze from the disc surface with sandpaper or emery cloth

4   Front brake disc - inspection, removal and installation

Warning: *Dust created by the brake system may contain asbestos, which is harmful to your health. Never blow it out with compressed air and don't inhale any of it. An approved filtering mask should be worn when working on the brakes. Do not, under any circumstances, use petroleum-based solvents to clean brake parts. Use brake cleaner or denatured alcohol only!*

Inspection

Refer to illustrations 4.4a, 4.4b, 4.5a and 4.5b

1   Loosen the wheel lug nuts, raise the vehicle and support it securely on jackstands. Remove the wheel(s).

2   Unbolt the brake caliper and remove the brake pads (see Section 2). It's not necessary to disconnect the brake hose. After removing the caliper, suspend it out of the way with a piece of wire. Don't let it hang by the hose and don't stretch or twist the hose.

3   Visually check the disc surface for score marks and other damage. Light scratches and shallow grooves are normal after use and may not always be detrimental to brake operation, but deep score marks - over 0.015-inch - require disc removal and refinishing by an automotive machine shop. Be sure to check both sides of the disc. If pulsating has been noticed during application of the brakes, suspect disc runout. Be sure to check the wheel bearings to make sure they're not worn out (see Chapter 1).

4   To check disc runout, place a dial indicator at a point about 1/2-inch from the outer edge of the disc **(see illustration)**. Set the indicator to zero and turn the disc. The indicator reading should not exceed the runout limit listed in this Chapter's Specifications. If it does, the disc should be refinished by an automotive machine shop. **Note:** *Professionals recommend resurfacing of brake discs regardless of the dial indicator reading (to produce a smooth, flat surface that will eliminate brake pedal pulsations and other undesirable symptoms related to questionable discs).* At the very least, if you elect not to have the discs resurfaced, remove the glazing from the surface with sandpaper or emery cloth using a swirling motion **(see illustration)**.

5   The disc must not be machined to a thickness less than the minimum allowable thickness. The minimum thickness is cast into the center portion of the disc **(see illustration)**. The disc thickness can be checked with a micrometer **(see illustration)**.

Removal and installation

Refer to illustrations 4.6, 4.7a and 4.7b

6   Unbolt the front brake caliper mount from the steering knuckle **(see illustration)**.

7   Unscrew the retaining screws and remove the disc **(see illustrations)**.

8   Installation is the reverse of removal. Be sure to tighten the caliper mount bolts and the caliper lock bolts to the torque listed in this Chapter's Specifications. Tighten the wheel lug nuts to the torque listed in the Chapter 1 Specifications.

4.5a The minimum thickness limit is cast into the disc

4.5b Use a micrometer to measure the disc thickness at several points near the edge

4.6 Before you can remove the brake disc, you must remove the brake caliper mount-to-steering knuckle bolts (arrows) and detach the mount

4.7a Remove the brake disc retaining screws - they're usually very tight, so you may need to use an impact screwdriver

4.7b Once the screws are removed, slide the disc off the hub

9   Depress the brake pedal a few times to bring the brake pads into contact with the disc. Bleeding of the system isn't necessary unless the brake hose was disconnected from the caliper. Check the operation of the brakes carefully before placing the vehicle into normal service.

5   Rear brake shoes - replacement and adjustment

Refer to illustrations 5.5a through 5.5gg, 5.9a and 5.9b
Warning: *Drum brake shoes must be replaced on both wheels at the same time - never replace the shoes on only one wheel. Also, the dust created by the brake system may contain asbestos, which is harmful to your health. Never blow it out with compressed air and don't inhale any of it. An approved filtering mask should be worn when working on the brakes. Do not, under any circumstances, use petroleum-based solvents to clean brake parts. Use brake cleaner or denatured alcohol only!*
Caution: *Whenever the brake shoes are replaced, the return and hold-down springs should also be replaced. Due to the continuous heating/cooling cycle that the springs are subjected to, they lose their tension over a period of time and may allow the shoes to drag on the drum and wear at a much faster rate than normal. When replacing the*

rear brake shoes, use only high quality, nationally recognized brand-name parts.
1   To ease installation of the brake assembly during the removal procedure, lay out all parts in an assembled order on a rag near the work area.
2   Loosen the wheel lug nuts, raise the rear of the vehicle and support it securely on jackstands. Block the front wheels to keep the vehicle from rolling.
3   Release the parking brake.
4   Remove the wheels. **Note:** *All four rear brake shoes must be replaced at the same time, but to avoid mixing up parts, work on only one brake assembly at a time.*
5   Follow the accompanying photos **(see illustrations 5.5a through 5.5gg)** for the brake shoe replacement procedure. Be sure to stay in order and read the caption under each illustration. **Note:** *If the brake drum cannot be easily pulled off the axle and shoe assembly, make sure that the parking brake is completely released, then apply some penetrating oil at the hub-to-drum joint. Allow the oil to soak in and try to pull the drum off. If the drum still cannot be pulled off, the brake shoes will have to be retracted. This is accomplished by first removing the two plugs from the backing plate. With the plugs removed, pull the lever off the adjusting star wheel with one small screwdriver while turning the adjusting wheel with another small screwdriver, moving the shoes away from the drum, which should now come off (see illustrations 5.9a and 5.9b).*

9

5.5a Remove the screws that attach the drum to the axle flange (you'll probably need to use an impact screwdriver to avoid stripping the screw heads)

5.5b Slide the drum off the axle flange

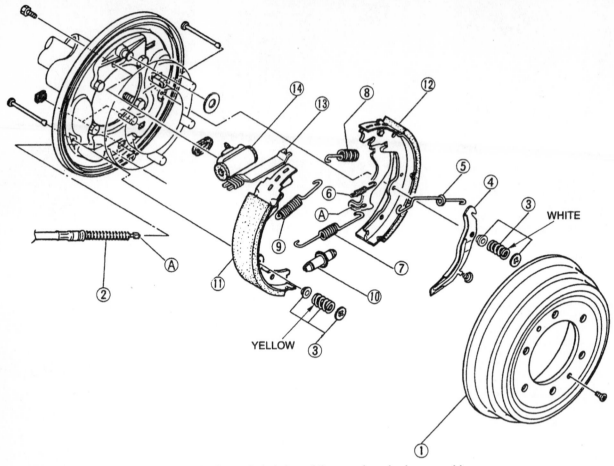

5.5c An exploded view of the rear drum brake assembly

1 Brake drum
2 Parking brake cable
3 Brake shoe hold-down spring, washer and seat (yellow spring - primary shoe; white spring - secondary shoe)
4 Parking brake adjusting lever
5 Adjusting lever link
6 Pull-off spring
7 Shoe-to-shoe spring
8 Return spring
9 Return spring
10 Adjuster
11 Primary brake shoe
12 Secondary brake shoe
13 Parking brake link
14 Wheel cylinder assembly

5.5d Remove the brake shoe hold-down springs with a brake spring removal tool or a pair of pliers (don't mix them up - the yellow spring goes on the primary shoe and the white spring goes on the secondary shoe)

5.5e Remove the adjusting lever . . .

5.5f . . . and remove the adjusting lever link (note which end of the link hooks over the anchor pin)

5.5g Unhook the upper end of the secondary shoe return spring from the anchor pin (diagonal cutting pliers are being used here because they grip the spring well) . . .

5.5h . . . and unhook the lower end from the secondary shoe

5.5i Unhook the primary shoe return spring from the anchor pin and detach the other end from the primary shoe

5.5j Pry off this small E-clip from the parking brake pivot pin

5.5k Remove the large washer from the anchor pin

5.5l Unhook the pull-off spring from its hole (arrow) in the secondary shoe

5.5m Spread the shoes apart and remove them as an assembly

5.5n Remove the parking brake link (don't lose the spring on front end of the link)

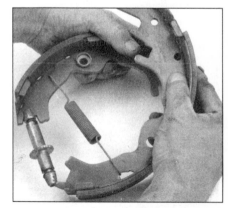

5.5o Overlap the upper ends of the shoes like this and remove the adjuster,. . .

6   Before reinstalling the drum, check it for cracks, score marks, deep scratches and hard spots, which will appear as small discolored areas. If the hard spots cannot be removed with fine emery cloth or if any of the other conditions listed above exist, the drum must be taken to an automotive machine shop to have it turned. **Note:** *Professionals recommend resurfacing the drums whenever a brake job is done. Resurfacing will eliminate the possibility of out-of-round drums. If the* drums *are worn so much that they can't be resurfaced without exceeding the maximum allowable diameter (cast into the drum), then new ones will be required. At the very least, if you elect not to have the drums resurfaced, remove the glazing from the surface with medium-grit emery cloth using a swirling motion.*

7   Install the brake drum on the axle flange.

8   Install the wheels and lug nuts, tightening the lug nuts finger tight.

9

5.5p . . .then remove the spring

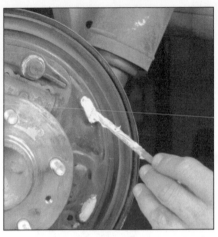

5.5q Lightly coat the shoe contact areas on the backing plate with high-temperature brake grease

5.5r Lubricate the adjuster screw with high-temperature brake grease

5.5s Install the shoe spring . . .

5.5t . . .and the adjuster

5.5u Install the parking brake link, . . .

5.5v . . .then install the shoes, shoe-to-shoe spring and adjuster as a single assembly

5.5w Install a new E-clip over the parking brake pivot pin

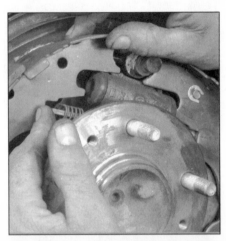

5.5x Make sure the slot at each end of the parking brake link is properly seated against its respective notch on each shoe (and make sure the spring is installed on the front end of the link)

5.5y Also make sure the shoe-to-shoe spring and the adjuster are properly installed

5.5z Attach the rear end of the pull-off spring to the secondary shoe

5.5aa Install the large washer on the anchor pin

5.5bb Hook the lower end of the secondary shoe return spring into the shoe, then - holding it in place with your thumb - attach the upper end to the anchor pin (a brake spring installation tool, shown here, greatly simplifies this step)

5.5cc Hook the front end of the primary shoe return spring into the shoe and attach the rear end to the anchor pin

5.5dd Hook the upper end of the adjusting lever link over the anchor pin, . . .

5.5ee . . . hook the lower end of the link into its notch (arrow) in the parking brake lever and install the spring seat, spring and washer, then install the front seat, spring and washer on the primary shoe (not shown)

5.5ff Make sure the spring (arrow) attached to the parking brake adjusting lever is properly seated between the lever and the secondary shoe

5.5gg Compare your work to this photo and make sure everything is properly installed

9

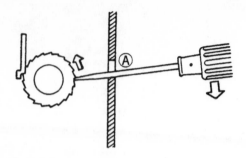

5.9a To adjust the rear brakes, remove the two plugs from the backing plate, place a screwdriver against the adjuster through hole A, turn the adjuster in the direction of the arrow marked on the backing plate until the wheel is locked, . . .

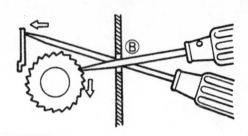

5.9b . . .then, using hole B, push the pawl lever of the self-adjuster and back off the star wheel so the drum rotates freely without dragging

9   The rear brakes are self-adjusting. They require adjustment only after the shoes have been replaced or the adjusting lever has been moved for some other service procedure. To adjust them, remove the two hole plugs from the backing plate, place a screwdriver against the adjuster through hole A **(see illustration)** and turn the adjuster in the direction of the arrow marked on the backing plate until the wheel is locked. Then, using hole B, push the pawl lever of the self-adjuster and back off the star wheel until the drum rotates freely without dragging **(see illustration)**. Repeat this adjustment on the other wheel.

10   Adjust the parking brake cable (see Section 13).

11   Lower the vehicle to the ground and tighten the lug nuts to the torque listed in the Chapter 1 Specifications. Check brake operation before driving the vehicle in traffic.

6   Wheel cylinder - removal, overhaul and installation

Note: *If an overhaul is indicated (usually because of fluid leakage or sticky operation) explore all options before beginning the job. New*

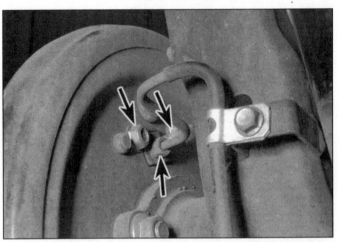

6.4 Working from the back side of the brake backing plate, disconnect the brake line fitting and remove the wheel cylinder mounting bolts (arrows)

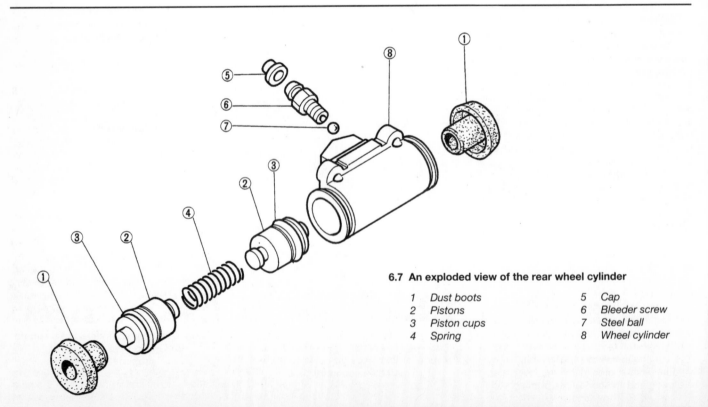

6.7 An exploded view of the rear wheel cylinder

1	Dust boots	5	Cap
2	Pistons	6	Bleeder screw
3	Piston cups	7	Steel ball
4	Spring	8	Wheel cylinder

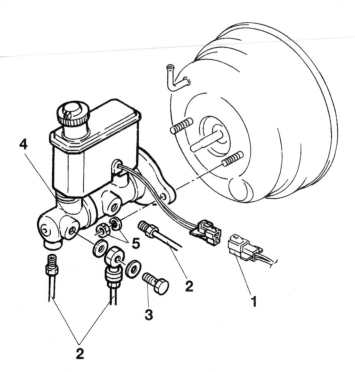

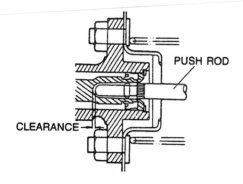

7.6 Check the master cylinder-to-booster pushrod clearance and adjust it as required

7.2 Mounting details of the brake master cylinder

1	Fluid level sensor connector	3	Banjo bolt
2	Brake lines	4	Brake master cylinder
		5	Mounting nut and washer

wheel cylinders are available, which makes this job quite easy. If it's decided to rebuild the wheel cylinder, make sure that a rebuild kit is available before proceeding. Never overhaul only one wheel cylinder - always rebuild both of them at the same time.

Removal

Refer to illustration 6.4

1   Loosen the wheel lug nuts, raise the rear of the vehicle and support it securely on jackstands. Block the front wheels to keep the vehicle from rolling.

2   Remove the brake shoe assembly (see Section 5).

3   Remove all dirt and foreign material from around the wheel cylinder.

4   Unscrew the brake line fitting **(see illustration)**. Don't pull the brake line away from the wheel cylinder.

5   Remove the wheel cylinder mounting bolts.

6   Detach the wheel cylinder from the brake backing plate and place it on a clean workbench. Immediately plug the brake line to prevent fluid loss and contamination. **Note:** *If the brake shoe linings are contaminated with brake fluid, install new brake shoes.*

Overhaul

Refer to illustration 6.7

7   Remove the bleeder screw, cups, pistons, boots and spring assembly from the wheel cylinder body **(see illustration)**.

8   Clean the wheel cylinder with brake fluid, denatured alcohol or brake system cleaner. **Warning:** *Do not, under any circumstances, use petroleum-based solvents to clean brake parts!*

9   Use compressed air to remove excess fluid from the wheel cylinder and to blow out the passages.

10   Check the cylinder bore for corrosion and score marks. Crocus cloth can be used to remove light corrosion and stains, but the cylinder must be replaced with a new one if the defects cannot be removed easily, or if the bore is scored.

11   Lubricate the new cups with brake fluid.

12   Assemble the wheel cylinder components. Make sure the cup lips face in.

Installation

13   Place the wheel cylinder in position and install the bolts.

14   Connect the brake line and tighten the fitting. Install the brake shoe assembly.

15   Bleed the brakes (see Section 12).

16   Check brake operation before driving the vehicle in traffic.

7   Master cylinder - removal, overhaul and installation

Removal and installation

Refer to illustrations 7.2 and 7.6

1   Push the brake pedal down several times to expel the vacuum from the brake booster.

2   Unplug the electrical connector for the fluid level sensor **(see illustration)**.

3   Unscrew the brake lines from the primary and secondary outlet ports of the master cylinder. Plug the ends of the lines to prevent the entry of dirt and moisture. Place newspapers under the connections to catch the brake fluid that will spill out.

4   Remove the nuts which secure the master cylinder to the brake booster.

5   Remove the master cylinder from the vehicle. Brake fluid will damage painted surfaces, so don't spill any on the vehicle. If the cylinder is to be overhauled, proceed to Step 7.

6   Installation is the reverse of the removal Steps with the following additions:

a)   **Note:** *Whenever the master cylinder is removed, the entire hydraulic system must be bled. The time required to bleed the system can be reduced if the master cylinder is filled with fluid and bench bled (see below) before the master cylinder is installed on the vehicle.*

b)   Insert threaded plugs of the correct size into the cylinder outlet holes and fill the reservoirs with fresh brake fluid. The master cylinder should be supported in such a manner that the brake fluid will not spill during the bench bleeding procedure.

c)   Loosen one plug at a time, starting with the rear outlet port first, and use a large Phillips screwdriver to push the piston assembly into the bore to force air from the master cylinder. To prevent air from being drawn back into the cylinder, the appropriate plug must be tightened before allowing the piston to return to its original position.

d)   Stroke the piston three or four times for each outlet to ensure that all air has been expelled.

e)   Since high pressure is not involved in the bench bleeding procedure, an alternative to the removal and installation of the plug with each stroke of the piston is available. Before pushing in on

9

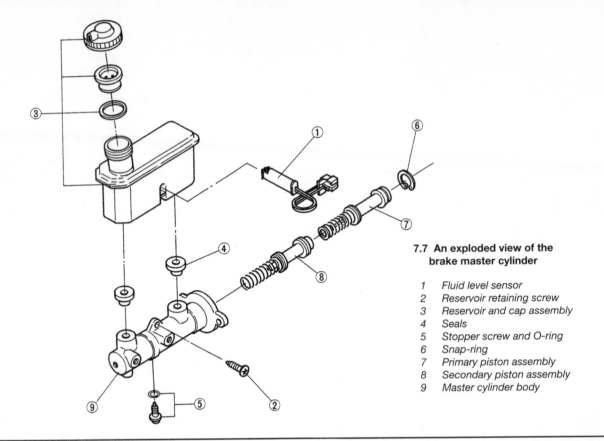

7.7 An exploded view of the brake master cylinder

1   Fluid level sensor
2   Reservoir retaining screw
3   Reservoir and cap assembly
4   Seals
5   Stopper screw and O-ring
6   Snap-ring
7   Primary piston assembly
8   Secondary piston assembly
9   Master cylinder body

the piston assembly, remove one of the plugs completely. Before releasing the piston, however, instead of installing the plug, simply place your finger tightly over the hole to keep air from being drawn into the master cylinder. Wait several seconds for the brake fluid to be drawn from the reservoir to the piston bore, then repeat the procedure. When you push down on the piston it will force your finger off the hole, allowing air inside to be expelled. When only brake fluid is being ejected from the hole, install the plug and go to the other port.

f)   Refill the master cylinder reservoirs and install the diaphragm and cap.
g)   Bleed the brake system as outlined in Section 12.
h)   Using a hand-held vacuum pump, apply 20-in Hg of vacuum to the power brake booster and check the distance from the outer end of the booster pushrod to the front face of the brake booster assembly. Now measure the depth from the master cylinder mounting flange to the bottom of the master cylinder piston and subtract the previous measurement from it. Turn the pushrod adjusting screw in or out as required to obtain the clearance listed in this Chapter's Specifications **(see illustration)**.
i)   Test the brakes carefully before driving the vehicle in traffic.

Overhaul

Refer to illustrations 7.7, 7.9, 7.10, 7.11 and 7.12

Note: *Before deciding to overhaul the master cylinder, check on the availability and cost of a new or factory-rebuilt unit and also the availability of a rebuild kit.*

7   Remove the master cylinder. Clean the exterior of the master cylinder and dry it with a lint-free rag. Remove the reservoir cap and pour out any remaining brake fluid **(see illustration)**.
8   Place the master cylinder in a vise with the vise jaws clamping on the mounting flange.
9   Use a large Phillips screwdriver to depress the piston assembly, then remove the snap-ring from the retaining groove at the rear of the master cylinder **(see illustration)**.
10   Remove the primary piston assembly from the cylinder bore **(see**

7.9 Use a Phillips head screwdriver to push the primary piston into the cylinder, then remove the snap-ring

illustration). Inspect the seal for damage.
11   Remove the secondary piston assembly from the cylinder bore. It may be necessary to remove the master cylinder from the vise and invert it, carefully tapping it against a block of wood to expel the piston **(see illustration)**. Inspect the seal for damage.
12   If fluid has been leaking past the reservoir grommets, carefully pry the reservoir from the body with a screwdriver **(see illustration)**. Remove the seals and discard them.
13   Inspect the surfaces of the cylinder bore and pistons for corrosion, wear and damage. If these are evident, replace the complete master cylinder assembly. Do not hone the master cylinder bore.
14   If these main components are in good condition, then the original assembly is worth overhauling.
15   If the rubber seals are swollen or very loose on the pistons, suspect oil contamination in the system. Oil will swell these rubber seals

7.10 Remove the primary piston assembly from the cylinder

7.11 Tap the master cylinder against a block of wood to eject the secondary piston assembly

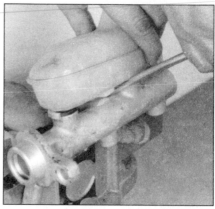

7.12 If you must remove the reservoir (to replace leaking seals or a broken reservoir), remove the retaining screw and gently pry the reservoir off with a screwdriver or prybar

and if one is found to be swollen it is reasonable to assume that all seals in the brake system need attention.

16   Purchase a repair kit which contains all the necessary seals and other replaceable parts. Some repair kits will contain a complete primary piston assembly.

17   Wash all the internal components in clean brake fluid, brake system cleaner or denatured alcohol. Do not use any other type of fluid. Mineral spirits or solvent must never be allowed to come in contact with hydraulic cylinder components.

18   Lubricate the new reservoir seals with brake fluid and press them into the master cylinder body. Make sure they are properly seated.

19   Inspect the reservoir cap and reservoir for cracks or damage and replace if necessary.

20   Lay the reservoir on a hard surface and press the master cylinder body into the reservoir, using a rocking motion.

21   Lubricate the cylinder bore with clean brake fluid.

22   Dip the secondary piston assembly into clean brake fluid and push the piston into the cylinder, so the spring will seat against the closed end of the cylinder. Ease the seals into the bore taking care that they do not roll over.

23   Reinstall the master cylinder in a vise so that the open end of the cylinder is facing up. Dip the primary piston assembly into clean brake fluid and then push the piston, spring end first, into the master cylinder.

24   Depress the piston and install the snap-ring. Make sure the snap-ring is seated correctly in its groove.

25   Bench bleed the master cylinder as described in Step 6.

---

8   Power brake booster - removal and installation

1   The power brake booster unit requires no special maintenance apart from periodic inspection of the vacuum hose and the case.

2   Dismantling of the power unit requires special tools and is not ordinarily done by the home mechanic. If a problem develops, install a new or factory rebuilt unit.

Removal

Refer to illustration 8.4

3   Remove the master cylinder (see Section 7).

4   Loosen the clamp and disconnect the vacuum hose where it attaches to the check valve on the power brake booster. Remove the check valve from the booster **(see illustration)**.

5   On V6 models, you'll have to remove the windshield wiper arms, the wiper motor and the link to remove the booster (see Chapter 12).

6   From the passenger compartment, remove the cotter pin and pull out the clevis pin from the top of the brake pedal assembly.

7   Remove the nuts securing the booster to the firewall.

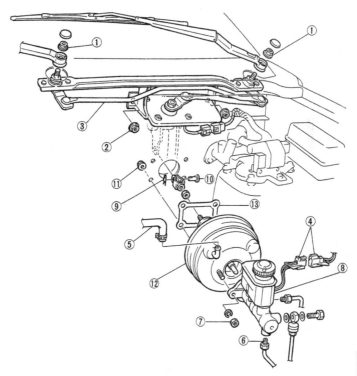

8.4 Mounting details of the brake booster assembly

1	Windshield wiper arm retaining nuts (must be removed on V6 models only)	6	Brake line
2	Wiper motor retaining nuts (must be removed on V6 models only)	7	Brake master cylinder mounting nut
3	Wiper motor link (must be removed on V6 models only)	8	Master cylinder and reservoir assembly
4	Fluid level sensor connector	9	Clip
5	Brake booster vacuum hose	10	Clevis pin
		11	Brake booster mounting nut
		12	Power brake booster assembly
		13	Gasket

9

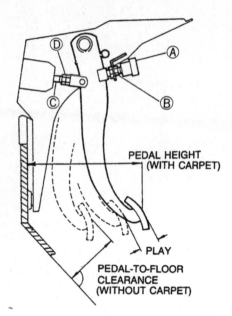

9.1 Brake pedal adjustment details

A   Brake light switch   *B   Locknut*

8   Working in the engine compartment, lift the booster unit away from the firewall and out of the vehicle.

Installation

9   Installation is the reverse of the removal Steps with the following additions.
10   Carefully test the operation of the brakes before placing the vehicle in normal service.
11   Check the pushrod length as described in Step 6 of Section 7.
12   When adjustment is complete, reinstall the master cylinder and check for proper operation before driving the vehicle in traffic.

9   Brake pedal - adjustment

Pedal height

Refer to illustration 9.1

1   Verify that the distance from the center of the upper surface of the pedal pad to the carpet **(see illustration)** is as listed in this Chapter's Specifications.
2   If the pedal height isn't correct, adjust it as follows:
3   Disconnect the electrical connector for the brake light switch (see previous Section).
4   Loosen locknut B and turn switch A until it doesn't touch the pedal.
5   Loosen locknut D and turn rod C to adjust the height.
6   Turn the brake light switch until it contacts the pedal, then turn it an additional 1/2-turn. Tighten locknut B.

Pedal freeplay

7   Depress the pedal a few times to eliminate the vacuum in the system.
8   Gently depress the pedal again by hand and check the freeplay (the distance between the point at which the valve plunger contacts the stopper plate and the point at which the power piston starts to move) and compare your measurement to the freeplay listed in this Chapter's Specifications.
9   If the pedal freeplay isn't correct, adjust it as follows:

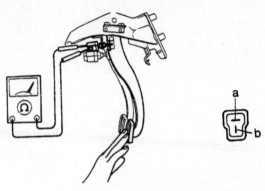

10.3 Hook up an ohmmeter to the terminals of the switch and verify that there's continuity when the brake pedal is depressed and no continuity when the pedal is released

10   Loosen locknut D of operating rod C, then turn the rod to adjust the freeplay.

Pedal-to-floor clearance

11   Verify that the distance from the floor panel to the center of the upper surface of the pedal pad is the same as the dimension listed in this Chapter's Specifications when the pedal is depressed.
12   If the pedal-to-floor distance isn't correct, check for the following problems: Air in the brake system (see Section 12); malfunction of the automatic adjuster (see Section 5); worn pads or shoes (see Sections 2 and 5, respectively).

10   Brake light switch - check, adjustment and replacement

Check

Refer to illustration 10.3

1   Look up under the dash and locate the brake light switch at the top of the brake pedal.
2   Unplug the electrical connector for the switch.
3   Connect an ohmmeter to the terminals of the switch **(see illustration)** and verify that there's continuity between terminals A and B when the pedal is depressed, but no continuity between then when the pedal is released.
4   If the brake light switch doesn't perform as described, try adjusting it. If it still doesn't work properly, replace it.

Adjustment

5   Adjust the brake pedal height (see Section 9).
6   Unplug the electrical connector for the brake light switch.
7   Loosen the brake light switch locknut **(see illustration 9.1)**.
8   Turn the brake light switch locknut until it contacts the pedal, then turn it an additional 1/2-turn.
9   Tighten the locknut.

Replacement

10   Unplug the electrical connector, loosen the locknut and remove the switch.
11   Installation is the reverse of removal. Be sure to adjust the switch.

11   Brake hoses and lines - inspection and replacement

Inspection

1   Brake hoses and lines should be inspected when recommended in the maintenance schedule and whenever the vehicle is raised. See Chapter 1 for inspection intervals and procedures.

11.2a To disconnect a front brake hose from a metal brake line, remove this U-clip from the bracket on the wheel well, then, using a backup wrench, disconnect the threaded fitting between the hose and the line (there's another U-clip and bracket on the strut housing)

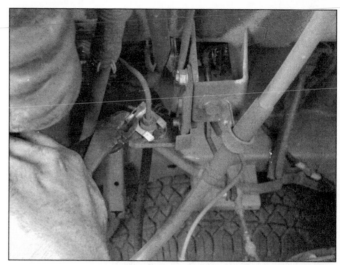

11.2b To disconnect the rear brake hose from the metal brake line, remove this U-clip from the bracket on the underside of the body, then, using a backup wrench, disconnect the threaded fitting between the hose and the line (the other end of the hose is connected to a metal line at a similar bracket on top of the axle housing)

Replacement

Brake hoses

Refer to illustrations 11.2a and 11.2b

Note: *The following procedure applies to either front brake hose between the bracket on the wheel well and the caliper, or the single rear hose between the bracket on the underside of the body and the bracket on top of the axle housing.*

2   Use a pair of pliers to remove the U-clip from the bracket **(see illustrations)**, then detach the hose from the bracket.

3   Using a back-up wrench, disconnect the brake line from the hose fitting.

4   Remove the U-clip from the strut housing and detach the hose from the bracket.

5   Unscrew the inlet banjo bolt from the caliper. Discard the sealing washers.

6   To install the hose, place a new sealing washer on each side of the hose fitting, install the inlet banjo bolt and tighten it securely.

7   Insert the hose into the bracket on the strut housing and secure it with the U-clip.

8   Without twisting the hose, install the hose fitting in the frame bracket.

9   Using a back-up wrench, attach the brake line to the hose fitting.

10   Install the U-clip retaining the female fitting to the frame bracket.

11   When the brake hose installation is complete, there should be no kinks in the hose. Make sure the hose doesn't contact any part of the suspension. Check this by turning the wheels to the extreme left and right positions. If the hose makes contact, remove it and correct the installation as necessary.

12   After installation, check the master cylinder fluid level and add fluid as necessary. Bleed the brake system (see Section 12) and test the brakes carefully before driving the vehicle in traffic.

Metal brake lines

13   When replacing brake lines be sure to use the correct parts. Don't use copper tubing for any brake system components. Purchase genuine steel brake lines from a dealer parts department or auto parts store.

14   Prefabricated brake line, with the tube ends already flared and fittings installed, is available at auto parts stores and dealer parts departments. These lines are also bent to the proper shapes.

15   When installing the new line make sure it's securely supported in the brackets and has plenty of clearance from moving or hot components.

16   After installation, check the master cylinder fluid level and add fluid as necessary. Bleed the brake system (see Section 12) and test the brakes carefully before driving the vehicle in traffic.

12   Brake hydraulic system - bleeding

Refer to illustration 12.8

Warning: *Wear eye protection whenever bleeding the brake system. If the fluid comes in contact with your eyes, immediately rinse them with water and seek a physician's advice.*

Note: *Bleeding the hydraulic system is necessary to remove any air that manages to find its way into the system when it has been opened during removal and installation of a hose, line, caliper or master cylinder.*

1   It will probably be necessary to bleed the system at all four brakes if air has entered the system due to low fluid level, or if the brake lines have been disconnected at the master cylinder.

2   If a brake line was disconnected only at one wheel, then only that caliper or wheel cylinder must be bled.

3   If a brake line is disconnected at a fitting located between the master cylinder and any of the brakes, that part of the system served by the disconnected line must be bled.

4   Remove any residual vacuum from the brake power booster by applying the brake several times with the engine OFF.

5   Remove the master cylinder reservoir cover and fill the reservoir with brake fluid. Reinstall the cover. **Note:** *Check the fluid level often during the bleeding operation and add fluid as necessary to prevent the fluid level from falling low enough to allow air bubbles into the master cylinder.*

6   Have an assistant on hand, as well as a supply of new brake fluid, an empty clear plastic container, a length of 3/16-inch plastic, rubber or vinyl tubing to fit over the bleeder valve and a wrench to open and close the bleeder valve.

7   Beginning at the right rear wheel, loosen the bleeder valve slightly, then tighten it to a point where it is snug but can still be loosened quickly and easily.

9

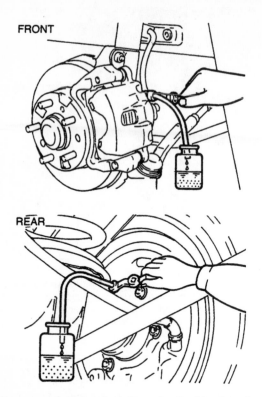

12.8 Place one end of the tubing over the bleeder valve and submerge the other end in brake fluid in the container (front, above; rear, below)

8   Place one end of the tubing over the bleeder valve and submerge the other end in brake fluid in the container **(see illustration)**.

9   Have the assistant pump the brakes slowly a few times to get pressure in the system, then hold the pedal firmly depressed.

10   While the pedal is held depressed, open the bleeder valve just enough to allow a flow of fluid to leave the valve. Watch for air bubbles to exit the submerged end of the tube. When the fluid flow slows after a couple of seconds, close the valve and have your assistant release the pedal.

11   Repeat Steps 9 and 10 until no more air is seen leaving the tube, then tighten the bleeder valve and proceed to the left rear wheel, the right front wheel and the left front wheel, in that order, and perform the same procedure. Be sure to check the fluid in the master cylinder reservoir frequently.

12   Never use old brake fluid. It contains moisture which will deteriorate the brake system components.

13   Refill the master cylinder with fluid at the end of the operation.

14   Check the operation of the brakes. The pedal should feel solid when depressed, with no sponginess. If necessary, repeat the entire process. **Warning:** *Do not operate the vehicle if you are in doubt about the effectiveness of the brake system.*

13   Parking brake - adjustment

Refer to illustration 13.3
Note: *Adjust the rear brakes (see Section 5) before adjusting the parking brake cable.*

1   When you pull up on the parking brake lever, it should take about five to seven clicks of the lever to apply the parking brake system. If it takes more than that, adjust the parking brake system.

2   Before adjustment, start the engine, put the vehicle in reverse and depress the brake pedal several times while moving backwards. Stop the engine.

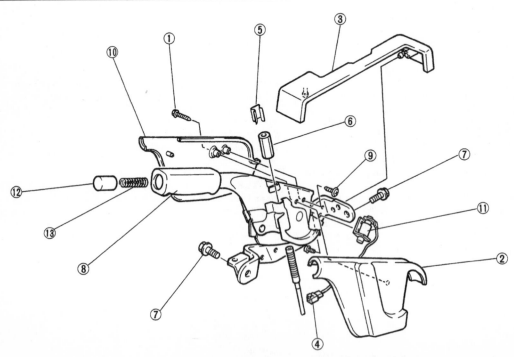

13.3 An exploded view of the parking brake lever

1	Screw	5	Clip	10	Cover
2	Cover	6	Adjusting nut	11	Parking brake switch
3	Cover	7	Bolt	12	Button
4	Parking brake switch connector	8	Parking brake lever	13	Spring
		9	Screw		

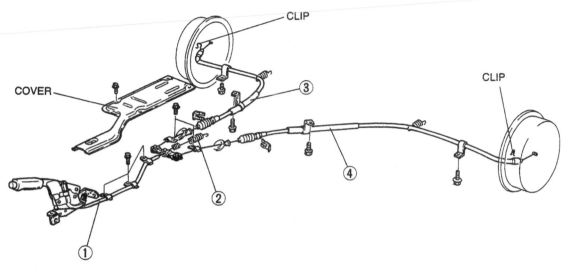

14.5a Routing details of the parking brake cables

1	Front parking brake cable	3	Paring brake cable (left)
2	Spring	4	Parking brake cable (right)

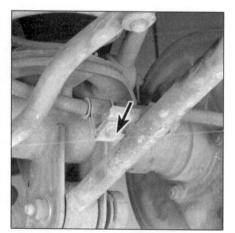

14.5b Detach the parking brake cable bracket (arrow) from the lower suspension arm

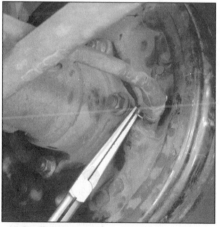

14.5c Remove the retaining clip from the parking brake cable at the backing plate

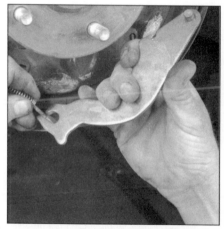

14.5d Remove the brake shoes and disconnect the cable from the parking brake lever

3   Remove the cover retaining screw and the cover from the parking brake lever **(see illustration)**.

4   Remove the adjusting nut clip and turn the adjusting nut at the front of the cable.

5   Turn the ignition switch to On, pull the parking brake lever one notch, verify that the parking brake warning light illuminates and verify that the rear brakes don't drag.

14   Parking brake cables - removal and installation

Refer to illustrations 14.5a, 14.5b, 14.5c, 14.5d and 14.5e

1   Release the parking brake and remove the parking brake lever adjusting nut.

2   Remove the rear seat and floormats (see Chapter 11).

3   Block the wheels firmly, raise the vehicle and place it securely on jackstands.

4   Remove the rear brake shoes and detach the parking brake lever(s) (see Section 5).

9

14.5e Loosen the adjustment nut(s) (arrows) and slip the cable(s) out of the bracket(s)

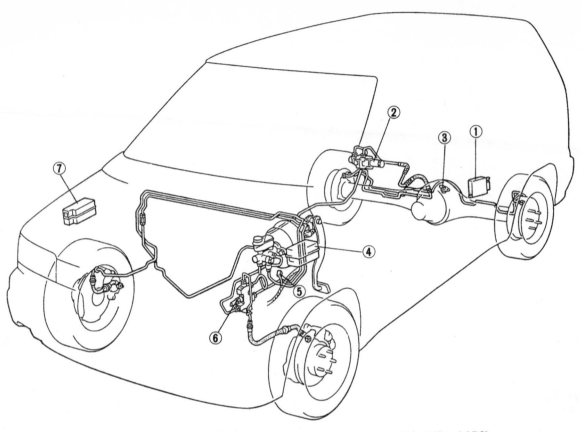

16.1 Schematic of the Rear-Wheel Anti-Lock Brake System (Rear Wheel ABS)

1	Control unit	5	Check connector
2	Hydraulic unit	6	Pressure differential switch
3	Speed sensor	7	ABS fuse
4	ABS relay		

5   Working from underneath the vehicle, disconnect the parking brake cable(s) in the order shown **(see illustrations)**.

6   Working from inside the vehicle, disconnect the cable from the parking brake lever (see Section 13).

7   Installation is the reverse of removal.

8   After installing a new cable, or cables, adjust the parking brake lever stroke (see Section 13), then depress the brake pedal a few times and verify that the rear brakes don't drag while rotating the wheels.

15   Load Sensing Proportioning Valve (LSPV) - general information

The Load Sensing Proportioning Valve (LSPV), which is used only on 1989 models, regulates hydraulic pressure to the rear brakes in accordance with the amount of weight present in the rear of the vehicle. When the load is light, pressure to the rear brakes is decreased to avoid locking up the wheels. When the load is heavy, the valve senses the lower ride height and directs more hydraulic pressure to the rear brakes.

Because of the special tools, test equipment and skills required to diagnose and service the LSPV system, we don't recommend servicing it. If you're experiencing difficulties with the LSPV system, take

the vehicle to a Mazda dealer service department. **Warning:** *Any suspension modifications that alter the distance between the rear axle and the frame will alter the accuracy of the LSPV system, which could lead to inadequate braking force and an accident.*

16   Rear Wheel Anti-Lock Brake System (Rear Wheel ABS) - general information

Refer to illustration 16.1

1   A Rear Wheel Anti-Lock Brake System (Rear Wheel ABS) is used on all 1990 and later models. The system consists of a control unit (computer), hydraulic unit (anti-lock brake valve), a speed sensor on the differential, an ABS relay, a check connector for troubleshooting, a pressure differential switch and an ABS fuse **(see illustration)**.

The ABS control unit prevents rear wheel lockup by sensing the drop in rear wheel speed and modulating hydraulic pressure to the rear brakes accordingly.

Because of the complexity of this system, we don't recommend any attempt to service it at home. If you're experiencing difficulties with the rear wheels locking up during braking, take the vehicle to a Mazda dealer service department or other qualified repair shop.

Chapter 10
Suspension and steering systems

Contents

10

Specifications

General

Power steering fluid type..	See Chapter 1

Torque specifications

Ft-lbs

Front suspension

Strut upper mounting nuts...	22 to 27
Strut-to-steering knuckle bolts/nuts...	69 to 86
Damper rod-to-upper strut mount nut...	47 to 59
Compression rod rear nut..	103 to 127
Compression rod bushing-to-frame bolt..	61 to 76

Torque specifications (continued)

Ft-lbs

Front suspension

Compression rod-to-lower arm bolt	76 to 93
Control arm-to-steering knuckle balljoint stud nut (2WD)	87 to 116
Control arm-to-frame pivot bolt and nut (2WD)	94 to 108
Control arm-to-steering knuckle balljoint stud nut (4WD)	116 to 137
Balljoint-to-control arm through bolt/nut (4WD)	94 to 127
Balljoint-to-control arm bolts (4WD)	75 to 101
Control arm-to-frame pivot bolt and nut (4WD)	
1990	75 to 101
1991 on	102 to 126
Stabilizer bar link bolt and nut	
2WD	Tighten so that 1/2-inch of thread is exposed above nut
4WD	Tighten so that 1/4-inch of thread is exposed above nut
Stabilizer bar bushing and clamp bolt	37 to 45

Rear suspension

Stabilizer bar bushing clamp bolt	23 to 38
Stabilizer bar link bolt	Tighten so that one-quarter inch of thread is exposed above nut
Shock absorber bolt and nut (upper and lower)	56 to 76
Panhard rod upper bolt and nut	94 to 127
Panhard rod lower bolt and nut	108 to 127
Upper suspension arm bolts and nuts	94 to 127
Lower suspension arm bolts and nuts	101 to 127

Steering

Steering wheel nut	29 to 36
Intermediate shaft-to-steering gear pinch bolt	13 to 20
Steering gear clamp bolts	54 to 69
Steering gear mounting bracket-to-subframe bolts	46 to 69
Tie-rod end-to-steering knuckle nut	43 to 58

1.1a The front suspension components on a 2WD model

1	Stabilizer bar	5	Tie-rod end
2	Stabilizer bar bushing and bracket	6	Compression rod
3	Strut assembly	7	Control arm
4	Stabilizer-to-control arm link	8	Rack-and-pinion steering gear

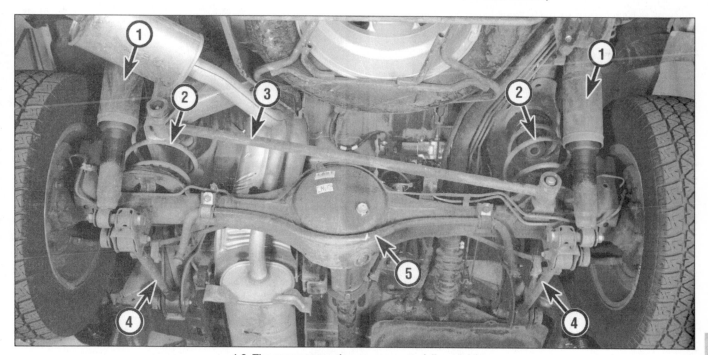

1.1b The front suspension components on a 4WD model

1	Stabilizer bar	4	Control arm
2	Stabilizer bar bushing and bracket	5	Balljoint
3	Tie-rod end	6	Strut assembly

1.2 The rear suspension components (all models)

1	Shock absorber	4	Lower suspension arm (upper suspension arms not visible in this photo)
2	Coil spring		
3	Panhard rod	5	Stabilizer bar

10

1   General information

Refer to illustrations 1.1a, 1.1b and 1.2

The front suspension **(see illustrations)** consists of MacPherson struts, control arms and stabilizer bars. 2WD models use a forged control arm and a compression rod; 4WD models use an A-arm type control arm. The steering knuckles are located by the control arms and the struts. Both front control arms are connected via the stabilizer bar.

The rear suspension **(see illustration)** consists of a live axle located by a Panhard rod and four trailing arms (two upper and two lower arms). The axle is suspended by a pair of shock absorbers and a pair of coil springs. The shocks are bolted between the axle and the body; the coil springs are located between the top of the axle and the body.

2.4 To detach the brake hose from the strut bracket, remove this U-clip

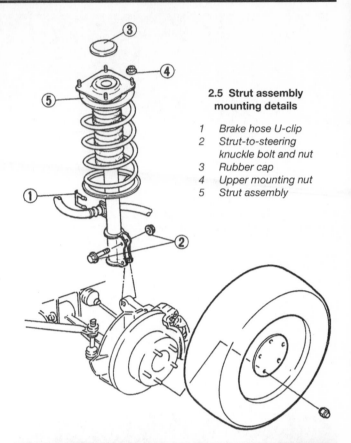

2.5 Strut assembly mounting details

1   Brake hose U-clip
2   Strut-to-steering knuckle bolt and nut
3   Rubber cap
4   Upper mounting nut
5   Strut assembly

The rack-and-pinion steering gear, which is mounted on the crossmember under the engine, actuates the tie-rods, which are attached to the steering knuckles. Power assist is standard and the steering column is designed to collapse in the event of an accident.

Frequently, when working on the suspension or steering system components, you may come across fasteners which seem impossible to loosen. These fasteners on the underside of the vehicle are continually subjected to water, road grime, mud, etc., and can become rusted or frozen, making them extremely difficult to remove. In order to unscrew these stubborn fasteners without damaging them (or other components), be sure to use lots of penetrating oil and allow it to soak in for a while. Using a wire brush to clean exposed threads will also ease removal of the nut or bolt and prevent damage to the threads. Sometimes a sharp blow with a hammer and punch will break the bond between a nut and bolt threads, but care must be taken to prevent the punch from slipping off the fastener and ruining the threads. Heating the stuck fastener and surrounding area with a torch sometimes helps too, but isn't recommended because of the obvious dangers associated with fire. Long breaker bars and extension, or "cheater", pipes will increase leverage, but never use an extension pipe on a ratchet - the ratcheting mechanism could be damaged. Sometimes tightening the nut or bolt first will help to break it loose. Fasteners that require drastic measures to remove should always be replaced with new ones.

Since most of the procedures dealt with in this Chapter involve jacking up the vehicle and working underneath it, a good pair of jackstands will be needed. A hydraulic floor jack is the preferred type of jack to lift the vehicle, and it can also be used to support certain components during various operations. **Warning:** *Never, under any circumstances, rely on a jack to support the vehicle while working on it. Whenever any of the suspension or steering fasteners are loosened or removed they must be inspected and, if necessary, replaced with new ones of the same part number or of original equipment quality and design. Torque specifications must be followed for proper reassembly and component retention. Never attempt to heat or straighten any suspension or steering components. Instead, replace any bent or damaged part with a new one.*

2   Strut assembly - removal and installation

Refer to illustrations 2.4, 2.5, 2.6 and 2.8

Removal

1   Loosen the front wheel lug nuts.
2   Raise the vehicle and support it securely on jackstands.
3   Remove the front wheel.
4   Detach the brake hose from the bracket on the strut **(see illustration)**.

2.6 Remove the strut upper mounting nuts (on this model the ignition coil mounting bracket must also be removed)

5   Remove the strut-to-steering knuckle nuts and bolts **(see illustration)**.
6   Open the hood and remove the four strut upper mounting nuts **(see illustration)**, disengage the strut from the steering knuckle and detach it from the vehicle. **Warning:** *Don't unscrew the large nut in the center of the strut mount.*
7   Inspect the strut and coil spring assembly for leaking fluid, dents, damage and corrosion. If the strut is damaged, see Section 3.

Installation

8   To install the strut, place it in position with the upper mounting studs extending up through the holes in the strut tower. Make sure the white mark on the mounting flange is facing in and toward the front of the vehicle **(see illustration)**. Install the nuts and tighten them to the torque listed in this Chapter's Specifications.

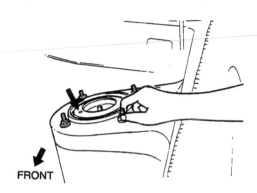

2.8 When installing the strut assembly, make sure the white mark (arrow) on the strut mounting flange is facing forward and toward the inside as shown

3.3a Install the spring compressor according to the tool manufacturer's instructions and compress the spring until all pressure is relieved from the upper seat

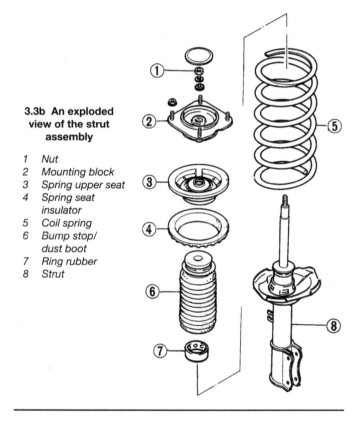

3.3b An exploded view of the strut assembly

1 Nut
2 Mounting block
3 Spring upper seat
4 Spring seat insulator
5 Coil spring
6 Bump stop/ dust boot
7 Ring rubber
8 Strut

3.4 Remove the damper shaft nut - to prevent the mounting block from turning, brace a screwdriver or prybar across two of the mounting studs

9   Attach the strut to the steering knuckle, then insert the strut-to-steering knuckle bolts and nuts. Tighten the nuts to the torque listed in this Chapter's Specifications.
10   Attach the brake hose to the strut bracket and install the clip.
11   Install the wheels and lower the vehicle. Tighten the lug nuts to the torque listed in the Chapter 1 Specifications.

3   Strut - replacement

Refer to illustrations 3.3a, 3.3b, 3.4, 3.5a, 3.5b, 3.5c, 3.7, 3.10 and 3.11

Warning: *Disassembling a strut is a potentially dangerous job - pay close attention to what you're doing or you could get hurt! Use only a high quality spring compressor and carefully follow the manufacturer's instructions furnished with the tool. After removing the coil spring from the strut assembly, set it aside in a safe, isolated area (a steel cabinet is preferred).*

Note 1: *If the struts or coil springs exhibit the telltale signs of wear (leaking fluid, loss of damping capability, chipped, sagging or cracked coil springs), explore all options before beginning any work. The strut assemblies are not serviceable and must be replaced if a problem develops. However, strut assemblies complete with springs may be available on an exchange basis, which eliminates much time and work. Whichever route you choose to take, check on the cost and availability of parts before disassembling anything.*
Note 2: *You'll need a spring compressor for this procedure. Spring compressors are available on a daily rental basis at most auto parts stores or equipment yards.*
1   Remove the strut(s) (see Section 2).
2   Mount the strut assembly in a vise. Line the vise jaws with wood or rags to prevent damage to the unit and don't tighten the vise excessively.
3   Following the tool manufacturer's instructions, install the spring compressor (which can be obtained at most auto parts stores or equipment yards on a daily rental basis) on the spring and compress it sufficiently to relieve all pressure from the upper seat **(see illustrations)**. This can be verified by wiggling the spring.
4   Loosen the damper shaft nut with a socket wrench **(see illustration)**. To prevent the mounting block and damper shaft from turning, wedge a prybar between two of the mounting studs.

10

3.5a Remove the mounting block . . .

3.5b . . .followed by the spring upper seat

3.5c The bearing in the mounting block should turn smoothly - if it doesn't, replace the mounting block

3.7 Slide the bump stop/dust boot off the damper shaft

5   Remove the nut, mounting block and upper seat **(see illustrations)**. Inspect the bearing in the mounting block for smooth operation **(see illustration)**. If it doesn't turn smoothly, replace the mounting block. Check the rubber portion of the mounting block for cracking, separation from the block and general deterioration. If any of these conditions are present, replace the mounting block.

6   Check the insulator in the upper seat for cracking and hardness, replacing it if necessary.

7   Slide the bump stop/dust boot off the damper shaft **(see illustration)**. Also remove the ring rubber.

8   Carefully lift the compressed spring from the assembly and set it in a safe place, such as a steel cabinet. **Warning:** *Keep the ends of the spring facing away from your body!*

9   To begin assembly, install the ring rubber and bump stop/dust boot - extend the damper rod as far as it will go and slide the boot and bumper down to the strut body. Make sure the dust boot properly engages with the ring rubber.

10   Carefully place the coil spring onto the lower seat, with the end of the spring resting in the lowest part of the seat **(see illustration)**.

11   Install the rubber insulator into the upper spring seat. Install the upper seat and mounting block, making sure the flat in the D-shaped hole in the mounting block matches up with the flat on the damper shaft and the "out" mark on the mounting block faces the same direction as the flanges for the strut-to-knuckle bolt holes **(see illustration)**.

12   Install the damper shaft nut and tighten it to the torque listed in this Chapter's Specifications. Use the technique described in Step 4 to prevent the shaft from turning.

13   Install the strut(s) (see Section 2).

3.10 When installing the spring, make sure the end of the lower coil seats in the recessed portion of the lower seat

---

4   Stabilizer bar (front) - removal and installation

Removal

Refer to illustrations 4.2, 4.3 and 4.4

1   Loosen the lug nuts on both front wheels, raise the vehicle and support it securely on jackstands. Remove the front wheels.

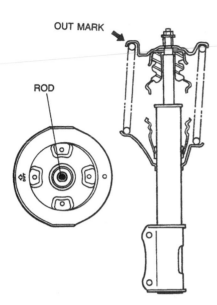

OUT MARK

ROD

3.11 When you install the upper seat and mounting block, making sure the flat in the D-shaped hole in the mounting block matches up with the flat on the damper shaft and the "out" mark on the mounting block faces the same direction as the flanges for the strut-to-steering knuckle bolt holes

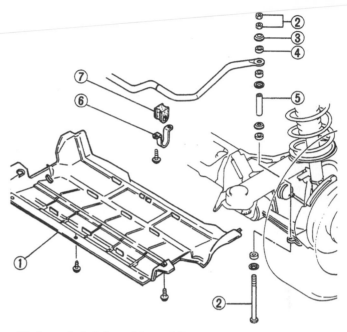

4.2 An exploded view of the stabilizer bar assembly (2WD model shown, 4WD models similar)

1	Engine undercover	6	Stabilizer bar
2	Nuts and link bolt		bushing bracket
3	Retainer	7	Stabilizer bar bushing
4	Rubber bushing	8	Stabilizer bar
5	Spacer		

4.3 Stabilizer bar -to-control arm link nuts, retainer, bushing, spacer and bolt (2WD model shown, 4WD models similar)

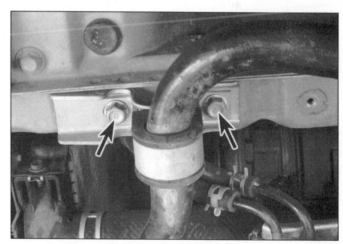

4.4 Stabilizer bar bushing bracket bolts (arrows) (2WD model shown, 4WD models similar, except brackets are mounted on the front of the frame and face forward)

2   Remove the engine undercover **(see illustration)**.
3   Remove the nuts from the stabilizer bar-to-control arm link bolts **(see illustration)** and pull off the retainers, rubber bushings, spacers and link bolts. Be sure to note the order in which these parts are removed so that you don't get them mixed up during reassembly.
4   Remove the bolts from the stabilizer bar bushing brackets **(see illustration)**.
5   Remove the stabilizer bar, clamps and bushings.
6   Inspect the bushings for wear and damage and replace them if necessary. To remove them, pry the bushing clamp off with a screwdriver and pull the bushings off the bar. To ease installation, spray the inside and outside of the bushings with a silicone-based lubricant. Do not use petroleum-based lubricants on any rubber suspension part!

Installation

7   Assemble the bushings and brackets on the stabilizer bar. Place the bar in position and install the bracket bolts and the link bolts.

Tighten the link bolts securely but don't tighten the bracket bolts completely yet.
8   Install the wheels and lower the vehicle. Tighten the lug nuts to the torque listed in the Chapter 1 Specifications.
9   Tighten the bushing bracket bolts to the torque listed in this Chapter's Specifications.

10

---

5   **Compression rod (2WD models) - removal and installation**

Refer to illustrations 5.2a, 5.22b and 5.4

1   Loosen the wheel lug nuts, raise the front of the vehicle and support it securely on jackstands. Apply the parking brake and block the

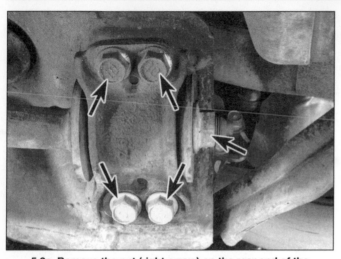

5.2a Remove the nut (right arrow) on the rear end of the compression rod - don't remove the bushing bracket bolts (arrows) until you've disconnected the stabilizer bar link and the compression rod-to-control arm bolts

rear wheels to keep the vehicle from rolling off the jackstands. Remove the wheels.

2 Remove the nut from the rear end of the compression rod **(see illustrations)**.

3 Disconnect the stabilizer bar from the compression rod (see Section 4). Be sure to note the order in which the nuts, retainer, bushing and spacer are arranged on the link bolt to ensure correct reassembly.

4 Remove the compression rod-to-control arm bolts **(see illustration)**.

5 Remove the compression rod bushing bracket bolts and remove the rod.

6 Inspect the rubber bushing for cracking, deterioration and leakage. If it's worn or damaged, replace it.

7 Installation is the reverse of removal.

---

6 Control arm (2WD models) - removal and installation

Removal

Refer to illustration 6.4a, 6.4b and 6.5

1 Loosen the wheel lug nuts, raise the front of the vehicle and support it securely on jackstands. Apply the parking brake and block the

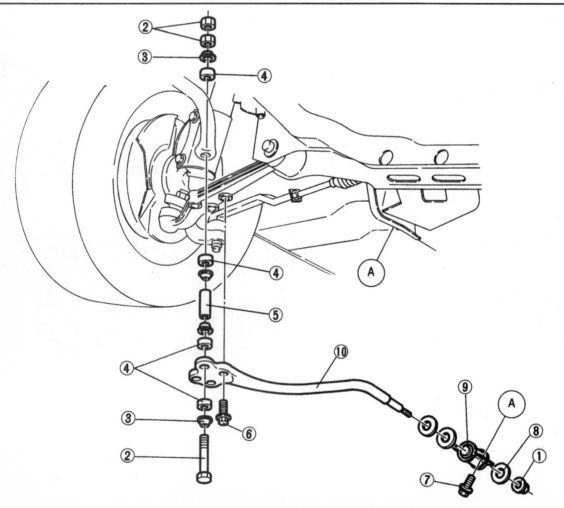

5.2b An exploded view of the compression rod assembly

1	Compression rod rear nut	6	Compression rod-to-control arm bolt
2	Stabilizer bar link bolt and nuts	7	Compression rod bushing bracket bolt
3	Retainers	8	Washer
4	Rubber bushings	9	Fluid-enclosed rubber bushing
5	Spacer	10	Compression rod

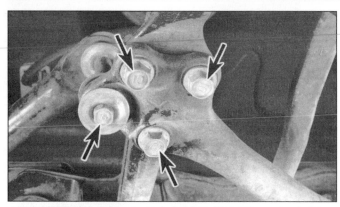

5.4 To disconnect the compression rod from the control arm, remove the stabilizer bar link bolt (arrow) and the three compression rod-to-lower arm bolts (arrows)

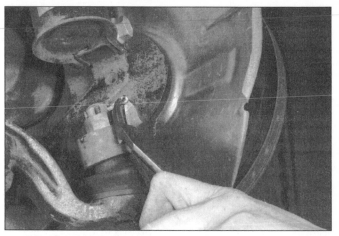

6.4a Remove the cotter pin from the castellated nut, then unscrew the nut

6.4b Rap the knuckle sharply with a hammer right next to the balljoint stud until the stud pops loose

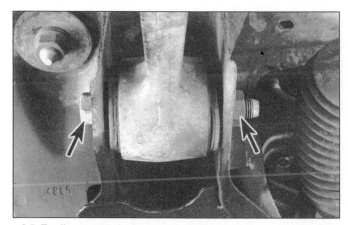

6.5 To disconnect the inner end of the control arm, remove the nut and pivot bolt (arrows)

rear wheels to keep the vehicle from rolling off the jackstands. Remove the wheel.

2   If only one control arm is being removed, disconnect only that end of the stabilizer bar. If both control arms are being removed, disconnect both ends (see Section 4).

3   Remove the compression rod (see Section 5).

4   Remove the balljoint stud-to-steering knuckle nut **(see illustration)**, then pop the balljoint stud loose from the knuckle by striking the knuckle sharply with a hammer **(see illustration)**.

5   Remove the control arm pivot bolt and detach the control arm **(see illustration)**.

6   The control arm bushings are replaceable, but special tools and expertise are necessary to do the job. Carefully inspect the bushings for hardening, excessive wear and cracks. If they appear to be worn or deteriorated, take the control arm to a dealer service department or other repair shop to have new bushings installed.

7   Installation is the reverse of removal.

8   Drive the vehicle to a dealer service department or an alignment shop to have the front wheel alignment checked and, if necessary, adjusted.

---

7   Control arm (4WD models) - removal and installation

Refer to illustrations 7.3a, 7.3b, 7.5a and 7.5b

1   Loosen the wheel lug nuts, raise the front of the vehicle and support it securely on jackstands. Apply the parking brake and block the rear wheels to keep the vehicle from rolling off the jackstands. Remove the wheel.

10

7.3a To disconnect the control arm from the balljoint, remove this control arm-to-balljoint through-bolt (lower arrow) and the two bolts and washers on top of the control arm (upper arrows)

2   If only one control arm is being removed, disconnect only that end of the stabilizer bar. If both control arms are being removed, disconnect both ends (see Section 4).

3   Remove the control arm-to-balljoint nut, washer and bolt from the control arm **(see illustrations)**.

4   Remove the other two control arm-to-balljoint bolts and washers.

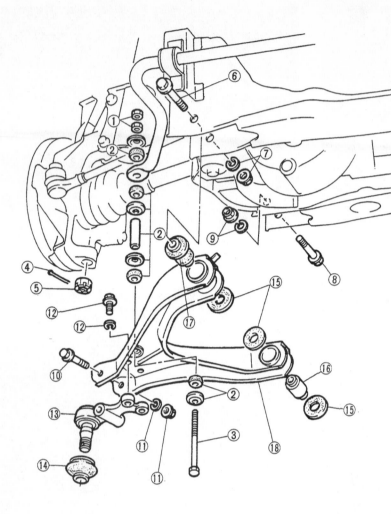

7.3b An exploded view of the control arm and balljoint assemblies (4WD models)

1	Stabilizer link nuts
2	Stabilizer link retainer, bushing and spacer
3	Stabilizer link bolt
4	Cotter pin
5	Balljoint nut
6	Control arm front pivot bolt
7	Pivot bolt nut and washer
8	Control arm rear pivot bolt
9	Pivot bolt nut and washer
10	Control arm-to-balljoint through-bolt
11	Through-bolt nut and washer
12	Control arm-to-balljoint upper bolt and washer
13	Balljoint
14	Balljoint dust boot
15	Pivot bolt rubber washers
16	Rear pivot bushing
17	Front pivot bushing
18	Control arm

5   Remove the control arm inner pivot bolts, nuts and washers **(see illustrations)**.
6   Remove the control arm.
7   Installation is the reverse of removal).

---

8   Balljoint - check and replacement

Check

Refer to illustration 8.3

1   Raise the front of the vehicle and support it securely on jackstands. Apply the parking brake and block the rear wheels to keep the vehicle from rolling off the jackstands.
2   Visually inspect the balljoint seal for damage and deterioration. If these conditions are noticed, the balljoint should be replaced.
3   Place a large prybar between the control arm and the steering knuckle and try to lever the steering knuckle up and down **(see illustration)**. If any play is evident, replace the balljoint.

Replacement

4   Loosen the wheel lug nuts, raise the front of the vehicle and support it securely on jackstands. Apply the parking brake and block the rear wheels to keep the vehicle from rolling off the jackstands. Remove the wheel.

2WD models

5   The balljoint is an integral part of the control arm on these models; you'll have to replace the control arm (see Section 6).

7.5a Remove the front inner pivot bolt (arrow), nut and washer from the control arm . . .

4WD models

Refer to illustration 8.7

6   Disconnect the stabilizer bar link from the control arm (see Section 4).
7   Remove the cotter pin **(see illustration)** from the balljoint stud nut and remove the nut.
8   Use a puller to separate the balljoint stud from the steering knuckle.

7.5b . . .remove the rear inner pivot bolt (arrow), nut and washer from the control arm and remove the control arm

8.7 On 4WD models, remove the cotter pin from the balljoint stud nut and remove the nut, then separate the balljoint stud from the steering knuckle with a puller

9.4b . . . then unstake the spindle nut and remove the nut

9   Pull the control arm and balljoint down to remove the balljoint stud from the steering knuckle, then unbolt the balljoint from the control arm.
10   Position the new balljoint on the control arm and install the bolts. Tighten the bolts to the torque listed in this Chapter's Specifications.
11   Insert the balljoint into the steering knuckle, install the nut, tighten it to the torque listed in this Chapter's Specifications and install a new

8.3 To check a balljoint for wear, insert a prybar between the control arm and the steering knuckle and try to lever the steering knuckle up and down - if there's any play evident, replace the balljoint (procedure shown on 2WD model, procedure for 4WD models similar)

9.4a To remove the hub from the steering knuckle on 2WD models, remove the grease cover . . .

cotter pin. It may be necessary to tighten the nut some to align the cotter pin hole with an opening in the nut, which is acceptable. Never loosen the nut to allow cotter pin insertion.
12   Reattach the stabilizer bar-to-control arm link (see Section 4).

All models

13   Install the wheel, lower the vehicle and tighten the lug nuts to the torque listed in the Chapter 1 Specifications. It's a good idea to take the vehicle to a dealer service department or alignment shop to have the front end alignment checked and, if necessary, adjusted.

10

9   **Steering knuckle and hub (2WD models) - removal and installation**

Refer to illustration 9.4a, 9.4b and 9.4c

Removal

1   Loosen the wheel lug nuts, raise the vehicle and support it securely on jackstands. Remove the wheel.
2   Remove the brake caliper and support it with a piece of wire as described in Chapter 9. Also remove the caliper mounting bracket.
3   Remove the brake disc (see Chapter 9).

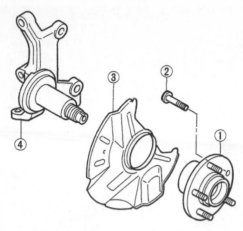

9.4c An exploded view of the steering knuckle and hub assembly

1	*Hub assembly*	3	*Dust shield*
2	*Wheel stud*	4	*Steering knuckle*

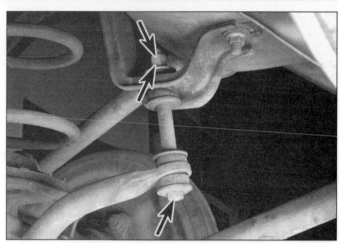

11.2a To disconnect the stabilizer bar from the body, remove these nuts (arrows), note the order in which the various retainers, bushings and spacers are installed and pull out the link bolt (left link assembly shown, right side identical)

4   If you're only replacing the hub assembly, remove the spindle nut grease cover, unstake the spindle nut and remove the nut **(see illustrations)**, discard the old hub and install a new unit (the hub isn't re-buildable). If one or more of the wheel studs must be replaced, they can usually be pressed out and back in again with a C-clamp and two sockets, but if they are stubborn, a hydraulic press will be required. Installation is the reverse of removal. If you're removing the entire steering knuckle, proceed to the next step.

5   Disconnect the tie-rod end from the steering knuckle arm (see Section 18).

6   Separate the control arm from the steering knuckle (see Section 6).

7   Remove the strut-to-knuckle nuts and bolts and pull the top of the knuckle out of the strut flange **(see illustration 2.5)**.

Installation

8   Position the top of the steering knuckle between the strut flanges and install the strut-to-knuckle bolts and nuts (but don't tighten them completely yet).

9   Reattach the control arm to the steering knuckle (see Section 6).

10   Reattach the tie-rod end to the steering knuckle (see Section 18).

11   Tighten the strut-to-knuckle bolts to the torque listed in this Chapter's Specifications.

12   Install the hub with a new nut, if removed. Although the spindle on this design isn't a bearing surface, a little grease will make it easier to press the inner race of the hub bearing onto the spindle.

13   Install the brake disc, caliper mount and caliper assembly (see Chapter 9).

14   Tighten the hub nut to the torque listed in the Chapter 8 Specifications.

15   Install the wheel and hand tighten the wheel lug nuts. Lower the vehicle and tighten the lug nuts to the torque listed in the Chapter 1 Specifications.

---

10   Steering knuckle and hub (4WD models) - removal and installation

Removal

1   Loosen the wheel lug nuts, raise the front of the vehicle and support it securely on jackstands. Apply the parking brake and block the rear wheels to keep the vehicle from rolling off the jackstands. Remove the wheel.

2   Remove the hub nut (see Chapter 8).

3   Remove the caliper and suspend it out of the way with a piece of wire, then remove the caliper bracket and brake disc (see Chapter 9).

4   Remove the strut-to-knuckle nuts and bolts (see Section 2). Don't drive out the bolts at this time.

5   Separate the control arm balljoint from the steering knuckle (see Section 8).

6   Push the driveaxle out of the hub (see Chapter 8). Hang the driveaxle with a piece of wire to prevent damage to the inner CV joint.

7   Support the knuckle and drive out the two strut-to-knuckle bolts with a soft-face hammer. Remove the steering knuckle assembly from the strut.

8   If the hub and/or hub bearing needs to be replaced, take the hub/knuckle assembly to a dealer service department or other repair shop. The hub and bearing assembly must be pressed out of the knuckle with special tools.

Installation

9   Position the knuckle in the strut and insert the two bolts and nuts, but don't tighten them at this time.

10   Install the driveaxle in the hub.

11   Connect the control arm to the steering knuckle (see Section 7).

12   Tighten the strut-to-knuckle nuts to the torque listed in this Chapter's Specifications.

13   Install the brake disc, caliper mount and caliper (see Chapter 9).

14   Tighten the hub nut to the torque listed in the Chapter 8 Specifications.

15   Install the wheel, lower the vehicle and tighten the lug nuts to the torque listed in the Chapter 1 Specifications.

---

11   Stabilizer bar (rear) - removal and installation

Refer to illustrations 11.2a, 11.2b and 11.3

1   Raise the rear of the vehicle and place it securely on jackstands.

2   Remove the nuts, bolts, retainers, rubber bushings and spacers at each end of the stabilizer bar **(see illustrations)**.

3   Remove the bolts from the stabilizer bar brackets **(see illustration)** and remove the stabilizer bar.

4   Inspect all of the rubber bushings. If they're cracked or deteriorated, replace them. Inspect the retainers (the big washers) used on the link bolts. If they're bent or damaged, replace them.

5   Installation is the reverse of removal. Be sure to install the various retainers, bushings and spacers in the correct order and tighten all fasteners securely.

---

12   Panhard rod - removal and installation

Refer to illustrations 12.3a, 12.3b and 12.4

1   Raise the rear of the vehicle and place it securely on jackstands.

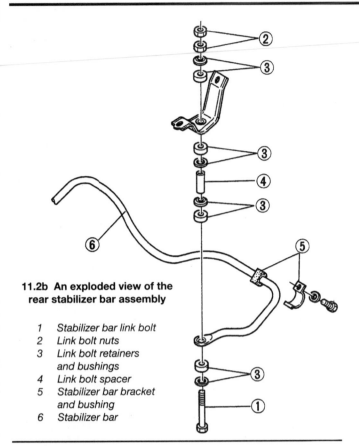

11.2b An exploded view of the rear stabilizer bar assembly

1   Stabilizer bar link bolt
2   Link bolt nuts
3   Link bolt retainers and bushings
4   Link bolt spacer
5   Stabilizer bar bracket and bushing
6   Stabilizer bar

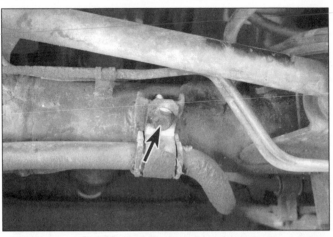

11.3 To disconnect the stabilizer bar from the rear axle, remove each bracket bolt (arrow) (right side shown, left side identical)

12.3a Remove the Panhard rod nut and bolt (arrow) from the body bracket

2   Place a floor jack under the differential and raise the axle to simulate normal ride height.

3   Remove the Panhard rod to body bolt **(see illustrations)**.

4   Remove the Panhard rod to axle housing nut **(see illustration)**.

5   Inspect the rubber bushings. If they're dried or cracked, have them pressed out and replaced by a dealer service department, an automotive machine shop or the repair shop.

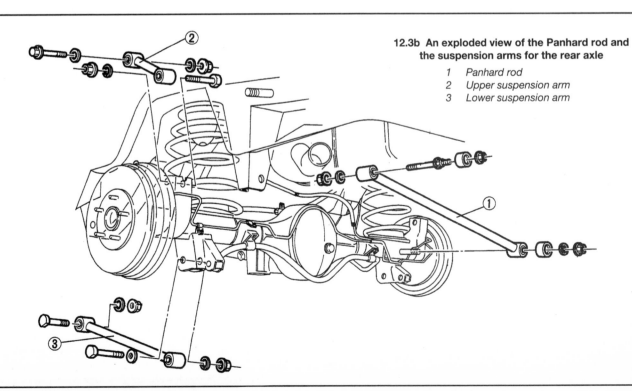

12.3b An exploded view of the Panhard rod and the suspension arms for the rear axle

1   Panhard rod
2   Upper suspension arm
3   Lower suspension arm

10

12.4 Remove the Panhard rod nut (arrow) from the axle housing bracket

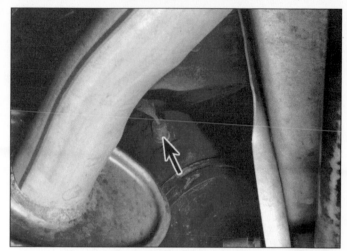

13.3 On models equipped with the Automatic Load Leveling (ALL) system, remove this air line fitting (arrow) from each shock

13.4 To disconnect the upper end of the shock from the body, remove this nut (arrow) from the upper shock mounting stud

13.5 To disconnect the lower end of the shock from the axle housing, remove this nut (arrow) and bolt from the lower shock mounting bracket on the axle

6   Installation is the reverse of removal. Be sure to tighten the bolts and nuts to the torque listed in this Chapter's Specifications.

---

13   Shock absorbers - removal, inspection and installation

Refer to illustrations 13.3, 13.4 and 13.5

Removal

1   Raise the rear of the vehicle and place it securely on jackstands.
2   Place a floor jack under the differential housing to support the axle assembly and raise the axle slightly to remove the load from the upper and lower shock absorber bolts.
3   On models equipped with Automatic Load Leveling (ALL), disconnect the air line fitting from the shock absorber **(see illustration)**.
4   Unbolt the shock-to-axle bolt and nut **(see illustration)**.
5   Unbolt the shock-to-body nut **(see illustration)**.
6   Remove the shock absorber.

Inspection

7   Holding each shock upright, grasp it at each end and pump it in and out several times. The action should be smooth, with no binding or dead spots. Check for fluid leakage. Replace a shock if it's leaking, or if the pumping action is rough. Always replace shocks in pairs.

Installation

8   Hold each shock in position and install the bolts. **Note:** *Raise or lower the jack as necessary to align the lower bolt holes.* After the upper and lower mounting bolts have been installed, raise the jack to simulate normal ride height and tighten the nuts securely.
9   If the vehicle has ALL, reattach the air line fittings and tighten them securely. After a brief test drive, check for air leaks with a soapy water solution.

---

14   Coil springs (rear) - removal and installation

Removal

1   Loosen the rear wheel lug nuts, raise the rear of the vehicle and support it securely on jackstands. Remove the wheels.
2   Support the axle housing with a floor jack under the differential. On models equipped with Automatic Load Leveling (ALL), disconnect the air line fitting from the shock absorbers **(see illustration 13.3)**.
3   Detach the lower end of the Panhard rod from the axle housing (see Section 12).
4   Detach the lower ends of the shock absorbers from the axle (see Section 13).
5   Secure the coil springs to the axle with chains to prevent them from flying off as the axle is lowered (make sure there is enough slack in the chain to allow the coil springs to extend fully). Carefully lower the

15.4 Remove the upper arm rear pivot bolt and nut (arrow) from the axle bracket - when you reattach the rear end of the upper suspension arm, make sure the flat side of the nut is facing toward the rear as shown

15.5 Remove the upper suspension arm front pivot bolt (arrow), washer and nut and remove the suspension arm from the vehicle

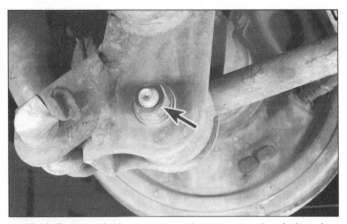

15.10 Remove the lower suspension arm rear pivot bolt and nut (arrow)

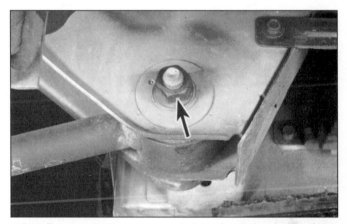

15.11 Remove the lower suspension arm front pivot bolt and nut (arrow) and remove the lower suspension arm from the vehicle

jack, supporting the axle until all compression is relieved and remove the coil springs.

Inspection

6   Inspect the bump stoppers and spring seats at the upper and lower ends of each coil spring. If a bump stopper is cracked or distorted, replace it.
7   Check the springs for breakage, nicks and cracks. Replace a spring if you notice any of these conditions.

Installation

8   To install the coil springs, make sure they're seated properly (the ends with the larger diameter coils must face down),loop the safety chains through the springs then carefully raise the axle back into position with the jack.
9   The remainder of installation is the reverse of removal.

---

15   Suspension arms (rear) - removal and installation

---

1   Raise the rear of the vehicle and support it securely on jackstands placed beneath the frame rails. Block the front wheels.
2   Position a floor jack under the differential and raise it slightly.
3   Secure the coil springs to the axle housing with chains to prevent them from flying off their seats in the event of a jack failure.

Upper arm
Refer to illustrations 15.4 and 15.5

Removal

4   Remove the upper arm-to-rear axle pivot bolt and nut **(see illus-**

tration).
5   Remove the upper arm-to-frame bracket pivot bolt and nut **(see illustration)** and remove the upper arm from the vehicle.
6   Inspect the bushing in each end of the arm. If either one is cracked or deteriorated, replace the upper arm assembly.

Installation

Note: *Refer to illustration 12.3b for proper assembly of upper suspension arm bolts, washers and nuts.*
7   Position the forward end of the suspension arm in the frame bracket. Install a new pivot bolt and nut with the nut on the inner side of the frame bracket, but don't fully tighten the nut at this time.
8   Place the other end of the arm into its mounting bracket on the axle housing. It may be necessary to jack up the rear axle to align the holes. Install a new pivot bolt and nut with the nut on the outer side of the bracket. Make sure the flat side of the nut faces toward the rear as shown in illustration 15.4. Don't tighten the bolt yet.
9   Raise the axle to simulate normal ride height and tighten the fasteners to the torque listed in this Chapter's Specifications.

Lower arm
Refer to illustrations 15.10 and 15.11

Removal

10   Remove the lower arm-to-axle bracket pivot bolt and nut **(see illustration)**.
11   Remove the lower arm-to-frame bracket pivot bolt and nut **(see illustration)**, then remove the arm from the vehicle.
12   Inspect the rubber insulators bonded to the washers. If either insulator is dried, cracked or deteriorated, replace it. Inspect the bush-

10

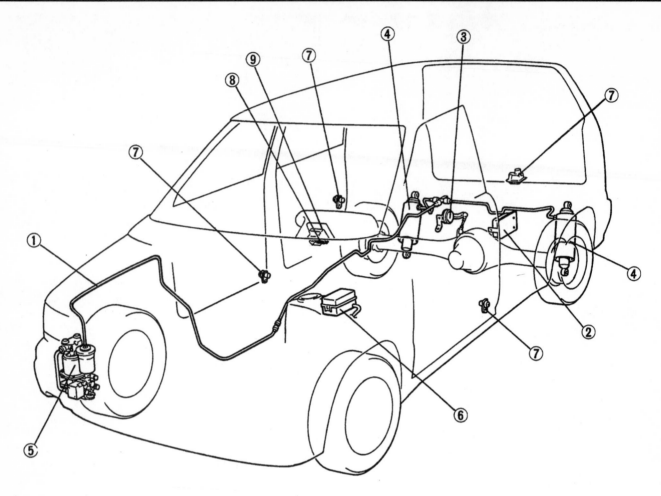

16.1 Automatic Load Leveling (ALL) system used on models equipped with the towing package

1	Air lines	6	Compressor relay
2	Control unit	7	Door switch
3	Height sensor	8	Speed sensor
4	Rear shock absorber	9	ALL indicator
5	Compressor assembly		

ing in each end of the arm. If either one is cracked, dried out or deteriorated, replace the lower arm assembly.

Installation

Note: *Refer to illustration 12.3b for proper assembly of lower suspension arm bolts, washers and nuts.*

13   Position the lower arm in the frame mounting bracket and install a new pivot bolt, washer and nut, with the nut facing in. Don't tighten the nut completely at this time.

14   Position the trailing end of the lower suspension arm into the rear axle bracket and install a new pivot bolt, washer and nut with the nut facing in.

15   Raise the axle to simulate normal ride height, then tighten the pivot bolt nuts to the torque listed in this Chapter's Specifications.

16   Automatic Load Leveling (ALL) system - general information

Refer to illustration 16.1

1   The Automatic Load Leveling (ALL) system **(see illustration)** is used on all models equipped with the towing package. The ALL system detects changes in ride height at the rear of the vehicle caused by load changes and automatically adjusts the rear vehicle height accordingly to maintain the correct front-to-rear attitude of the vehicle.

2   Because of the complexity of this system, any service should be handled by a dealer service department or other repair shop.

17   Steering system - general information

Refer to illustration 17.1

Warning: *Whenever any of the steering fasteners are removed, they must be inspected and, if necessary, replaced with new ones of the same part number or of original equipment quality and design. Torque specifications must be followed for proper reassembly and component retention. Never attempt to heat or straighten any suspension or steering components. Instead, replace any bent or damaged part with a new one.*

All vehicles covered by this manual have power rack-and-pinion steering systems **(see illustration)**. The components making up the system are the steering wheel, steering column, rack-and-pinion steering gear, tie-rods and tie-rod ends. The power steering system has a belt-driven pump to provide hydraulic pressure.

In the power steering system, the motion of turning the steering wheel is transferred through the column to the pinion shaft in the rack-and-pinion assembly. Teeth on the pinion shaft are meshed with teeth on the rack, so when the shaft is turned, the rack is moved left or right in the housing. A rotary control valve in the rack-and-pinion unit di-

17.1 The power steering system

1   *Steering gear boot*
2   *Steering column*
3   *Steering gear*
4   *Power steering pump*
5   *Drivebelt*

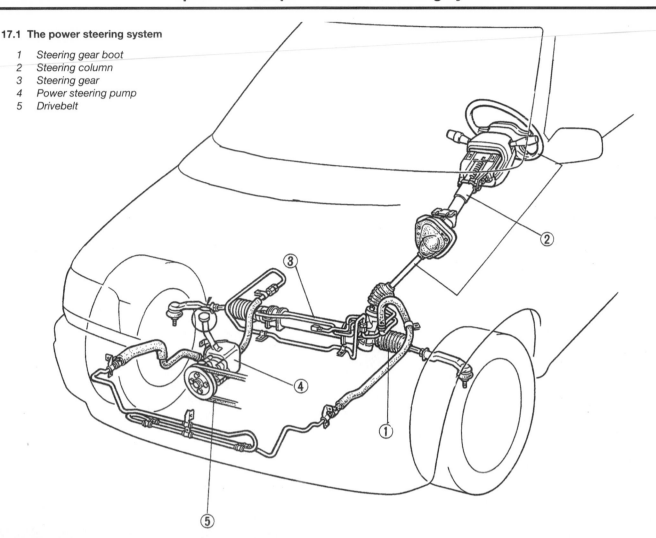

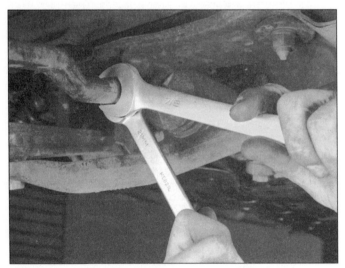

18.2 Back off the tie-rod end jam nut

rects hydraulic fluid under pressure from the power steering pump to either side of the integral rack piston, thereby reducing the required steering force. Depending on which side of the piston this hydraulic pressure is applied to, the rack will be forced either left or right, which moves the tie-rods, etc. If the power steering system loses hydraulic pressure it will still function manually, though with increased effort.

The steering column is a collapsible, energy-absorbing type, designed to compress in the event of a front end collision to minimize injury to the driver. The column also houses the ignition switch lock, key warning buzzer, turn signal controls, headlight dimmer control and windshield wiper controls. The ignition and steering wheel can both be locked while the vehicle is parked.

Because disassembly of the steering column is more often performed to repair a switch or other electrical part than to correct a problem in the steering, the upper steering column disassembly and reassembly procedure is included in Chapter 12.

18   Tie-rod ends - removal and installation

Refer to illustrations 18.2, 18.3 and 18.4

Removal

1   Loosen the wheel lug nuts, raise the front of the vehicle and support it securely on jackstands. Apply the parking brake and block the rear wheels to keep the vehicle from rolling off the jackstands. Remove the wheel.
2   Loosen the tie-rod end jam nut **(see illustration)**.
3   Mark the relationship of the tie-rod end to the threaded portion of the tie-rod **(see illustration)**. This will ensure the toe-in setting is restored when reassembled.
4   Remove the cotter pin and loosen the castellated nut on the tie-rod end balljoint stud, then disconnect the tie-rod end from the steering knuckle arm with a puller **(see illustration)**. Remove the nut and detach the tie-rod end from the steering knuckle.

10

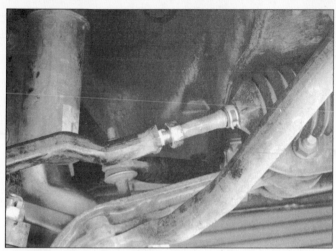

18.3 Mark the relationship of the tie-rod end to the threaded portion of the tie-rod - this will ensure the toe-in setting is restored when reassembled.

18.4 Separate the tie-rod end from the steering knuckle with a puller (note that the nut has been loosened, but not removed - this will prevent the components from separating violently)

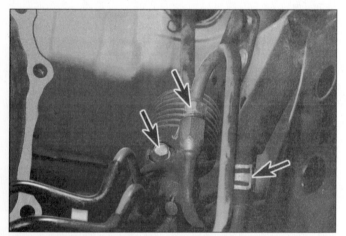

20.3 Disconnect the power steering line fittings (right arrows) and remove the steering coupler pinch bolt (left arrow) - this photo was taken from the engine compartment (with the engine removed) for illustrative purposes, but access to these components is actually gained from under the vehicle (2WD model shown)

5   Unscrew the tie-rod end from the tie-rod.
6   While the tie-rod end is removed, inspect the steering gear dust boot. If it's torn or deteriorated, replace it (see Section 19).

Installation

7   Thread the tie-rod end onto the tie-rod to the marked position and connect the tie-rod end to the steering arm. Install the castellated nut and tighten it to the torque listed in this Chapter's Specifications. Install a new cotter pin.
8   Tighten the jam nut securely and install the wheel. Lower the vehicle and tighten the lug nuts to the torque listed in the Chapter 1 Specifications.
9   Have the front end alignment checked by a dealer service department or an alignment shop.

19   Steering gear boots - replacement

1   Loosen the wheel lug nuts, raise the vehicle and place it securely on jackstands. Remove the wheels.
2   Remove the tie-rod end from the steering gear (see Section 18).
3   Remove the jam nut (see Section 18) and outer boot clamp.

4   Cut off the boot inner retaining ring and discard it.
5   Remove the boot.
6   Slide a new retaining ring onto the inner end of the new boot and install the boot onto the end of the steering gear.
7   Make sure the boot isn't twisted, then tighten the retaining ring.
8   Install the outer clamp and tighten it.
9   Install the tie-rod end jam nut and the tie-rod end (see Section 18).

20   Steering gear - removal and installation

Removal

Refer to illustration 20.3

1   Loosen the front wheel lug nuts, raise the front of the vehicle and support it securely on jackstands. Apply the parking brake and block the rear wheels to keep the vehicle from rolling off the jackstands. Remove both front wheels.
2   Separate the tie-rod ends from the steering arms (see Section 18).
3   Place a drain pan or tray under the vehicle, positioned beneath the steering gear. Using a flare-nut wrench, disconnect the pressure and return lines from the steering gear **(see accompanying illustration and illustrations 20.5c and 20.10)**. Plug the lines to prevent excessive fluid loss.

2WD models

Refer to illustrations 20.5a, 20.5b and 20.5c

4   Mark the relationship of the steering shaft to the pinion shaft on the steering gear, then remove the coupler pinch bolt **(see illustration 20.3)**.
5   Support the steering gear and remove the steering gear mounting bolts **(see illustrations)**.
6   Carefully lower the steering gear and mounting bracket assembly. After lowering the steering gear assembly from the vehicle, remove the steering gear clamp bolts and clamps and separate the steering gear from the mounting brackets.

4WD models

Refer to illustrations 20.7 and 20.10

7   Remove the intermediate shaft-to-steering gear pinion shaft pinch bolt and the steering column mounting bolts **(see accompanying illustration and illustration 20.3)**. Pull the steering column/intermediate shaft assembly back to detach the coupler from the steering gear.

20.5a To detach the steering gear assembly from the subframe, remove these four bolts (arrows) from the front of the subframe. . .

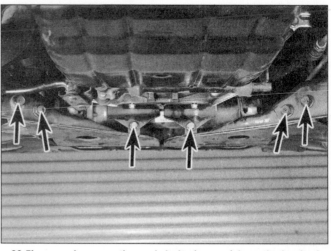

20.5b . . .and remove these six bolts (arrows) from the back of the subframe

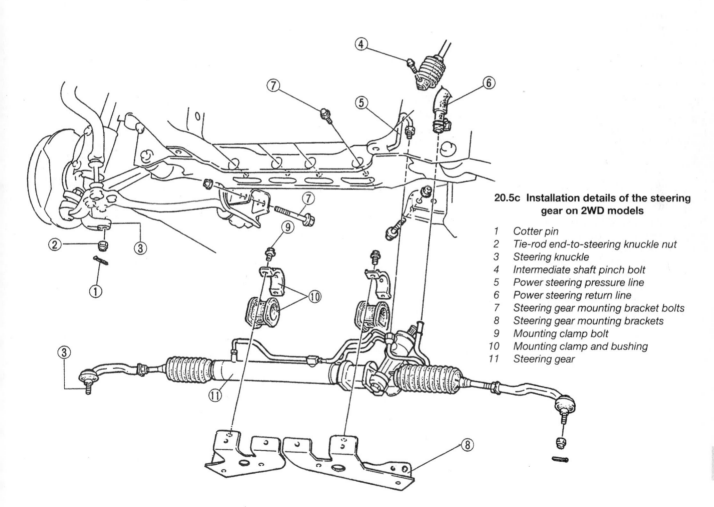

20.5c Installation details of the steering gear on 2WD models

1   Cotter pin
2   Tie-rod end-to-steering knuckle nut
3   Steering knuckle
4   Intermediate shaft pinch bolt
5   Power steering pressure line
6   Power steering return line
7   Steering gear mounting bracket bolts
8   Steering gear mounting brackets
9   Mounting clamp bolt
10 Mounting clamp and bushing
11 Steering gear

10

---

8   Remove the front driveshaft (see Chapter 8).
9   Unbolt the front differential and joint shaft assembly from the crossmember (see Chapter 8) and slide the assembly to the rear as far as possible.
10   Remove the steering gear mounting bolts **(see illustration)**, turn the steering gear housing 90-degrees and slide it towards the rear of the vehicle. Maneuver the steering gear to the left and out from under the vehicle.

Installation (all models)

11   Installation is the reverse of removal.
12   Fill the power steering pump with the recommended fluid (see Chapter 1), bleed the system (see Section 22) and recheck the fluid level. Check for leaks.
13   Have the front end alignment checked by a dealer service department or an alignment shop.

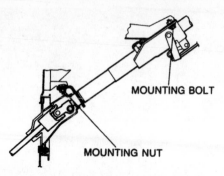

20.7 On 4WD models, remove the steering column mounting bolts after removing the intermediate shaft pinch bolt, then move the column back to detach the intermediate shaft from the steering gear

MOUNTING BOLT

MOUNTING NUT

---

21   Power steering pump - removal and installation

Removal

Refer to illustrations 21.3, 21.4, 21.6 and 21.7

1   Disconnect the cable from the negative battery terminal.
2   Remove the pump drivebelt (see Chapter 1).
3   If you're planning to install a new pump, remove the pulley BEFORE you remove the pump mounting bolts **(see illustration)**.
4   Position a drain pan under the vehicle. Using a suction pump, re-

move as much fluid from the pump reservoir as possible, then disconnect the return line **(see illustration)**.
5   Using a flare-nut wrench, disconnect the pressure line from the pump **(see illustration 21.4)**. Unplug the electrical connector from the power steering pressure switch.
6   Remove the pump mounting bolts **(see illustration)** and detach the pump from the engine, being careful not to spill the remaining fluid.
7   Installation is the reverse of removal **(see illustration)**.
8   Fill the reservoir with the recommended fluid (see Chapter 1) and bleed the system, following the procedure described in Section 22.

---

22   Power steering system - bleeding

1   Following any operation in which the power steering fluid lines have been disconnected, the power steering system must be bled to remove air and obtain proper steering performance.
2   With the front wheels turned all the way to the left, check the power steering fluid level and, if low, add fluid until it reaches the Cold mark on the dipstick.
3   Start the engine and allow it to run at fast idle. Recheck the fluid level and add more if necessary to reach the Cold mark on the dipstick.
4   Bleed the system by turning the wheels from side-to-side, without hitting the stops. This will work the air out of the system. Don't allow the reservoir to run out of fluid.
5   When the air is worked out of the system, return the wheels to the straight ahead position and leave the engine running for several minutes before shutting it off. Recheck the fluid level.

20.10 Installation details of the steering gear on 4WD models

1   Cotter pin
2   Tie-rod end-to-steering knuckle nut
3   Power steering hose clip bolt
4   Power steering pressure hose
5   Power steering return hose
6   Power steering pressure and return lines
7   Intermediate shaft pinch bolt
8   Steering column mounting bolt and nut
9   Intermediate shaft and steering shaft
10 Front driveshaft flange nut and washer
11 Front driveshaft
12 Steering gear mounting clamp bolt
13 Steering gear mounting clamp and bushing
14 Front differential mounting bolt
15 Steering gear

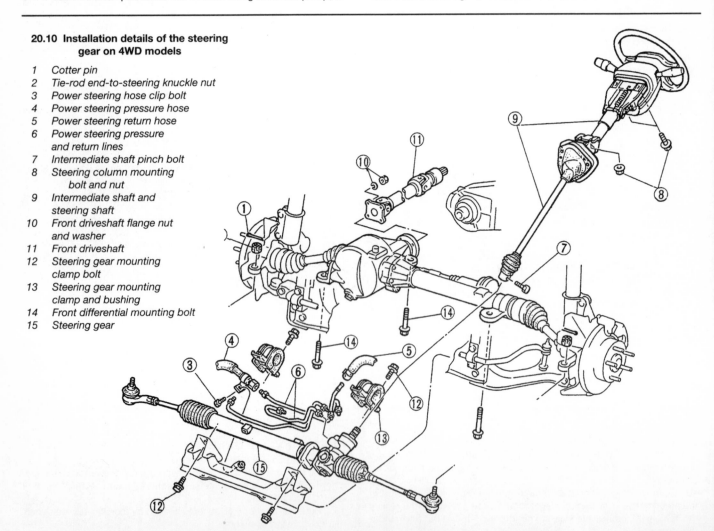

21.3 With one of the power steering pump pulley holes in this position (about 7 o'clock), insert a punch through the hole and wedge it into the notch in the mounting bracket, then break the pulley nut loose

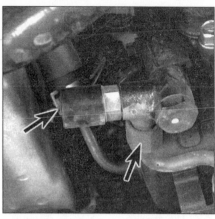

21.4 Disconnect the power steering pump return line (upper arrow) first and allow it to drain, then disconnect the pressure line fitting (lower arrow)

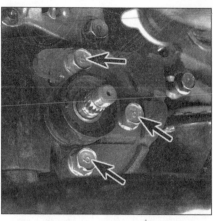

21.6 Remove the power steering pump mounting bolts (arrows)

6   Road test the vehicle to be sure the steering system is functioning normally with no noise.

7   Recheck the fluid level to be sure it's up to the Hot mark on the dipstick while the engine is at normal operating temperature. Add fluid if necessary.

23   Steering wheel - removal and installation

Refer to illustrations 23.3a, 23.3b, 23.4 and 23.5

Warning: *On 1994 models, the following procedure is DANGEROUS! The steering wheel on this vehicle is equipped with an air bag. DO NOT attempt to remove the steering wheel until you have read* Air Bag - General Information *in Chapter 12. Failure to observe the Warnings can result in accidental deployment of the air bag and serious physical injury.*

1   If equipped, have the air bag module disabled and removed from the steering wheel by an automotive repair facility or dealer service department.

2   Disconnect the cable from the negative battery terminal.

3   Remove the horn pad retaining screws and remove the horn pad from the steering wheel **(see illustrations)**. Disconnect the horn wire as you remove the pad.

4   Remove the steering wheel retaining nut, then mark the relationship of the steering shaft and hub to simplify installation and ensure

21.7 Installation details of the power steering pump assembly

1   *Drivebelt*
2   *Pulley retaining nut*
3   *Pulley*
4   *Pressure switch electrical connector*
5   *Pressure line and fitting*
6   *Return hose*
7   *Power steering pump assembly*

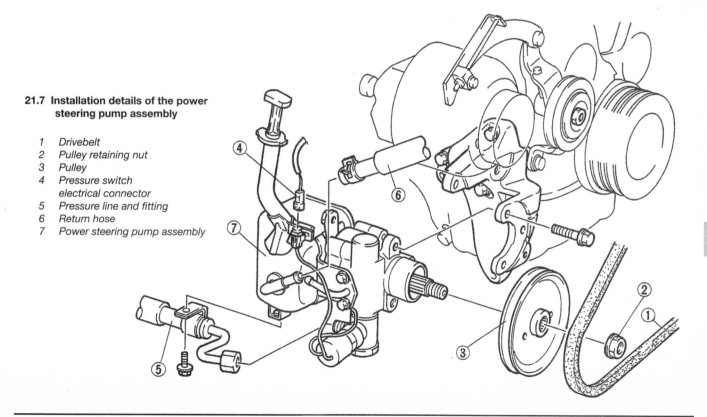

10

23.3a Remove the horn pad retaining screws from the steering wheel . . .

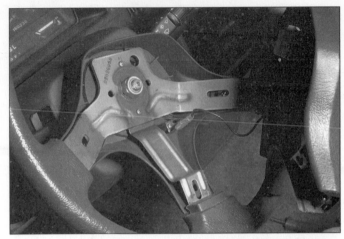

23.3b . . .then remove the horn pad and detach the horn wire

23.4 After removing the steering wheel retaining nut, paint an alignment mark on the steering shaft and the steering wheel to ensure that the wheel is reinstalled correctly

23.5 Use a steering wheel puller to remove the wheel from the steering shaft

steering wheel alignment **(see illustration)**.

5   Use a puller to disconnect the steering wheel from the shaft **(see illustration)**. DO NOT beat on the steering shaft!

6   To install the wheel, align the mark on the steering wheel hub with the mark made on the shaft during removal and slip the wheel onto the shaft. Install the hub nut and tighten it to the torque listed in this Chapter's Specifications.

7   Reattach the horn lead, press the horn pad into place on the steering wheel and install the pad retaining bolts.

8   Connect the negative battery cable.

9   Take the vehicle back to the repair shop or dealer service department that removed the air bag module and have the module reinstalled and re-enabled.

---

24   Wheels and tires - general information

Refer to illustration 24.1

All vehicles covered by this manual are equipped with metric-size fiberglass or steel belted radial tires **(see illustration)**. The use of other size or type tires may affect the ride and handling of the vehicle. Don't mix different types of tires, such as radials and bias belted, on the same vehicle, since handling may be seriously affected. Tires should be replaced in pairs on the same axle, but if only one tire is being replaced, be sure it's the same size, structure and tread design as the other.

Because tire pressure affects handling and wear, the tire pres-

sures should be checked at least once a month or before any extended trips (see Chapter 1).

Wheels must be replaced if they're bent, dented, leak air, have elongated bolt holes, are heavily rusted, out of vertical symmetry or if the lug nuts won't stay tight. Wheel repairs by welding or peening aren't recommended.

Tire and wheel balance is important to the overall handling, braking and performance of the vehicle. Unbalanced wheels can adversely affect handling and ride characteristics as well as tire life. Whenever a tire is installed on a wheel, the tire and wheel should be balanced by a shop with the proper equipment.

---

25   Front end alignment - general information

Refer to illustration 25.1

A front end alignment refers to the adjustments made to the front wheels so they are in proper angular relationship to the suspension and the ground. Wheels that are out of proper alignment not only affect steering control, but also increase tire wear. The adjustments normally required are camber, caster and toe-in **(see illustration)**.

Getting the proper front end alignment is a very exacting process, one in which complicated and expensive machines are necessary to perform the job properly. Because of this, you should have a technician with the proper equipment perform these tasks. We will, however, use this space to give you a basic idea of what is involved with wheel

METRIC TIRE SIZES

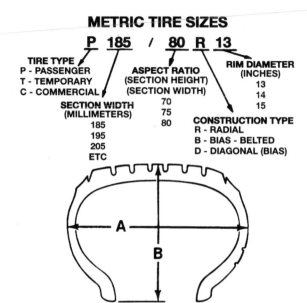

P 185 / 80 R 13

TIRE TYPE
P - PASSENGER
T - TEMPORARY
C - COMMERCIAL

ASPECT RATIO
(SECTION HEIGHT)
(SECTION WIDTH)

SECTION WIDTH
(MILLIMETERS)
185
195
205
ETC

70
75
80

RIM DIAMETER
(INCHES)
13
14
15

CONSTRUCTION TYPE
R - RADIAL
B - BIAS - BELTED
D - DIAGONAL (BIAS)

24.1 Metric tire size code

| A | Section width | B | Section height |

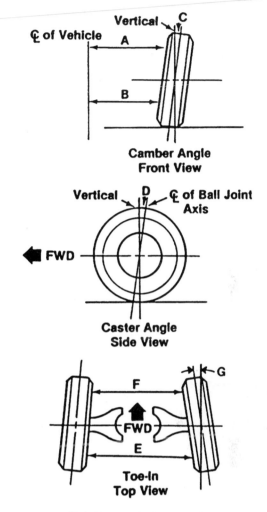

**Camber Angle
Front View**

**Caster Angle
Side View**

**Toe-In
Top View**

25.1 Front end alignment details

A minus B = C (degrees camber)
E minus F = toe-in (measured in inches)
D = caster (expressed in degrees)
G = toe-in (expressed in degrees)

alignment so you can better understand the process and deal intelligently with the shop that does the work.

Toe-in is the turning in of the wheels. The purpose of a toe specification is to ensure parallel rolling of the wheels. In a vehicle with zero toe-in, the distance between the front edges of the wheels will be the same as the distance between the rear edges of the wheels. The actual amount of toe-in is normally only a fraction of an inch. Toe-in adjustment is controlled by the tie-rod end position on the tie-rod. Incorrect toe-in will cause the tires to wear improperly by making them scrub against the road surface.

Camber is the tilting of the front wheels from vertical when viewed from the front of the vehicle. When the wheels tilt out at the top, the camber is said to be positive (+). When the wheels tilt in at the top the camber is negative (-). The amount of tilt is measured in degrees from vertical and this measurement is called the camber angle. This angle affects the amount of tire tread which contacts the road and compensates for changes in the suspension geometry when the vehicle is cornering or traveling over an undulating surface.

Caster is the tilting of the top of the front steering axis from verti-

cal. A tilt toward the rear is positive caster and a tilt toward the front is negative caster. Camber and caster are adjusted by changing the position of the strut upper mounting block in the four mounting stud holes.

10

NOTES:

Chapter 11 Body

Contents

1 General information

These models feature a welded body that is attached to a separate frame. Certain components are particularly vulnerable to accident damage and can be unbolted and repaired or replaced. Among these parts are the body moldings, bumpers, hood, doors, liftgate and all glass.

Only general body maintenance procedures and body panel repair procedures within the scope of the do-it-yourselfer are included in this Chapter.

2 Body - maintenance

1   The condition of your vehicle's body is very important, because the resale value depends a great deal on it. It's much more difficult to repair a damaged body than it is to repair mechanical components. The hidden areas of the body, such as the fenderwells, the frame and the engine compartment, are equally important, although they don't require as frequent attention as the rest of the body.

2   Once a year, or every 12,000 miles, it's a good idea to have the underside of the body steam cleaned. All traces of dirt and oil will be removed and the area can then be inspected carefully for rust, damaged brake lines, frayed electrical wires, damaged cables and other problems.

3   At the same time, clean the engine and the engine compartment with a steam cleaner or water soluble degreaser.

4   The fenderwells should be given close attention, since undercoating can peel away and stones and dirt thrown up by the tires can cause the paint to chip and flake, allowing rust to set in. If rust is found, clean down to the bare metal and apply an anti-rust paint.

5   The body should be washed about once a week (or when dirty). Wet the vehicle thoroughly to soften the dirt, then wash it down with a soft sponge and plenty of clean soapy water. If the surplus dirt is not washed off very carefully, it can wear down the paint.

6   Spots of tar or asphalt thrown up from the road should be removed with a cloth soaked in solvent.

7   Once every six months, wax the body and chrome trim. If a chrome cleaner is used to remove rust from any of the vehicle's plated parts, remember that the cleaner also removes part of the chrome, so use it sparingly.

3 Vinyl trim - maintenance

Don't clean vinyl trim with detergents, caustic soap or petroleum-based cleaners. Plain soap and water works just fine, with a soft brush to clean dirt that may be ingrained. Wash the vinyl as frequently as the rest of the vehicle.

After cleaning, application of a high quality rubber and vinyl protectant will help prevent oxidation and cracks. The protectant can also be applied to weatherstripping, vacuum lines and rubber hoses, which often fail as a result of chemical degradation, and to the tires.

11

4   Upholstery and carpets - maintenance

1   Every three months remove the carpets or mats and clean the interior of the vehicle (more frequently if necessary). Vacuum the upholstery and carpets to remove loose dirt and dust.
2   Leather upholstery requires special care. Stains should be removed with warm water and a very mild soap solution. Use a clean, damp cloth to remove the soap, then wipe again with a dry cloth. Never use alcohol, gasoline, nail polish remover or thinner to clean leather upholstery.
3   After cleaning, regularly treat leather upholstery with a leather wax. Never use car wax on leather upholstery.
4   In areas where the interior of the vehicle is subject to bright sunlight, cover leather seats with a sheet if the vehicle is to be left out for any length of time.

5   Body repair - minor damage

See color photo sequence

Repair of minor scratches

1   If the scratch is superficial and does not penetrate to the metal of the body, repair is very simple. Lightly rub the scratched area with a fine rubbing compound to remove loose paint and built up wax. Rinse the area with clean water.
2   Apply touch-up paint to the scratch, using a small brush. Continue to apply thin layers of paint until the surface of the paint in the scratch is level with the surrounding paint. Allow the new paint at least two weeks to harden, then blend it into the surrounding paint by rubbing with a very fine rubbing compound. Finally, apply a coat of wax to the scratch area.
3   If the scratch has penetrated the paint and exposed the metal of the body, causing the metal to rust, a different repair technique is required. Remove all loose rust from the bottom of the scratch with a pocket knife, then apply rust inhibiting paint to prevent the formation of rust in the future. Using a rubber or nylon applicator, coat the scratched area with glaze-type filler. If required, the filler can be mixed with thinner to provide a very thin paste, which is ideal for filling narrow scratches. Before the glaze filler in the scratch hardens, wrap a piece of smooth cotton cloth around the tip of a finger. Dip the cloth in thinner and then quickly wipe it along the surface of the scratch. This will ensure that the surface of the filler is slightly hollow. The scratch can now be painted over as described earlier in this Section.

Repair of dents

4   When repairing dents, the first job is to pull the dent out until the affected area is as close as possible to its original shape. There is no point in trying to restore the original shape completely as the metal in the damaged area will have stretched on impact and cannot be restored to its original contours. It is better to bring the level of the dent up to a point about 1/8-inch below the level of the surrounding metal. In cases where the dent is very shallow, it is not worth trying to pull it back out at all.
5   If the back side of the dent is accessible, it can be hammered out gently from behind using a soft-face hammer. While doing this, hold a block of wood firmly against the opposite side of the metal to absorb the hammer blows and prevent the metal from being stretched.
6   If the dent is in a section of the body which has double layers, or some other factor makes it inaccessible from behind, a different technique is required. Drill several small holes through the metal inside the damaged area, particularly in the deeper sections. Screw long, self tapping screws into the holes just enough for them to get a good grip in the metal. Now the dent can be pulled out by pulling on the protruding heads of the screws with locking pliers.
7   The next stage of repair is the removal of the paint from the damaged area and from an inch or so of the surrounding metal. This is easily done with a wire brush or sanding disk in a drill motor, although it can be done just as effectively by hand with sandpaper. To complete the preparation for filling, score the surface of the bare metal with a

screwdriver or the tang of a file or drill small holes in the affected area. This will provide a good grip for the filler material. To complete the repair, see the Section on *filling and painting*.

Repair of rust holes or gashes

8   Remove all paint from the affected area and from an inch or so of the surrounding metal using a sanding disk or wire brush mounted in a drill motor. If these are not available, a few sheets of sandpaper will do the job just as effectively.
9   With the paint removed, you will be able to determine the severity of the corrosion and decide whether to replace the whole panel, if possible, or repair the affected area. New body panels are not as expensive as most people think and it is often quicker to install a new panel than to repair large areas of rust.
10   Remove all trim pieces from the affected area except those which will act as a guide to the original shape of the damaged body, such as headlight shells, etc. Using metal snips or a hacksaw blade, remove all loose metal and any other metal that is badly affected by rust. Hammer in the edges of the hole to create a slight depression for the filler material.
11   Wire brush the affected area to remove the powdery rust from the surface of the metal. If the back of the rusted area is accessible, treat it with rust inhibiting paint.
12   Before filling is done, block the hole in some way. This can be done with sheet metal riveted or screwed into place, or by stuffing the hole with wire mesh.
13   Once the hole is blocked off, the affected area can be filled and painted. See the following subsection on *filling and painting*.

Filling and painting

14   Many types of body fillers are available, but generally speaking, body repair kits which contain filler paste and a tube of resin hardener are best for this type of repair work. A wide, flexible plastic or nylon applicator will be necessary for imparting a smooth and contoured finish to the surface of the filler material. Mix up a small amount of filler on a clean piece of wood or cardboard (use the hardener sparingly). Follow the manufacturer's instructions on the package, otherwise the filler will set incorrectly.
15   Using the applicator, apply the filler paste to the prepared area. Draw the applicator across the surface of the filler to achieve the desired contour and to level the filler surface. As soon as a contour that approximates the original one is achieved, stop working the paste. If you continue, the paste will begin to stick to the applicator. Continue to add thin layers of paste at 20-minute intervals until the level of the filler is just above the surrounding metal.
16   Once the filler has hardened, the excess can be removed with a body file. From then on, progressively finer grades of sandpaper should be used, starting with a 180-grit paper and finishing with 600-grit wet-or-dry paper. Always wrap the sandpaper around a flat rubber or wooden block, otherwise the surface of the filler will not be completely flat. During the sanding of the filler surface, the wet-or-dry paper should be periodically rinsed in water. This will ensure that a very smooth finish is produced in the final stage.
17   At this point, the repair area should be surrounded by a ring of bare metal, which in turn should be encircled by the finely feathered edge of good paint. Rinse the repair area with clean water until all of the dust produced by the sanding operation is gone.
18   Spray the entire area with a light coat of primer. This will reveal any imperfections in the surface of the filler. Repair the imperfections with fresh filler paste or glaze filler and once more smooth the surface with sandpaper. Repeat this spray-and-repair procedure until you are satisfied that the surface of the filler and the feathered edge of the paint are perfect. Rinse the area with clean water and allow it to dry completely.
19   The repair area is now ready for painting. Spray painting must be carried out in a warm, dry, windless and dust free atmosphere. These conditions can be created if you have access to a large indoor work area, but if you are forced to work in the open, you will have to pick the day very carefully. If you are working indoors, dousing the floor in the work area with water will help settle the dust which would otherwise be in the air. If the repair area is confined to one body panel, mask off the

surrounding panels. This will help minimize the effects of a slight mis-match in paint color. Trim pieces such as chrome strips, door handles, etc. will also need to be masked off or removed. Use masking tape and several thicknesses of newspaper for the masking operations.

20   Before spraying, shake the paint can thoroughly, then spray a test area until the spray painting technique is mastered. Cover the repair area with a thick coat of primer. The thickness should be built up using several thin layers of primer rather than one thick one. Using 600-grit wet-or-dry sandpaper, rub down the surface of the primer until it is very smooth. While doing this, the work area should be thoroughly rinsed with water and the wet-or-dry sandpaper periodically rinsed as well. Allow the primer to dry before spraying additional coats.

21   Spray on the top coat, again building up the thickness by using several layers of paint. Begin spraying in the center of the repair area and then, using a circular motion, work out until the whole repair area and about two inches of the surrounding original paint is covered. Remove all masking material 10 to 15 minutes after spraying on the final coat of paint. Allow the new paint at least two weeks to harden, then use a very fine rubbing compound to blend the edges of the new paint into the existing paint, Finally, apply a coat of wax.

6   Body repair — major damage

1   Major damage must be repaired by an auto body shop. These shops have the specialized equipment required to do the job properly.
2   If the damage is extensive, the frame must be checked for proper alignment or the vehicle's handling characteristics may be adversely affected and other components may wear at an accelerated rate.
3   Due to the fact that all of the major body components (hood, fenders, etc.) are separate and replaceable units, any seriously damaged components should be replaced rather than repaired. Sometimes the components can be found in a wrecking yard that specializes in used vehicle components, often at a considerable savings over the cost of new parts.

7   Hinges and locks - maintenance

Once every 3,000 miles, or every three months, the hinges and latch assemblies on the doors, hood and the liftgate should be given a few drops of light oil or lock lubricant. The door latch strikers should also be lubricated with a thin coat of grease to reduce wear and ensure free movement. Lubricate the door and the liftgate locks with spray-on graphite lubricant.

8   Fixed glass - replacement

Replacement of the windshield and fixed glass requires the use of special fast-setting adhesive/caulk materials and some specialized tools and techniques. These operations should be left to a dealer service department or a shop specializing in glass work.

9   Hood - removal, installation and adjustment

Refer to illustration 9.3 and 9.12

Note: *The hood is heavy and somewhat awkward to remove and install - at least two people should perform this procedure.*

Removal and installation

1   Open the hood and support it in the open position with a long piece of wood.
2   Cover the fenders and cowl with blankets or heavy cloths to protect the paint.
3   Scribe or draw alignment marks around the bolt heads to ensure proper alignment on reinstallation **(see illustration)**.

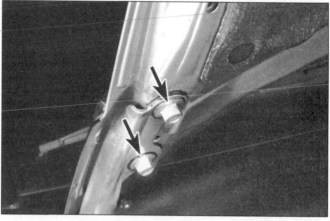

9.3 Carefully paint a mark (arrows) around the hinge and the bolts to maintain the correct alignment of the hood when it is reinstalled

4   Disconnect the windshield washer hose on the passenger side of the hood.
5   Have an assistant hold onto the hood on one side while you hold the other side.
6   Remove the hood-to-hinge assembly bolts on your side of the hood, then hold your side of the hood while your assistant removes the hood-to-hinge bolts on the other side.
7   Lift the hood off.
8   Installation is the reverse of the removal steps with the following additions:
   a)   Align the hood and hinges using the alignment marks made in Step 3.
   b)   Be sure to tighten the bolts securely.

Adjustment

9   The hood can be adjusted to obtain a flush fit between the hood and fenders.
10   Loosen the hood retaining bolts.
11   Move the hood from side-to-side or front-to-rear until the hood is properly aligned with the fenders at the front. Tighten the bolts securely.
12   Loosen the bolts securing the hood latch assembly **(see illustration)**
13   Move the latch until alignment is correct with the hood latch striker. Tighten the latch bolt securely.
14   The hood latch assembly, as well as the hinges, should be periodically lubricated with white lithium base grease to prevent sticking or jamming.

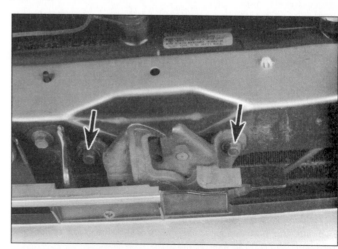

9.12 Loosen the two latch bolts and move the assembly up or down

11

These photos illustrate a method of repairing simple dents. They are intended to supplement *Body repair - minor damage* in this Chapter and should not be used as the sole instructions for body repair on these vehicles.

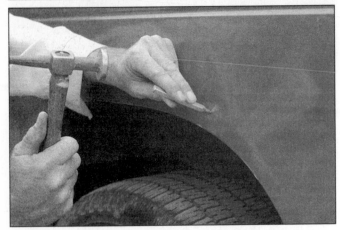

1   If you can't access the backside of the body panel to hammer out the dent, pull it out with a slide-hammer-type dent puller. In the deepest portion of the dent or along the crease line, drill or punch hole(s) at least one inch apart . . .

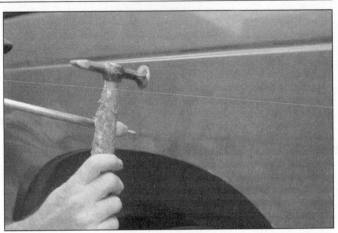

2   . . . then screw the slide-hammer into the hole and operate it. Tap with a hammer near the edge of the dent to help 'pop' the metal back to its original shape. When you're finished, the dent area should be close to its original contour and about 1/8-inch below the surface of the surrounding metal

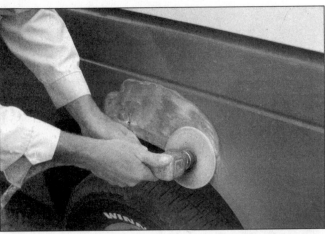

3   Using coarse-grit sandpaper, remove the paint down to the bare metal. Hand sanding works fine, but the disc sander shown here makes the job faster. Use finer (about 320-grit) sandpaper to feather-edge the paint at least one inch around the dent area

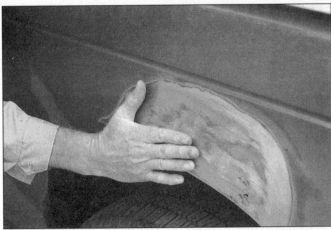

4   When the paint is removed, touch will probably be more helpful than sight for telling if the metal is straight. Hammer down the high spots or raise the low spots as necessary. Clean the repair area with wax/silicone remover

5   Following label instructions, mix up a batch of plastic filler and hardener. The ratio of filler to hardener is critical, and, if you mix it incorrectly, it will either not cure properly or cure too quickly (you won't have time to file and sand it into shape)

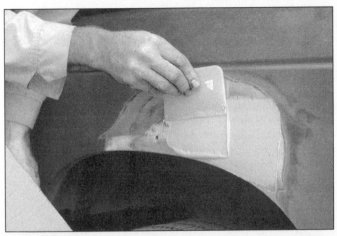

6   Working quickly so the filler doesn't harden, use a plastic applicator to press the body filler firmly into the metal, assuring it bonds completely. Work the filler until it matches the original contour and is slightly above the surrounding metal

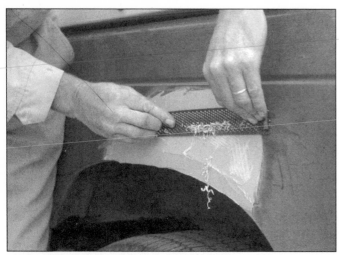

7   Let the filler harden until you can just dent it with your fingernail. Use a body file or Surform tool (shown here) to rough-shape the filler

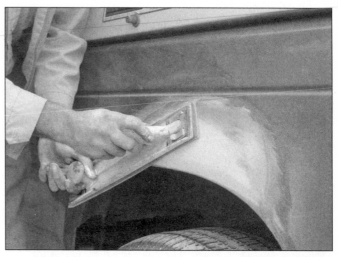

8   Use coarse-grit sandpaper and a sanding board or block to work the filler down until it's smooth and even. Work down to finer grits of sandpaper - always using a board or block - ending up with 360 or 400 grit

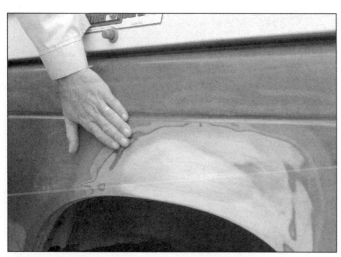

9   You shouldn't be able to feel any ridge at the transition from the filler to the bare metal or from the bare metal to the old paint. As soon as the repair is flat and uniform, remove the dust and mask off the adjacent panels or trim pieces

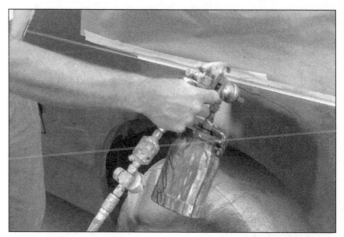

10   Apply several layers of primer to the area. Don't spray the primer on too heavy, so it sags or runs, and make sure each coat is dry before you spray on the next one. A professional-type spray gun is being used here, but aerosol spray primer is available inexpensively from auto parts stores

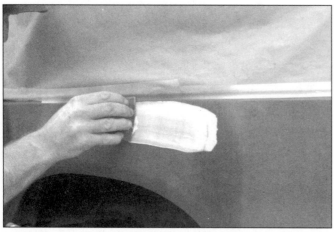

11   The primer will help reveal imperfections or scratches. Fill these with glazing compound. Follow the label instructions and sand it with 360 or 400-grit sandpaper until it's smooth. Repeat the glazing, sanding and respraying until the primer reveals a perfectly smooth surface

12   Finish sand the primer with very fine sandpaper (400 or 600-grit) to remove the primer overspray. Clean the area with water and allow it to dry. Use a tack rag to remove any dust, then apply the finish coat. Don't attempt to rub out or wax the repair area until the paint has dried completely (at least two weeks)

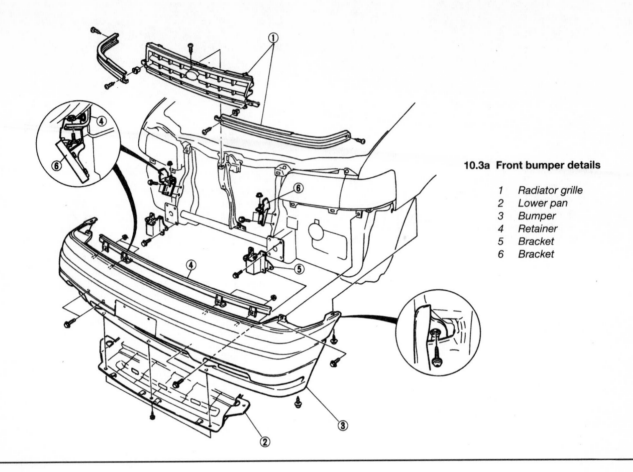

10.3a Front bumper details

1   *Radiator grille*
2   *Lower pan*
3   *Bumper*
4   *Retainer*
5   *Bracket*
6   *Bracket*

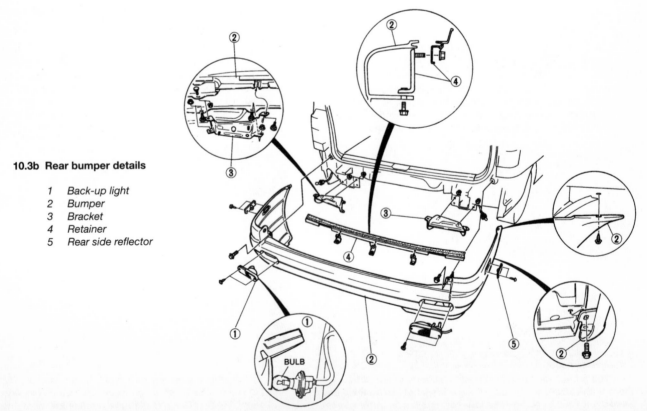

10.3b Rear bumper details

1   *Back-up light*
2   *Bumper*
3   *Bracket*
4   *Retainer*
5   *Rear side reflector*

BULB

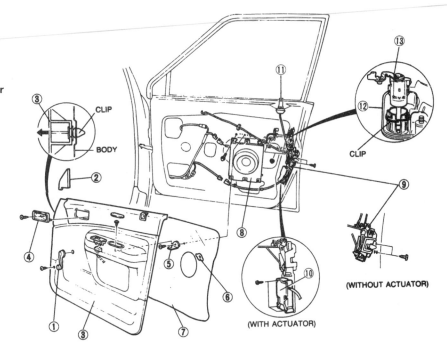

11.2a Details of the front door and components

1   Regulator handle
2   Inner garnish
3   Front door trim panel
4   Inner handle
5   Bracket
6   Sealing pad
7   Door screen
8   Speaker
9   Door lock assembly
10 Door lock actuator
11 Door lock knob
12 Outer handle
13 Key cylinder

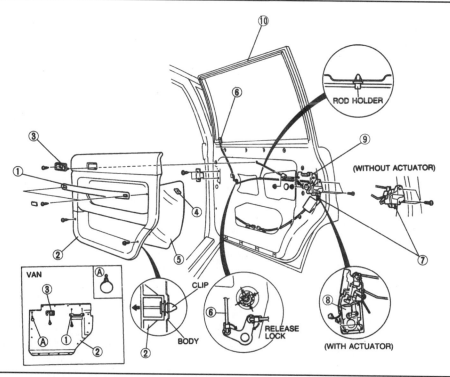

11.2b Details of the rear door and components

1   Pull handle
2   Rear door trim panel
3   Inner handle
4   Sealing pad
5   Door screen
6   Door lock knob
7   Door lock assembly
8   Door lock actuator
9   Outer handle
10 Weatherstrip

10   Bumpers - removal and installation

Refer to illustrations 10.3a and 10.3b

1   Detach the bumper cover (if equipped).
2   Disconnect any wiring or other components that would interfere with bumper removal.
3   Support the bumper with a jack or jackstand. Alternatively, have an assistant support the bumper as the bolts are removed **(see illustrations)**.
4   Remove the retaining bolts and detach the bumper.
5   Installation is the reverse of removal.

6   Tighten the retaining bolts securely.
7   Install the bumper cover and any other components that were removed.

11   Door trim panel - removal and installation

Refer to illustrations 11.2a through 11.2e, 11.3, 11.4 and 11.5

1   Disconnect the negative cable from the battery.
2   Remove all door trim panel retaining screws and door pull/armrest assemblies **(see illustrations)**.

11

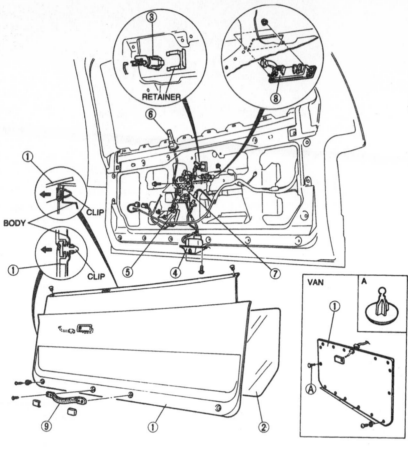

11.2c Details of the liftgate and components

1   Liftgate lower trim panel
2   Liftgate screen
3   Key cylinder
4   Liftgate lock assembly
5   Liftgate lock actuator
6   Liftgate lock knob
7   Remote controller
8   Outer handle
9   Assist handle

3   On manual window regulator equipped models, remove the window regulator crank **(see illustration)**. On power regulator models, pry off the control switch assembly and unplug it.

4   Disengage the trim panel-to-door retaining clips. Work around the outer edge until the panel is free **(see illustration)**.

5   Once all of the clips are disengaged, detach the trim panel, unplug any wire harness connectors and remove the trim panel from the vehicle **(see illustration)**.

6   For access to the inner door, carefully peel back the plastic watershield.

7   Prior to installation of the door trim panel, be sure to reinstall any clips in the panel which may have come out during the removal procedure and remain in the door itself.

8   Plug in the wire harness connectors and place the panel in position in the door. Press the door trim panel into place until the clips are seated and install the armrest/door pulls. Install the manual regulator window crank.

---

12   Door - removal, installation and adjustment

Refer to illustrations 12.1a, 12.1b, 12.4, 12.5 and 12.7

1   Remove the door trim panel (see Section 11). Disconnect any wire harness connectors and push them through the door opening so they won't interfere with door removal **(see illustrations)**.

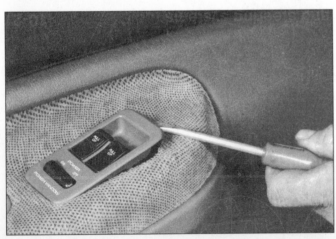

11.2d Carefully pry the power window switch up and disconnect the electrical connector

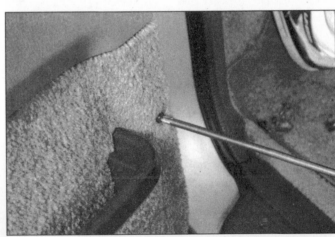

11.2e You might have to pull the carpet away a slight amount in order to expose the two screws

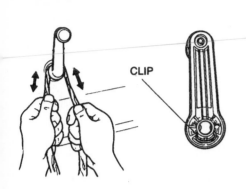

11.3 Use a rag and pry the clip down until it disengages from the shaft

11.4 Carefully pry the door trim panel off the door.

11.5 Lift the door trim panel up and then off the door

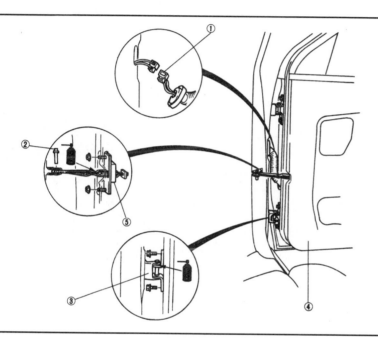

12.1a Details of the front door mounting assembly

1   Harness connector
2   Check pin
3   Hinge
4   Front door
5   Door check

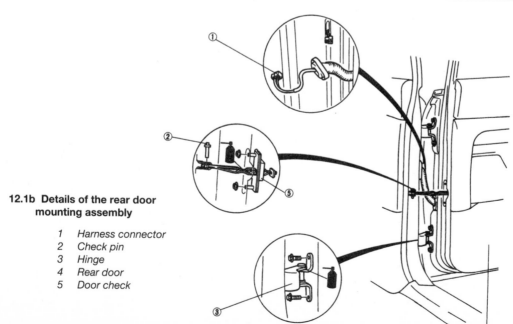

12.1b Details of the rear door mounting assembly

1   Harness connector
2   Check pin
3   Hinge
4   Rear door
5   Door check

11

12.4 Remove the check pin by tapping from the bottom

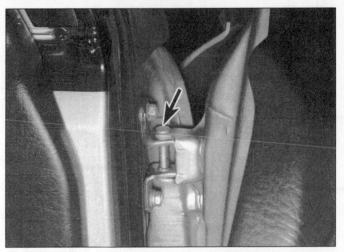

12.5 Sometimes it is easier to remove the hinge pin (arrow) thereby not altering the adjustment of the door

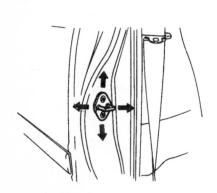

12.7 The door lock striker can be adjusted sideways or up and down

13.2a Carefully pry the circlip up and off the hinge pin

13.2b Remove the pin from the upper hinge

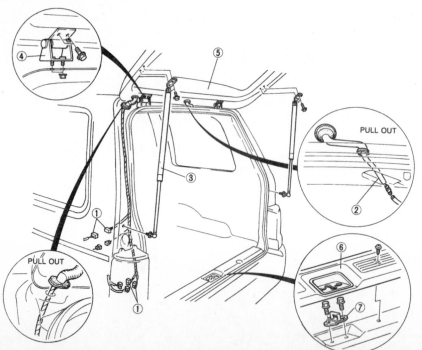

13.3a Details of the liftgate damper assembly

1   Harness connector
2   Washer pipe
3   Stay damper
4   Hinge
5   Liftgate
6   Mat end set plate
7   Door lock striker

13.3b Carefully remove the pivot assembly from the body of the liftgate door jamb using an open end wrench

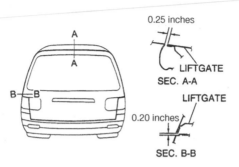

14.7 Check the gap of the liftgate in relation with the top of the hood (Section A-A) and with the side of the body (B-B) to make sure they are uniform

14.8 Loosen the bolts and move the striker to the proper position to align the liftgate

2   Place a jack or jackstand under the door or have an assistant on hand to support it when the hinge bolts are removed. **Note:** *If a jack or jackstand is used, place a rag between it and the door to protect the door's painted surfaces.*

3   Scribe around the door hinges.

4   Disconnect the check strap **(see illustration)** by tapping the retaining pin up with a small hammer.

5   Remove the hinge-to-door bolts or drive out the pins **(see illustration)** and carefully lift off the door.

6   Installation is the reverse of removal.

7   Following installation of the door, check the alignment and adjust it if necessary as follows:

 a) Up-and-down and forward-and-backward adjustments are made by loosening the hinge-to-body bolts and moving the door as necessary.

 b) The door lock striker can also be adjusted both up-and-down and sideways to provide positive engagement with the lock mechanism. This is done by loosening the mounting bolts and moving the striker as necessary **(see illustration)**.

---

13   Liftgate damper - removal and installation

Refer to illustrations 13.2a, 13.2b, 13.3a and 13.3b

1   Open the liftgate and support it.

2   Use a small screwdriver and pry the small circlip **(see illustration)** off the pin and force the pin out of the hinge **(see illustration)**.

3   Use an open end wrench to detach the lower end of the strut **(see illustrations)** from the body.

4   Installation is the reverse of removal.

---

14   Liftgate - removal, installation and adjustment

Refer to illustrations 14.7 and 14.8

1   Open the liftgate and cover the upper body area around the opening with pads or cloths to protect the painted surfaces when the liftgate is removed.

2   Disconnect all cables and wire harness connectors that would interfere with removal of the liftgate.

3   Paint or scribe around the hinge flanges.

4   While an assistant supports the liftgate, detach the support struts (see Section 13).

5   Remove the hinge bolts and detach the liftgate from the vehicle **(see illustration 13.3a)**.

6   Installation is the reverse of removal.

7   After installation, close the liftgate and make sure it's in proper alignment with the surrounding body panels **(see illustration)**. Adjustments are made by moving the position of the hinge bolts in the slots.

To adjust it, loosen the hinge bolts and reposition the hinges either side-to-side or fore-and-aft the desired amount and retighten the bolts.

8   The engagement of the liftgate can be adjusted by loosening the lock striker bolts, repositioning the striker and retightening the bolts **(see illustration)**.

---

15   Latch, lock cylinder and handles - removal, installation and adjustment

Refer to illustrations 15.2a, 15.2b and 15.3

Note: *Refer to illustrations 11.2a, 11.2b and 11.2c for views of the door mechanisms.*

1   Remove the door trim panel and plastic shield (see Section 11) from either the front door, rear door or liftgate.

Latch

2   Disconnect the operating rods from the latch **(see illustrations)**.

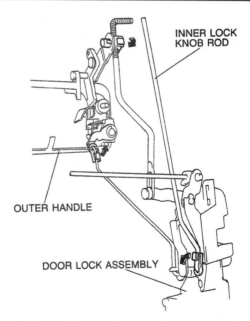

15.2a The rod(s) can be removed from the door lock and latch assembly by forcing the clip(s) (arrows) off the rod(s) and spinning them out of the way (front door shown, others similar)

11

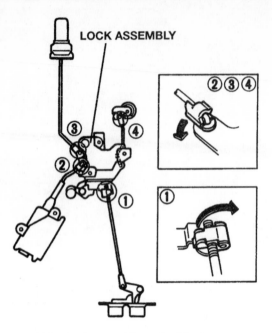

15.2b Lock assembly on the liftgate

1	*Liftgate lock assembly*	3	*Locking knob*
2	*Actuator*	4	*key cylinder*

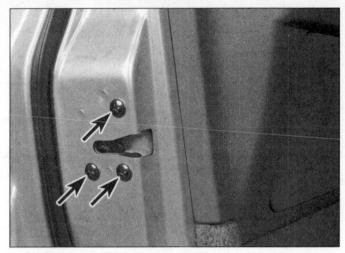

15.3 Remove the three mounting screws (arrows) from the lock assembly

3   Remove the three latch retaining screws located in the end of the door **(see illustration)**.
4   Detach the latch assembly and lift it from the door.
5   Installation is the reverse of removal.

Lock cylinder

6   Remove the outside door handle (see Step 12).
7   Detach the lock cylinder from the handle assembly.

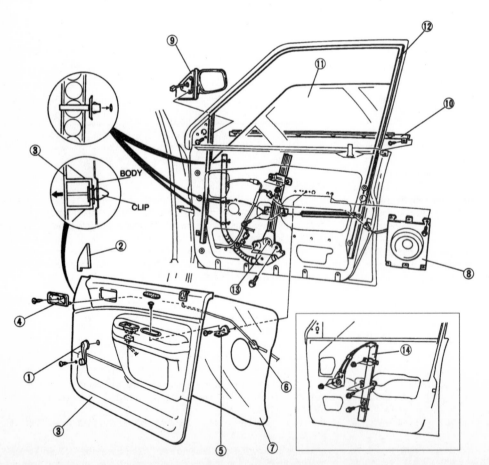

16.5 Exploded view of the window regulator and glass on the front door

1   *Regulator handle*
2   *Inner garnish*
3   *Front door trim*
4   *Inner handle*
5   *Bracket*
6   *Sealing pad*
7   *Door screen*
8   *Speaker*
9   *Door mirror*
10   *Front beltline molding*
11   *Front door glass*
12   *Glass channel*
13   *Power window regulator*
14   *Manual window regulator*

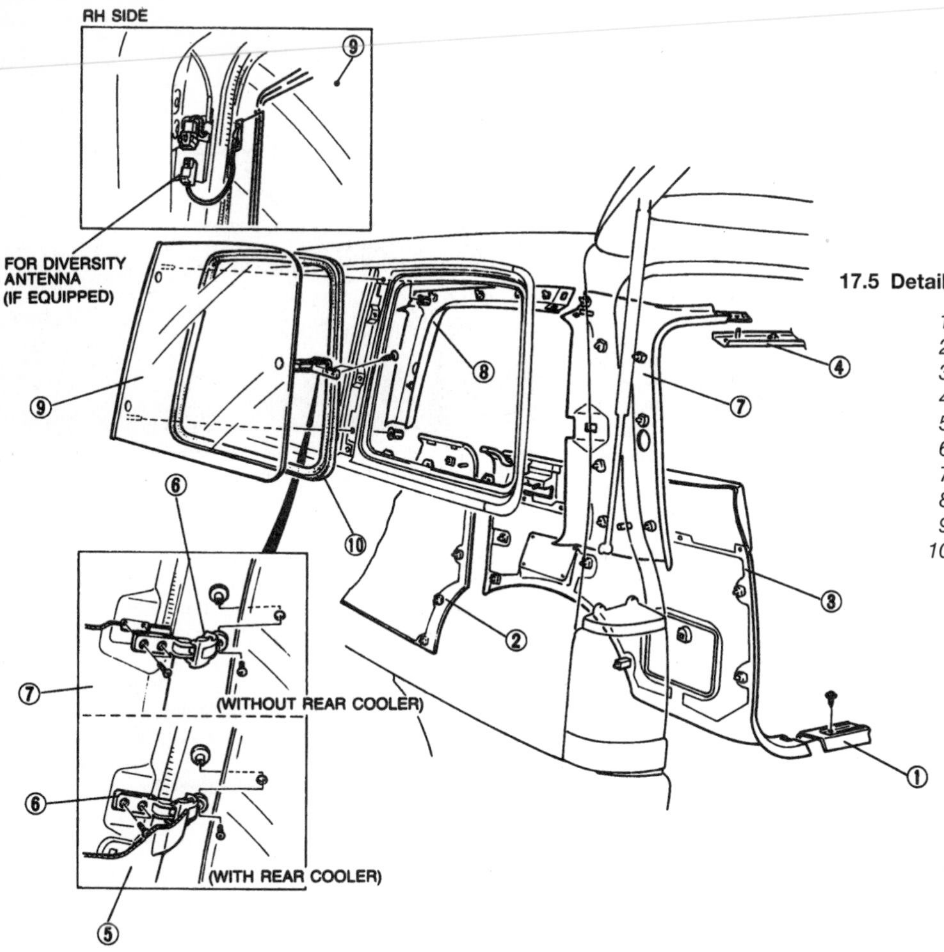

RH SIDE

FOR DIVERSITY ANTENNA (IF EQUIPPED)

(WITHOUT REAR COOLER)

(WITH REAR COOLER)

17.5 Details of the rear quarter glass

1   Rear molding
2   Trim panel A
3   Trim panel B
4   Rear header trim
5   Rear cooler trim
6   Rear quarter glass lock
7   D pillar trim
8   B pillar trim
9   Rear quarter window glass
10 Weatherstrip

8   Installation is the reverse of removal. **Note:** *On models equipped with electric door locks, tape the switch harness to the actuator to prevent it from interfering with the door glass.*

Inside handle

9   Disconnect the operating rod from the handle **(see illustrations 15.2a and 15.2b)**
10   Remove the retaining screws and lift the handle from the door.
11   Installation is the reverse of removal.

Outside handle

12   Disconnect the operating rods, remove the two retaining nuts and lift the handle off the door.
13   Installation is the reverse of removal.

16   Door window glass and regulator - removal, installation and adjustment

Refer to illustration 16.5

1   Disconnect the cable from the negative terminal of the battery.
2   Remove the door trim panel and the plastic water shield (see Section 11).
3   Remove the door outer weatherstrip.

Window glass

4   Lower the window so that the mounting bolts can be reached through the access hole. On power windows, temporarily reconnect the battery cable to accomplish this.
5   Remove the retaining bolts **(see illustration)**.

6   Lift the window glass up and out of the door window slot, then tilt it and remove it from the door.
7   Installation is the reverse of removal. To adjust the position of the regulator and glass guides so the glass runs smoothly, loosen the attaching bolts, check the window operation, then retighten.

Regulator

8   Remove the attaching bolts and lift the window regulator assembly out of the door (withdraw the regulator mechanism through the access hole) **(see illustration 16.5)**. On power window models, unplug the electrical connector.
9   Installation is the reverse of removal. To adjust the position of the regulator and glass guides so the glass runs smoothly, loosen the attaching bolts, check the window operation, then retighten.

17   Rear quarter glass - removal and installation

Refer to illustration 17.5

1   Remove the rear, right side trim panel B from the trunk area (see Section 23).
2   Remove the plugs from the right side emergency handle and remove the screws. Remove the handle from the passenger compartment.
3   Remove pillar B trim panel from above the glass area (see Section 23).
4   If the window is equipped with an antenna, disconnect the electrical connector.
5   Remove the screws from the window glass hinge **(see illustration)**.

11

18.2 Carefully pry the trim plate off the instrument cluster bezel without scratching the surface

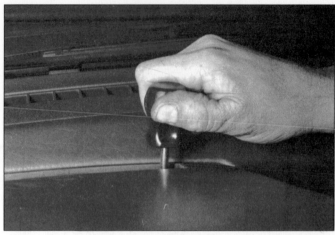

18.3 Use a short Phillips screwdriver to remove the upper screws from the bezel

6   Remove the side mount screws from the window glass and remove the glass.
7   Installation is the reverse of removal.

---

18   Instrument cluster bezel - removal and installation

Refer to illustrations 18.2, 18.3, 18.4 and 18.5
1   Disconnect the negative cable at the battery.
2   Use a flat-bladed screwdriver and pry the trim plate from the top

of the cluster bezel **(see illustration)**.
3   Use a short Phillips screwdriver and remove the screws from the upper section of the instrument cluster bezel **(see illustration)**.
4   Remove the screws from the lower section of the bezel **(see illustration)**.
5   Pull the instrument cluster bezel partially out and disconnect the electrical connectors **(see illustration)**.
6   Lift the instrument cluster bezel from the passenger compartment.
7   Installation is the reverse of removal.

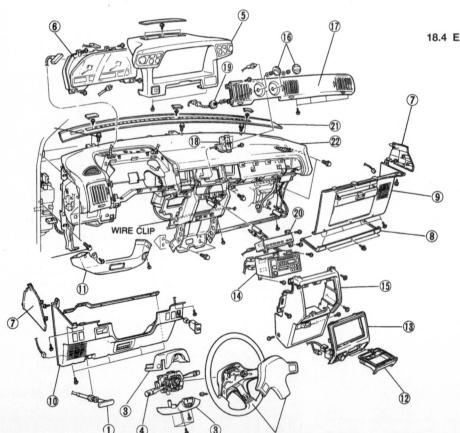

18.4 Exploded view of the instrument panel

1   Hood release handle
2   Steering wheel assembly
3   Column cover
4   Combination switch
5   Instrument cluster bezel
6   Instrument cluster
7   Side panel
8   Right undercover panel
9   Lower right panel assembly
10   Lower left panel assembly
11   Duct number 3
12   Ashtray
13   Audio panel assembly
14   Audio unit
15   Lower center panel assembly
16   Knob
17   Switch panel assembly
18   Temperature control adjustment
19   Blower control
20   Mechanical airflow mode control
21   Upper garnish panel
22   Dashboard

18.5 Be careful not to pull on the electrical connectors while trying to reach them from the backside

19.13 First, use a small screwdriver and pry the cover off the garnish and . . .

19   Dashboard trim panels - removal and installation

1   The dashboard panels are held in place by a combination of screws and clips **(see illustration 18.4)**.

Lower panel assemblies

2   Use a screwdriver and pry the side cover(s) off, then remove the screw(s) and detach the side cover(s) from the dashboard.
3   Remove the right side undercover panel screws and panel.
4   Remove the four screws from the top and the four screws from the bottom of the right lower panel and slide the panel horizontally (toward the door) until it separates from the dash assembly.
5   Remove the three screws from the top and the four screws from the bottom of the left lower panel and slide the panel horizontally (toward the door) until it separates from the dash assembly.
6   Remove the hood handle by loosening the cable nut and dropping the handle assembly from the slotted portion of the panel.
7   Remove the right and lower panel assemblies from the vehicle.
8   Installation is the reverse of removal.

Center panel

9   Remove the lower panel assemblies (see Steps 2 through 7).
10   Remove the screws from the center panel **(see illustration 18.4)**.
11   Pull the panel out partially and disconnect the electrical connector for the cigarette lighter. Remove the center panel from the vehicle.
12   Installation is the reverse of removal.

Instrument panel garnish

Refer to illustrations 19.13 and 19.14
13   Use a small flat-bladed screwdriver and carefully pry the panel covers off the instrument panel garnish **(see illustration)**.
14   Use a deep socket and remove the mounting bolts **(see illustration)**.
15   Carefully lift from the end of the garnish and separate it from the panel clips.
16   Installation is the reverse of removal.

Switch panel assembly

Refer to illustration 19.19
17   Remove the instrument cluster bezel (see Section 18) and the lower panel assemblies (see Steps 2 through 7).
18   Pry the control knobs off the switch panel assembly.
19   Remove the screws from the lower portion of the switch panel assembly and lift it off **(see illustration)**.
20   Disconnect any electrical connectors from the back of the assembly.
21   Installation is the reverse of removal.

Dashboard

22   Remove the instrument cluster bezel (see Section 18) and the lower panel assemblies (see Steps 2 through 7). Also, remove the lower panel assemblies, the center panel, the switch panel assembly

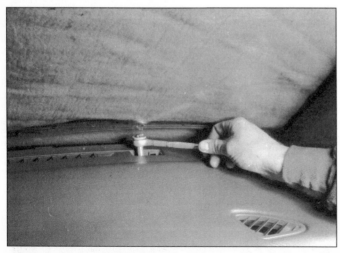

19.14 . . . then use a deep socket and remove the retaining bolts

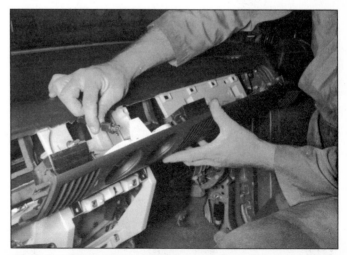

19.19 Remove any bulb assemblies from the switch panel before lifting the assembly from the dashboard

11

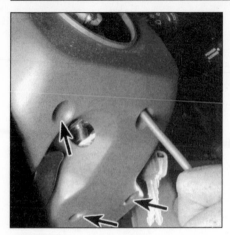

20.3 Remove the screws (arrows) from the lower section of the steering column cover

20.4 Separate the column covers

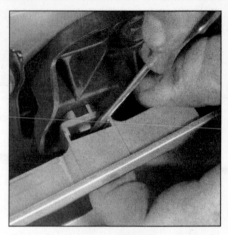

21.1a Push down on the tab to release it from the grille

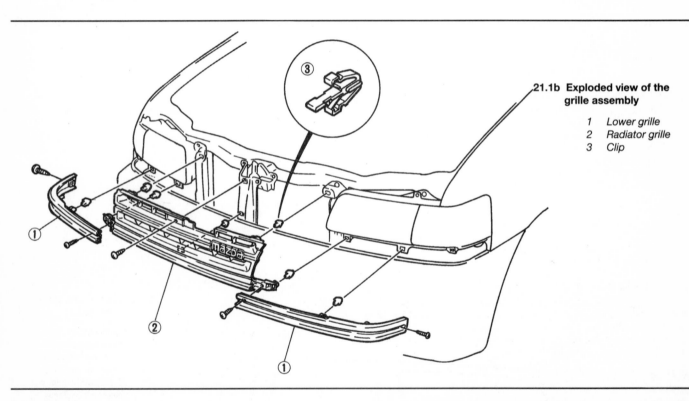

21.1b Exploded view of the grille assembly

1   Lower grille
2   Radiator grille
3   Clip

and the instrument garnish (see Steps 9 through 21).

23   Remove the instrument cluster (see Chapter 12).

24   Remove the radio (see Chapter 12).

25   Remove the duct number 3 **(see illustration 18.4)**.

26   Remove all the dashboard screws and lift the dashboard from the vehicle.

27   Installation is the reverse of removal.

---

20   Steering column cover - removal and installation

Refer to illustrations 20.3 and 20.4

1   Disconnect the negative cable from the battery.

2   Remove the steering wheel (see Chapter 10).

3   Remove the screws **(see illustration)**.

4   Separate the cover halves **(see illustration)**.

5   Installation is the reverse of removal.

21   Radiator grille - removal and installation

Refer to illustrations 21.1a and 21.1b

1   Push down on the grille clips **(see illustrations)** and carefully pull the radiator grille out.

2   To install the grille, insert the clips into the grille and when they are all aligned properly, press firmly until the assembly is entirely installed.

---

22   Outside mirror - removal and installation

Refer to illustrations 22.1 and 22.2

1   Pry off the cover panel **(see illustration)**.

2   Remove the retaining screws and lift the mirror off **(see illustration)**. On power models, unplug the electrical connector.

3   Installation is the reverse of removal.

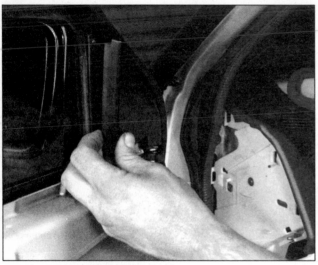

22.1 Carefully pry the trim panel off the door

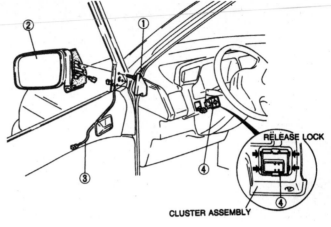

22.2 Details of the power mirror

1	Inner trim panel	3	Wire harness
2	Outside mirror	4	Mirror switch

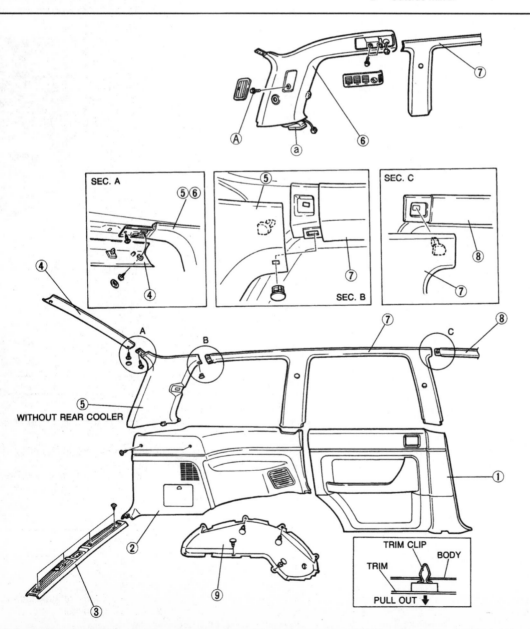

23.1a Interior trim panels (left side)

1   Rear side trim A
2   Rear side trim B
3   Mat end set plate
4   Rear header trim
5   D pillar trim (without rear air conditioning [cooler])
6   Rear air conditioning trim (with rear air conditioning [cooler])
a   Rear cooler duct
7   B pillar trim
8   A pillar trim
9   Wheel house rear trim

11

23   Interior trim panels - removal and installation

Refer to illustrations 23.1a and 23.1b

1   The interior trim panels are held in place by a combination of screws and clips **(see illustrations)**.

2   When removing the trim panel B, first remove the upper pillar trim panels B and D. **Note:** *Do not use excessive force to remove the trim panels. The trim panel clips will separate from the body with a steady movement.*

24   Seats - removal and installation

Front seat

Refer to illustration 24.1

1   Remove the bolts securing the seat track to the floorpan and lift the seat from the vehicle **(see illustration)**.

2   Installation is the reverse of the removal. Tighten the retaining bolts securely.

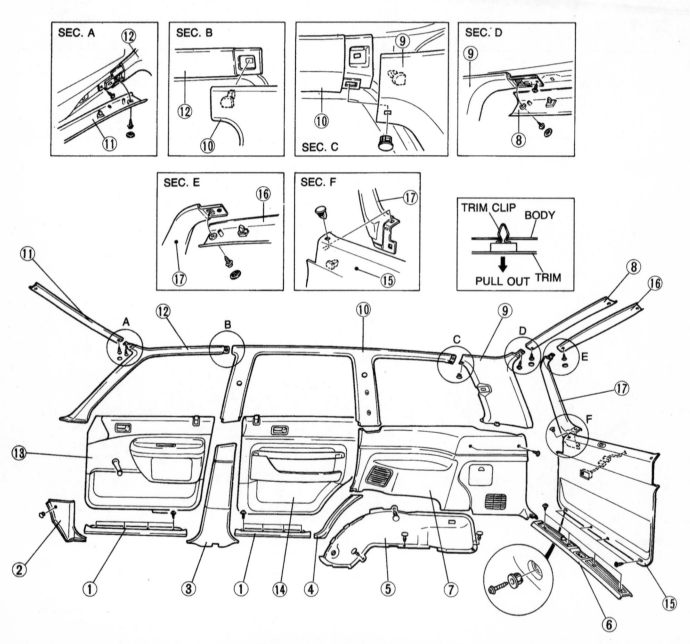

23.1b Interior trim panels (right side)

1	Scuff plate	7	Rear side trim B	13	Front door trim
2	Front side trim	8	Rear header trim	14	Rear side door trim
3	B pillar lower trim	9	D pillar trim	15	Liftgate lower trim
4	Tire house trim	10	B pillar trim	16	Liftgate upper trim
5	Tire house rear trim	11	Front header trim	17	Liftgate left/right trim
6	Mat end set plate	12	A pillar trim		

Middle seat

Refer to illustration 24.3

3   Pull on the release handle and lift the front section of the seat to release it from the floor. Swing the seat up and to the rear of the vehicle and remove it from the passenger compartment **(see illustration)**.
4   Installation is the reverse of removal. Tighten the retaining bolts securely.

Rear seat

Refer to illustration 24.5

5   Remove the bolts securing the seat track to the floorpan and lift the seat from the vehicle **(see illustration)**.
6   Installation is the reverse of the removal. Tighten the retaining bolts securely.

25   Seat belt check

1   Check the seat belts, buckles, latch plates and guide loops for obvious damage and signs of wear.
2   Check that the seat belt reminder light comes on when the ignition key is turned to the Run or Start position.
3   The seat belts are designed to lock up during a sudden stop or impact, yet allow free movement during normal driving. Check that the retractors return the belt against your chest while driving and rewind the belt fully when the buckle is unlatched.
4   If any of the above checks reveal problems with the seat belt system, replace parts as necessary.

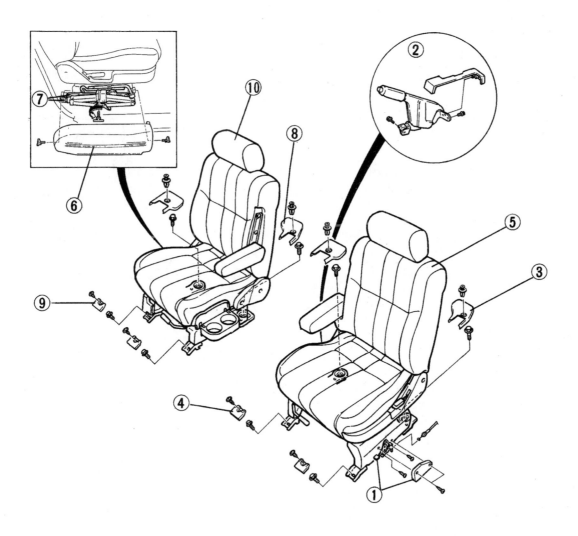

24.1 Front seat mounting details

1	Fuel filler lid opener	6	Jack cover
2	Parking brake lever	7	Jack handle
3	Seat set bracket cover	8	Seat set bracket cover
4	Leg cover	9	Leg cover
5	Front seat	10	Front seat

11

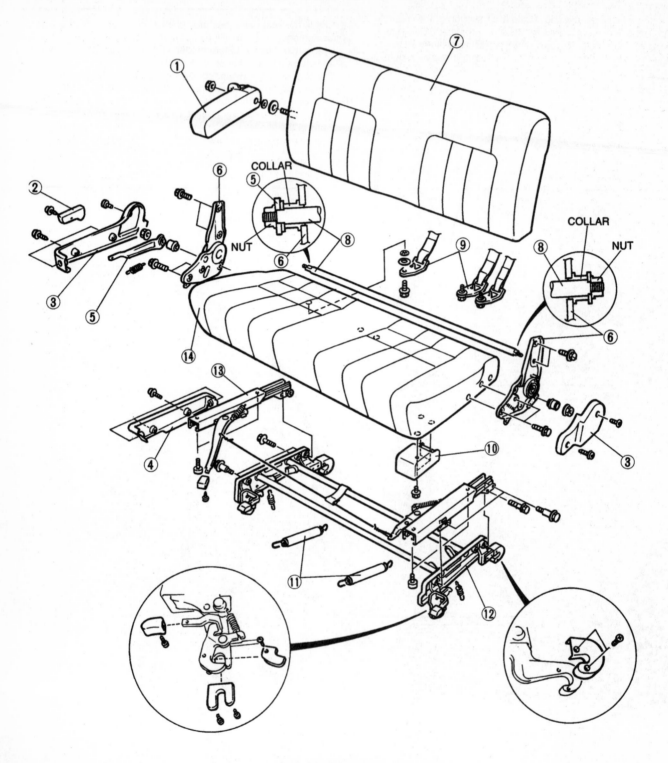

24.3 Middle seat mounting details

1	Armrest	6	Reclining knuckle	11	Return spring
2	Knob	7	Seat back	12	Seat set bracket
3	Side cover	8	Shaft	13	Slide adjuster
4	Lower side cover	9	Seat belt	14	Seat cushion
5	Knuckle lever	10	Slide protector		

24.5 Rear seat mounting details

1	Safety stand	10	Seat back	19	Cable unit
2	Hinge assembly	11	Bolt cap	20	Lever assembly
3	Knuckle lever	12	Seat belt	21	Hook guide cover
4	Knuckle cover	13	Double folding lever	22	Hook cover
5	Knuckle	14	Double folding vessel	23	Hook spring
6	Lever	15	Cushion trim and pad	24	Bush
7	Back board	16	Reclining cable	25	Hook assembly
8	Pulley cover	17	Double folding cover	26	Cushion frame
9	Cable	18	Double folding hook cover		

11

NOTES

Chapter 12 Chassis electrical system

Contents

1   General information

Warning: *To prevent electrical shorts, fires and injury, always disconnect the cable from the negative terminal of the battery before checking, repairing or replacing electrical components.*

The chassis electrical system of this vehicle is a 12-volt, negative ground type. Power for the lights and all electrical accessories is supplied by a lead/acid-type battery which is charged by the alternator.

This chapter covers repair and service procedures for various chassis (non-engine related) electrical components. For information regarding the engine electrical system components (battery, alternator, distributor and starter motor), see Chapter 5.

2   Electrical troubleshooting - general information

A typical electrical circuit consists of an electrical component, any switches, relays, motors, fuses, fusible links or circuit breakers, etc. related to that component and the wiring and connectors that link the components to both the battery and the chassis. To help you pinpoint an electrical circuit problem, wiring diagrams are included at the end of this book.

Before tackling any troublesome electrical circuit, first study the appropriate wiring diagrams to get a complete understanding of what makes up that individual circuit. Trouble spots, for instance, can often be isolated by noting if other components related to that circuit are often routed through the same fuse and ground connections.

Electrical problems usually stem from simple causes such as loose or corroded connectors, a blown fuse, a melted fusible link or a bad relay. Visually inspect the condition of all fuses, wires and connectors in a problem circuit before troubleshooting it.

The basic tools needed for electrical troubleshooting include a circuit tester, a high impedance (10 K-ohm) digital voltmeter, a continuity tester and a jumper wire with an inline circuit breaker for bypassing electrical components. Before attempting to locate or define a problem with electrical test instruments, use the wiring diagrams to decide where to make the necessary connections.

Voltage checks

Perform a voltage check first when a circuit is not functioning properly. Connect one lead of a circuit tester to either the negative battery terminal or a known good ground.

Connect the other lead to a connector in the circuit being tested, preferably nearest to the battery or fuse. If the bulb of the tester lights up, voltage is present, which means that the part of the circuit between the connector and the battery is problem free. Continue checking the rest of the circuit in the same fashion.

When you reach a point at which no voltage is present, the problem lies between that point and the last test point with voltage. Most of the time the problem can be traced to a loose connection. **Note**: *Keep in mind that some circuits receive voltage only when the ignition key is in the Accessory or Run position.*

3.1a One fuse block is located under the left side of the instrument panel

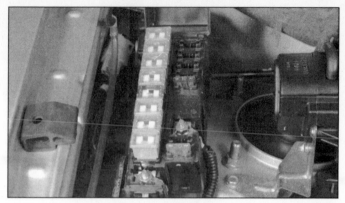

3.1b A second fuse block is located under a flip-up cover in the engine compartment

Finding a short circuit

One method of finding shorts in a circuit is to remove the fuse and connect a test light or voltmeter in its place. There should be no voltage present in the circuit. Move the electrical connectors from side-to-side while watching the test light. If the bulb goes on, there is a short to ground somewhere in that area, probably where the insulation has been rubbed through. The same test can be performed on each component in a circuit, even a switch.

Ground check

Perform a ground test to check whether a component is properly grounded. Disconnect the battery and connect one lead of a self-powered test light, known as a continuity tester, to a known good ground. Connect the other lead to the wire or ground connection being tested. If the bulb goes on, the ground is good. If the bulb does not go on, the ground is not good.

Continuity check

A continuity check determines if there are any breaks in a circuit - if it is conducting electricity properly. With the circuit off (no power in the circuit), a self-powered continuity tester can be used to check the circuit. Connect the test leads to both ends of the circuit, and if the test light comes on the circuit is passing current properly. If the light doesn't come on, there is a break somewhere in the circuit. The same procedure can be used to test a switch, by connecting the continuity tester to the power in and power out sides of the switch. With the switch turned on, the test light should come on.

Finding an open circuit

When diagnosing for possible open circuits it is often difficult to locate them by sight because oxidation or terminal misalignment are hidden by the connectors. Merely wiggling a connector on a sensor or in the electrical connector may correct the open circuit condition. Remember this if an open circuit is indicated when troubleshooting a circuit. Intermittent problems may also be caused by oxidized or loose connections. Electrical troubleshooting is simple if you keep in mind that all electrical circuits are basically electricity running from the battery, through the wires, switches, relays, fuses and fusible links to each electrical component (light bulb, motor, etc.) and then to ground, from which it is passed back to the battery. Any electrical problem is an interruption in the flow of electricity to and from the battery.

---

3   Fuses - general information

Refer to illustrations 3.1a and 3.1b

The electrical circuits of the vehicle are protected by a combination of fuses and circuit breakers. The fuse boxes are located under the instrument panel on the left side of the dashboard and in the engine compartment **(see illustrations)**.

Each of the fuses is designed to protect a specific circuit, and the

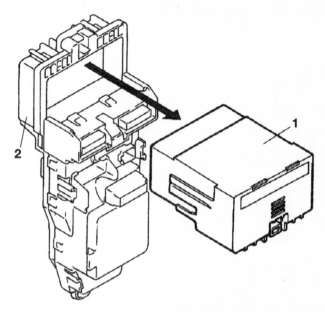

4.1 The Central Processing Unit (CPU) is located on top of the fuse block, under the dash

1   CPU   2   Fuse block

---

various circuits are identified on the fuse panel cover.

Miniaturized fuses are employed in the fuse boxes. These compact fuses, with blade terminal design, allow fingertip removal and replacement. If an electrical component fails, always check the fuse first. A blown fuse is easily identified through the clear plastic body. Visually inspect the element for evidence of damage. If a continuity check is called for, the blade terminal tips are exposed in the fuse body.

Be sure to replace blown fuses with the correct type. Fuses of different ratings are physically interchangeable, but only fuses of the proper rating should be used. Replacing a fuse with one of a higher or lower value than specified is not recommended. Each electrical circuit needs a specific amount of protection. The amperage value of each fuse is molded into the fuse body.

If the replacement fuse immediately fails, don't replace it again until the cause of the problem is isolated and corrected. In most cases, the cause will be a short circuit in the wiring caused by a broken or deteriorated wire.

---

4   Central Processing Unit (CPU) - general information

Refer to illustration 4.1

1   These models are equipped with a Central Processing Unit (CPU)

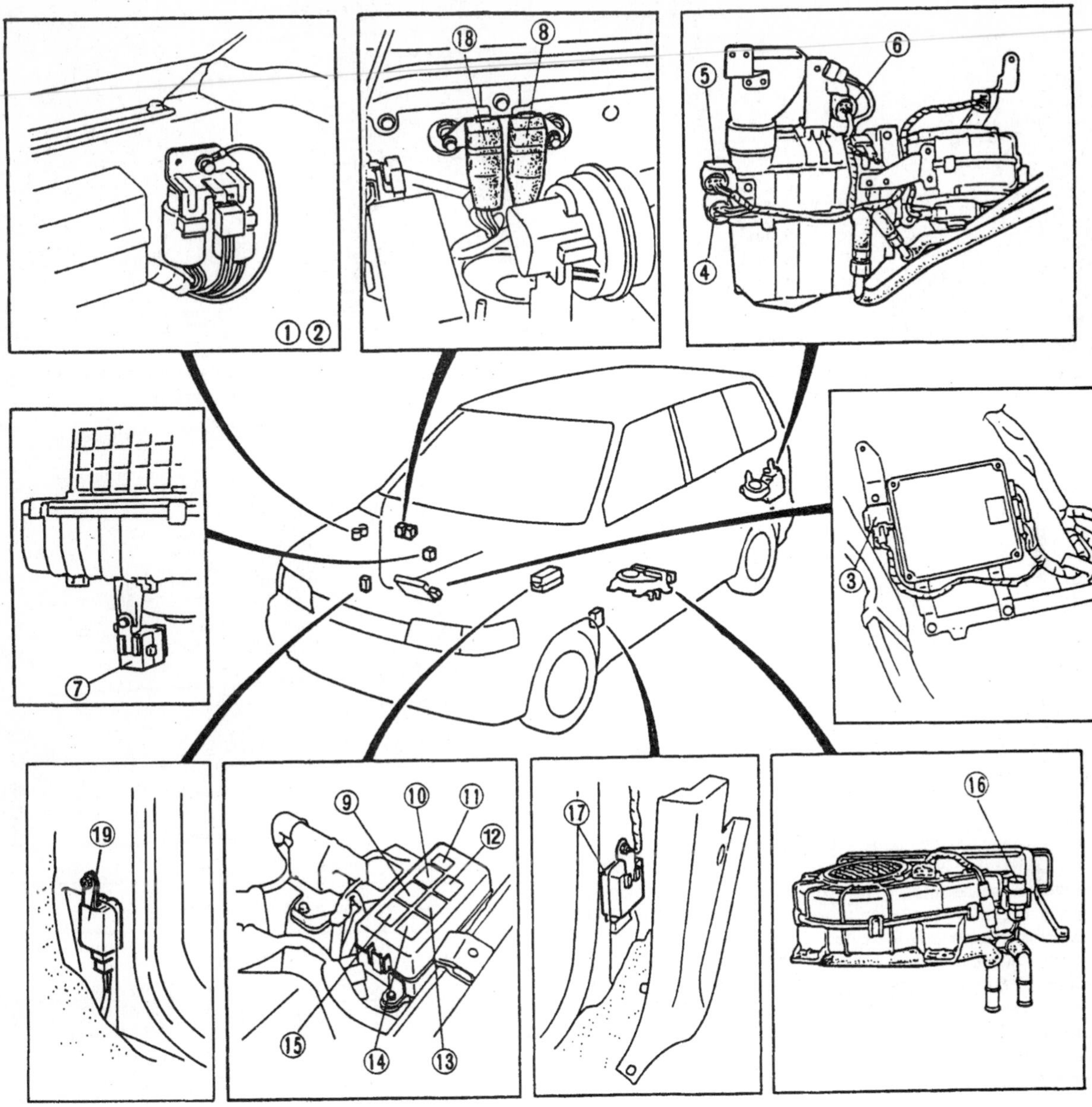

5.2a Typical relay and related component locations

1	Air conditioning relay	8	4WD change relay number 2	14	Rear window defroster relay
2	Air conditioning condenser relay	9	EGI main relay	15	ALL (four-cylinder engine) or kick-down (V6 engine) relay
3	Circuit opening relay	10	Day Light Running (DLR) relay (Canadian models)	16	Rear heater motor blower motor relay
4	Rear cooler relay number 1	11	Horn relay	17	Turn signal/hazard flasher unit
5	Rear cooler relay number 2	12	Blower motor relay	18	4WD change motor number 1 relay
6	Rear cooler relay number 3	13	Rear wheel ABS relay	19	Brake light relay
7	Door lock timer				

located behind the driver's side kick panel, next to the fuse box **(see illustration)**. The CPU is a compact unit which performs many functions that are normally controlled by relays and other electronic devices.

2   Special equipment is required to check the CPU, so if a fault is suspected take the vehicle to a dealer.

5   Relays - general information

Refer to illustrations 5.2a, 5.2b and 5.2c

Several electrical accessories in the vehicle use relays to transmit the electrical signal to the component. If the relay is defective, that

component will not operate properly.

The various relays are grouped together in several locations under the dash and in the engine compartment for convenience in the event of needed replacement **(see illustrations)**.

If a faulty relay is suspected, it can be removed and tested by a dealer or other qualified shop. Defective relays must be replaced as a unit.

6   Turn signal/hazard warning flasher - check and replacement

Refer to illustration 6.1

1   The turn signal/hazard flasher is a small square shaped unit lo-

12

5.2b The engine compartment relay block is clearly marked on the cover

5.2c Flip the cover up for access to the relays

6.1 The turn signal/hazard flasher unit is located under the driver's kick panel

7.3 Use a screwdriver to lift the release lever to loosen the harness strap, the loosen the combination switch clamp screw (arrow)

cated under the drivers side kick panel **(see illustration)**.

2   When the flasher unit is functioning properly, and audible click can be heard during its operation. If the turn signals fail on one side or the other and the flasher unit does not make its characteristic clicking sound, a faulty turn signal bulb is indicated.

3   If both turn signals fail to blink, the problem may be due to a blown fuse, a faulty flasher unit, a broken switch or a loose or open connection. If a quick check of the fuse box indicates that the turn signal fuse has blown, check the wiring for a short before installing a new fuse.

4   To replace the flasher, remove the kick panel, remove the screw and detach the flasher, then unplug the connector.

5   Make sure that the replacement unit is identical to the original. Compare the old one to the new one before installing it.

6   Installation is the reverse of removal.

7   Combination switch - removal and installation

Refer to illustrations 7.3, 7.4a and 7.4b

1   Disconnect the negative cable at the battery.

2   Remove the steering wheel (see Chapter 10) and the steering column cover (see Chapter 11).

3   Trace the wiring harness down the steering column to the connector. Release the wiring retainer clamp and unplug the connector, then loosen the clamp screw

4   Remove the turn signal canceling cam and slide the switch up off the column **(see illustrations)**.

5   Installation is the reverse of removal.

7.4a Lift the turn signal canceling cam off

7.4b Slide the combination switch off the steering column

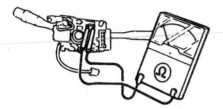

8.2a Use an ohmmeter to check the terminals with the switch in each position

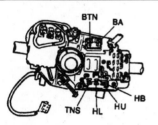

Position \ Terminal		HB	HL	HU	BA	BTN	TNS
Headlight	Low beam	O—O	O		O	O—O	
		O		O			
	High beam	O—O		O		O—O	
		O		O			
Passing			O—O				
Tail, Parking						O—O	

O——O: Indicates continuity

8.2c Headlight, dimmer and passing switch terminal location and continuity check chart - continuity should be as specified in each switch position

8 Steering column switches - check and replacement

Refer to illustration 8.2a through 8.2f and 8.3

1   Remove the combination switch (see Section 7).
2   Use an ohmmeter to check each switch in each position for continuity (see illustrations).

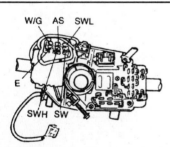

Position \ Terminal			AS	W/G	SWL	SWH	E	SW
Wiper switch	OFF	One touch OFF	O		O			
		ON			O		O	
	INT				O		O	
	I (Low)				O		O	
	II (High)					O	O	
Washer switch ON							O—O	

O——O: Indicates continuity

8.2e Wiper/washer switch terminal location and continuity check chart - continuity should be as specified in each switch position

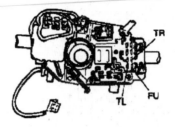

Position \ Terminal	FU	TL	TR
Left	O—O		
Right	O		O

O——O: Indicates continuity

8.2b Turn signal switch terminal location and continuity check chart - continuity should be as specified in each switch position

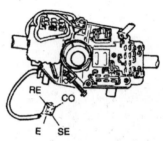

Position \ Terminal	SE	RE	CO	E
Off				
Set	O			O
Resume		O		O
Coast			O—O	O

O——O: Indicates continuity

8.2d Cruise control switch terminal location and continuity check chart - continuity should be as specified in each switch position

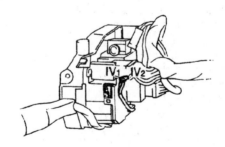

Position \ Terminal	IV₁ — IV₂
Slow	0— 1 kΩ
Fast	40—60 kΩ

8.2f Wiper variable interval switch terminal location and resistance chart - continuity should be as specified in each switch position

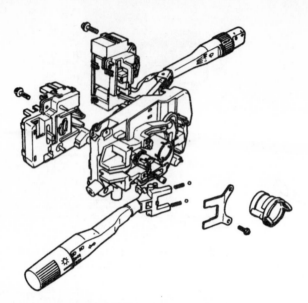

8.3 Combination switch details

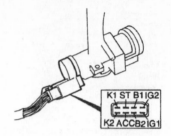

Position	Terminals							
	B1	B2	ACC	IG1	IG2	ST	K1	K2
LOCK							○——○	
ACC	○———————○						○——○	
ON	○——	——○——	—○——	——○			○——○	
		○——		——○——	——○			
START	○—			—○			○——○	
		○——		——○——		——○		

○———○: Indicates continuity

9.4 Ignition switch terminal location and continuity check chart - continuity should be as specified in each switch position

9.5a Remove the ignition switch screw. . .

9.5b . . .then release the clips on both sides to detach it

3   Replace any faulty switch with a new one. Remove the retaining screws, detach the switch and lift it off the combination switch **(see illustration)**.

---

9   Ignition switch and lock cylinder - check and replacement

---

1   Disconnect the negative cable at the battery.
2   Remove the steering wheel (see Chapter 10).
3   Remove the steering column cover (see Chapter 11).

Ignition switch

Refer to illustrations 9.4, 9.5a and 9.5b

4   Unplug the electrical connector and use an ohmmeter to check the switch for continuity with the key each position **(see illustration)**.
5   If the switch is faulty, remove the retaining screw and detach the clips to separate it from the steering column **(see illustrations)**.
6   Installation is the reverse of removal.

Lock cylinder

Refer to illustration 9.7

7   The lock cylinder assembly is clamped to the steering column by

9.7 Use a chisel to make slots in these two bolts, then unscrew them with a screwdriver

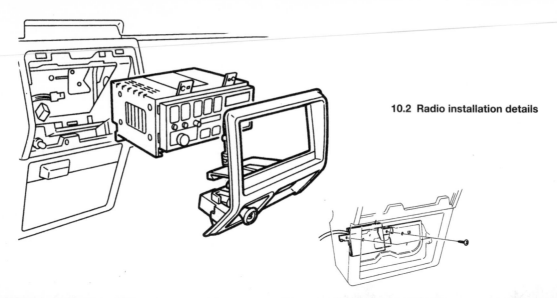

10.2 Radio installation details

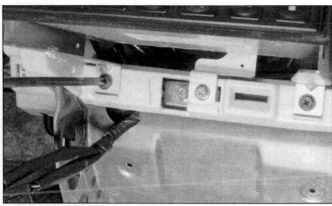

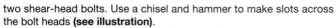

10.3 Remove the radio screws

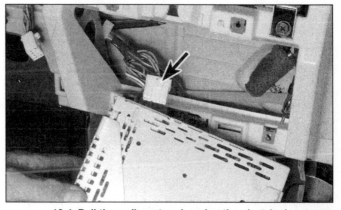

10.4 Pull the radio out and unplug the electrical connectors (arrows)

two shear-head bolts. Use a chisel and hammer to make slots across the bolt heads **(see illustration)**.

8   Use a screwdriver to unscrew the bolts, then separate clamp and remove the assembly from the steering column.

9   Place the new switch in position , then install the clamp and bolts. Tighten the bolts until the heads break off.

10   Radio and speakers - removal and installation

1   Disconnect the negative cable at the battery.

Radio

Refer to illustrations 10.2, 10.3 and 10.4

1   Disconnect the negative battery cable.

2   Detach radio cover panel **(see illustration)**.

3   Remove the radio retaining screws **(see illustration)**.

4   Pull the radio out, unplug the electrical connector and remove the assembly from the vehicle **(see illustration)**.

5   Installation is the reverse of removal.

Speakers

Door speakers

Refer to illustrations 10.7

6   Remove the door trim panel (see Chapter 11).

7   Unplug the electrical connector, remove the screws, and detach the speaker **(see illustration)**.

8   Installation is the reverse of removal.

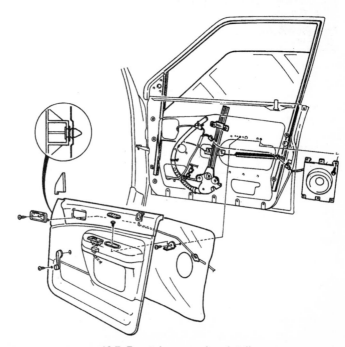

10.7 Front door speaker details

12

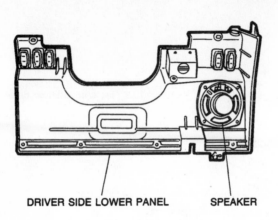 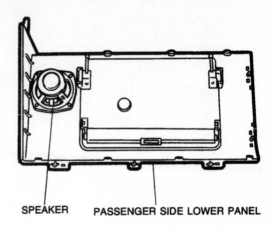

DRIVER SIDE LOWER PANEL   SPEAKER   SPEAKER   PASSENGER SIDE LOWER PANEL

10.9 The front speakers are mounted on the back side of the lower panels

10.10 Remove the speaker screws (arrows)

Front speakers

Refer to illustrations 10.9 and 10.10

9   Detach the lower panel (see Chapter 11) and unplug the electrical connector **(see illustration)**.
10   Remove the screws and detach the speaker **(see illustration)**.
11   Installation is the reverse of removal.

Rear speakers

Refer to illustration 10.13

12   Remove the rear trim panel(s) (see Chapter 11).
13   Remove the screws, pull the speaker out, unplug the electrical connector and remove the speaker from the vehicle **(see illustration)**.
14   Installation is the reverse of removal.

11   Radio antenna - removal and installation

Refer to illustration 11.2

1   Disconnect the negative cable at the battery.
2   Use snap-ring pliers to unscrew the antenna-to-fender mounting nut **(see illustration)**.
3   Remove the radio and unplug the antenna power and radio lead connectors (see Section 10).
4   Detach the inner fender panel, remove the retaining bolt and lower the antenna from the vehicle.
5   Installation is the reverse of removal.

12   Instrument cluster - removal and installation

Refer to illustrations 12.4a, 12.4b, 12.5 and 12.6

1   Disconnect the negative cable at the battery.

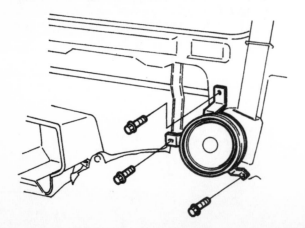 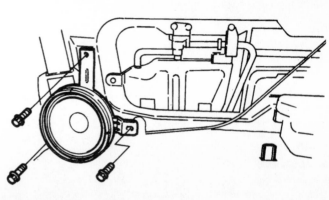

10.13 Rear speaker details

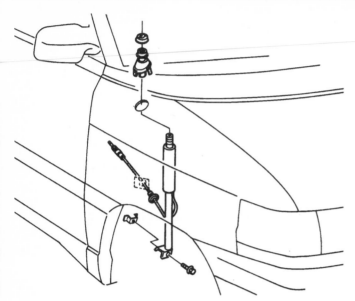

11.2 Antenna installation details

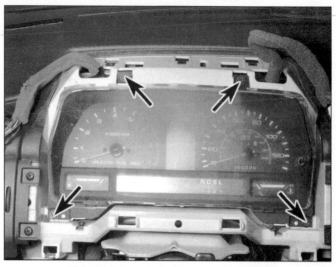

12.4a Instrument cluster screw locations

12.4b Use needle-nose pliers to detach the clip from the
automatic transmission shift indicator cable

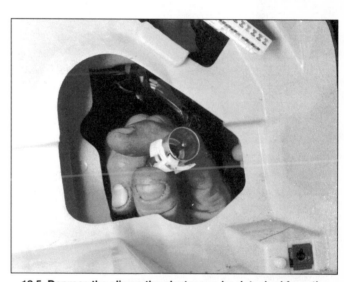

12.5 Depress the clip so the cluster can be detached from the
speedometer cable

2   Remove the steering column covers (see Chapter 11).
3   Remove the instrument cluster housing (see Section 13).
4   Remove the cluster retaining screws **(see illustration)**. On automatic transmission-equipped models, use needle-nose pliers to detach the clip, then disconnect the shift indicator cable **(see illustration)**.
5   Pull the cluster out and reach up behind it and press the tab on
the speedometer cable collar to detach the cable **(see illustration)**
6   Remove the retaining screws, then pull out the instrument cluster
and disconnect the electrical connectors **(see illustration)**.
7   Pull the cluster out for access, unplug the electrical connectors
and remove the cluster from the vehicle.
8   Installation is the reverse of removal.

**13   Instrument cluster housing switches - check and
replacement**

Refer to illustrations 13.2, 13.3a and 13.3b
1   Disconnect the cable from the negative terminal of the battery.
2   Remove the instrument cluster housing assembly **(see illustration)**.

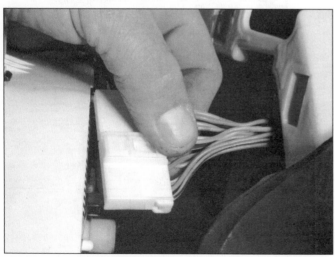

12.6 Pull the cluster back, depress the clips and unplug
the connectors

12

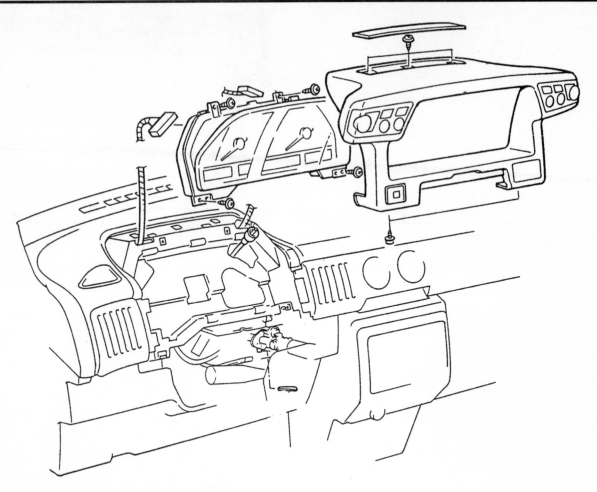

13.2 Cluster switch housing details

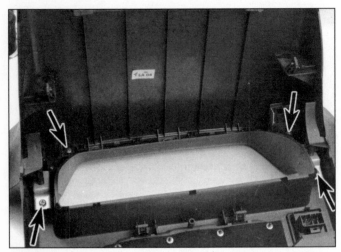

13.3a Remove the screws (arrows) and separate the housings

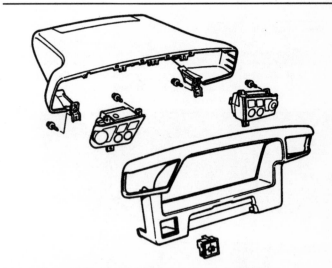

13.3b Bezel, housing and switch details

3   Remove the screws and separate the bezel from the cluster housing **(see illustrations)**.

Check

Refer to illustrations 13.4a, 13.4b, 13.4c and 13.4d

4   Use an ohmmeter to check the cluster housing switches for continuity **(see illustrations)**. Replace any switch which fails the continuity check.

Replacement

Refer to illustrations 13.6a and 13.6b

5   The switch cluster assemblies themselves can be separated from the bezel after removing the screws.

6   The switches are removed by releasing the clips and detaching them from the housing **(see illustrations)**.

7   Installation is the reverse of removal.

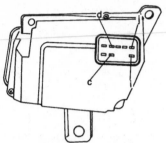

RIGHT CLUSTER ASSEMBLY

Switch	Terminals			
	c	d	i	j
ON	O——O		O——O	
OFF			O——O	

O——O: Indicates continuity

13.4a Hazard warning light switch terminal location and continuity check chart - continuity should be as specified in each switch position

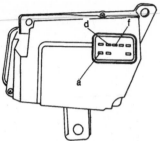

RIGHT CLUSTER ASSEMBLY

Switch	Terminals		
	a	d	f
ON	O——O		O
OFF	O——O		

O——O: Indicates continuity

13.4b Cruise control switch terminal location and continuity check chart - continuity should be as specified in each switch position

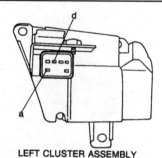

LEFT CLUSTER ASSEMBLY

Switch	Terminals	
	a	d
ON	O——O	
OFF		

O——O: Indicates continuity

13.4c Rear washer wiper switch terminal location and continuity check chart - continuity should be as specified in each switch position

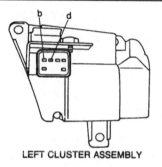

LEFT CLUSTER ASSEMBLY

Switch	Terminals	
	b	d
ON	O——O	
OFF		

O——O: Indicates continuity

13.4d Rear wiper intermittent switch terminal location and continuity check chart - continuity should be as specified in each switch position

13.6a While pressing on the switch, use a screwdriver to depress the clips to detach it

13.6b Some switches can be detached by pressing on the release clip with your finger

14.2 Unscrew the speedometer cable collar with a wrench

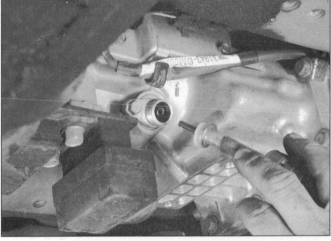

14.3 Withdraw the cable from the driven gear

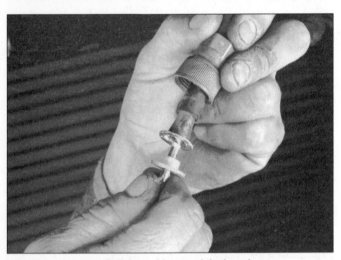

14.4 Pull the cable out of the housing

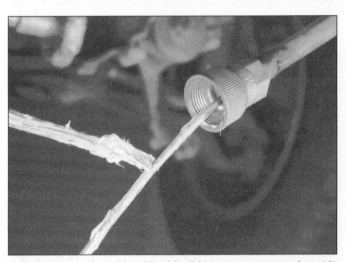

14.5 Lubricate the cable with white lithium grease as you insert it into the housing

14 Speedometer cable - replacement

Refer to illustrations 14.2, 14.3, 14.4 and 14.5

1   Raise the vehicle and support it securely on jackstands.
2   Use a wrench to unscrew the speedometer collar **(see illustration)**.
3   Withdraw the cable **(see illustration)**.
4   Pull the cable out of the housing **(see illustration)**.
5   Lubricate the length of the new cable with white lithium grease and insert it into the housing until it seats in the speedometer **(see illustration)**.
6   Insert the cable into the drive housing and tighten the collar securely.

15 Headlight bulb - replacement

Refer to illustrations 15.3 and 15.4
Warning: *Halogen gas filled bulbs are under pressure and may shatter if the surface is scratched or the bulb is dropped. Wear eye protection and handle the bulbs carefully, grasping only the base whenever possible. Do not touch the surface of the bulb with your fingers because the oil from your skin could cause the bulb to overheat and fail prematurely. If you do touch the bulb surface, clean it with rubbing alcohol.*
1   Open the hood.
2   Disconnect the negative battery cable from the battery.

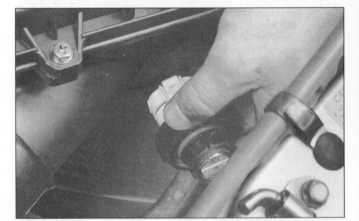

15.3 Turn the retaining ring counterclockwise and pull the bulb assembly out of the headlight housing

3   Rotate the retaining ring counterclockwise (viewed from the rear) and withdraw the bulb assembly from the headlight housing **(see illustration)**.
4   Squeeze the clips and unplug the bulb holder from the electrical connector **(see illustration)**.
5   Remove the retaining ring from old bulb and transfer it to the new one, without touching the glass with your bare fingers.

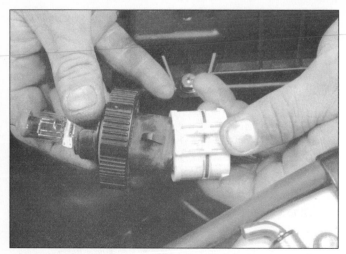

15.4 Depress the clip and unplug the electrical connector from the bulb holder

16.1a Use a Phillips head screwdriver (arrow) to adjust up-and-down position

16.1b Side-to-side position is adjusted at the corner of the headlight

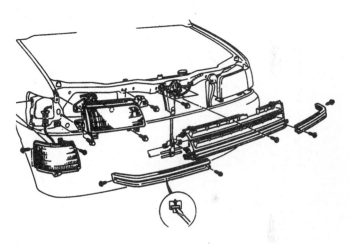

17.2 Grille and parking light details

6   Insert the bulb assembly into the headlight housing and tighten the retaining ring.
7   Connect the electrical connector. Test headlight operation, then close the hood.
8   Have the headlight adjustment checked and, if necessary, adjusted by a dealer service department or service station at the earliest opportunity.

16   Headlights - adjustment

Refer to illustrations 16.1a and 16.1b
Warning: *The headlights must be aimed correctly. If adjusted incorrectly they could momentarily blind the driver of an oncoming vehicle and cause a serious accident or seriously reduce your ability to see the road. The headlights should be checked for proper aim every 12 months and any time a new headlight is installed or front end body work is performed. It should be emphasized that the following procedure is only an interim step which will provide temporary adjustment until the headlights can be adjusted by a properly equipped shop.*
1   Headlights have two adjusting screws, one behind the headlight housing controlling up-and-down movement and one at the upper corner of the headlight controlling left-and-right movement **(see illustrations)**.
2   There are several methods of adjusting the headlights. The simplest method requires a blank wall 25 feet in front of the vehicle and a level floor.
3   Position masking tape vertically on the wall in reference to the vehicle centerline and the centerline of both headlights.

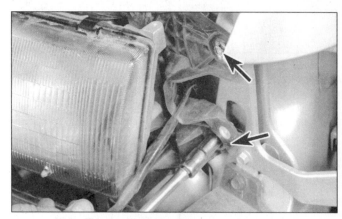

17.4a The headlight housing has two bolts on the side (arrows) . . .

4   Position a horizontal line in reference to the centerline of all headlights. **Note**: *It may be easier to position the tape on the wall with the vehicle parked only a few inches away.*
5   Adjustment should be made with the vehicle sitting level, the gas tank half-full and no unusually heavy load in the vehicle.
6   Starting with the low beam adjustment, position the high intensity zone so it is two inches below the horizontal line and two inches to the right of the headlight vertical line. Adjustment is made by turning the adjusting screw behind the headlight as necessary to raise or lower the beam **(see illustration 16.1a)**. The other adjusting screw should be used in the same manner to move the beam left or right.

12

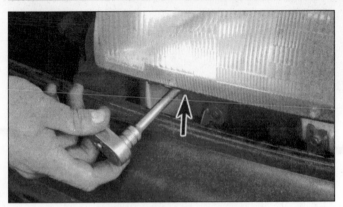

17.4b . . . and one underneath

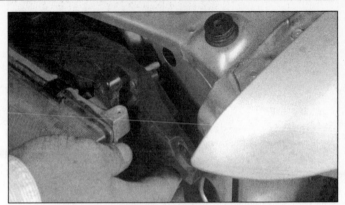

17.4c Lift the housing up and rotate it back to remove it

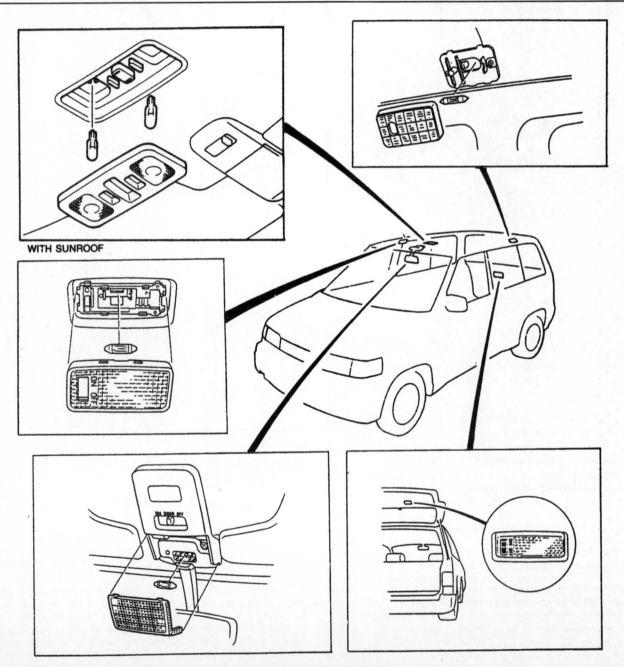

WITH SUNROOF

18.1 Interior light bulb details

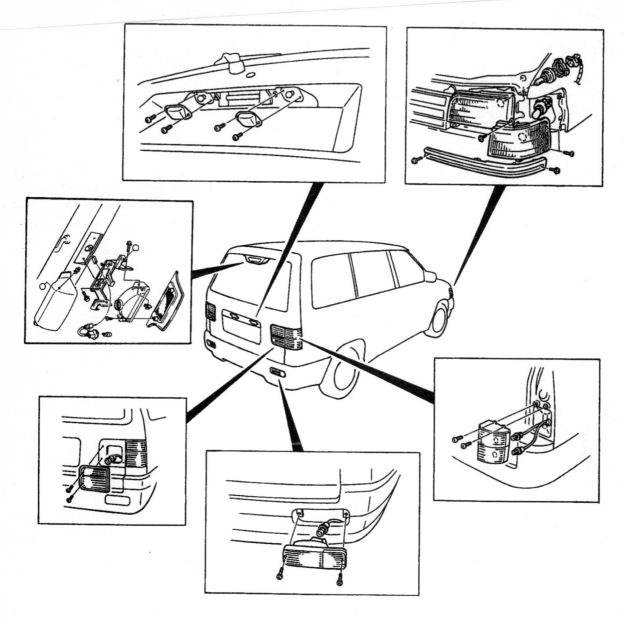

18.3 Exterior light bulb details

7   With the high beams on, the high intensity zone should be vertically centered with the exact center just below the horizontal line.
Note: *It may not be possible to position the headlight aim exactly for
both high and low beams. If a compromise must be made, keep in
mind that the low beams are the most used and have the greatest effect on driver safety.*
8   Have the headlights adjusted by a dealer service department or
service station at the earliest opportunity.

17   Headlight housing - removal and installation

Refer to illustrations 17.2, 17.4a, 17.4b and 17.4c
1   Disconnect the negative battery cable.
2   Remove the radiator grille and parking light assemblies **(see illustration).**
3   Unplug the headlight bulb connectors (see Section 15).

4   Remove the three bolts and detach the headlight housing **(see illustrations).**
5   Installation is the reverse of removal.

18   Bulb replacement

Refer to illustrations 18.1, 18.3 and 18.4
1   The lenses of many lights are held in place by screws, which
makes it a simple procedure to gain access to the bulbs **(see illustration).**
2   On some lights the lenses are held in place by clips. The lenses
can be removed either by unsnapping them or by using a small screwdriver to pry them off.
3   Several types of bulbs are used. Some are removed by pushing in
and turning them counterclockwise **(see illustration).** Others can sim-

12

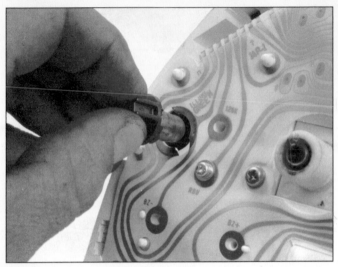

18.4 Instrument cluster bulbs can be replaced after removing the cluster

19.2 Remove the two nuts, detach the air conditioning hose clamp and move the hose out of the way

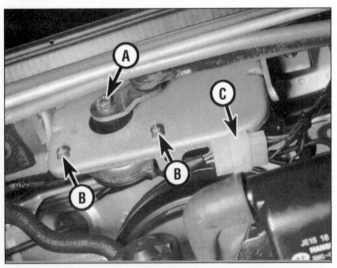

19.3 Remove the nut (A), detach the arm, then remove the bolts (B) from the back side, unplug the connector (C) and lower the wiper motor from the bracket

ply be unclipped from the terminals or pulled straight out of the socket.
4   To gain access to the instrument panel lights, the instrument cluster will have to be removed first **(see illustration)**.

---

19   Wiper motor - removal and installation

Refer to illustrations 19.2, 19.3 and 19.4
1   Disconnect the negative cable at the battery.

Windshield wiper motor

2   Remove the retaining nuts and detach the air conditioning hose bracket, then move the hose out of the way **(see illustration)**.
3   Remove the retaining nut, detach the wiper arm from the motor shaft, then remove the four retaining bolts, unplug the electrical connector and remove the wiper motor from the vehicle **(see illustration)**.

Rear wiper motor

4   Flip up the cover, remove the wiper arm retaining nut and remove the wiper arm **(see illustration)**.
5   Remove the nut and washers from the wiper arm shaft. Note the

order in which they are arranged for ease of installation.
6   Open the liftgate and remove the trim panel.
7   Unplug the electrical connector, remove the retaining bolts and lower
the motor from the liftgate **(see illustration 19.4)**.
8   Installation is the reverse of removal.

---

20   Rear window defogger - check and replacement

Refer to illustrations 20.4 and 20.7
1   The rear window defogger consists of a number of horizontal elements baked onto the glass surface.
2   Small breaks in the element can be repaired without removing the rear window.

Check

3   Turn the ignition switch and defogger system switches On.
4   Ground the negative lead of a voltmeter to terminal B and the positive lead to terminal A **(see illustration)**.
5   The voltmeter reading should be between 10 and 15 volts. If the reading is lower, there is a poor ground connection.
6   Contact the negative lead to a good body ground. The reading should stay the same.
7   Connect the negative lead to terminal B, then touch each grid line at the mid-point with the positive lead **(see illustration)**.
8   The reading should be approximately six volts. If the reading is O, there is a break between mid-point "C" and terminal "A".
9   A 10 to 14 volt reading is an indication of a break between mid-point "C". Move the lead toward the break; the voltage will change when the break is crossed.

Repair

10   Repair the break in the line using a repair kit recommended specifically for this purpose, such as Mazda Repair Kit No. 2835 77 600 (or equivalent). Included in this kit is plastic conductive epoxy.
11   Prior to repairing a break, turn off the system and allow it to de-energize for a few minutes.
12   Lightly buff the element area with fine steel wool, then clean it thoroughly with rubbing alcohol.
13   Use masking tape to mask off the area of repair.
14   Mix the epoxy thoroughly, according to the instructions on the package.
15   Apply the epoxy material to the slit in the masking tape, overlapping the undamaged area about 3/4-inch on either end.
16   Allow the repair to cure for 24 hours before removing the tape and using system.

19.4 Rear wiper details

1. Wiper arm cover
2. Wiper arm and blade assembly
3. Seal cap
4. Outer bushing
5. Liftgate trim panel
6. Water shield
7. Wiper motor
8. Interior trim panel
9. Washer tubing
10. Washer fluid reservoir
11. Washer pump
12. Washer nozzle

RELEASE
LOCK

LOCK

BODY

BODY

Ⓐ BODY Ⓑ

FUEL-FILLER LID
OPENER CABLE

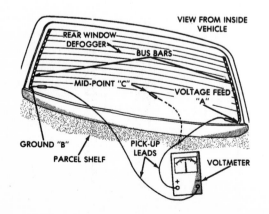

20.4 Rear window defogger test points

VIEW FROM INSIDE
VEHICLE

REAR WINDOW
DEFOGGER

BUS BARS

MID-POINT "C"

VOLTAGE FEED
"A"

GROUND "B"

PICK-UP
LEADS

PARCEL SHELF

VOLTMETER

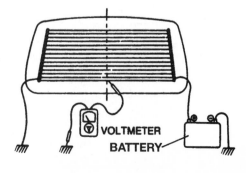

VOLTMETER

BATTERY

**20.7 Check the center of the heating elements - the meter should
read 6 volts**

12

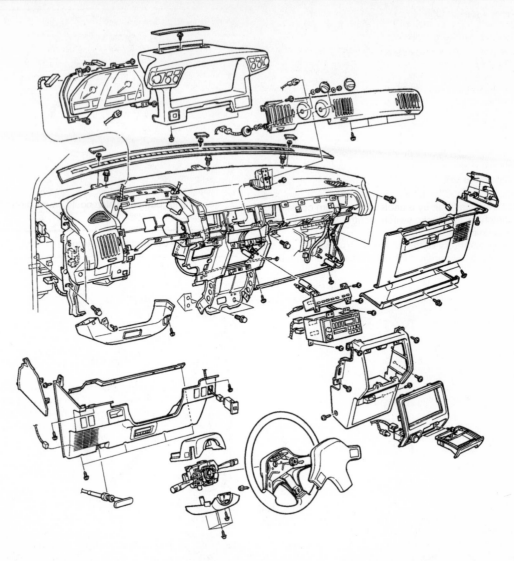

21.2 Instrument panel details

Color	Code	Color	Code
Blue	L	Natural	N
Black	B	Orange	O
Brown	BR	Pink	P
Dark Blue	DL	Red	R
Dark Green	DG	Purple	PU
Green	G	Tan	T
Gray	GY	White	W
Light Blue	LB	Yellow	Y
Light Green	LG	Violet	V

26.3 Wiring diagram color codes

21 Instrument panel - removal and installation

Refer to illustration 21.2

1   Disconnect the negative cable at the battery.
2   Remove the dashboard panels **(see illustration)**.

3   Remove the radio and the dashboard mounted speakers (see Section 10).
4   Remove the instrument cluster housing and the cluster (see Section 13).
5   Remove the tilt steering column bolts.

6   Remove the hood release handle.

7   Remove the attaching bolts and carefully lift the instrument panel back for access to the electrical connectors.

8   Unplug the electrical connectors and disconnect any component which would interfere with removal. Lift the instrument panel from the vehicle.

9   Installation is the reverse of removal. Make sure none of the wiring is crimped when the instrument panel is rotated back into position.

22   Cruise control system - description and check

The cruise control system maintains vehicle speed with a vacuum actuated servo motor located in the engine compartment, which is connected to the throttle linkage by a cable. The system consists of the servo motor, clutch switch, brake switch, control switches, a relay and associated vacuum hoses.

Because of the complexity of the cruise control system and the special tools and techniques required for diagnosis, repair should be left to a dealer service department or a repair shop. However, it is possible for the home mechanic to make simple checks of the wiring and vacuum connections for minor faults which can be easily repaired. These include:

a) Inspect the cruise control actuating switches for broken wires and loose connections.

b) Check the cruise control fuse.

c) The cruise control system is operated by vacuum so it's critical that all vacuum switches, hoses and connections are secure. Check the hoses in the engine compartment for tight connections, cracks and obvious vacuum leaks.

23   Power door lock system - description and check

The power door lock system operates the door lock actuators mounted in each door. The system consists of the switches, actuators and the associated wiring. Diagnosis can usually be limited to simple checks of the wiring connections and actuators for minor faults which can be easily repaired. These include:

a) Checking the system fuse and/or circuit breaker.

b) Checking the switch wiring for damage or loose connections.

c) Checking the switches for continuity.

d) Removing the door panel(s) and checking the actuator electrical connections for looseness or damage. Inspect the actuator rods (if equipped) to make sure that they are not bent, damaged or binding. The actuator can be checked by applying battery power momentarily. A solid click indicates the solenoid is operating properly.

24   Power window system - description and check

The power window system operates the electric motors mounted in the doors which lower and raise the windows. The system consists of the control switches, the motors (regulators), glass mechanisms and associated wiring.

Diagnosis can usually be limited to simple checks of the wiring connections and motors for minor faults which can be easily repaired. These include:

a) Inspect the power window actuating switches and wiring for broken wires and loose connections.

b) Check the power window fuse/and or circuit breaker.

c) Remove the door panel(s) and check the power window motor wires to see if they're loose or damaged. Inspect the glass mechanisms for damage which could cause binding.

25   Air bag - general information

The 1994 models are equipped with the Supplemental Restraint System (SRS), more commonly known as an air bag. This system is designed to protect the driver from serious injury in the event of a head-on or frontal collision up to 30 degrees of the centerline of the vehicle. It consists of an air bag inflator module in the center of the steering wheel, a crash arming sensor and a forward discriminating sensor mounted at the front, a discriminating sensor and a Diagnostic Energy Reserve Module (DERM) located inside the passenger department.

On vehicles equipped with an air bag, DO NOT attempt to remove the steering wheel without first having the air bag disabled or removed from the steering wheel by an automotive repair facility or dealer service department. Failure to do so can result in accidental deployment of the air bag and serious physical injury.

26   Wiring diagrams - general information

Refer to illustration 25.3

Since it isn't possible to include all wiring diagrams for every model year covered by this manual, the following diagrams are those that are typical and most commonly needed.

Prior to troubleshooting any circuit, check the fuses and circuit breakers to make sure they're in good condition. Make sure the battery is fully charged and check the cable connections (see Chapter 1). Make sure all connectors are clean, with no broken or loose terminals.

Refer to the accompanying table for the wire color codes applicable to your vehicle **(see illustration)**.

12

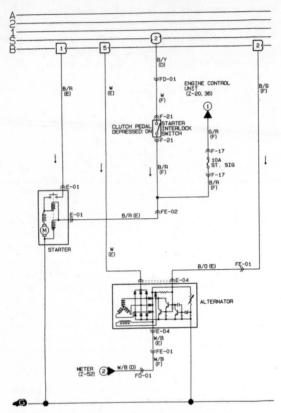

Typical charging and starting circuit wiring diagram (manual-transmission models)

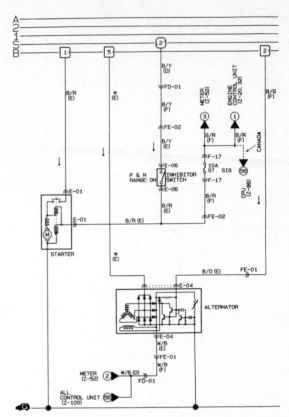

Typical charging and starting circuit wiring diagram (automatic-transmission models)

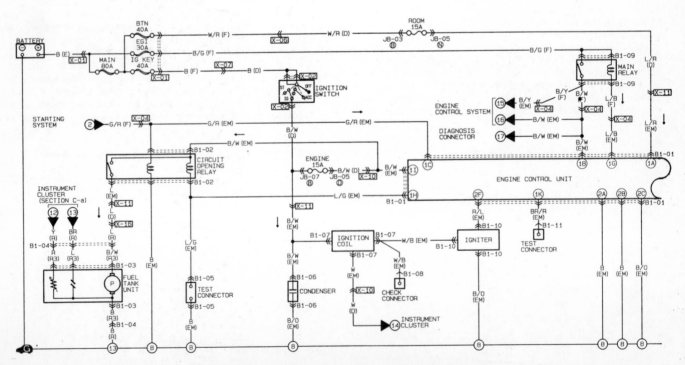

Typical four-cylinder engine control wiring diagram (1 of 3)

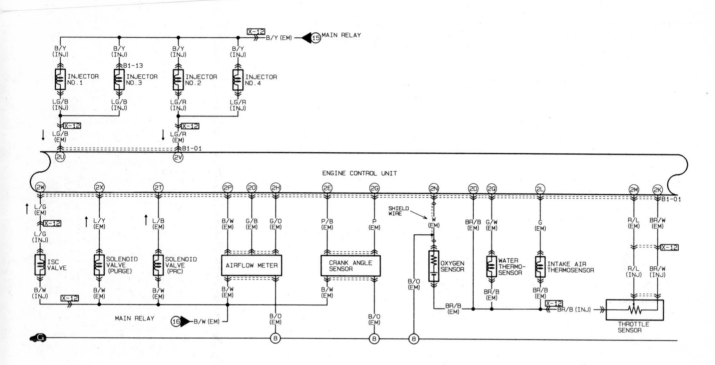

Typical four-cylinder engine control wiring diagram (2 of 3)

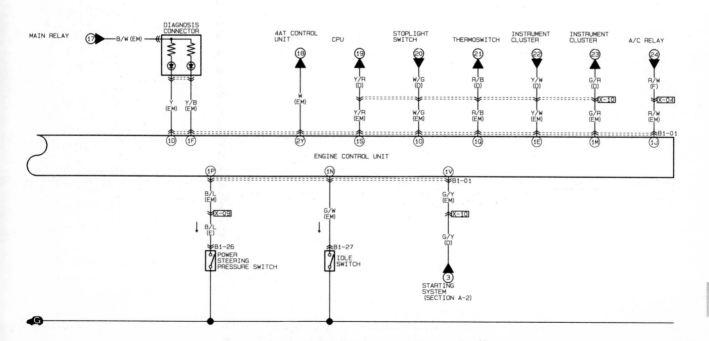

Typical four-cylinder engine control wiring diagram (3 of 3)

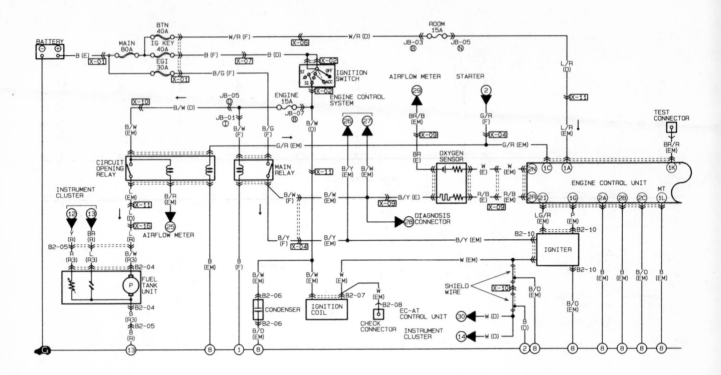

Typical V6 engine control wiring diagram (1 of 3)

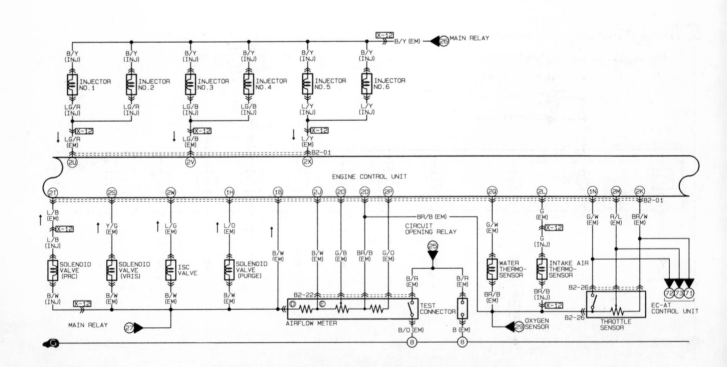

Typical V6 engine control wiring diagram (2 of 3)

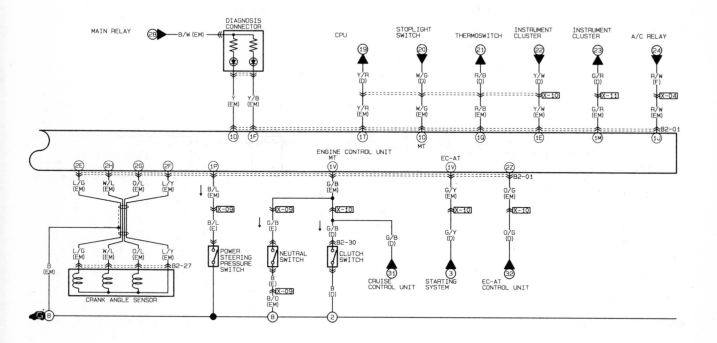

Typical V6 engine control wiring diagram (3 of 3)

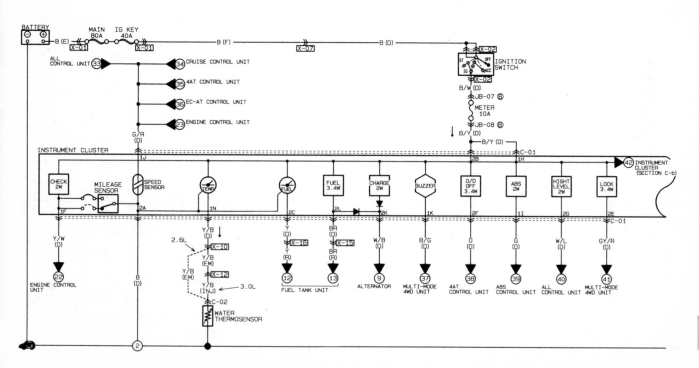

Typical instrument cluster wiring diagram (1 of 2)

12

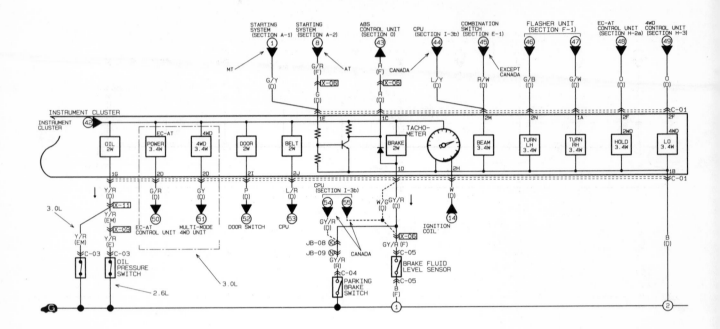

Typical instrument cluster wiring diagram (2 of 2)

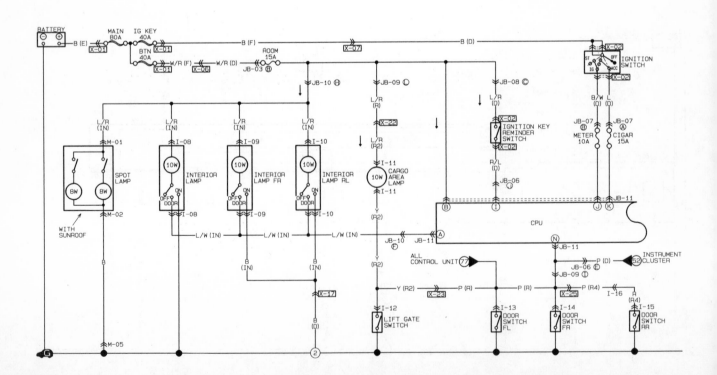

Typical interior lights and Central Processing Unit (CPU) wiring diagram (1 of 2)

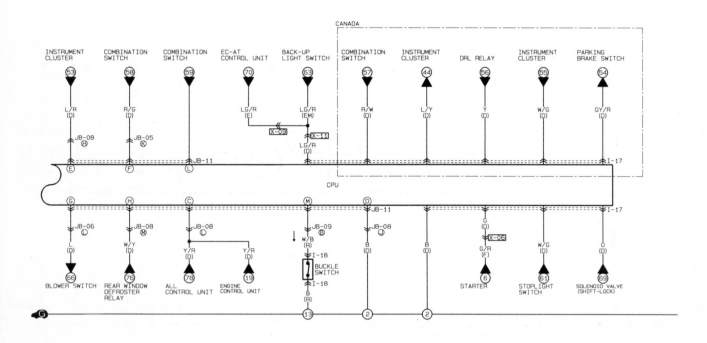

Typical interior lights and Central Processing Unit (CPU) wiring diagram (2 of 2)

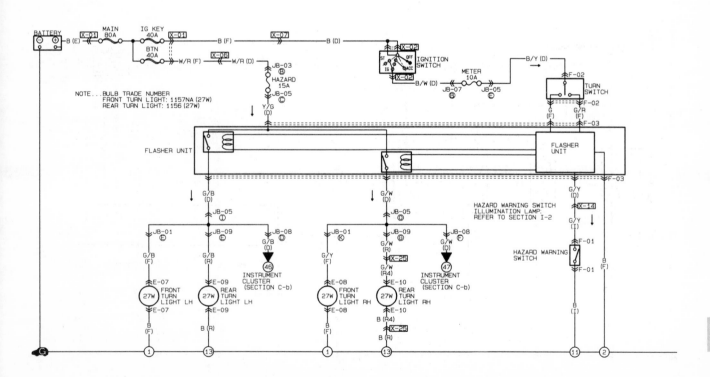

Typical turn signal/hazard flasher wiring diagram

12

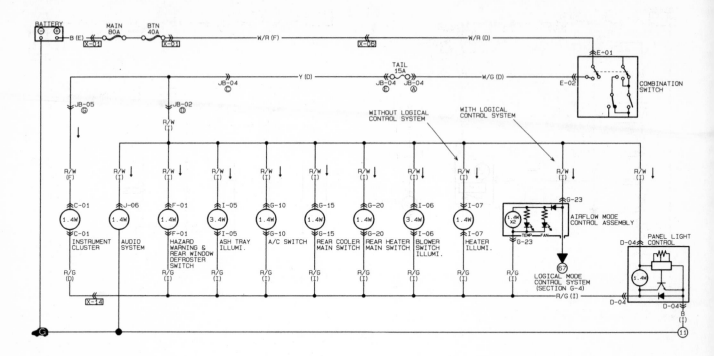

Typical interior lighting wiring diagram

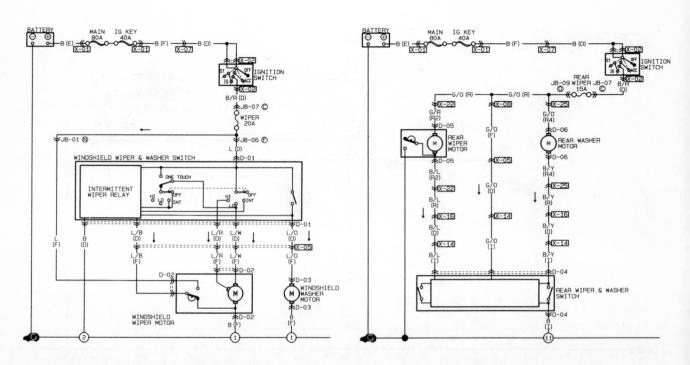

Typical windshield wiper/washer wiring diagram   **Typical rear wiper/washer wiring diagram**

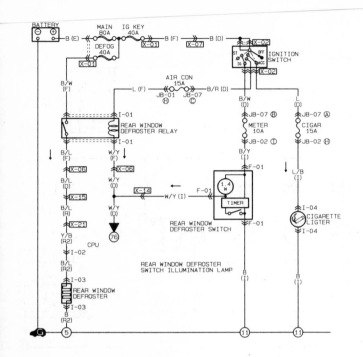

Typical rear window defroster and cigarette lighter wiring diagram

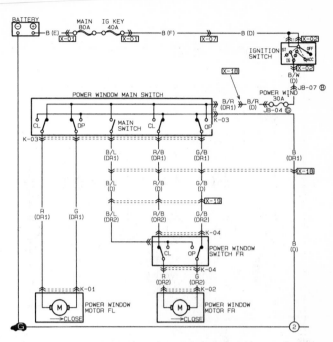

Typical power window wiring diagram

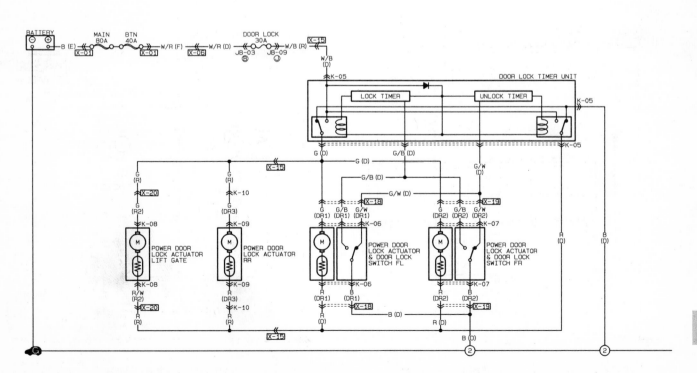

Typical power door lock wiring diagram

12

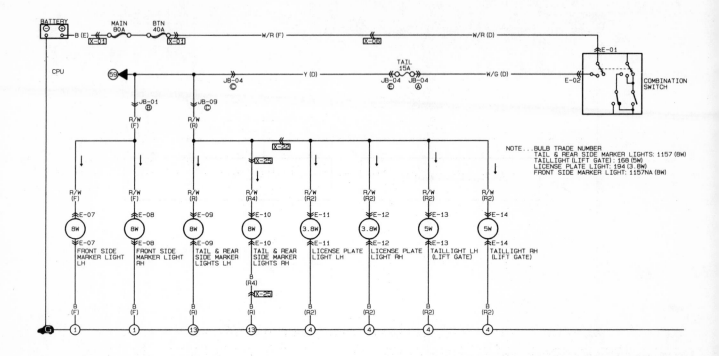

Typical rear and side lighting wiring diagram

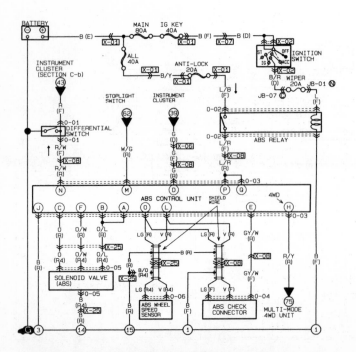

Typical Anti-lock Brake System (ABS) wiring diagram

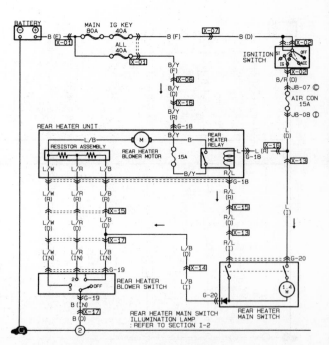

Rear heater wiring diagram

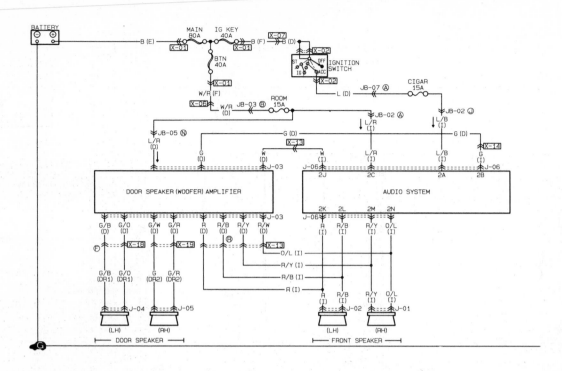

Typical audio system wiring diagram

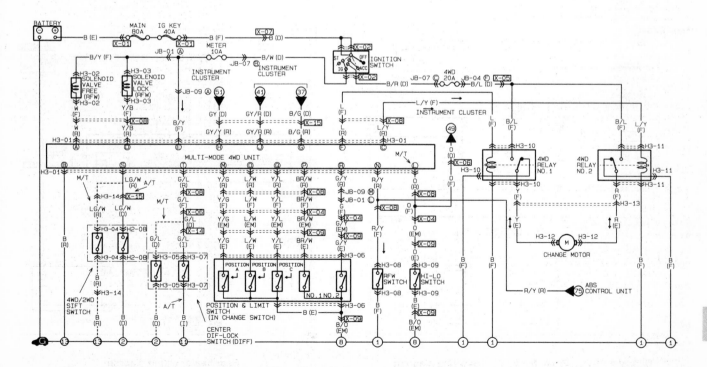

Typical multi-mode 4WD system wiring diagram

Index

Index

Index

Index

Index

Haynes Automotive Manuals

NOTE: New manuals are added to this list on a periodic basis. If you do not see a listing for your vehicle, consult your local Haynes dealer for the latest product information.

ACURA
*12020 **Integra** '86 thru '89 **& Legend** '86 thru '90

AMC
    Jeep CJ - see JEEP (50020)
14020 **Mid-size models,** Concord, Hornet, Gremlin & Spirit '70 thru '83
14025 **(Renault) Alliance & Encore** '83 thru '87

AUDI
15020 **4000** all models '80 thru '87
15025 **5000** all models '77 thru '83
15026 **5000** all models '84 thru '88

AUSTIN-HEALEY
    Sprite - see MG Midget (66015)

BMW
*18020 **3/5 Series** not including diesel or all-wheel drive models '82 thru '92
*18021 **3 Series** except 325iX models '92 thru '97
18025 **320i** all 4 cyl models '75 thru '83
18035 **528i & 530i** all models '75 thru '80
18050 **1500 thru 2002** except Turbo '59 thru '77

BUICK
    Century (front wheel drive) - see GM (829)
*19020 **Buick, Oldsmobile & Pontiac Full-size (Front wheel drive)** all models '85 thru '98
    Buick Electra, LeSabre and Park Avenue; **Oldsmobile** Delta 88 Royale, Ninety Eight and Regency; **Pontiac** Bonneville
19025 **Buick Oldsmobile & Pontiac Full-size (Rear wheel drive)**
    Buick Estate '70 thru '90, Electra '70 thru '84, LeSabre '70 thru '85, Limited '74 thru '79
    Oldsmobile Custom Cruiser '70 thru '90, Delta 88 '70 thru '85,Ninety-eight '70 thru '84
    Pontiac Bonneville '70 thru '81, Catalina '70 thru '81, Grandville '70 thru '75, Parisienne '83 thru '86
19030 **Mid-size Regal & Century** all rear-drive models with V6, V8 and Turbo '74 thru '87
    Regal - see GENERAL MOTORS (38010)
    Riviera - see GENERAL MOTORS (38030)
    Roadmaster - see CHEVROLET (24046)
    Skyhawk - see GENERAL MOTORS (38015)
    Skylark '80 thru '85 - see GM (38020)
    Skylark '86 on - see GM (38025)
    Somerset - see GENERAL MOTORS (38025)

CADILLAC
*21030 **Cadillac Rear Wheel Drive** all gasoline models '70 thru '93
    Cimarron - see GENERAL MOTORS (38015)
    Eldorado - see GENERAL MOTORS (38030)
    Seville '80 thru '85 - see GM (38030)

CHEVROLET
*24010 **Astro & GMC Safari Mini-vans** '85 thru '93
24015 **Camaro V8** all models '70 thru '81
24016 **Camaro** all models '82 thru '92
    Cavalier - see GENERAL MOTORS (38015)
    Celebrity - see GENERAL MOTORS (38005)
24017 **Camaro & Firebird** '93 thru '97
24020 **Chevelle, Malibu & El Camino** '69 thru '87
24024 **Chevette & Pontiac T1000** '76 thru '87
    Citation - see GENERAL MOTORS (38020)
*24032 **Corsica/Beretta** all models '87 thru '96
24040 **Corvette** all V8 models '68 thru '82
*24041 **Corvette** all models '84 thru '96
10305 **Chevrolet Engine Overhaul Manual**
24045 **Full-size Sedans** Caprice, Impala, Biscayne, Bel Air & Wagons '69 thru '90
24046 **Impala SS & Caprice and Buick Roadmaster** '91 thru '96
    Lumina - see GENERAL MOTORS (38010)

24048 **Lumina & Monte Carlo** '95 thru '98
    Lumina APV - see GM (38035)
24050 **Luv Pick-up** all 2WD & 4WD '72 thru '82
*24055 **Monte Carlo** all models '70 thru '88
    Monte Carlo '95 thru '98 - see LUMINA (24048)
24059 **Nova** all V8 models '69 thru '79
*24060 **Nova and Geo Prizm** '85 thru '92
24064 **Pick-ups** '67 thru '87 - Chevrolet & GMC, all V8 & in-line 6 cyl, 2WD & 4WD '67 thru '87; Suburbans, Blazers & Jimmys '67 thru '91
*24065 **Pick-ups** '88 thru '98 - Chevrolet & GMC, all full-size pick-ups, '88 thru '98; Blazer & Jimmy '92 thru '94; Suburban '92 thru '98; Tahoe & Yukon '98
24070 **S-10 & S-15 Pick-ups** '82 thru '93, Blazer & Jimmy '83 thru '94,
*24071 **S-10 & S-15 Pick-ups** '94 thru '96 Blazer & Jimmy '95 thru '96
*24075 **Sprint & Geo Metro** '85 thru '94
*24080 **Vans - Chevrolet & GMC**, V8 & in-line 6 cylinder models '68 thru '96

CHRYSLER
25015 **Chrysler Cirrus, Dodge Stratus, Plymouth Breeze** '95 thru '98
25025 **Chrysler Concorde, New Yorker & LHS, Dodge** Intrepid, **Eagle** Vision, '93 thru '97
10310 **Chrysler Engine Overhaul Manual**
*25020 **Full-size Front-Wheel Drive** '88 thru '93
    K-Cars - see DODGE Aries (30008)
    Laser - see DODGE Daytona (30030)
*25030 **Chrysler & Plymouth Mid-size** front wheel drive '82 thru '95
    Rear-wheel Drive - see Dodge (30050)

DATSUN
28005 **200SX** all models '80 thru '83
28007 **B-210** all models '73 thru '78
28009 **210** all models '79 thru '82
28012 **240Z, 260Z & 280Z** Coupe '70 thru '78
28014 **280ZX** Coupe & 2+2 '79 thru '83
    300ZX - see NISSAN (72010)
28016 **310** all models '78 thru '82
28018 **510 & PL521 Pick-up** '68 thru '73
28020 **510** all models '78 thru '81
28022 **620 Series Pick-up** all models '73 thru '79
    720 Series Pick-up - see NISSAN (72030)
28025 **810/Maxima** all gasoline models, '77 thru '84

DODGE
    400 & 600 - see CHRYSLER (25030)
*30008 **Aries & Plymouth Reliant** '81 thru '89
30010 **Caravan & Plymouth Voyager Mini-Vans** all models '84 thru '95
*30011 **Caravan & Plymouth Voyager Mini-Vans** all models '96 thru '98
30012 **Challenger/Plymouth Saporro** '78 thru '83
30016 **Colt & Plymouth Champ** (front wheel drive) all models '78 thru '87
*30020 **Dakota Pick-ups** all models '87 thru '96
30025 **Dart, Demon, Plymouth Barracuda, Duster & Valiant** 6 cyl models '67 thru '76
*30030 **Daytona & Chrysler Laser** '84 thru '89
    Intrepid - see CHRYSLER (25025)
*30034 **Neon** all models '95 thru '97
*30035 **Omni & Plymouth Horizon** '78 thru '90
*30040 **Pick-ups** all full-size models '74 thru '93
*30041 **Pick-ups** all full-size models '94 thru '96
*30045 **Ram 50/D50 Pick-ups & Raider and Plymouth Arrow Pick-ups** '79 thru '93
30050 **Dodge/Plymouth/Chrysler** rear wheel drive '71 thru '89
*30055 **Shadow & Plymouth Sundance** '87 thru '94
*30060 **Spirit & Plymouth Acclaim** '89 thru '95
*30065 **Vans - Dodge & Plymouth** '71 thru '96

EAGLE
    Talon - see Mitsubishi Eclipse (68030)
    Vision - see CHRYSLER (25025)

FIAT
34010 **124 Sport Coupe & Spider** '68 thru '78
34025 **X1/9** all models '74 thru '80

FORD
10355 **Ford Automatic Transmission Overhaul**
*36004 **Aerostar Mini-vans** all models '86 thru '96
*36006 **Contour & Mercury Mystique** '95 thru '98
36008 **Courier Pick-up** all models '72 thru '82
36012 **Crown Victoria & Mercury Grand Marquis** '88 thru '96
10320 **Ford Engine Overhaul Manual**
36016 **Escort/Mercury Lynx** all models '81 thru '90
*36020 **Escort/Mercury Tracer** '91 thru '96
*36024 **Explorer & Mazda Navajo** '91 thru '95
36028 **Fairmont & Mercury Zephyr** '78 thru '83
36030 **Festiva & Aspire** '88 thru '97
36032 **Fiesta** all models '77 thru '80
36036 **Ford & Mercury Full-size,** Ford LTD & Mercury Marquis ('75 thru '82); Ford Custom 500,Country Squire, Crown Victoria & Mercury Colony Park ('75 thru '87); Ford LTD Crown Victoria & Mercury Gran Marquis ('83 thru '87)
36040 **Granada & Mercury Monarch** '75 thru '80
36044 **Ford & Mercury Mid-size,** Ford Thunderbird & Mercury Cougar ('75 thru '82); Ford LTD & Mercury Marquis ('83 thru '86); Ford Torino,Gran Torino, Elite, Ranchero pick-up, LTD II, Mercury Montego, Comet, XR-7 & Lincoln Versailles ('75 thru '86)
36048 **Mustang V8** all models '64-1/2 thru '73
36049 **Mustang II** 4 cyl, V6 & V8 models '74 thru '78
36050 **Mustang & Mercury Capri** all models Mustang, '79 thru '93; Capri, '79 thru '86
*36051 **Mustang** all models '94 thru '97
36054 **Pick-ups & Bronco** '73 thru '79
36058 **Pick-ups & Bronco** '80 thru '96
36059 **Pick-ups, Expedition & Mercury Navigator** '97 thru '98
36062 **Pinto & Mercury Bobcat** '75 thru '80
36066 **Probe** all models '89 thru '92
36070 **Ranger/Bronco II** gasoline models '83 thru '92
*36071 **Ranger** '93 thru '97 & **Mazda Pick-ups** '94 thru '97
36074 **Taurus & Mercury Sable** '86 thru '95
*36075 **Taurus & Mercury Sable** '96 thru '98
*36078 **Tempo & Mercury Topaz** '84 thru '94
36082 **Thunderbird/Mercury Cougar** '83 thru '88
*36086 **Thunderbird/Mercury Cougar** '89 and '97
36090 **Vans** all V8 Econoline models '69 thru '91
*36094 **Vans** full size '92-'95
*36097 **Windstar Mini-van** '95-'98

GENERAL MOTORS
*10360 **GM Automatic Transmission Overhaul**
*38005 **Buick Century, Chevrolet Celebrity, Oldsmobile Cutlass Ciera & Pontiac 6000** all models '82 thru '96
*38010 **Buick Regal, Chevrolet Lumina, Oldsmobile Cutlass Supreme & Pontiac Grand Prix** front-wheel drive models '88 thru '95
*38015 **Buick Skyhawk, Cadillac Cimarron, Chevrolet Cavalier, Oldsmobile Firenza & Pontiac J-2000 & Sunbird** '82 thru '94
*38016 **Chevrolet Cavalier & Pontiac Sunfire** '95 thru '98
38020 **Buick Skylark, Chevrolet Citation, Olds Omega, Pontiac Phoenix** '80 thru '85
38025 **Buick Skylark & Somerset, Oldsmobile Achieva & Calais and Pontiac Grand Am** all models '85 thru '95
38030 **Cadillac Eldorado** '71 thru '85, **Seville** '80 thru '85, **Oldsmobile Toronado** '71 thru '85 **& Buick Riviera** '79 thru '85
*38035 **Chevrolet Lumina APV, Olds Silhouette & Pontiac Trans Sport** all models '90 thru '95
    General Motors Full-size Rear-wheel Drive - see BUICK (19025)

(Continued on other side)

Listings shown with an asterisk (*) indicate model coverage as of this printing. These titles will be periodically updated to include later model years - consult your Haynes dealer for more information.

Haynes North America, Inc., 861 Lawrence Drive, Newbury Park, CA 91320-1514 • (805) 498-6703

Haynes Automotive Manuals (continued)

NOTE: New manuals are added to this list on a periodic basis. If you do not see a listing for your vehicle, consult your local Haynes dealer for the latest product information.

GEO
   Metro - *see CHEVROLET Sprint (24075)*
   Prizm - *'85 thru '92 see CHEVY (24060), '93 thru '96 see TOYOTA Corolla (92036)*
 *40030 **Storm** all models '90 thru '93
   Tracker - *see SUZUKI Samurai (90010)*

GMC
   Safari - *see CHEVROLET ASTRO (24010)*
   Vans & Pick-ups - *see CHEVROLET*

HONDA
 42010 **Accord CVCC** all models '76 thru '83
 42011 **Accord** all models '84 thru '89
 42012 **Accord** all models '90 thru '93
 42013 **Accord** all models '94 thru '95
 42020 **Civic 1200** all models '73 thru '79
 42021 **Civic 1300 & 1500 CVCC** '80 thru '83
 42022 **Civic 1500 CVCC** all models '75 thru '79
 42023 **Civic** all models '84 thru '91
 *42024 **Civic & del Sol** '92 thru '95
 *42040 **Prelude CVCC** all models '79 thru '89

HYUNDAI
 *43015 **Excel** all models '86 thru '94

ISUZU
   Hombre - *see CHEVROLET S-10 (24071)*
 *47017 **Rodeo** '91 thru '97; **Amigo** '89 thru '94; **Honda Passport** '95 thru '97
 *47020 **Trooper & Pick-up**, all gasoline models Pick-up, '81 thru '93; Trooper, '84 thru '91

JAGUAR
 *49010 **XJ6** all 6 cyl models '68 thru '86
 49011 **XJ6** all models '88 thru '94
 *49015 **XJ12 & XJS** all 12 cyl models '72 thru '85

JEEP
 *50010 **Cherokee, Comanche & Wagoneer Limited** all models '84 thru '96
 50020 **CJ** all models '49 thru '86
 *50025 **Grand Cherokee** all models '93 thru '98
 50029 **Grand Wagoneer & Pick-up** '72 thru '91 Grand Wagoneer '84 thru '91, Cherokee & Wagoneer '72 thru '83, Pick-up '72 thru '88
 *50030 **Wrangler** all models '87 thru '95

LINCOLN
   Navigator - *see FORD Pick-up (36059)*
 59010 **Rear Wheel Drive** all models '70 thru '96

MAZDA
 61010 **GLC Hatchback (rear wheel drive)** '77 thru '83
 61011 **GLC (front wheel drive)** '81 thru '85
 *61015 **323 & Protogé** '90 thru '97
 *61016 **MX-5 Miata** '90 thru '97
 *61020 **MPV** all models '89 thru '94
   Navajo - *see Ford Explorer (36024)*
 61030 **Pick-ups** '72 thru '93 Pick-ups '94 thru '96 - *see Ford Ranger (36071)*
 61035 **RX-7** all models '79 thru '85
 *61036 **RX-7** all models '86 thru '91
 61040 **626 (rear wheel drive)** all models '79 thru '82
 *61041 **626/MX-6 (front wheel drive)** '83 thru '91

MERCEDES-BENZ
 63012 **123 Series Diesel** '76 thru '85
 *63015 **190 Series** four-cyl gas models, '84 thru '88
 63020 **230/250/280** 6 cyl sohc models '68 thru '72
 63025 **280 123 Series** gasoline models '77 thru '81
 63030 **350 & 450** all models '71 thru '80

MERCURY
   See FORD Listing.

MG
 66010 **MGB** Roadster & GT Coupe '62 thru '80
 66015 **MG Midget, Austin Healey Sprite** '58 thru '80

MITSUBISHI
 *68020 **Cordia, Tredia, Galant, Precis & Mirage** '83 thru '93
 *68030 **Eclipse, Eagle Talon & Ply. Laser** '90 thru '94
 *68040 **Pick-up** '83 thru '96 & **Montero** '83 thru '93

NISSAN
 72010 **300ZX** all models including Turbo '84 thru '89
 *72015 **Altima** all models '93 thru '97
 *72020 **Maxima** all models '85 thru '91
 *72030 **Pick-ups** '80 thru '96 **Pathfinder** '87 thru '95
 72040 **Pulsar** all models '83 thru '86
 *72050 **Sentra** all models '82 thru '94
 *72051 **Sentra & 200SX** all models '95 thru '98
 *72060 **Stanza** all models '82 thru '90

OLDSMOBILE
 *73015 **Cutlass V6 & V8** gas models '74 thru '88
   For other OLDSMOBILE titles, see BUICK, CHEVROLET or GENERAL MOTORS listing.

PLYMOUTH
   For PLYMOUTH titles, see DODGE listing.

PONTIAC
 79008 **Fiero** all models '84 thru '88
 79018 **Firebird V8** models except Turbo '70 thru '81
 79019 **Firebird** all models '82 thru '92
   For other PONTIAC titles, see BUICK, CHEVROLET or GENERAL MOTORS listing.

PORSCHE
 *80020 **911** except Turbo & Carrera 4 '65 thru '89
 80025 **914** all 4 cyl models '69 thru '76
 80030 **924** all models including Turbo '76 thru '82
 *80035 **944** all models including Turbo '83 thru '89

RENAULT
   Alliance & Encore - *see AMC (14020)*

SAAB
 *84010 **900** all models including Turbo '79 thru '88

SATURN
 87010 **Saturn** all models '91 thru '96

SUBARU
 89002 **1100, 1300, 1400 & 1600** '71 thru '79
 *89003 **1600 & 1800** 2WD & 4WD '80 thru '94

SUZUKI
 *90010 **Samurai/Sidekick & Geo Tracker** '86 thru '96

TOYOTA
 92005 **Camry** all models '83 thru '91
 92006 **Camry** all models '92 thru '96
 92015 **Celica Rear Wheel Drive** '71 thru '85
 *92020 **Celica Front Wheel Drive** '86 thru '93
 92025 **Celica Supra** all models '79 thru '92
 92030 **Corolla** all models '75 thru '79
 92032 **Corolla** all rear wheel drive models '80 thru '87
 92035 **Corolla** all front wheel drive models '84 thru '92
 *92036 **Corolla & Geo Prizm** '93 thru '97
 92040 **Corolla Tercel** all models '80 thru '82
 92045 **Corona** all models '74 thru '82
 92050 **Cressida** all models '78 thru '82
 92055 **Land Cruiser FJ**40, 43, 45, 55 '68 thru '82
 92056 **Land Cruiser FJ**60, 62, 80, FZJ80 '80 thru '96
 *92065 **MR2** all models '85 thru '87
 92070 **Pick-up** all models '69 thru '78
 *92075 **Pick-up** all models '79 thru '95
 *92076 **Tacoma** '95 thru '98, **4Runner** '96 thru '98, & **T100** '93 thru '98
 *92080 **Previa** all models '91 thru '95
 92085 **Tercel** all models '87 thru '94

TRIUMPH
 94007 **Spitfire** all models '62 thru '81
 94010 **TR7** all models '75 thru '81

VW
 96008 **Beetle & Karmann Ghia** '54 thru '79
 96012 **Dasher** all gasoline models '74 thru '81
 *96016 **Rabbit, Jetta, Scirocco, & Pick-up** gas models '74 thru '91 & Convertible '80 thru '92
 96017 **Golf & Jetta** all models '93 thru '97
 96020 **Rabbit, Jetta & Pick-up** diesel '77 thru '84
 96030 **Transporter 1600** all models '68 thru '79
 96035 **Transporter 1700, 1800 & 2000** '72 thru '79
 96040 **Type 3 1500 & 1600** all models '63 thru '73
 96045 **Vanagon** all air-cooled models '80 thru '83

VOLVO
 97010 **120, 130 Series & 1800 Sports** '61 thru '73
 97015 **140 Series** all models '66 thru '74
 *97020 **240 Series** all models '76 thru '93
 97025 **260 Series** all models '75 thru '82
 *97040 **740 & 760 Series** all models '82 thru '88

TECHBOOK MANUALS
 10205 **Automotive Computer Codes**
 10210 **Automotive Emissions Control Manual**
 10215 **Fuel Injection Manual, 1978 thru 1985**
 10220 **Fuel Injection Manual, 1986 thru 1996**
 10225 **Holley Carburetor Manual**
 10230 **Rochester Carburetor Manual**
 10240 **Weber/Zenith/Stromberg/SU Carburetors**
 10305 **Chevrolet Engine Overhaul Manual**
 10310 **Chrysler Engine Overhaul Manual**
 10320 **Ford Engine Overhaul Manual**
 10330 **GM and Ford Diesel Engine Repair Manual**
 10340 **Small Engine Repair Manual**
 10345 **Suspension, Steering & Driveline Manual**
 10355 **Ford Automatic Transmission Overhaul**
 10360 **GM Automatic Transmission Overhaul**
 10405 **Automotive Body Repair & Painting**
 10410 **Automotive Brake Manual**
 10415 **Automotive Detailing Manual**
 10420 **Automotive Eelectrical Manual**
 10425 **Automotive Heating & Air Conditioning**
 10430 **Automotive Reference Manual & Dictionary**
 10435 **Automotive Tools Manual**
 10440 **Used Car Buying Guide**
 10445 **Welding Manual**
 10450 **ATV Basics**

SPANISH MANUALS
 98903 **Reparación de Carrocería & Pintura**
 98905 **Códigos Automotrices de la Computadora**
 98910 **Frenos Automotriz**
 98915 **Inyección de Combustible 1986 al 1994**
 99040 **Chevrolet & GMC Camionetas** '67 al '87 Incluye Suburban, Blazer & Jimmy '67 al '91
 99041 **Chevrolet & GMC Camionetas** '88 al '95 Incluye Suburban '92 al '95, Blazer & Jimmy '92 al '94, Tahoe y Yukon '95
 99042 **Chevrolet & GMC Camionetas Cerradas** '68 al '95
 99055 **Dodge Caravan & Plymouth Voyager** '84 al '95
 99075 **Ford Camionetas y Bronco** '80 al '94
 99077 **Ford Camionetas Cerradas** '69 al '91
 99083 **Ford Modelos de Tamaño Grande** '75 al '87
 99088 **Ford Modelos de Tamaño Mediano** '75 al '86
 99091 **Ford Taurus & Mercury Sable** '86 al '95
 99095 **GM Modelos de Tamaño Grande** '70 al '90
 99100 **GM Modelos de Tamaño Mediano** '70 al '88
 99110 **Nissan Camionetas** '80 al '96, **Pathfinder** '87 al '95
 99118 **Nissan Sentra** '82 al '94
 99125 **Toyota Camionetas y 4Runner** '79 al '95

Over 100 Haynes motorcycle manuals also available

5-98

---

* Listings shown with an asterisk (*) indicate model coverage as of this printing. These titles will be periodically updated to include later model years - consult your Haynes dealer for more information.

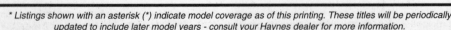

Haynes North America, Inc., 861 Lawrence Drive, Newbury Park, CA 91320-1514 • (805) 498-6703